Fraternally
N. Stacy

MEMOIRS

OF THE

LIFE OF NATHANIEL STACY

Preacher of the Gospel of Universal Grace.

COMPRISING

A BRIEF CIRCUMSTANTIAL HISTORY OF THE RISE AND PROGRESS OF UNIVERSALISM IN THE STATE OF NEW YORK, AS IDENTIFIED THEREWITH.

"And what thou seest write in a book, and send it to the churches."

COLUMBUS, PA.:
PUBLISHED FOR THE AUTHOR, BY ABNER VEDDER.
PRINTED BY W. HEUGHES, MONROE HALL, ROCHESTER. N.Y.

1850.

Entered according to Act of Congress,
BY NATHANIEL STACY,
In the Clerk's Office of the District Court of the United States for Western Pennsylvania, Dec. 1, 1849.

CONTENTS.

CHAPTER IV.

CHAPTER V.

CHAPTER VI.

CHAPTER VII.

CHAPTER VIII.

CHAPTER IX.

CHAPTER X.

CHAPTER XI.

CHAPTER XII.

CHAPTER XIII.

CHAPTER XIV.

CHAPTER XV.

CHAPTER XVI.

CHAPTER XVII.

CHAPTER XVIII.

APPENDIX.

PART I.---EXHIBITING THE AUTHOR'S PECULIAR DOCTRINAL VIEWS.

PART II.---MISCELLANEOUS POETRY.

INSCRIPTION.

To the Central Association in the State of Michigan, and to the Chautauque Association of Universalists in the State of New York, the following sheets are humbly, but most respectfully inscribed. The great length of time that has passed since the call for these memoirs was made by the Central Association in Michigan, and reiterated by that of Chautauque, has consigned to the grave many, and perhaps most of those peculiar friends who felt the deepest interest therein. But nevertheless, those bodies still exist, and some few individual members, who, with the author, are permitted to live a little longer on borrowed time, have been spared to see the accomplishment of the task; and for the peculiar manifestation of their confidence, and the numerous tokens of their kindness, the author can make no other return than humbly offering to their patronage this fruit of his humble labors.

Unaccustomed to write, and disinclined to authorship, he was well aware that the task would be a severe one; and when the work was first commenced he felt serious doubts that it would ever be completed by his own hand; but through the tender mercy of God, his life has been spared to a sufficient period to see the end. The task, though laborious for him, has by no means been so unpleasant as he anticipated. Indeed, it has been rather pleasing to review the scenes of childhood, and retrace the vivacious steps of youth—it was almost like living over again the life which can never otherwise be recalled;—and especially, it has afforded much pleasure to retrospect the days of the infancy of our cause, to trace its onward progress, and mark the hand of God in its establishment and prosperity.

I anticipate much disappointment for many of my readers. Those, however, best acquainted with me, could expect nothing more than an unvarnished detail of such facts as came within the sphere of my action and observation; and such will experience no great disappointment, for this has been my aim. With this object solely in view, the volume might have been swelled to ten times its present size; but I have selected and abridged according to the best of my judgment. By some strange and unaccountable means, the idea that I was preparing a work of the kind has got widely circulated, and many, no doubt, have anticipated something extraordinary—some wonderful detail of miraculous events, and, perhaps, some strange developments of the mysteries of Providence! Such will feel a disappointment, which, although I am very sorry, I cannot prevent.

In dates of certain events, I may have been inaccurate in some instances, though I think not. I had kept minutes in most cases; and I have been, in a few instances, assisted by the "Historical Sketches and Incidents" of Rev. S. R. Smith.

In the course of the narration, I have often used the term *Partialist*, not invidiously, but as the most appropriate appellation to distinguish those of all sects, indiscriminately, who advocate the doctrines of a partial salvation, from those who believe in universal, efficient grace, and in the final destruction of sin, and the universal holiness and happiness of all moral intelligences.

Such, however, as the work is, it is deferentially submitted to the examination of the fraternity of Universalists, and to a candid and charitable public, with a most fervent prayer that it may be no injury to the cause of religion, but that it may, in some small degree, be subservient to the advancement of the truth, as it is in Christ Jesus. THE AUTHOR.

Columbus, Warren Co., Pa., June, 1849.

INTRODUCTION.

During my residence in the State of Michigan, at the session of the Central Association in Ann Arbor, 1837, a resolution was passed, requesting me to give to the world the memoirs of my life, together with a history of the rise and progress of Universalism in the State of New York, as far as connected therewith; and the Clerk of the Association was directed to address me on the subject. He immediately complied with the request; and although I was fully aware that the task would be, to me, a severe one, and quite contrary to my inclination, yet the kind manner in which the resolution was got up, and the persuasive tone of the communication, overcame my reluctance, for the moment at least, and drew from me an answer of compliance.

Before it appeared in the printed minutes of the Association, however, I began to regret exceedingly that I had given the least encouragement for any such expectation. I never had any ambition to appear before the world as an author. The epidemic, (I do not know that I can give it a more appropriate appellation,) of authorship, which has raged of late years with such alarming violence among the advocates of our doctrine, and indeed among the would-be literati of the world, both religious and profane, had not as yet seized me. Perhaps the reason was, I never thought myself qualified to write profitably, either for the instruction or the amusement of mankind; indeed, I had little inclination to amuse, had I the gift, unless I could, with it, bestow something upon my fellow-creatures more profitable.

I had in early life embraced the doctrine of God's Universal Grace. I embraced it upon the strongest convictions of incontestible evidence—I embraced it with my whole heart, and entered into it with all the zeal of an enthusiast. I was never contented nor satisfied until I began to publish it to the world; and I was never so happy as when proclaiming in the ears of man, and defending, with all the efforts of my feeble talents, the GREAT SALVATION. But still I was of a diffident and retiring temperament. I wished to do my work with as little noise as possible—to make no parade, no ostentatious show; I wished not to excite any particular notice. My desire was to have my voice heard, my doctrine freely advocated and strongly defended, and myself unobserved, and as much out of sight as possible. And, with such feelings as these, to attempt to write the history of my own life—to have my name emblazoned before the world upon the title-page of a book, as its author; and myself the hero of the tale, relating my own wonderful adventures, and telling to the world the vast importance of my life; appeared to me too severe a task to undertake. It looked too egotistical to a mind that never entertained a very exalted opinion of its own talents or wisdom. I, therefore, shrunk from the task, and was fast coming to a resolution to relinquish it entirely, and let my friends wait for the events of my life until my biographer should gather up such fragments as were within his reach, which he should esteem of sufficient interest to publish to the world, when a voice from the East again shook my resolution.

I had many dear friends within the limits of the Chautauque Association, in the State of New York; with some of whom I had been intimately associated from the commencement of my labors in that State, and for whose judgment as well as piety I had the highest reverence. At the next session of that body, after the resolution calling for the memoirs of my life had been passed in Michigan, the council passed a resolution to the same effect, urging its importance. Individual friends, also, would insist on the obligation I was under to do it. I had been long in the ministry—my travels in promulgating the doctrine had been very considerable—I was one of the first who advocated the doctrine of Universalism in Central and Western New York, and quite the first who devoted his whole time undividedly to the cause. There were many particulars very interesting, at least, to Universalists, relative to the first planting of the doctrine in that region, which would be inevitably lost unless I recorded them, for no one else living knew them, or, at least, knew them so correctly as I did; and I must feel under a deep obligation, for the gratification of my numerous friends, as well as for the prosperity of the cause of divine truth, to give them to the world. Moreover, in despite of my efforts to the contrary, my name being identified with the rise of Universalism in the State of New York, had become known almost as far as the banner of Universal Grace waved in our land; and hundreds who had never seen me were anxiously inquiring for the memoirs of my life, and would never be satisfied without them. These, and such-like arguments, were urged to induce me to commence the work; and they had the effect to produce a renewed resolution; and again I promised my friends that, if God should spare my life and health, and, in his good providence, afford me an opportunity, I would enter upon the task.

But my reluctance led me to defer the commencement as long as possible, and to accept of almost any trifling incident as an excuse. My mind has undergone many trials on the subject. I know that I am, and ever have been, willing, perfectly willing, to encounter any labor within my ability to perform, and to endure any privation that I am capable of enduring, for the advancement of the cause of divine truth; but I am equally opposed to doing, or attempting to do, any thing to wound the cause, to deter its progress, or weaken its influence. Could I do justice to the cause? Would the incidents of my life honor it, or disgrace it? I had reason to believe that my labors had not been wholly useless; indeed, I had seen more fruit, vastly more, than I could have anticipated. But would a rehearsal of these things profit the cause? Could I adopt such a style in relating them as would be interesting and profitable? I could give a dry, unvarnished relation of facts, in such language as I could command; and I had many friends so partial toward me, that I had no reason to doubt it would be interesting and entertaining to them; but would it not be stale and barren of interest to the stranger? Such were my cogitations; and it was with difficulty I could come to any conclusion. In the mean time, it became necessary, in the providence of God, that I should change the place of my residence, and remove from Michigan; and I willingly received this as an excuse—as an indication of divine Providence, that the memoirs of my life were not called for in the world.

But, in my recent tour through New York to New England, there has been so much said to me on the subject—so many inquiries whether or not the memoirs of my life were published, (for the thing had got noised abroad, even as far as that,) or when they would be forth-coming, that I began to revolve the subject again in my mind, and once more to resolve. I have, indeed, like Youug's man of the world, "Resolved, delayed—and chid my impious delay—resolved, and re-resolved;" and there is quite a probability that I "shall die the same." But I have, at length, on this first day of January, in the year of our Lord, 1845, and on the first month of my 67th year, gone so far as to brace up my resolution with all possible determination; and, brushing up my rusty memory, have gathered around me the scattered fragments of my long—yes, long life, for Heaven has already lengthened out my life far beyond my youthful expectation—and I have seated and forced myself to the arduous and thankless task of writing a book! yes, and a book about myself! *O tempora! O mores!* But I have taken my pen in hand, and must not look back: it is not my habit. I have begun; but whether or not I shall be able to finish, is known only to Him who "calleth the things that are not as though they were." Should I make as tardy progress toward the completion of my design, as I have done in fixing my resolution to commence the work, my life must be lengthened out far beyond the common age of man, to enable me to bring it to a close; and death will close the eyes of many expectants, ere they behold the wonderful thing.

But how shall I do it? What style shall I use, to make the world think that I am "A bonnie gude writer, an' a muckle wise mon?" I hate egotism, and I hate prolixity; and so does every body else. But I sadly fear I shall commit myself in both, before I complete my task. I would take the method of Dr. A. Clarke, and write in the third person; but it would require too much labor for me to write "*The subject of these memoirs*," when one single letter would express just as much. But I have serious fears, if I do not adopt that style, and this manuscript should ever be so unfortunate as to fall into the hands of the printer, he would be compelled to purchase an extra supply of the letter I, to meet the demand. What shall I do, then? Ah, I have it! I will write the truth. I will write in as brief and concise a manner as I think the subject will admit of, and in my own plain, homely style; and leave the result in the hand of that Being whose honor I revere, whose glory I seek, and whose approbation I desire above all other considerations. I will do this, and let the critic growl, and the connoisseur curl his lip, if they please.

My object shall be, not merely to gratify my numerous and dear friends, for whose happiness I would cheerfully relinquish my own ease and encounter any privation and any labor within the compass of my ability; but to advance the truth of God, to cast, in my old age, another mite into the treasury of the Lord, and to be, if possible, even to my last breath, instrumental in uprooting those unhallowed prejudices which prevent the knowledge and enjoyment of the truth as it is in Jesus, engendered by a false religious education, and fostered, I have too much reason to fear, by the time-serving policy of a pampered priesthood; and to extend yet farther the saving knowledge of God's Universal Grace to a needy world.

If the publication of the incidents of my life, connected as they are with the rise and progress of Universalism, will tend to the accomplishment of this desirable object, I shall be amply rewarded for all my toil, and for all the solicitude, almost to vexation, which I have experienced since the first intimation that such a work was desired.

NATHANIEL STACY.

CHAPTER I.

Parents—Native place—Their Occupation—My father's marriages—Removal to New Salem—Commences farming—Ignorance of agriculture—Campaigns in the revolutionary war—Bunker Hill—Cherry Valley—Col. Stacy prisoner—Gideon Day killed—State of learning; no schools—Maternal instruction—Parents Universalists; hearers of John Murray—Universalist Preachers—Mr. Rich, Mr. Lathe, Mr. Barnes—Advanced age and death of Parents.

The world generally expect, when one undertakes to give the history of his life, that he will begin with an account of his pedigree; and much of the popularity of his book depends upon his lineal descent. If he can trace his ancestry back through a long line of honorables, to some mighty monarch, some noble lord, some brave general, some profound philosopher or sage, some eminent divine or celebrated poet, his work is sought after with insatiable avidity, and swallowed without stopping to taste. But if he be a humble, unassuming man, and his ancestors laid no claim to honorable titles, great wealth, or high literary fame, people are apt to exclaim, "What fellow is this?" and cast his book aside as an unwelcome intruder upon the literary world.

Alas! here, again, I am unfortunate. I can not trace my

> "Ancient, but ignoble blood,
> Creeping through scoundrels ever since the flood;"

but must be content to trace my origin only a little way back, from very obscure and humble individuals.

My parents were both natives of the town of Gloucester, Mass.; and my father was bred to a seafaring life. It is well known, that the inhabitants of the capes on both sides of Massachusetts Bay, Cape Ann and Cape Cod, generally follow the sea for a livelihood, and are trained to it almost from infancy. Fishing on the Grand Banks, whaling, and coasting, in their proper seasons, are their employment from the time they can be of any use aboard a vessel, until age renders them incapable, or, growing weary of their calling, they remove back into the country. Such was the occupation of my father. He entered shipboard at the age of seven years, and followed a seafaring life until forty; passing through all its stages, from a cabin-boy to that of skipper, or commander of a fishing-vessel. His business was fishing on the banks of Newfoundland in the proper season, and coasting the remainder of the year. In the course of his life, he made some foreign voyages; but the former was his most constant employment. His name was Rufus; and his most common appellation, from the earliest of my remembrance, by all his familiar acquaintances, was *Uncle Rufus.* His father's name also was Rufus; and this is nearly all I can tell of his ancestry. He informed me that he supposed he was of Scotch, or Irish descent; but his ancestors, as well as those of my mother, were among the earliest settlers of New England, and, for many generations, had been inhabitants of the town of their nativity. My father was twice married. For his first wife, he married Elizabeth Allen, by whom he had two children, a daughter and a son, who were mere infants at the time of her death. He shortly after married a second wife, by the name of Anna Day, with whom he lived to an advanced age. At the age of forty, or thereabout, growing tired of a seafaring life, either from the gathering storm of the Revolution, which was fast approaching, or from some other cause, he left the seacoast and removed about one hundred miles back into the country, to the town of New Salem, (then called Hampshire, now Franklin Co.,) which was then very new but rapidly being settled; where he purchased a lot of new land, and, with all his ignorance of agriculture, commenced as a farmer. So great was his ignorance of every kind of land employment, it may well be supposed that he made but slow progress in his new vocation, and acquired but a meagre and scanty living for his growing family.

I have often heard my mother tell an anecdote, illustrative of his profound ignorance of the nature of crops, which he attempted to raise. She had previously lived in the country with a brother-in-law, for some years, and, being an observing woman, had acquired quite a knowledge of agriculture. My father had sown a small piece of ground to flax. It had come up finely, grew well, and looked very promising. Near the time when it became ripe enough to pull, he one day came into the house with a sombre countenance, quite dejected, and remarked to her, "We shall have no flax this year." "Why?" asked my mother, "I thought it looked well." "So it does," he replied, "but there is no flax in it. I have broken off several stalks, and they are all hollow." My mother could not repress a hearty laugh; and informed him, that the flax was the bark of the stalk—that it did not grow inside.

His ignorance of farming, and the consequent disadvantage he labored under in performing every kind of work pertaining thereunto, together with the troubles of the revolutionary war which soon followed, kept him in a state of poverty; and it was with severe toil that he was able to provide the absolute necessaries of life for his family. He was called out several times in his country's defense. He was a patriot, and an ardent friend of rational civil liberty. He was in the battle at Bunker Hill; and also at Cherry Valley, when it was ravaged and burnt by the combined forces of the Tory Butler, and the celebrated Indian commander Brandt. There a brother-in-law of his, Col. William Stacy, was made prisoner; and another brother-in-law, Gideon Day, was killed; but my father gained the fort, and escaped. Col. Stacy was carried into Canada, prisoner of war, where he remained until peace was settled between the contending nations, and the dogs of war called in. The first event that I can distinctly recollect, was the return of Col. Stacy from captivity.

The circumstances which I have briefly noticed, together with the newness of the country, the disorganized state of society, or rather the total absence of primary schools, prevented my father from giving his children that early education which, under other circumstances, he probably might have done. My parents laid no claim to learning; but still they were not wholly uneducated. They could read and write, and understood figures sufficient to transact the ordinary business of life; and my father, as was necessary in his business, understood navigation. But the facilities for obtaining an education in those days, were not as they are now. O, how often have I thought, could I have had the privileges in my youth that young men now enjoy, that I too might have known something. But my parents had little time to teach their children, even as far as they were capable. Their whole time was necessarily engrossed, day and night, (for the midnight lamp has often witnessed, at least, the toils of my mother,) to provide their children bread, and something to cover their bodies, and shield them from the winter's cold blast. And how much gratitude do I owe them! When I think of their toils, their privations, and their solicitude on my behalf, my heart swells within me almost to bursting. I am now a parent; but never until I sustained that character, could I appreciate their kindness. How little do children think of the unceasing solicitude, the agonizing pain and anxiety, that parents endure on their account. But my mother—never had children a better and kinder mother—early endeavored to instil into our minds the principles of reverence toward God, and justice, truth, and benevolence toward man. Nor did she teach by precept alone; her *example* was constantly before us. Her soul was a fountain of benevolence. She was a faithful companion, the unwearied nurse of the sick, the comforter of the afflicted, and a peace-maker in her neighborhood. I never knew her to have the least difficulty with a neighbor; nor do I remember that the tongue of slander ever attempted to assail her. Kind reader; call not this fulsome panegyric; it is but a feeble tribute to departed worth, but the gentle breathing of the heart of filial piety toward one of the best of parents. On each returning Sabbath, at least, long before we knew a letter, our mother would teach us the Assembly's Catechism, and to answer numerous questions from the Bible; and, as early as possible, fitted us for meeting, and encouraged our attendance at church.

But my parents were liberal in their religious sentiments. Although I knew it not for many years—until Universalist preachers began to come into our region of country and publish the Great Salvation—they were some of the earliest hearers of John Murray, in Gloucester, and became rationally convinced of the truth of his doctrine. But when they removed into the country, as the doctrine was unknown, or if known was very unpopular, they said nothing about their peculiar tenets; attended the Congregationalist meetings, became what were then called half-covenant people, had their children baptized, and educated them religiously, in the Orthodox school. But after a lapse of some years, there came into our region, occasionally, strange preachers of a strange doctrine, which produced considerable excitement, and called forth all the bitter censures, denunciations, and condemnations of the standing order as they were called, (the Orthodox Congregationalist,) were capable of expressing. But, notwithstanding their unpopularity, and the cry of heresy, delusion, and danger, my parents would improve every opportunity they had to hear them. The preachers to whom I allude were Caleb Rich, Zephaniah Lathe, and Thomas Barnes. From this time, I began to learn that my parents were Universalists; and they no longer attempted to conceal their faith, but freely advocated it on every proper occasion. And when I became capable of reading, I found, among the few books and pamphlets of my father, some of the writings of Shippy Townsend; and once, on his return from a visit to Cape Ann, he brought home a volume of original hymns, by James and John Relly. These were all the Universalist books I read, until I became fully established in the faith of a world's salvation.

My parents both lived to an advanced age; and lived and died in the faith they so early embraced. My father, by the time he arrived at middle age, lost his hearing to a great degree. As early as I can remember, it was necessary to talk to him very loud to enable him to understand; but his sight remained good until he advanced beyond eighty. He was a man, though of small stature, of a vigorous and healthy constitution, of very industrious habits, and, uniformly, while able to labor, enjoyed good health; but when his sight failed him, his physical powers soon failed, and he was reduced to quite a helpless condition. The last time I saw him, he was 84 or 85 years of age. He took me by the hand to welcome me home; and before he let go my hand said, "I hope I shall die before you leave." He repeated this wish several times during my stay; and said, his mother once told him that she hoped he would live until he was willing to die; and then added, "she has had her prayer answered. I have lived long enough—as long as I can be any comfort to myself, or any body else; and I now wish to depart." But he lived several years longer. He had arrived within one month of the completion of ninety years, when he was "gathered to his fathers."

I never visited the land of my nativity, after the death of my venerated father, until last fall: and lo! the destroyer had left his foot-prints there! The hand of desolation and death had been laid upon my old acquaintances, and a new generation had sprung up in their places, whom I knew not. But a solitary individual of my father's family still remained in the town—an aged widow, my half-sister; who remarked to me, one day during my visit, "This is my birth-day—set it down in your memorandum;—to-day I am eighty-five years old."

The rest of our family, though mostly in the land of the living, were widely scattered, from Vermont to Illinois.

After the death of my father, which occurred in February, 1824, my mother chose to spend the evening of her life with my youngest sister, who married a man by the name of Abel Thompson, and resided in Bridgewater, Windsor Co., Vt.; arrangements were accordingly made, and she went thither; where, in accordance with her desires, she breathed her last in the arms of her daughter. I visited her twice only, after her removal there. She, too, was a person of vigorous constitution, and retained the use of her physical and intellectual powers more perfect than almost any other person I ever knew. The last visit I ever made her, was during her eighty-fifth year; she was then able to ride around with me among our relatives and friends, had the perfect use of her limbs, nor could I discover that her intellectual faculties were impaired. Her memory was bright, and she could relate events both of former and latter years with equal facility and correctness; and my sister has informed me, that she retained the use of her limbs, and the faculties of her mind to the last. She departed this life, after a brief sickness, in the month of February, 1837, in the 92d year of her age.

Thus, kind reader, have I given you a brief account of my parentage. And now allow me to ask, what can you expect to find interesting, instructive, useful, or even amusing, in the life of an individual who originated in such obscurity, and under such disadvantageous circumstances? But you have asked for it, and you shall have it; though you must not expect that I shall frighten you with an exposition of all my follies, nor bewilder you with all the eccentric flights of a wild and volatile imagination.

CHAPTER II.

Birth of the author—Diminutive stature—Tenacity of early impressions—Deplorable consequences of a wrong education—First schools—Learns the alphabet in one day—School books—Proficiency—School teacher—Specimen of pronunciation—First spelling book; Dilworth's; Perry's; Webster's—Goes from home to live—Commits to memory the third chap. of Matt.—Eldest brother goes to Ohio—His return—Death of youngest brother, and feelings on the occasion—Father puts eldest brother in possession of all his property—Discontent—Subsequent course—Goes an apprentice to a blacksmith—Health declines—State of health—Hypochondria—Strange phantasma—Health improves—Stature and weight—Commences study of arithmetic—Proficiency—Religious convictions—Thoughts turned toward an education—Academy—Importunes his father for his freedom—Obtains it—Resolution—Habit of profane swearing—Cause of reform—Hires out to labor—Wages—Goes to Vermont—Enters as clerk in a store—Goes to Boston with a drove—Returns to New Salem—Goes to a common school—First term at the Academy.

My mother had seven children, four sons and three daughters. They ranged in the following order: Rufus, Anna, Ezekiel, Martha, Nathaniel, Mary, and Michael. The youngest died at the age of seven years; the others were all living at the commencement of the year 1844. But ere the earth had completed her annual circuit, two of them, my second brother and second sister, slept in death. The third son is the subject of these memoirs. And—reader, can you believe it? —as I have been informed, nothing extraordinary took place at his birth—no lambent flame played round his infant head, presaging future greatness—no wonderful phenomenon was visible in the planetary universe; but his birth-place was a log cabin—all was still, and nature kept on in her wonted course peacefully and as undisturbed as though nothing more than a common personage had been introduced on this mundane sphere! Nor have I ever been informed that there was any early development of intellectual genius, or greatness; or that any thing peculiarly characterized his youth, except his diminutive stature, which argued poorly for his future usefulness. I have heard my mother—who was herself of very small stature—say, that the fore part of the first pair of breeches she made for me, measured the exact length of her middle finger! Dreary, indeed, must my future prospect in life have been, in the view of my parents and friends. Of what use could such a pigmy be in the world? But to me it produced no concern. I was full of life and glee; and, I presume, a very wayward and roguish child. Indeed, I have been so told; and I can well remember the chidings and corrections of my poor mother, whose heart, no doubt, I have often made bleed by my waywardness. I possessed, I suppose, what phrenologists would call a sanguine, nervous physical temperament—was as light and volatile as air, as nimble as a cat, and as passionate as a wasp; but incapable of retaining my resentment long, or meditating revenge—I could strike and kiss the same moment. And, attracting the notice of every body who saw me, by the smallness of my stature, I became talkative and saucy to every one. O, what a mistake do many well-meaning people make, by talking to such children—by applauding their roguish tricks, and encouraging their boldness and impudence. They subject them to many necessary corrections and chastisements, and help them to contract habits which, if they are ever so fortunate as to abandon, will, nevertheless, cause them much shame, and many heart-burnings, and require strong efforts to overcome. Habits, formed in very early life, make very lasting and almost indelible impressions; and false principles, imbibed in youth, exert an influence almost or quite as lasting as life. A great responsibility, therefore, rests upon parents and guardians of children; and also upon every individual who holds any intercourse with them, or indulges in fondling or playing with them. It was fashionable in my early youth to indulge in telling and listening to stories about witches, hobgoblins, and ghosts; and I had a good old aunt, whom I loved above all people in the world, next to my mother, who possessed an extraordinary faculty for telling such stories; and I well remember my solicitude to hear, and the vast delight I took in listening to them, until my hair seemed to stand erect on my head, and my blood to curdle in my veins, and I would not dare to move five feet from my friends, especially if it were dark. I believed every word true as Holy Writ; and if I stepped out of doors in the dark, I expected most likely to see some apparition, or that old Nick would come with his cloven foot to carry me off for some of my ugly tricks; or that some witch would stick forks into my flesh, or make me fly over the barn, or put a witch-bridle into my mouth, and ride me off; for if they could turn a young calf into a horse, and make him jump over a great river, they could as easily make a horse of me, small as I was. And to confirm these impressions, some of my earliest reading was the "History of New England," comprising a detailed and circumstantial account of the Salem witchcraft. And although the stories made me shudder, I would select them to read, as the most entertaining and interesting of the whole history.—This made me timorous; it did not reform me, but it made me a coward. When I became quite a youth, and thought myself old enough to go into company, if I was caught out alone after dark, I was terrified beyond measure, and constantly looking around expecting to see some supernatural agent that would injure me in some way, or perhaps carry me off bodily; and I was in indescribable agony until I reached home, or found company. And these impressions were indelible. In riper years, after I became fully satisfied of the fallaciousness of all such representations, and abjured the whole theory; and even after my confidence in God and his divine government had given me courage to go any where and every where, by day and by night, and to encounter any danger where duty called; I have often detected myself under the influence of these early impressions. In approaching a dark swamp in the dead of night, or passing some dilapidated and deserted building, or going by some burying-ground; my eyes, in spite of my efforts to the contrary, would wander in search of some ghost. O, how cautious ought parents, and guardians, and, indeed, every body else, to be in the education of children, not to make such impressions upon their pliant minds, and thereby injure their mental improvement, and subject them to so much agonizing pain. But to return to my narrative in detail.

I had no other chance for education but such as I have named, until I was seven years old. I had never seen a school-house, nor entered a room where school was taught, of any description, nor had I learned my letters. My mother, as I have already observed, had learned me many valuable lessons, the impress of which has never been entirely obliterated, but has benefited me through a long life; as well as some which have been a serious trouble to me; and she often attempted to learn me the alphabet; but my heedlessness, rudeness, and frowardness, as often defeated her intentions. But now a school was to be set up in the neighborhood. We had no school-house—such a thing had never been thought of; but a neighbor, having a tolerably large house, would prepare a room, and a teacher was hired for four weeks! I now began to feel anxious to learn my letters, and was highly elated with the idea of going to school. I well remember the day, when my eldest brother took me in hand, and learned me my letters; it was the Sunday previous to the commencement of the school. I learned them all in one day, and never forgot them afterwards; and I attended willingly and joyfully every day through the term, and greatly lamented when the school closed. I may presume I learned fast, considering the elementary books used for our instruction, which consisted, exclusively, of the New England Primer, the Psalter, (Psalms of David, in a volume by themselves, purposely for the use of schools,) and the Bible. You may well conclude we were a backward set of scholars, though some were approaching the age of twenty one; but the older members of my father's family could read, and some of them could write and cypher a little; and this was the case with many of the older scholars. The height of my ambition and pride may be easily conceived, when, before the close of the four-weeks' school, I gained the head of the whole school in spelling. I strutted around, and felt as important as though I measured six feet; and ever after that I was extremely fond of school, and always improved every opportunity afforded me. Schools were set up, about this time, in every neighborhood or district throughout the town, for a short term in the winter season; and, in some of the most populous districts, summer schools were taught by females. We had uniformly, after this, a school taught in our district from one to three months, in the winter; but never a summer school, during my minority; nor did I ever attend a common school one day in the summer season. But I paid some attention to my books during the interim of schools; and, as the time for the commencement of school approached, my pulse beat higher, and I was always one of the first on the ground, and never lost a day, if it was possible to avoid it, during the term, were it long or short. There was no play, no pastime, that could, in my estimation, equal the enjoyment of school. This feeling continued through the whole process of obtaining the limited education I acquired. I shall never forget the deep melancholy and regret that I experienced, when I closed my last term at the academy, that I could not pursue my studies and continue in school as long as there was any thing for me to learn. But, alas! I had not the means, nor any friendly hand to assist me; nor health, nor strength to obtain sufficient means to defray the expenses through the routine necessary, in those days, to acquire a liberal education. I had, therefore, to content myself where I was, and with tears left the school-room, and bade farewell to academical studies. But to return.

My inclination for reading and study was not encouraged as much by my father as my mother. He thought it necessary to keep his children all at work, with all possible diligence, in order to obtain a subsistence; and, indeed, so it was. He had a sterile farm, and lacked the knowledge of cultivating it to the best advantage; and with all our diligence and economy, we could but just struggle through the year, without sinking into abject poverty. He allowed us to attend school very steadily during its term in our own district. But alas for our means of efficient instruction! No school-house was built for some three or four years after schools were set up; but schools were kept in one room of a dwelling-house, and an illiterate neighbor employed as a teacher, who possessed some little tact in the management of children, but no other qualification for a school-teacher. Do you wish to have a specimen of his pronunciation, and to see the advantages I enjoyed for acquiring the rudiments of language, and imbibing first principles? You shall have it—*a b*, ab; *e-b*, eeb, (pronounced long e,, or double-e,)—and so of the rest. The letter *z*, we were taught to pronounce *ezzard*; consequently, it was *a-z*, azzard; *e-z*, ezzard; &c. There, reader! do you not think I enjoyed superior advantages, in my youth, for literary attainments? He was a tolerable writer, however, and possessed some little knowledge of figures. He taught our school, I believe, not more than three terms; and we were after that privileged with a teacher of more correct elementary education. But it takes children quite as long to unlearn what they have learned wrong, as it does to learn all correctly in the first place. Hence, the importance of obtaining competent teachers for the instruction of our children; who thoroughly understand what they profess to know. Our new teacher had quite a task to correct our bad habits, and to set us right. Spelling-books now began to be introduced into our school. The first spelling-book I ever saw was Dilworth's; in which, in the division of words into syllables, he made two syllables of *tion*—thus, *na-ti-on*, for *nation*. The next was Perry's. This was the first spelling-book my father ever bought for his children; and we thought, when we got Perry's spelling-book, that we soon should become very learned people! After this followed Webster's, with his series of elementary books; and we soon began to make some more correct and profitable advances. It is but reasonable to suppose, however, that a child possessing no better advantages than I did, attending school only from one month to three in a year; under such teachers, too, as my first were, and having to apply my hands diligently to manual labor all the rest of the year—could make but very slow progress in learning.

I lived mostly at home with my parents; but at the age of eleven, my father put me out to live with a man in a neighboring town; where I lived one season; or rather, I went in the spring, and remained until the first of the next winter.—But there was no school in that place that I could attend; and as the time approached for the commencement of our school, I became uneasy; and, taking advantage of the absence of my master and mistress, I packed up my clothes and returned to my father's. I complained, too, that they left me alone too much; which they did. They would frequently go from home, and leave me entirely alone until late in the evening, and sometimes all night; which, with my timorous habits, alarmed and terrified me extremely. But the man never came after me; and I persuaded my parents to let me remain at home—a matter which was settled without any difficulty. There was one thing that occurred, while I lived in that family, very much to my profit; and I name it to encourage parents to early teach their children to commit suitable pieces to memory, especially passages of Scripture. The lady with whom I lived was a good reader, and she also encouraged me to read in my leisure moments. She had been on a visit to her brother's, Dr. H., of Pelham; and on her return told me, that the Doctor had been trying, for a long time, to make his son John commit to memory the third chapter of Matthew, but he could not do it. "Now," said she, "I know you can do it; and if you will learn it in a week, I'll give you six coppers; and besides, I'll brag of you over John." This was a great temptation. It tempted both my acquisitiveness and my ambition. I wanted the coppers, and I also wanted to excel. I promised her I would try. Accordingly, I did so, and succeeded. Before the week expired, I had it perfectly, and never forgot it. I, therefore, gained the victory and obtained the reward. And I also obtained a greater benefit than either; for it helped me more to learn to read, than any thing I had ever before done; and inclined me to love to read the Bible, and commit passages to memory. It taught me how easy it was to lay up in my memory such pieces as pleased me, both in prose and poetry; and I soon learned quite a number of hymns, &c. By the time I arrived at the age of sixteen, I became a tolerable reader and speller, and could write a legible hand. Our school, too, was assvming a better character. But an occurrence had taken place in my father's family and circumstances, which rendered me unusually discontented and uneasy.

It is well known that, soon after the revolutionary war, and the establishment of our national independence, a number of the military officers entered into company and purchased a tract of land in Ohio, called the New England purchase, and commenced the first settlement in that now-flourishing State, at Marietta. Col. William Stacy, my uncle, (I call him uncle—he was cousin to my father, and married my mother's sister,) was one of the company; and in the summer or fall of 1788, according to the best of my recollection, removed there with his family; and my eldest brother, Rufus, went with him. This was a source of great anxiety and disquietude to our parents; for this new settlement, being on the extreme frontier, far removed beyond any other important settlement, was constantly exposed to the ravages of the exasperated Indians, who were daily watching an opportunity to make inroads upon them, and exterminate them, if possible. They were under the necessity of fortifying themselves in the surest manner possible, of maintaining a constant guard, of keeping their arms by them, day and night, in all their avocations; and, at night, all to collect and sleep within their stockades, or fortifications; and, notwithstanding these precautions and their sleepless vigilance, the savages picked off numbers of them. The second year that my brother remained there, the inhabitants formed a resolution to plant a settlement some forty miles up the Muskingum river. Accordingly, they went up with a sufficient force for a guard, erected a block house, and about forty young men went on and commenced operations. They established a rigid discipline among themselves, and adopted every necessary precaution, as they supposed, to secure themselves against surprise by the savages. Two of Col. Stacy's sons, John and Philemon, were of the number. The Indians, it is evident, watched their motions, but were careful not to show themselves until they had lulled them into a fatal sense of security. The company began to grow lax in their discipline, and became more and more careless, until the Indians came suddenly upon them, and killed the whole company, except two who alone made their escape to Marietta, and gave the alarm. I said killed the whole company. This is not correct. Philemon Stacy escaped the shot of the Indians by crawling under a bunk in the block house; he was, therefore, made prisoner, and carried to Canada; there he was purchased and liberated by a namesake, and sent back; but died before reaching his family in Marietta. Soon after this melancholy transaction, my brother, becoming discouraged about ever finding a peaceable home in that country, returned to his native land. His return was hailed, by my parents, and indeed by the whole family, as one of the most joyful events they had ever experienced. We had all given him up for lost; knowing his exposure, and hearing frequently of the depredations the Indians were making upon the frontier settlements, we supposed most probably he would fall a prey to their savage ferocity. And what added to our joyful excitement, was that he came suddenly upon us, not having had the least intimation that he was on his return home, or that he ever designed to come home; and supposing, if he were still alive, that he was seven hundred miles from us. We all felt as though our cup of joy was filled to the brim—as though nothing could be added. But we were soon made to realize, that if our joy was beyond increase, we were not elevated above the reach of sorrow and mourning. In less than one month after this joyful event, my youngest brother, the idol of the family, suddenly sickened and died; and my sorrow now was as excessive as my previous joy. I was a very sensitive being, capable of enjoying much and of suffering much; and from the moment he was taken sick, I had a presentiment that he would never recover; and my feelings were inconsolable—I remember them well. Even before his case was considered alarming, by my parents or any one else, ashamed to expose my feelings before the family, I would go behind the house alone, and weep my sorrows there.

These events inclined my father to make different arrangements from what he had previously calculated. His youngest son, who he undoubtedly expected would be the prop of his declining years, had been taken from him, and his eldest son had been, as it were, almost raised from the dead; and he resolved that the latter should never again leave him, if it could possibly be prevented. He, therefore, made him a proposal, which was accepted; and that was to give him, my oldest brother, all he possessed in the world, if he would obligate himself to provide for him and my mother in old age. He, therefore, gave him a deed of his farm, together with all his stock, farming utensils, &c., and took a lease back, during the life of himself and my mother. At the same time he gave my second brother, who had arrived at the age of eighteen, his time; but made no provision for me, only I was to remain at home and work, without any obligation on the part of my brother, either written or verbal, to give me a cent, or provide me with apparel, at the age of twenty-one. My brother soon married, and began to have a family, with a great prospect of having a numerous one, as actually proved to be the case.—Young, inconsiderate, and giddy as I was supposed to be, and really was, I soon began to have some serious thoughts and reflections on my dreary prospects. I had slender opportunity for schooling; must stay at home and work hard for my brother eight years; and yet he was under no obligation to give me any thing, not even a suit of clothes, unless he chose to do so. And, indeed, I saw but little prospect of his being able, with all his diligence and economy, to do more than to support his own family, and provide for our parents. And this was probably all he ought to do; for he had but a small patrimony from my father: one hundred acres of inferior land, with poor buildings, and but little improvements; a small stock of cattle, and a slender set of farming utensils, comprised the whole. This was the cause of my uneasiness; and, as I now approached the age of fourteen, I began to importune my father and brother to put me to some trade; my mother joined her voice with mine, and we prevailed. Though small in stature, I had a pretty good constitution, and had, thus far, been healthy. Different trades were spoken of, but I had little choice; I wanted some trade, and I liked the blacksmith's as well as any. I would have preferred obtaining an education; but, under present circumstances, that was hopeless: my father had no great taste for it, had he been able, and my brother had as much as he could well turn his hands to. A place was, at length, found with a blacksmith; and I went off with a light and cheerful heart to my new home, with sweet hope sparkling bright before me. Phrenologists say I have a pretty large development of hope, and I presume that is the case; for I have lived on hope, rather than fruition, the greater part of my life; at least, in respect to temporalities; but I have been happy, or have, in the aggregate, enjoyed more happiness than unhappiness.

I found my new home agreeable, a worthy, steady man for a master, and a kind and affectionate woman for a mistress. She was a second wife, and had no children; but my master had, by a previous marriage, a daughter a little older than myself, a fine and pleasant girl, who always treated me as kindly as a sister could have done; and I spent the winter, (I went in the fall season,) very pleasantly. I worked in the shop mornings and evenings, and went to school days. I was lively and buoyant, fond of company; and they indulged me in visiting, associating, and playing with the youth of my own age, with whom I soon formed happy and agreeable acquaintances. This was one of the happiest winters of my youthful days. But, on the next spring, my health began to fail; before midsummer I was wholly unable to work; and my mother came and took me home. For several succeeding summers, my health failed me so that I was unable to labor for the most part of the time. In the fall season, my strength would recruit, and I enjoyed very tolerable health through the winter; but as soon as warm weather commenced, I again sunk into a feeble and sickly condition. It was the opinion of many of my friends, that I was consumptive, and would live but a short time; and the physician to whom they applied expressed the same opinion to them. I was not ignorant of their opinion; and it had a tendency, no doubt, to make me exceedingly nervous and hypochondriacal. I dreaded the approach of night; it seemed as though the curtains of death were drawn around me; for I had no expectation that I should live to see the light of another day. I would plead with my mother not to go to bed; and she, always disposed to indulgence, would sit by me hour after hour when her wearied frame required rest and sleep. O, how often have I called to remembrance her maternal kindness, while my heart has bled with conscious remorse at the recollection of my own ingratitude and folly! We feel impatient with people laboring under hypochondria, and vexed at their conduct; for it really seems to us as though they might reason with themselves and overcome it, and banish those strange vagaries from their minds. And it now seems to me as though *I* might have done it; and indeed it seemed so then, each morning. For when I awoke in the morning, and found myself in the land of the living, and saw the rising sun smile upon the earth, and all nature reviving and rejoicing under his genial influence; and the whole animal creation rejoicing and happy, my own feelings partook of the exhilarating influence; I felt cheerful, and could join in the laugh at my strange vagaries of the last evening, and verily thought that I should no more experience them. But, alas! when the sun had passed his meridian and began to sink in the west, an irresistible melancholy would invariably creep upon me; and, as the darkness of the night closed in, in despite of all my efforts to resist it, my soul would sink in the horrors of despair, and I felt as though the frost of death had seized upon the fountain of life. It was a reality to me then, and continued so, until wearied and exhausted nature sank, and the light of another morning dispelled the fearful gloom. O, how much did I suffer! and how much do others suffer under that strange and soul-chilling disease. We do not compassionate them enough. To show its strange operations, I must be indulged in relating an incident. My mother had gone from home, and was to be absent all night. This was dreadful to me, for it seemed as though I could not live an hour out of her presence—and no one else could have the patience with me that she exercised. My eldest sister was at home, but I could not prevail on her to sit up with me as long as my mother had done—she hurried me off to bed, with all the fearful apprehensions of immediate death upon me! I lay trembling a while; but, at length, dropped to sleep. My sleep, however, was short—I awoke—it was dark, and no living being was to be seen! I verily believed I was dying—nearly in the last struggle of expiring nature. I leaped from my bed, ran to where my sister slept, and begged of her to get up and make me some hot drink, for I was certainly dying! nor would I be refused, nor give her any peace, until she complied. After she had made me the tea—it was a matter of indifference what kind—I found I was not yet dead; and consented to go to bed, where I slept quietly until the next morning, when I could join in the laugh about it, as heartily as any one else.

These feelings are as strange, as mysterious, as unaccountable to me now, and were even then, as they are to any one who never experienced them; but they were solemn realities to me at the time. I thought, in the morning, that I should no more experience them. I believed that I could successfully resist them, and I was resolved to do it; but when night came, their death-like feelings again assailed me, and I could no more resist them, than I could prevent the setting of the sun. The bare recollection of these scenes is appaling; and they are as fresh in my memory as though they were the transactions of the last night. The terrific phantoms, the ghostly visages that surrounded me, the frightful chasms that yawned before me, the ponderous mountains of horrid darkness which were about to roll upon me, were enough to curdle the blood in the stoutest heart! I sometimes slept with my brother, and as I saw these fearful objects, I would often cringe and curl up to his back, till he would fret, and push me off; but I dare not tell him what I saw; for I knew he would only laugh at, and deride me.

I have, perhaps, been tediously minute in describing these phantasma, and my feelings under them; but I have done it, kind reader, in the hope that it may excite commiseration for the unhappy victim of them, and soften that harshness of judgment and treatment which they are too apt to meet with from those who are so fortunate as to escape that unhappy experience. I know not that there was more than one soul living that really pitied my sufferings; and that was my mother. Ah, mother! how much is comprehended in that endearing name! Who can endure as much as a mother for her child? Who can exercise that unremitted, that untiring patience? Who can love as strongly, as ardently, as enduringly! Who can forgive follies and crimes, and overlook insults and indignities like a mother! Would to God I had known, at that age, as much of the strength and nature of a mother's love as I think I have since learned—could I willingly have caused her one sigh, one groan, one tear? Alas, my folly, my forwardness cansed her many!

For something like three summers, my health was exceedingly miserable. I would gain a little in the cold season and was able to attend school; but in the summer I became emaciated, and reduced to a mere skeleton. I grew but little, as may be well supposed, when the reader is informed that at the age of eighteen I weighed but eighty pounds. But from that time—and indeed from the age of seventeen, my health began greatly to improve ; my hypochondria left me entirely ; and I gradually gained health and strength until I possessed a healthy, firm and vigorous constitution, and was able to endure as much labor and fatigue as almost any other person. I gained in stature, too ; but never arrived at an enormous size, as the greatest number of pounds I ever weighed was only 125 !

The winter after I left the place where I was apprenticed to a trade, I was able to attend school, and to apply myself very closely to study. I then began to study arithmetic. The book at that time mostly in use in common schools, as well as in academies, was Pike's Abridgment ; and that was the book I used. My teacher was a very good arithmetician, and he took unbounded pains with me. I began in simple addition, went to school but three months, and closed in single position. But my evenings, as well as days, were devoted to study ; and many of them in company with my teacher, who was always ready to instruct me. I saw—I felt the necessity of a close application, and a diligent improvement of my time ; and my teacher boasted of me, which raised my ambition and stimulated exertions to excel. My parents could not afford me candles to study by night ; but I would collect pine knots to make a light on the hearth, and then lie down on my breast with my book and slate before me, and then cypher for hours. This was the only school term that I ever devoted to arithmetic ; but together with other studies, I occasionally learned it, both in common school and the academy, and became so familiar with Pike's rules and characters, that I could take his book, and, without any other instruction, answer any question throughout its pages. In the winter of 1803, I taught a district school in the town of Worcester, Mass. Two young men came to me and wished to enter school. I had previously learned that they had both been school-teachers, and observed to them that I could, probably, be of little or no benefit to them, as I made no pretensions to the higher branches of literature ; and enquired what branches they wished to pursue. They replied, English grammar and arithmetic. I asked them how far they had cyphered ? They replied, through Pikes's Abridgment. "Well, (I said,) that is as far as I make any pretensions, and I cannot engage to teach you." They modestly observed, they did not come to impose on me, nor on the school ; they wished to review their studies, and doubted not that I could be of benefit to them. They came; and brought with them, Pike's full volume. I soon found that they needed much instruction in branches that they had already studied, and attempted to teach; and when I found them approaching the extent of my arithmetical knowledge, I borrowed one of their books, and found I could study enough in one evening to last them a whole week; and had no difficulty in teaching them through the whole term. But to return to my narrative:

My health was such, that I gave up all expectation of being ever able to learn the blacksmith's trade, or follow it, if I could learn it: and indeed I had little expectation of living many years. I thought much of death, and underwent many fearful apprehensions in regard to futurity. I knew that I was a sinner—I had been taught so, and I felt the conviction of its truth; and became fully sensible that, while in sin, there was no hope of happiness here or hereafter. But how to obtain deliverance, I knew not. I wished to be religious; but religion, as I had been taught, was gloomy and forbidding —it was not desirable to live by; we only needed it when we came to die. It would spoil all our happiness in life; but without it we could not be happy after death. It required us to renounce all recreations, however civil and innocent they might appear; to suppress all youthful vivacity, and maintain in the spring-tide of life, the gravity of age! My nature, both the physical and moral constitution which heaven had bestowed upon me, would not admit of such a course; and with my utmost exertions I *could not* attain to it. I was naturally buoyant, full of life and vivacity, and when not depressed with the fearful malady before named, (hypochondria,) I was cheerful, and even vain, in spite of every effort to be otherwise. This was a source of great disquietude, and discouragement. I began seriously to think that religion was infinitely beyond my reach, and I must be a reprobated heir of future woe! I had the opportunity, to be sure, of hearing occasionally a discourse from some one of the Universalist preachers, before named; for, as I have remarked, my parents went, and they suffered their children to go likewise; and I would at the time, receive some encouragement; but my judgment was feeble; I had not power to shake off the prejudices of education, and I dare not trust my judgment, nor indulge in hope. I had been taught that I was natural, and could not discern spiritual things; for I was born totally depraved, and must have a radical change of *nature* before I could be, in the least degree, permitted to trust my own judgment in religion or spiritual things. Under these impressions, and with the prospect of an unchangeable eternity at hand, it may be well supposed that my feelings were indescribable, and my sufferings, at times, almost beyond endurance! My disease lingering, but beyond the skill of the physician—my body wasting and drawing near the grave, and not a gleam of hope to light up the pathway through the dark valley of the shadow of death—

> "But darkness, death, and long despair,
> Reign'd in eternal silence there!"

I believed in God—I believed in a future existence, or thought I did—I had been so taught. I tried to reverence the divine name; but, alas! my reverence was mingled with slavish fear. I looked upon God as an angry, vindictive judge, who would sentence me to everlasting burnings for sin, and for not performing that which I was totally unable to perform, without his special grace, which he had seen fit to withhold! Oh how often, when retrospectieg this part of my life, and calling to remembrance those exercises of mind, those agonizing horrors, have I groaned in bitterness of sou! over the false, the perverse, the wicked education of children! How they have been taught to look upon the best, the dearest, the tenderest Friend that high Heaven can bestow, even Heaven itself, as the most implacable and inexorable enemy! How the uncreated fountain of changeless love has been covered over with the murky, impervious cloud of malignity! and the pliant and susceptible mind has been driven, with fearful apprehensions, from that bosom in which alone it could find peace, and be joyful! I have wondered, from my soul, that there are not ten thousand religious maniacs in the world, where there is only one. And the deplorable consequences arising from a false religious education have fixed my zeal in the cause of divine truth, and led me to more unwearied exertions to disabuse the human understanding of its fatal errors, and root out—out of the world, these blasphemous creeds, the fruitful source of the false religious education of our youth.

As my health recruited, and I began to rise above the phantasma of hypochondria, my mind acquired its regular buoyancy and cheerfulness, and those agonizing fears concerning my future destiny gradually wore off. I began to entertain hopes of living awhile longer; and although I still felt unsafe, unprepared to die, I hoped to have opportunity to make preparation ere the awful hour should come. I was uncommonly fond of youthful company, and of all the recreations and amusements, called civil, practiced by young people in those days; in which I indulged with as much hilarity as my companions. But in my retired moments I found sufficient subjects for serious thought and reflection, not only in regard to the future, but the present. Here I was again, at work with my brother, as far as I was able; and no calculations made by me, or for me by any body else, in regard to future livelihood or means of support. I had given up trying to learn a trade, from want of health and bodily strength sufficient to work at it; and I was unable to perform any kind of labor equal to the generality of boys of my age; nor was there much encouragement to hope that I ever should be stronger. My thoughts and desires were, therefore, directed toward an education sufficient to enable me to obtain some profession, or means of livelihood without manual labor. I had no friend who was able and willing to assist me; I persuaded myself, however, that if I could prevail on my father to give me my time, I could get along some way. I could work some, earn a little; and I knew that my mother would aid me all she could—would help me at least to a few articles of clothing, and I could do with as few as possible; I could manage, if my health continued to improve, so as to go a term to the academy; and this, I hoped, would enable me to teach a common-school; and then I should have better means of prosecuting my studies. There was, a short time previously, an academy opened in our town, which is still in existence, aud has proved a valuable institution. The legislature granted to the town a tract of land in the then province of Maine, for the support of the academy; and when the proceeds of the land became available, it was to become a free-school for the children of the town; but those benefits did not become available during my minority.

After reflecting upon and maturing my plan, I laid siege to my father, with all the earnestness and zeal that I supposed the importance of my design justified, to give me my time. He at first ridiculed the idea; but I have always been pretty persevering and untiring in the pursuit of any object which I had determined on, and which I verily believed was justifiable—was right; and I persevered until I probably were out his patience, and finally obtained my object. And now behold a yonth, not quite seventeen years of age, with health and strength not sufficient to enable him to do the moiety of the work of some boys at twelve, not weighing over seventy-four pounds—strut out into the world, a man for himself! But you may rest assured I felt as large as life. I had obtained my liberty—I was my own man, and could pursue my own course, and my own object, without the interference of any body. The world appeared bright before me; my health was improving; and hope swelled, in my youthful bosom, mountain high. I built castles in the air, without number; for if one exploded before it arose, I had another immediately to supply its place. But, young, frivolous, and inexperienced as I was, I in the outset adopted some rules for my future conduct, and among them one to which I have inviolably adhered through life, thus far; which was, never to allow myself, on any occasion, to make bets, nor gamble in any form, nor play at any games of chance for any earthly consideration. And this resolution, formally, and seriously, and religiously made at the commencement of my career in life, has been of the utmost advantage to me; for whenever a temptation of the kind presented itself, my solemn resolution came up before me, and appealed to my conscience with sufficient force to save me from this vortex of ruin, both of body and soul. I had learned, while very young, to play at cards for amusement, which was a very popular practice; and although, after forming the foregoing resolution, I did occasionally indulge in this amusement, yet I never did in a single instance violate this solemn engagement, which I might have done had it not been for that timely precaution; for I had frequent temptations set before me. But, though I was thoughtful and fortunate enough to avoid one evil, I was not equally so in every other respect. I was now a man, or was to act as a man, and must therefore assume manly habits; and among the most important, and most easily acquired, was that of profane swearing. And although I had been forbidden to practice it, and had never been accustomed to hear it in my father's family, yet I was now at liberty, was in the world for myself, and must try to act like other people. Alas for the habits and customs of mankind! If they would reflect seriously upon the vulgarity, the folly, not to say the wickedness of profane swearing—if they would consider the pernicious effects of their examples upon unthinking youth, upon the rising generation, they would resolutely reject the habit, and hold it in the utter abhorrence it so justly demerits. But because men indulge in it, boys—thoughtless boys, think that to be like men they must swear too! This certainly was the case with me. And although it was with some difficulty I could acquire the habit, (for I really had conscientious scruples about it—my religious feelings instilled by early education, and fostered by a long season of feeble health, were not wholly obliterated,) I at length prevailed, and became a tolerable adept at harsh language. True, I could not go as far as some, and even some of my own age. I could not take oaths. My reverence and fear of God would not permit me to lightly and irreverently use the sacred name; but I could say, swear, curse it, and damn it, with a pretty good grace. But still not this, without compunctions of conscience, and often very unhappy feelings after I had done it; and I have been seriously led to question whether or not any one ever could. I have wondered at the infatuation of men, in pursuing a course so unnecessary, so impolitic, so pernicious in its effects, and which is always followed, I believe, with so much mental pain. But I did not follow it a great while. I met with a check from an unexpected source, which made me ashamed and entirely broke up my habit. I was at work with a man who I supposed would be pleased with some big and manly words. My work vexed me a little, and I damned it with all my might. He dropped his work, and looked up reprovingly and said, "Swear not at all." I felt rebuked, mortified, and ashamed; and said within myself, If he is not pleased with such words, surely no one will be; and I will no longer make myself miserable, nor render myself ridiculous by using such language. And from that moment I broke off from the habit; I felt a justification, a happiness immediately in so doing, which I would not have exchanged for all the popularity of profane swearing that the world could award. But, to return again from my wanderings:

I had now obtained my freedom, and must do something for myself. I had no longer a right to a home in my father's house unless I purchased it, any more than a stranger. I had no money, no resources, was poorly clad, and must provide for myself. I, therefore, let myself to my brother and a neighbor to work, alternately a week with each, for six months, at the enormous wages of twenty shillings, ($3,33,) per month. Was not this an auspicious beginning in the world? and could not one, under such circumstances, afford to build castles in the air? But I worked my time out; and in the fall of the year had procured some new clothes and had a few shillings in my pocket. But my volatile mind would not permit me to pursue what would probably have been my best course, that is, to have staid at my father's, and attended the district school through the winter, (for our schools had assumed a much better character than when I first began to go to school,) but I must try something new—something more congenial with my character as a man.

I had a sister who had married, and resided in Vermont, about one hundred miles distant; and I resolved to go to the new State and try my fortune there. I accordingly performed the journey, walking on foot in company with a brother of my brother's wife. I was received very kindly by my brother-in-law, whose name was Shaw, and was made welcome to a home there for a season; but I had not been there more than a week, when his brother, who kept a small store in the neighborhood, wanted to engage me as a clerk, if I should answer his purpose. I could write a very tolerable hand, was competent in figures, and had, the previous winter, commenced the study of English grammar. He made an examination of me, and pronounced my learning sufficient. Accordingly, I engaged, and remained with him until September following. I then assisted him in collecting, and driving to Boston, a drove of cattle and sheep; and after they were sold, I returned to my native town. I remained there during the winter following, boarded at a neighbor's, and attended a district school. We had, for the times, a good teacher; and I made some proficiency in English grammar. But, alas! to what disadvantage were we subjected, in comparison to present facilities.

CHAPTER III.

Second journey to Vermont—Capt. Shaw—First attempt to teach school—Success—Elder Wm. Graw—Religious awakening and fears renewed—Commences reading the Bible, and obtains relief—Engages as post-rider—Universalist association—Mr. Ballou—Benoni Shaw; his previous religious profession—Association holden in the Court-House—conduct of the sheriff—Mr. Ballou preaches in Barnard—Mr. Young visits Bridgewater—Three preachers only reside in Vt.—Second term of school-teaching—Return to Mass.—Labors on the turnpike in Hardwick—Visits Billerica, and works on a farm—Return to New Salem—Term at the Academy—Enters as clerk of the store of Joel Amsden Dana—Became personally acquainted with Mr. Ballou—Iclination to preach—Ellis Blake's suicide—Feelings on the occasion—Clergy.

In the autumn of this year, 1798, I again went to Vermont; with a trembling hope that I might obtain a place as school-teacher in some small district of that new country, and succeed in making myself useful in that employment. I went directly to my friend Capt. Job Shaw, who was always ready to find me employment, and to help me all in his power, whenever I needed; and entered for a short season as clerk in his store. I had been there but a short time, before a gentleman came to engage me to teach a school, by friend Shaw's recommendation, as I supposed. I presume, however, he felt much hesitation when he came to see me, for his conduct manifested it. To see a chap scarcely up to his knees in height, who it seemed could hardly possess strength of body or mind sufficient to manage a child of ten years old, offer himself as a school-teacher, appeared, no doubt, to him as preposterous and presumptuous in the extreme. However, he at length did his errand; and we agreed that I should enter the school on trial. The school was described to me as pretty numerously attended—near the centre of the town—some quite large scholars—and, worst of all, had been badly managed for a few years, and had obtained the character of a very bad school ; I should, therefore, with the best management and skill, have a hard task of it ; and he had his doubts whether I should be able to succeed : and his doubts were not stronger than my own. But I had never yet tried my skill ; and neither myself nor any one else could determine how I would succeed until I had made the experiment ; I moreover felt very anxious to take that method to help myself along in life, if I should possess the requisite qualifications ; and I resolved, at any risk, to make the trial. I engaged, therefore, for very small wages, and with the express understanding, that if I could not succeed, I should have the privilege of peaceably leaving the school without any hard feelings on either side. I was to demand no wages, if I could not succed to their satisfaction.

The time arrived, and I went with trembling steps to enter upon my new vocation. I had not yet attained to my twentieth year ; unskilled in the knowledge of man, unacquainted with the ways of the world ; and my stature, my beardless face, white hair, and very light complexion, would indicate to a stranger that I had only seen a still less number of years ; indeed, had I called myself only fifteen, no stranger would have disputed me. When I entered the school-house, I found it well filled, and probably one-third of the scholars were heavier than myself, and several were actually older. I felt diffident, and even fearful of the result of my undertaking, and should probably have quailed under the suspicious and scrutinizing gaze of the scholars, and given up in despair ; but I had previously settled matters with myself—had anticipated all this, and made up my resolution to proceed at all hazards. I introduced myself with as much dignity as I was master of,—established the rules and regulations of the school—tried to impress on the minds of the scholars the object and design of their being placed there, and the importance of a close application to study and a faithful improvement of their time ; assuring them of my readiness to cheerfully devote every moment of my time, and every faculty I possessed to their benefit ; and nothing could afford me so much pleasure, and so high gratification, as to see them advance in their studies, and appealed to the intelligence and good-will of the older scholars to help me in maintaining good regulations in school, and carrying into effect the important and interesting design, by a faithful observance of every minute regulation of the school, and a close application to study. My appeal was not in vain ; for I instantly obtained their good feelings, and their faithful co-operation. I determined to be master of the school, if I remained in it ; and I resolved to govern it, if at all, not by a rigid, tyrannical discipline, but by gaining the confidence of my scholars, and securing, from good-will to me, their ready and cheerful obedience to all my regulations ; and my success was equal to my most sanguine desires—not to say expectations, for they were very faint. I laid down as few laws, or rules for the regulation of the school, as I thought would possibly answer ; and I never allowed the least breach or infringement of those laws with impunity, by young or old, great or small. I never resorted to corporeal punishment, save in very few instances ; I could generally humble the most obstinate by talking ; and if that would not do alone, some trifling inconvenience, for a very short time, would uniformly bring to submission. I had not been in school three weeks, before it had the name of being under the best discipline of any school in town, and of advancing with the greatest rapidity. I was so successful, that I was one of the happiest boys in the world—I loved my scholars like children ; and had every reason to believe that they regarded me with equal affection. We established evening schools for exercising in spelling and in other branches ; I spent all the time with my scholars, by day and by night, that I could keep them together, and was never so happy as when engaged in teaching them ; and when it became necessary to close the school, my engagement being out, it was with the utmost reluctance we parted. We all, both scholars and teacher, wept on the occasion.

This proved one of the happiest winters of my early life. My employers were so happily disappointed, (though certainly not more so than myself,) that they called a district meeting at the close of the school, and voted me one dollar per month in addition to my wages, and engaged me for the next winter. This did me vastly more good than to have received the highest wages which the best teachers commanded ; while they agreed to give me the highest wages for the next winter.

During the winter, I boarded with a Baptist preacher[*] by the name of Graw. He had a numerous family that attended my school, the oldest of whom were about my age. I associated with them very pleasantly, spending a good deal of time there in addition to what was necessary as a boarder; for the Elder was always social and pleasant, ever made me welcome to his house, and seemed to take great satisfaction in my calls. He was a zealous man, a rigid Calvinist, possessed a good English education and good speaking talents, with a heavy, strong, thundering voice; and he would pour out the wrath of God, without mixture, upon the devoted head of the impenitent sinner! "They call me a hell-fired preacher," he would say, "and they say right—I mean to be a hell-fired preacher." He talked to me much on the subject of religion; and I very generally attended his meetings. He was rather egotistical, and boasted of the victories he had gained in argument over preachers of other denominations, and especially the Universalists—(for there were a very few Universalists, and two or three preachers of the order, in Vermont, even in those days)—and would often repeat to me his argument. His conversation, his preaching, and his arguments, had a very powerful effect upon me. I verily thought the Elder must be right; I had never studied the Bible very closely, but he had. And, moreover, he was one of the few favorites of Heaven—God had given him the assurance of his election to eternal life, and he was divinely instructed. His doctrine ascribed to God *infinite sovereignty*. He was infinite in knowledge, wisdom, and power, if not in goodness; and I had no right to determine what the goodness of God should do, or ought to do, for sinful man. God had certainly created them, and he had a sovereign right to dispose of them according to his own will—for his own glory. They had no right to complain. The Elder could also quote a great deal of Scripture in support of his theory. I thought, therefore, it must needs be so; and I became exceedingly alarmed. I would try every expedient likely to shake off these feelings; I would reason the subject—"what can I do? —if I am so happy as to be one of the elect, I shall surely be brought in; but if, on the other hand, I am one of the rebrobate—if I was not included in the covenant of grace, if I am not one of Christ's purchased possession, if he never died for me, all my tears, and groans, and all my exertions, can avail nothing; I must, in despite of all my efforts, at last sink down in unutterable and endless woe! I can not convert myself—I can do nothing of myself, so Elder Graw says. The grace of God must alone convert me, must fit me for heaven—I can do nothing, for I am totally depraved —every thought, word, and action, is infinite evil in the sight of God, and even my prayers are an abomination! This was a deplorable dilemma; on whichever horn I seized, it afforded me no hope, no consolation! I must work or be damned—I had no power to work; and if I tried to work, I should be damned for trying! I felt myself sinking down into a state of total despair. But I studiously kept all these feelings to myself; and strove, as much as possible, to shake them off, by mixing in company with my young and thoughtless companions. But, alas, they stuck to me with an unyielding tenacity, until sleep would be driven from my eyes and slumber from my eyelids! Thus I labored for weeks, and for months. I strove to make myself reconciled to my fate, be it what it might—would say, it all must be right, under the divine government. God is infinite in all his perfections, and has an undoubted right to control the affairs of his own dominions; and I *will* submit. If I am finally to be saved, according to his purpose, I shall be; if otherwise, I cannot help it—God has decreed it. I supposed I believed the Bible; and I verily thought that it taught the doctrine of Calvinism. I tried to reverence the divine name—I would say to myself, I will be reconciled to God. But, alas! I would find myself dissatisfied with his plan, and inwardly complaining from the bitterness of my soul. Why did Heaven create me? Why not have let me slept in eternal unconsciousness? Then, surely, I could not have offended him, nor been in danger of endless sufferings! But, woe to me! here I am, brought into existence without any wish of my own; an existence which, at best, subjects me to the agonizing fears of endless misery; and, most probably, chained down by the unchangeable decree of Jehovah to ceaseless, excruciating burnings! And every feeling of reconciliation would vanish in a moment; and all the reverence for the divine character which I could entertain, was that kind of reverence which the most servile fear produces toward the most inexorable tyrant! Alas! it is not strange that Calvinism has driven its thousands into despair and madness—it is rather strange that an individual can continue under its influence for a moment, and not be driven to insanity!

At length, worn out with these ceaseless harrowings of mental agony, I resolved, sink or swim, live or die, saved or damned, to risk the heinous crime of lifting up my soul in secret prayer to God, for light; and to give myself to the study of the Bible, natural and carnal as I was; to try to find the truth therein contained; although I had been studiously taught that I could not understand it, beeause I was a *natural man*; and it was infinitely dangerous to attempt it. But, blessed be God, I soon found relief. I learned from the sacred oracle a very different doctrine from that I had been taught by man. I could find it no where recorded, that the Father made a covenant with the Son, that on condition he would come into the world, and suffer, and die, to fulfil the broken law and to satisfy the claims of divine justice, which required the endless damnation of the whole human race, that he, the Father, would give him, the Son, a certain select number, as a reward for his obedience, &c. But I did find, on the Holy Record, that "God *so loved the world* that he gave his only-begotten Son, that whosoever believeth in him should not perish, but have everlasting life. For God sent not his Son into the world to condemn the world; but that the *world, through him, might be saved.*." (John, 3: 16, 17.) That the "Father loveth the Son, and hath given all things into his hand." (John 3: 35.) That He gave him "The heathen for thine inheritance, and the uttermost parts of the earth for thy possession." (Ps. 2: 8.) That "It is a light thing," saith the Lord, "that thou shouldest be my servant to raise up the tribes of Jacob, and to restore the preserved of Israel: I will also give thee for a light to the Gentiles, that thou mayest be my salvation unto the end of the earth." (Isa. 49: 6.) That he, Christ, "by the grace of God should taste death for *every man.*" (Heb. 2: 9.) That he "gave himself a ransom for *all, to be testified* in due time." (1 Tim. 2: 6.) That "He is the propitiation for our sins; and not for ours only, but also for the sins of the *whole* world." (1 John 2: 2.) That Christ came down from heaven to do the Father's will; and that the Father's will was, that of *all* he had given to Christ, he should lose nothing, but raise it up again at the last day. (John 6 :38, 39.) That "God commendeth his love toward us, in that, while we were yet sinners, Christ died for us." (Rom. 5: 8.) That God "will have all men to be saved, and to come unto the knowledge of the truth." (1 Tim. 2: 4.) And that God says, under the solemnity of an oath, that he "has no pleasure in the death of the wicked, but that the wicked turn from his way and live." (Ezek. 33: 11.) That he "worketh all things after the counsel of his own will." (Eph. 1 : 11.) That "whatsoever the Lord pleased, that did he in heaven, and in earth, in the seas, and all deep places." (Ps. 135 : 6.) "Saying, my counsel shall stand, and I will do all my pleasure." (Isa. 46 : 10.) &c., &c. O, how precious were these truths to my panting soul. How I could press the sacred volume to my throbbing heart, and thank the God of my salvation, for the life he had given me—for existence—for all things! and how cheerfully submit to every dispensation of his government, however afflictive, since he had destined me, and not only me, but all my friends and the whole human race, to be infinite gainers by that existence! I loved God with all my heart—I knew I loved him; and my soul was filled with love for all mankind—for every thing that God had made. I did then, indeed, reverence the divine name, unmingled with slavish fear; for "perfect love casteth out fear." O, how I longed to proclaim this truth—this glorious news of free salvation—to the sin-sick and despairing world, and set the captive free; for I verily believed that the world, or a great share of it, was laboring under the same yoke of bondage which had galled me to the quick, and driven me nearly to raving madness! But I was diffident—exceedingly bashful. I had never been talkative on the subject of religion. I had buried my feelings, as much as possible, in my own breast, and put on as cheerful an appearance as I could, to secrete the sad exercises of my own mind, and avoid observation. But I could not help speaking of the joy of my heart to some friends; and was so enthusiastic in my expressions to my beloved friend, Capt. Shaw, that he exclaimed, "Why, Nat, you are crazy!" I wrote some—not for publication, for I dared not show it to many; and I began to express my feelings in poetry.—Poetry! yes, gentle reader, I wrote poetry. But the world has not been blessed with as much of it as it probably would have been, had not some of my fastidious friends had the impertinence to more than hint to me, that it was not the best poetry they ever saw. And although I supposed it was because they could not appreciate the excellency of it as well as I could, it no doubt had a tendency to make me a little more diffident about exposing it, and to dampen the ardor of my muse. But you shall have some of it before I have done with you; and probably some, too, which several of our splenetic editors declined publishing; but it will do well enough for my book.

In the spring of the year, after the close of the school of which I have been speaking, I was induced, by the persuasion of several highly esteemed friends, to undertake to distribute newspapers through this section of country. There was but one newspaper then, I believe, published in the county of Windsor, and that was called "The Vermont Journal," published in Windsor, by Alden Spooner. Post-offices were not then, as now, established in every town, village, and hamlet through the country, and it was with difficulty that people could get the news of the day through that medium. I had my fears with regard to the result; but the earnest solicitations of my friends overruled them, and I undertook it for six months. My friend, Capt. Shaw, went with me to Windsor, and became my bail to the printer. I purchased a horse, and set out upon my new avocation; but, alas, it was a wearisome job, and proved an unprofitable speculation. My residence was at my friend Shaw's, in Bridgewater, about twenty miles from the printing-office; and I occupied three days in each week on my ride. I would leave home on Monday morning, ride to Windsor, get my papers, and return the same day, distributing them through Hartland and Woodstock. The next day, I would leave home in the morning, go as far as White river, in the town of Bethel, on one road, and return on another, and distribute the papers through North Bridgewater, Barnard, and parts of Bethel and Woodstock; and the third day, go to Plymouth and return. The remainder of the week, I was in the employment of Capt. Shaw, which paid for my board and horse-keeping. Thus I had established my route upon as frugal a plan as possible; but notwithstanding this, and all the economy I was master of, (though, by-the-by, I was never a good financier,) I found myself at the close of the engagement involved in a debt, which took more than all my wages of the next winter to cancel. I had to make out a large sum to the printer; and I had no other resource but the small sums on my subscription list, scattered all over the country. And, before the payments became due, numbers of my subscribers were beyond my reach. Others were slack, and availed themselves of all possible means to evade payment. And one Barlow—he was called a justice of the peace, but a *disturber* of the peace would have been a more appropriate appellative—took measures, successfully, to cheat me out of almost all my dues in the town of Barnard. I discovered, long before the close of my engagement, that the business would not do for me, and made my arrangements to quit it; and I had reason soon to congratulate myself on my success, poor as it was. A young man wanted the route; and I took him round once with me, to introduce him to my patrons and properly initiate him into the business, although I formed the route for myself, in the beginning. But before he had been in the business as long as I had, he found himself in prison for the debt he had incurred. He did not take the precaution that I did, to keep in the good graces of the printer. Whenever I received any sum, however small, even if it did not exceed fifty cents, I paid it immediately into the hands of the printer. This course gained me his confidence; and he would say to me, "Do the best you can—I will not trouble you—you do better by me than any other of my post-riders;" and he was as good as his word. He never sued me, nor even threatened, but waited patiently, and took any thing I could turn out to him.

Though my summer's work was pecuniarily unprofitable, it was, no doubt, to my spiritual advantage. My solitary rides afforded me time and opportunity for thought and reflection; and, before the close of the season, my mind became very well established in the doctrine of God's universal grace, and I was happy. As fall approached, probably in the month of August, I saw a notice in the paper that I was distributing, that a Universalist Association would be holden at the Court-house in Woodstock, in September. On discovering this, my heart leaped for joy. Though I had heard a few Universalist preachers when quite a boy, yet I had not felt sufficient interest in the doctrine, or my judgment was not sufficiently matured, for it to make much impression. I had, during the intense exercise of my mind on the subject of religion, striven to recal to my recollection some of their arguments and illustrations, to get some views of the theory, but to very little purpose; I could get no important relief thereby. But now I felt as though I could hear and understand—as though the seed would not fall on stony ground, or by the way-side, and I hoped not among thorns. As the time drew nearer, my heart beat higher; but, alas! I could get no one to supply my place on the post-route, and, consequently, could only get to the meeting on the last day.

I shall not attempt to describe the sensations I experienced on approaching and entering the house of worship, for it would be impossible. It seemed as though light beamed in matchless glory from above, and heaven had thrown wide open its portals of beauty! The words of the speaker were like a precious healing balm to my soul. There were but three preachers present. Our venerable father, Hosea Ballou, now living in Boston; Mr. William Farwell, and Mr. Walter Ferris. Both of the latter have long since been numbered with the congregation of the dead. Mr. Ballou preached, and one of his discourses was on the parable of the rich man and Lazarus; and it swept away the last vestige of doubt and darkness from my mind. I followed the clergymen around as closely as possible, so as to catch every word—ventured into the council-chamber, in the intermission, where they, together with many other friends, were assembled, and where, also, the excellent choir, led by the celebrated teacher, Mr. West, performed several excellent pieces adapted to the occasion; and the preaching, and the singing, and the social converse, so enraptured my soul, that, young and bashful as I was, I could hardly refrain from crying out, in the language of the celestial messenger, "Glory to God in the highest, and on earth peace, good-will toward men." And I really felt as the entranced disciples did at the transfiguration of the Savior, "It is good for me to be here." And my astonishment was excited beyond measure, when I came to look around among the attendants who thronged the room, and saw several of my acquaintances, who appeared as happy as myself, and whom I had supposed to be violently opposed to the doctrine; and to whom, consequently, I had never dared to express a thought, after I became favorably impressed with a belief of its truth. Among them was a brother of my friend, Captain Shaw, Benoni, whom I supposed to be very rigid in his Partialist faith. Benoni Shaw, together with his four brothers who resided in that country, were, I believe, members of what was called the New-light Congregational Church; with Mr. Seth Ransom as their pastor. They were all, as I thought, rather bigoted; but Capt. Job, with whom I boarded, I considered the most liberal. I was told, that when a brother of Benoni's wife, Mr. Noah Winslow, embraced the doctrine of Universal Salvation, he charged his wife if Noah came there not to harbor him, nor associate with him and by no means sit at table with him. But now I saw this same Benoni at a Universalist Association, with his eyes, his ears, and his heart wide open. I heard him speak of the truth of the doctrine, and with rapture! And he, ever after that, was a warm and hearty believer, and a fearless advocate of it, and a bright and practical exemplar of its moral influence. He departed this life rejoicing in its strength.

I now felt myself in a new world; and although among old acquaintances, surrounded by new friends, bound together by stronger ties than I had ever before experienced. This meeting had a very happy effect in this country. Besides its tendency to lead many into the belief of the truth, who had never before entertained a favorable opinion of it, and to establish those who were wavering, it brought together congenial minds, and introduced them to an acquaintance with each other, which served to strengthen and embolden them in the cause, to extend their influence, and enlarge the sphere of their action; by which means the cause of divine truth advanced with greater rapidity.

An incident occurred at this meeting, which, I think, is worth recording; because it shows the bitterness of spirit which actuated the opposers of this great salvation, and the effect of a calm, dignified, and fearless perseverance in the spirit of kindness. I was not an eye-witness; but I was told of it; indeed, it was a subject of common observation and remark, and had a very salutary effect upon the reasonable part of community; for it led them to make a comparison between the influence of the two doctrines. The friends of Universalism had applied to the proper authorities for the use of the Court-house for the meeting, and obtained their consent; and the doors were accordingly opened. But the sheriff of the county, one Rice, a bigot, without religion, as his character too plainly testified, undertook to frighten them away, by placing himself before the door with a drawn sword in his hand; no doubt thinking that the importance of his office, and a little blustering, would break up the meeting. But, at the appointed hour, the clergy, with Mr. Ballou at their head, walked deliberately to the house, and, as they approached the door where this wonderful majesty of law had placed himself and was flourishing his broad-sword, Mr. Ballou, with his wonted urbanity and pleasantness, addressed the little man in the language of the Savior; " Peter, put up thy sword into his place," and walked by the shame-smitten sheriff into the house. I was told that he hung down his head, and, without uttering a word, walked off to his house, probably with a less-exalted opinion of his own importance than when he placed himself at the Court-house door.

From this time my mind was perfectly satisfied in regard to the doctrine of the Gospel, and the ultimate destiny of our moral race: I had no doubt. I saw clearly the paternity of the divine character, the immutability of the divine nature, the absolute sovereignty of Jehovah,—and the impossibility of the least failure of his gracious designs. And although, in the exceeding deficiency of my own wisdom, I could not comprehend the means, nor analyze their fitness to the object designed, yet I felt that I knew they were sufficient, for God had given his word; and that was all that I sought to know. For I read, in the divine word, this positive, unconditional declaration: "*God, our Savior, will have all men to be saved, and come unto the knowledge of the truth,*"—and that the mystery of his will, according to his good pleasure which *he had purposed in himself*, was, that in the dispensation of the fulness of times he might gather together, in one, *all things in Christ*, both which are in heaven and which are in earth, even in him." I was consequently relieved from a ponderous load which, for a long season, had borne me down almost to distraction. I was now also blest with friends, who were before unknown to me as such, with whom I could associate, and to whom I could speak with confidence of the Great Salvation. About this time, too, (I think immediately after this meeting,) Mr. Ballou entered into engagements to preach steadily, a portion of the time, in Barnard—and although the distance was ten miles, or more, from my residence, I improved the opportunity, as often as possible, to hear him. And during the following winter I also had the privilege of hearing Mr. Joab Young, a Universalist preacher who resided in the State. There were, at this time, three preachers only, who resided in the State of Vermont: William Farewell, in Barre; Joab Young, in Stafford; and Walter Ferris, in Monkton; and I presume not more, if as many, organized societies in the State; but the doctrine began to advance rapidly: a spirit of earnest inquiry was abroad; for the galling yoke of Partialism began to sit extremely uneasily upon the lacerated necks of its votaries.

At the proper season, the following winter, I commenced school again, according to engagements the previous spring; and I know not but I accomplished the task with equal satisfaction both to myself and my employers. On the following spring, however, I found myself not quite even with the world, in a pecuniary point of view; for my previous summer's miscalculation had involved me in a debt that I was not quite able to liquidate ; but my creditor, the printer, gave me liberty to pursue my own course to obtain the means. I therefore left Vermont, and returned to my native state ; resolved, if possible, to find means to pay my debts, and pursue my studies somewhat farther. I had no means, however, bnt to engage in manual labor, my health and strength had much improved, and I felt able to do tolerable work. I soon found employment on a turnpike road, then being made from Boston to Northampton, where I worked in the town of Hardwicke, until the haying season commenced, when the hands were dismissed to attend to that important branch of husbandry. I then started for the canal, which was then being cut from Merrimack river to Boston harbor, with a design to find employment there for a season. Several of my town's people were at work on it ; and from their representation, I concluded I should find an agreeable employment and good wages. But on my arrival, I at once became disgusted ; not simply with the employment, I could have endured that ; but with the society I should be compelled to associate with, and the habits I should be likely to contract ; I therefore turned away, and let myself for half a month to a farmer in the town of Bilerica, to work at haying. I told him I should be awkward, for I had never mowed any ; however, he praised my skill, and appeared quite satisfied with my labor ; and before my time was out with him, I had several applications, and higher wages offered than he gave me. I accepted one of them, and engaged for a month only ; but before my time was out with this man, whose name was Bradstreet, he solicited me very earnestly to remain with him. He said he had pretty much made up his mind to go into the mercantile business ; and if I would remain with him, he would set up a store, employ me as clerk, and give me any reasonable chance I would propose. I had done some writing for him while in his employ, which he approved ; and it was with some difficulty I could excuse myself from accepting his friendly offers. But the fact was, I was in a state of mind ill calculated to qualify me to settle down in any kind of business permanently. There was no business which I thought myself qualified to pursue, that seemed satisfactory. My mind was on the Gospel—I longed to proclaim the glad tidings of Universal Salvation to a sinful world,—a deliverance to all them that were bound—bound down to the most abject slavery, by the heart-chilling and non-reforming dogma of endless woe ! I longed to be instrumental in dissipating the impervious cloud of darkness that hung with fearful gloom over the moral horizon, and freeing souls of immortal desire from their bondage of slavish fear. And although I could not indulge the most distant hope of ever being able in the least degree, to be useful in the ministry, still, the inward desire burned so fervently in the soul, as to render every other calling or employment insipid and undesirable. But I loved the truth too well ;—I regarded the prosperity of the cause too highly to willingly do any thing, or attempt to do any thing, to retard its progress, or bring it into disrepute. I considered my talents infinitely inadequate, and my information and literary attainments vastly too limited, to be in any degree useful to the cause ; and, besides, my unconquerable timidity and bashfulness would be insuperable obstacles in the way, were I otherwise qualified. These feelings totally forbade every hope of the kind, and imposed a veto upon any attempt to qualify myself for the ministry : for such an attempt would only be a subject of just ridicule to the opposer, and would wound the Redeemer in the house of his friends. These thoughts and feelings, however, were buried deeply in my own breast, not daring to breathe the most distant hint of them to the most trusty friend I had on earth. But in every place where I went, I would try, in a timorous way, to find Universalists—to find congenial minds with whom I could commune on the subject nearest my heart. I tried in the family of Mr. Bradstreet, in Bilerica ; but I found little sympathy. The man inclined to be chraitable and liberal, though orthodox ; but his wife had no charity for such heretics. But I found, in a near neighbor, a Mr. Smith, and his aged mother who resided with him, minds with whom I could sympathize ; they were strong and bold in the doctrine of God's Universal Grace ; and thither I often retired in my leisure moments to hold sweet counsel, and converse on the subject of the Great Salvation.

When the time for which I had engaged with Mr. Bradstreet had expired, I put the pittance I had earned in my pocket, and returned to my native town, and entered another term in the academy ; and I entered, as I calculated, for the last time. In the embarrassed circumstances under which I labored, and consequently the length of time I must sacrifice to obtain a liberal education, I considered the attempt preposterous ; and I therefore only now entered to complete an education sufficient to enable me to transact the ordinary business of life with correctness and respectability, in the humble circle in which I moved. I had not the vanity to aspire to distinction ; but I desired to be as useful in my humble sphere as my abilities would enable me to be ; and to obtain a competency for the necessaries of life. I therefore concluded I would study the art of surveying, and then go into some newly-settling country, where I could find considerable employ ; as with that, and teaching common school, which I had commenced pretty successfully, I imagined I could maintain myself, and probably be as useful to society as in any other way. I accordingly purchased books and implements, and completed my study ; and, after obtaining the theory, practised for a short time with a surveyor, who was employed in perambulating the town lines. I had but just completed my terms of study and service, and returned to my father's house to make some farther arrangements to put my designs into execution, when a merchant, by the name of Amsden, from the neighboring town of Dana, called, and wanted to engage me as a clerk in his store. He did not wish, however, to engage me, unless I designed to make that profession a business for life. He wanted a clerk who would realize that he was in an employment he was to follow for a livelihood, and would consequently feel interested in making himself thoroughly acquainted with the business in all its branches ; that he might be both profitable to himself and his employer. And he proposed not to pay wages for the first three months—he would board me, and furnish me with some articles of clothing, if I needed ; and after that, if we were agreed, he would pay good wages. Well, I was about as well prepared for one kind of business as another. My mind was fluctuating and unsteady—no business actually pleased me ; and none that was lawful, and useful to society, disgusted me ; I might as well sell goods as any thing else, and I had had a little experience too in that kind of business ; so, after a little reflection, I engaged to go. There was one circumstance that had quite a bearing to incline me to accept of his proposals ; the man was himself a Universalist ; and my residence would bring me into the immediate neighborhood of Mr. Ballou. Mr. B. then lived in Dana, and preached a part of the time in a meeting-house within a stone's throw of the store I was going to tend ; I should, therefore, have an opportunity of becoming personally acquainted with him, and the privilege of hearing him preach the glad tidings of salvation. And this constituted no little inducement for me to close in with the opportunity.

Very soon after I took up my residence in Dana, I became familiarly acquainted with Mr. Ballou. Mr. Amsden and he were great associates, their residences a short half-mile apart; and when Mr. B. was at home, they were often together. Mr. B. made frequent calls at the store, which gave me an opportunity of seeing him, and hearing him converse; his social, affable habits made him an agreeable companion for all with whom he associated, both young and old; and I soon felt myself easy and happy in his society. But he was at home only during a moderate proportion of his time. His ride, at that time, extended from Barnard, in Vt., to Gloucester, on Cape Ann, upon the Atlantic; and he performed it, if I rightly recollect, once in two months, preaching often, perhaps nearly every day, at intermediate places. His residence was nearly in the centre of his circuit, so that he supplied the desk in Dana as often as once a month. I enjoyed a privilege, therefore, which I prized very highly, at least, in the commencement; but alas, I did not improve it as I ought. I was young, and fond of young company and merriment; and there was a great opportunity of indulging my vivacious propensities; for I was in the midst of a large circle of very respectable young people, of both sexes. But I forgot not my faith, though I treated it with so much lightness in my conduct. I was happy, extremely happy, when the time came for Mr. Ballou to preach in the town, and my seat was never vacant in the church; I listened with such greedy attention to every word, and manifested such deep interest in his discourses, that it was observed by others, and my friends would sometimes say to me, "You must preach." And although their words would pierce my soul, and awaken up the imperishable desire for ever burning there, I would try to treat them with the utmost levity; and I consequently entered more freely into the amusements of my young companions, to repel and drive away those desires, and to convince my acquaintances that I had no such thought, or, at any rate, that I was very unfit to enter upon so holy a vocation. For I knew very well that I was wholly unfit—that I lacked every qualification and every grace requisite to the sacred calling; and when I felt the strongest yearnings of soul to preach the Gospel, I would try to cool my ardor by repeating these lines of Cowper:

"The pulpit—
And I name it fill'd with solemn awe, which bids
Me well beware with what intent I touch
The holy thing."

I treated my desires, as the unfruitful longings of a vain mind, and tried to extinguish them by light and vain conversation, and frivolous amusements, which often made my soul shudder, on reflection. I suppose I had a native propensity to preach; for I very well remember, when a mere child, that after returning from meeting, I would frequently call the children around me, get into a chair, and go through with all the exercises I had been witnessing, with as much solemnity as though it had been a reality. And now, if I could keep the desire in some degree of subjection while awake, I could not while sleeping; for I oftentimes found myself preaching when asleep, sometimes under the most ludicrous circumstances, which would mortify me beyond measure;—sometimes I would make a total failure, and leave the congregation with shame; and at others, would be quite successful. I have often felt sorely vexed with myself, that I could hardly go to sleep without being harrassed with such dreams. All these things had a tendency to make me more reckless in my demeanor, until I felt ashamed to own I was a Universalist. Whenever a person would ask me, "Are you a Universalist?" —(for I could not help speaking of it whenever a convenient opportunity was presented,) I would answer, "No; for were I a Universalist I should be a better man. I am convinced of the truth of the doctrine; but, alas! I do not believe it strongly enough to be denominated a Universalist."

An occurrence took place while I lived with Mr. Amsden (for I completed my apprenticeship, or probationary term of three months, and then engaged for one year, and fulfilled that engagement also,) which had a tendency to enstamp a greater degree of solemnity upon my feelings than I had lately experienced, and to check the rudeness of my conduct. I had formed an agreeable acquaintance with a young man, a little my junior, by the name of Ellis Blake, a clerk in McCarty's store, in the town of Petersham, about six miles distant. We had often visited each other, on business or otherwise, and had formed quite an attachment. He came one day to the store which I was tending, on business; and, as was usual in those days, I set liquor before him; and I noticed that he drank more freely than was his usual habit, for he was always temperate. He had transacted his business, and stepped out of the store; soon afterward I heard very loud and angry words, and I thought one of the voices sounded like Blake's. I had never found him quarrelsome, but quite the reverse; and concluded I must be under a mistake. Still the conversation continued, and grew louder, and more fierce and blustering. I at length stepped to the door, and was astonished to see Ellis Blake in close and violent quarrel with a petulent old man by the name of Woodward, and stripped ready to fight. I immediately ran to him, soothed down his ruffled passions, and got him into the store; but I perceived he was intoxicated. I however soon got him on his horse, and he went home. Shocking to relate, before the sun set that night, I heard that he was dead! It appears that he rode home as fast as his horse would carry him—went into the store where McCarty was—wept, and said he was unwell, that his horse had thrown him; and McCarty told him to go into the house—that he merely passed through the house, and from thence directly to the barn, where he drew off his coat, and, with his silk bandano pocket-handkerchief, hung himself! He was dead when they took him down; although McCarty followed him within a few minutes to the house, and thence to the barn, toward which he was seen to go.

I had never met with an occurrence in my life which struck me with so much horror, or excited in me more gloomy sensations. My religious faith now came to my aid, quickly dispelling the gloom which had oppressed me, and presenting to my mind a brilliant light beyond the confines of the grave. Oh, thought I, how could we endure occurences of this nature, without the glorious hope of immortality? and that, universal—for every individual of our mortal race! I wrote a short elegy on his death, with a few reflections, which I mustered courage enough to show to Mr. Ballou.—He applauded the verses and the sentiments; and I was compelled repeatedly after that, by his request, to recite or exhibit them to our mutual friends. Does the reader wish to know what they were?—Well, you may have them, for I may as well fill up a little space, and close a chapter with them, as any thing else. And you must have, as the biographer of General Marion said, "the real" Nathaniel Stacy; you can make nothing else of him, more or less. This was not the first poetry I had written; but it was the first I had courage to show.

ELEGIAC LINES.

WRITTEN ON THE DEATH OF ELLIS BLAKE.

Hark—youths, and mark the doleful, saddening sound!
 Such solemn tidings reach our listening ear!
A blooming youth, so soon by death cut down!
 Bow o'er his urn, and drop the soothing tear.
His limbs so active, and his visage mild;
 At once, by his own hand, their beauty fled—
The silken halter round his neck confined,—
 The humble stanchions bear the youthful dead!
O, see his kindred weeping o'er his clay,
 Bow to the powerful hand that bears the rod—
"The Lord doth give, the Lord doth take away;
 And blessed be the eternal name of God!"
O, victor, death! to thee we all must bow;
 Kings, peasants, beggars, to thy dart must yield!
But short's thy race, resign thy power must thou,
 When our great Captain drives thee from the field.
Thy fatal dart again thou shalt not fling;
 Nor shall the grave a conqueror be—
We'll sing in triumph, "Death, where is thy sting?
 O, grave! where is thy boasted victory?"
Then shall all be united to the head,—
 Christ is our Head, and we the members be:
We'll sing, "Eternal glory to our God;"
 And in his praises spend eternity!

To this homely poem I appended the following reflections: "Here we may view the uncertainty of life, and the certainty of death, in some form. Our life is not our own, but a few breaths lent us by our all-wise and bountiful Creator; and he has an undoubted right to recal them when he sees fit. It should be a matter of indifference to us whether he makes use of our own hands to accomplish his eternal purpose, or any other method; but it should teach us to submit patiently to the decrees of Heaven, make virtue our guide—

'Wait the great teacher, Death; and God adore.'"

I was rather more of a Predestinarian, when I wrote the above, than I am now.

CHAPTER IV.

The author enters an apprentice to a clockmaker—Mr. Ballou's visit to the shop—Conversation—Engagement to study with Mr. Ballou—Scarcity of Books on the doctrine—No periodicals—No commentaries—An illiterate ministry—Analogy of divine means to introduce special dispensations—First attempt to preach—Renewed Resolution—Meetings in New Salem—Accompanies Mr. Ballou to Mr Babbit's ordination, Jericho, Vt.—Remains with Mr. Babbit, and itinerates in that country—Preaches in Moretown, Bolton, Montpelier, Jericho, Essex and Westford—Opposition—Controversy—Journey to Rutland—Visits Mr. Ferris and Mr. Rich—Preaches in Hinesburgh, New Haven and Salisbury—Engages to teach school—Introduction to, and conversation with, an Episcopal clergyman—Return to Onion River—Visit to Mr. Ballou, in Barnard—Returns to Salisbury and commences school—Delivers his first funeral discourse at the burial of two children in one grave—Association with Methodists—Execution of a Methodist preacher—Preaches in Salisbury, the adjacent towns, and in Benson—Controversy in the midst of a discourse—Success and prospects of the doctrine in Addison county.

At the close of my engagements with Mr. Amsden, he offered to recommend me to some mercantile house in Boston, where I could obtain higher wages; or he would assist me, if I wished, to set up business for myself. But, no—I had done enough at this business—selling goods, by no means, satisfied my mind. It was attended with too much care; and I very well knew it required a better calculator, and a more accurate financier, than myself to insure success; and I could not confine my mind to it. I wanted some employment that would not require much calculation, and would afford a mere competency, while it afforded me time for reading and reflection. There was a clockmaker who had set up his business opposite to the store that I was in; and I formed an idea that his business would be the kind I wanted. I could work at the bench, and think; and, indeed, I could place a book before me, and occasionally look at it while at work, after I had learned my trade; and when I had finished a clock, I could sell it; and get a living in this way, without much care or anxiety. And I was satisfied I could soon be master of the trade; for I had, during my clerkship, taken many opportunities of running into his shop and working; for he allowed me to handle his tools as much as I pleased, and seemed to take satisfaction in showing me the use of them. And, discovering my inclination, he made me an offer, that if I would work for him one year, he would board me, and learn me the trade. This I at once accepted, and immediately, at the close of my engagement with Mr. Amsden, entered upon my apprenticeship. And I was truly the best satisfied with this business of any I had hitherto tried; and my time rolled cheerfully on. I enjoyed the same opportunity of Mr. Ballou's society, and of hearing him preach, as before; and I felt as though I was better improving my privilege.

I had accomplished about one-half of the time of my apprenticeship, and thought I was making pretty good proficiency—had got so that I could make every part of a clock, and put it together; and was congratulating myself on having discovered the means of a livelihood more congenial with my feelings than any I had hitherto tried; when, one day, while at work alone in the shop, Mr. Ballou came in, and, in his usual pleasant and familiar manner, began to handle my tools and inquire the use of them. After conversing a while about the business, he turned to me, and said, with an unusually serious air, "Brother Stacy, what are you tinkering here for?" I looked at him with some degree of surprise, for we had been talking about the business and its prospects, and answered; "Why, Brother Ballou, to get a living." "But," said he, "you will never follow this business for a living." "Well," I replied, "I do not know that I shall. I have tried many ways to support myself, and like none of them very well.—My mind is too unstable to be successful in any thing; and I do not know that I shall succeed in this business; but, at present, I like it better than any that I have before tried."—"Well," said he, "you will not follow this—this is not your business." "What is my business, then, Brother Ballou?" "Preaching," he replied. I was thunder-struck. I know not how I looked; but I felt as though I must sink into the earth. What, (thought I,) sent him here to make such a remark?—Does he mean to insult me? Surely he can not be in earnest; for he certainly knows that I never could succeed so as to be of any use in the ministry. If I should have the temerity to attempt it, I should only disgrace the profession. And I have certainly never given him a hint that I ever felt an inclination to preach, nor any one else. On the whole, I concluded he meant it for a joke; but my feelings were ill prepared to relish a joke on that subject. I must, however, turn it off as well as I could; and therefore, after looking at him earnestly a moment, I broke out in as boisterous a laugh as I could well make, and exclaimed, "Preaching! I should make noble work of preaching, shouldn't I?" "Ah!" said he, still looking serious, "you may laugh, and make as light of it as you please; but you have got to preach the Gospel. You acknowledge you have tried different kinds of business, and feel satisfied with none; and you never will feel satisfied until you commence preaching." His serious look, and his language, indisposed me to laugh any more; and I said, "if you are really serious, Brother Ballou, I will ask you seriously, how you suppose I should succeed in attempting to preach, when you certainly must know that I am destitute of every qualification requisite for a preacher of the Gospel?" "But," he asked, "have you never had a desire to preach?" I replied, "Why—yes—I must confess that I have, many times, most seriously wished that I had the ability, the grace, and the necessary literary qualifications; and then I should rejoice, above all things, in the privilege of proclaiming the glad tidings of the Gospel to the world." "Well, I knew it," he replied; "and did you never dream of preaching?" I answered, "yes; I must acknowledge I have many times." "Very well; I was sure you had," he said, "Heaven has designed you for a preacher, and you will never be satisfied until you enter upon the work." "But, Brother Ballou!" I replied, "I have not the qualifications—my learning is not sufficient; and I have never made myself sufficiently familiar with the Bible to defend the doctrine, in the face of its enemies, successfully. And, besides all that, I have not confidence enough to speak in public; and were every other qualification ample, I should only wound the cause, were I to attempt it." "Your learning will do," he replied, "you can study the Bible, and practice will overcome your diffidence. You are welcome to my house, to the use of my books, as long as you need them, and to all the assistance I can give you." Thus we conversed for a long season; I raising objections and difficulties, and he removing them, until, at last, they were overcome; and, with much trembling, I accepted his generous offer. I settled with the man for whom I worked, and, the next week, entered Mr. Ballou's study.

But, alas, for the books to assist me in acquiring a knowledge of the theory of Universalism, save the holy Bible itself! His study, nay the world, did not contain them. His library, at that time, was very limited. There were no works extant, or scarcely any, on the doctrine of Universalism, except the Bible. True, Winchester's Dialogues, and his Lectures on the Prophecies, were published. The Dialogues I had read, but the Lectures I had never seen. I also read Petitpierre, on Divine Goodness, and, shortly after this, Relly's Union; and these, I believe, were all the books I ever read on the theory of Universalism, except the Bible, before I commenced preaching. But the Bible was my study, and Mr. Ballou my commentator.

When I look around me now, and see the facilities which young men enjoy to prepare them for the ministry, and help them along in the commencement of their labors, and compare them with the privileges which I enjoyed, and those of my brethren who entered the ministry before me, or about the same time, I envy them not; but, while I bless God for their advantages, I am filled with astonishment at the success which attended our labors. As before remarked, there was scarcely a work extant on the subject of Universal Salvation—not a periodical in the wide world devoted to the cause, or that would dare to admit a word in favor of it in its columns. There was not a living preacher in America, (for Mr. Winchester was dead,) who had ever put pen to paper, to write a word on the doctrine, except their discourses; and very few of them were written, and fewer still found their way to the press. And, with all these embarrassments, we had to confront a well-disciplined and learned ministry; a popular and well-organized church, with a pampered and influential priesthood at its head, ready to scorn, frown, or brow-beat every thing that opposed their favorite dogmas, or their spiritual pride, or their temporal interests; while there was scarcely a preacher in our ranks who professed the advantages of an education! Is it not, then, supremely astonishing that we succeeded at all? No—no! for the work was of God, not of man. And this is the course which God always pursues to manifest his own power, to reveal and establish his own truth, and display his own glory. When about to reveal a new dispensation, or establish a truth not hitherto made known, contrary to the traditions and prevailing prejudices of the world, Divine Wisdom ever chooses "The foolish things of the world to confound the wise," "the weak things of the world to confound the things which are mighty; and base things of the world, and things which are despised, hath God chosen, yea, and things which are not, to bring to nought things that are: that no flesh should glory in his presence." When God would deliver the children of Israel from the iron oppression of Pharaoh's arm, he took a refugee, an outcast from the house of Pharaoh, a wanderer in a strange land, keeper of the flocks of Jethro, priest of Midian; and sent him to Egypt, to confound the wisdom of Pharaoh's magicians, and overthrow the gigantic power of that monarch. When he would deliver his terror-stricken people from the exterminating power of the Philistine host, he took a stripling from the sheep-fold, to kill the boasting Goliah of Gath, and scatter his army. And when the Savior of the world would make bare his mighty arm for the deliverance of our fallen race, he passed by the wise, the great, and the renowned, and selected humble, illiterate fishermen to be the first recipients and promulgators of that truth which, in its progress, should overset kingdoms, demolish empires, and overturn the existing order of things throughout the whole world; and renovate, reform, and remodel it upon a permanent basis of righteousness. It is not strange, then, when God would reform the wandering and back-slidden church, and bring it out of the wilderness, that he should make use of such means to re-establish his own truth; and to convince the world that the truth and the power were of God, and not of man. Indeed, it would have been strange had it been otherwise.

I remained with Mr. Ballou but a short period; and, when at home, my time was devoted to the careful study of the Scriptures, hearing Mr. Ballou's comments on them, (for he was always ready to assist me, and answer any question I proposed to him,) to arranging discourses on particular subjects, and writing sketches of sermons. I also traveled with him to his appointments, very generally, that I might enjoy the benefit of his private conversation, as well as his public discourses; for he had now done riding to Vermont and Cape Ann; and his circuit, if I mistake not, was wholly confined to the county of Worcester, the towns of Dana, Brookfield, Charleston, Oxford, Sturbridge, &c.

It was in the month of October, 1802, if I rightly recollect, in the 24th year of my age, that I entered the study of Mr. Ballou. I had been with him not to exceed one month, when, one Sunday morning, being his appointment in Dana, after we had reached the village, and called at the house of our friend Amsden, Mr. Ballou was seized with a violent pain in the head, and came to me with his hand on his forehead, saying, very mournfully, "Brother Stacy, you must preach to-day; for I am in such violent pain, I can not." It was a dark, lowery morning; very few had assembled, and, in all probability, the congregation would be composed wholly of our particular friends. I looked at him to see if he was really in earnest; and seeing that he looked quite serious, I replied, "Why, I guess you can preach, well enough; and, besides, you know I can not make an attempt at beginning here, among my familiar acquaintances,—I should be confounded, and break down at once. Moreover, if you had any idea of setting me to preach to-day, you should have informed me before we left home. I have some manuscripts which I could have taken for assistance; but I have now not a scroll of writing with me. I cannot attempt to go into the desk to-day." "I am glad," he said, "you have no writing with you; it would only be a trouble to you. You must learn to preach extemporaneously; and the better way is to begin in the first place." "But," I answered, "I cannot attempt it to-day; and I never can begin here. I must go among strangers in the first place; I shall feel less embarrassment there, I'm sure. Here every body knows me, and I shall certainly break down under their suspicious gaze." "No," he said, "this is the very place; and this is the time for you to begin. There will be but a small congregation, to-day, and these, all our special friends. They know you are designing to preach, and they all want to hear you; and they will be ready to overlook your diffidence, make every allowance, and pardon every blunder; and when once you have made your *debut*, the way will be broken, and you will begin to feel a freedom. And, besides, you may say just what you please, and I'll get up and prove it all true, by Scripture;" and with that he turned away, leaving me confounded, and almost stupified. In a few moments he returned, with some half-dozen of our friends, who surrounded me with, "Brother Stacy! come, preach to-day;—this is your time to begin—the very best time you ever can have; and when once you have made a beginning, the worst will be over; and the sooner you begin the better." By their united importunity, I was at length led, "like an ox to the slaughter," into the desk! But Belshazzar's knees could never smite together more violently, when he saw the hand-writing upon the wall, than did mine when I arose to address the congregation! They were all my intimate acquaintances, and they gazed at me with astonishment. They had, indeed, been made acquainted with my determination to try to preach; but they did not expect it that day, nor, probably, ever expect that I should attempt to make my debut in that place. I was not, however, afraid of their censure; I knew they were friends to the cause, and friends to me. But I felt my own insufficiency, my own nothingness; and the absolute preposterousness of attempting to teach those whose experience was so much greater than mine, and whose knowledge must, consequently, far exceed that of mine. But notwithstanding that, I felt no regret that I had resolved to enter the ministry; no inclination to give up exertions to become a useful laborer in the vineyard, but rather a renewed resolution to persevere; and I devoutly prayed for strength, and boldness in the good cause. The congregation took their seats, and I arose, and with a trembling voice read a hymn, or rather a psalm, for we used Watts' psalms and hymns. And here I made a blunder in the outset—I read a psalm and called it a hymn; and the choir would not have found it had not Mr. Ballou corrected the mistake. This added to my embarrassment, and I began to fear that I should not be able to tell where my text might be found, nor read it right, if I could find it myself. However, they sung, and I arose, made a short prayer, and put out another hymn correctly. After the choir had concluded singing, I again arose, and it was well that I had a desk to lay my bible on, and to lean against, otherwise I felt sure I could not have seen a letter, and it is very questionable whether I should have been able to stand up. But I opened the bible and read, I guess, intelligibly, the 8th verse of the 40th chapter of Isaiah: "The grass withereth, and the flower fadeth; but the word of our God shall stand forever." I spoke probably twenty or twenty-five minutes; but I attended to every proposition of my text, and finished my discourse. Mr. Ballou then arose and closed the service; and it appeared to me, that I never heard so fervent and pathetic a prayer uttered by mortal man before. I heard no more of Mr. Ballou's headache—he was well enough, as far as I could discover, when he got me into the desk; for he made no complaint in the afternoon, but preaehed like an Apostle. I told him afterwards, and I always believed it, that his headache was feigned; though I could never make him own, or deny it. After we had left the meeting-house, I asked Mr. Ballou how I got along with my discourse? For, said I, it is nearly impossible for me to recollect any thing I said. O, he replied, you did very well—I thought you sometimes made rather long pauses between your sentences; but you preached a better sermon than Mr. Babbit did the other day. This I set down for what it was worth; for I supposed it was said merely to encourage me. Mr. Babbit had been preaching about two years; and the discourse he alluded to, was called a very good discourse. But Mr. Ballou used every possible means he could devise to inspire me with confidence, encourage, and help me along.

The way was now broken, I had opened my mouth in public, as an advocate of the doctrine of God's Universal Grace; and I must now strive to keep my armor bright for the contest, and be always ready to defend the truth against the attacks of its enemies, and to answer such calls to speak in public, (for I dare not call it preaching,) as I should receive. I therefore applied myself closely to the study of the inspired word, to watchfulness and prayer, that I might be found clad with "the whole armor of God; and having done all, to stand." For I now resolved, God being my helper, to devote my life, with all the talents he had given me, to the promulgation of the Gospel, with all faithfulness and perseverance, to the end.

My second attempt to address a congregation was at my own father's house. All this was entirely contrary to my calculations, when I commenced my study, and consented to try to preach. I designed to study with Mr. Ballou until I thought myself pretty well prepared, then get him to give an appointment somewhere among entire strangers, at least, for the first time; where, I concluded, I should feel less embarrassment than among acquaintances. But Providence otherwise had ordered it; I had commenced among intimate acquaintances, and it seemed to be necessary I should persevere among them. I went home on a visit soon after my first attempt; but the news of my attempt had preceded me, and curiosity, if nothing more, was excited; the neighbors and my old associates wanted to hear, and they would not be denied; nor was it so difficult a task to make up my mind to gratify them, as it was to commence speaking in the first instance. An appointment was therefore given out; and I endeavored to impress on the minds of my auditors the solemn importance of religion, as well as to illustrate and defend the despised doctrine of Universalism. My third and fourth were delivered at the house of a near neighbor of my father; and my fifth at the house of a brother-in-law, in another part of the town.

The above-named were all, or nearly all, the discourses I delivered before I left Massachusetts and went to Vermont. Mr. Babbit, whose name has been mentioned, had accepted an invitation from a small society in Jericho—or rather from an individual of that society, Mr. John Thompson, father of the celebrated Dr. Thompson, author of the Thompsonian theory of physic—to settle with them, for a season, and had removed his family into that town. Mr. Thompson agreed to furnish him with a house and barn, provisious for his family, keeping for a horse and cow, and fuel for his fire, for one year, in addition to what he would receive from the societies to which he engaged to preach. The society had applied for his ordination, and Mr. Ballou was chosen as one of the council. In December, 1082, he started for the place, and I accompanied him. Mr. Babbit was anxious that I should remain with him. There was a great field for labor around him, and numerous and urgent calls for preaching more than he could possibly supply; for there was no other preacher of the order in all that part of the state. I was young, just entered upon the ministry, and this was a right field for my labors; I should grow up with the young societies, &c.

I therefore consented to remain; and spent the winter in in that region. My first discourse in Vermont was delivered January 20th, 1803, at the house of Esq. Hazleton, in Moretown, on Onion River. I made Mr. Babbit's residence my home, Mr. Thompson extending his charity also to me; but I extended my labors up Onion River as far as Montpelier, and through the towns of Moretown, Bolton, Jericho, Essex, and Westford. I had as many calls as I could well attend to; but, during the winter, also found some opportunity for reading; and Mr. Babbit was a tolerable cemmentator for me. I also wrote out some discourses in full.

Although I suffered much from diffidence, in my public exercises, yet I found that I gradually gained confidence, could command my feelings, and my recollection better, and began to feel more encouraged that I should be able to overcome my timidity entirely ; and the constant opposition I met with, from opposers of the doctrine, had a very great tendency to enable me to do so, in a great measure. I was but a boy, inexperienced ; and this encouraged opposers to make attacks upon me, on every occasion. I scarcely delivered a discourse, or even entered a house to warm or refresh myself, but I had to meet an opposer in argument. I sometimes felt a little abashed at the first onset ; but my confidence in the truth of the doctrine, and my zeal for its promulgation, would soon inspire me with courage, and I would defend it, if not with the skill, yet with all the boldness of a veteran.

One evening, at the close of a discourse delivered in a well-filled school-house, in the town of Westford, three men came upon me altogether, with their denunciations of the doctrine I had advanced, and in a clamorous manner began to ask me questions. I said to them, "Gentlemen, have the goodness to speak one at a time, and give me time to answer, and I'll wait on you with pleasure, as long as you desire ; but there must be some order, or I cannot give intelligible answers." They seemed a little ashamed at their unpoliteness, and concluded to adopt that course, though they all seemed resolved to have a stroke at me. One of them stepped forward and put a number of questions, which I answered as well as I could ; and so answered, as at least to confound him. When he drew back, the second came, who also, soon gave place to the third. This was a valiant soldier, filled with holy wrath against such heresy and heretics—his zeal was warmed to a high degree, and his voice trembled with emotion, as he stepped into the arena, with the courage of a Napoleon, determined to have me down, by fair play, or by foul. His arguments were hard almost as brick-bats, but made no impression on me, and very little, I apprehended, on any member of the audience ; for they were heated so highly, that they exploded before reaching the object at which they aimed. I endeavored to keep cool, though it was rather difficult amidst such showers of hot balls ; but I treated his arguments with all the candor, at least, they merited. As defeat seemed to stare him in the face, he resolved to make one bold and irresistible effort, which, undoubtedly, he designed should close all argument, and for ever seal up the mouths of Universalists ; and he took (reader, don't be surprised out of your senses) this invulnerable position, wkich I give in his own unmistakable language: "If you have proved the salvation of all men, you have not proved that all women will be saved!" There, reader! will you ever dare again to open your mouth, in favor of Universal Salvation? Will you not now give it up, and come to the conclusion, almost, that it is right for some people to be endlessly miserable, inasmuch as their attachment to that cherished and beloved dogma is so violent, that they would thrust women into their hell, or even rather go there themselves, than have it fail! This remark tended more to confound me than any thing the man had said; for I felt such a degree of astonishment, mingled with disgust, that my first impression was to treat it with silent contempt. But, thinking it possible that there might be some in the congregation (for none had withdrawn) weak enough to take it for argument, I thought it best to leave no possible chance for misconception. I therefore looked at the man for a moment with indignation, for his whole demeanor had merited nothing but contempt—and replied, "I am truly astonished, sir, that a man professing to be a gentleman, and a Christian, should condescend to resort to so mean a subterfuge. Your remark is unworthy a reply, it merits only contempt: but for the sake of those that stand by, I will merely remark that the Apostle says, 'There is neither Jew nor Greek, there is neither bond nor free, there is neither male nor female; for ye are all one in Christ Jesus.'" The man, manifestly, turned away ashamed; the congregation broke out into a laugh, and the controversy closed.

Mr. Babbit had some business to transact in Rutland, near a hundred miles to the south; and in the month of March I volunteered to go and do it for him. This enabled me to visit Mr. Ferris and Mr. Rich, whose places of residence lay on the route. Mr. Rich had accepted the invitation of a society recently organized in the town of New Haven, Addison county, to settle with them, and a few weeks previous to this had removed his family from Warwick, Mass., to that place. Mr. Ferris furnished me with letters of introduction to friends in the town of Salisbury, where I delivered a lecture on my way out, and made an appointment for a Sabbath on my return. In Salisbury, on my return, I was solicited to teach their school, the ensuing summer; and as it became necessary to resort to some means to provide the necessaries of life, (for I had not probably received to the amount of five dollars for all my labors since I entered the ministry, although

I had traveled many hundred miles,) and as there appeared also a promising field for my sacerdotal operations, I readily entered into an engagement to teach their school for four months, commencing the first of May. On this journey, I also delivered discourses in New Haven, at Mr. Rich's ; and in Monkton, or rather Hinesburgh, in the neighborhood of Mr. Ferris'. In New Haven I met Richard Carrique, who soon after this became a preacher, and labored in the connection for many years, with acceptance and good success. Mr. Rich remarked to me, after I had delivered my discourse in his house, in which I suffered an unusual embarrassment, probably on account of his presence—that he perceived the "root of the matter was in me," "but (said he) you need more experience ;" and he gave me much good counsel and fatherly advice. He was an old and faithful laborer, and a good man. He was one of the earliest preachers of the doctrine in America, and though not a learned man, was a sound reasoner, and an able advocate of the truth. At Hinesburgh, after meeting, Mr. Ferris introduced me to a Mr. Catlin, an Episcopalian clergyman, who was present. He said he did not do it before meeting, lest it should embarrass me. It might have done so ; but as it was I enjoyed an unusual degree of freedom in my discourse, which much flattered me that I should soon be able to conquer my unhappy diffidence. Mr. Catlin gave me an invitation to call on him ; and as I should pass his residence the next morning, I agreed to do so. I called and spent some hours with him the next day, and enjoyed a very agreeable interview. He showed me a discourse in MS., which he had delivered from the same text that I made use of the evening before ; and on comparing the discourses, they proved very similar. But he must oppose Universalism a little, as it appeared in the sequel, merely to try my strength. He brought another MS. which he had written and delivered, on the subject of the sheep and goats, in Matt. 25th, which he had treated in the common Orthodox way, making it a representation of a day of final judgment, &c., laying great stress upon the Greek word rendered, *everlasting* and *eternal.* He asked me if I was a Greek scholar ; and being informed that I was not, he went and got his Greek Testament, and manifested much solicitude to show me that the original word was the same, in reference both to punishment of the wicked and life of the righteous. I remarked, that although not a Greek scholar, I was aware of the fact he stated ;

and I considered the words of equal import; and the different conditions to which they were applied, in that parable, of equal duration. Well, how could I get along, then, with the doctrine of Universal Salvation? "Mr. Catlin," said I, "will you answer me, frankly, two or three questions?" "Yes." "Well, sir, is our immortal salvation of grace—pure grace? or is it a reward for works that we have done?" "Oh, it is of free grace, to be sure, not a reward for the works of the creature." "Well, sir, will you have the goodness to read your text again, or hear me read it? 'Come, ye blessed of my Father, &c.—For I was an hungered and ye gave me meat, &c. And inasmuch as ye did it unto one of the least of these, my brethren, ye have done it unto me.'" Now, is not the eternal life, actually and truly a reward for those deeds of benevolence and charity? Is there any thing like free grace, in the bestowment of this blessedness?" "No; I must confess there is not—it is plainly a reward for works." "Well, sir, is the doctrine you have drawn from this text correct, then?" He answered, with a smile, "No; I must confess it is not." And then he began to talk more freely with me on the doctrine of God's Universal Grace; and finally acknowledged that he was as strong in the faith of it as I was. He had been making it the special subject of his study for some time, and had become fully convinced of the truth; but he hesitated about declaring it publicly. He did not know that the time had fully come to publish it to the world; perhaps they would make a bad use of it—it might lead to licentiousness, &c. I replied, that course might do for him, but it would never answer my feelings. I could not be a hypocrite; if I preached at all, I must openly and boldly preach what I believed God had revealed as his truth; and leave the event in the hands of infinite Wisdom. Nor had I any fear that that truth which converted me, and made me love God, and all his works—love righteousness and hate sin, would have a bad effect upon others.

This interview constituted a subject for thought and reflection during my ride to Jericho. It is probable, quite probable, that there are many, perhaps hundreds of the popular clergy in America, in the same situation of Mr. Catlin; who are rationally convinced of the truth of Universal Salvation, but from some cause, either the fear of losing their popularity or their salaries, or the dread of meeting opposition, or the timidity produced by that slavish fear, under whose influence they have so long groaned; think it "better to be on the safe side," to secure the favor of both parties; and say, "Good Lord and good devil," and thus play the hypocrite—bury the treasure they have found among the rubbish of human creeds and formularies—and, in mingling with the opposers of divine truth, if they do not inveigh against it with virulence, say nothing publicly in favor of it, but, by all means, say enough to make the world think they are no Universalists. Alas! whatever they may think, they are not Universalists. Their understanding, probably, is convinced that the Bible teaches the doctrine; for they very well know that it does not teach endless misery; they know that the most erudite and learned among them can not successfully defend his theory against an illiterate stripling to whom God has taught his sacred truth. But this truth has never reached their hearts; if it had, they would never make the puerile plea, that they feared it would lead to licentiousness—they would know better, and find a refutation of it in their own hearts; nor could they resist the inclination to "proclaim it upon the house-top"—they would feel, that if they "should hold their peace, the stones would cry out." I saw Mr. Catlin once after this, at Mr. Ballou's, in Barnard; and indulged a hope that he was coming out in defense of the Gospel, but he never did, or he never united with our connection; and I heard no more of him.

I had made several appointments in the region of Onion River, to fulfil on my return, previous to my journey to Rutland. These I felt under solemn obligation to attend to: for I had never, yet, disappointed a congregation by failing to fulfil my appointments. I knew well that nothing, scarcely, could operate more to the disadvantage of a cause, than to have its advocates manifest an indifference and carelsesness in fulfilling their appointments. I was aware that I could not preach very well; but I set out with the resolution to make amends for that deficiency, as far as possible, by a scrupulous punctuality in attending all appointments which I made. And I have, through the whole period of my ministry, of over forty years, made but very few disappointments considering the extent of my itineracy. I have traveled, repeatedly, through storms, and over roads which most people would think unendurable and impassable, for miles on miles, to meet appointments, when I was confident people would think it a hardship to travel a half-mile to attend meeting. But that would not excuse my neglect. I had made the appointment—God had given me health and strength to endure the fatigue, and I must be there; that people might be sure, when I made an appointment, they need fear no disappointment, if they felt disposed to attend. I have very often heard people say, that they were more disappointed in seeing me on the ground, than they would have been at my absence

This had been a very cold winter. I noticed, during the months of January and February, forty days or more, that it snowed more or less every day; or rather the air was filled with a kind of frost, and if the sun showed his face at all, it was a pale face, looking despiaringly through a gloomy and frosty atmosphere. It was not warm enough, during the period I have mentioned, to form an icicle on the south side of a building. But through this freezing atmosphere, and amid a still more chilling moral frost, produced by the soul-freezing influence of human creeds, the belief in God's free, universal grace enkindled sufficient warmth of zeal in my breast to keep me alive, and propel me forward in the good cause.

I had now spent nearly four months, itinerating in this region, and proclaiming free grace to all to whom Providence gave me access. I had formed many agreeable acquaintances, among whom I may name Mr. John Thompson, of Jericho; Esq. Knickerbocker, of Essex; Esq. Hazleton, of Moretown; Capt. Hazleton, of Westford; and many others; and I had reason to believe, I had seen some fruits spring up under my feeble labors. But the time had now arrived (the latter part of April) when it became necessary to take leave of this section of the Redeemer's vineyard, and bid farewell to the friends I have named, never more to meet them in the flesh; for I have never since been able to visit that section of country, although I have earnestly desired it.

I returned to Salisbury sufficiently early, before commencing my school, to afford me an opportunity to cross the mountain and visit my friends, in Windsor county. Some time during the preceding winter, Mr. Ballou had removed his family from Dana, Mass., to Barnard, and settled with the united societies of Woodstock, Bridgewater, Barnard, and Bethel. I made him a short visit, went to Bridgewater, where two of my sisters resided, and where I had spent parts of several years, in early life. Here, by the request of friends, I preached one Sunday, and delivered a lecture at the house of my old friend, Captain Shaw, by the special request of his lady. She was not at that time a Universalist, but a special friend to me ; and, many years afterward, I had the pleasure of meeting her in the State of New York, and of finding her happy in the faith of a world's salvation. On my return to Addison county, I also spent one Sunday in Rochester, where I had a brother, and gave two discourses to respectable congregations. I believe there had never been a discourse delivered in that town by a Universalist preacher. I reached Salisbury in season to commence my school, according to engagement.

The ensuing summer, my time was employed in my school, in which, I believe, I was tolerably successful. I also preached in that and the neighboring towns on Sundays, and delivered lectures occasionally. I had been there but a few days when I was called, for the first time, to administer the consolations of the Gospel to souls in heavy and deep affliction. Mr. Abner Moore, one of the members of the district, and one of the few Universalists in that place, lost two children, all that he had, in one day, by that fatal disease, dysentery; and they were buried in one grave. This was an uncommon and mournful circumstance; much sympathy was manifested for the afflicted family, and a numerous and mixed congregation assembled on the occasion. I had never before been called to deliver a funeral discourse, and I felt some degree of embarrassment, as well as great sensibility for the afflicted family. I have always been much subject to the influence of sympathy on such occasions, and frequently found it difficult to so control my feelings as to allow me utterance. But I devoutly prayed for strength, and received it. I read for a text, Rev. 21 : 4. Good attention was given to the discourse of the stripling; and I had reason to believe that the result was favorable to the cause of divine truth. I had several other calls to attend and officiate at funerals, during the summer, in that and the neighboring towns.

My school was large, and a majority of the district were Methodists. I boarded around among them, united in their family worship, and soon cultivated a social and friendly intercourse, and received numerous expressions of Christian charity, although they considered me in great error in doctrine. There was a society, or class, as they called it, organized in the place, and they had regular circuit preaching on Wednesday, each week, at four o'clock, P.M.; and I uniformly so arranged my school as to dismiss it early enough to attend; and was generally introduced to the preacher, and in most cases treated with civility. There were several different preachers on the circuit, during my residence there, and among them one who was an exception to the gentlemanly character they generally manifested. His name was Mitchell; and he was as coarse-featured, thin-faced, and raw-boned, as one of Pharaoh's lean kine; rather below the medium stature, a little round-shouldered, and wore a very short and narrow calico loose-gown. He appeared as though he had almost hallooed and hooted his life away. I did not reach the place of his meeting until services had commenced. They uniformly held their meetings in a room of a private house. As I entered the room, a Methodist friend arose and placed a chair for me in front of the speaker, and within six or eight feet of him. He was reading a hymn when I entered. After they had sung, he kneeled down and delivered something which I suppose he would have called a prayer; but it was rather a tissue of execrations upon the heads of such as had the temerity to think and believe differently from his divinityship. He arose and sang again, and then named, for a text, 1 Pet. 4 : 18. "And if the righteous scarcely be saved, where shall the ungodly and the sinner appear?" He remarked, that he should, in the first place, show who the righteous were, and how difficult it would be for even them to be saved; secondly, describe the sinner, and the ungodly, and show where they would appear. He proceeded; and, to be brief, undertook to prove that none were righteous but those who believed and acted like himself; in a word, that none were righteous but Methodists; and it would be with the utmost difficulty that any, even of them, could get to heaven. During his discourse, he paid great attention to me. I had not been introduced to him; but it was evident he knew who I was—some of his friends, no doubt, had described me to him; for, repeatedly, when he had quoted a passage of Scripture, he would look earnestly at me, and even point at me, and say, "Don't you remember it?" I was on the point of answering him vocally; but I very well knew, although his impudence deserved it, that if I did so, it would be represented that I went there to make disturbance in their meetings, notwithstanding I uniformly attended, and had had no occasion to behave disorderly before. For I felt interested in all religious meetings, and wished to hear different opinions advanced with all the force of argument they could claim; for I had no fears that truth would suffer by investigation. Truth was what I wanted; and, to obtain it, I felt a desire to "Prove all things, and hold fast that which is good." And I felt no more inclination to disturb the meetings of others, nor infringe on their privileges, than those of my own order. But he would, without turning his eyes from me, repeat the question, "Don't you remember it?" and continued to repeat it, until I gave him a token, either by an inclination, or a shake of the head, that I did, or did not, as the case might be. After he had finally settled the destiny of *his* righteous, he began with sinners and the ungodly. Sinners, meant the ordinary sinners among mankind; but the ungodly were false teachers—those who were propagating false doctrines, and leading souls blindfold down to hell! And then, leaning forward so as to almost thrust his finger in my face, and raising his voice almost to a scream, he exclaimed, "If the righteous are scarcely saved, where do *you* expect to appear?" I now had to exert my patience and fortitude to the utmost, to keep my seat. I could not answer this question by a motion of the head, as before; but I resolved still to give no occasion for censure by disturbing the meeting, and therefore kept my seat. But to show him my perfect contempt of such unchristian, ungentlemanly, and insolent treatment, I smiled, disdainfully, in his face. His face instantly reddened with passion—his eyes seemed to flash fire! he leaped, it appeared to me, three feet from the floor, and smiting his fist on the Bible, his eyes steadfastly fixed on me, and mine on him with the same contemptuous smile–he exclaimed, with a voice like thunder, "I'll tell you where you'll appear—you'll appear in *hell*, with the liquid streams of fire and brimstone pouring down your throat, to all eternity!" Although I kept my seat, yet I said within myself, You and I, sir, will have a reconsideration and review of this matter, after meeting. When he closed, however, he made no pause between Amen and ordering all to leave the room without delay, but Methodists, in order to hold a class-meeting. I have often had the opportunity of witnessing the advantage which illiterate, low, vulgar, and abusive Methodist preachers take of their class-meeting arrangement, to escape rebuke for their insolent conduct. But although I implicitly obeyed the order of his ghostly highness, I resolved to wait the close of class-meeting, for an introduction to him; and did wait until long after dark; but fearing, if I did not go home, he would keep the poor Methodists all night, I concluded to retire. However, though I felt disappointed at the time, it was probably quite as well in the result;

for his own brethren took him in hand, and rebuked him sharply for his unchristian and uncivil conduct. And it proved, as such vile and malignant opposition always does prove, for the advancement of the cause they designed to overthrow. The effect was altogether to my advantage; for a respectable portion of the Methodists seemed to double their exertions to make me feel their charity and kindness, afterward.

I held meetings regularly once a month, in the house where I taught-school; and soon after I commenced my labors there, I gave appointments in other parts of the town of Salisbury, and in the adjacent town of Middleborough. In the fore part of July, I received a request to preach in the town of Benson, about twenty miles distant, and I made an appointment accordingly. Here I found a number of Universalists, and among them some of my old friends from Dana, Massachusetts. My meetings were well attended; and I continued to preach there as often as once in two weeks, during the time of my engagement in Salisbury. I rode there on Saturday afternoon, and back on Sunday evening, or started early enough on Monday morning to reach home in season to begin my school. The cause here was, at least, sufficiently prosperous to excite the fears of its enemies, and I had frequent and warm controversies with opposers, in almost every imaginable form; one of which is certainly worth recording. I was preaching in a barn—curiosity, if nothing more, had drawn together a vast congregation, for that country—the barn was literally filled, every part of it. They had erected a little staging for me, on one end of the floor, on which I stood, and was laboring with all my might to prove that God, our heavenly Father, would have all men to be saved, and come unto the knowledge of the truth, when a man, past the meridian of life, who was seated nearly in the centre of the floor before me, looked up at me, and, in a voice sufficiently audible to be heard by the whole congregation, said, "Have I not chosen you twelve; and one of you is a devil?" Had any one told me beforehand, that I should meet with such an interruption, it would doubtless have embarrassed me—probably completely unmanned me; for I had not yet been able to overcome my embarrassing diffidence; nor have I yet, completely, after almost half a century's experience. But I was astonished at myself, on reviewing the scene—for instead of embarrassing, it at once inspired a degree of boldness I had never before experienced—I felt as strong as Sampson. I stopped, looked at the man, and said,

"I thank you, sir, for reminding me of that objection; it might have slipped my memory; and I wish to remove all possible objections, real or imaginary, which can be brought to the doctrine of God's Universal Grace." The man appeared confounded and ashamed; and replied, "I ask pardon, sir—I'm sorry I spoke and interrupted you—have the goodness to pay no attention to it, but go on with your discourse." "No," I said, "I will take the liberty to break off *here*, and answer the objection, lest it should be forgotten, and then resume my discourse." The man seemed really in trouble, and again asked pardon, and requested me to proceed with my discourse. I replied, "you have done no one any injury, sir, by your interruption, but rather conferred a favor—I'll answer the objection now." I then took up the case of Judas, and labored on it, probably, twenty or thirty minutes; and then resumed my discourse where I left it, and finished it much to my own satisfaction. I never had before experienced so much liberty of speech. As soon as I dismissed the congregation, the man arose, and requested the people to wait a moment, and indulge him in the privilege of speaking. He addressed himself to me, and said, "I feel ashamed of my conduct—I have violated the laws of the land, and the rules of civility—and feel under obligation to make this confession, and to humbly ask your pardon, and the forgiveness of this congregation. But," continued he, "I have been highly gratified and instructed, by your explanation of that passage—I feel satisfied with it; and now, if you will have the goodness to give your views on another passage, and the people will consent to stay and hear, I shall be very much obliged;" and he named the parable of the Rich man and Lazarus. The congregation instantly resumed their seats; and I arose and spoke to them another half hour or more. The man then arose, thanked me and the congregation, and requested me to go home with him; and, from that time, as long as I remained in that country, he was one of my hearers, and most devoted friends. He was a Baptist, and came to my meeting, fired with a mad sectarian zeal, resolved, no doubt, to put a stop to the spread of this soul-destroying heresy, as he honestly esteemed it, but was slain by his own sword. This resulted highly favorable to the cause of divine truth in that place.

In the course of the summer, I had the satisfaction of planting the doctrine in several places, where it had never before been proclaimed; and of witnessing the awakening of a spirit of inquiry among the people, to a considerable extent. I procured all the assistance possible; made one exchange with Mr. Rich, of New Haven; and, in the course of the summer, Mr. James Foster, a little my senior both in years and in ministerial labors, made me a visit, and delivered several discourses among us. And before I left the place, I was instrumental in engaging Mr. Ballou to make one tour and preach, in all the places I had visited, with some additional places. The doctrine was new in that, and, indeed, almost every other part of the country, and strange as well as new, especially to people educated strictly in the doctrines of the Westminster Catechism; and it required a vast amount of patient and persevering labor to uproot the strong prejudices of education, and free the mind from the manacles of human creeds; and to give it courage to think for itself. The doctrine, too, addressed itself not, like Methodism, to the animal passions, but to the rational understanding; and hance could only reach the heart and reform the character, through the understanding. It could not, therefore, like the terrifying and fear-exciting doctrines of divine wrath and endless woe, make those rapid and all-sweeping strides, which Methodism was then making, in many places; but its progress, though gradual, was permanent and sure. And so much, at least, was effected in that region of country, as to create a strong desire for the continuance of preaching among them; and when my labors closed, they urged me, very strenuously, to return and take up my abode among them.

CHAPTER V.

Author starts for Association—Falls in company with Mr. Kneeland—Mr. Kneeland's and Mr. Ballou's genius contrasted—Mr. Kneeland's course, anecdotes concerning him—The convention—Preachers' names—Mr. Winchester's tomb-stone—Number received into fellowship—Letter of fellowship—Noah Murray—Samuel Smith—Confession of Faith—Visits his native place—Tour to Vt.—Return to Mass.—Teaches school—Tour to Vermont—Preaches for Rev. Thos. Fessenden—Congregationalist ministers in Walpole, Surrey, Alstead, and Charlestown, Universalists—Sufferings in body and mind, on return journey, from Benson, Vt., to Williamsburgh, Mass.—Itinerating in Mass.—Singular introduction at Oxford—General Convention, 1804—Mr. John Murray—Mr. Palmer—Modification of the name of the Convention—Engagement to teach school in Worcester, Mass.—Illiberality of a clergyman—Success in school—Singular influence of educational habit.

Having finished my school, early in September, and settled with the trustees of the district, I crossed the Green Mountains, on my way to the Association, or Convention, as it was called, (now changed to the General Convention of the United States,) which met that year in Winchester, N. H. On my way, I delivered discourses in Rochester and Bridgewater; and in Barnard, joined company with Mr. Ballou, and delegates from the societies to which he ministered. Mr. Ballou and lady, with several others, rode together in a carriage; Mr. Dean, a young man then preparing for the ministry, and a delegate from the society in Barnard, and myself, were on horseback. Mr. Ballou had previously sent an appointment for an evening lecture, at the house of a Mr. Burroughs in the town of Surrey; and when we arrived at Bellows' Falls, in Walpole, the company with whom Mr. B. traveled were unwilling to take the road by Burroughs' on account of its roughness; he, therefore, requested me to go that way and supply his place. I told him I would willingly go that way, and inform the people that he would not be there, and excuse him as well as I could; but I could not supply his place, nor would I promise to try to preach. The people would be sadly disappointed; and no one living could fill his place, in their estimation, and it would be but mockery for me to try. However, go the other way they would; and Mr. Dean and myself went to Burroughs', where we found a numerous congregation awaiting. When we informed them that Mr. Ballou would not be there, they manifested so much disappointment, and even dissatisfaction, (as I expected they would,) that I could not have preached, had no other preacher been present. But as good Providence would have it, Mr. Farwell, one of the oldest preachers in our connection, and Mr. Kneeland, were already on the ground; and Mr. Kneeland consented to deliver a discourse—and he did deliver one, the least interesting and instructive that I ever heard from a Universalist minister. He repeated a text, but could not tell the people where to find it, not having furnished himself with a Bible; but his discourse and his text were utter strangers to each other, and never were so happy as to have an introduction. The reader may be curious to know, whether this was the celebrated Abner Kneeland, author of the Greek and English testament, and who afterwards figured so conspicuously as an Atheistical lecturer, and editor of an Infidel periodical? Yes, the identical personage. But Mr. Kneeland was then young in the ministry, having attempted to preach the doctrine of Universal Salvation but very few times. He had belonged to the Baptist connection, and had publicly improved in that church for a season; but, I think, had never been regularly initiated into the ministry, according to the rules of their discipline. He then barely possessed a respectable English education, and had very limited understanding of the doctrine he wished to inculcate. Mr. Kneeland was a very singular man, for a great man. He was naturally a scholar, and made rapid advance in every science he attempted to study. After he became regularly established in the faith and ministry of our order, he entered upon the study of the languages, and obtained, very soon, a good knowledge of the Latin, Greek, and Hebrew, without any assistance, I believe, except what he obtained solely from his authors; and I have been informed, no doubt correctly, that he obtained a knowledge of several other languages. But he never possessed the faculty of original thought—he never originated a single idea; it was all borrowed; and he was generally the echo of the last author he read. In this respect he was exactly the reverse of Mr. Ballou. Mr. Ballou was perfectly an original genius—he never borrowed any thing, not a single idea, from any man, or any author, save the inspired word. His theory was his own ; such as he had formed, independently of any man, or any church, by a careful and faithful study of the Sacred Scriptures.

At the time I have been speaking of, Mr. Kneeland had formed no acquaintance with Universalist preachers ; he had probably never heard three discourses on the doctrine ; and it appears to me, that he said he had never heard a preacher of our order. But he had read Mr. Winchester's writings, and became a convert to his theory of Universalism. He was a perfect Winchesterian. Whatever Mr. Winchester had published, that Mr. K. believed in, that he preached ; and he could illustrate and defend that, and nothing else. He had a great itching for authorship too. He had previously published a definition spelling-book ; though I believe it never got into very extensive use ; and he was even now collecting scattered fragments of Mr. Winchester's writings, most of which had been published in a periodical in Philadelphia, many years before, and compiling them into a book which he afterwards published, under the title of the *Columbian Miscellany.*

Mr. Kneeland was now on his way to the General Convention of Universalists, with a design to unite with them ; and he did so. Here he became acquainted with Mr. Ballou, heard him preach, and had conversation with him ; and it was not six months from this time before he renounced Winchesterianism and became a complete Ballouite ; and preached Mr. Ballou's theory with as much zeal as he ever did Mr. Winchester's, with vastly more eloquence and soundness of argument. He continued in this faith until he left the ministry, went into the mercantile business, broke down, resumed his sacerdotal functions, and settled as pastor of the society in New Hartford, Oneida county, N. Y. There he was so unfortunate as to fall in with Dr. Joseph Priestly's writings on Materialism. This was something new to Mr. K., and he devoured it at once, and became a most zealous Materialist. He preached it with all his eloquence ; and defended it by all the arguments he was master of, both in private and in public ; and he continued to do so, to the great disadvantage of the cause of divine truth, in that region, until he removed to Philadelphia. He remained in New Hartford not quite a year, I think, before he received a call from Philadelphia. Thither he removed; and there he resumed the publication of his beloved theory of Materialism, both in the desk, and through the medium of a periodical which he there established. While Mr. Kneeland resided in Philadelphia, (for he remained there several years,) the celebrated Robert Owen visited that city, and lectured on his theory of social community. Mr. K. attended his lectures, became personally acquainted with him, and a convert to his system of social community; and, no doubt, became tinctured with his Atheistical sentiments; for shortly after that, Mr. K's hearers began, from the tenor of his discourse and some particular expressions he made use of, to distrust his fidelity to the Christian religion. And after he removed to the city of New York, before he finally abjured all religion, he was once or twice called to account by some of his parishioners, for his sceptical remarks, and a presentment was once made to the Association.

Mr. Kneeland was also a visionary man. In the summer of 1826, before Mr. K. renounced religion, and while he was yet officiating as pastor of a church in New York, I visited him; and he was then actually engaged, with several others he had induced to join in the enterprise, in planting a community upon the Owen plan, some forty miles up the North River. And this was not the most impracticable nor ridiculous project he was engaged in. He, with a number of others, had formed a company to raise money, and other treasures, from the bottom of the bay, which had been sunk there in the time of the revolutionary war. They had procured a diving-bell, and were actually engaged in the business; and their operations were guided by a little girl, about twelve years old, who, by looking into a tumbler of clear water, could see the treasures in the bottom of the ocean, and tell them exactly where to dive for them. She could see the wreck of a British ship, which lay at the bottom of the bay, and also the kegs of gold which lay among the rubbish on the bottom of the wreck. They had dived several times, had brought up some pieces of ordinance, and other things, but had not yet got the gold; they however should have it soon. And this was not all: she could tell—indeed, she could tell almost every thing, present, past, or future! and see things at a vast distance. She could see a boat full of wedges of gold, which was buried in the earth, near the bank of the North River, about forty miles above New York, by the famous Captain Kidd, in the time of his piracy; and the river, by a washing away of the bank, in consequence of a curve in that place, had laid one end of the boat bare—she could see it, perfectly plain, in the city of New York! And Mr. K. actually took passage in the boat with me, up the river, ostensibly for the purpose of visiting his Owen community, but really to find that boat and get the gold. He had the little girl and her father in the boat with him, and pointed them out to me; but requested me not to talk with them; the little girl, he said, was bashful, and, moreover, their expedition was a secret—(he told it to me in confidence.) I took the liberty to question him on the subject—asked him if it were not possible, and even probable, that he was deceived? That they were practicing an imposition on him? No, he answered, he was positively sure that she was honest—that she could actually tell what she pretended to tell—he had proved her to his full satisfaction; she had told many, very many things which he had taken pains to trace out; and she had described them accurately—to the very letter. And among others, she had minutely described a man who came ten or twelve miles to New York—she described his dress, and the color of the horse he rode; related when he started from home; how he progressed on his journey, at what time he arrived in the city, and where he might be found; and he (Mr. K.) went himself, and saw the man, and found every particular circumstance had been accurately described by her! How then could I doubt that Mr. K was on a sure track to wealth and fame? I did doubt, however, for, from some cause, I am very incredulous in such matters. But Mr. K. congratulated himself gloriously, on his auspicious prospects, and told me many wonderful things he designed to do for the cause of Universalism, when he came in possession of this immeasurable wealth. When I parted with him, in the vicinity of his boat-full of gold, (it was the last time I ever saw him,) I requested him to write and let me know how he succeeded with his enterprise. He promised to do so. A few months afterwards I received a letter from him (the last he ever wrote me) in which he just alluded to the circumstance, and said, "but we shall know who the Governor is, after election." However, I never learned "who the Governor" was. Soon after this, he renounced all religion, left the connection, and broke off all correspondence with us.

At the convention of 1803, a great majority of the preachers in the United States were present; and they made not a very formidable procession, even then. If my memory is not treacherous in this particular, and I think it is not, there were but twenty-one preachers in the whole connection previous to that meeting; and there were four who received letters of fellowship at that time. It can not, I apprehend, be uninteresting to the reader to see the names of those veterans in the Christian warfare, who enlisted at this early period, and dared to raise the standard of Universal Grace in the face of well disciplined and countless hosts, who, in mighty phalanx, were resolved, by all the means within their power, (for their maxim was, the end justifies the means) to crush every innovation upon their theological establishments;—the names of those men who fearlessly risked their reputation, their interest, their earthly *all*, (for several of them certainly expended a handsome property in their devotion to the cause,) without the least prospect of temporal fee or reward—who suffered every hardship and privation, that human nature could endure and survive, solely for the love they bore to the cause of Christ, the cause of Universal reconciliation to God, and the final beatitude of our whole race. Such names should ever stand in bold relief, upon the faithful page of history; that unborn ages, as they rise in the enjoyment of spiritual freedom, may be taught to cherish, in grateful remembrance, the instruments that laid the foundation of the inestimable privileges, they are born heirs to. Here they come—besure, they were not all equally influential, nor equally worthy; but, at the time I speak of, they were all enrolled in the little army of Universalists; and most of them have received their discharge, and are gathered home to enjoy the fruition of their hope. A very few remain; but their gray hairs show that the time of their service is nearly expired: JOHN MURRAY, CALEB RICH, THOMAS BARNES, ZEBULON STREETER, ZEPHANIAH LATHE, WILLIAM FARWELL, DAVID BALLOU, HOSEA BALLOU, JACOB YOUNG, GEORGE RICHARDS, EDWARD TURNER, SOLOMON GLOVER, WALTER FERRIS, EDWIN FERRIS, EBENEZER PAINE, CORNELIUS G. PERSON, JOSHUA FLAGG, MILES T. WOOLEY, JAMES BABBIT, NATHANIEL SMITH, JAMES FOSTER. ADAM STREETER, and ELHANAN WINCHESTER, died previous to this meeting; and at this session a contribution was made to erect a stone at the grave of the lamented Winchester. This, to me, was a season of unprecedented felicity. I had never been enabled to attend but part of an Association, since the one I have before mentioned, in Woodstock; and at that I enjoyed the satisfaction of hearing only one discourse, and that was from Mr. Barnes. But now I had met nearly all the preachers of our order; and I should have the unspeakable happiness of hearing several of them preach! My feelings were so excited in anticipation, that I could scarcely eat or sleep for days, and even weeks, before the meeting. And when I was actually permitted to meet the brethren, face to face; to feel the warmth of their fraternal hands—to listen to the gracious words that fell from their lips—to hear their songs of praise and thanksgiving, and to mingle with them in the joyful season of devotion, as one of their number, was indeed overwhelming! I "knew not whether I was in the body, or out of the body;" but one thing I did know—that I was in the spirit! What rendered the season more exquisitely delightful to me, probably, was, I had been but a short time in the ministry, not quite a year; and most of that time I had spent at quite a distance from any of my ministering brethren, and had not enjoyed even the privilege of associating with but very few who dared to name the name of Universalism: I had been exposed, alone, to the buffitings of opposers, and had to meet with vastly more frowns than smiles, and with more censures, rebukes and curses, than with tokens of kindness, or words of encouragement. This rendered the meeting doubly interesting and joyful, as well as all other meetings of the Association for years, from similar causes. I looked forward with earnest anticipations for the time to arrive, traveled with tireless steps and sleepless eyes to the appointed place, and remained in extacy until the close of the meeting; but then, alas, the time of trial came! I had to part with the brethren, and go off alone to my thankless labor; to meet the frowns of the enemy of the holy cause, the curses of those I loved, and the fatigues and privations unavoidable to my calling. I have wept for miles, after parting with the brethren; and felt like a child when whipped to his task, by a father's rod.

At this session of the Convention, four brethren received letters of fellowship, viz., Noah Murray, Abner Kneeland, Samuel Smith, and Nathaniel Stacy. I have still, in a good state of preservation, my letter of fellowship, written by Geo. Richards, and signed by Zebulon Streeter, Moderator, and Edward Turner, Clerk; dated Sept., 1803. Mr. Murray was a convert from the Baptists, with whom he preached a number of years; but, many years before this, he had renounced the doctrine of Partialism, and had been proclaiming the doctrine of Impartial Grace; but never, until this time, had met and united with the Association. But, at this session, he not only received a letter of fellowship, but ordination was conferred upon him; and he continued faithfully to proclaim the glad tidings of free grace to all mankind, until he closed his earthly pilgrimage. His residence was in the town of Athens, Tioga Point, Pa. A few years after his death, I visited the surviving members of his family, at Athens, among whom was his venerable widow, who, in the full enjoyment of the faith and hope which sustained him, in the hour of his departure, was waiting that deliverance which she has long since experienced.

Samuel Smith proved an unprofitable member. He traveled about in many places, among the societies and brethren, attempting to preach, but wounding the cause wherever he went. A short time after I visited the State of New York, Smith came into, and was about, that country two or three months. I saw him, I believe, but once, and felt little inclination to encourage his meetings. From thence he went to Connecticut, and soon after made shipwreck of his faith, (if he ever had any, which to me was very questionable,) at an exciting Methodist meeting; and the last I ever heard of him was through a very singular letter from him, addressed to a friend in New Berlin, Chenango Co., New York, which afforded abundant evidence that he never entertained any correct views of the doctrine of Universalism. The ultimate course of the other two, the world has already learned, or will soon be apprised of. Such were the four who received the fellowship of the Association, in 1803. Two of them have certainly paid the debt of nature; and, it may be safely presumed, that only one of them remains a tenant of this earthly ball.

There was a measure called for, at this time, which, in its adoption by the council, produced considerable argument in the discussion, and no little sensation among the brethren; which was, the adoption of a written creed or confession of faith. It became absolutely necessary, to save Universalists in New England, and particularly in New Hampshire, from clerical oppression. In those days, the Presbyterians and Congregationalists were denominated the *Standing Order*; and they had a legal right to tax every individual in the parish, for the support of the clergy; and the only remedy the individual had to avoid paying such tax to them, was to join some other sect, and bring a certificate from them to the Standing Order, that he had joined that society, and actually paid taxes to them. This had been done in one or more cases, in the State of New Hampshire; but, nevertheless, the Standing Order proceeded to collect the tax. Resistance was made, and the case was finally carried up to the Supreme Court, which decided that there was no such order known as Universalists, for they had no creed or profession of faith to distinguish them from the Standing Order; and they were, consequently, compelled to pay taxes to them. Our brethren felt afraid of creeds. They had read, seen, and experienced, as they supposed, the distracting, illiberal, and persecuting effects of human creeds; and they wished to avoid the vortex of that whirlpool into which they had seen so many drawn to inevitable destruction. The Bible was a sufficient creed—it was all the creed they wanted—all they needed—it was sufficiently definite—and each one had an equal right to construe it for himself, while he did not deny its inspiration and authority. They felt no inclination to take upon themselves a "yoke, which neither they nor their fathers had been able to bear." They had so far lived without a creed; and they had lived in perfect union. Now, they very much feared, should they go to making creeds, they would become divided, and, like others who had gone before them, begin to cherish an exclusive and persecuting spirit. But what should be done? They sympathized deeply with the persecuted brethren in New Hampshire; and wished, if possible, to relieve them. A committee was appointed the previous year to prepare a confession of faith, and a platform, or constitution; of which Mr. Walter Ferris was a member; and he now presented one so unobjectionable, that it was difficult to find where the most fastidious could object to it, or how it could lead to division. A motion was made to adopt it; and probably the longest and warmest debate ensued, that had ever been known in that deliberative body. It was, however, conducted throughout with the kindest feelings, but with much earnestness and considerable sensibility; tears and smiles by the attentive auditors, alternately followed the pathetic appeals of the speakers on each side. Among its warmest advocates were George Richards, Hosea Ballou, Walter Ferris, and Zephaniah Lathe; and among its opposers, Edward Turner and Noah Murray. I distinctly recollect a metaphor in one of Mr. Murray's arguments, and Mr. Lathe's reply. Mr. Murray said, in allusion to the confession of faith, "It is harmless now—it is a calf, and its horns have not yet made their appearance; but it will soon grow older—its horns will grow, and then it will begin to hook." Mr. Lathe arose, and replied, "All that Br. Murray has said would be correct, had he not made a mistake in the animal. It is not a calf; it is a dove; and who ever heard of a dove having horns, at any age?" But the confession was adopted without alteration, I believe, as reported by the committee, through Mr. Ferris. The opposition yielding, it passed, (if my memory well serves me,) by the unanimous voice of the council, with a resolution appended to it to this effect, that *no alteration should ever be made, hereafter, to the confession of faith.* These articles have been published repeatedly, and are contained in the "Modern History of Universalism," by Mr. Whittemore; but it may be gratifying to my readers, notwithstanding, to see them here; and, as they are short, I feel disposed to satisfy their curiosity.

"ARTICLE I.–We believe in one God, whose nature is love, revealed in one Lord Jesus Christ, by one holy spirit of grace; who will finally restore the whole human family to holiness and happiness.

ARTICLE II.—We believe that the Scriptures of the Old and New Testaments, contain a revelation of the character of God, of the duty, interest, and final destination of mankind.

ARTICLE III.—We believe that holiness and true happiness are inseparably connected; and that believers ought to be careful to maintain order, and practice good works; for these things are good and profitable to men."

To the above creed no one could reasonably object, who believed in the final restitution of man, let his views of future retribution be what they might.

At the close of the meeting, I proceeded to Massachusetts, made a visit of a few weeks in my native town, preached a few discourses, among which were two on funeral occasions, in families of my early and most intimate associates; and then returned to Vermont, where I tarried about one month. During this tour, I supplied the desk of Mr. Ballou, in Bethel, one Sabbath; made a tour with him as far as Calais; preached in the towns of Rochester, Randolph, and Bridgewater; and then returned to New Salem, where I had engaged to teach a district school, commencing on the first of December. On my way from Vermont to Massachusetts, I called on the venerable father in Israel, Zebulon Streeter, and delivered a lecture in his dwelling-house, to a respectable congregation. It was with some difficulty I could make up my mind to address a congregation in the presence of an old veteran, one who, I was sensible, could discharge the duty to so much better advantage to the cause than myself. I was not afraid of being censured —I shrank not from his criticism; for I felt grateful for every correction of a defect in enunciation, language, gesture, or any inconsistency in doctrine; but I felt that a waiting congregation should always be served with the best ability, and the soundest and most cogent arguments—I wanted good to be done, and the greatest possible good; and as I never had a very exalted opinion of my own talents, I felt that the congregation were sufferers whenever I attempted to preach, while others of greater strength and more experience were present. These were, and invariably have been my feelings. up to the present time. I have marveled greatly, many times, when I have heard young and inexperienced preachers contending earnestly about *their right* to preach; and sometimes with those of vastly greater experience than themselves, as though they had a *right* to be heard—to display their *splendid talents*, without any regard to the feelings of the congregation, or the advancement of the cause. "Thinks I to myself," their ambition is very different from mine. But my venerable brother Streeter treated me with great tenderness and fatherly affection, gave me good counsel, and encouraged me in my resolution to persevere. He had never before heard me speak publicly.

During this winter, (1803—4,) I taught school in the district where I first went to school; and quite a number of my scholars, (for the school was large,) were my old school-mates. But my school was a good one; and the winter glided pleasantly away. My Sundays were mostly employed in preaching in New Salem, and the adjacent towns of Dana and Hardwick. I did not lose sight of the holy cause in which I was engaged; and whatever I did—whatever business was necessary for me to engage in, or labors to perform, I designed should be subservient to it.

In the latter part of April, 1804, having finished my pedagogic term, I started again on a tour through Vermont; though I designed to tarry but a short time, having resolved to spend the ensuing summer in Massachusetts, that I might enjoy the privilege of associating more frequently with my older brethren in the ministry; and, therefore, left an appointment for a Sunday in the town of Williamsburgh. On my way, I called, as usual, on my friend Burroughs, in Surry; and, by his earnest solicitation, accepted a letter of introduction from him to Rev. Thomas Fessenden, pastor of the Congregational Church in Walpole. Mr. Fessenden had long been their settled minister, and enjoyed the confidence of the people of his charge, probably to as great an extent as any clergyman ever did. He was advanced in years, and a few Sundays previous to the time of which I speak, was attacked with a paralytic fit in his desk; from which he had not yet sufficiently recovered to leave his room. Mr. Burroughs said, they had had no preaching since Mr. Fessenden's sickness; and he felt confident Mr. F. would be very glad to have me preach in his desk the next Sunday. He said Mr. F. was a Universalist, or a Restorationist, although in the Congregationalist connection; and would rather have his desk filled by a Universalist than a preacher of any other denomination. I was diffident, and felt quite doubtful as to the reception that I should meet with, but reluctantly took the letter and presented it to Mr. F. I found him able to sit up, and even walk about the room, but could only speak in a loud whisper. He received me cordially and politely, and inquired if I was in regular standing in the Universalist connection. Being answered in the affirmative, he inquired, whether or not I believed in the utility of church order and ordinances, and having received the assurance that I did, he said that was all he required; and it was very kind in Mr. Burroughs to influence me to call on him; his people had been destitute of preaching for several Sabbaths, and would be highly gratified in having a meeting; and he would immediately take measures to give general notice. This was on Wednesday; and Mr. F. ordered my horse to be taken care of, and requested me to make myself at home in his study, during the week. He inquired, if I was in the habit of writing my discourses. I answered, I had written some, but not generally. I was in the habit of itinerating, and was ill convenienced to commit much to writing. He replied, "Well, it is a good thing to be able to extemporize; but it is also profitable to write some. You have now time to write one discourse, at least, and I would advise you to do so. I am in the habit of writing generally; and it will be quite as acceptable to the people you will preach to, next Sunday, to hear you read, as to speak extemporaneously." I promised to write one discourse, and, accordingly, I did write.

Early on Sunday morning, Mr. Fessenden called to me and asked, "Have you written a discourse?" "Yes, sir," I replied. "Well, get it, and read it to me," he rejoined. "O, my dear sir, do excuse me—it will not bear criticism. I have not had the advantages of an education; and although I am willing, and even desire you to criticise my doctrine, I feel too diffident of the language and method of the discourse, to try to read it to you—pray, sir, excuse me," I replied. "No," said he, "Mrs. Fessenden and I will be your only hearers. We want to hear a sermon. I can not go to meeting; and she must stay to take care of me. The most learned men are not always the most useful men. Go, get the sermon, and read it." I went, and, with a tremor through my whole frame, brought the manuscript; and, at his bidding, took a seat, and read it as well as I could. When I closed, the first one to break silence was Mrs. Fessenden, who said, "There has not been so good a discourse as that delivered in our meeting-house, for a long while." This brought up my head; I had not before dared to look up. "It is a good sermon, and well written," responded Mr. Fessenden. This was worth a ruby to me. Mr. F. was a learned man, and an aged minister; and, if he approved of the discourse, it might be acceptable to others, and be the means of doing some good. It inspired me with confidence, and I went to the church with increased fortitude. I had never before entered a meeting-house, for the purpose of preaching in it, since my first attempt. My sanctuaries of worship had been private dwellings, school-houses, barns, and the grove—that splendid temple made by God's own hand; and when I looked around upon the gathering congregation, (the house was large, and the assembly numerous,) I might have quailed under the stern gaze of so many prying eyes, had not the encouraging remark of Mr. F., who, I thought, was certainly as good a judge of matter and diction as any of them, strengthened and supported me.

My visit at Mr. Fessenden's was both agreeable and profitable. I found him and his lady well established in the faith of Universal Restitution, upon Mr. Winchester's theory, and fearless advocates of the doctrine. Mr. F. told me he had been well established, himself, for about twelve years; that when he first embraced the faith, he began to modify his discourses in conformity to it, without directly naming the doctrine; and progressed and enlarged by degrees, until he was enabled to freely and fully declare his doctrine without alarming his church, or losing his standing as pastor; and now, he said, there were not a dozen members of his church, (and it was large,) who believed in the dogma of endless misery. It is a singular fact, that about the same time that Mr. Fessenden came into the faith of the Final Restitution, three other clergymen, of three adjacent towns, of the same denomination, embraced the same faith: Mr. Howe, of Surry; Mr. Mead, of Alstead; and Mr. Dan Foster, of Charlestown. And they all, except Mr. Mead, so managed as to retain their standing in the Congregational Association, and to remain in the pastoral charge of their respective churches, notwithstanding they fearlessly advocated the doctrine. Mr. Foster also published a treatise on the subject, in reply to Dr. Strong, of Hartford, Connecticut, who had written against Dr. Huntington's posthumous work. I found Mr. Foster's book in the library of Mr. Fessenden; as also the work of Dr. Chauncy, which I had never before seen. Mr. F. was not able to talk long at a time; though, during my stay, we had considerable conversation, and I received from him much good counsel. My visit was rendered much more agreeable on account of the kindness and maternal attention of his excellent lady. She was a native of the same town as myself; a daughter of the first settled minister in New Salem, Rev. Mr. Kendall; and was well acquainted with my parents. She manifestly received me with the affection of a mother. She was a woman of more than ordinary talents, and rejoiced heartily in the faith of the Great Salvation. Several times, during my stay, when people came in, and I was introduced as a Universalist preacher, arguments on doctrinal subjects were introduced; but I could never get an opportunity to reply; for either Mr. F. or his wife would take up the argument, and defend the doctrine with as much zeal, and vastly more ability, than I could possibly have done.

On taking leave of this excellent family, on Monday morning, Mrs. F. presented me with a number of small articles of apparel, such as cravats, &c.; and they very affectionately invited me to call as often as convenient, with the assurance that I should ever be welcome to their hospitality, and every other assistance they could render me. But, alas! it was the first and the last time I ever enjoyed the pleasure of visiting them; for I never afterward passed through that country, until the fall of 1843, many—many years after these good people were numbered with the great congregation of the dead. And such alterations had been made, by the hand of time and the hands of man, in that region of their habitation, that I could not certainly recognize the locality of their ancient dwelling-place.

One object of this tour was to make a short visit to Mr. Ballou and other friends in Windsor county, as well as to fulfil a promise my friends in Addison had drawn from me when leaving them; I had also made some appointments in that county by letter. In fulfilling these engagements, I preached one Sunday in Rochester; lectured in Salisbury and Middleborough; preached one Sunday, and delivered one lecture, in Benson. On Wednesday morning, I was more than one hundred miles from Williamsburgh, the place of my appointment for the next Sunday; and I was an entire stranger to the country through which I must travel. I had, at the solicitation of friends, particularly in Addison county, traveled two hundred miles to visit them, and deliver my message. They had manifested great satisfaction in the opportunity of hearing me preach, had urged me, with the utmost earnestness, to stay longer; solicited me, with all apparent sincerity, to make them another visit as soon as possible; thanked me times without number, and expressed their gratitude in the warmest terms possible; but, alas! they never thought to inquire how I was, pecuniarily, prepared to meet the expenses of my journey; nor if my horse would ever need a shoe, or myself a change of apparel. My ministerial labors had ever been sparingly rewarded; and it was right, no doubt, for they were worth but little—I so considered them myself; all I ever had received, I esteemed as a charitable donation. But now I felt the need of something, more than I ever had before. My earnings in school-teaching, the previous winter, had been exhausted in the payment of some small debts I had been obliged to contract, and in furnishing myself with a few articles of necessary wearing apparel; and the few shillings I had started on my journey with, were nearly exhausted. I had the confidence to name to them my destitute condition, but not one of them put a cent into my hand. I never was exactly like the unjust steward, who said, "Dig I can not, and to beg I am ashamed." I was ever ashamed to beg; but I could dig, with good-will, if I had opportunity. But now I had no chance; it would require the whole, or nearly the whole time between this and the next Sunday to reach the place of my appointment. What was to be done? I felt very unwilling to cause a disappointment; I therefore moved forward, though with rather a despairing heart, at first; but soon gathered courage and strength from the reflection, that if God had allotted me a work to perform, he would either provide means to feed me on the way, or give me strength to perform the journey without it. It required me to be on the way two nights; and I had barely change sufficient in my pocket to pay for my horse-keeping and my lodging, and furnish me with a single meal. And with this I performed the journey, without making my condition known to any person, or asking the charity of strangers. On the last day, long after every cent was spent, in crossing the Green Mountains from Adams through Savoy to Williamsburgh, I felt quite exhausted, and thought my poor beast felt faint and weary too; and, on looking around and beholding the abundance that rewarded the labors of the industrious husbandman, even in that cold and mountainous country, I could scarcely refrain from repining at my lot, and thinking that, if this was an allotment of Providence, it was a severe one; and, for a moment, a fearful despondency seized my soul! But it was momentary only; for, on looking around, I saw a good fresh turnip by the wayside, that somebody had dropped. I alighted, picked it up, and proceeded but a few rods, when I came to a spot of good fresh grass by the way. I here let my horse feed, stretched my weary limbs on nature's verdant carpet, and ate my turnip. I then arose refreshed, both in body and in mind. My desponding feelings had entirely left me; and a holy calmness, an unshaken confidence in an all-wise and bountiful Providence, with a conscientious conviction that I was in the way of duty, accompaied and cheered me to the end of my journey. I arrived at the house of Mr. Washburn, father of Mrs. Ballou, some time after noon; but could wait, without feeling any inconvenience, until their usual tea-time; and then ate a hearty meal, without experiencing any injury. Several times, in the course of my journey, I was on the point of inquiring for Universalists, with a design to make my condition known. But I was so young, or looked so young—a mere beardless boy—that no one would readily believe I was a preacher; and I thought it most probable I should only expose myself to insult, and bring a stain on the cause I felt so zealous to support; and I would rather starve myself than do either.

The next Sunday, I delivered my message to a respectable

congregation: and they made me a liberal contribution; so that I was able to return to my father's house, encouraged, and in comfortable circumstances.

The ensuing summer, in accordance with my previous design, I spent in Massachusetts. I had one regular monthly appointment in the town of Medway, where I was recommended by Mr. Turner; and the rest of the time was employed in different places, by appointments, from time to time, as circumstances called for them I supplied Mr. Turner's and Mr. Flagg's places occasionally, during their absence on journeys or to other societies. A rather odd and amusing incident, which occurred on one of these occasions, I will briefly relate: I had agreed to supply for Mr. Flagg, in the town of Oxford, one Sunday; and on my way thither, on Saturday, was overtaken by night, some six or seven miles before reaching the place. There was no public-house before reaching the village; and I had no acquaintance in that region of country. There was no alternative, therefore, but to put up at a private house, among strangers, or to persevere until I reached Oxford. I chose the latter, and pressed forward as fast as my jaded beast could carry me. When I reached the village, there was no light in any house save the tavern, and they were on the point of extinguishing theirs. I therefore simply called for entertainment, and, without making any inquiry, or any remark in reference to my business, retired to rest. On Sunday morning I arose—knew no one, and was unknown to all. I told the landlord I would breakfast with him. Meantime I inquired what denomination owned the meeting-house, which stood a few rods from the tavern. My host answered, "The Universalists." "Do they have preaching there to-day?" "Yes." "Who preaches with them?" "Mr. Flagg." After breakfast, he inquired if I would have my horse. I replied, that I thought of attending meeting there that day. Nothing more was said, and I retired to my chamber, adjusted my apparel, and prepared for church. Bye-and-bye the first bell rang, and soon people began to assemble; many of whom appeared to have come a great distance. I occasionally walked through the crowd, to see if any came with whom I was acquainted, and to hear what was said. The inquiry was repeatedly made, "Is Mr. Flagg come?" "Has the preacher come?" No one knew, but thought he was at Capt. Davis', his usual stopping-place. Soon, however, word came from Capt. Davis that the preacher was not there ; and they began seriously to fear they would be disappointed that day. Much anxiety was manifested ; the day was pleasant ; and a numerous congregation were assembling. They had preaching but once a week, and they very much deprecated a disappointment; however, Mr. Flagg might have stopped somewhere, and thought he would be in season yet. Presently the second bell rang ; and they began walking back and forth, from the public-house to the meeting-house. No preacher was to be found, and they were quite in despair ; I could, once in a while, see some one look quite earnestly at me ; but nobody addressed me, and I said nothing. As the bell began to toll, I went into my chamber, put my Bible and psalm-book under my arm, so as to have them in fair sight, and walked deliberately down, and through the crowd, and directed my steps toward the meeting-house. As I walked through the room, not a word was said ; but all eyes were riveted on me, in apparent astonishment, and without a word being spoken, in my hearing, a simultaneous move was made, and they all followed me to the church. I walked into the house, made my bow to the congregation as I passed, and ascended the pulpit. When I turned around, if I ever saw amazement, wonder, and doubt, depicted upon the countenances of an assembly, I saw it then. Mr. F. had never told them of the proposed change ; and there was, at that time, not a soul present who had the least knowledge of me. The house was immediately filled, and I arose and commenced service ; while profound and breathless attention prevailed. During the intermission, I was surrounded by many, and two or three had joined the congregation, with whom I had a limited acquaintance : and, taking it altogether, we had a happy, and, I trust, profitable, meeting. The singularity of my introduction excited attention, and had rather a beneficial tendency. At the close of the meeting, Capt. Davis, the treasurer of the society, handed me five dollars. This, at that time, was the regular salary of our Universalist preachers, in those old societies ; and as much a lawful tender, for a Sunday's preaching, as was six cents for an almanac. In the course of this season, I preached in the towns of Medway, Wrentham, Oxford, Charleston, Brockfield, Grafton, Milford, Dana, Williamsburg, New Salem, Massachusetts ; and Smithfield, Rhode Island.

The Association, or as it was called in the platform, or constitution adopted the preceding year, "The General

Convention of Universalists in New England," held its annual session, in the fall of 1804, in the town of Sturbridge, Mass. At this meeting, I for the first, and last, and only time in my life, saw the venerable apostle of Universalism in America, Rev. John Murray, and heard him deliver two discourses; he came in company with a man from the city of New York, by the name of Palmer, who also delivered one discourse. It was interesting, indeed, to me, to see and hear Mr. Murray. I had heard my parents often speak of him, after they boldly avowed their faith in Universalism; and describe the manner of his preaching; and I had imbibed a high veneration for the man, and had a strong desire to hear the word of truth from his lips; nor were my anticipations disappointed. His manner, to me, was pleasing, and his eloquence captivating. He appeared to possess a perfect government over his own passions; riveted the attention of his hearers; carried them with him through his whole discourse, and made them feel the sensibilities of his own soul; would bring tears into their eyes, or excite their risibility, with as much ease as the words flowed from his opening lips. Mr. Palmer delivered a very good discourse; but of him I never afterwards heard anything. I believe he never pretended to devote his time to the ministry; and he never associated much with our denomination, nor became a member of the convention.

Mr. Wooley had traveled, the preceding summer, as far as Otsego, in the state of New York, and had preached in different towns in that section of country. He attended this meeting, and brought quite a favorable report of his success, and the call for the preached word in that country. He expressed great confidence, that could that region be supplied with preaching, the truth would spread with great rapidity, and societies would spring up in every direction. And to favor the cause in that State, and dispose societies there organizing to unite more readily with the great body of Universalists, by his suggestion the name of the convention underwent a modification; it was resolved, in council, that it should thereafter be entitled "*The General Convention of Universalists of the New England States, and others.*"

By the persuasion and influence of a man in the town of Worcester, with whom I became acquainted, I engaged to teach a district school, for five months, in that town, commencing the first of November. To show the narrowness and illiberality of bigoted souls, and their hostility to a doctrine they dare not attempt to refute in an open and ingenuous manner, as well as their malignant persecution of those they dare not meet in open discussion, I must here be permitted to relate an incident: The laws of Massachusetts required a school-teacher to procure a certificate of his moral character from the select men of the town where he resided, or had last resided, and of his literary qualifications from the settled minister of the town in which he taught. I had taught the previous winter in Massachusetts; but as it was in my native district, nothing was said about a certificate, and I never applied for one. But now I was going among strangers, and it was necessary I should be supplied with legal credentials. I readily obtained my credentials from the select men; and knowing that sectarian prejudice might have an unfavorable influence on the feelings of the clergyman in Worcester, should they learn my religious tenets; I concluded it might be essentially to my advantage to obtain one from the settled minister in New Salem; and I entertained no doubt that he would readily give me one, inasmuch as he and I had always been acquainted from boyhood, and certainly, until we became preachers, on terms of cordiality and friendship. He was considerably my senior; but we were natives of the same town, and in early life associated much together. I therefore applied to him with all confidence; but alas! I applied in vain; he would not give me one; and said, if the clergymen in Worcester knew their duty, they would neither of them give me one. It was perfectly obvious that, knowing he had now the advantage of me, he meant to use his prerogative to crush me, if in his power. However, he had not time, if he had the inclination, to interpose his influence with the clergymen of Worcester, before I presented myself before his reverence, Dr. Austin, a rigid Calvanistic divine; and in less than half an hour obtained the necessary credential.

My school was very large, for a district school, averaging seventy or eighty during the whole term; and as I had no assistant, it required my whole attention, and occupied my whole time, day and evening; so that I made no appointments to preach, nor did I deliver one discourse, during the five months of my engagement. Besides, there were very few in that place who felt any interest in the cause of Universalism; there was but one solitary individual who felt any sympathy for the doctrine in the district; and that was Mr. Williams, by whose influence I was employed, and with whom I boarded. The rest of the district were all, or nearly all, members of the Orthodox churches, either that of Dr. Austin, or Dr. Bancroft; but they were uniformly very civil and friendly to me, and took every opportunity to express their perfect satisfaction in my management of the school.

I had, this winter, a most ample illustration of the power and influence of habit—at least, educational habit; and how easily one can be led, with the most innocent feelings, and conscientious submission, into practices which another, educated under different circumstances, would shudder at the thought of. The community with whom I resided were a friendly, social people, fond of parties for conversation and amusement; and both old and young had their weekly or semi-weekly parties, during the whole winter. For a while, the young people gave me repeated, polite, and even urgent invitations to attend their parties; but I excused myself on the ground of the necessity of employing the evening in preparing for my school the next day. And, indeed, it was necessary to do much in that way; besides, I had little inclination for such amusements as they indulged in—dancing, playing, and the like; I could enjoy much more alone, in my little chamber, in reading and meditation. After trying, a few weeks, to induce me to join their social parties, the young people gave up their importunities; and I enjoyed my retirement peaceably for a short time. But when the older, married people, saw that I did not choose to associate with the young in their amusements, they began to invite me to meet with them; and pleaded the importance of it, as a means of cultivating an acquaintance with my employers, and giving satisfaction. They alleged, that none but the respectable part of community assembled with them; and their recreations were civil and inoffensive. Well—I agreed to go; and one evening, in company with Mr. Williams and his lady, I went nearly a mile, but within the limits of the district. We were greeted with politeness; and soon a large assembly of middle-aged ladies and gentlemen were assembled. After their teams were taken care of, and the company were comfortably warmed before a cheerful, blazing fire upon the hearth of a large square room, our kind hostess placed a table in the centre of the floor. I supposed it was their practice, as I afterwards learned it was, uniformly to provide supper for their guests; but I was a little surprised that they should get it so early in the evening; for we had not yet been assembled half an hour. However, I concluded it might be their custom to spread their entertainment at an early hour of the evening, and thereby render it convenient for their guests to retire at their own pleasure; and I began to applaud the custom. But I was soon undeceived—the table was set, brilliant lights placed upon it, and a pack of cards thrown thereon! and immediately the people surrounded it, male and female, as they were first introduced into our strange world, and began to shuffle the cards, and to deal them out. They politely offered me a card; but I told them, I should beg to be excused; as I was unacquainted with the game. They expressed some doubt, and began to rally me on the subject—said I was superstitious—they only played for amusement; and Mr. B. (that was their minister) would not scruple to take a card, whenever he met with them, &c. I told them, I did not consider myself superstitious—I really did not know how to play cards—that, although when quite a boy I had known sufficient to play, after a sort, at what we used to call All-fours, yet, for many years, I had scarcely seen a card, and had actually forgotten all I ever knew about them. "O, well, if I had ever known any thing about playing, they could very readily show me again." I replied, that I thought I should be rather a dull scholar; and as I really had no time to spare from other important duties and studies, I should ask to be entirely excused. So I sat mostly alone during the evening; for those who were not actually engaged in the game, felt so deeply interested in the result, that they would say little or nothing about anything else. The good lady of the house, however, commiserated my lonely condition, and came and seated herself by me, and kindly inquired, if I ever played chequers;—for their whole thoughts were exclusively on some sort of game. I told her I had sometimes tried to play. Well, would I play a game with her? Why, madam, I think it will afford you but dull amusement, for I really profess no skill in that game. She insisted, however, that I should play, and brought out her chequer-board, and we commenced the game. But I was so unfortunate as not to get a king, before she had taken every "man" from me. She gave me a pretty sharp reprimand for carelessness, or wilfully wrong movements—said she knew I could play better, if I would try; and set her chequers again. But again I had no better success—she " skunked " me a second time. She was now almost vexed—said I did not try—she would place the chequers again; and I must try to do better. I observed, that I was perfectly aware it could be no amusement for her to play with me—I had told her so in the first place. I felt very grateful to her for her endeavors to entertain me; but as it would be no gratification to her, to play at a game where she could have no competition, I would not insist on her trying it any longer. She would try it once more; and I should try to do better. Well, madam, I will use what skill I have. But, alas! she "skunked" me the third time! and, in total despair, put her board and chequers away, and went back to the card-table. So I enjoyed my own thoughts, in quietness, the remainder of the evening.

Card-playing is considered by many, and probably by most religious people, as the most heinous crime that mortals can be guilty of; and I verily look upon it as one of the most foolish, and even the most dangerous amusements, that a rational mind can indulge in. It certainly consumes time that might be, and ought to be, more profitably employed. No information whatever is obtained; no sociable or instructive conversation can be enjoyed; but the mind is wholly engrossed with black and red spots, and the most grotesque pictures ever drawn on paste-board, and exhibits the most intense solicitude about—nothing! I could but marvel, to see so many well-dressed, polite, respectable, and apparently well-educated, and well-informed gentlemen and ladies, spending the precious hours of life, evening after evening, in this, worse-than-useless manner. And the astonishment of the reader will surely equal mine, when I inform him, that all of these, with only two exceptions, were professors of religion, and members in good standing of one or the other of the Orthodox churches in Worcester! But they meant no hurt by this practice, if they meant no good. Nothing would have tempted them to gamble, as they called it—i.e., to play for the consideration of any gain—not even one cent. Their game was mere recreation, to pass away a social—or, as I should call it, an *unsocial* hour; and they considered it perfectly harmless and innocent. I met with them no more; and they never again urged me to do so; they unquestionably discovered that it was no amusement for me, but rather a dull entertainment. I found, however, that it was a uniform practice among them, whenever they met together, by day or by night, to introduce card-playing; and every man, or at least every family, kept a pack of cards. There was a shoemaker who worked in a shop a few yards from the house in which I boarded, a zealous professor of religion, and a member of Dr. Austin's church, and whom I could, at any time, make zealously mad, by introducing an argument in favor of Universalism; who also kept small articles in his shop for sale, such as pins, needles, writing paper, quills, &c., and whenever I wanted any small articles of stationery, I stepped into his shop. This man always kept a pack of cards lying on his bench; and I have repeatedly seen him lay down his work, with a half-finished seam, when a neighboring boy came in, and take up his cards, and go to playing with as much zeal as he would anathematize Universalism, as a licentious doctrine, if I chanced to say a word in favor of it. So strangely—so singularly are we influenced by our educational habits! I could but reflect, most seriously and solemnly, on the vast responsibility of parents, in regard to the education of their offspring.

CHAPTER VI.

Author starts on a tour to Vermont—Visit to Mr. N. Foster—Mr. F's former religious sentiments—His conversion to Universalism, and its moral effects—Visits Benson—Leaves Benson on a tour to the state of New York—Meeting in Whitehall, and Fort Ann—Incidents in Fort Ann—Meetings in the house of Mr. Gilbert Harris—Visits his brother in Canajoharie—Interview with Elder Elliot—Journey to Sangerfield, Oneida county—Delivers his first discourse in Sangerfield—Solicitation to remain longer—State of feeling among the inhabitants of the country, and progress of the doctrine—Begins to itinerate through the counties of Oneida, Chenango, &c.—Visit to his brother, and meeting in Otsego—Meets Mr. Wooley—Conference in Burlington—Germ of the Western Association—Opposition—Confab with Mr. B. Morse—A bow drawn at a venture—Desultory discussion with Rev. Mr. Knapp—Singular question—First discourse in Hamilton village—Judge Paine—Amusing anecdote—First meeting in Madison—Interview with Elder Morton—Curious anecdote of Elder M.—Challenge—First meeting in Whitestown—Organization of the first society in Oneida county—Singular remark of Polycarpus Smith—A regular circuit—Joseph Tenny and his book—Two societies organized—Growth and prospects of the cause.

About the middle of April, 1805, having closed my school in Worcester, I once more started on a journey to the State of Vermont, but on a different route from that I had before traveled. I had previously received a very pressing solicitation from an old gentleman residing in Wilmington, by the name of Foster, who, from my earliest remembrance until within a few years, had been a resident of New Salem, and had uniformly served as a tithing-man in the Congregational Church, and whose main business was to take care of the boys, and keep them in order, on Sundays. He was a most rigid Partialist—equally rigid in his sentiments and discpline of the boys—and we all stood in fear and dread of him. He had removed to Wilmington, Vermont, a few years prior to the time to which I allude; and I had not seen him until the session of the Association, in the autumn of 1803. As I then rode up to the house where we stopped, in Winchester, New Hampshire, I saw a man approaching from an opposite direction, who resembled Mr. Foster; but surely, (thought I,) that can not be uncle Nathan; for I should as soon expect to see one arise from the dead, as to see him at a Universalist meeting. However, as we approached each other, I saw that he was the identical man. Still, I concluded he must be on a journey, and our meeting purely accidental. We both dismounted and secured our horses; and, looking again so as to be sure of his identity, I walked toward him and addressed him by name. He instantly recognized me, and, with a countenance reflecting cheerfulness and happiness, took my hand with unusual warmth. Such was not his former appearance. He had uniformly worn a gloomy countenance, and exhibited discontent and peevishness in his demeanor. After inquiring concerning his health and family, I said to him, "Mr. Foster, are you on a journey?" He responded, "No, no farther." I then said, "I believe there is a religious meeting to be holden here, to-morrow and next day." He answered, "Yes, there is." "But," I said, "you have not come to attend this meeting, Mr. Foster, have you?" "Yes," he replied. I next inquired, "But do you know what kind of meeting it is, Mr. Foster?" "Yes," said he, "it is a Universalist Association.' "But you are not a Universalist, Mr. Foster!" I said. "Yes, thank God, I am," he rejoined. I clenched his hand again, and thanked God for his deliverance; and the big tears started in the eyes of the good old man. We had, indeed, a happy meeting—what a change had come over him! He was completely metamorphosed from a gloomy, sour, crabbed Partialist, to one of the most cheerful, pleasant, and happy beings I ever met with. I said to myself, "If the knowledge of divine truth can work wonders like this—can thus renew a man, in his old age—God grant that it may speedily prevail over all Christendom." He was perfectly sensible of the full and complete change wrought upon himself. "O," said he, "how strange—how unutterably strange—I have lived in darkness so long, when the truth is so clearly taught in the Bible! How much I have lost! O, if I were young, how earnestly I would preach the Gospel to mankind!" And he did preach. His mouth was full of argument, and his tongue dwelt on praise, wherever he went. He so lived, and so died. Both were equally astonished at meeting each other. He had not until then heard that I was a Universalist; and he would probably have thought me the last being of our mortal race, who would attempt to preach it. But before we parted, I had to make him a promise, should Providence permit, that I would at some future period make him a visit, and preach in his neighborhood; and this was the first opportunity which presented.

I went to Wilmington, tarried one Sunday, and delivered two discourses in that town. From thence, I pursued my journey to the town of Benson, where I had been, repeatedly, requested to take up my abode. But, after spending three Sundays, and looking around with some thought of fixing upon a location, I did not feel exactly satisfied; moreover, I had an undefinable presentiment that I was not altogether in the right place; and my mind was involuntarily and irresistibly drawn westward. I had a brother residing in the town of Canajoharie, in the State of New York, whom I had not seen for a number of years; and I informed my friends, in Benson, that I felt it a duty to make him a visit. They again requested me to return and settle with them; but I made no engagement, telling them simply that I would be governed by the indications of Providence. If I found that God had a work for me to do whither I was going, I would try to do it; if not, I would probably return to Benson, in a few weeks.

My first stop, after leaving Benson, was at White Hall, at the head of Lake Champlain. Here I stayed two days, and delivered a discourse in the dwelling-house of Capt. Hinman, who, in consequence of a spinal injury, had been confined to his house, for two or three years. In the township of Fort Ann, a short day's ride from this place, I had a cousin living who was as dear to me as a sister, and whom I had not seen for many long years. She married a man by the name of Goodell. On them I called, and tarried several days, at their urgent solicitation. They were Baptists; and although we conversed freely and much on the subject of religion, and although I expressed my feelings and sentiments as plainly as language would enable me, without saying they were Universalism, they did not, for several days, understand me, nor did they suspect that I was a preacher. There was a gentleman residing within a few miles, with whom I had formed an acquaintance in Benson; and, during my stay, I took the opportunity to make him a short call. He requested me to appoint a meeting; and I told him, if a house and congregation could be obtained, I should be very happy to give them a discourse. The second day after this conversation, a man by the name of Gilbert Harris came to Mr. Goodell's to graft some fruit-trees; and, while employed in this business, I walked out to see the operation, and made some remarks upon the improvement of fruit thereby. "Yes," said he, with a significant look at me, "this is doing what every preacher of the Gospel ought to do—taking away falsehood, and supplying its place with the truth." And then, laying aside his pruning knife, he informed me that the gentleman I have alluded to had been to see him on the subject of having a meeting; and requested me to appoint a time to preach at his house. My friend Goodell stared at me with amazement; and said, "Why didn't you tell *me* you were a preacher?" He not only learned, now, that I was a preacher, but also learned what, probably, were my sentiments; for he knew that Mr. Harris was a zealous Universalist. I made an appointment at the house of Mr. H., and Mr. Goodell and wife accompanied me there; I had designed not to return, but proceed from thence on my journey. A good congregation were in attendance; and, after meeting, many of them surrounded me, and pressed their solicitations with so much earnestness, that I consented to return back with Mr. G., and remain over the next Sabbath. I did so, and a very numerous congregation came together, my friend Goodell and wife among the number. They had had some Universalist preaching in that section of country, and there were some among them who were not ignorant of the doctrine, but quite able to defend it, and many others earnestly inquiring after truth. They made a small contribution to assist me on the way, and then separated, with apparently gratified feelings. Here I parted with my friend Goodell and his wife, who still maintained their usual kindness toward me, if they did not feel more sympathy for the doctrine which I taught than they had ever done before.

The next morning, I again pursued my lonely journey to the west. I found my brother in Canajoharie, as I anticipated; and although he and his wife were exceedingly gratified, and expressed overmuch joy at my arrival, (it being the first family connection who had visited them in their new home,) yet they had no inclination to hear much about my doctrine, nor to have me preach in the place. They were Free-Will Baptists—my sister-in-law was a member of Elder Elliott's church, and my brother a constant attendant on his meetings, probably with an intention also of becoming a member. They had been informed that I had commenced preaching; but my brother told me it would be useless to appoint a meeting in that place, as no one thereabout would willingly hear the doctrine. However, he was mistaken; for on a subsequent visit I had a request to preach there, and did preach several discourses to very respectable congregations, for those times; and I soon found some believers in the truth of the Great Salvation. On my second visit, some five or six weeks afterward, I had a short interview with his preacher, Elder Elliott. The Elder, hearing I was there, and fearful, no doubt, that I should corrupt the principles of my brother and his wife, and lead them astray, called purposely to give me battle. We held a pretty brisk conversation in the presence of my brother's wife, (he being absent,) probably for an hour; when the Elder, manifestly finding more difficulty in his way than he had anticipated, became extremely excited and impatient, and arose, walked rapidly across the floor a few times, then, turning on his heel, he addressed me in a stern, determined, and almost defiant manner, as follows: "Mr. Stacy! I will tell you plainly, if there is not something more done for our salvation than Christ has done, or ever will do, we shall all be damned." I looked at him with some degree of surprise, no doubt; for I was truly astonished to hear such a statement from an old preacher of the Gospel of Christ, as he professed to be, and merely replied; "Well, Elder, if such be the fact, I am inclined to think it is a *gone case* with us all; for if I mistake not, I have read in the Scriptures, that Christ is our only Savior; that 'His own arm brought salvation; and his own righteousness sustained him; and of the people there was none with him;' that 'There is none other name given, under heaven, among men, whereby we must be saved;' and that, 'By grace are ye saved, through faith; and that not of yourselves, it is the gift of God; not of works, lest any man should boast.'" The Elder seemed not inclined to say any more to me, and soon took his leave. But it had a very salutary effect on my sister. She remarked, after he had retired, that she was very much surprised to see the Elder manifest so much passion, and hear him make so singular a remark. This led her to reflect upon the subject, and to examine it with more prayerful attention, in all probability, than any thing I could have said to her, under other circumstances; and it was not long before both she, and my brother also, became fully convinced of the truth of the doctrine, and lived and died rejoicing in the faith of Universal Salvation. But to return to the thread of my narrative.

As before remarked, my brother said it would do no good to appoint a meeting, for nobody would hear. "Well," said I, "if people do not wish to hear, I have no wish to hold them by the button, if I could; and if they wish not to hear in this place, there are other places where they do; and I am going to Sangerfield, to see if the people there are equally bigoted." I had several old acquaintances in Sangerfield, and one relative, a sister's son. My brother said, if I would wait a few days, until he got his work in a state to leave, he would go with me. I did so, and we went together; the distance being nearly fifty miles. I had not been in Sangerfield one hour, before I was requested to give them a discourse. An appointment was consequently given out for a meeting in a little hamlet, called the Huddle, (now Waterville,) for the next day. The doctrine was an entire new thing to a large majority of the people in that country; and curiosity, if nothing else, drew together as many people as could possibly be convened in a school-house. It was on the sixth day of June, 1805, that I delivered my first message in Western New York, as it was then denominated. Breathless and profound attention was given; and I felt confident, from appearances, that some minds had discovered, at least, the glimmerings of a light they had never before seen. Some excitement was produced, and a good deal of conversation was elicited; and before many of the congregation separated, they sent a deputation to me with a request that I would preach next Sunday. To this I acceded, and told my brother that he might return home, and as soon as I could find opportunity I would make him a visit; but I was satisfied the Lord had a work for me to do in this region, and I was resolved to stay and perform it according to the best of my ability. To this he consented, with manifest reluctance. I was satisfied he would rather I did not preach at all. But I told him I should remain; and as long as there was such an inclination to hear, I would proclaim the glad tidings of free salvation to all who would hear me.

The next Sunday the congregation was very considerably enlarged; such was the case generally, wherever the doctrine was first introduced. The name, Universalism, was a strange name for a religion. And the thought, that any mortal man should have the presumption to publicly declare, that all mankind would finally be saved, was astonishing! and curiosity was on the tiptoe, to hear what could be said on such a theme. It was said, too, that they used a Bible, and had the temerity to attempt to pray! No wonder, then, that people should be very curious to witness such an anomaly, and see the Heaven-daring wretch, who should make such a mockery of sacred things! For two or three discourses in any place, the congregations would be quite numerous.

But then their fears would begin to be excited, the prejudices of their religious education would operate, the alarm would be sounded by the clergy, and the congregation would suddenly drop down to not more than half-a-dozen frequently, and sometimes entirely dwindle out. But, in most instances, some would get such a hold of the truth as to continue faithful, "through good, and through evil report;" and then, by an untiring perseverance, the cause would gradually, but permanently, grow. The people, after recovering a little from their first alarm, would occasionally drop in again; and, bye-and-bye, the congregation would increase to a respectable number of constant hearers, and permanent supporters. The congregation would be composed mostly of men; very few women would dare venture in. I have frequently addressed quite a respectable congregation, for numbers, and not a woman among them. This, at first thought, seems strange; when we would suppose, from the natural benevolence, kindness, sympathy, and tenderness of the female heart, that the doctrine of the universal paternity and benevolence of the Divine character would exactly meet their desires, and be a most grateful revelation to the goodness of their natures. But they were more difficult than men to persuade to hear and examine the doctrine, and probably for the very reason of their superior benevolence. They had heard the doctrine, if they had ever heard it at all, distorted and misrepresented by the popular clergy—condemned as a delusion of the devil, and calculated to "lead souls, blindfold, down to hell!" Their early religious education disposed them to place implicit confidence in the learning, piety, and divine knowledge of the clergy; whose decision was as infallible, in their estimation, as is that of the Pope among Papists. They, therefore, trembled at the prevalence of a doctrine fraught with such woeful consequences to the human race, and felt conscientiously obligated to use all means, not only to avoid its snares, but to arrest its progress; and that very benevolence, so congenial with the doctrine of divine truth, and which now leads almost every female of sound intellect to embrace it, and employ all means within her sphere of action to promulgate it among the sons of sorrow; forbade them to give the least countenance to it, or to those who were engaged in its extension, lest they should be accessory to the spread of a delusion which would endanger the eternal welfare of a single soul. This, and nothing else, I am satisfied, was the main reason of the shyness and opposition of females to the doctrine. For when once a woman did become acquainted with it, and believed, her joy, her courage, her zeal, and her faithfulness, exceeded greatly that of the other sex. How could it be otherwise? What could make a mother rejoice more? How could her maternal heart fail to swell with the most intense sensations of gratitude? How could her tongue be silent, and not vibrate with the "high praises of God," when she could look around upon her offspring—those objects of her tenderest love and greatest solicitude, for whose salvation, if no other means would secure it, she would cheerfully relinquish the hopes of heaven for herself, and submit to endure eternal burnings—when she could look upon them with faith, a faith of assurance founded upon the word of God, and a "hope, like an anchor of the soul, both sure and steadfast," and contemplate them as the heirs of an immortal inheritance, secured by the *will* of their heavenly Father, and sealed by the precious blood of Christ! Oh my soul, praise the Lord!

Before the congregation separated, they requested another Sunday's preaching; and a request was made for a lecture in the adjacent town of Brookfield. I consented to both, and gave the messenger from Brookfield an appointment for the next Thursday. Here an old gentleman from Hamilton, by the name of Murdock, met me, with a request for a meeting in his place; and on the next Sunday, I had a call to go to another settlement in the town of Sangerfield, six miles from the village, and hold a meeting. To all these calls I gave a ready and cheerful assent, and received good attention at each place. I continued to preach in these towns on Sundays, and lectured in different neighborhoods, for four or five weeks; when I bethought me, it was about time to make my brother the promised visit, and inform him of my success in the great work Heaven had appointed for me; for I verily thought I could discover manifest tokens of divine approbation, and a blessing actually attending my feeble efforts; I had, moreover, received a request to visit the north part of the town of Otsego, and hold a meeting, which I could easily accomplish, as the place lay directly on my way. Leaving appointments to fill on my return, allowing myself to be absent one Sunday, I started on my tour, called on my friend in Otsego, left with him an appointment for the next Sunday, and visited my brother in the intermediate time. I found my brother a little more favorable to the cause; and he began to think it possible that a meeting might be acceptable to the people in that place. However, I had not time then, but told him he might feel round among the inhabitants; and when I came again, I would hold a meeting, if they desired it. At that time, too, I had the interview with Elder Elliott, before recorded.

I returned to Otsego according to engagement; and on Sunday had a barn full of hearers. Oh, a barn is a most delightful place to hold a meeting! I always remember, when I enter one on such an occasion, that a stable was the birth-place of the Savior of the world. After meeting, that day, Mr. Wooley came to see me. He had preached some ten miles off; but hearing of my appointment, had hurried through his services as fast as possible, mounted his horse, and, soon after the close of my meeting, reached the place. I went with him to the town of Hartwick, his place of residence; and where he had organized a small society; which was then the only society of Universalists west of the Hudson river, if not the only society in the State of New York.

Mr. Wooley, Mr. Edwin Ferris, and myself, were the only preachers of Universal Salvation then in the State of New York, except in the city; and Mr. Ferris was scarcely known as such, at that time. He had united with the connection, and preached a few years in New England; but he had married, and some time in 1802, or 1803, removed into the town of Unadilla, Otsego county, purchased a lot of new land, and begun to work upon it. He had held some meetings in the vicinity, called himself a Christian preacher, (not a Christ-ian, for the sect was not known, at least not known in that section of country, at that time,) but said little or nothing about his peculiar tenets. Mr. Wooley came to the State, I believe, in 1804, preached the doctrine boldly in every place where he could find access; and organized the society in this place, probably in the winter or spring of 1805. He introduced me to several members of his society, whom I found to be worthy and excellent people, and strong, and bold in the faith; several of them were originally from the State of Rhode Island, and were made converts to the under the preaching of the venerable John Murray; and before leaving them I agreed, by the request of Mr. Wooley and the society, to preach with them the second Sunday in July. At this time, also, our Hartwick friends, with Mr. W. and myself, made arrangements to hold a general meeting of the friends of the cause—a conference, if you please—for mutual consultation upon measures for its advancement, as well as for religious worship; and the place agreed upon, as the most eligible, was Burlington, Otsego county; and the time, the Wednesday after my meeting in Hartwick. The Presbyterians had erected a meeting-house in Burlington, and we could have the use of it for the occasion, which would be a liberal accommodation, although the house was in an unfinished state; and we had a few friends in the neighborhood, who would cheerfully supply our temporal necessities while among them. Letters were accordingly written to our most influential friends scattered through the country; and Mr. W. and myself would give all the notice we could, in our itinerations. I spoke to Mr. Wooley of Mr. Ferris. He had not seen him in this country—did not know where he lived, and seemed little inclined to hunt him up, or give him notice of our proposed meeting. I expressed my surprise—told Mr. W. that we surely ALL should be together on the occasion, there were so few of us in the country; and expressed my earnest desire that he should be notified, if possible, and attend the meeting at Burlington; and I was at a loss to account for his indifference about it. Mr. Ferris and he had formerly been acquainted, and they had had some misunderstanding. Mr. W. was a man of rather jealous temperament, as I afterward learned by experience; and I had no inclination to renew acquaintance, or have him associate with us.

I returned to my appointments in Hamilton, Sangerfield, and Brookfield, and gave as general notice of our meeting in Burlington as lay in my power. I also made arrangements for further labors. On the second Sunday in July I went to Hartwick, according to engagement; delivered my message, and ascertained that no notice had been sent to Mr. Ferris; nor could I find any person who could inform me where he lived. Several persons had heard of such a man, and believed he lived some where on Butternut Creek, either in the town of Butternuts, or not far below. I told my friends I was resolved to find him, if he could be found, and to use all the influence I could exert to induce him to attend the meeting; as we surely needed all the strength we could muster, to meet so formidable a host of opposers as we anticipated. I had never seen Mr. F.; but I had heard a good report of him at the east, where he had labored; and I had enjoyed a very particular acquaintance with his brother Walter, of whom I had a very exalted opinion both as a Christian and an able preacher of the Gospel. I therefore started early on Monday morning, resolved to spend all the time I could spare between then and our meeting on Wednesday in seeking for him, if it were necessary. Directing my course to the town of Butternuts, I made inquiry at every place where I thought information might be obtained; but I could hear nothing of him until I got near the south line of the town, and within three miles of his residence; there I found a man who knew him, and who informed me where he resided. I reached his dwelling early in the afternoon. He was not within when I arrived; but his wife directed me where I might find him. I introduced myself to him, told him my business, and he wept tears of joy. He had not seen a preacher, and but very few people, who could sympathize with him in faith, since he left New England. He had heard that Mr. Wooley was in the country; but I soon found that he had as little inclination to renew acquaintance with Mr. Wooley, as Mr. Wooley had with him—their antipathy was mutual. However, he readily agreed to accompany me to the meeting; and the next day we rode to Burlington. Individuals from a great distance attended, and we made up a numerous and respectable congregation. Public worship was holden on Wednesday, and Mr. Ferris and Mr. Wooley delivered each a discourse. A council was organized by appointing Mr. W. moderator, and Mr. Abel Gardner, (layman,) clerk; and a number of resolutions were passed, the most important of which was, that it was expedient to organize an association in the State of New York. Consequently, delegates were elected to attend the next meeting of the Convention in New England, to present the doings of this meeting, and to ask the appointment of a committee from that body to meet with us on the first Wednesday and Thursday in June, 1806, and assist in the organization of an association; and Mr. Wooley and myself were appointed said delegates. There was a man at this meeting by the name of Fowler, who had been a Methodist preacher, but had become converted to the faith of Universalism, and for several years after this preached around in the country, more or less; but his preaching did not prove very profitable; and for reasons not necessary to name, he was never received into formal fellowship.

Mr. Smith, in his "Historical Sketches," says, that this conference "was attended by two or more delegates from each of the respective societies," &c. Here he labors under a trifling mistake. But one single society existed in all central and western New York—the society in Hartwick. Preaching had not yet been introduced into Whitestown, and no organization had yet been attended to in the field of my special labor. The society in Hartwick attended nearly en masse, and individuals promiscuously came in from all, or nearly all towns and places where preaching had been introduced.

This meeting was attended with happy consequences. It diffused information abroad, both of the doctrine, and the state of the cause. It encouraged our friends, by showing that we were resolved to maintain order, and persevere—that we were determined to permanently plant the standard of Universal Grace, and, by all the weapons of divine warfare Heaven had placed within our reach, to manfully defend it. It gave strength and stability to the doubtful, and encouragement to those seeking after truth; and, what proved equally as beneficial and advantageous to the cause—it alarmed sectarians and awakened up oppositon and discussion. From this time, and indeed from the commencement of our labors in the state of New York, but more especially after this meeting, which had a tendency to bring us more into public notice, we met with warm opposition from every quarter, from all Partialist denominations, and in every imaginable form, except a fair one. Few of the clergy would condescend to hold an argument with us. They seemed to think that the most successful way, at least the safest for them, would be to rail against the doctrine in their public discourses, to misrepresent it, to slander and abuse its advocates, and to treat us with the utmost contempt, as entirely beneath notice—to sneer, or frown us down; but they would encourage their deluded and enthusiastic emissaries to attack and abuse us at every opportunity.

My most common practice was, at the close of my discourses, especially in new places, to give liberty for remarks, or inquiry; and whether I did or not, I was most sure to meet with opposition from some quarter. And not only did I meet opposers at public meetings; but at almost every house where I chanced to call; at the corners of the streets, and on the public highway. It was a good thing for me; it admonished me never to lay aside my panoply, but to keep the weapons of my warfare polished and bright. Among the most zealous and virulent of my opposers, was an old gentleman by the name of Benjamin Morse, who resided in the town of Sangerfield. This man was, originally, from Connecticut; a dissenter from the Presbyterian church, because it had not fire enough for his zeal. He was what they called a "new light;" and as great a Pharisee as I ever met with. He sought me out, followed me from house to house, attacked me in the most abusive manner, and would denounce the most awful imprecations upon my head. For a season, I treated him with the deference and respect due to his age; and several times had the success to cool down his holy wrath, and make him ask pardon for abuse. But he would soon forget it, and, the next time I met him, come again upon me like a hungry lion. At length I told him, I had hitherto treated him as a youth ought to treat a man of gray hairs, but I found it of no use; and I resolved, in future, to treat him in his own way—to "answer a fool according to his folly;" and he must remember the old adage, "If you begin with children, you must take children's play." Shortly after this, while I yet made my home in Sangerfield, I had a call to attend the funeral of a child in Brookfield; and Mr. Morse's house was situated on my way. On my arrival at the place of appointment, I saw Mr. M. in the congregation. Nothing, however, passed between us at the time; but on my return, the next day, when I was in sight of his house, I saw the old gentleman walk deliberately from his door down to the road; and when I came up, he stood leaning upon his fence. "Stop," he said, "I want to talk with you; get off and walk into the house." "I can not alight, Mr. M., I have an appointment a-head, and have little time to spare." "But I want to talk with you," he replied. "Well, Mr. M., I will sit here and talk with you a very few minutes; but I can not go into the house." "I was at your meeting yesterday," he said. "I saw you there," said I; "and I was quite surprised to see you in such an unhallowed congregation." "I did not know who was going to preach, until I got there." "Well, sir, you were not obliged to stay, after you found out; the same road that you came was open for your return." "Oh, I was not afraid of you hurting me; but your doctrine is false—it's a damnable heresy." "How do you know that, Mr. M.?" "Because the Bible says, 'He that believeth shall be saved, and he that believeth not *shall be damned.*'" "Are you a believer, Mr. M., according to the import of those words?" "Yes, thank God, I am." "Your words prove nothing to me, Mr. M.; if you are a believer, you can prove it by something more convincing than mere assertion. Can you exhibit the signs which follow the believer?" "Why, what are they?" "Do you not know sir? An old man, whose hairs have blossomed for the grave—one who has long made high and loud professions of discipleship to the Great Teacher, and who can anathematize with so much assurance every one who has the temerity to dissent from his creed,—and not know what conspicuous signs our Savior said should follow those who believed!" The old gentleman, with a lowered voice, said, "I do not now recollect." "Well," I replied, "'these signs shall follow them that believe;

in my name shall they cast out devils; they shall speak with new tongues; they shall take up serpents; and if they drink any deadly thing, it shall not hurt them; they shall lay their hands on the sick, and they shall recover.' Can you do these things, Mr. M.?" The old gentleman's countenance changed at once; he dropped his head, and looked confounded; and merely replied, "I never tried." "Well, now is your time to try, Mr. M. I will produce a sick person for you to heal, and deadly poison for you to drink; and if the sick recover by the laying on of your hands, and the poison does not injure you, I will then acknowledge you are a believer; otherwise, I shall take the liberty of pronouncing you an old impostor, and a hypocrite; and most solemly warn you never again to call yourself a believer." The old gentleman was so completely confounded, he could not reply. He had never had any just conception of the meaning of the passage; indeed, he did not seem to know that the words I quoted were connected with the words he had repeated. He hemmed, and stammered, and changed color; but at length, looking at me, stammered out, "Are you a believer?" "I have never told you that I was, Mr. M." Then, turning on his heel, he cried out, "Physician heal thyself," and left me. I was encouraged to hope, now, that I had so completely stopped his mouth, that he would no more assail me; for there was no use in trying to reason with him; and all he seemed to know of the Scriptures was a few detached passages, which Partialists had converted into cant phrases to sling at Universalists: but I was mistaken. He repeatedly assailed me after that; and soon after I was married, and fixed my residence in Brookfield, he took occasion to call on my wife, (who was not then a believer,) in my absence, and warned her against the doctrine; and he went so far as to advise her to leave me, and no longer endanger her salvation by living with such a heretic! I had heard a story about the old gentleman; and some of my friends told me, if I would tell him of it, he would quit me, and never again trouble me. It was not long before the old man called again, and I happened to be at home; when he soon began his abuse. I said to him "Mr. Morse, I feel it my duty to ask you a few serious questions, and beg you will give me candid replies. I am sorry to be under the necessity, but duty impels me. "I am ready," he said, "to answer any question that you are disposed to ask, that I am able to answer." "Well, sir, you can answer them perfectly easy, if you feel disposed to do so." [Here I must inform the reader, that the old gentleman was a shoemaker by trade; and also, that he had been telling me some stories about Michael Coffin, who was once a Universalist preacher, but who had been expelled from the connection years before that time.] "The first question I wish to propose, Mr. M., is, how long is it since you experienced religion, and have squared your conduct by the holy precepts of the Gospel?" "Ever since I was sixteen years old—thank God," he replied. "How long is it, Mr. M., since you made a pair of birch-bark shoes for a man, instead of leather; and obliged him to take them because the obligation did not say *leather shoes?*" The old gentleman started from his seat, evidently in a violent passion, and walked rapidly across the floor, and, in quite an angry tone, cried out, "I don't know any thing about birch-bark shoes." "I don't know that you do, Mr. M.—don't get mad." "If you say I ever made a pair of birch-bark shoes for any man, you shall prove it." "I have not said so, Mr. M; I merely asked you a question—don't be offended. But supposing you did so, which would be the worst, think you, in the sight of God, to do as you say Coffin did, or to cheat a man out of his just dues?" The old gentleman turned toward me with his fist doubled, and said, "If you say I have cheated a man out of his just dues, you shall prove it." "I have not said so, Mr. M.;—why are you so offended? But we should do well to remember the old adage, 'Those who live in glass houses, should be careful how they throw stones.'" The old gentleman discovered he could not frighten me, and soon left; and as my friends predicted, it entirely broke up his haunt—he never afterwards molested me.

But every imaginable means was resorted to in order to silence, and put me down, and stop the progress of the doctrine—arguments, threats, ridicule, and even flattery! Some said, "Such a fellow ought not to be suffered to go at large. The law ought to make provision to arrest and confine such disturbers of the public peace." Children were indulged, or perhaps taught, to insult me in the streets, by throwing sticks, and crying out, "There goes a Universalist preacher!—Halloa, you, Universalist preacher!" One man came to me, a man in good standing in society, and a member of the Congregationalist church, and in a wonderfully complaisant manner complimented me on my happy talent for public speaking; and said, that a number of the brethren had heard me preach, and were highly pleased with my manner; and if I could only consent to preach the doctrine they believed, as they were now destitute of a preacher, I would give great satisfaction, and command almost any salary I would name. I looked at him with indignation ; for I saw more of the devil in him than I had seen in any one before, and rebuked him sharply—told him, if he supposed I was preaching to please people, or for the sake of salary, he was greatly deceived in his man—that his threats, his sneers and his flatteries, were equally despicable in my view; and he would find them as unavailing to turn me from my course, as his arguments were to refute the doctrine I preached. I would answer him in the language of the inspired Peter—"Whether it be right in the sight of God, to harken unto you more than unto God, judge ye." The man left me, rebuked, and evidently ashamed.

I had repeated invitations to call at the houses of opposers, and discourse with them ; and being desirous of improving every means in my power to advance the cause of Divine truth, I accepted such invitations as often as possible, whenever I thought I should not be abused beyond endurance. A Mr. B—t, an influential member of the Presbyterian church in Sangerfield, had several times manifested a great desire for a conversation, and very earnestly requested me to make him a visit. He wanted a long conversation—he had a great regard for me, and verily thought he could show me the error of my way so clearly, that I would forsake it. He had a great many passages of Scripture he wanted to read, which he thought I could not reconcile with the doctrine of Universalism. He wanted, at least, half a day's conversation, &c. &c. My friends said he would treat me civilly, and several of them would accompany me ; I agreed therefore to make him an afternoon visit ; and the time was appointed. The day arrived, and I went in company with some five or six who were desirous of hearing the discourse ; and we found as many, or more, of his special friends already assembled, and among them the before-mentioned Benjamin Morse, who was father-in-law to Mr. B—t ; making quite a respectable congregation of hearers, for those days, and that place. We were received very civilly ; and Mr. B—t soon got his Bible, which he had prepared for the occasion by turning down a vast number of leaves. The first passage he introduced was the parable of the rich man and Lazarus ; and was very anxious to know, how I could reconcile that passage with the doctrine of Universal Salvation ? After a few remarks, in which I succeeded in showing him it was a parable, or a figurative passage, I observed, "We must seek a solution of it, as well as of all other figurative passages, by carefully examining the context, in all its bearings; as well as parallel texts." He still held the Bible in his hand—I had none in mine: "Now, sir," I said, "we will examine the context, and see how the Savior introduces the parable, and what his leading discourse was about. Please to look after me, and see whether I repeat right;" and I began, "'The law and the prophets were until John; since that time the kingdom of God is preached, and every man presseth into it; and it is easier for heaven and earth to pass, than one tittle of the law to fail. Whosoever putteth away his wife, and marrieth another, committeth adultery; and whosoever marrieth her that is put away from her husband, committeth adultery'—Do I read right, sir?" The man raised not his eyes, but changed color, looked confused, and after a long pause, drawlingly answered, "Y-e-s." I was surprised at his manner; and on looking around, observed his wife's face blood-red, and nearly every one in the room with the muscles of their faces disturbed, evidently with suppressed laughter. What, in the name of reason, (thought I,) does all this mean? I felt confused, and hurt; and looked round on the company disapprovingly, and then proceeded with my reading, and exposition of the parable. Mr. B—t made no objection to the exposition; but seemed quite satisfied with it. Nor did he once attempt to dispute my interpretation of any one of the numerous passages he introduced, nor offer an argument against my doctrine; but seemed to listen attentively to all I said; though I could not help observing that he appeared somewhat embarrassed, and conducted quite differently, all the afternoon, from what I anticipated; nevertheless, he treated me kindly; and we parted in a friendly manner. On my way to a friend's house, where I was going to stop for the night, he said, "Why, you gave Mr. B—t a most tremendous shot." "I gave Mr. B—t a shot! How—what do you mean, sir?" "Why, don't you know?" "Certainly not—I had no design to injure his feelings; and if I gave him a shot, as you say, I am totally ignorant how." "But, do you not know his situation?" "No; I am acquainted with no peculiarities of his circumstances." "Why did you stop, then, in that particular spot in the parable, and ask him if you read right?" "Because I wanted to fix his attention closely on the subject; and I was then going to enter on the parable he had introduced for examination." "Well, everybody in the house supposed you knew he was the identical character there spoken of, and that you did it intentionally, because of that; they supposed that you knew he was living with a second wife, his first wife being yet alive. He is the *man* who has *put away his wife, and married another.*" "Well," I replied, "this was not dreamed of by me. Surely the bow was drawn at a venture; and if he was hit, the Lord directed the arrow; and I hope it may prove a salutary wound." Mr. B—t had been vociferous in his condemnation of Universalism on account of its licentious tendency; but I heard no more from him after this—he was peaceable as a lamb.

After I had delivered two or three discourses in Hamilton, in the neighborhood called Colchester, or rather Graham's Corners, it began, as usual, to produce some excitement, and stir up opposition. They had a settled Presbyterian clergyman, an aged man, by the name of Knapp, who held his meetings at the centre of the town, about three miles from the place of my meetings. Several of his hearers had attended my discourses, and become favorably impressed with the doctrine advanced. The old gentleman became alarmed, and told them, if they would get me to deliver a discourse in a certain school-house, near the centre of the town, he would attend the meeting and refute the doctrine in their presence. Poor man! he little knew what the doctrine was, as he afterwards found out. I was requested to make the appointment; which I accordingly did, without being informed of Mr. K.'s engagement. On the appointed day, I repaired to the house of a friend, near the place of appointment, to put out my horse, when he informed me that it was quite probable Mr. Knapp would attend meeting; and asked me, if I should feel intimidated if he were among my hearers? I replied, I thought not—I had no fears from the opposers of the doctrine, but really desired that all such would attend, and examine for themselves. He did not tell me, however, that Mr. K. had engaged to attend, for the express purpose of argument, nor hint that he had any such object in view. I requested the gentleman, however, if Mr. K. did come in, to introduce him to me; as I always wished to treat a clergyman with the respect due to his profession. Soon the people assembled, and filled the house to excess. The exercise was delayed for a season with the expectation of Mr. K's arrival; but as I heard nothing of him, and the people began to manifest some uneasiness, I arose and opened the meeting. At the close of prayer, an old gentlemen who stood near me pointed out Mr. K. He had come in during prayer, and taken his seat near the centre of the house. On being informed who he was, I called him by name, and invited him to a seat by my side;

this he declined, however, and I proceeded with my services. I took for a text, 2 Luke 10 : 4, and labored with all my powers to show the listening congregation the nature of those good tidings which the angel published to the shepherds, the certainty of their universal publication, and the salvation which would surely be produced thereby. The whole congregation, (and many of Mr. K.'s hearers were among the number,) gave profound attention. As soon as the text was named, Mr. K. took out his Bible, and was very busy with it through the whole of the discourse. I supposed he was looking up my proof-texts, and watching to see if I did not mutilate the word of God; and to favor him as much as possible, I would quote book, chapter, and verse, as accurately as my memory would serve. The services closed—the congregation were dismissed, but not a soul moved—the house was as still as the chamber of death—the people looking toward each other, and then toward Mr. K.; and for several minutes this, to me, strange scene continued. I felt surprised at this unusual circumstance, but concluded to wait the event with equal silence. At length, probably to break the wearisome spell, some individual called for a contribution. Mr. K. then spoke—"Yes," he said, "there will be opportunity for those who wish to contribute; but before it is taken, I wish the privilege of making a few remarks." The congregation, as with one consent, took their seats, and Mr. K. proceeded: "The young man has said a great deal; and much that he has said is true. His exhortation is good, and I could wish we might all profit by it. But this doctrine of Universal Salvation *is not true*; for in view of that, I desire to know what he, or any one else, can do with the passages of Scripture that I shall now read." I then learned the use the old gentleman had been making of his Bible. I had noticed he had turned down a number of leaves; and he now turned them up, in succession, and commented as he read, beginning with Mal. 4: 1. "For behold the day cometh that shall burn as an oven," and proceeding through many of the parables in the Evangelists, he closed with his comment on the twentieth chapter of Revelations. He spoke nearly as long as I had, and the most profound attention was given him. When he closed, I arose, and, addressing myself to Mr. K., thanked him, most sincerely, for his attendance, and for his faithfulness. I remarked, it was not often that I found such a manifestation of faithfulness; for, in most cases, those who were placed as shepherds of the flock would flee when they saw the supposed wolf coming, and ensconcing themselves behind the impregnable bulwark of their own pulpits, entirely out of his reach, would there growl their disapprobation, and thunder anathemas upon his head. But he, as a faithful guardian and guide of the people of his charge, had come to meet the enemy, and arrest, in its infancy, the error to which he supposed them exposed. I felt grateful, too, on another account. He had afforded me an opportunity to answer his objections in the audience of the people; and thus, I hoped and trusted to advance the cause of divine truth. I then took up the texts in the order he had read them, (for he had not read a single passage which was not perfectly familiar in my memory,) and gave my opinion on them; and probably occupied about as much time as he had, in his comments; the people, all the while, listened with breathless attention—such was the excitement to hear the discussion. But there was evidently some alarm felt by some of Mr. K.'s church. I had scarcely closed my comment on the last passage, introduced by Mr. K., when some person cried out in an agitated tone to me, "What's become of Judas?" I answered suddenly, "He has gone to his own place." "Where's that?" he inquired. Another answered, before I had time to speak, "To hell, Christ says." I responded, "He does not say a word like that." "He does," was the quick reply. I asked, "Please, sir, show me the place in the Bible where Christ says that hell is Judas' place?" He replied, "Christ called him a devil, and hell is the place for devils." I further inquired, "Do you believe, sir, that the old serpent, which is the devil and satan, are one and the same character?" "Yes," he answered. Then I asked, "Well, sir, what has become of Peter?" "I don't know," said he. I replied, "Our Savior said to Peter, 'Get thee behind me, satan; thou art an offense unto me.' Now if Judas has gone to hell because he was a devil, Peter must also have gone there, because he was a satan; and we lose two of Christ's disciples. What shall we do in such a case, sir?" By this time silence prevailed again—no reply was made. I then took up the case of Judas, and spoke pretty freely; for God gave me great freedom of utterance. After I had closed, I waited a few moments for some response; but none was made. I then addressed Mr. K., as follows: "We have kept the people here a long while, and they have surely manifested a great share of patience. Much has been said on both sides of the question, but the argument has not been brought to a crisis. Probably the people have not yet been able to discover where the truth lies. Now, if you will answer me two or three plain questions, we will at once let this waiting and patient congregation see where the truth is, without detaining them many minutes longer." "I am willing," he said, very pleasantly, "to answer any question I am able to answer." "Well, sir, the questions shall be plain, such as you can easily answer, and such as will admit of a direct answer. Do you believe, sir, that it is the will of God that all men should be saved?" He replied, "It is the will of God, that all who accept of the overtures of mercy, who close in with the offers of salvation, who repent and believe the Gospel, should be saved." I rejoined, "Mr. K., will you have the goodness to answer my questions directly? and then you can make as many remarks as you please, afterwards. Do you believe that it is God's *will* that all mankind should be saved? I do not ask you if they will be saved, but whether or not you believe it is God's *will* to save them?" He spoke a second time in a very similar manner, wholly evading an answer to the question. I then said, "Mr. K., I must confess that I am such a blunder-head, I do not understand which you mean, yes or no; have the goodness to tell me?—I simply ask for your belief; and you can certainly tell me what you believe about it, if you please. Do you believe it is the will of God, that all men should be saved, or not?" He now began to grow a little petulent, and answered rather peevishly, "It is God's will to save as many as he pleases." "Mr. K.," said I, "if you are unwilling to answer the question, please to say so, and I will dispense with this, and ask another; but, if you are willing to answer the question, I wish you would, so that I, and these people, can understand you. Do you believe, that it is the will of God, that all men should be saved, and come unto the knowledge of the truth?" The old gentleman now felt quite excited, and replied in an angry tone, "I'll answer you when I please—and I sha'nt before." "Very well, Mr. K.," I replied, "this is all the answer I need; for you know, sir, that you can not answer it, either in the affirmative or negative, and maintain your doctrine. You know, sir, that, if you answer it in the affirmative, you have already acknowledged the sovereignty of God—that 'He worketh all things after the counsel of his own will;' and if you answer in the negative, you know, sir, that you flatly contradict the word of God, which says, 'God, our Savior, will have all men to be saved, and come unto the knowledge of the truth;' therefore, go which way you will, sir, you are down." While I was speaking, the old gentleman arose and took his hat; and, as I closed my remarks, he turned to me and said, "I am very sorry, that a young man of such talents—so capable of doing good in the world as you are, should embrace such an error, and so fatally deceive the people;" and, without giving me a chance to reply, he shot out of the door with all the nimbleness of youth. Thus ended the controversy—thus concluded this threatened overthrow and remediless explosion, that the doctrine of God's Universal Grace, in the hands of an illiterate stripling, was to receive from an aged and learned Orthodox divine. It was astonishing to witness the visible manifestation of feelings among the different individuals composing the congregation. Mr. Knapp's special friends, (for many of his church were in attendance, to witness the overthrow of Universalism,) immediately followed his example; and left the house with disappointment, mortification, and chagrin imprinted deeply upon their countenances, muttering their dissatisfaction blended with anathemas on my poor head; while the faces of another part of the congregation brightened up with a smile of hope, that the impervious cloud which had hitherto obscured their prospects was beginning to vanish, before the light of a *truth* that they had never before seen. The hat was then passed round, and a liberal contribution taken up. It was the first I had received since I crossed the Hudson river.

It was curious, indeed, to witness the different views and feelings which agitated the minds of different individuals; and frequently not a little perplexing and vexatious to listen to their remarks, and meet their questions. As I have before had occasion to remark, curiosity, for a short season, drew together quite a numerous congregation in almost every place where appointments were first made; and they were truly mixed congregations—people of every faith and no faith, grave and frivolous, sober and intemperate, civil and profane—all assembled together to see a being that could hardly be considered as belonging to the human species, a Universalist! And to hear what strange, what marvelous, and incredible stories he had to tell. Some thought all my professed faith a mere hoax; that my proceedings were mere matter of sport; that I was only trying to see how I could vex and discomfit the Orthodox; and to them it was a scene of hilarity. Others supposed me mad—that I was a pitiable maniac, and knew nothing what I said, nor considered the consequences of my conduct; while others considered me honest and sincere in my profession, but woefully deluded, and mourned sincerely over my fate, and the fate of those who were deceived by my arguments.—Some, strange as it may seem, although they knew that I received little or nothing for my services, believed or pretended to believe me hypocritical, and that I was trying to deceive others for gain! But a few, among the many, were able to discover some glimpses of the divine light, which led them to follow on, until they reached the desirable goal of a well-grounded hope. Among the first class named, was a man with whom I tarried after my casual discussion with the Rev. Mr. Knapp. He was educated in the Baptist school—his parents were Baptists; but he had paid no attention to the subject of religion. He thought, no doubt, that the Baptists were right, if there were any truth in religion; but to him it was all a matter of indifference. He had heard of my meeting, and he attended; and it was a source of great hilarity. He felt wonderfully pleased with my success in the discussion with Mr. K., and invited me home with him. And the conversation that we had, my apparent sincerity, &c., led him to think it *possible* that I was sincere, notwithstanding it seemed very strange to him; and the next morning, while going to a pasture together to catch my horse, he looked at me with great earnestness and said, "Mr. Stacy, do you really believe the doctrine that you preach?" I was amazed. I replied, "Why, Mr. D., what, in the name of reason, do you suppose would tempt me to preach—solemnly to preach, in the name of religion, a doctrine I do not heartily believe? What could induce me to expose myself to the scorn and derision of the popular world—to sacrifice every earthly consideration, and receive, most certainly, the hatred and malice of the bigoted and superstitious, and all the persecution they are able to inflict, without the most distant hope of temporal gain or emolument! Is it possible, sir, that you, or any other man, can suppose me insincere?" My reply seemed to strike him with much force. He began to look serious and thoughtful; and, as he has repeatedly said since, (for he has often referred to the circumstance,) it made him feel ashamed. But he did not absent himself from my meetings; he attended every opportunity. The light soon began to beam upon his understanding, and effect a visible reformation; and he faithfully persevered until he obtained a hope, which has been "an anchor to his soul," through all the labors and trials of life; which has borne him up and consoled him amid the most trying bereavements, in the death of a beloved and very promising son, under circumstances the most afflicting, just as he was entering upon the stage of manhood; and more recently, the amiable companion of his youth. Under all these afflictions he has never doubted, but has found an abundant source of consolation in a well-established faith in the Gospel of Universal Grace, and a permanent support upon a well-grounded hope of a glorious immortality for the whole Adamic family; and his head is now blossoming for the grave, while he is peacefully and cheerfully awaiting his entrance into that blessed mansion, where his beloved ones have entered before him.

In a very short time after the interview with Rev. Mr. Knapp, I had a request to make an appointment, in what was called Paine's Settlement, now Hamilton village. This was then the most populous part of the town; and the Baptist sect predominated. They had, for those times, a pretty numerous and wealthy community, and had built them a very good meeting-house; into this, however, I was not permitted to enter; and, indeed, some vigorous measures were taken to prevent the spread of my pernicious doctrine among them. A meeting of the church was called, as I was informed, for consultation; and they came to the conclusion that the most advisable course would be, to have some of their most able members attend, and give battle to the deceiver on the spot. And, as their settled preacher, Elder Hosmer, was under the necessity of being absent, (or, as some shrewdly suspected, was disposed to be absent,) it was agreed that Judge Paine, one of the deacons of the church, and one of their most zealous and talented members, should attend and oppose me. All this arrangement, however, was carefully concealed from me, and my friends, until after the event.

The only place that could be obtained for my meeting was a ball-room, in a public-house. The room was quite large, but at an early hour was literally filled; and profound attention was given to the new and strange doctrine. I delivered a discourse from 1 John, 4: 8. My general practice was, to give liberty for remarks, or questions, at the close of a discourse, and wait a reasonable time for those who wished to speak, before dismissing the congregation; but as no one manifested a disposition to speak at this time, I waited but a few minutes, then dismissed the congregation, and retired to the sitting-room below. I had been seated, however, not five minutes, when a friend came to me and said, "You must go back again, for Judge Paine is tearing your sermon all to pieces." I arose and followed him; and when we entered the chamber, Judge Paine was standing nearly in the centre of the room, harangueing the people, very few of whom had left, in a very loud and earnest manner, and warning them in a most solemn tone to beware of the doctrine they had been hearing—it was damnable heresy, and would lull them into carnal security, and lead them down to perdition! The divine law was out against the sinner—he had broken the law of God—it was infinite transgression—the penalty of the law was infinite, and its threatenings endless punishment; &c. The people were standing closely round the Judge; and, being like Zaccheus, short in stature, I could not see him; I therefore stepped upon a bench where I could have a fair view of him, and listen more understandingly to his discourse. I had been in this position but a moment before his eye caught me; and, in an instant, his voice faltered—he lost sight of his subject—was evidently much embarrassed, and began to stammer. To relieve him from his unpleasant predicament, I said, "When you have finished your remarks, Judge, I should like to ask you two or three questions." "Well," he replied, "I don't know but I am through now." "Well, sir, do you expect salvation by the deeds of the law?" He replied, "No." "Then, sir, what does all your discourse amount to?" "I should like to ask you a question," he said. "Well, sir, I am ready to hear it." He proceeded, "You have been endeavoring to prove to us, that God loves all the works of his hands, have you not?" "Yes, sir." "Well, the question I wish to propose is, does God love the devil?" "It is truly a singular question, sir, but I am prepared to answer it directly: If the devil be a creature of God, he loves him; for 'God is love,' and he loves all that he has made; he can not hate. As the author of Wisdom says, 'Thou lovest all the things that are, and abhorrest nothing that thou hast made; for never wouldst thou have made any thing, if thou hadst hated it.' But it is not so much my purpose to speak of the origin of the devil, as his end." "His end!" he repeated, "you do not believe the devil will have an end, do you?" "Yes, certainly, sir; don't you?" "No, I don't." "Do you believe the Bible, sir?" "Yes." "Will you believe the devil will be destroyed, if I will prove it by the express words of the Bible?" "Yes, to be sure I will; but that you can't do." "Listen then, sir, (I quote Hebrews 2: 14.) 'Forasmuch then as the children are partakers of flesh and blood, he also himself likewise took part of the same, that through death he might destroy him that hath the power of death, that is, *the devil;*' and not only so, but we are assured that he will destroy all his works; for John says, 'For this cause was the Son of God manifested, that he might *destroy the works of the devil.*'" By the time I had finished these quotations, the Judge had got his hand on the handle of the door. "Stop, Judge," said I, "do not go yet; hear me a little further, if you please; I have a number more passages to the point, I wish to quote." "It will do no good," said he, "for you and I to talk any more." "But please answer me one question, at least, before you go. Do you believe the devil will be destroyed?" "No," he replied. "I was afraid, sir, you did not believe the Bible, by your previous conversation." By the time I had finished the last remark, the Judge had shut the door after himself pretty hard.

These brief, casual controversies had a very favorable effect. They produced a degree of excitement, were subjects of conversation among the people in their private circles, and increased a desire to hear, and an inclination to investigate. The people began to discover that the arguments of their spiritual leaders, were not so pungent and powerful, in support of their theories, as they had supposed them to be, when opposed by an illiterate stripling. Individuals who had been habitually taught to pay superior reverence to the clergy, and to the leaders of the church, and to receive their *ipse dixit* on spiritual things as divine oracles and the end of all controversy, began to assume the unwelcome boldness to ask questions, and to criticise their answers; and to indulge sometimes in witty and humorous remarks. I must be permitted, in illustration, to relate a short anecdote.

There was a young gentleman, an attorney-at-law, who had set up in his profession in the village, and boarded with Judge Paine. He, among others, came to hear the new doctrine proclaimed, and was a hearer of the discourse between the Judge and myself. On the following morning, while at breakfast, the young attorney addressed the Judge, in a very serious manner, and said, "Why, Judge, they are circulating very bad stories about you, which I am sorry to hear." The Judge, with much surprise, replied, "Circulating bad stories about me! What in the world are they?" "Why," replied the lawyer, "the report is very currently passing the round, that you have become a deist!" "That I have become a deist!" replied the Judge, "why, this appears to be one of the last things that could have been thought of about me! what in the world could it have originated from?" "Why," replied the lawyer, with a shrewd look, "they say, that you denied the Bible, yesterday." This was sufficient—the Judge now understood him—dropped his head, and said no more. Nor did he ever after that, I believe, attempt to hold an argument with the most feeble advocate of Universalism. I afterward enjoyed a long and friendly acquaintance with him, though I do not recollect seeing him again at my meeting. Many years after, when in conversation with a gentleman in regard to the different denominations in the town, the Judge remarked, "We have to lament, that the Universalist society in this town, comprises men of the brightest talents, of the greatest respectability, and moral worth, of any we have among us."

About this time, two gentlemen, Col. Cleveland and Dr. A. B. Sizer, from the third township, (now Madison,) attended my meeting in Hamilton, and requested an appointment for their place. I had now found labor enough to perform in the vineyard of Christ; and I had zeal enough to drive me ahead with all my might; and, blessed be God, I had health and strength to do much, in my own way. I allowed them to give out the appointment; they did so, and had sufficient influence to get the use of the Baptist meeting-house, at what was called the Indian Opening; not a solitary building then stood where the flourishing village of Madison has since grown up. This meeting-house was owned by a Close-communion Baptist congregation, and Elder Salmon Morton, a rigid Calvinist, and a violent and obstinate polemic, was their preacher.

Elder Morton was alarmed, and came forth in a high state of perspiration, with his coat on his arm, to make an attack. It was on the 19th of July; but he did not enter the house until after services had commenced; and consequently, I had no introduction to him, till after meeting. I delivered my message, and the Elder then arose and merely notified the congregation that he would deliver a discourse from the same text on the next Sabbath. I descended from the desk, was introduced to the Elder; and we walked together to the house of Dr. Sizer, in company with a number of other gentlemen, where we held a long, and somewhat spirited conversation. I was sitting on one side of the room, and the Elder on the opposite side, in pretty earnest conversation, while a death-like silence was observed by our auditors; when the Elder suddenly arose and stepped toward me with his fist doubled. As he came toward me, I involuntarily arose; for what purpose I knew not, for I neither felt anger nor fear; but an individual whose position was nearly between us, said, "Elder Morton, don't get mad." The Elder stopped, as suddenly as he arose, and very pleasantly said, "I am thinking of the passage which says, 'Be ye angry, and sin not;'" and, with a smile, turned and again took his chair. This produced quite a laugh in the assembly; and we soon closed our debate, and parted quite amicably.

But the Elder could not withhold his rage against the doctrine of Universal grace. It destroyed all his ambitious hopes of exultation over his fallen enemies, all the exquisite pleasure he anticipated in beholding their endless writhings in the agonies of unquenchable fire of hell, all the delightful music of the hopeless groans of damned spirits! He inveighed against it in every discourse, and in every place, with all the bitterness of his Christian (?) soul; and his common appellation for it was "Stacy's doctrine." His bitterness, and his obstinacy may be illustrated, by a brief anecdote. He had been preaching one day, with all his eloquence against Stacy, and Stacy's doctrine, and most solemnly warning the people against giving it the least countenance; and at the close gave liberty for remarks, exhortations, &c. An individual arose and requested the privilege of asking the Elder one question. He remarked, it was rather an odd question; but he wanted the Elder should allow him the privilege. Leave was granted, and he proceeded—"You have said a great deal to day, against Stacy's doctrine; now, Elder, if you should hear a voice from heaven, and know it to be the voice of God, which should tell you that Stacy's doctrine was true, and yours false, would you believe it?" "No!" said the Elder.

Shortly after this, Elder Morton requested my friends in Madison to invite me to hold a meeting with him, and preach each a discourse from the same text. They informed me of it; and, in passing the Elder's house, not many days afterwards, I called on him, informed him of what I had heard, and asked him if it was correct? He said it was—he wished to have such a meeting. Well, I said, it will be quite agreeable to me; and you may choose the text and preach first, or I will choose the text and deliver the first discourse, as shall best accommodate your feelings. "Oh," he said, "I wish to choose the text." Very well, you will then deliver the first discourse, and give me the privilege of closing. Well—he would do that; and named the text. (Mark 3: 19.) I told him, I liked the text well; and we agreed on a time and place for the meeting. It was to be holden on Wednesday, 13th November, and at the Presbyterian meeting-house, in Madison, if that could be obtained. The reason of its being put off so long was, the Elder wished for sufficient time to give very general notice; for he anticipated giving Universalism its death blow; and I had to make a journey to New England, in September, to attend the General Convention; so the meeting was necessarily deferred until after my return.

A gentleman from Whitestown, attended meeting one Sunday, in Hamilton, and made a very earnest request for an appointment in the town of his residence ; assuring me, that he could procure a large congregation ; among whom I would find quite a number of respectable and influential gentlemen, already well established in the faith. I gave him an appointment, and accordingly, on the 20th of August, 1805, delivered my first message in that town. No meeting-house could be procured, and no school-house could hold the congregation that assembled. We were, therefore, compelled to occupy a barn ; and it was literally filled. As my friend had informed me, there was a much larger number than I had ever found before in any one place, in this country, who had already embraced the true Gospel ; and many more, who were seriously disposed to inquire. They manifested a strong desire to have stated preaching ; and immediately adopted measures for it, by circulating a subscription paper for its support. I left with them another appointment ; and on my second visit they organized a society, which, if my memory will serve me, consisted of between thirty and forty male members ; all, I think, heads of families. This was the second society organized in Central New York. But the members were widely scattered over a large territory, comprising the towns of Whitestown, Westmoreland, Clinton, New Hartford, Utica, Paris, Deerfield, and Litchfield, where now exist a number of societies, and where no less than five Universalist meeting-houses have since been erected.

It was certainly a source of amusement, if not of instruction, to witness the varied feelings manifested by different individuals composing a congregation, on the introduction of the doctrine into any place ; to mark the effect of educational prejudices, and the fears of any innovation upon their religious creeds and practices. In Whitestown, as in almost all other places, the first congregation was composed of all classes and all kinds of people, and of all religious denominations ; and among them was an old sedate professor of the Presbyterian faith, by the name of Polycarpus Smith. After the close of meeting, a brother-in-law of his, a Mr. Dewey, addressed him among a number of bystanders in a familiar manner. "Well, uncle Carp., what do you think of such preaching as this?" "What do I think?" said the old gentleman, "Why, it beats all! I never heard such a sermon before, in all my life—I never heard so much Bible in one discourse before. It is every word true—it must be true, for it is all Bible." And then, looking round upon the people, he added, "But it won't do to believe it—don't one of you believe it, for your souls!"

I had now a regular circuit established through the towns of Whitestown, Sangerfield, Brookfield, Hamilton and Madison, with regular appointments in each place. But I diverged to the right, and to the left, as I received calls to deliver lectures, and generally delivered several discourses in the course of the week, besides my Sunday appointments.

An incident occurred in the course of this summer, which I must not omit, as it was the means of producing a book, some few years afterwards; and it is quite probable that some people were surprised that it received no attention from me at the time; though none disapproved of my course in respect to it, who were acquainted with the author, and the particular circumstances that gave rise to it.

There was an individual residing in the town of Sangerfield by the name of Joseph Tenney, a very restless and troublesome member of the Presbyterian church, a great egotist and pedant, who considered himself one of the most profound controversialists of the age; and who was so bigoted, and so obstinate in his own way, that he kept the church to which he belonged in constant turmoil so long as they suffered him to hold a standing within its pale. This man sent word to me, by a friend, that he wished the privilege of attending a meeting of mine, to take notes of my discourse, and reply to it. I told my friend, that Mr. Tenney, or any other man, had always an unquestionable right to attend any meeting of mine; and, so far from objecting to his taking notes, I would rather wish all my hearers to take notes, and carefully examine the doctrine I advance, comparing it with the standard of divine truth, and thereby test its soundness; and I had no possible objection to Mr. T. replying to my discourse, if he felt disposed so to do. "But," said I, "my manner of speaking is extemporaneous, and my delivery very rapid; and I am inclined to think Mr. T. is hardly expert enough as a penman so keep up with me; however, he may try, if he choose. This was all the arrangement we ever made. I had never yet seen Mr. T., but had heard so much of him, that I felt no inclination to engage in a discussion with him in any form. A few weeks after this, I delivered a lecture in a neighborhood where I was in the practice of preaching occasionally; and Mr. T., with several of his brethren, came prepared with pen and paper, to take notes. They all, I believe, took down the text; and Mr. T. continued to write for ten minutes, perhaps, and then laid down his pen, which he never after resumed, except to note some passage of Scripture that I quoted. At the close of my discourse, he requested to be allowed to ask me several questions, to which I acceded; and I answered them as briefly and as plainly as I could. He then wanted I should agree on a time when I would attend and hear a reply. I told him I was quite indifferent about hearing a reply—that he had a right to reply, if so disposed, and to reply in the presence of as many as he could induce to attend—that I had as many engagements as I could well attend to, and it would be difficult to fix on a time when I could wait on him, consistently with my present engagements. "But," said I, "you may appoint your own time and place; and I will attend provided other engagements do not interfere. But it is of little consequence whether I attend or not; as it is more than probable I shall never attempt to offer a rejoinder. The people have heard what I have said, and now I am quite willing that they should hear what you have to say in reply; and then judge for themselves, without another word from me on the subject." He then appointed a time to deliver his discourse, in the Baptist meeting-house in the village. When the time arrived, it so happened I had a leisure day, but had previously taken up my residence in the town of Brookfield, and was boarding with Col. N. Hasket, about seven miles distant from the place of appointment; I, however, persuaded the Colonel to go with me, and we rode over. Before reaching the place, we met Col. Norton, one of the deacons of the Baptist church in Sangerfield, with whom I had previously enjoyed some friendly acquaintance. He said to me, "Are you going to attend Joe Tenney's meeting?" "Yes, sir." "Well," he replied, "I would not go; there is no such thing as holding a fair argument with him. If you begin you will never find a stopping-place; and he will abuse you in every shape he possibly can. I would have nothing to do with him." He told me an anecdote about him: he had been trying hard to get into a controversy with the Baptists, on the subject of baptism; indeed they had some controversy; but the Baptists becoming disgusted with the course he took, declined taking any farther notice of him. On a certain day, however, when several were to be baptized, Mr. T., having prepared a lengthy polemical dissertation on the subject, came, with paper in hand, and placed himself on a bridge, in a conspicuous situation; and as soon as the ceremony closed, he called the attention of the congregation, and began reading; and so intent was he in reading his production, that he did not notice the situation of the congregation, until every soul had left the ground but Elder Butler, who had been officiating, and who was then pastor of the church; but he stood alone, listening with profound attention to Mr. T.'s arguments. The fact was, people had no confidence in Mr. T., and paid no attention to his reading, but moved off with as much unconcern as though nothing was being said. When Mr. T. looked up, and saw the Elder standing alone, and the people all off, or moving off in different directions, he remarked, "Well, I don't know but I may as well stop reading, for the people are gone." "Never mind, Mr. T." said the Elder, "read on, I'll hear you." But Mr. T. folded up his paper, and walked off.

I thanked the Deacon for his counsel—told him I should have no controversy with Mr. T.; I should never attempt to reply to him; but as I had promised to attend and hear him, if I could make it convenient, I felt it my duty to be present. We called on Esq. Dyer, who resided near the meeting-house, who also gave me the same advice as Deacon Norton, and insisted on it, that my best course would be not to go to the house at all; and the Esquire himself actually refused to go with us. However, at a late hour, we saw Mr. T. and a few others enter the house, and the Col. and I walked over. There were probably not twenty persons assembled, notwithstanding Mr. T. had used all his influence to get a great congregation. He began reading his discourse, and continued until nea rnight; when Col. H. whispered and said, "We must be going, or we shall have to be out in the dark." And it was evident Mr. T. had not read half he had got written, for he had not yet mentioned my discourse, nor alluded to it. In his printed book, he has reversed the order of his discourse. At this meeting, he began with an attempt at a general refutation of the doctrine of Universalism, and criticised upon such authors as he had read in defense of it; and probably was reserving his strictures on my discourse to close up with. He commented upon Winchester, upon Huntington, and upon Bishop Newton, &c. The Colonel growing very impatient, whispered to me a second time, and said, "*I* must go soon." I then arose, and observed to Mr. T., that I had made it convenient to attend; that we came in season, and waited more than one hour after the appointed time before he arrived: that it was now drawing near night, and I was under necessity of returning to Brookfield that evening; and, moreover, it appeared probable from the quantity of matter he seemed to have before him, that he would not be able to finish the reading of it before dark; and as he had not yet touched my discourse, I could feel under no obligation to remain longer; and, besides, it would be of no consequence, as I should never attempt to reply to him; he might, therefore, as well read it to the people in my absence, as in my presence. But I thought it proper to make these remarks before I withdrew. He proposed then to adjourn; and appoint another day to finish it, provided I would name a time when I could attend. I told him, I could not; but would say, as before, that he might appoint his own time, and if I was at leisure, I would attend. But, I said, if the people here are willing to stay, perhaps you may as well finish now. But, how could he determine whether the people would stay or not? Why put it to vote—request those who wish the meeting now to close, to rise. He did so, and every soul in the house rose up; but before the congregation separated, he named another day to meet and finish his discourse. It was not convenient for me to attend his next meeting; nor do I know who did attend, or whether a soul was present. I heard no more about it for several years; not until some person put into my hand a book published by Joseph Tenney, purporting to be the substance of a discourse delivered by myself, together with a reply, and a refutation of the doctrine of Universal Salvation. I read it, and found it to contain a garbled misrepresentation of my discourse, as well as an unfair and uncandid representation of the authors he named; and his arguments against the doctrine, I considered unworthy of notice. Some of my friends urged me to reply. But I had made up my mind never to enter into any controversy with Mr. T., in any shape whatever; and I felt confident that the influence of the little book would never, for a moment, retard the progress of divine truth. Nor did it, as far as my knowledge extends; and certainly the whole transaction, in the region where it took place, was altogether favorable to the cause.

During this summer, I traveled very considerably, preached on Sundays, and lectured often on week-days, in the towns of Hartwick, Otsego, Burlington, Hamilton, Brookfield, Madison, Whitestown, Westmoreland, and Deerfield; and two very respectable societies were organized, one in Whitestown, already mentioned, and one in Hamilton, which have now existed for above forty years. The society in Whitestown, however, which for many years past has been known as the New Hartford society, and which built the first Universalist meeting-house, west of the Hudson river, has become nearly extinct by being divided into several others. Certainly no less than four others, or at least parts of others, have grown out of it, viz.: Utica, Clinton, Marshal, and Litchfield. Numbers had been converted from the Orthodox faith, (erroneously so called,) whose main distinguishing-point of doctrine is the dogma of endless punishment, to the soul-cheering doctrine of Universal Reconciliation and Salvation. Several excommunications from Baptist and Presbyterian churches had already taken place; for the heresy of Universalism; and numbers, who had never before found a religious home, united with us; and for strength of mind, respectability of character and moral worth, our societies would lose nothing in comparison with any other societies, or churches, of any denomination; nor did they lack for zeal in Christian order, and social worship. Both the societies, in Whitestown and Hamilton, or a good proportion of their members, manifested a strong desire to come into church order and fellowship, and to enjoy the privileges of the Christian ordinances; which I strongly recommended; and do still recommend, as a most efficient means of improvement and growth in divine life. I had not received ordination, and, therefore, did not consider myself legally nor properly authorized to take the oversight of a Christian church, or administer its ordinances. The societies in Whitestown and Hamilton desired to be adopted into the young but growing family of Universalism; and therefore prepared letters to the General Convention of Universalists in New England, requesting the fellowship of that body; and earnestly recommended me as a suitable candidate, and requested my ordination to the evangelic work of the ministry.

CHAPTER VII.

Delegates from the State of New York attend the convention—Visit to Wilmington—Committee appointed to assist in organizing an Association in the State of New York—Father Z. Streeter—Ordination—Visit to New Salem—Return to New York—Churches organized in Whitestown and Hamilton—Persecution --A vile slander—Elder Joy Handy—Extract of a letter from Elder S. King—A preaching race—Author marries—Brief account of his family—Removes to Brookfield, New York—Incident on the journey—Loses his horse—Slender remuneration for ministerial labors—Impossibility of regular salary—Author's established principles on the subject of salary.

Early in the month of September, Mr. Wooley and I, agreeably to an appointment at the conference in July, started on our mission. We had now three societies to represent—he the one in Hartwick and vicinity, and I those in Whitestown and Hamilton. We presented our letters and credentials; and the report we were enabled to give of the success of our labors, the prosperity of the cause, and the promising aspect of the condition of things in the State of New York, was truly a subject of great joy to the hearts of the faithful who had assembled at our happy annual convocation, and readily obtained a favorable response to our request for assistance to organize an Association in the State of New York. A committee of three were appointed; and, at my request, Mr. H. Ballou stood at the head; Mr. William Farwell and Mr. Joshua Flagg were associated with him.

The convention met this year in Westmoreland, New Hampshire. On my way thither I passed through Wilmington, Vermont, called on my old friend, Mr. Foster, and held a meeting with the few brethren on Sunday; and Mr. F. accompanied me to the convention. As we rode up to the place of appointment, with my heart and my eyes full, the first person I saw, before I had dismounted from my horse, was the venerable father in Israel, Zebulon Streeter, who exclaimed with a smile, "There comes my boy!" I leaped from my horse, and Oh! with what heart-felt joy and affection did I grasp the extended hand of this aged saint. It was the last time I ever met him. And since that time I have never been able to attend but four sessions of that convention. Previously, my joy was so full in anticipation of meeting my beloved brethren again, in whose hearts I could well believe reigned triumphantly the spirit of Christian love, and the soothing influences of whose sympathy I could so fully realize, after having, alone and at so great a distance, for a whole season experienced the unmerciful buffetings of the storms and tempests of sectarian wrath, that the approaching meeting caused me to weep for joy.

The letters from the societies which I had been instrumental in organizing, were presented, and their petitions readily granted; the societies were received into fellowship, and I received ordination. Mr. C. G. Person was ordained at the same time; and by our request, Hosea Ballou delivered the sermon on the occasion. He chose for a text, Mark, 16 : 15, 16. Mr. Joab Young made the consecrating prayer, Father Streeter presented the holy Bible and administered the charge, and Mr. Kneeland, if I mistake not, gave the right hand of fellowship. This was the first and the last time I ever suffered myself to pass through the solemnities of ordination. To me it was a most imposing, and deeply affecting scene—too solemn to be often and triflingly repeated. Once being solemnly set apart and consecrated to the work of the ministry, by prayer, "and the laying on the hands of the presbytery," appears to me quite sufficient. To call for the solemnities of ordination every time a preacher changes his place of residence, or his pastoral charge, has always appeared to me as trifling with one of the most sacred institutions of the Christian church.

After the close of the convention, I went to New Salem, Massachusetts, made my parents a short visit, preached two Sundays in that town, and in October I returned to New York, and resumed my labors on the circuit I had previously established. Soon after my return, the brethren both in Whitestown and Hamilton adopted measures, in accordance with their previously expressed desires, to organize into a church relation. We adopted the profession of faith sanctioned by the General Convention; and I drew up a disciplinary constitution, and a form of covenant, to which the members subscribed, and which, I believe, the church in Hamilton still retains; although they have seen cause to amend the confession of faith, or rather to expunge it, and substitute the apostolic confession alone—"I believe that Jesus Christ is the Son of God"—as abundantly explicit and sufficient; leaving the mind free and untrammeled for investigation and growth in divine knowledge. A respectable number, (I may say, between twenty and thirty in each place,) subscribed to the covenant, and among them several females, who, even at that early day, had the faith and the confidence to publicly own the despised name of *Universalist*, and subscribe the covenant, in defiance of the popular odium which a vain or a superstitious world endeavored to heap upon it; and we found ourselves abundantly refreshed and strengthened in attending to the ordinances of the Christian institution. I was now enabled to extend my labors still farther, and also into intermediate places where I had not heretofore been able to find entrance, lecturing, and occasionally preachlng, that fall, in Utica, Paris, Bridgewater, Westmoreland, and Springfield; and, while on a visit to my brother, I also had opportunity to deliver one discourse in the town of Canajoharie.

Fully aware, when I entered upon the ministry, of the unpopularity of the doctrine of God's Universal Grace, and the array of prejudice it was destined to encounter, and the low and vile means which ever have been and would continue to be resorted to, to oppose it, by vilification, slander, sneers, and all the measures of persecution which the equitatable laws of our blessed country would admit of—I solemnly resolved, God being my helper, so to steer my course through the mists, and clouds, and storms that would hover over and around my way, as never to lose sight of my polar star, nor be put off my course; nor be ever under the necessity of paying any attention to the stories and slanders that malicious and vituperative tongues should indulge in fabricating and retailing respecting me; and thus far I had been successful. I had been called a fool, a hypocrite, an infidel, trying to deceive mankind in the name of religion, and thereby to disturb and break up churches. I had been called a low-bred, ignorant blockhead, who knew not what I was about—a knave, a witty, cunning knave, just such as the devil always chose to build up his cause, (for sectarians have always accorded to him more wisdom than they have to the Lord, in the choice of his servants,) and they suspected, bye-and-bye, I would commit some crime that would undeceive the people in regard to my real character; and they were not slow in praying for it. Elder Morton, whom I have had occasion to name already, and whom I must notice again, said he "was never glad of hearing of any man getting drunk but once; but when Stacy got drunk, I was heartily glad of it." But none of these things moved me. When my friends mentioned them to me, I would generally reply, "If they have called the Master of the house 'Beelzebub,' they will, of course, call those of his household as ignominious names. If you are not already satisfied about my character, watch me closely, and see if these things be so. I shall take no notice of them —if I can not outlive them, I must fall under them." But now I was destined to encounter a more formidable and aggravating report.

Shortly after my return from New England, I discovered a change of demeanor among some of my friends. They did not meet me with their wonted cheerfulness, nor give me their hands so warmly as formerly; nor so heartily and urgently invite me to their houses; but seemed to manifest an unusual shyness, and a suspicious look. I was never of a jealous temperament, and was resolved not to indulge any unfounded suspicion; it might have no meaning on their part—might all originate in my own feelings; I would, therefore, try to regulate my own conduct properly, and maintain my usual friendly feelings toward them, use the same freedom I had always done, and wait the event. A few weeks passed in this way, when a good old brother, who was a brother indeed, and whose name I can never repeat without feelings of profound gratitude, Benjamin Stetson, of Sangerfield, was kind enough to undeceive me and put me in a way to restore confidence. He asked me, if I did not discover that there was a difference in the appearance and conduct of some of my former friends, and an unusual shyness toward me? I told him that I sometimes thought I did; but as I was unwilling to indulge any jealousy, I had been inclined to impute it all to my own distempered imagination. "No," said he, "it is a reality—they are afraid of you; there is a very bad story in circulation about you; and I have been resolved to tell you of it, the first opportunity I could find. If it be true, you ought not to attempt to preach; and if it be false, you ought to have an opportunity to clear yourself, and chastise your calumniators." I thanked him most heartily; for I felt a sudden and great relief, even before he told me the substance of the story. But he continued: "The story is this. It is reported that you were sent for, while boarding in Sangerfield, to attend a funeral in Brookfield; that the messenger, on arriving at your usual place of boarding, did not find you at the house, but was informed that you were at a neighboring house; that he went where he was directed, and found you at the card-table, playing cards with several others. He felt astonished, and so nearly confounded at the event, that he seriously thought of going away without doing his errand; believing that the people who sent him would hardly be willing that a gambler should officiate on the mournful occasion, knowing him to be such; but, after a little reflection, he concluded to do his errand, and say nothing about it until after the funeral. He accordingly informed you what he came for, and you readily agreed to go; but you noticed his embarrassment, and addressed him in the following language—'I suppose, sir, you are surprised to see me playing cards; you, probably, dare not play—you are afraid of God; but we neither fear God, man, nor the devil!' This story," continued Mr. S., "was reported while you were absent in New England, and has been circulated very industriously to your disadvantage. And as you were once actually called from Sangerfield to Brookfield to attend a funeral, many were disposed to give implicit credit to the story, without taking the trouble of making any further inquiry. I was fearful," he added, "that no one had been friendly enough to inform you of it." "This," said I, "Brother S., is the very first hint I ever had of it. Well has the poet said,

> ''Tis slander,
> Whose edge is sharper than a sword, whose tongue
> Outvenoms all the worms of Nile.'

It is of no use, Brother S., for me to contradict it—to tell you there is not a word of truth in the whole of it; but thus much I will say—that, with your assistance, *you shall know* whether it be so or not; and all I want of you now, is, to give me the name of your author." He did so; and I immediately called on the man, and rebuked him sharply; for, although he was a member of a Baptist church, he stood in such a relation to me as to be under the most solemn obligation not to circulate slanderous reports about me; but should have come and whispered my faults into my own ears. I made the man tremble, and humbly ask forgiveness. I told him, however, as it respected myself, I cared little about his assisting to spread the story; but I wanted he should be more faithful to his duty; and all I required of him at present was, to inform me who told him the story. This he readily did, and voluntarily offered to assist me in tracing the story to its origin. The story now rested upon the shoulders of his own minister, Elder Joy Handy.

In the course of a few days, I made it convenient to call at Elder Handy's house. He was not within; but his wife told me he was at work on his farm, and directed me to the place. I went and found him. I had previously formed an acquaintance with Elder Handy, and had uniformly received polite treatment; but his holy wrath against Universalism must now be gratified, even at the expense of my reputation. Oh, how much mischief sectarian bigotry is capable of doing! "Father, forgive them, for they know not what they do." After a few moments' talk on common topics, I inquired of him, if he had ever heard any thing disreputable of my character. The Elder answered rather hesitatingly "Why, no—not as I particularly recollect." I then related the story to him circumstantially, and observed, that I did not know but he might have heard of it, as I understood it was in quite general circulation; and asked him, if he had ever heard any thing like that about me. He again hesitated, and, as I thought, manifested a little confusion, for I looked at him pretty steadily in the eye; but at length he answered to the effect, that it did seem as though he had heard something like it; but he could hardly recollect—he paid very little attention to it—he did not know but I allowed such things. By this time, old Adam came pretty near getting the advantage of me; and I said, with some degree of earnestness I presume, "Elder Handy! this indifference will not answer your purpose. Whether you have ever heard such a story or not, *you* have reported it. I have now come to you, sir, in a Christian spirit, I hope and trust, to ask an explanation, and to obtain Christian satisfaction—that satisfaction which one Christian has a right to demand of another, and which a Christian is under obligation to give. I ask nothing but Christian satisfaction; but if I can not have that, the law is open, and I will have legal satisfaction. If you *heard* the story, all I want of you is, to assist me in tracing it to its origin; and if you refuse that, I shall treat you as its author. You shall know, sir, whether I allow of such things or not." By this time the Elder began to look quite serious; said he would go to the house, and talk with Mrs. Handy about it; perhaps she might recollect something more definitely. We accordingly went to the house; and before I left them, they could recollect all about it, even to the most trivial circumstance. They could not only remember who told them, the time when, how the subject was introduced; but the identical spot in the room occupied by the speaker when he related the story to them. There had been but two alterations of the story in its circulation; and those were in regard to the time and place of transaction. The scene was now transferred from that place to Massachusetts; and the time, before I ever came into the western country.

The fact was, a Baptist preacher by the name of King, a resident of the town of Wendell, Mass., adjoining the town of my nativity, had made a tour through this country in my absence, and visited Elder Handy, in Brookfield; and, hearing of me in this country, and of the progress of Universalism, in order to give vent to his malignity—to destroy my influence, and check the progress of the doctrine, had descended to the meanness and wickedness of altering a story which he might have heard about another person, and applying it to me. I informed Elder H., and his lady, that I should go to New England the first good sleighing; and I should depend on them giving me their testimony in writing concerning this report, with their own signatures; as I should certainly visit Elder King, and call on him for an explanation. This they expressed their entire readiness to do; and added, "We now believe that Elder King must have labored under a mistake; and we are not only willing, but desirous, to do all in our power to help you to put this matter right." Immediately, while every circumstance of the story was fresh in my mind, I prepared a writing, something in the form of an affidavit, and presented it to Elder H. and lady for signature. The Elder remarked, I had got the story correct; but he did not so well like the form of the instrument; he would rather write a letter with his own hand, and he and Mrs. H. would sign it; and he would deliver it to me unsealed, and I might carry it to Elder King. I told him, the form was a matter of indifference with me; so that the story should be correctly reported, and Elder K. should clearly understand us. He therefore prepared his letter with great care and exactness—relating every circumstance as he had previously told it to me; and in addition, gave me a higher recommendation than I should have dared to ask of any man; remarking to Elder K. that he was confident there must be some unhappy mistake about it, for he had every reason to disbelieve it; and he and Mrs. H. both signed the letter, and handed it to me in good season.

It was wonderfully amusing to see how quick the tongue of slander was silenced, the moment I began to make a stir, and to inquire into the origin of this story—to witness the stillness of death among those who had been the most officious and vociferous in its propagation, and had chuckled secretly at the prospect of my downfall, and the overthrow of Universalism in consequence. Not a word more was said in favor of it—they were all ready to declare, they never did believe a word of it, but were always confident it was a shocking mistake!

At the time appointed, I went to New England, and carried my unsealed letter. The step-mother of her who, on this visit, became my wife, was a member of Elder King's church. I took an early opportunity to show her Elder Handy's letter, and asked her what she thought of it? The old lady was shocked, mortified, and vexed beyond measure. She wondered what Elder King could mean, by reporting such a story; when she was confident he must know, or certainly ought to have known, there was not a word of truth in it. She would go with me herself to Elder King; and she was sure he would readily give me satisfaction. We accordingly went, but we found not the Elder at home. He had gone on a short mission, but would be at home in a few days. Elder K. was a widower, but his housekeeper was a member of his church; I therefore read Elder K.'s letter to her, and left it in her care, to deliver it to him as soon as he returned. I told her how long I expected to remain in New Salem, when I intended to return to New York; and I should certainly expect to hear from Elder K. before that time. The old lady, Mrs. Clark, urged the importance of it also, in very strong terms, and we left. The time elapsed, but Elder K. never made his appearance, nor could I hear a syllable from him; and the day before I left the country I addressed a letter to him, couched, I presume, in pretty strong terms, and closed by giving him my place of address, and assuring him in the most peremptory manner, that if I did not hear from him within one month, at farthest, he might expect to hear from me, in a more disagreeable way. This letter I left in the care of my mother-in-law, to be forwarded immediately; and in less than a month, I received a letter from him, of which the following is an extract:

"I am satisfied that the report of your being found playing cards, when called to attend a funeral, and the speech you are said to have made on that occasion, *is not true.* It is but justice to you, and *satisfaction* to myself, to declare, that I am *very sorry* that I reported the story. I am also unhappy if any unfavorable impressions have been made on any minds by my means, and wish they may be done away. I further say, that I have never, that I recollect, heard any thing unfavorable to your moral character, saving this unfounded affair. Please to give my love to brother and sister Handy—I regret the trouble I have given you all in this business, and thank you all for your exertions to bring things right.

"Your friend and humble servant, "SAMUEL KING."

This letter I exhibited to my friends, and made it as public as I could, without committing it to the press; and it proved satisfactory to all—totally stopped the further circulation of the story in all that county, and had a tendency to make our enemies more cautious in fabricating and circulating slanderous reports about Universalist preachers. And the whole transaction had a very favorable effect upon the progress of divine truth, in its infancy in this country; indeed all the efforts of its enemies, however malignant and bitter, to suppress it, seemed to terminate in its favor, and advance its popularity and its progress. It seemed to be an illustration of what the Apostle said in respect to himself and his coadjutors, that whatever their characters might be, they could "do nothing against the truth, but for the truth." God, in his goodness, overruled all their vile machinations, to the advancement of the truth they intended to suppress, and for the upbuilding of the Redeemer's kingdom in this new and flourishing part of his vineyard. Although I felt well satisfied at the time, and have never seen cause to change my opinion, that Elder King did not make a *full* confession of his guilt—that he perfectly knew, when he was relating the story to Elder Handy, that he was telling a positive and wilful falsehood about me; still his confession answered my purpose, and made him an unwilling instrument in advancing the cause he designed to destroy; and I felt perfectly willing to leave the rest for him to settle between his own conscience and his God. But to return to my narrative more consecutively:

As the time drew nigh when Elder Morton and myself were to hold our meeting, considerable excitement was manifested on the subject, both by friends and opposers. It was a subject of conversation for a considerable distance around, and preparations were made to attend the *preaching race*, as some were pleased facetiously to denominate it; for no such occurrence had ever taken place in all that region of country. My friends expressed a good deal of symyathy for me, and indulged not a little fear. I stood alone and but a stripling; and my opponent was a man of years and experience, and stood high in his denomination as a man of sound talent, and a shrewd and successful controversialist. He would also be surrounded with friends and assistants; for, indeed, clergymen and laymen of every religious sect, however opposed to each other on every other point of doctrine, agreed in the soul-cheering (!) anticipations of endless misery for some immortal souls; and, therefore, like the factions in Jerusalem, who, when closely beseiged by the Romans, would cease to kill each other, and unite to fight the common enemy—my opponents would, with spirited unanimity, strive together against Universalism. But I must stand entirely alone, in respect to human help—not a brother preacher to assist or encourage me, nor one to hold up my head during the battle—not a preacher of the order, nor one who had the least sympathy for the doctrine within forty or fifty miles. I told them, however, not to fear; the cause was not mine, but the Lord's—that "He had chosen the weak things of this world, to confound the things which are mighty"—that the "race was not always to the swift, nor the battle to the strong."

The day at length arrived; and a vast concourse of people assembled. Some, with ardent expectations that Universalism would that day receive its overthrow, were already exulting with invidious smiles, and verily hoping, that the damnable heresy would be scouted from the country; some, with seriously inquiring minds, to know what *truth* was; some, with "trembling hope" for my success; and many from mere curiosity, feeling quite indifferent how the argument terminated. I was on the ground in season, with a few of my faithful friends accompanying me. We met at the house of Rev. Mr. Woodworth, the Presbyterian clergyman, where we found several clergymen of his own denomination, some from quite a distance, who had come purposly to attend the meeting; one Baptist preacher was there besides Elder M., and some Methodists. The people soon assembled, and filled the church to excess. It was a large, high house, with galleries on the sides, all in an unfinished state; but temporary seats, above and below, compactly fixed over the whole area; and every seat was filled, and many had to stand up during the whole exercise. The services were to commence precisely at ten o'clock; but the hour passed, and Elder M. still delayed. I spoke to him about commencing—observed, the day is short, and we shall probably need all the time we can have; and the people are waiting. Still he delayed. I again reminded him of the importance of commencing his exercise. In a few moments I discovered he was missing, and inquired of Mr. Woodworth if he knew where Elder M. was? He replied, he did not; but thought it possible he had gone to the meeting-house. I remarked to my friends, that we would go and see. We did so, and found him in the desk, and just prepared to commence his services. I took this as a manifest indication of his design; which was, to treat me with the utmost contempt, and to take every advantage he possibly could, by consuming time, and in every other way. However, I said to myself, God will manage these matters, and overrule all for his glory, and the good of the cause; and I very contentedly took my seat with the congregation, although Elder M.'s own father, who was also a member of his church, came to me and urged me to go into the desk, saying, "You have as good a right there as Salmon has." I mention this, to show, that such unchristian conduct can not escape notice, and will excite sympathy for the abused, even among honest opposers. The Elder commenced by reading his text, after the ordinary ceremonies of singing and prayer; but he did not attempt to illustrate the doctrine of it, or make any further use of it than of any other text which he quoted to prove endless misery. The whole of his discourse consisted of a violent philippic against, and a wilful or profoundly ignorant misrepresentation and perversion of the doctrine of Universalism; and a most ungentlemanly, not to say unchristian, abuse of its advocates; and he closed with a filthy and obscene poem, (not the one appended to Lemuel Haynes' notorious sermon against Universalism, but vastly more filthy, if possible) which he intended as a caricature of Universalism. It proved as I feared—he lengthened out his services so as to use up all the time he possibly could, occupying more than two hours, and bringing it to nearly two o'clock when he closed. But his own malice defeated his object. Every step he took was so apparently unjust and unchristian, that he enlisted the sympathies of the whole congregation in my favor; and undoubtedly procured me a more patient and favorable attention than I should have otherwise received.

When he closed, I arose, and notified the congregation that after an intermission of fifteen minutes, services would be resumed. The congregation went out, for the sake of exercise; and I stepped into a friend's house and took a morsel of refreshment. The time had not expired when I returned; but found the people assembled and in their seats—not one, I presume, was missing. Near the desk sat Elder M. and his associate, and just by them six Presbyterian ministers. As I passed, I spoke to Elder M., and invited him into the desk with me. He looked ashamed, and declined the invitation. We had a good choir of singers in attendance, but I remarked, as the time had nearly all been consumed, and so little remained for me to occupy, I should only read one hymn for an introduction, and must dispense with further singing. When the hymn was read, it made every eye in the congregation stare; and many significant glances were exchanged from one to another. I cast my eye upon the circle of clergymen who sat before me, and they were looking and winking at each other, with suppressed smiles and thoughtful countenances. I read from Watts; but I was afterwards told by several, that they would actually have believed I made the hymn, as I read it, had not the singers found it in their books, and sang it. It was the cause of more speculation than I ever before heard on a similar subject; and it seemed as though Dr. Watts wrote it specially for the occasion. I read it as emphatically as I could; and the choir caught the spirit, and sang it with life. In order that the reader may have, as nearly as possible, the whole scene before him, and enter into the spirit of the occasion, I will take the liberty to insert the hymn, distinguishing the words on which I laid a particular emphasis. It is the 18th Ps., 1st part, C.M.

1. The Lord appears my helper now,
 Nor is my FAITH afraid
What all the sons of EARTH can do,
 Since HEAVEN affords its aid.

2. 'Tis safer, Lord, to hope in thee,
 And have my GOD MY FRIEND;
Than trust in MEN of high degree,
 And on THEIR truth depend.

3. Like bees, my foes begirt me round,
 A large and angry swarm;
But I shall all their rage confound,
 By THINE ALMIGHTY ARM.

4. 'Tis through the LORD my HOPE is STRONG,
 In HIM my lips rejoice;
While his SALVATION is my song,
 How CHEERFUL is my voice.

5. Like angry bees they girt me round;
 When GOD APPEARS, they fly;
So burning thorns, with crackling sound,
 Make a fierce blaze, and die.

6. Joy to the saints and peace belong;
 The Lord protect their days;
Let Israel tune immortal songs
 To his ALMIGHTY GRACE.

I was perfectly aware that the opposers, and especially those wise and knowing divines who surrounded me, eagerly anticipated my total break-down upon the text; and if I failed to show its harmony with the doctrine of God's universal and triumphant grace—that it did not contain, in itself, nor support, the doctrine of endless misery—whatever I might say besides, or however I might dispose of other passages quoted by Elder M., they would claim a complete victory. I had not time to follow Elder M.

through the whole of his incoherent and wandering harangue, had I been so disposed; I therefore formed my resolution, at once, to confine myself exclusively to the text; and remarked, in the outset, that the short time which the gentleman had allowed me, rendered it impossible for me to follow him through all the devious windings of his long discourse, and notice all the passages he had brought up as objections to the doctrine he had misrepresented; nor was I inclined, if I had time, to reply to all his invidious remarks, or retaliate his personal abuse. I would rather follow the instructions of the Savior of the world, *when I was reviled, not to revile again.* Elder M. was looking me in the face, but when I made the last remark, I fixed my eye upon him, and he dropped his head; and I know not that he looked at me again, during my discourse. I occupied a reasonable time on the text, which brought it to very near night; but had the success so to engage the attention of the congregation, notwithstanding many of them were far from home, and the seats to which they had so long been confined were not the most agreeble, that a profound stillness prevailed; and I know not that one left the house, until I dismissed the assembly, and thanked them for their attention.

So far from gratifying the enemies of the doctrine, by its total overthrow and fatal explosion, this meeting had an efficient tendency to advance it in the country round about, and to build up a society in Madison, and establish regular preaching in that town; and it was the last attack that Elder Morton ever made upon me, personally. Some years afterwards, when Mr. Dean came into the country, and was employed part of his time with the society in Madison, the Elder made several furious attacks upon him; and once preached *at* him from the text, "O, full of all subtlety, and all mischief, thou child of the devil, thou enemy of all righteousness! wilt thou not cease to pervert the right ways of the Lord?" And which of them gave the challenge, I can not now tell, but they once held a public debate, which I attended one afternoon and evening; and that, I believe, finished Elder Morton's public and open warfare against Universalism; for I do not recollect hearing of his making an attack upon a Universalist preacher after that time.

When once I had surmounted the barriers to an entrance on the Gospel ministry, and had actually made my *debut* upon that solemn stage, I fully resolved, God being my helper, to faithfully and exclusively devote my life, with the feeble talents Heaven had bestowed, to the great and holy cause I had espoused, and to suffer no engagements which I might make, nor connections which I might form, to divert my attention from it, or serve as a hindrance to my usefulness. My whole soul was engaged in it; for here I had found the happiness, the peace of mind, and the stability of purpose and pursuit, which I had for years sought in vain, in other callings, but which had hitherto eluded my pursuit. I looked for an exemplar among the early christians and first preachers of the Gospel of reconciliation, and none appeared more amiable, more zealously devoted to the cause, more self-sacrificing, and worthy of imitation, that the great Apostle of the Gentiles. His whole life was exclusively devoted to the cause. He suffered no persecution to discourage him, or cause him to relinquish his calling, or falter in his race. He made it as little expensive as possible to his hearers and friends, working with his own hands to minister to the wants of himself and those who accompanied him; and he encumbered himself with no connection that would, for a moment, divert his attention from his high and holy calling. Although he did not condemn the institution of marriage, he more than intimated, as I thought, that preachers of the Gospel, at least, had better remain in a state of celibacy; in order to be the most useful: "He that is unmarried careth for the things of the Lord, how he may please the Lord; but he that is married careth for the things of the world, how he may please his wife." This looked to me truly philosophical; and I made up my mind not to entangle myself with the bonds of wedlock. It required no small resolution and fixedness of purpose; for I had always been remarkably fond of society, and of virtuous female association; and to exclude myself entirely from their society, and from the refining and polishing, as well as the exhilarating, influence of their manners and conversation, appeared to me almost impossible; but this I must do, at least in a very great measure, or be very liable to be drawn into the vortex of connubial connection, which I thought it my duty to avoid. I therefore put on as cold, frigid, and misanthropic a manner and habit toward the female sex as lay in my power; and for a few years persevered in this course, shunning, as much as consistent with politeness and common civility, the society of unmarried females. But alas! the tax was too severe on my feelings; although I felt happy in religion, I still felt a loneliness, a solitude in the midst of a world of living beings. I wanted the union of a heart that felt all that I could feel, that could be a faithful repository of my most secret thoughts, that could fully sympathize with me in all my trials, and cares, and anxieties, and sufferings, and fully share all my hopes and my joys. And in the spring of 1804, immediately after the close of my winter's school in New Salem, I fell in company with a young woman, who, I verily thought, would make me such a companion. She was a native of the same town as I was; her parents, like mine, being among the earliest settlers of the township. They settled, however, in parts of the town remote from each other, some eight miles apart; and very little intercourse was enjoyed between the neighborhoods, either by old or young. In consequence of residing in that part of the town for a short season, in youth, I had seen her when a child of ten or eleven years, but had hardly heard her name mentioned since then until the time alluded to. I had never taken the veil, nor the oath of celibacy; and, fortunately, my resolution was not like the laws of the Medes and Persians, which admitted of no revocation; I therefore sought an interview, and ventured to spend some seasons, from time to time, in her company. She was by no means a believer in my doctrine, nor did she manifest strong prejudices against it; she had never heard much about it. Her parents were members of the Congregational church, and she had been bred up in that religion; but had never made any personal profession. Her mother had been dead a few years, when I became acquainted with her, and her father had married a second wife, who was a very rigid Baptist. The name of the young woman was Susan Clark, the youngest daughter and youngest child of Percy Clark; whose family originally consisted of twelve children. Mr. Clark was, at that time, in point of property, above the mediocrity of society around him, a shoemaker by trade, but also a successful farmer. He brought up his family in habits of industry; and also gave them as good opportunities for education, in primary or common schools, as the country at that time afforded. I was sensible, if I did marry, and calculated to be made happier thereby, and live in cordiality and peace with a companion, I must marry "*an help-meet*"—one who could work, who was willing to work, and who would not feel disgraced by being found with her needle or her distaff in her hand. It would not secure my own happiness, much less the happiness of my companion, to take one, even if the oppportunity were afforded me, from what are erroneously called the higher walks of life—who had never been accustomed to housewifery, and knew not how to make a loaf of bread, or to perform any kind of hand-labor—however exalted her intellect, or however refined her education; for I had no means of supporting such an one, much less of gratifying her pride or vanity; and it would be but involving her and myself in eternal disquietude, mortification, and wretchedness. But the person I had found appeared to me every way calculated to constitute the companion my heart sighed for, to sooth the rough current of life, and enable me to bear, with more fortitude, the peltings and buffetings of those storms I was destined to meet, and must encounter, in the voyage of life.

After a sufficient lapse of time to enable me to become fully acquainted, as I believed, with the character and disposition of the object of my choice; and seriously viewing the proceeding in all its bearings, as far as my ability would enable me; and prayerfully seeking Divine aid to direct my steps, I with much trembling proposed marriage. I well considered the consequences of practicing the least deception in regard to my future prospects. I told her, if she married me, she knew that she would, by that act, be united for life to a devoted preacher of a very unpopular doctrine; who possessed no estate, no property; and who resolved, at all hazards, to devote his life to the cause he had espoused; whose prospects of subsistence for himself and family depended wholly upon the small amount of labor he would be able to perform amidst his professional engagements, and the voluntary subscriptions of the societies to whom he would preach, which never had been, and probably never would be, very liberal; her temporal prospects, therefore, were any thing but flattering. I sometimes felt so conscience-smitten with regard to my endeavors to allure a confiding female from a "father's house, where was bread enough and to spare," where she could enjoy every rational privilege and comfort in the bosom of a fond and doting parent—to follow the fortunes of what the unbelieving world called "a wild and thoughtless adventurer"—to be doomed, most surely, to hard toil, and perhaps extreme poverty, in a new and strange country, far from her father's house, and from all her friends and acquaintances—that I even shuddered with horror, and severely condemned myself for attempting to win her affection. But I felt that I could not be happy without her; that the world would be too thorny, and barren of rational enjoyment, for me ever to think of threading its "'wildering mazes" alone; and I silenced my conscience with the old doctrine, "Matches are made in heaven;" I was, therefore, not to be blamed for the decree, nor could I successfully resist it. But in view of all these prospective trials, and inconveniences, and disadvantages, my suit was not rejected; and the time now approached when I was to return to New England, to consummate the engagement, and enter the married state. Accordingly, the earliest sleighing time, which happened about the middle of January, 1806, I started for New Salem; and on the thirtieth day of that month the nuptial knot was tied, in her father's house. I was in my twenty-eighth year, and she in her twenty-third.

Nor have I, for a moment of my life, seen cause to repent of the engagement. We have lived long together, and probably have experienced as few discordant feelings as generally fall to the lot of people, struggling through the trials of this mortal life. She has been a faithful companion and "help-meet," assisting to bear the almost insupportable burdens allotted me in my arduous, and, by the world, thankless calling, not only by her caresses and encouraging counsel, but by her incessant labor. Her needle, and her spinning-wheel, and her loom, have been, by turns, employed in procuring the bread that we needed, and the clothing necessary for our rising family. We have been blessed with eight children, three sons and five daughters. Six are still living, but two, our third son and third daughter, have been taken home to a better Father's house. All our surviving children are now married, (1848,) and are comfortably and pleasantly settled in the world; and, blessed be God, have thus far sustained a respectable standing in society.

Two of our friends from Brookfield, (Col. N. Haskel, and his brother Jesse,) went down with teams, and removed our effects; and on the 17th day of February, we found ourselves in one of the apartments of the spacious dwelling-house of Col. Haskel, where we first commenced the untried business of housekeeping.

But I must relate an incident which occurred on our journey; because it had a very salutary and lasting effect on the feelings of my companion, and greatly assisted in preparing her head and her heart for what I now most ardently desired, her fully embracing and feeling all the influence of the doctrine I believed and advocated; and I took every possible opportunity to place her in the way of means calculated to make proper impressions, and to do this as much as possible without obviously manifesting a design; for more could be done this way, and done effectually, than by the most cogent argument I could use.

A most horrible transaction had occured the previous winter, which produced a fervid excitement through the length and breadth of the land, by means of advertisements in almost every newspaper published in the United States. A man, by the name of Arnold, in the town of Burlington, Otsego county, N. Y., had whipped a child to death! He had fled; and all the sensibilities of the human heart were awakened. Compassion for the little innocent sufferer, sympathy for the bereaved and distressed mother, enkindled an equal horror and resentment against the unfeeling, barbarous monster who could perpetrate so foul and awful a deed! Advertisements flew on the wings of the wind; messengers scoured the country in every direction, until he was taken, brought back, and lodged in jail. He had his trial, was condemned to be executed, and was actually led to the gallows, the July preceding; but had been respited by the Governor, who had this winter presented his case to the legislature; and they were, at the time I speak of, acting upon it. My companion had partaken of the excitement very feelingly. She was a great lover of children, and the least cruelty practiced upon them excited her indignation even to revenge. She had read the heart-rending story of the poor child's sufferings till her heart bled with pity, and burned with indignation against her savage and cruel murderer; and nothing could satisfy her but his protracted death, wherein he should feel as much pain, in proportion to his strength to bear it, as the poor innocent child did. Hanging was too good for him,—he ought to be whipped to death; and she could see it done—she would exult in seeing him cut into shreds.

On our journey, we passed through Cooperstown, where Arnold was confined in jail, awaiting the action of the legislature on his case. I had to make some stay in the vicinity, and fulfil an appointment left on my way down; and I proposed to her to go to the jail, and see this monster in human shape. She was horror-struck at the idea of beholding such a monster; but finally concluded to go in. It was a good time to make the impression I desired. He had just received a paper from Albany, containing the proceedings on his case, and the present appearance was hopeless; the probability was that the legislature would not commute his punishment, but would appoint an early hour for his execution. He was, therefore, in a state of hopeless despair! and the deep dolorous groans that escaped from his dark cell, as we entered the jail, mingled with the rattling of his chains as he writhed about; were enough to appal the boldest spirit, and draw sympathy from a heart of stone!

His wife was by his side; and a Methodist preacher, who had been praying with him, was just holding him by the hand to take his leave. I entered his cell and spoke to him, and talked with him a few minutes about his present prospects, and also his future hopes; he was heartless, hopeless, and gloomy in the extreme, incapable of receiving any encouraging hope; a groan accompanied every word, and his poor wife wept aloud! I looked at my companion, and her countenance was softened down, it had entirely lost that stern, rigid expression of revenge which it had uniformly worn, when speaking of him, and exhibited nothing but sensibility and compassion, while tears trembled in both eyes. This was as I would have it. I strove, as well as I could, to administer a ray of comfort to the wretched man, and his weeping wife, and bade them farewell. When we had left the jail, I said to my wife, do you want to see Arnold hung. "No," she said, bursting into tears, "he has suffered enough; I wish they would let him go." And true it was: although his cruelty to the child was unparalleled, and savage in the extreme, yet the intensity of his sufferings in twenty-four hours was inexpressibly and immeasurably beyond all that the child could have endured. But the legislature did, contrary to his expectations then, commute his punishment, and sent him to the penitentiary, where he closed his life.

This scene had the effect on my companion that I most sincerely desired; it embued her heart with a feeling of compassion, even toward guilty sufferers, which she never before experienced, and which was as abiding as her existence. And, this, and similar scenes which fell in her way, prepared her to listen with deep attention to the doctrine of God's divine compassion for a world of sinners, and formed her heart, as well as prepared her understanding, to embrace at last the doctrine of Universal Grace and Salvation, as fully and as heartily as myself.

Arrived, at last, at the spot where I had agreed to fix my residence for a season, and blessed with a companion who would sympathize in all my feelings, and participate in all my hopes and joys, except in religion, and who certainly felt no repugnance to that, I felt myself in a more eligible situation to enjoy contentment and happiness than I had ever been before; and I felt stronger and better prepared to meet the buffetings of opposition, and endure the labors and trials of life. But I was destined immediately to meet with a serious misfortune, under my present circumstances; one which almost deprived me of every means of fulfilling my engagements, or procuring the means of subsistence. A horse was almost as necessary to me as my very life. I had to travel, monthly, more than one hundred and fifty miles to meet my regular engagements on Sundays; besides week-day lectures, and casual calls. The day following my arrival home, my horse received a kick from another, from the effects of which he died. In this horse, I lost more property than I was worth in the world; for I was still indebted for him; and as yet I had no means of making payment, much less of purchasing another; for during the four years I had been preaching, I had scarcely received sufficient to keep my wardrobe in decent repair, and defray the necessary expenses of traveling; nor could I have done that, had I not employed a portion of my time in teaching school, and practiced the most severe economy. What was now to be done? I felt a momentary despondency, and my wife shed tears. I had not yet acquired friends sufficiently numerous and strong to purchase me another horse, or even to assist me much about it. What friends I had were widely scattered; and the societies and congregations to which I preached (for as yet there were but three societies in existence, in central New York,) were too poor, or thought they were, to pay more than their meagre subscriptions. However, my desponding feelings soon subsided: I said to myself, "The Lord will provide;" and took courage. I had now regular monthly appointments, besides in the town where I resided, in Hamilton, Madison, Whitestown, Sangerfield, and Hartwick; and my friends, sometimes one, and then another, furnished me a horse for a trip, for a few weeks; when my good old brother Stetson, who always stood by me like a guardian angel, sold me a horse, and agreed to wait on me until I could pay him for it; which took me several years.

Oh, how little do our young brethren, who enter the ministry in the present day, know or dream of the labors, the trials, embarrassmnnts, obstacles, and discouragements which bestrewed my path, and, indeed, that of nearly every other preacher of the order, in those days! I often hear them complain of their hardships, their meagre salaries, and the scanty remunerations they receive for their services; and I often think, had they lived in those days, they would feel that such complaints and repinings are, manifestly, ingratitude to God. They find societies organized to their hands, calling for their services, and holding out moderate, if not ample compensation. And even congregations which they occasionally supply, where no societies are organized, have learned that when the Apostle said, "He that preaches the Gospel shall live of the Gospel," he did not mean that they should eat, drink, and wear nothing else. What would they think, if they had to go time after time, and preach sometimes to large congregations, assembled merely out of curiosity to hear what "this babbler would say;" and at other times, to half a dozen; and so continue for months, while the people considered that they were doing the preacher overmuch honor, and quite as much as they could afford to do, to spend time to give him a hearing, without once thinking that he needed any thing else? And to be obliged, in doing this, to ride whole days without money enough in their pockets to buy a meal of victuals, or a mess of oats for their horse; and even compelled to pawn their pocket-knife, to get through a turnpike-gate, to go to the place of appointment; and then take a circuitous route back, to avoid the gate, so as to get home again, because they got not enough for their services to pay the toll? Why, they would at once say, *they would not do it.* But some one must have done it, or there would now have been no societies, no congregations to hear and support them. All this I have done; and all this was necessary to be done, in order to clear the ground, and plant the seed which has come up, and is now producing a luxuriant crop.

Mr. S. R. Smith, in his "Historical Sketches," recently published, seems to insinuate, that the early preachers themselves were, in a measure at least, the cause of their own pecuniary embarrassments and sufferings, by preaching against "fat salaries," &c. It may be so; but salaries were out of the question among Universalist preachers, under the state of society in this country at the time to which I allude, whether they preached against salaries or not. I know not that I ever preached a word against salaries; I *know* I never did against a reasonable salary; but I certainly did not preach for the sake of salary; I hope and trust I had a higher and a holier object in view than mere salary. I ever felt very willing to receive what my friends freely gave, and was always very thankful for it; but I never could make that kind of contract about preaching that I would about bartering commodities. It was always the hardest thing in the world for me to talk about salary; and I ever got rid of it with as few words as possible. After societies were formed, and in circumstances to do something for their preachers, and began to learn that preachers were subject to the same temporal wants as other people, and began to say something about paying me for my labors, my uniform practice was to make them name the amount of salary themselves. I would say to them, "I have a family to support, and if I devote my time to the work of the ministry, I must depend on that for their support. Now you certainly know, as well as I do, what will be necessary to do that; and so much I should be glad to realize." They would name a certain amount, in proportion to the time they wished me to improve among them. "Well, can you raise that ?" "Yes, we think we can." "Well, that will satisfy me." Sometimes it would be subscribed, and sometimes not; and when subscribed, it was never expected, by me, that it would all be paid; and I was scarcely ever disappointed in that respect. Could I this moment receive the arrearages of salary voluntarily offered by societies to whom I have preached during my ministerial labors, it would count thousands of dollars. But whether it would make me really any happier, is quite problematical; nevertheless it would surely ease the labors and burdens of old age, if wisely improved. Some who subscribed were actually unable to pay without injury to their families, others were negligent; and I would never allow legal process to be resorted to for the purpose of collecting a subscription for me. An incident occurred, in the society in Whitestown, in an early day, which is worth relating. That society, immediately after organization, availed themselves of the provisions of the statute, and became a body-corporate, so that they could hold property, collect their dues, &c. They had raised a sum by subscription for my services, and collected it all, or all that could be reasonably collected, except a sum of four dollars. This was against a man of property, a professed Universalist, and a constant attendant at meeting, but a slack man in paying his debts generally. The trustees said to me one day, "We have tried to get Esq. E's subscription for you, but he is never ready to pay it, and never will be, until he is sued; for he always has to be sued before he pays a debt. You need it, and we have concluded to sue for it. "Well, brethren," I said, "you can sue him, I very well know, and can collect it; and you may do it as soon as you please; and when you have done so, use it yourselves, for I will never receive a cent of it; I will never, knowingly, receive any thing for preaching that is collected by stress of law—I will starve first." Whether they ever told him what I said, I know not; but a short time after that he paid it, voluntarily, and I was glad to receive it.

Brother Smith surely knows much about the labor, trials, and embarrassments that attended the early ministry of the word in the State of New York, but he knows not all, by experience; times had materially altered, when he came on the stage, from what they were when I first commenced itinerating in the State. Although he penetrated the west farther than any of us had previously done, still those very inhabitants had emigrated from the east, and more or less of them from sections where the doctrine had been preached, and were therefore better prepared to give a Universalist preacher at least a civil reception, than the inhabitants of Central New York were when we first broke in among them.

CHAPTER VIII.

Organization of the Western Association in the State of New York—Complaint against Mr. M. T. Wooley—His trial and expulsion—Anecdote of Mr. Flagg—Proceedings printed in a pamphlet—Haynes' sermon and Ballou's letter—New societies—General Convention, 1806—Confab with a Dutchman and Yankee school-master in Watervliet—Interview with Mr. Lansing—Mr. Vandenburg-Confab with Elder William Underwood-Mr. Underwood's conversion—Removal to Whitestown-Interview with Elder Calvin Winslow—Mr. Winslow's conversion, excommunication from the Methodists, character, &c.—Society organized in Western—Appointment between Whitesboro' and Rome—Encounter with a termagant—Association in 1807—Flattering prospects, and increased opposition—Whitestown society invite Mr. Ballou to settle with them—Mr. Dean engages to settle in Whitestown.

As the season approached that would call our ministering brethren from the east to preach with us, and counsel and assist us in organizing an Association, my heart beat high in anticipation of peculiar felicity. I could hardly wait its arrival. All preparations in our power were made for the coming event, to render it as satisfactory as possible to the visiting committee, and profitable to the glorious cause, by securing as large a congregation as we could induce to attend. Delegates from three societies, (for only three yet existed within the limits of my knowledge in the State of New York,) were appointed. Information of the meeting was widely extended through all the country, with earnest invitations, both to friends and opposers, to attend, and as ample provision was made for their entertainment as circumstances would admit. Here let it be remembered, that although Brookfield, Sangerfield, and Madison have been named as stations for preaching, yet they were all included in the Hamilton society, whose appellation, in its organization, was "The Universalist society of Hamilton and vicinity." The place for the meeting was appointed in Columbus, Chenango county; not because more Universalists, or friends to the cause, were there, or even as many as in other places; but because it was the most central location we could obtain, where we could find any accommodation. No Universalist society was, at that time, thought of there; but Mr. Wooley had preached there a few times; and there were a few families in the immediate vicinity who were ready to do all they could for the accommodation of those who should assemble; and whose liberality was generous and ample. The country was new and thinly settled, at that time, and no meeting-house had been erected in that region by any denomination. But two brothers, by the name of Lamb, (the youngest of whom is now a judge, and still occupies the same house,) had just built a house, designed for a tavern, with a pretty extensive ball-room, which they generously offered and we gratefully accepted, as the most eligible place that could be found. And, here we assembled, on the sixth day of June, 1806, and were met by the delegation from the General Convention. Mr. Ballou, Mr. Farwell, and Mr. Flagg; and a young man by the name of Paul Dean, who had commenced preaching something like a year before, and had received a letter of fellowship from the General Convention, at its sesion in September previous, accompanied Mr. Ballou from Barnard, Vermont. And here was organized the first Association of Universalists in the State, which then and there received the appellation of "The Western Association of Universalists in the State of New York;" and this was the third organization of the kind effected in America. Four discourses were delivered on the occasion, one by Mr. Flagg, one by Mr. Dean, and two by Mr. Ballou. A numerous congregation, for the time and place, were in attendance; and in the afternoon of the first day, and both parts of the second, we were compelled to repair to the adjacent forest for our religious exercises, the chamber not being sufficiently capacious to hold a tenth part of the congregation. The weather was fine for the season; and we found ourselves comfortably accommodated, with the verdant and waving foliage of a dense forest to screen us from the scorching rays of a summer sun, and the trunks and fragments of fallen trees, mostly for our seats; and here we listened with intense interest and fervent gratification to the preaching, which, it appeared to me, was almost sufficiently piercing to penetrate the dark vault of the tomb, and powerful enough to raise the dead to life. Heaven's richest spiritual blessings were bestowed with a liberal hand; and my anticipations of felicity on the occasion would by no means have been extravagant, had it not been for one occurrence, which I shall hereafter have to record.

This meeting gave courage, confidence, and strength to our friends, and alarmed our enemies. Such a congregation of Universalist preachers, it was thought, could scarcely have been collected together in the wide world! Why, there were six of them together! And, unexpectedly to me, in addition to the societies already named, a delegation from a society in Delaware county, (I suppose, under the preaching of Mr. Ferris, though he was not present,) presented credentials, and were received into fellowship; which made four societies, duly represented. What think you, brethren in the ministry? Would such a meeting as that be a subject of extreme congratulation and encouragement to you at the present day? But so it was to us, then. We felt that it was the "Lord's doing, and marvelous in our eyes." We received it as a pledge of divine approbation, and sure confirmation that the cause would prosper in our hands; and, like Paul when he met the brethren at "Appii Forum, and the Three Taverns," we "thanked God, and took courage."

But, alas! while citizens of this changeable and changing world, we may always look for an alloy to our anticipated enjoyment. Mr. Wooley, whom I have already named as the instrument of the organization of the first Universalist society west of the Hudson river, had been, at least, imprudent in his conversation and conduct. He was a man of jealous temperament, and frequently, on that account, abused his best friends. He hailed my coming into this country with the utmost apparent sincerity and cordiality; introduced me to his society; and, in the strongest manner, insisted on my preaching with them. But soon after our meeting at Burlington, for causes unknown to me, and which I had not wisdom enough to divine, unless it was on account of my influencing Mr. Ferris to meet with us, and which he never saw fit to speak to me about, or in any way attempt to explain, he became decidedly unfriendly. I was left to learn it from our mutual friends; for, in my presence, he still continued to manifest his former friendship. But I could often hear of his unfriendly remarks in regard to me, of the invidious epithets that he used, and his untiring efforts to render me ridiculous, and destroy my influence; and I was advised, several times, to enter a complaint against him to the Association. But I uniformly answered, "No —I extremely regret Br. Wooley is taking such a course; for the cause will be injured thereby. We are weak, at best, and need all our united and friendly co-operation to advance the cause of divine truth. But I will try to outlive all these unjust aspersions, and pray that Brother Wooley may neither hurt himself, nor the cause in which we are engaged; for I feel assured that he can not seriously injure me, if I do not hurt myself." He even went so far as to represent, in a letter that he prepared for the society in Hartwick to the General Convention, that my labors were injurious to the cause in that section of country, and advised the Convention not to grant me ordination; and presented this letter to the clerk of the society for his signature; but he would not sign it. He said, however, that he had sufficient influence in the Convention to prevent my ordination; and he would do it. But on his return from the Convention, which was several weeks before I returned, on being asked if I was ordained, said, "Yes, that hellish club of Free Masons have put him as far forward as possible." Still, Mr. Wooley was on the committee of ordination before which I was examined; and so far from raising any objections to my ordination, or manifesting any unfriendly feeling toward me in the council, every word and every act of his were in my favor, and he promoted my ordination with all the influence he possessed. His conduct was most inexplicable, and a source of the greatest trial I ever experienced in all my ministerial labors. I could, with the utmost fortitude, bear the opposition, the scoffs, the sneers, the vituperations, and the calumnies of enemies, and almost thank God that I was worthy to suffer persecution for the cause of Christ; but when professed friends, and especially one engaged in the same work, holding fellowship with the same church, bound together by the sacred ties of faith, of Christian sympathy, of clerical fellowship, and whose bonds should have been strengthened by a consideration of the vast importance of the work in which we were engaged, and the opposition we were doomed to encounter from a malignant and cruel foe; when such an one turned his heel against me, and, like Joab, while saluting me with a brother's kiss, had a dagger concealed under his cloak, to stab me "under the fifth rib," was more than I felt able to bear. And, had I not been fully aware that Mr. Wooley's influence was, with himself, more imaginary than real—that the friends of the cause did not entertain so high an opinion of his talents and usefulness as he did—that his standing in the denomination was not the most exalted, I should certainly have sunk under the burden. Moreover, in addition to his treatment of me, he was engaged, about this time, in the puerile and visionary pursuit of digging for treasures in the earth. He and several others had formed a company, and engaged the services of one of those impostors who, by looking into a mysterious glass, or rather stone, pretended to be able to discover hidden treasures, or lost things, and even foretell future events; and he was leading them about from place to place to dig for subterraneous wealth, which he could plainly see by looking into his dark hat, having this stone in the crown. Mr. Wooley's friends had admonished him of the impropriety of the course he was pursuing, of the injury the cause would sustain by it, and its disadvantage to himself in particular. They represented to him the great probability that this man was a gross impostor, and practicing this deception upon his too-credulous employers to gratify his idleness and his avarice. But this only vexed Mr. Wooley, and led him to make some very unwise and unchristian expressions.

Without the least previous knowledge of mine, or even a hint that such a thing was in agitation, at an early session of the council after its organization, a gentleman residing in Columbus, and an ardent friend to the cause, presented a written complaint, founded upon the circumstances above related. This was a source of grief, and indeed of mortification to the whole council, and a severe drawback upon our enjoyment. But it was just; the council were obliged to receive the complaint, and Mr. Wooley was called to answer to it. He pleaded that he was not prepared to meet the allegations and defend himself, neither could he be during this session; and wished to appeal to the General Convention for his trial, at its next session. This request was readily granted; but at the next session of the General Convention, Mr. Wooley did not appear. The case was called up, the evidence examined, and Mr. W. was suspended from fellowship for one year; but the privilege granted him to appear at the next meeting of the Convention, to vindicate and clear himself from the charges brought against him, if he should be able. The next Convention, however, Mr. Wooley did not see fit to attend, either personally or by proxy; and hearing nothing from him, the hand of fellowship was finally withdrawn; and he never afterward took any measures to renew his standing in the connection, although he continued to hold meetings for several years, more or less, after his expulsion.

The position of Mr. Wooley left me substantially alone in this region; for Mr. Ferris was too deeply engaged in his secular affairs to pay much attention, or devote much time to preaching. But, strange as it may appear, Mr. Wooley manifested more friendship after this, than he had at any time since his alienation; and was of more service to me, in recommending my labors, and trying to introduce me into different places to proclaim the word.

At the time the committee was appointed, by the General Convention, to visit us in New York and organize an Association, I requested Mr. Flagg, whose time was not so closely occupied as some others, to make arrangements to remain a season in our country, even all summer if he could, as there was a "great and effectual door opened" for the preached word, "and many opposers," and laborers but few and feeble. He made his arrangements accordingly, and did remain among us somewhat over one month. During that time, he preached to great acceptance in many places, delivered an address to the friends in Columbus, on the fourth of July, which was highly extolled; and was earnestly solicited to remain longer; but, for reasons known only to himself, declined, and returned to New England in the month of July.

There is an anecdote in regard to Mr. Flagg, which I think worth relating, and which is at least amusing, and not wholly without instruction. While in Cooperstown, where Mr. Flagg had been preaching, he fell in company with Mr. Aplin, a rigid Calvinist, and deacon of the Presbyterian church, with whom he had a desultory controversy. The deacon soon found himself in difficulty; and becoming vexed, which is generally the case with violent opposers, when they find themselves so crossed in argument that they can not extricate themselves, began to rail against the doctrine because of its licentious tendency; "Why," said he, "if I believed your doctrine, Mr. Flagg, I should feel no restraint—I would give loose to all my passions and propensities, and gratify them to the full extent—I would steal, murder, rob, or do any thing I felt disposed to do." Mr. Flagg was sometimes pretty severe, especially on a bigoted, uncivil, and stormy opponent; and being a large, stern-looking man, he fixed his piercing eye on the deacon, and replied, "Deacon A., I believe it—I believe every word you say—I believe you have as corrupt a heart as you say you have; and God knows what a rascal you are; and he has hid the truth from your eyes, to prevent you from committing those atrocious crimes." The deacon quailed under the stern gaze and severe rebuke of Mr. F., and withdrew from the contest; no doubt ashamed of the horrible confession he had unwittingly made.

After the close of the Association, which adjourned to the first Wednesday and Thursday in June, 1807; then to hold a session in New Hartford, Oneida county; Mr. Ballou went with me to my residence in Brookfield, where he delivered a discourse. From thence he went to New Hartford and Utica, preached in each of those places, and then returned to his residence in Barnard, Vermont. After Mr. Flagg returned to Massachusetts, I was again left alone, even more solitary than ever before, in this enlarging field of operation; for I could no longer associate with Mr. Wooley, as I had, in some measure, heretofore always done, notwithstanding his unkind treatment; and, indeed, the friends in this immediate region would no longer countenance his attempts to hold meetings among them; therefore, if he preached at all, it must have been in some remote place. About this time, or soon after this, he made some journeys into the Genesee country, and preached in several places, then far west of my travels. Mr. Ferris traveled none, of any account, and preached but little. But I had enjoyed "a feast of fat things," which renewed my strength, and gave me fortitude and courage to meet the opposition, although alone, and fight, fearlessly, the battles of the Lord, under the unfurled banner of his love. We adopted the practice at our first Association, of publishing our proceedings in a pamphlet, accompanied by a general epistle, or circular letter, to the societies, which was distributed among our friends, and also among as many of our opposers, as we could induce to read it, gratuitously; and this practice was continued until periodicals were so established in our denomination as to supersede the necessity, or even utility, of this course. And this practice proved a very efficient means of advancing the cause, by diffusing information, not only in regard to our order, but also in respect to doctrine, among many who had not the moral courage to attend our meetings, even when convenient for them to do so.

Some time in the course of the previous year, Mr. Ballou had delivered a discourse in the meeting-house in West Rutland, Vermont, where the mulatto, Rev. Lemuel Haynes, was settled, which called forth Haynes' memorable discourse against Universalism. This discourse was immediately published, and republished, through several editions, and circulated with the rapidity of lightning, almost, through the length and breadth of our country. It was extolled from the pulpit, and recommended by many newspapers, as a complete exposition, refutation, and explosion of Universalism; and highly applauded in an Orthodox periodical, the first I ever saw, entitled, if my memory serves me, the "Christian Panoplist," and recommended to the perusal of *all*, but especially to such as had not *time to read* the Bible in reference to the subject! I found it in almost every place where I went; it was thrown in my face by almost every saucy boy, quarrelsome man, and petulent old woman that I met. It happened, very fortunately, that Mr. Ballou brought with him into that country, a few of his letters addressed to Haynes on the subject. I therefore purchased one of Haynes' pamphlets, attached it to Mr. Ballou's letters, and got five hundred printed; and scattered them through the country, wherever I went. This had the desired effect. It not only put a stop to the exultation of opposers over Haynes' production, in that region; but it showed so plainly the absurdity of that tissue of low satire and black-guardism, as well as the unchristian and uncivil course pursued by the author, that it actually produced a reaction, and led hundreds to reflect; and paved the way for them to burst the manacles of bigotry and superstition, and come into the liberty of the Gospel. Thus was the wrath of man made to praise the Lord. Mr. Ballou also brought with him a few copies of his "Treatise on Atonement," then just published, and a few copies of his "Notes on the Parables," first edition, in pamphlet form. These were of immense value to the cause; for as yet, no books, or nearly none, on the subject of Universalism, were to be found in all that country; while it was being inundated with Partialist writings of almost every description. I believe I had found one copy of Dr. Huntington's posthumous work, "Calvinism Improved," and perhaps two or three copies of "Winchester's Dialogues;" and I do not recollect of meeting with any other works in favor of Universalism, in the hands of any individual in all that region of country.

During the year intervening between the sessions of our Association, my labor was as incessant as in any period of my life. I regularly supplied the societies and congregations in Hamilton, Sangerfield, Whitestown and Hartwick, and lectured several times in the course of the week, extending my travels very considerably beyond their former limits. I found also many more places, within the limits of my former travels, and even beyond them. The doctrine of the Great Salvation was this year introduced into the towns of Paris, Bridgewater, Deerfield, Litchfield, Westmoreland, Rome, Western, Floyd, Eaton, and Norwich, besides the villages of Utica, Whitesboro', and Clinton; and various other neighborhoods in the towns of Hamilton, Madison, and Sangerfield, where I could never before gain admittance; for the Gospel, in order to succeed, must be carried to every man's door. I cheerfully answered every call I could possibly find time to attend to, even from the smallest settlement; and felt abundantly rewarded if I could get ten or a dozen willing to listen to my message; and in the course of the year, a number of respectable congregations were got up in different places, and societies organized in the towns of Madison, Eaton, and Western.

In September, this year, (1806) the General Convention held its session in the village of Hoosick Falls, N. Y. My wife had two brothers residing in that region, one within the limits of the town of Hoosick, and the other near the mouth of the Mohawk River, in Watervliet. She therefore accompanied me; and we spent the Sunday after the Convention in Watervliet. The inhabitants of this place, with the exception of one or two families, were Dutch, and very bigoted and superstitious. But at the request of a few friends, an appointment for a meeting was given out; and, contrary to my expectations, quite a respectable congregation, for numbers, assembled. This, I believe, was the first discourse ever delivered by a Universalist in that place, and it produced somewhat of an excitement; and after the close of the exercise, several individuals manifested quite a pugnacious spirit, and unceremoniously commenced an attack. Among the most forward was an old Dutchman, by the name of Canute, quite a shrewd and intelligent man. But the old gentleman soon became very angry, and indulged in unmeasured abuse. This so disturbed my sister-in-law, in whose house our meeting had been held, and where we still remained, that with some spirit she interrupted the conversation, by saying, "Mr. Canute, Mr. Stacy is my brother!" The old gentlemen rather petulently replied, "Vel, den, sho wash Cain prother to Apel." This produced some risibility; and I had to tell my sister not to be disturbed—Mr. C. could not offend me. But a more formidable antagonist now interposed, a bigoted, self-conceited Yankee school-master. He charged me with taking advantage of Mr. C., because he did not understand the English language. "Perhaps, sir," said I, "you would like to take Mr. Canute's place." No sooner was this said, than Mr. C. withdrew, and the Yankee school-master, with all the pomposity of a pedant, and the assurance of a bravado, seated himself before me, *foot to foot and knee to knee*, and resumed the argument. But in less than half of the time which Mr. C. occupied, he arose and left the house in a rage. He was totally ignorant of the Scriptures, and destitute of all knowledge of the nature of an argument. During the meeting, I noticed a young man manifestly giving profound attention to the discourse; he also remained during the discussion, and paid close attention; but did not introduce a word, *pro* or *con*. On the next day, this young man, (he was a Dutchman,) came and very civilly accosted me, saying, that he attended my meeting yesterday, and also heard the discussion between me and Mr. Canute, and the school-master; and he understood me to say, that the phrase *endless punishment* could not be found in the Bible; and that there could not a word be found, either in the English or Greek Testament, that primarily and necessarily meant endless, when applied to punishment. He said, he was a professor of religion, and an inquirer after truth. He had supposed that endless punishment was a prominent doctrine of the Bible; but if it were not so, he certainly wished to know it. And as he felt incapable of holding an argument, he had persuaded a gentleman of learning to accompany him; and, if I felt willing, he wished us to discuss the question in his presence. He said, he was a gentleman and a Christian, and would use me politely, if I would permit him to introduce him to me. I replied, I should be very happy to discourse with him; and he invited him into the room, and introduced him. If my memory be correct, (but I am not very positive, in this particular,) his name was Lansing. He also was a Dutchman. I found him to be a man of classical education, and a gentleman; and he certainly demeaned himself like a Christian. He immediately directed my attention to the twenty fifth chapter of Matthew—the parable of the sheep and the goats. But in less than twenty minutes, I made him acknowledge, that the word *aionion*, applied both to the happiness of the righteous and the punishment of the wicked, did not necessarily mean endless; but actually was, in most cases, applied to things of limited duration; and, as he could find no word stronger than that, applied to punishment, he gave up the argument in my favor, and pursued no further the subject of endless punishment with me.

A number of years after the above-mentioned incident, at a meeting of the Western Association, in Hamilton, a gentleman by the name of Vandenburg applied for a letter of fellowship; and after examination, in which he was found worthy, and his request granted, he took occasion to remind me of the foregoing circumstance. He told me he was the young man who desired the interview, and observed, that the discourse and the discussion to which he listened at that time, resulted in inducing him to enter into a close and critical examination of the Bible on the subject; and it was but a short time before he became firmly established in the doctrine, and felt an irresistible desire to proclaim it to the world. He was shortly after solemnly ordained to the sacred work of the ministry of reconciliation, in the town of Pompey, Onondaga county, N. Y., near which, I believe, he still resides; and remains faithful to his divine Master, and his holy profession. This, and similar circumstances which frequently occurred, always renewed my courage, and inspired a spirit of perseverance. I discovered that, although seed might be sown under the most untoward and unpromising circumstances, yet there might be spots of good ground to receive some small part of it, which would germinate, and in due time yield a profitable harvest.

On my second visit to the town of Litchfield, Herkimer county, in the autumn of this year, an occurrence took place of some interest, which, like almost every attempt of the opposers to crush the truth, proved essentially advantageous to the establishment of the cause in that place. I had previously delivered a single lecture within the limits of that town, in the dwelling-house of James Gage, Esq.; but now the appointment was made for a meeting in a school-house in one of the most populous settlements in the town, and in close proximity to the Presbyterian meeting-house, the center of that society. There was also a Baptist society and church in the immediate vicinity, and a clergyman of the order residing in the neighborhood. This invasion upon their premises alarmed them. Something must be done. The prowling wolf was about to venture into the midst of their flocks, and even in their presence attempt to seize their sheep! A meeting was called, as I was subsequently circumstantially informed, and measures adopted to effectually oppose and drive the presumptuous intruder from their borders. Pilot and Herod were that day made friends. The consultation was mutual between the two denominations, and the result was, that Elder William Underwood, the Baptist minister, with the aid of two deacons, one Baptist and one Presbyterian, should attend the meeting, and give battle to the stripling, whom they understood was a mere boy. All this, however, was kept a profound secret from me, at the time, and also as much as possible from my friends. At length the day arrived, and a crowded congregation filled the house. The Elder with his two aids, one on each side, placed himself on the other side of the room, directly opposite to me. I was not introduced to them, and consequently was unable to distinguish them from others, until they arose for combat. The text I made use of was Mark, 16 : 15, 16. They considered this as a knock-down text, and sufficient, of itself, to refute Universalism. However, I had the temerity to approach it, and delivered a pretty long discourse upon it, with as much freedom of speech as I ever enjoyed. At the close, I gave liberty for remarks, or questions, and took my seat. But my opposers were not quick to rise. The deacons began to jog Mr. Underwood, and whisper "Come, get up," as the Elder subsequently informed me. But he whispered back, "What shall we do? This is something new—we are not prepared for it." But they replied, "Something must be done—get up and oppose it." So up Mr. U. arose, and stammered out something, and quoted two or three passages of Scripture. But his discourse was short, and, I thought, his arguments very feeble. I replied briefly, however, to what he said. He then remarked, that there was a boy in the house, who had committed to memory a poem which he thought very descriptive, and very clearly illustrated Universalism; and he motioned that the boy be called upon to rise and repeat it. No remark was made in reply, and the boy was placed upon a bench, and commenced repeating the same obscene satire, mentioned heretofore as the closing exercise of Elder Morton. When the boy had repeated one stanza, I arose and stopped him; and told the congregation, that I had once heard that filthy production, and must be excused from hearing it a second time—it was too obscene to be repeated in public; but if they chose to hear it, I would retire until the boy had concluded his exhibition; and then return and answer questions, candidly proposed, as long as they desired. The faces of the clergyman and deacons were instantly suffused with shame, and the boy was pulled off the bench. No farther questions were proposed, nor opposition attempted; and, after waiting a reasonable time, I dismissed the congregation. I had a few words of conversation with the Elder and his deacons after the people were dismissed; and it was perfectly evident that they, too late, discovered that the course they had taken was calculated to have a contrary effect from what they designed.

From this time, I saw no more of Mr. Underwood for nearly three years; although I frequently held meetings in Litchfield, and sometimes in his immediate neighborhood; but he never again attended my meeting, until he became an advocate of the faith he once attempted to destroy. After Mr. Dean's settlement in New Hartford, we frequently lectured in Litchfield; and I was told that Mr. Underwood attended his meetings several times; and had several interviews with him. About three years after the above-mentioned interview with Mr. U., and after my removal to the town of Hamilton, a neighbor of mine, Mr. Stevens, deacon of the Presbyterian church, and a rigid, sour sectarian, sent his son very early one morning to my house, with a request that I should immediately call there. This was unaccountably strange! I could never persuade the deacon to hold any more intercourse with me, than a Jew would hold with a Samaritan. "What," said I to the boy, "does your father wish of me?" "There is a minister," he replied, "that wishes to talk with you." "What minister is it?" I inquired. "Mr. Underwood," said he. "Well," said I, "you may return my answer, that I will come as soon as I have taken breakfast." When the boy had gone, I told my wife who this Mr. Underwood must be, and, said I, "you must go with me; for no doubt I have got to have a severe battle." We went—but instead of a battle, and to the very great astonishment of the deacon and his wife, all I had to do was to sit and hear the Elder preach Universalism, with all the eloquence he was master of, for the period of half a day. He said, "I am not a Universalist; but I have found some flaws in my former creed, and I have abandoned all creeds, and am resolved to search impartially, and, God being my helper, to follow on till I find the truth." I merely replied, "You are doing well, Brother Underwood—God speed you—you will end right." This was in the winter. I was, at this time, under engagement to preach one Sunday in each month in Litchfield, about six miles from the residence of Mr. U., and on a Sunday in the fore part of the following summer, being a little behind time in the morning, when I arrived at the school-house where our meetings were holden, Mr. Underwood had opened the meeting by prayer. He declined my invitation to him to preach, but cheerfully associated in the other exercises of worship, and openly avowed his faith in the final Restitution. I went home with him after meeting, and for the first time visited his family. I found his wife also in the faith, and rather in advance of her husband; and they both affirmed, that they felt vastly happier, more reconciled to the divine government, loved God better, and felt a more expansive and enduring affection for mankind than they did, or could, in their former faith, or even thought it possible to experience. He was a man then passing the meridian of life; had been a Baptist preacher for many years; but he had now entered a new and a more delightful field of labor. After a suitable season, he joined the Universalist connection, became a zealous and useful laborer in the vineyard, and lived and died rejoicing in the faith.

On the first of January, 1807, by the urgent solicitation of the society in Whitestown, I removed my family into that town. This, however, caused no alteration in my labors and itinerations. I continued to supply the societies with whom I had before labored nearly in the same ratio, devoting a little more time, however, to Whitestown and vicinity. I had received several urgent calls to hold a meeting in the town of Eaton, Madison county, but hitherto had found no opportunity to answer them. In the month of March, however, I sent them an appointment, and with much labor and fatigue, over roads well surcharged with mud, I was enabled to fulfil the engagement. The distance was about twenty miles, and the hour of appointment had passed by, fifteen or twenty minutes before I arrived, which caused considerable solicitude by my friends. As I came within sight of the schoolhouse, in what was called Log City, then the most populous settlement in the town, I discovered quite a large concourse of people in front of the house, and suddenly two individuals emerged from the crowd, and met me at the distance of thirty or forty rods. They said some fears had been indulged, and some impatience manifested; and they wanted me to make no delay, lest the people should begin to retire. Therefore, one took my horse, and the other, without introducing me to an individual, conducted me into the house. I noticed a gentleman, very active and officious in seating the people, (who soon filled the house, though the principal part found seats of some sort,) and trying to arrange things for the convenience of the congregation, who, on completing his task, seated himself on the other side of the room, directly opposite to me. His movements naturally arrested my attention, and his location in the assembly rendered him an object of my special attention. I could not detect his eyes turned from me during the whole discourse; and his emotions were more visible than I had ever before witnessed in any man living. Sometimes, his sides would shake with laughter, and, at others, tears would run in rivers down his cheeks. As soon as the congregation were dismissed, he crowded his way to me, and, taking me by the hand most cordially, said, "I wish to introduce myself to you, sir, as a Methodist preacher, by the name of Calvin Winslow." He then gave me a most pressing invitation to go home with him—he resided about a mile distant. This I had to decline, as I had other engagements for the evening; but, before I left the town, I made him a visit.

Mr. Winslow was a popular preacher among the Methodists, and had been a most virulent enemy of Universalism. He was an illiterate man, but possessed strong natural talents, was quite eloquent in his way, and could be cuttingly satirical; and he failed not to employ this talent freely upon Calvinism and Universalism. I will give an illustration. In a sermon, not long previous to my first acquaintance with him, after belaboring Calvinism with all the vindictive feelings of an enraged soul, he closed by exclaiming, "Here, Calvinism! get out at the back door, to black damnation—to your mother hell!" Then turning upon Universalism, he whipped that with the lashes of his fiery tongue, as long as he could find expressions bad enough, when, with a bitter sneer, he wound off by saying, "And you, Universalist, how you'll look, after you have been in hell forty nine thousand years, and helped Winchester build a bridge across the impassable gulph—how you'll look like a parcel of scorched toads, hopping about in heaven, and singing praises to hell-fire!"

But God had prepared Mr. Winslow to feel a different spirit, at that time. He had just buried a beloved child, and his feelings were very tender and susceptible. On my visit to him, I was accompanied by several others who wished to hear the discussion, for they expected to hear a warm controversy. I found him very little inclined for disputation, but quite disposed to make inquiry. He did, indeed, commence a trifling controversy; but in an exceedingly mild way; and manifested no disposition to continue it, but turned the conversation wholly to inquiry, without attempting a reply. Our friends who went with me were very much disappointed at the result of our meeting, but the interview was a very pleasant one. He informed me of his afflictive bereavement. We united in prayer, and separated with the kindest feelings. From that time, Mr. Winslow sought every opportunity to associate with me, often attended my meetings; and we several times held meetings together, he improving one part of the day, and I the other; and we often exchanged visits, until the Methodists became quite jealous of him. Our friendly intercourse continued notwithstanding; and at every opportunity he propounded questions for investigation on important doctrinal points; and I could plainly discover, from time to time, a progressive improvement in thought; and report said, his preaching became vastly more liberal.

Some time in the summer of 1809, Mr. Winslow called at my house, and immediately, even before taking his seat, said, "Brother Stacy, there is but one thing that prevents me from being a Universalist; and that is, the unalterable state of the soul after death. All men are certainly not prepared for heaven before death, nor have we any evidence that all are converted at the hour of death. Now if I could be convinced that there could be a saving change wrought upon the soul after death, I should be compelled to be a Universalist." "Well, sit down, Br. Winslow," said I, "if that is your last and only difficulty, you have got to be a Universalist, or I a Methodist, before we part. For if the Bible does positively teach, that there is to be *no alteration* after death, I will renounce Universalism. And now, let me hear your strongest proofs and arguments in favor of the sentiment, that there is no change to the soul after the death of the body." The reader will doubtless be astonished, especially when he considers that Mr. W. had been a preacher for many years, and the boast of his denomination, on learning that the first proof he named was, "There is no repentance in the grave." "Why, Brother Winslow, do you quote that as Scripture?" "Yes, surely." "But do you not know, that there is no such passage in the Bible?" "Well, if I have not got the words exactly, there is something nearly like it." "Well, there is something near enough—the words you probably allude to are in the ninth chapter of Ecclesiastes, and read thus: "Whatsoever thy hand findeth to do, do it with all thy might; for there is no work, nor device, nor knowledge, nor wisdom in the grave, whither thou goest." "Well, that is as strong as though the word repentance was there." "Just as strong, Brother Winslow; and I am perfectly willing you should add the word repentance to it, if it will suit your argument any better." "Well, that surely teaches, that there can be no saving change after death." "We will look at it, Brother Winslow. You suppose that this refers to the state of the soul after the death of the body, do you not?" "Yes, certainly." "Now, permit me to ask you one question. Can we either enjoy happiness, or experience misery, without knowledge?" "No, certainly." "We will now read your text according to your supposition of its meaning: '*For there is no work, nor device, nor knowledge, nor wisdom to the soul, after death.*' How do you like it, Brother Winslow?" "I do not like it at all." "Well, you must not have it so, then; but take it as the sacred penman has given it to you. You now see, that according to your application of the text, if it prove any thing, it proves too much for you; because it proves the annihilation of the soul!" "Well, I will give up that text, but I have others." "Please to name them." "As a tree falleth, so it lieth; and as death leaves us, so judgment will find us." In short, he went from this to the eighth chapter of John; and quoted, erroneously, "If ye die in your sins, where God and Christ are, you never can come;" and then from Revelations, "He that is unjust, shall be unjust still," &c.; reciting every passage wrong that he attempted to quote. I carefully followed him, turning to every passage he attempted to quote, and read them correctly, giving him my views upon each text. I then took the affirmative of the question—There is an alteration after death; and quoted 1 Pet. 3: 18, 19, 20; and 4: 6; Rom. 14: 7, 8, 9; Heb. 2: 14; and concluded with the fifteenth chapter of first Corinthians, when Mr. Winslow, faithful to himself and his word, declared that he was fully convinced of the truth of the Final Restitution; and manifested exceeding great joy in his deliverance from Partialism. A few weeks after this interview, he authorized me to give out an appointment for him in connection with mine, in the town of Eaton, with the annunciation that he would there fully declare his sentiments. This produced a very considerable excitement; for it was obvious that Mr. W's preaching had undergone a change—the Methodists had become jealous of him, and much speculation had been indulged in regard to his private sentiments. The annunciation, therefore, that he would openly avow and explain his doctrinal sentiments, called together an unusually large congregation; and, in their presence, on the seventeenth day of September, 1809, he boldly avowed his faith in the final salvation of the whole human family, through Jesus Christ our Lord. It was a refreshing season, and much good was done in our holy cause. "Is this Universalism?" said an old gentleman by the name of Hatch to me, who had never dared to venture out to a meeting of the kind before. "Surely," I replied, "this is Universalism." "Well," said he, "if this is Universalism, then I have been a Universalist for many years, for this is exactly according to my faith; but I knew not what to call myself." And from that time he became one of my constant hearers.

Immediately after this public declaration of his faith, the Methodists took up a labor with Mr. Winslow, and, in a very unfriendly manner, excommunicated him from the connection. Previously to this step, however, he had addressed a very affectionate letter to the Conference, informing them of his change of sentiment, and requesting a peaceable withdrawal. They took no notice of this letter, but thundered their bitterest anathemas upon his head, and delivered him up to satan, not for the salvation of his soul, like Paul of old, but to be tormented in hell world without end. He soon joined our Association, and was for several years a successful and profitable fellow-laborer. But he was an unfortunate man. He had a good heart—never man had better; but his unconquerable appetite for ardent spirits overpowered his judgment, and he became an inebriate! Long and affectionately did the Association labor to restore and preserve him, for all loved him; but our labor proved fruitless. Several times he came with deep contrition of heart—he was always sincere—and, with tears streaming from his eyes, confessed his sin, and begged forgiveness; but alas! his resolution was easily overcome, perhaps by the next decanter of spirits placed before him; and this, in his day, was too common and too dangerous a practice. The Association was at length compelled—but it was done with feelings of heart-felt sorrow and commiseration for his infirmities—at its session in 1817, I think, to withdraw from him the hand of fellowship; and he never afterward attempted to preach. "The voice of my brethren," he said to me, "is the voice of God, in this respect—I shall never try to preach again."

From my first visit to Eaton, I continued them monthly, delivering one or more lecture each time; and before our Association in June, they organized a small society, which was at that time received into fellowship.

Soon after my removal to Whitestown, I received a pressing solicitation to visit the town of Western, north of Rome. Methodism had made very considerable progress in that town; and it had done some good. It had exposed the absurdities of Calvinism, and, in a good degree, liberated the mind from the prejudices of education; and in several instances, certainly excited a freedom of thought and investigation which it could not restrain. Several, who had early united with the Methodists, had thoroughly tried that system and found it entirely inadequate to answer the desires of the soul; or, to use Scripture metaphor, "The bed was so short, that a man could not stretch himself on it; and the covering so narrow, that he could not wrap himself in it." Some had already discovered a more ample plan of salvation, and others were earnestly seeking. My time was so constantly taken up, that I could not answer their call until March; but from that time I visited them as often as I could find opportunity, generally preaching several times, and in several different places, in the course of each visit; and in the course of the summer following, a society was organized in that town. "Come," said a gentlemen, when I presented a constitution for a society,—"Come, sister U., you and I were the first to join a Methodist class in this place; and now let us be the first to join a Universalist Society." But sister U. was not then quite ready. However, she soon became ready, and joined with a full and glowing heart.

There was a gentleman who kept a public-house between

Whitesboro' and Rome by, the name of Putnam—(Col. Putnam.) This gentleman had several times attended my meetings in Whitestown, and requested that I would, at some convenient time, make an appointment in his neighborhood. On my way to Western, on one of my visits to that town, I called on Col. P., to make arrangements for a lecture, on my return. The Colonel was not in his house, but his wife directed me to a lot where he was at work, and I went and found him. He dropped his work, and returned with me to the house. We were conversing on the subject of a meeting when we entered the house, and took seats. Mrs. P. was washing the shelves in the bar; and I felt a little surprised that he did not introduce us to each other; but no such ceremony was performed. I could discover her occasionally stop work, and listen to our conversation. At length she turned round, and, with a face suffused with scarlet, said, "Is this Mr. Stacy?" "Yes," answered the Colonel, and then formally introduced us. Addressing me, she then said, "If I had known who you were, I would not have told you where Mr. P. was." "Why, madam?" I asked. "Because I consider you a very great deceiver, and a very dangerous man; spreading your damnable doctrine in the world, and leading souls down to hell. You must know that my husband is very dear to me; and you have enticed him away after your corrupt doctrine, and are trying to lead him astray, and will be the means of him being damned at last. I do not wish to have him go after you. I don't wish you to have an opportunity to deceive him any more. I wish you would leave the house, and never call here again." "I presume, madam, the Colonel is a man capable of judging for himself in these matters; and will not easily be deceived by a stripling, as I am." "No, he is not; you have deceived him—you are now trying to deceive him; and I wish you would leave the house." All this, and much more, was said in a high state of excitement and vehemence of passion. Indeed, her menaces and grimace, led me very seriously to apprehend she would actually come at me, even in the presence of her husband, to put me out of the house by force. The Colonel manifested great mortification—used his utmost endeavors to calm her passions and cool her temper; but all in vain. Nothing that he or I could say had any other effect but to inflame her passions, and excite her volubility in the use of the most invidious language she was mistress of. He finally said, he would consult his neighbors; and an appointment would be given out for a meeting somewhere in the neighborhood; and I left the house, thankful to escape with the hair on my head.

On my return, I rode up to the house, and not seeing the Colonel, felt some hesitation about entering; however, I concluded to venture, hair or no hair. I hitched my horse in the shed, and entered the bar-room. The house was small, consisting of but two rooms on the ground, one serving for a bar-room, and the other for a kitchen. As I entered, I saw Mrs. P. sitting alone in the bar-room, with her elbows on her knees, and her face dropped between her hands, so as to completely cover it. I looked at her, but she moved not; I thought it possible she was asleep. I walked across the floor as heavily as I could —threw my hat and whip on the table, with as much noise as I could make, and turned toward Mrs. P.; but no movement was yet discoverable. I then took several turns across the floor, with as heavy a tread as my light frame could well make; but without arousing her, or scarcely perceiving any signs of life. I then turned my face toward her, and vociferated, "Mrs. P!" She then slowly raised her head. She had not been asleep; but evidently had seen me ride up, and had fixed herself in that position to avoid an interview. She looked sour enough; but I ventured to inquire, "Is the Colonel within?" She answered coldly, "He is somewhere about—he'll be in soon." This was all the conversation we had. She did not ask me to be seated; but, notwithstanding, I did take a seat. The Colonel soon came in; and as we were about to repair to a near neighbor's where a meeting had been appointed, he asked her if she would go to meeting with us. She replied, gruffly, "No; I am going to prayer meeting." I delivered my message; and remained with the gentleman at whose house the meeting was holden, through the night; and the next morning left the neighborhood with a whole skin; and I have no recollection of ever having seen either Col. P. or his wife since. Although I often passed his house, after that, I had no inclination to cultivate a further acquaintance with his lady; and for some reason, either through mortification at the conduct of his wife, or her influence over him, he never afterwards attended my meetings. This was the most severe rebuff I ever had from a lady, face to face. I was once told, that after I had left the house of a friend on whom I had called, his wife threw a chair against the door after me, with violence; but fortunately the door stopped it, so that I escaped unscathed.

As the season for the meeting of our Association drew near, I exerted myself to arouse the feelings of the brethren and sisters, (for we had a few faithful sisters even at this early period) and to urge the importance of attending meeting themselves, and encouraging others to attend. Delegates were appointed in the few societies organized, and letters and credentials made out. The Presbyterian meeting-house in New Hartford, was obtained for the occasion; and it was well filled. The delegates from the societies were punctual in their attendance, as well as many other individuals; and numbers from all the region where the doctrine had made any advances came to our "yearly feast;" besides many, whom curiosity led to hear something about that strange "sect, which was everywhere spoken against;" and not a few of the Pharisees of the land appeared in our assembly—came in, no doubt, to "spy out our liberty." But whatever were their object or feelings, we were gratified with their attendance; feeling a confidence that the all-wise Governor of the universe, would overrule the whole for the advancement of the cause of divine truth. Mr. Ballou again met with us, and was accompanied by Mr. Dean, and Mr. Richard Carrique, who were appointed as a delegation from the General Convention in New England. Mr. Carrique was a young man of very promising talents, who had commenced his ministerial labors in the State of Vermont, a short time previous to this. Discourses were delivered, on the occasion, with powerful effect, by the three brethren from the east; and nothing took place to mar the pleasantness of the meeting, except the clandestine distribution of a large number of Haynes' filthy discourses against Universalism, over the seats of the meeting-house, during the intermission of the second day, by some malignant hand; and even this, Mr. Ballou so ingeniously noticed, and so kindly but severely rebuked, in his closing address, that the injury designed to be inflicted recoiled with tenfold violence upon the offender, and enstamped visible marks of shame upon the faces of the abetting party.

This—and indeed all our annual associations—but this in particular, was a season of great rejoicing and encouragement to our friends, and to the lovers of truth in this region of country. They saw the standard of God's Universal Grace so firmly planted in this new but thriving country, that they now considered it beyond the power of the enemy to uproot it. A spirit of deep and thrilling interest was excited; and the opposing clergy began to see that they had something more to do, to stop the progress of the doctrine, than merely to treat it with contempt. They began, more zealously, to open their batteries against it; but they were careful generally, to ensconce themselves safely behind the ramparts of their own pulpits, where they felt secure from an onset. However, the more they railed against the doctrine, the more they excited the people to inquire into its claims for truth, and consequently the faster it spread.

Our friends began to see the vast necessity of more labor in this part of the vineyard. One feeble individual was very incompetent to supply a tithe of the calls that were constantly pouring in, from every quarter, for the preached word. And indeed, so strong did our friends in Whitestown and vicinity feel, that they even thought of establishing here a ministerial emporium. They, or some of them, suggested the idea of engaging several of our preachers to settle in their town, and so radiate from this center, to spread the glad tidings of the Great Salvation toward the four cardinal points! And so zealous were they, that they could hardly be persuaded that such a scheme was impracticable. They felt exceedingly anxious, at any rate, to engage the labors of Mr. Ballou; and soon after the session of the Association, addressed a letter to him on the subject. In his reply, he gave them to understand, that he considered that my field of labor, and he could not consent to settle there, to discommode or disturb me. As soon as they made this known to me, I assured them that so far from being discommoded or disturbed, by the removal of Mr. Ballou, or any other approved preacher of Universal Salvation, into this place; I should consider it an important acquisition, and most desirable; and if it would facilitate such an object, I would most cheerfully give up Whitestown to him, and every other place where I was preaching, if it would be any inducement for him to come; that the field was extensive enough for him and me; and, indeed, it needed many more laborers; and nothing could gratify me more than to have Mr. Ballou settle in Whitestown; and I immediately wrote him to that effect. But they did not succeed in obtaining his valuable labors. I then suggested to them the probability of their being able to obtain Mr. Dean, They therefore opened a correspondence with Mr. Dean, which eventuated in his settlement in that place.

CHAPTER IX.

Introduction of the doctrine into Sullivan—Homer—Society organized in Homer—Author turns pedagogue again—Common Schools—Sectarian bigotry—Commences School—School-house burned—Prosecution of supposed incendiary—Removes to Hamilton—Purchases and builds—Association, 1808—Mr. Ballou's last visit—Mr. Babbit—Mr. Ferris—Encouraging prospects—First discourse in Norwich Court-house—Society formed in Norwich—Matthew Long, Esq.—Appointment in Bainbridge—Society in Bainbridge—Extensive circuit—Mr. J—d—his malignant opposition, and conversion—Mr. Tylor, his sickness, death, and funeral—Association, 1809—Mr. Wm. Baker—Extension of the doctrine—Accessions to the ministry—First meeting August, desultory conversation and discussion at the close—Sally Murdock, her sickness and death—Triumphs of her faith—Dialogue between Mr. Holmes and his Minister, on the beforementioned occasion—Another testimony in the case of Mrs. Beach—And yet another, Mrs. Woodhull.

The Association, at its session in New Hartford, 1807, adjourned to meet in Hartwick, Otsego Co., in 1808. In the year intervening, I labored alone in this enlarging field—not a single preacher of the order, that I now recollect, visited this section of country during the whole period. I traveled constantly during the summer and fall, supplying the places already named, even extending my ride as far as Sullivan, Madison Co., and Homer, now Cortland Co. Homer was then a newly settled country. There was but one solitary house where the flourishing village of Cortland now stands, and that was the residence of a friend of ours by the name of Hubbard, long since gathered home to his fathers. On my first visit to Homer, I delivered one discourse at the old village, and another at Port Watson. Port Watson was then very new, but contained as many families as did the old village. I subsequently visited Homer several times in the course of the summer and fall; and organized a society in the place, which in after years I regularly supplied for a considerable space of time.

Our friends were hardly as liberal in contributing for the

support of a preacher as they were in attending meetings; and as I began to have a family to provide for, I was again compelled to resort to my pedagogic employment, to produce the necessaries of life. There was no law then in the State regulating common schools, nor for several years afterwards. Each neighborhood, at their own option, organized themselves into a district, built their own school-house, hired their teacher, judging for themselves of his qualifications, and paid in proportion to the scholars each family furnished. They had a good school-house, for those times, in the neighborhood where I resided; and after their annual school meeting in the fall, the trustees applied to me to teach their winter school; and I readily engaged.

An occurrence here took place, worth recording, because it affords a vivid illustration of the deplorable effects of a bigoted adherance to sectarian creeds. Soon after my engagement, I learned that there was a dissatisfaction among some of the inhabitants of the district, on account of the trustees engaging me to teach the school. I went immediately to the trustees and requested to be released. They replied, they could not release me, as there was no objection founded upon any reasonable cause—that there were few who owned right in the house, that had made any objection; and those who had, objected solely on account of religious sentiments; a bigotry and superstition which they considered injurious to community to indulge in. I pleaded, that I had had some experience in teaching; and I had always found it a task sufficiently severe and difficult where a district were united; and to go into a school where there was already a dissatisfaction existing, and growing out of the cause they had named, which set at defiance all my ability to remove, was a vortex into which I should not willingly be drawn; and I was, therefore, resolved not to enter the school. They remarked, that old Mr. L—s, who had no children to send, and who was the only man that owned any right in the house, who would be opposed were they not influenced by him, was the instigator of all the disturbance; and to yield to his whim—to be dictated by him in a thing in which he could have no interest, except the gratification of religious prejudices, they thought would be unjust to society, and involve themselves in greater difficulty than to proceed according to their own sense of duty, in defiance of his displeasure and threats. They also thought that he would eventually withdraw his objections; but whether he did or not, they were resolved to have the school go on; and if I did not fulfil my contract with them, they should prosecute me for damage. The trustees were not Universalists, but they were not sectarian bigots. Their reasoning was good; and I was ill able to pay damage for non-compliance; I therefore concluded to go into the school. Previous to the commencement of the school, they had several meetings, to try to reconcile Mr. L—s, but to no effect. Mr. L—s was not a member of the church, I believe, but an adherent to old Connecticut Presbyterianism, and as bigoted as though he had subscribed to fifty creeds. The school-house stood on his land; and he swore that his land should not be "made a den of thieves"—and that if I attempted to enter the school-house, to teach school, he would burn the house. This he repeatedly said, both in private conversation, and in their public meetings. However, the time arrived, and I commenced school; and in less than a week the house was filled to inconvenience with scholars. The dissatisfied party united with others in an adjoining neighborhood, and established another school; and all things seemed restored to tranquility. I had kept school just three weeks; and as I held meetings every Sabbath, my common custom was to dismiss the school at twelve o'clock on Saturday; but as my meeting was to be holden in the neighborhood the next day, and as I had a large number of scholars studying arithmetic, I devoted an hour or more to them after dismissing the school, at this time. December had commenced —the day was sunny; the snow had fallen some four or five inches in the course of the day; and before we separated, I told the scholars to bring in some snow, throw it on the hearth, and on the floor around the hearth, as we had kept a pretty heavy fire, so as to quench any coals which might have dropped into the crevice, between the hearth and floor. This was carefully done; and I raked up the coals on the hearth, covered them with ashes, and locked the door with my own hands, and left the key at a neighbor's, the usual place. I resided in an apartment of the house of a friend, by the name of Stillman, about half a mile from the school-house, and in plain sight of it. Near nine o'clock in the evening—my wife had gone to bed, and I had drawn my boots, and sat reading—I heard Mr. Stillman go to his door and open it; and then with a hurried step he approached my door, saying as he opened it, "The school-house is on fire!" I stepped to the door, and behold the building was in flames, the rafters nearly naked. We drew on our boots and hurried to the scene; but long before we reached the spot, the whole roof fell in. The alarm had early been given; and although we heard it not, others had, and a large concourse of people were already on the spot. I will not attempt to describe my feelings; but they were anything but pleasant. I considered it impossible that the house should have taken fire from the coals left upon the hearth; and it was still more seriously to be deplored, that there should exist, and so long be cherished, so malignant a spirit as to burn a school-house, with a large number of valuable school-books, and other appendages, merely because a Universalist preacher was employed as a teacher in it!

With these reflections, I approached the spot. By the time we had arrived within fifty rods of the school-house, it was light as day around us. We met an old gentlemen by the name of Dewey, on horse-back; he discovered, no doubt, by the appearance of my countenance, that my mind was not at ease, and said, "Mr. Stacy, don't feel troubled—nobody blames you. We are all satisfied, how the house took fire—go and examine faces, and see who looks guilty." The next man we met, was old Mr. L—s. "Well, (said I,) Mr. L—s, the house is burned, it seems." The old gentleman snapped out as spiteful as an adder, "Yes, and by devilish carelessness, I believe." I made no reply, but passed on. I soon learned by the general conversation, what was the opinion of the people in general, about the cause of the fire; and felt not a little gratified, to find among the inhabitants of the district, a fixed determination that this unpleasant event should, by no means, break up the school. And their actions were as spirited as their words. This was on Saturday evening; and on the Wednesday morning following, they had a spacious room, in a dwelling-house not sixty rods from where the school-house stood, conveniently fitted up, and I resumed teaching.

Early on the Monday following, this Mr. Dewey, whom I have before named, entered a complaint, and obtained a warrant for Mr. L—s; but behold, he had absconded! and he kept out of sight, and hearing, for more than two weeks. When he did return, however, he was arrested, and examined, and laid under bonds for trial. The evidence was clear against him, as words could make it; but he was an old man, one of the first settlers in the place, and, save his petulancy, and his malignant hatred of Universalism, was quite inoffensive; his case excited the commiseration of the inhabitants generally, after the first paroxism of disgust had passed; and it was so managed, that he was never brought to trial.

The society in Hamilton had long expressed a strong desire for me to remove, and settle permanently in that town, and offered to purchase a small lot of land for me, and help me to build, if I would settle among them. This was a strong inducement; for I thought I could employ a portion of my time in cultivating a little farm, both to the advantage of my health, and the support of my family; and with less interference with my profession, than any other employment; and I must do something besides preach, or my family must suffer for the necessaries of life. Accordingly, I made the necessary arrangements, and in the month of April, 1808, removed my family to Hamilton, Madison Co., where we resided twenty-two years.

The society purchased, or rather helped me to purchase, twelve acres; eight or nine under improvement; and in the course of the ensuing summer and fall, I built a house on it. I now felt a degree of satisfaction, in regard to temporal things, and measurable safety for the support of my family, which I had never before enjoyed. I had now a permanent home; and every hour I could get to work, and every improvement I made, would advance the interest and improve the comfort of my family. And I would work on my land, when at home, during the day; read at night, and meditate and reflect while riding to my appointments. This, reader, was the course I had to pursue for many long years—and this was necessary, in order to plant the doctrine of God's free and universal grace, permanently and surely, in a world benighted and stupified, under the long and tyrannical reign of anti-christian creeds.

The joyful time of our annual Convention arrived, and with delightful anticipations we assembled, to bring up our yearly offerings of praise to the altar of the Lord. Our Associations frequently reminded me of the Jewish feast of tabernacles, when the tribes of Israel assembled from the different lands of their sojourn, to bring up their offerings to the temple, and hold a season of festivity and rejoicing in commemoration of their deliverance from Egyptian bondage. We too, had experienced a moral bondage more galling than that of the Israelites in the land of Egypt, from which the Lord, by his mighty word, had delivered us; and we felt the full beatitude of our spiritual freedom.

We obtained the use of the Baptist meeting-house, in the village of Perth, town of Hartwick, for the session of our Association, this year (1808); and it was literally filled at every exercise, during this session. Mr. Ballou met with us, for the third and last time; but I can not now recollect who were his colleagues, or whether he had any, on the committee from the General Convention, this year. About this time, Mr. James Babbit removed from Vermont into the town of Duanesburg, in this State, and commenced preaching in that town; and he also attended this association. Mr. Ferris, for the first time, took his seat in this council; and delivered one discourse.

This, like the previous meetings of our Association, and all subsequent meetings, certainly for many years, was a season of rejoicing, of refreshing and encouragement. There was in those days, no competition for precedence, or pre-eminence—no jealousies, nor heart-burnings toward each other; we met in perfect harmony. Our souls were absorbed in the love of the truth; we had no selfish ends to gratify, and no places of preferment to quarrel about; no heavy salaries were offered, nor popular applause rendered to tempt impostors to intrude upon us—we were glad to give place to those among us who could be the most useful to the great cause, which was the engrossing object of our whole souls. Indeed, we were willing to be led by the most feeble hand to the rich banqueting-house of our conquering Leader, while "His banner over us was love."

From this time, I felt a peculiar renewal of strength. The cause had prospered beyond my most sanguine expectations; and the Lord was sending more laborers into his vineyard. Mr. Ferris began to travel and preach, more than he had heretofore done; and Mr. Babbit had removed within our limits—we could now count *three* preachers—Universalist preachers in the State of New York!—and our societies were increasing in numbers, and in strength. We had had an accession of two or three, since our last Association. But this, so far from diminishing my sense of responsibility for individual exertion, rather increased it. I felt an increased obligation to be faithful; and as the field of operation enlarged, my zeal to improve it became more fervid; and during that year my travels were still farther extended.

In June of that year, the lodge of Free-masons in Norwich, Chenango Co., having passed a resolution to celebrate the festival of St. John the Baptist, sent a committee to engage my services on the occasion. The seat of justice for the county of Chenango had recently been established at Norwich, and they were, at this time, erecting a court-house; it was in an unfinished state, but the master-workman agreed to prepare the court-room for the services. He did so; and made it very convenient for a numerous congregation. I there delivered the first discourse that was ever delivered in that house, either on law or gospel. But I have preached many sermons in that house since that time. A society was organized there, shortly afterwards, and I preached to them once a month for several years.

At this celebration, I met a very dear friend, Matthew Long Esq., with whom I had formed an acquaintance in Wilmington, Vt. I had learned that he had removed into that region, somewhere, but had been unable to learn in what town he had fixed his residence. But he, with two or three others of the fraternity, came from Jericho, now Bainbridge, to attend the celebration. Our meeting was quite a joyful one, and to me very unexpected; and it tended very much to advance the cause of our religion. Esq. Long had found a few friends of truth, even in Jericho; and I could not resist his importunity to give him an appointment, and visit his town. Consequently, in August following, I took a tour through that region; delivered five discourses in different parts of the town of Jericho—one in the academy in Oxford; and preached on Sunday, on my return, in Norwich court-house. From that time, I often visited Jericho and Oxford; and in June following, delivered a festival discourse to the Masonic lodge, in Jericho. The cause advanced with rather unusual rapidity in Jericho; several converts were obtained from Orthodox churches; and in a short time, a society was organized, which I regularly supplied as often as once a month, for a season, until they could obtain preaching from some other source. My travels were very laborious this year, extending from Whitestown, north, (and occasionally, to Western)—to Jericho, south; and from Otsego and Hartwick, east, to Homer, west. This tour, at least requiring two hundred and fifty miles ride, I made generally once a month, supplying at the same time a large number of places in the intermediate country.

At the time of my removal into Hamilton, the members of the society residing in the town were not numerous; and these were promiscuously scattered through every neighborhood. There were but two families in my immediate neighborhood, who professed any faith in Universalism, save a widow lady, at the funeral of whose husband I had officiated the previous autumn. The majority of my neighbors were bitterly, and some madly opposed to my doctrine; and among the latter class, a brother-in-law of the above-mentioned widow; who subsequently told me, that at the time of my removal into town he would have united with others, in order to prevent me by physical force—mobbing, if no other means could have been effectual—from settling in the place.

Many times, when reflecting upon my success amidst such malignant opposition, I have been astonished, and deeply impressed with reverential awe, on the manifest interposition of Providence in my behalf, or rather in behalf of the progress of the glorious Gospel, of which I was the feeble advocate. It was so in the case of Mr. J—d, the man above alluded to; and in numerous other instances.

The substance of the following I had from the lips of Mr. J—d, not a year after my settlement in the town; but not until he had become a hearty believer in the doctrine of God's Universal Grace, and one of my warmest friends and most liberal supporters. He attended the funeral of his brother-in-law, the previous fall; but the sermon stung him to madness; and nothing prevented him from leaving the congregation but his regard for the feelings of the widow and her family. From that moment he was resolved to put me down, at all events. He knew he would not be allowed to do it by physical force; for the law protected me in the enjoyment of my religious opinions, and in preaching equally with other denominations; he had no other resource, therefore, but argument; and for that, he did not, as yet, feel himself fully qualified; but he could be; and he resolved to be so, fully and completely. He knew the Bible was all in his favor; and he resolved to study it, until he was completely armed for the contest. He therefore went at it in earnest, with the sole design to find weapons to break down Universalism.

On my removal into the place, being apprised of the prejudices of my neighbors, and observing their shyness, and their carefulness to keep at a distance, I resolved to use my best endeavors to change their feelings, and at least, to draw them into a friendly, neighborly intercourse. For this purpose I called often, and solicited calls, especially among the most shy and fearful; and soon succeeded, in most cases, to produce a more friendly manifestation of feeling. Among others, I called on Mr. J—d, and transacted some little trifling business with him. He expressed a desire to have a lengthy conversation with me, on the subject of my doctrine; but observed, "we have not time now." Well, Mr. J—d, I replied, any time when you have leisure, call on me, or let me know, and I will call on you; and will devote any length of time you desire. Several times in the course of the season, he made similar remarks to me; but he was a very busy man, and never found opportunity for the desired discussion. But before the season closed, we had a conversation; and he then remarked, that he wanted to talk with me on the subject of religion; but not with the same feelings, or sentiments, as formerly. He then informed me of what I have, in substance, related above; and said, that every time he opened his Bible to find weapons against Universalism, he found sharper against his own creed,—and, in despite of his efforts to avoid it, strong proof in favor of the doctrine he so much wanted to destroy. He would feel confounded, and almost vexed, and shut his book. But after a while, would try it again, and would meet with a similar repulse—and after wearying himself a long time in this way, he took his Bible with a very different resolution, and that was, to find what it did teach irrespective of creeds; and it was not long before the truth, in all its harmony, and beauty, and glory, beamed with divine clearness upon his understanding! And now he was able to rejoice in full assurance of the "Restitution of all things, which God hath spoken by the mouth of all his holy prophets, since the world began."

During this summer, while building a house on my own land, we resided in a house with an old gentleman and his wife, by the name of Tylor. The old gentleman had never made a public profession of religion, though he was a very constant attendant at meeting—but his wife had, for years, been a member of the Presbyterian church. They were friendly people, and had never manifested that acrimony which I had met with in many other families; besides, several of their sons, who all had families, and were living in other parts of the town, were giving a listening and favorable ear to the doctrine. During our residence in his house, the old gentleman became very much attached to me and my family; and after our removal into our own house, scarcely failed a day in calling and chatting awhile, and playing with our little boy; nevertheless, he never attended my meetings except on funeral occasions; and never manifested any sympathy for the doctrine. Early the summer following (1809,) the old gentleman was taken sick; and very soon his disease assumed a fatal tendency; and all hope of his recovery was given up. I visited him nearly every day, from tho commencement of his sickness, and endeavored, by all means in my power, to administer to his temperal comfort; but carefully avoided all doctrinal conversation. I frequently conversed with him on the subject of religion, and the consolations of a Christian hope, in the approaching hour of dissolution, and always found him reconciled and cheerful; but I sedulously avoided alluding either to his, or my creed. Soon he began to request me to pray with him, with which I most cheerfully complied. At length he said, "I want you to pray with me every day, it makes me feel so comfortable." I did so, always when about home. And his wife told me he would always manifest a degree of impatience, if I was not there at the time expected; and when off at my appointments, he would often inquire if it was not time for me to return. One day, his wife said to me, "I fear Mr. Tylor is stupid—there he lies; he can live but a few days at most; and he manifests no anxiety about his soul. I have tried to make him willing for Mr. N.—[Mr. N. was the Presbyterian clergyman] to come and talk with him; but he does not want him. I wish you would converse with him, closely, about his future hopes." Why, (said I,) Mrs. T., he is as well prepared to die, as any man I ever saw. He is perfectly at peace with God and man, reconciled to the Divine will, believes in Christ, as the Savior of sinners, and hopes for eternal salvation through His mediation; and what can you desire more? But if you wish, I will talk with him in your presence. We went into the room together—I said to him, How do you feel to-day, Mr. Tylor? "Oh," he said, holding out his hand with his usual smile, "I am here yet; and as comfortable as could be expected." You are very sick, said I, are you not? "Yes, I am very sick." Have you any hopes of recovery? "No, none at all; I can live but a few days, at most." And how do you feel about dying—have you any fears in regard to your future state? "None at all—I feel perfectly reconciled to the Divine will, have no wish to alter it—I am as ready and as willing to die now, as I ever can be." In what, or in whom do you trust for future happiness? "In the Lord Jesus Christ—I believe in him, and I trust in his merits for salvation." Much more was said; I talked as long as I thought he could bear it, without injury; but the foregoing gives the important substance of our conversation. I then turned to Mrs. T., and asked, "What can you want more? Can you expect it possible to find a soul in better preparation?" But she was not satisfied. She at length prevailed on him to have Mr. N. visit him and pray with him. Mr. N. came; and after a rather lengthy visit, (at which, however, I was not present, having gone on my parochial duties,) pronounced him one of the most hardened sinners he ever saw on a death-bed!

I had assisted Mr. Tylor in settling his temporal concerns, had written his will, and, by his urgent request, was named in the will as the executor. One day, while several of his children were present, adverting first to the arrangement of his temporal concerns and the prospect of his immediate dissolution, he very feelingly addressed me, and requested me to preach his funeral sermon. This was very unexpected to me, and probably equally so to all present. He had never attended my meeting, except on funeral occasions, and I presume had never heard me more than twice on such occasions, at most; but had always been a constant attendant on the Presbyterian meeting. I however replied, that should I outlive him, and God in his providence should enable me, I would willingly attend the solemn duty, provided it should be agreeable to his surviving family. He then asked his wife, and children present, if they were willing, and they all replied in the affirmative; and several times before his death, he repeated this request in the presence of his wife.

One of my regular appointments was in the town of Homer, distant about forty miles. Before leaving on Saturday morning, I called to see Mr. Tylor, and, as usual, attended prayer with him, and found him very low. He said, "I'm very sorry you are going away; I am afraid I shall not live until you return." I replied, "I would forego my visit there on your account; but I preach with them only once in a month, and a disappointment makes so long an interval that it is quite discouraging to them." "Well," said he, brightening up with a smile, "return as soon as you can; I feel now as though I should live to see you again." I replied, "I will ride out to day, and to-morrow make my services as short as propriety will admit; then start directly on my way back, and, Providence permitting, I will be here by Monday at noon." "Well, be as spry as you can," he responded. "I will, Mr. Tylor, and I have a hope we shall see each other again in the flesh." But, alas! our hope was fallacious—he died before the next morning.

I was faithful to my promise; made the utmost expedition in my power, and arrived at the house of Mr. Tylor a little before twelve o'clock on Monday: but they were too expeditious for me. I could not even see the corpse, the procession was just moving away from his house to the grave, as I came in sight of his premises. The old lady and the opposing part of the family took advantage of my absence, and hurried the funeral so as to prevent a compliance with the request of the deceased, and save themselves the pain of hearing a Universalist. But it was all overruled for good, and, as such unchristian proceedings uniformly have done, tended to advance the cause they were designed to overthrow. The discourse delivered on the occasion, together with the accompanying exercises, and the well-known non-conformity to the last request of the deceased, tended to excite far more sympathy for the persecuted doctrine, and inquiry into its merits, than any discourse I could have delivered.

The Presbyterian clergyman, Mr. N., who had prejudged the deceased, was, of course, called to officiate. His text was Eccl. 9: 10. "For there is no work, nor device, nor knowledge, nor wisdom in the grave, whither thou goest." He represented the deceased as an old hardened sinner, dying in a state of impenitence, and therefore beyond the reach of mercy! The hymns he selected for the occasion were enough to curdle the blood in a sympathetic heart, and drive a fearful soul into utter despair. For his first, he selected from Watts, second book, 52d hymn, which commences with

"Death! 'tis a melancholy day
To those that have no God;
When the poor soul is forced away,
To seek her last abode."

For the second, he read the 88th hymn of the first book, which closes with the following stanza:

"There are no acts of pardon past,
In the cold grave to which we haste;
But darkness, death, and long despair
Reign in eternal silence there."

And for his third, the 91st hymn of the same book, which contains the following stanza:

"Behold the aged sinner goes,
Laden with guilt and heavy woes,
Down to the regions of the dead,
With endless curses on his head."

The whole congregation were disgusted, except a few malignant spirits; and the feelings of the mourners abused and outraged insufferably. The widow subsequently told me with great manifestation of sensibility, that she blamed herself severely for not complying with her husband's request, by waiting for my return; that her feelings were tantalized and wounded beyond any thing she ever before experienced, or could have dreamed of; and the whole neighborhood felt shamefully abused by this scandalization of the character of their deceased neighbor. Mr. Tylor had lived a sober, moral life—was a close observer of the Sabbath, and a constant attendant on religious worship; and through a long life had maintained as inoffensive a character as flesh and blood could maintain; and he was respected by all his acquaintances. But all this obloquy upon his memory—all this tantalization of the feelings of his bereaved family—all this abuse of his neighbors, he had incurred simply because he had not bowed to the idol of Presbyterianism, had associated with a Universalist near the close of his life, and requested him to officiate at his funeral.

The fourth session of our Association, (1809,) was holden in Norwich, Chenango county. Mr. Dean and Mr. Carrique attended as a delegation from the General Convention; and the three preachers in the State, Mr. Ferris, Mr. Babbit, and myself were present, making the formidable number of five! Mr. Ballou was again appointed on the committee, but being about this time, I believe, making arrangements to remove from Barnard, Vermont, to Portsmouth, New Hampshire, he could not well attend. It was a disappointment to many expecting friends; but notwithstanding we enjoyed a happy and profitable season. Our meeting for pubiic worship was holden in the court-house, and a vast concourse of people, for those days, assembled. Several societies had been organized since the last meeting of this body, which were here represented by authorized delegates. Our two visiting brethren from the east, though young, were able advocates of the Great Salvation; and acquitted themselves, on this occasion, to the great satisfaction of the waiting congregation, and the furtherance of the cause of truth in that region. At this Association, too, we were encouraged by the prospect of an accession to the ministry; and the addition of even one to our little band was abundant cause of gratulation. Mr. William Baker, a Methodist local preacher, attended this meeting, made a pathetic declaration of his conversion to the faith of Universal Salvation, and asked for a letter of fellowship as a preacher of the unlimited grace of God. But as he was a total stranger to most, or all of us, and had no letter or credentials commendatory of his moral or Christian character, we thought it prudent to require a certificate of regular dismission from his former connection, or, at least, some testimonials of his moral character; and therefore postponed any further action in regard to his request, except cordially greeting him, and advising him to improve his talent wherever God, in his providence, should open a door, until such credentials could be obtained. He succeeded in obtaining his vouchers, and, at the next session of the council, received a letter of fellowship. But, alas! he was of little service to the cause; although a man of irreproachable moral habits, yet he possessed no strong intellectual faculties; was vacillating in his opinions, and not finding sufficient encouragement to satisfy his own mind, he, in a few years, left the ministry, and shortly afterward renounced the faith, and united with the Baptists. I visited him once after his renunciation, but used no argument to reclaim him. I merely remarked to him, that neither his faith nor mine made or altered the truth—truth was eternal and unchangeable, and independent of all faith; and, if he were happy, it was all I felt solicitous about in his case. But, alas! he had lost his wonted cheerfulness, and a gloomy despondency had settled on his countenance.

The cause now began to assume a still more important and encouraging aspect, in this western country. In the course of this year, (I mean by the year the time intervening between the sessions of our Association, as from June, 1809, to June, 1810,) I had the happiness of introducing the doctrine into a number of towns, mostly within the limits of my former travels, but where it had never before been proclaimed by me, and very seldom, if ever, by any one else; viz., Sherburne, Smyrna, Butternuts, Nelson, Smithfield, and Augusta; and we had the prospect of soon obtaining an important accession to the ministry in that country. If I mistake not, Mr. Dean, in the course of his visit this year, made an engagement to settle with the society in Whitestown; and, in the fall of this year, Mr. Winslow, to whom I have had occasion heretofore to allude, became converted to the faith, and commenced preaching the Great Salvation.

I must be permitted to interlard my otherwise dry history with occasional anecdotes, illustrating our mode of operation, showing the diversified geniuses we met with among our opposers, and their varied mode of attack; for we scarcely ever held a meeting, especially in a new place, without being attacked in some form. On my first visit to Augusta, after delivering my message, I gave liberty for remarks as usual; but no one manifested an inclination to speak, the congregation were dismissed, and I repaired to the house of a friend about one hundred rods distant. But my hearers did not all forsake me; to this place a number followed, enough, at any rate, to closely line a large room; and here they were ready enough to break silence with question after question, from different individuals, which probably kept me talking for more than one hour. Among the company was a man who had been pretty officious in proposing difficulties, as he no doubt supposed, and seemed resolved to get me entangled by some means, not being very scrupulous as to the kind. He said to me, in rather a gruff manner, "I suppose sir, you profess to believe in Christ." I replied, "I should not engage in the ministry of his Gospel, and make all the sacrifices I am compelled to make in consequence, and expose myself to all the obloquy and persecution I am destined thereby to meet with in the discharge of that arduous and solemn duty, without an unshaken faith in the Savior of the world." "Well, sir," said he, "can you show your faith by your works—by the signs which he said should follow those who believed on him?" "I think I can, sir." He then looked around significantly upon the company, no doubt thinking he had at length entrapped me; but I was well aware of his wiles; and fixing my eye steadily upon him, felt prepared for the opening of his heaviest battery, and awaited the attack. "Well," said he, "Christ says, He that believeth in my name shall cast out devils, &c. Can you work those miracles?" "Yes." His eyes then glared with utter astonishment, and he proceeded to state his questions more definitely. "Can you heal the sick, by laying your hands on them?" "Yes." "Can you raise the dead?" "Yes." "Can you drink poison, and not be hurt by it?" "Yes." "Can you let a poisonous serpent bite you, and feel no injury?" "Yes." I had during these questions and answers kept a close watch of the company, to see that no one left the room until I should have an opportunity to explain; and after I had answered Yes to several of his questions, I noticed an old lady fetch a deep sigh, and begin to rise. I broke in upon his questions enough to say to her, "Madam, have the goodness to keep your seat—you do not now understand me. If you will be so kind as to wait until I have an opportunity to explain myself, you will leave with very different views from what you will if you leave now;" and the old lady quietly took her seat again. After he had proposed the foregoing questions he stopped, with apparently breathless astonishment at my presumption, and fixed his eye sternly upon me. I then said, "Sir, I have answered all your questions directly and plainly; and, with your permission, I will now endeavor to explain myself."

"I firmly believe that the immediate disciples of our blessed Lord, and the first preachers of his Gospel, during the apostolic age had power to work miracles literally; but after that period, when Judaism was abolished, and the truth of the Gospel fully attested, they were no longer necessary, nor has any one had the gift of miracles since; and all who have pretended to have such gift, from the Pope of Rome down to the most ignorant quack in religion, have been impostors. But, sir, there is a spirituality in these things. The Savior says, 'The flesh profiteth nothing; my words, that I speak unto you, they are spirit, and they are life.' Now, I do not pretend to do these things literally; but, if I am a preacher of the Gospel of Christ, I can do them spiritually. You asked me, if I could lay my hands on the sick, and heal them. I answered, Yes. Now, there are other ailments besides physical. Sin is represented as a disease in the Scriptures. 'The whole head is sick, and the whole heart is faint.' Christ is the great Physician, and his truth the medicine. 'If ye believe the truth, the truth shall make you free,' [*well.*] If I am a preacher of Christ's Gospel, I am commissioned by him to administer this medicine. If I can, therefore, lay my hands upon the sick, that is, if I can approach them so as to communicate to them the knowledge of the *truth*, they will be restored to health. You asked me, if I could raise the dead. Although Christ did not enumerate this among the signs that were to follow the believer, yet I answered in the affirmative; for 'the wages of sin is death'—all have sinned, therefore all have become dead. But our Savior has said, 'He that heareth my word, and believeth on him that sent me, hath everlasting life, and shall not come into condemnation, but *is passed from death unto life.*' Now if I be a preacher of the Gospel, I am authorized to teach men the knowledge of the truth whereby they are enabled to believe on God; and, therefore, I am instrumental in raising them from the dead. You asked me, if I could drink poison without hurting me. I answered, Yes. I recollect of reading that, in ancient times, when the family of the prophet had become very much enlarged, and there was a dearth in the land, he sent out his servants to gather herbs for pottage; and some of them being ignorant and unskilful in the use of many varieties, gathered the wild gourd; and when it was served to the guests, some of them discovered the danger, and cried out, 'O, thou man of God, there is death in the pot;' and Elisha called for meal, which he cast into the pot, and they could then eat of it without injury. Now there are, even in this age, many unskilful servants gathering herbs to seeth and make pottage; and they are exceedingly apt to gather much of the wild gourd; but I have the meal of Elisha, to sprinkle into the pot; and can therefore eat at their tables without harm. You asked me, if I could take up poisonous serpents, &c. I answered, Yes. The serpents that I can take up are those very animals which emit this poison that I have been speaking of; and I can handle them with all the pleasure imaginable; and their bite is as harmless to me as the bite of a fly." By the time I had concluded my explanatory remarks, the faces of my audience had assumed a very different appearance from what they were at the commencement; and that of my catechizer, especially, had lost its rigidity; he smiled approvingly, and said, "I believe you are right, sir."

Among the stale and stereotyped remarks of opposers, no one was more common and popular than "Universalism will do to live by, but it will not do to die by." But a dispensation of divine Providence, which occurred in Hamilton this year, (1810,) in the month of January, imposed an everlasting silence upon this senseless saying, in that vicinity. There was a widow, by the name of Murdock, who had quite a numerous family, nearly or quite all of whom became early attendants at Universalist meetings; and she soon united with the church, and subsequently one of her sons. Among the members of her family was a fine girl, whose name was Sally; and, for a year or two, she was as constantly at meeting as any member of the family, or indeed any other person. But an excitement, or a revival as it was called, was got up among the Presbyterians; and great exertions were made to induce people, especially the youth, to attend their meetings, and considerable effect was produced; and among the subjects was the young lady above named. She, consequently, forsook our meetings; for every terror was brought into requisition to frighten them from Universalist meetings, and to rivet the manacles of Partialism upon them in the morning of life. She, however, did not unite with the church, but, for a year or more, was a constant attendant on their meetings, related her experience, and was, by their leaders, pronounced a true convert, and an heir of salvation. During this period I had frequent conversations with her on the subject of religion, at the home of her mother where I often visited; but I never introduced the subject of peculiar sectarian opinions, nor ever inquired of her the reason of forsaking our meetings. Our conversation embraced the subject of experimental and practical religion, and nothing more. After the lapse of about a year, she again ventured to go to our meeting; from that time she occasionally came with the rest of the family; but no explanation took place—nothing was said by me, nor any of her relatives, directly to her to indoctrinate her into our faith, or to persuade her to attend our meetings, but she was left to her free and uncontrolled choice.

In the fall of 1809, she was taken sick. She was away from home when attacked, nursing the sick. A mortal sickness was prevailing extensively in the town; and when carried home she told her mother, and the family, that she felt sure she should not recover. However, they felt no alarm for several days, and even weeks; but her fever, after continuing a long while, assumed a more malignant aspect, and they soon gave up all hope of her recovery. I had heard of her sickness, but being very busily engaged, and supposing that a visit from me would add little or nothing to her enjoyment, especially as I was informed that Mr. N., the Presbyterian clergyman, was very constantly at her bed-side, I did not make it convenient to call. But on the Sunday before she died, her brother came to me after meeting, and said his sister was evidently near her end, and had manifested a strong desire to see me. I went home with him, and there learned what had just transpired.

In order for the reader fully to understand, it will be necessary to digress a little here, and introduce, briefly, another circumstance. A man by the name of Holmes, who had long held a conspicuous standing in the Presbyterian church, had seceded from their faith and embraced the doctrine of God's Univeral Grace, and was at this time, under admonition for his heresy. Mr. H. was a very worthy man, and they regretted much to lose him. They therefore labored long and patiently with him; and as they had been very unfortunate in losing several of their most valuable members in the same way, they resorted to every expedient their best wisdom could devise to prevent his egress. Many letters had passed between him and his pastor, and every opportunity for conversation between them was faithfully improved. Mr. H. did not forsake their meetings, nor the communion-table until requested to do so; he faithfully attended all their church-meetings for disciplining himself, and was always in his seat on the Sabbath; so that he could be accused of no dereliction of duty, except that of forsaking his creed—heresy was all the crime they could accuse him of. He was always very ready to defend his own cause in church-meetings, and he and his minister were very sure to have a discussion during intermission on Sundays.

This Mr. H. was a neighbor of the widow Murdock, and on Saturday night previous to my visit to the sick young lady, Mr. H. and his wife watched with her. Mr. H. was very deaf, and all be could do was to sit by the fire and wait upon his wife, while she attended upon the patient. In the course of the night, the sick girl said to Mrs. H. "I wish you would ask Mr. H. to come to the bed—I want to talk with him." He went; and what I shall now relate, I received from his own mouth. She commenced by asking him several important doctrinal questions, which he answered according to the best of his ability; but felt very much astonished at the tendency of her questions, as he and all her acquaintances supposed her to be a strict Presbyterian in sentiment. After answering her questions, he asked her several, which she readily and satisfactorily answered; which led him to ask her, emphatically, "Sally, what does this mean? Are you a Universalist? and are you willing to have your name go through good report and through evil report as such?" She answered unhesitatingly, "I am. I have always been afraid of it, and have avoided the meetings lest I should be led astray. But since I have been brought on to a sick-bed, which is undoubtedly my death-bed, I have become fully settled and established in the faith of Universal Salvation; and it has been my support through the bodily sufferings I have experienced, and it is my solace and my comfort in the hour of approaching death. It has reconciled me to God, enabling me to bow, without a murmuring thought, to his divine will. I have rejoiced in it, and do rejoice; and I can no longer keep it a secret. I shall probably never see my grandfather again, (her grandfather was a worthy old gentleman, had long been a decided Universalist, and was the first who requested a meeting of the order in the town,) but I wish you to inform him, that I believe the doctrine without the shadow of doubt, and that I die rejoicing in the faith; and I wish all my friends, and the world to know it." The foregoing is the substance, and as nearly as I can remember in the same words, as related to me by Mr. Holmes within a day or two after it transpired.

The next day, Mr. H. went, as usual, to the Presbyterian meeting; and during the intermission, the following dialogue in substance took place, between Mr. H., and Mr. N. his minister.

Mr. N. Well, Mr. Holmes, what do you think of Universalism now? There is Sally Murdock, has been a Universalist—she has been through Universalism, has proved it, and renounced it; and is now on her death bed, as happy a person as I ever saw.

Mr. H. Have you seen Sally Murdock lately?

Mr. N. Yes, I have seen her several times since she has been sick—I was there the other day, and had a long conversation with her.

Mr. H. And you think she is reconciled and happy, do you?

Mr. N. The most so of any person I ever saw on a death-bed.

Mr. H. You really believe that Sally Murdock is a Christian, and an heir of salvation?

Mr. N. If Sally Murdock be not a Christian, I never saw a Christian.

Mr. H. Well, I am very happy to tell you what I think about it. He then related to him, circumstantially, the interview which he had with her the evening before. He said Mr N. was completely struck dumb! He had entrapped himself; and there was no escape. He had voluntarily, and even exultingly, pronounced Sally Murdock a Christian, and the most reconciled and happy person he had ever seen on a death-bed; and then to learn, (for he dared not to dispute the veracity of Mr. H.,) to learn that it was the very doctrine that he condemned—that he pronounced the doctrine of the devil, and which he had often said would not do to die by, that gave her this support, that made her thus reconciled and happy, and afforded her that consolation and hope in the hour of approaching dissolution, completely confounded him. Mr. H. said that he attempted no reply, but changed his countenance, choked, turned around, and walked away.

As before observed, I visited her on Sunday evening, and remained until nine o'clock. She was very feeble, and could talk but little herself; but enough, however, to express her faith, and tell me how happy it made her. By her request we united in prayer; I bade her farewell—and she died before morning. This was then a house of affliction; but, blessed be God, the inmates mourned not as those who have no hope. She had a sister, younger than herself, who was married a few years before this event, residing just out of the neighborhood, who was sick at the same time, and died an hour or two before Sally. Her remains were brought to the house of her mother, and, on the tenth day of January, 1810, I delivered a discourse at their funeral to a very large concourse of people. So numerous was the congregation that, notwithstanding the house contained three spacious rooms on the ground, besides other apartments, only a portion of the people could crowd into it; and although it was in the winter season, the weather however not tedious, they were compelled to take out a window in order to hear me, and I stood before it so as to address the people without as well as within. Although it was a deeply solemn and mournful occasion, yet I enjoyed a heart-felt satisfaction, in accordance with the desire of the deceased young lady, in publicly announcing to the world the triumph of her faith, in refutation of the trite saying, *Universalism will not do to die by.* At the same time, I was inexpressibly gratified in seeing, among the congregation, the face of Mr. N., the Presbyterian clergyman, so that he might hear this truth; although no doubt severely grating to the feelings of his *pious* Phariseeism.

This same testimony was confirmed in following years, by a number of instances; one or two of which I will take the liberty to record.

There was a young lady, daughter of Capt. Elisha Fuller, one of the earliest converts to Universalism in Hamilton, who had consequently been educated in the doctrine from childhood. She had never passed through the ordeal of Partialism, and consequently never experienced the heart-rending agonies of popular conviction; but "From a child" she knew "the Scriptures, which were able to make her wise unto salvation, through faith which is in Christ Jesus." She eventually married, and became a near neighbor of mine. While yet in the bloom of life, she was attacked with a fatal disease; and she soon, as well as her friends, gave up all hopes of her recovery. Her life had been a practical illustration of the superior excellency of our holy faith—she had always professed it, and, as far as circumstances would admit, had been a constant attendant on public worship; and her moral character bade defiance to the tongue of slander. I visited her nearly every day, when about home, during her sickness. I always found her patient, reconciled, cheerful, and happy—always ready to talk about the hopelessness of her case, her approaching dissolution, and the strength of her future hope—it seemed the theme on which she delighted most to meditate, and to converse. One day, while sitting by her bed-side, some lines from one of Watts' hymns came into my mind, and I repeated them:

"Why should we start and fear to die?
What tim'rous worms we mortals are?
Death is the gate to endless joy,
And yet we dread to enter there."

She looked into my face with a smile, and said, "I have none of that fear—none of that dread. I am ready and willing to go at any moment when I am called." One night the watchers thought she was dying, and called her husband who had laid down. On approaching her bed, he said, "Laura, we think you are dying." She raised her eyes, and exclaimed as loud as her feeble voice would enable her, "O, bless the Lord!" Thus she lived, and thus she died, rejoicing in the faith of God's Universal Grace; and added another convincing testimony to the superior excellency of that faith—to its holy influence in purifying the heart, in reconciling it to God, and in giving fortitude to the soul, filling it with "joy unspeakable and full of glory," in the hour of mortal dissolution.

One more; though many years afterwards. In the month of February, 1829, a gentleman by the name of Woodhull, though a resident of the town of Madison yet a total stranger to me, called at my house with an earnest request that I would visit him immediately—he even wanted I should be at his house that day. He said his wife was evidently in the last stage of consumption, could live certainly but a very short time; and she had so frequently expressed a desire to see and converse with me before she died—had set her mind so intently upon it—that she would not be put off another day; and he had come purposely after me, and was very anxious indeed that I should return with him. I could not learn from him the particular state of her feelings, nor wherefore she had this strong desire to have an interview; but, yielding to his importunities, I accompanied him home; and although a melancholy, it was nevertheless one of the most pleasant and agreeable interviews I ever enjoyed. For there I found a woman a little advanced of thirty years, in the prime of life, surrounded with all the conceivable causes of attachment to the world—a tender and provident husband, several promising young children, with every temporal comfort that her heart could desire—yet in ecstacies at the immediate prospect of death! She was a mere living skeleton, but yet possessed sufficient strength to sit up, and talk fluently; with eyes as bright as diamonds, and mind as clear as the light of heaven. After a formal introduction, she remarked, "We have had no personal acquaintance—you have never known me. But ever since this disease has been seated upon me, I have had an irrepressible desire to see and converse with you—a privilege which I felt I could not be denied; for you, sir, have been the instrument, in the hand of God, of bringing me out of darkness into his marvelous light; and I felt as though I could not die until I saw you, and informed you how unspeakably happy I am, in the enjoyment of that faith you advocate. You were the first man I ever heard preach the Gospel—the glad tidings of great joy—of salvation which shall be unto all people. O, I believe it with all my heart—I believe in the Lord Jesus Christ—that he is the Savior of the world—that he is able to save, and that he will have all men to be saved and come unto the knowledge of the truth. The belief of this has been a source of peace and joy since I first received the truth; and since I have been sick, it has been an anchor to my soul, sure and steadfast. It has enabled me to rejoice under the severest sufferings I have experienced, and to look forward, not simply with composure, but with rapture, to the hour of my deliverance. And now it seems as though my last request had been granted. I have seen you, and been able to bear witness in your presence to the truth of the doctrine you preach, and testify to its power to save. The Lord has given success to his word through your ministry, and may he still continue to bless you and prosper your labors." The substance of all this, and much more, she said, with a fervency of soul overflowing with love to God and man; for although but a shadow of physical life remained, she was alive in the spirit, and was able to talk, and did talk much more than I had an opportunity to do, so that she strengthened me much more than I did her. The Lord of life and glory had given her the strength of a Sampson, and she needed not the help of man. She said, she had experienced a momentary trial on account of leaving her children, but she had completely surmounted that trial; and she now felt not a single pang on that account—she should leave them in the hands of a heavenly Father whose love was infinitely stronger than hers, and whose wisdom and power would enable him to do all his love dictated. She had now no regrets, no fears, no anxiety, except on account of her impatience to be gone. She sometimes feared she was committing sin on that account. She said, "I asked my mother the other day, if she thought it was wicked to long to die."

I remained with her several hours, and heard her talk much more than I talked myself. At her request I prayed with her, or rather poured out my soul in grateful praise to Almighty God, for the faith, the hope, the joy, the light, and the life he had bestowed upon her. Before we separated, she requested me to visit her again, if she remained many days in the flesh, and as often as I could make it convenient; and to attend and preach at her funeral. I did make her one more visit, and found her faith, her hope, and her confidence unimpaired; and they held out to the utmost limits of her earthly pilgrimage. But, to her, the joyful day of deliverance at length came; and on the 24th day of March, in compliance with her request, I attended her funeral. Thus, did it please God, from time to time, to encourage and strengthen me in my arduous labors, giving me the assurance, that although feeble, yet they were not wholly in vain.

CHAPTER X.

Association in 1810—Prosperity of the cause—Mr. Dean's success; his character—Quarterly conference—Periodical, the "Religious Inquirer"—Mr. Fuller, Methodist preacher—Ill-health of my family—First visit to our native land—Desultory discussion with a preacher, at the close of a lecture in Augusta—Association in 1811—Female preacher, Maria Cook; anecdotes of her—Dr. Lewis Beers, his connection with Universalists, and subsequent course—First meeting in Cazenovia—Interview with Deacon M.—Long confab with sheriff Whipple—Dr. Ballard—First tour to the Genesee country—Interview with Elder James Parker—Meetings in Benton and Goreham—Preachers at the general meeting in Goreham—Elder Parker's conversion—State of the cause in that county—English settlement in Pittsford, their faith and manners—second tour through the Genesee country—Visit to Dr. Beers.

Our Association met in June 1810, in the town of Madison; and again Mr. Dean and Mr. Carrique attended as delegation from the General Convention of New-England. The Presbyterian meeting-house where Elder Morton and I had our preaching race, as it was facetiously called, a few years before, was opened for our accommodation, and a numerous congregation filled it. If no newly-organized societies were here represented, still an additional number of visiting brethren, from places where congregations had been collected, were in attendance; and loud and earnest calls, from various places where they had and where they had not had the privilege of hearing, were heard, and reiterated, for the preached word; and, thanks to the great Shepherd, we were becoming much better prepared to answer to such calls. Mr. Ferris was becoming much more zealously engaged. He was bred a Quaker, and still retained a strong predilection for many of their peculiarities; he went much by the movings of the spirit; and the spirit of preaching had now been given him, and he was laboring with renewed zeal, very extensively. Mr. Winslow was also itinerating through the length and breadth of the country; and Mr. Babbit was supplying the calls in Hartwick, Otsego, and vicinity;

and about this time removed his family into the town of Hartwick. Mr. Baker, too, having received the usual testimonials of fellowship, entered as extensively into the field of labor as his talents would enable him. But Mr. Dean, on his removal into this region, which took place not long after this, was altogether the brightest star of this constellation. His removal into this section of the Redeemer's heritage was hailed as the commencement of a more prosperous era; and indeed so it proved. He was a young man of prepossessing appearance, of brilliant speaking talents, and of indefatigable zeal and perseverance. He flew, as upon the wings of the wind, from place to place, proclaiming the word with the boldness of a veteran; challenged discussion, and even controversy, with clergymen of the Partialist sects, without distinction of denomination; met the opposer in open field, and conquered under the banner of the cross. Whatever Mr. Dean's course may have been since he left this State, he was, while here, certainly the most successful preacher we had ever had among us; and I very much question whether New York has ever had a more successful dispenser of the word, even up to the present time. I regretted extremely, his leaving the State; and I have great reason to believe that it would have been far better for him, and better for the cause of Universalism if he had never removed to Boston. But Mr. Dean was an ambitious young man; he wanted very much to excel, and aspired to notoriety. While riding together, one day—for he and I were often together, and traveled much together during his residence in this State—he said to me, "Brother Stacy, how old are you?" I answered, "I am thirty." "Well," said he, "by the time I am thirty years old, I mean to be able to preach as well as brother Ballou; I can spin as *fine* a thread *now* as he can, if it is not quite so strong." "That is right, brother Dean, I replied; trim your gallant ship, spread your sails, and launch out into the mighty deep; but permit me to fish around near the shore with my little boat—I may catch some small fish; I dare not venture out far into the great ocean."

In the course of this summer, in addition to my former travels, I visited and preached, more or less, in the towns of Manlius, Marcellus, and Richfield. And for mutual improvement among ourselves (the preachers,) as well as for the extension of the preached word, we this year commenced holding what we denominated a quarterly conference, in addition to our annual association, so as to assemble together at least once in three months. We met in different parts of the country, generally where they were the least accommodated with stated preaching, held meetings for public worship two days, and improved the intervening seasons in social conference. These meetings proved essentially advantageous both to preachers and to others. Our public exercises called together, generally, a large congregation; and as they were held on week-days, many who would think it a desecration of the Sabbath, to attend a Universal meeting on that day, would venture to attend these conferences; and, in our social interviews, important doctrinal subjects were discussed, and a free exchange of ideas and opinions indulged, which tended very much to enlarge and amplify our own thoughts and views, and more thoroughly equip us for the contest in which we were engaged.

These conferences became very popular, and large numbers flocked to them—(when I speak of large numbers and great congregations, let the reader bear in mind the time of which I write; he will then duly appreciate my language; for, in comparison with the present age, these congregations would hardly bear the qualification of *large*,)—and not unfrequently we could prevail on some of the most liberal and charitable of other sects to use freedom in our conferences, and unite with us in our devotional exercises; and this had a great tendency to increase their usefulness, by enabling us to make some little impression upon the almost invulnerable wall that separated us.

Commensurate with the advancement of the cause, was the increase of our zeal. Although our conferences were doing much, we were hardly satisfied, we wanted them to do much more; and I accordingly proposed to attempt the publication of a periodical, to be issued at the time of our conference meeting; something containing the minutes of our doings, and illustrating and defending the great doctrine we were trying to publish to the world, which would, in all probability, find its way, and carry light and instruction where the voice of the preacher could not be heard. We were in the habit of publishing yearly the doings of our association, accompanying the same with a circular letter, and we thought much good resulted therefrom; and I concluded that something of a similar kind, and perhaps on a little larger scale, might be profitably done at our conferences. The subject was deliberately weighed; and although of doubtful practicability in our infant state, we resolved to make the effort. A superintending and editorial committee was appointed, pledges given to try to furnish our proportions of matter for its columns, and a prospectus issued for a periodical in pamphlet form, containing at least, sixteen pages octavo, entitled the "Religious Inquirer;" to be published once in three months, immedietely subsequent to the meeting of our quarterly conference. Arrangements were accordingly made with a printer in Cooperstown, Mr. Prentis, and the first number published. We depended much on Mr. Dean's assistance to furnish matter for the work; but from some reason, Mr. Dean seemed much more inclined to talk than to write—we got not a scrap from his pen. Mr. Ferris and myself were obliged to furnish all the matter. Our enterprise, however, was so peculiarly unfortunate, we were compelled to relinquish it. We had received sufficient encouragement by promises, and no one complained that the work did not redeem the pledge we had given in the prospectus; but, alas! the purses of our friends were not as open as their mouths. We had involved ourselves in a debt of forty or fifty dollars, which we had to cancel from our own private purses, light as they were, with the help of one or two of our most liberal lay-brethren; and we dared not attempt to issue a second number.

At one of our conferences held in the town of Butternuts, after Mr. Winslow had removed his family into that town, a Methodist preacher by the name of Fuller called at Mr. Winslow's, where we held meetings every Tuesday evening, and we were formally introduced to him. I may here remark, that Mrs. Winslow never embraced the doctrine of Universalism, but retained her standing in the Methodist church; therefore, Mr. W.'s house was still a resort for Methodist circuit preachers. I took the liberty to inform Mr. Fuller of the object of our meeting, and remarked, that it was a free conference for christians of every denomination; we were always happy to have them attend, and use their liberty for improvement in exhortation, prayer, or in any way their religious feelings should incline them—we indulged not the presumption to say that we *knew* that we were right, and every one who differed from us was wrong—as our opinions were matter of *faith*, not absolute *knowledge*; we felt under obligation to hold ourselves open to the conviction of truth. And as we were satisfied truth could never suffer by investigation, we felt free to invite investigation on the all-important subject; and we should therefore be happy to have him remain with us, during our meeting; if consistent with his engagements. He replied that he was on a circuit, and had appointments before him for every day, and consequently could not turn aside from his engagements—and he had an appointment for a meeting that evening in the neighborhood. The excuse was reasonable; and to show our liberality, and gratify a real desire in my own mind, at least, I proposed suspending our conference for this evening, and attending Mr. F.'s meeting; and the proposition was readily agreed to. All this was said and done in Mr. F.'s presence; but he wished to get to the place where he should stop for the night, and immediately went on. At early candle-light we repaired to the place. Our company consisted of Mr. Winslow, Mr. Ferris and myself, and two young men who were very active in our conferences, but not preachers. The place of worship was a private dwelling-house; an old-fashioned one-story farm-house, consisting of a large kitchen, two front rooms, &c. The meeting was held in the kitchen, it being the largest and most convenient room; and we were the first who arrived. As we entered, Mr. F. was sitting alone in the room, by a stand suitably placed in the farther end of the same, with his Bible in his hand; he looked at us, but did not speak, and instantly arose, entered one of the square rooms and shut the door. We took convenient seats, and awaited the arrival of the congregation; and soon the room was decently filled. At length Mr. F. made his appearance, took his stand, read a hymn, and commenced what I supposed he would have called singing; but it was well there were not many small children there to be frightened. He then kneeled in the attitude of prayer; but such volleys of low scurrility and abuse I never before heard poured forth from the throat of a depraved mortal! Besides, he was the most illiterate and ignorant block-head, I ever heard attempt to address a congregation. His sole object seemed to be, to point us out, and heap execrations on our heads; and if he had used language that was decent, we could have borne it with some patience. After laboring for a long time to get at us, he at length exclaimed, "Oh Lord! we pray that thou wouldst rim-rap, center-shake, and annihilate the kingdom of the devil this evening." But this did not satisfy him; it did not hit us directly enough; he therefore took another splendid circumlocution, and came at us with a voice raised to its highest possible pitch; "Oh Lord! we pray that thou wouldst deliver us from atheism, from deism, from Universalism, and every other hell-hatched ism that prevails in the land." He had said what he wished then, and seemed quite satisfied. He immediately arose from his knees, sung again, after his fashion, and then named for a text,—"If it were possible, they shall deceive the very elect." His first object seemed to be to blackguard Calvinism, but the poor fellow knew no more about Calvinism than he did about the man in the moon. He stamped, raved, and foamed a long time about "'lection," but finally contented himself by saying, "but I don't believe that; but I'll tell you what I believe about 'lection." But instead of that, however, he raised his voice and said, "But some folks pretend to believe that everybody's 'lected. What! all going to heaven! liars, swearers, drunkards, thieves, robbers, whore-mongers, and all sich characters!—well, if everybody's going to heaven, I don't want to go there. But some folks may ax aint you to hard with the Universalists? But I don't believe I am; if all are 'lected, if all are going to heaven, it makes no difference what I do; I shall be well enough on it at last. But some may ax, isn't there some good folks among Universalists? I don't know; I've heard people tell about white crows, but I never see one." There, reader, was not that worth spending an evening to hear? Did we not get well rewarded for suspending our conference, by going to hear that rich exhibition of original eloquence? I have given you the pith and marrow of his whole discourse; and the poor fellow was so fearful we should make an attack upon him—poor soul! we could have found nothing to attack, had we diligently sought for it; there was nothing of him, in him, nor about him, that we could have distinguished from the mass of rubbish beneath our feet—but he was so fearful we should attack him, that there was no pause, not even that of a comma, between "Amen," and "Sister, what room shall we hold class-meeting in." The lady of the house pointed to the door, into which he darted, calling Methodists to follow him, and forbidding others to intrude upon their class-meeting. We therefore arose and left the house, and went back to Mr. Winslow's, ashamed enough of our adventure.

Our family now consisted of two children, a son and daughter; the youngest, born September, 1809, was a very feeble child; and my wife, from the time of its birth, had experienced a very poor state of health, and seemed gradually sinking. We had employed the most skilful physicians our place afforded, but nothing seemed to reach her case, or give any hopes of raising her again to health. I became fully satisfied that the seat of her difficulty was a derangement of the nervous system, and that traveling, if she could endure it, was the only effectual remedy. We had not, since we commenced housekeeping, visited our native land. My parents were both living, and she had a father, brothers, and a sister there. I proposed to her, a visit to that place; and although the thought seemed to interest her, I could hardly persuade her that she could endure fatigue. Her mind was gloomy and despondent, her spirit and ambition gone, and she could scarcely sit up an hour at a time during the whole day. I, however, made all necessary arrangements, procured as comfortable a carriage as our times afforded, and, contrary to the advice of my neighbors, who told me I was presumptuous, that I would never return with my wife alive; and, with great reluctance on her part to hazard the attempt, and a sick child, eleven months old, that required a constant nurse, and a little boy four years old, about the middle of August I started on a journey of two hundred miles, without any help to take care of my team, or the sick. Our first stage was four miles; and by the time she had accomplished it, my wife thought she was nearly gone; she had no idea of ever being able to be removed from that place. However, we carried her into the house and laid her on a bed; and after resting about two hours, she was able to take some refreshment, and proceed four miles farther, which completed our first day's journey. The next morning, contrary to the predictions of my friends, she felt stronger and better than when she left home; and in due season we were on our way again, and traveled sixteen miles that day. This was, indeed, too hard a day's journey for her, and she appeared to have but just the breath of life in her, when we reached the place of our destination. I had imprudently sent on an appointment for a lecture at that place, and I never allowed myself to make a disappointment, when it was possible to avoid it. But a gracious Providence favored my enterprise; the next morning she felt much recruited, and was able to proceed on her way with renewed courage. She had lived through these severe exertions, and began to be cheered with the hope of being able to accomplish her journey. Thus far a friend had accompanied us; but now he returned back, and I had, from henceforth, to take the whole charge of the establishment, sick family and all. We traveled ten miles the next day, which brought us among our friends in the town of Otsego, where we remained four or five days. We were here detained longer than we intended to stay, in consequence of a renewed attack on our feeble child, which we feared for a time would prove fatal. But it gave my wife time to rest from the fatigues of her journey thus far; and a kind Providence blessed the means used for the recovery of the child; we were enabled again to resume our journey with improved health, and renewed courage. My wife now appeared healthier and stronger than she had for months before, and from this time was able to ride as far in a day as I wished to drive my team. We were absent from home eight weeks; visited Ballston Springs on our route down, and also on our return; and the journey, with other means used, produced all the happy consequences I so ardently prayed for, and anticipated. My wife returned home cheerful and happy, with almost a new constitution; and the health of our child greatly improved. Our visit proved a very gratifying circumstance on another account. We found all the relatives we left, when we removed from that place, alive and well, and among them my wife's venerable father; but he lived but a little more than a year after that. The last we saw of him, he sat upon a large rock just before his door, with the big tears rolling down his aged cheeks, watching the receding movement of our carriage. It was a consoling reflection to us, after his departure, that we were permitted to visit him once, before he was gathered to his fathers.

On the 5th of January, 1811, I delivered an evening lecture in the town of Augusta, in a private dwelling-house. At the close of the discourse a man arose, who, I afterwards was informed, was a preacher, and commenced haranguing the people, and inveighing most bitterly against the doctrine I had advanced. His back was turned toward me, and he seemed designedly to overlook and treat me with neglect. I let him go on for a few moments, and then broke in upon his harangue, and remarked, "Sir, I am the person who has advanced the doctrine you so bitterly condemn; will you have the goodness to address me, and grant me the privilege of replying?" He then turned and addressed me, nearly as follows: "The law of God is out against the transgressor, and condemns him to everlasting punishment, if he does not repent. But your doctrine has a tendency to silence the conscience of the sinner, by taking away the penalty of the divine law, and therefore encourages him to go on in sin, with impunity," "Sir, I replied, will you inform me what the divine law demands of the sinner? What is the essential requisition of the law of God, upon all immortal beings?" He hesitated—"I will vary the question then, so that you can not help but understand me; does not the law demand of all moral beings, 'Thou shalt love the Lord thy God, with all thy heart, and thy neighbor as thyself?'" "Yes," he replied. "Well, sir, can any thing but this love to

God and love to man satisfy the demands of the Divine law? Can punishment do it?" The man evidently saw himself in difficulty; but he seemed determined to show out his pugnacity as bravely as Goldsmith's country school-master—

"E'en though vanquish'd, he could argue still,"

And drawled out "Yes—I will make a similitude. Our laws impose a penalty for the commission of crimes—for offences of a certain magnitude, imprisonment in the penitentiary for a term of years. Now when an individual is convicted of such a crime, and has received his sentence, and is shut up in the state-prison, the law is satisfied." "I must beg your pardon, sir, for a different opinion; I supposed the law never confined a man that it was satisfied with; I always supposed that the very imprisonment of the man showed the dissatisfaction of the law; that the moment the law was fully satisfied, the man would be liberated." He had discernment enough to see the inconsistency of his similitude, and said, "I will alter it—the law requires the death of the murderer; now when a man is found guilty of murder, and, in accordance with his sentence, is hung by the neck until he is dead, the law is satisfied." "I grant it; but permit me to vary the similitude. Suppose the murderer should be hung up between the heavens and the earth, and be always undergoing the pangs of death, but never die; would the law ever be satisfied?" "Why, no." The congregation saw he had entrapped himself; and many of them broke out into a loud laugh, which I had to reprove; and the man was struck dumb. I then addressed him and said, "Now, sir, you see a truth which you probably never before discovered, and that is, that the law of God, so far from demanding the endless punishment of the sinner, demands his obedience, and consequently his salvation, and will not be satisfied without it; and the punishment which the law inflicts on the disobedient, is evidence that the law is dissatisfied with the disobedient, and can only be satisfied when he is obedient, and punishment ceases; therefore, to argue endless punishment, is arguing the endless dissatisfaction of the law of God!" Controversies of this sort, in which our early preachers were almost constantly engaged, and which were the only kind I ever did engage in, uniformly proved essentially advantageous to the cause of truth; for they were generally conducted in the presence of many inquiring minds.

The uniform practice was to adjourn the Association, from year to year, to such place as petitioned for its session, without regard to central location, and disregarding our own convenience for the benefit of the cause; and we were generally compelled to make selections from the numerous requests presented. Our friends were soon made sensible of the salutary effects of those meetings in the region where they were held, and manifested a becoming zeal for the session; and were always ready to make ample provision, not only for members of the council, but also for all visitors during its continuance. Previous arrangements, therefore, were made by the society with whom we met—a committee was appointed expressly to wait on visiting brethren, and see that they were hospitably entertained—for many came from a great distance. Such was the excitement on these occasions, that it was not uncommon to see carriage-loads, individuals on horse-back, and even walking, from a distance of fifty, sixty, and sometimes a hundred miles. Universalists were scattered promiscuously through the length and breadth of the land; and there were but few in those days, in comparison with the great mass of Partialists, attached respectively to all the other sects. The reader may in some degree appreciate their feelings, though he can not fully, if he would, imagine himself in their position, located in a neighborhood where no one sympathizes with him, in his religious devotions; where, if he speak on the subject of his doctrine, he is sure to meet with nothing but frowns and execrations; where, if he attend church, he is a target for the most pointed, venomous shafts of the speaker's *holy* indignation; and where he probably has never had an opportunity to hear a single sermon that he considers even salted with Gospel truth; and then let him suppose that he hears of a meeting of preachers of that doctrine which he verily believes to be the Gospel of Christ, where a number are to assemble, and hold forth for two successive days; and he will have some faint conceptions of the feelings of those who attended our Associations—he may form some idea of the alacrity with which they made preparations for the journey—of the cheerfulness with which they sacrificed both time and money—and of the indescribable joy of heart with which they met and greeted each other. He may look around on such a congregation, and see the unmistakable evidences of the most perfect gratification—of joy in heart and peace of soul—delineated upon every countenance, in the complaisant smile, the glowing cheek, and the moistened eye, that meet him from every quarter. O, the blessedness of such a convocation! My old heart warms under this faint retrospective glance, and I almost wish to live life over again to renew the enjoyment of such blessed seasons. But, for some cause, under certain circumstances, I have very excitable materials in my moral composition, and I suppose every body did not feel as I did.

The sixth session of our Association, (1811,) was holden in Bainbridge, Chenango county, As no meeting-house could be obtained, our friends fitted up a newly-built barn in as convenient a manner as possible, for the occasion. Such meeting-houses as that, we often had to occupy; and we felt ourselves highly accommodated when we obtained a clean one; nor did we think it a disgrace for Christians to worship God in a barn, inasmuch as a stable was the birth-place of the Captain of our salvation. Mr. Dean then resided within the territorial limits of the Association, and was consequently with us; and five others, heretofore named, who were members of this ecclesiastical body, were present, and a single individual, Nathaniel Smith, bearing credentials of appointment from the General Convention, with two other preachers of the Great Salvation, who had never before appeared among us; and singular as the circumstance may appear, one was a female.

Maria Cook, then about thirty years of age, was escorted to that place by two gentlemen of the first respectability, from the town of Sheshequin, Bradford county, Pennsylvania, where she had been visiting for several weeks, and holding meetings. They introduced her to the council as a person of irreproachable morals, and with high encomiums upon her public labors. Some of our brethren and friends were a little fastidious about allowing a woman to preach, supposing St. Paul forbade it, where he says, *he suffered not a woman to teach, nor to usurp authority, &c.*, while others thought differently, believing he would not have applauded the labors of so many female *helpers in the Lord*, if he did not, under suitable circumstances, approve of their public ministration. But as the phenomenon of a female preacher appearing among us was so *extraordinary*, and curiosity was on tiptoe among the mass of the congregation, to hear a woman preach, our opposing brethren finally withdrew their objections, and she very cheerfully obliged us with a discourse. And there was not a sermon delivered with more eloquence, with more correctness of diction, or pathos, or one listened to with more devout attention; nor was there another delivered during the session so highly applauded by the whole congregation, as the one she delivered. And so excited and animated were many of the brethren by the novelty, and so highly pleased and edified with her public discourse, that a letter of fellowship for her, as a preacher of the Gospel, was almost peremptorily demanded. She, herself, appeared quite indifferent about it. But as she came well recommended, both as to her religious and moral character, and as she certainly exhibited sound faith and a becoming zeal for the promotion of the cause, was well educated and possessed more than ordinary speaking talents, an informal letter was presented to her, which she modestly accepted. This letter of fellowship, however, she destroyed in a few weeks afterwards, because she thought some of the preachers, especially Mr. Dean, did not treat her with that kindness which the letter betokened; and she conscientiously destroyed, (so she told me,) what she considered an insincere token of fellowship.

She there received numerous and earnest requests from the delegates from all the societies, and from nearly every visiting brother, to come to their respective societies and towns and hold meetings; and she readily complied with as many of these calls as her time and health would permit. She possessed no means of conveyance of her own, nor did she desire it; some friends always accompanied her, and helped her from place to place. Her meetings, for a season, were the most numerously attended of any preacher of any denomination, who had ever traveled through the country, and were certainly quite advantageous to the cause of truth, as they called out many who, had it not been for the novelty of the circumstance, could not have been induced to attend a Universalist meeting; and who, after obtaining some ideas of the doctrine from her discourses, were inclined to hear others; and her remuneration by contributions was far more liberal than any preacher of our order received, or perhaps any itinerant preacher of any denomination. But Miss Cook had numerous opposers to the course she pursued, irrespective of the doctrine she inculcated, and especially among her own sex, who thought it very improper, and even indecent for a woman to preach, and especially to itinerate as she did. She was quite sensitive; and the vituperations and uncharitable remarks which were constantly falling upon her ears considerably discomposed her, and soon began to give quite a tone to her public discourses, by leading her into long arguments in vindication of her right to preach; which would not unfrequently constitute the whole burden of her discourse. This rendered them rather stale and uninteresting; the novelty of the circumstance subsiding, invitations became less frequent, and her congregations vastly decreased in numbers. She however remained in the counties of Chenango, Madison, Oneida, Otsego, and Herkimer, something like a year. She then made a visit to the region of Troy; and quite a lengthy stay, (several months I believe,) among the Shakers; and then returned to her friends; for she had a mother, brothers, and sisters in Geneva and vicinity. After the lapse of a year or more, she made our part of the country another visit; but her reception was not so cordial and flattering as on her first tour; still she had many warm friends in different parts of the country. She preached but little; and, in the fall of the year, took up her residence among some friends in that part of the town of Otsego called Pierstown, with a design to spend the winter. But some malignant spirit, who wanted to spit his venom against Universalism in some form, and no doubt thinking that, by disturbing her, he should injure the feelings of some of her friends, and thereby ingratiate himself into the favor of the Orthodox aristocracy, entered a complaint to the proper authorities, stating that such a vagrant person was in town, and liable to become a town-charge. Nothing could have been more untrue. It was generally known that she had a sufficient income to maintain her, secured to her by the will of her deceased father—to amply provide her a support under any circumstances. Her brother, on whom I once called by her request, when traveling in Western New York, told me that, at any time when she wished to return home, he would send for her; and, at any time when she needed money, let him know it, and he would send it to her; notwithstanding, he and all her relatives were very much opposed to the course she was pursuing, and considered her under a mental derangement.

But a precept was issued by Esquire F., of Cooperstown, and put into the hands of a constable, who immediately went in pursuit of her. Her friends remonstrated with the officer—told him there was no possible necessity for disturbing her, that they would become responsible that she should not be chargeable upon the town—but all to no purpose; he had received his "letter of authority," and "haul her to prison" he would. He went where she had taken up her abode, and a ludicrous scene ensued. He was with a wagon; and he informed her, that the law required him to take her to Cooperstown, before Esq. F. She told him, he must do it then. "Well," said he, "will you take a seat in the wagon?" She replied, "No." "Well, how will you go?" She answered, "I will not go at all." "But the law requires me to carry you there." "Well, I have nothing to do with the law; and, if you have, you must do your duty." But how he should carry her, was the question, if she would not get into his wagon. "That," said she, "is your business—not mine." The man was completely put to his trumps—she moved not, nor would she move, or make any preparations. It was about five miles where he wanted to carry her. He was finally compelled, as a last resort, to take her in his arms, and set her in his wagon, to which she made no resistance. The friend who gave me the information, circumstantially, took his horse and followed them, to see that she met with no personal abuse; for he felt confident they never could extort an answer from her to a single question. The constable drove to the door of the office, stopped his team, and remarked, "This is Esq. F.'s office. Will you get out of the wagon, and walk in." She replied, "No; I have no business with Esq. F.; if he has business with me, let him come to me." No persuasion could make her move from the wagon; and the constable left her, went into the office, informed the magistrate of the circumstance, and asked him what he should do. The magistrate told him to bring her into the office. So he was again compelled to take her in his arms, carry her into the office, where he seated her in a chair; when the following dialogue ensued:

Magistrate. Miss Cook, inasmuch as a complaint has been entered, I have been obliged, by law, to issue a precept, and have you brought before me, not to abuse you, nor to injure your feelings, if I can avoid it; but to ask you a few questions, relative to your place of residence, means of subsistence, &c.

Miss C. You can ask me any questions you please; but I feel under no obligation to answer you, nor shall I answer any of your questions.

Mag. But will you not tell me your place of residence?

Miss C. No.

Mag. But the law requires it, madam, and I have but one course to pursue. If you will not answer the necessary inquiries, I shall be under the disagreeable necessity to commit you to jail, until you will answer.

Miss C. You can do as you please. I have seen demons in the seat of justice before now—I have a brother who acts in that capacity.

Not being able to obtain any thing like an answer to a single question he proposed, the magistrate wrote a *mittimus* for contempt of court, read it to her, and handed it to the constable.

Miss C. You have worded it right, sir, for you and all your proceedings are perfectly contemptible, in my view.

Constable. Miss Cook, will you walk out, and take a seat in the wagon?

Miss C. No.

The constable was, therefore, under the necessity of taking her into his arms again, and seating her in the wagon. He then drove to the jail, carried her into the building, and delivered her to the jailer. The keeper was a friendly man—his family resided in one part of the prison-house; and he told Miss Cook, that she was welcome to his table, and gave her liberty to visit any apartment of the prison, or other part of the building she was disposed to see. There she remained, perfectly contented and happy, for several weeks; and, while in these circumstances, she sent word to me, that she was preaching to the spirits in prison. After some weeks, finding they could neither drive nor flatter her to pay any respect to their authority, the magistrate hinted to the jailer to get rid of her the easiest way he could.

In the spring following, if my memory be correct, she made another visit to Troy, then returned to her friends, gave up traveling and preaching, and remained in retirement the rest of her life. I never saw her but once afterwards, which was many years since she had relinquished preaching. In the year 1829, I called on Mr. O. Ackley, in Hopewell, Ontario county, where I saw Miss Cook for the last time, and received from her tongue the most severe castigation that I ever received from any mortal, male or female. When I entered the house, I received as cordial and friendly greeting as I ever did, and that was as affectionate as I was in the habit of receiving from any person living; but she immediately remarked, "Now I know what I was sent here for." She then proceeded to inform me, that she had an irresistible presentiment that it was her duty to come to Brother Ackley's, and to come that morning; and so powerfully was it impressed upon her, that she had walked the whole distance of ten miles before breakfast. She felt confident she had a call from the Lord to perform some important duty; but what that duty was she had no distinct perception until she saw me; but now the whole was unfolded to her—it was to admonish, to exhort me, in the name of the Lord, to be more faithful to my duty. She said, preaching was no longer of any use—she had been convinced of it for a long while, and she was persuaded I must be also convinced. She firmly believed the doctrine—she believed it was God's truth, and would ultimately prevail—but it must be through other means than preaching. It must be done by work; that is, by organizing into an apostolic society—a community of interest, of property. This had been a favorite topic for many years; and she had made a number of efforts to get such a society established. She now said, that I had sufficient influence to establish such a society, and it was my imperious duty to do it—that my preaching was of no use, nor had it been for years—that I had been losing ground for a good while past—that the Lord had begun to curse me for neglect of duty, and he would still heap curses upon my head; and she devoutly prayed that he would curse me more and more until I would do my duty in that respect, &c., &c. This was the last interview I ever had with Miss Cook. She lived a number of years after this in retirement, and, indeed, pretty much secluded from the world: but lived and died in full faith of the ultimate universal purification and happiness of mankind.

Mr. Smith, in his "Historical Sketches," has made some very appropriate and just remarks, in relation to this eccentric woman.

The other individual, heretofore mentioned, was Dr. Lewis Beers, of the town of Spencer, Tioga county, but now Danby, Tompkins county, New York. It is not strange that Mr. Smith, in his "Historical Sketches," should have made some trifling mistakes in his notice of this individual, inasmuch as the incidents to which he alludes took place prior to his connection with the Universalist denomination; and as it is presumable that he never had much, if any, personal acquaintance with him.

Dr. Beers was an eminent and successful practitioner of medicine, a native of the State of Connecticut, and educated in the most rigid school of Presbyterianism; and I am strongly impressed with the belief, that he lived a number of years in the communion of that church. He was an early settler in that town; and by skill in the practice of his profession, and his successful financiering, had amassed a large property. His mind, however, was too inquisitive to be content with the incongruities of Calvinism, and his soul too capacious to be satisfied within the narrow limits of Partialism; and by dint of Biblical study, with the help of a few books that fell in his way, he arose, I am persuaded, without ever hearing a discourse from a Universalist preacher, above the fog of educational prejudice into the clear light of Gospel truth; and, without stopping to confer with flesh and blood, immediately began publishing it to the world. He had, I think, obtained Mr. Ballou's Treatise on Atonement; and, having ascertained the place of his residence, addressed him by letter, requesting information concerning the state of our organization, and what steps would be necessary for him to take in order to unite with the denomination of Universalists. Mr. Ballou immediately replied, (the Doctor showed me the letter,) and informed him of the existence of the "Western Association," which was the first knowledge he ever obtained of such an organization in the State of New York; and the session in Bainbridge, which he attended, was the first meeting of this body, after he obtained that knowledge.

Doctor Beers delivered one discourse at this meeting, which abundantly evinced the correctness and strength of his faith, and his ability to advocate it before the world; and, as he possessed ample credentials as to his religious and moral character, on his application a letter of fellowship, as a preacher of the Gospel, was most readily and cheerfully granted. It is presumable that Dr. B., at this time, had no knowledge whatever of the "New Jerusalem Church," and that he had never seen a volume of the writings of Swedenbourg, nor any other writings on the subject. From the time of our first acquaintance, we entered into an epistolary correspondence, which was continued for several years; and, in the fall of this year, I made him a visit, and delivered a number of discourses in his neighborhood. I had free access to his library while there, and found nothing of the kind among his books, nor was there a word passed between us on the subject; but, after he became a convert to Swedenbourgianism, it constituted one of the most common themes of his discourses. Some time in the spring of the year following, if I mistake not, I received through the post-office the first number of a periodical in pamphlet form, entitled, "The Halcyon Luminary," published by a company of gentlemen in the city of New York. It exhibited high literary merits, and its mechanical execution was in the first style. It was religious in its character, but professed to discard all sectarianism, to advocate liberty of thought and investigation; and it promised to give a key, which would fully and certainly unlock all the mysteries of divine Revelation, and deliver the church from the dense fog in which it had so long groped, and bring it out into the brilliant light and sun-shine of Gospel truth. I read it with considerable interest—and read it again; but there was something about it, notwithstanding its professed transparency, so inscrutable, so mystical, that it appeared to me, on the whole, to be itself in a more dense fog than that which it proposed to dispel from the atmosphere of the church; and I had so little faith in its ability to fulfil its high pretensions, that I made no return for it, nor interested myself in its favor, and consequently never received another number. How many of our preachers received it I am unable to say; but Dr. Beers did, and I shortly after received a letter from him, extolling the work beyond measure; and when I again visited him, in the fall of 1812, he had received all the numbers which had then been published, and was drinking deeply into its doctrine. He had obtained the "key" to the mysteries of Revelation, and was able to begin to explain the inspired word quite clearly, in his own estimation, at least, by the "science of correspondencies." Shortly after this—certainly within two years—he visited the city of New York, united with the "New Jerusalem Church," and received ordination at the hands of the clergy of that denomination. Subsequently, he built a meeting-house at his own expense, principally if not wholly, in his own neighborhood, collected something of a congregation, and organized a church to which he ministered. During his visit to New York, he procured the voluminous writings of Baron Swedenbourg, which comprised a vastly greater bulk than his extensive medical library. On his showing me the ponderous tomes which contained his theological lore, I remarked, "Br. Beers, I can never become a Swedenbourgian." "Why," he asked. "Because I could never find time to study the theory—I should rather undertake to acquire a knowledge of your medical profession than your theology—it would require less time and labor." He replied, "Well, you are about right."

This change of opinion, (if change of opinion it may be called) never interrupted, in any degree, our fraternal intercourse, for he never would acknowledge to me that he believed in endless misery or unhappiness in any form whatever; but said, as he understood it, the doctrine of the final restitution was not incompatible with the doctrine of the new church. I visited him repeatedly after this, and preached in his neighborhood and vicinity; and he made me a visit and preached for me one Sunday in Hamilton. On my first visit to him after he united with the Swedenbourgian church, I said to him, "Brother Beers, you have placed yourself in a very singular predicament, having united yourself to a church who probably would not acknowledge Universalism, as a Christian faith, without a formal withdrawal from us; and therefore stand as a visible member of the two churches, who hold no fellowship with each other. What are you going to do about it?" "I confess," he said, "there appears a discrepancy in my conduct; but I could not conveniently make known my views and wishes to the Association previous to the step I have taken. I think the Association had better withdraw fellowship from me." "But you know, Brother Beers, that we can not withdraw the hand of fellowship merely for opinion's sake, unless that opinion denies faith in the Christian religion. No, you must withdraw from us; and that you enjoy the privilege of doing, with or without giving your reason for the act, at your own choice." "But," said he, "I can not conscientiously do that, because that would be manifestation of feeling foreign to my heart; I have the same cordial fellowship for my Universal brethren that I ever had; I consider them right, in almost every point of doctrine, and the nearest right, by far, of any denomination of Christians except the New Jerusalem Church, and I shall always esteem it a privilege to unite with them in religious worship." "Well," I replied, "if you will not withdraw you must remain, for aught I see, in your present awkward position, unless you commit some crime; but look out, sir, if you commit crime, you will doubtless have to meet a double retribution; for we shall most certainly deal with you as a member of our church."

Such were the real feelings of Dr. Beers, no doubt; for his conduct evinced the sincerity of his profession. He remained, while I had any knowledge of him, a warm friend of Universalists and Universalism, and does, I presume, to the present day, if he is yet in the land of the living. But many years have passed since I have seen, or even heard from him; I know not whether he still remains a tenant of the earth, or whether he has gone to that brighter and better world he so firmly believed in, and so ardently anticipated. He was a good man, a practical Christian, and enjoyed the unlimited confidence of his friends and the high esteem of all his acquaintances.

In my itinerations in Madison county, particularly in the towns of Nelson, Smithfield, and vicinity, I had frequent interviews with a deputy-sheriff, by the name of Matteson, who became favorably impressed with the doctrine, and improved every convenient opportunity to hear it preached. He was a favorite of his principal, and being often with him, talked much about the new doctrine, and expressed a strong desire for the sheriff, J. Whipple Esq., to hear it. He succeeded at last in exciting a curiosity in the mind of the sheriff, and he sent a request to me, by Matteson, to make an appointment at his house. Cazenovia was then the seat of justice for Madison county, and Whipple of course resided there. Matteson very cheerfully made the application in behalf of the sheriff, and assured me, that I would receive kind and respectful treatment; and I gave him liberty to make the appointment. In the month of April, 1811, was delivered the first Universalist discourse ever preached in the village of Cazenovia. Whipple, however, was rather timid; fearful, probably, that it might eclipse his popularity to show too much favor to such an unpopular sect, and therefore, did not diffuse the information very extensively; but enough assembled to handsomely line a large square room in his dwelling-house. Not a child, or one in minority, nor a female, appeared in the congregation until I arose to commence service, when two women, one of them I afterwards learned was Mrs. W., just entered within the room; and, looking warily around as though fearful of some impending catastrophe, seated themselves near the door, cautiously keeping it open so as to secure a safe retreat, in case of an onset. I was pleased with my congregation, notwithstanding; they looked like men of respectability, and of mature judgment, and of sufficient understanding to comprehend what I had to say to them; and they gave very serious and close attention. The discourse was closed, the congregation were thanked and dismissed, and every soul left the room, leaving me entirely alone. Not more than five minutes elapsed, however, before Whipple returned, and said, Mr. M.—, one of the Deacons of the Presbyterian church, had been one of my hearers, and had expressed a wish to have some conversation with me. I requested Mr. W. to introduce him, as I should esteem it a privilege to gratify his desire. He withdrew, and in two or three minutes returned, followed by the Deacon, and nearly or quite every other individual that composed my congregation, except the women. We were introduced, and the Deacon remarked—that he wished to ask me a number of questions; but as he did not feel competent to enter into an argument, he wanted I should agree not to ask him a single question. I replied, that was quite an unusual and unequal way of holding a discussion; but as I was perfectly willing, and even desirous that everybody should know my opinion, and investigate and prove my doctrine, for I entertained no fears that it would suffer by investigation, I would cheerfully indulge him; and he might ask me as many questions as he was disposed to ask, and I would answer as many as I could. The Deacon was very mild and pleasant, exhibiting none of that ferocity so common among opposers of the doctrine, but demeaned himself like a Christian. We conversed an hour or more; the Deacon asked me a number of questions relative to the peculiarities of my doctrine; and then requested me to reconcile a large number of passages of Scripture therewith, which he considered as insuperable objections to the doctrine. The passages, as usual, consisted mostly of parables; and the Deacon listened with much patience, and some manifestations of surprise at my expositions; while a death-like stillness was maintained by our auditors. When the Deacon had exhausted the catalogue of passages which his memory retained, he seemed to sit in deep thought for a few moments, and then resumed, "Well, Mr. Stacy, your doctrine appears reasonable; but I can not believe it."

Stacy. Why, Deacon?

Deacon. Because I believe God is just—I believe he is a just as well as a merciful God.

S. Well, Deacon, so do I. I believe God is infinitely just—that his justice is inflexible—that it never did, and never will yield to mercy, nor relinquish one of its least demands; and because I so believe, I fully believe in the ultimate holiness and happiness of all intelligent beings.

Dea. I don't understand that—I don't see how that can be. I have always supposed, that if God dealt with us according to strict justice, not one soul could ever be saved.

S. Well, Deacon, you have certainly talked long enough with me, not to be afraid of me—to be afraid I will deal captiously with you; and now, if you will answer me a very few plain, simple questions—answer them just as you think, just as you feel, without the least reserve—I think I can make it appear perfectly plain to you, so plain that you can not help but understand me.

Dea. Well, I will try to answer.

S. Well, Deacon, Is it not perversely wicked and unjust for us to hate God, and hate man? And is not hatred of God, and hatred of man, the fruitful source of all our sins and consequent misery—the profound abyss of human depravity?

Dea. Well, I must confess I believe it is.

S. Then, sir, can a soul be miserable, who loves God with all his powers, and his neighbor as himself?

Dea. O, no; by no means. Love to God and love to man, constitute heavenly felicity.

S. And does not God righteously and justly demand this supreme love of all his intelligent creation?

Dea. Yes, certainly.

S. Then does not this love to God and love to man constitute the sum total of the demands of divine justice?

Dea. I think it does.

S. Now, Deacon, do you believe that God, in the economy of his wisdom, has devised any means by which his justice will be fully vindicated and satisfied ?

Dea. Most certainly.

S. Well, Deacon, you and I believe just alike. We are co-believers in the same glorious doctrine of the final Restitution.

Dea. I think not.

S. O yes—you are as clear a Universalist as I have found lately; and I profess to be a preacher of that doctrine.

Dea. I do not understand it so.

S. Well, Deacon, I'll try to make you understand it. You have acknowledged that you believe, first, That the infinite justice of God demands of all intelligent beings, that they should love God with all the heart, and each other as themselves; and that this constitutes the sum total of the requirements of the divine and just law of God; therefore, nothing but this love can satisfy the demands of justice—punishment can never do it, nor tend towards it, unless that punishment produce this love. Secondly, You believe that this love constitutes heavenly felicity—that no one, in the enjoyment of love is, or can be, miserable. Thirdly, You believe that God has devised efficient means whereby his justice will be fully satisfied; and as nothing but love will satisfy its demands, so it necessarily and unavoidably follows, that God has devised means whereby all mankind will eventually love God with all their powers, or justice will forever be dissatisfied; and, therefore, all intelligent beings will be partakers of heavenly felicity.

Sheriff Whipple, (with rather a boisterous laugh, and loud voice.) There, Deacon, you're down now—give it up—give it up.

The whole congregation broke out into rather a disagreeable laugh, and the Deacon dropped his head. I then resumed; "Now, Deacon, by reviewing this subject, you will be led to see what you probably never have before seen, that the justice and mercy of God are not conflicting attributes—that so far from opposing each other, they meet and embrace in the Gospel plan of salvation—that while justice inflexibly demands supreme love to God, and love to man, which the sinner, of himself could never yield, mercy, through our Lord Jesus Christ, steps in and enables him to comply with the demands of divine justice. Therefore, in the salvation of the whole human race, and in no other way, both justice and mercy can have their demands to the last fraction, and both be fully satisfied. The Deacon, at length, raised his head, and, with a pleasant smile, gave me his hand, and bade me good-bye. In subsequent years a small congregation was raised in Cazenovia, to whom I frequently preached; but I never again saw Deacon M.

Mrs. Whipple, notwithstanding she was a member of the Presbyterian church, and exhibited a great deal of caution and even shyness at first, was a lady of kind feelings; and eventually became quite sociable, and treated me with great politeness; and, after the congregation retired, we enjoyed a very pleasant interview. After we had partaken of some refreshment, which was liberally and cheerfully provided by Mrs. W., the Sheriff himself took me in hand.

Whipple. Well, Mr. Stacy, you have given us a good discourse, to-day—just what I believe, but it is not Christianity.

S. Not Christianity, Esquire! Then I have made a most capital mistake. I verily thought I was advocating the Christian religion in its purity.

W. No, that was not the Christian religion; but it was good—it was truth—just what I believe.

S. If it were not Christianity, Esquire, what do you call it?

W. Deism—I am a Deist.

S. A Deist! what makes you a Deist?

W. O, the inconsistencies of the Bible—a book so full of inconsistencies can't be true. I was educated strictly in Presbyterianism. My mother was a rigid professor, and a good woman; and she took much pains with my religious education; she made me learn the Catechism, and attend church strictly when I was young; but when I became old enough to read the Bible for myself, I found it so full of absurdities and contradictions, that I became fully satisfied it was a mere fiction—the invention of designing men—and I threw it aside; and I have paid no attention to it for many years.

S. Wherein do you find the greatest difficulty, in reconciling the Scriptures with reason and common sense, or with themselves?

W. O, they are full of contradictions; and a witness who contradicts himself is not to be credited.

S. But is there not some one idea, or sentiment, contained in the Bible, more difficult for you to reconcile than any other?

W. Yes; the notion of the Trinity is the greatest absurdity of all.

S. And are you sure that the common notion of the Trinity is contained in the Bible?

W. O, yes; the Bible is full of it—every where.

S. Well, sir; I have been a diligent student of the Bible for many years, and have not been able to find it there, nor do I believe it.

W. O, I knew you were a Deist by your preaching.

S. No; I am not a Deist—I firmly believe the Scriptures of the Old and New Testaments are a revelation from God, and contain no contradictions, nor absurdities, when rightly understood; but the doctrines of men, and the prejudices of education, have so misrepresented the Bible, that it is not surprising that a rational mind, who will not take the liberty to read it himself, independently of the teachings of others, should be led to reject it. No, sir; I have carefully examined the whole Bible; and the doctrine of Athanasian Trinitarianism can not be found there.

W. I am sure it is—I can find it in almost every part of the old book.

S. Well, sir, take the Bible, and show it to me if you can; and let us examine the Bible, and see what it does say about it.

The Bible was produced, down we sat, and continued our examination until long after the clock struck twelve. The Sheriff was not very conversant with the Bible; he had never read it much; but he was able to find some passages which he thought supported the doctrine of the Trinity, and I helped him to all such as are generally quoted in proof of it; and the result was, that he acknowledged that there was not sufficient evidence to establish the doctrine; and he seemed a little mortified that he should have been so confident, and promised to read the Bible again, more carefully.

The next morning I arose and went out into the sitting-room. The Sheriff and his wife slept in an adjoining bed-room, and, hearing me come into the room, called out, "Mr. Stacy, is that you?"

S. Yes, sir.

W. Well, I will get up then. I have not slept much; you plagued me so, last night, I could not sleep—I have been thinking it all over; and I have got a text for you now, that you can't get rid of so easily as you did them last night.

(By this time he had got into the room half dressed, and appeared quite confident and exulting.)

S. Well, Esquire, I am glad you have found another text—I want the truth; and I want to hear the strongest arguments, and the most direct proofs, that can be found in favor of that doctrine.

W. Well, I have got you down now; you can not explain this away so easily as you have done the others.

S. But, Esquire, what is it? Let us have it.

W. There are three persons in the God-head, the Father, the Son, and the Holy Ghost; and these three are one God, the same in substance, equal in power and glory. There, get rid of that if you can.

S. Well, Esquire, you have got it now in as plain words as can be spoken. I hardly know what I shall do with that text.

W. Ah! I knew there was something stronger than any thing we found last night. You plagued me so that I could not think, but after I went to bed it came to me.

S. Do you recollect where the text may be found, Esquire?

W. I don't exactly recollect where it is; but I can find it in a very little while—I read it not long since; but I guess you can tell where it is, if you are disposed; for I find you have the Bible almost by heart.

S. But I want you to find it, Esquire. Perhaps when we come to find it, and examine the context, we may not find it so difficult after all, as it now appears to be. My method for examining abstruse passages is to examine the context, learn the subject the writer is discoursing upon, then find collateral, or similar passages; and, by comparing them, I can generally very clearly understand the meaning of the writer, as I think. Now I wish you to find that passage, that we may examine it according to this rule.

W. Well, I can find it in a very short time; but I guess you can tell me where it is, if you have a mind to do so.

(Upon so saying, he started for his Bible; but I interrupted him.)

S. You need not get your Bible, Esquire. I can tell you exactly where you may find the text.

W. I thought you could, if you would. Where is it?

S. In the Primer.

W. In the primer! Why, is it not in the Bible?

S. Oh, no—It was never in the Bible, unless you, or some good Trinitarian, placed it there.

W. But I'm sure it's in the Bible, I believe I have read it there a great many times.

S. You say, sir, that you were educated a Presbyterian, that your mother was a member of the church, and was strict in her religious discipline; and if so, she made you learn the old Assembly's catechism—I presume she would call you up, at least, every Sunday, and with the primer in one hand and a rod in the other, so as to whip you if you did not answer right, would oblige you to answer all the questions of the shorter catechism.

W. Well, she did exactly so.

S. Well, sir, can you now recollect the answer to the following question, "How many persons are there in the God-head ?"

W. (Dropping his head and reflecting for a moment)—Well, I declare! I believe it is in the primer, after all; but it really appeared to me like Bible language, and I certainly thought it was there.

S. No doubt, and so do a great many other sectarian phrases probably appear to you, and to many other people, educated as you were, like Scripture. The prejudices of education are very powerful; and it requires a vigorous effort of mind to rise above them, so as to think and reason for ourselves. But I do seriously think, Esquire, if you will give yourself time to read the Bible once more, candidly, without prejudice, you will have a very different opinion of it, from what you now have.

He again promised me he would read the Bible once more; but whether he ever redeemed this promise, I am unable to say. I saw him at my meetings several times afterwards, and indeed a number of years afterwards; but never had enough intercourse with him to learn whether he ever renounced Deism; at any rate, he never attached himself to our denomination.

There was an old gentleman, by the name of Ballard, residing in the town of DeRuyter, Madison county, who had received the cognomen of doctor. He was what we vulgarly called, a root-doctor, of considerable celebrity, and extensive practice. He was an emigrant from the State of Rhode Island, was bred a Friend-Quaker, and retained many of their plain habits; but many years before this, had embraced the doctrine of Universal Salvation. He was rather an eccentric man fond of discussion, shrewd in argument, and acquired considerable notoriety on that account. He sought my acquaintance, often attended my meetings, and familiarly visited at my house. This man was in the habit of journeying to the Genesee country once or twice a year, to collect such roots and herbs as he could not find in the vicinity of his own residence. He informed me that he had found many Universalists in that country, and that they had organized societies, and held a general meeting once a year, which they called a Convention; and that he had informed them about me, and the state of the cause in our section of country; and they were very anxious that I should meet them at their next convention. This request was renewed with much earnestness through Dr. Ballard, who proposed to accompany me, and I consented to go. Their annual meeting was appointed to be held that year, (1811,) in that part of the town of Gorham which now constitutes the town of Hopewell, on the first Sunday and Monday following in October. The doctor and I arrived at the town of Benton, some twenty miles distant from the place of meeting, on the Friday preceding, and stopped at Esq. Benton's, one of our friends; for the doctor had searched out all the Universalists in that region, and seemed quite familiarly acquainted with the whole brotherhood. On our arrival, we were informed that Elder Parker, a Free-will Baptist, had an appointment for a lecture that evening at the house of our friend, in the immediate neighborhood, by the name of Gage; and although I was much fatigued, having preached the Sunday previous in the town of Butternuts, thirty miles east of my residence, and then traveled one hundred and ten miles west of it to reach this place; nevertheless, I proposed attending. At the hour appointed we repaired to the place; Elder Parker had arrived, and we were introduced to each other. He was a man on the down-hill of life, but of sound health, and vigorous constitution, and probably retained the use of all his physical and mental faculties as well as at any period of life, although he was in all probability advanced of sixty years; and withal I found him a social, companionable man, and, as I thought at the first introduction, possessing more than an ordinary share of kindness and charity, for a Partialist preacher. He was one of the earliest followers of the celebrated Jemima Wilkinson, was her principal agent in purchasing the tract of land in that country on which she and her followers settled, and removed with her from Rhode Island into their New Jerusalem. But several years previous to the time of which I am speaking, he had seceded from her connection; had united himself with the Free-will, or Open-communion Baptists, and had been ordained as Elder in that church.

We enjoyed a momentary and pleasant interview; and just as it became necessary to open the services of the evening, the Elder addressed me and said, "You will preach this evening." "Oh, no," I replied, "I am too much fatigued to preach; and, moreover, the meeting was expressly appointed for you; the people have assembled to hear a Baptist, and it would be an imposition on the congregation, to compel them to hear a Universalist, contrary to their voluntary inclination." "I was early taught," said he, "never to hold a man by the button, to hear me speak; these people have heard me often; you are a stranger whom they have never heard; and they will now be much better satisfied to hear you than they would to hear me; and I now tell you, if you do not preach, there will be no preaching this evening." "But will that be right, Elder?" He replied, "Right, or not right, I shall risk it—if you don't preach, there will be no preaching this evening." "Well," said I, "although I feel hardly able, in consequence of the fatigue of my journey; yet, rather than to have the people go away without anything being said, if you will pray, I will try to say something." To this he readily agreed, and we had a very comfortable meeting. I remained at Mr. Gage's all night; and the Elder and I slept together, or rather occupied the same bed; for we slept but little. He was full of his inquiries about my doctrine, and how I could reconcile such and such passages of Scripture with it; and I was as ready and as zealous to answer, as he was to to ask questions; and we talked the night away, in half the time, apparently, of an ordinary night.

The Elder informed me that he was on his way, designedly, to attend the Convention in Gorham; and consequently we rode together all the next day. In the course of the day, he introduced me to a number of friends, some of his faith, and some Universalists, and among them, to his wife, who was on a visit among several of her children in the town of Seneca. She was a second wife, a widow with a large family of children, when they were married. We arrived at the place of appointment a little before night—time enough, however, for notice to be given for an evening lecture; and I delivered a discourse in the dwelling-house of widow Spear.

I found the organization that our friends had affected in that country to consist merely of what we ordinarily denominate a society; but embracing in its territorial limits the whole county of Ontario, which, since that time, I believe has been divided into two, three, or more counties; and they appointed one or more trustees in each town where congregations had been collected. And these annual meetings; which were uniformly held two days, were, in addition to their exercises of social worship, for the purpose of appointing trustees and other officers, and transacting the necessary prudential business of the society. They generally collected together on Saturday, or within such a distance that they could assemble at an early hour the next morning; attended religious service on Sunday, and transacted their society business on Monday. None of the preachers, or those who improved in public, reached the place where I was on Saturday ; but when I reached the house where the meeting was appointed on Sunday, which was a school-house, nearly a mile distant, I found four; Mr. Billinghurst, Mr. Upson, Mr. Ross, and Mr. Moore. It was soon ascertained that the school-house would not hold a tithe of the people assembled and assembling, and a committee was appointed to seek some other place, and make the best preparations they could for the time being. The best accommodation they could find, however, was a little eminence in a forest close at hand, to which, by carrying the loose benches in the school-house, and collecting what chairs they could find in wagons, together with the help of the trunks of some fallen trees, they made passable seats for a portion of the congregation ; while the rest had to stand, sit, or lie on the ground, as it best suited them ; and for a pulpit, they drew a wagon into the center of the place designed to be occupied, on the most elevated part of the knoll.

I was formally introduced to the public speakers by my kind friend, Elder P., who appeared familiarly acquainted with them all ; and by them was told that I must occupy the whole day ; that being a stranger, and my intended visit having been announced through all the ramifications of their society, had brought together an unprecedented concourse of people ; and they would be only satisfied by having, at least, two discourses from me that day. It was in vain that I urged them to afford me some help ; if they would not preach, to assist me, at least, in some other parts of the exercise. It was in vain that I expostulated with them on the severity of the task they required of me, after the fatigues of a long journey, and preaching nearly every day, and now, in the open air, to address a congregation so large that it would require the utmost effort of my lungs to make them hear me. I could not get a single individual into my pulpit, nor a mouth opened, nor a tongue loosed to assist me. I therefore mounted the wagon—not, however, with such feelings as a condemned criminal would mount the cart under the gallows, for Heaven had inspired me with a courage, and a zeal, for the occasion. I looked around for my auditory, for they were on all sides of me ; and almost as far as I could see there was as dense a crowd of people as the trees would admit of, sitting, standing, leaning against trees, and lying on the ground, still as the house of death, with eyes and ears fixed to catch the word. And there I stood almost the whole of that day, hallooing as loud as my lungs enabled me, for I was obliged to shout to enable the people to hear, at such a distance; and talking to them of the Great Salvation through the mediation of our Lord and Savior Jesus Christ—a blessed day this!

At the close of the services, before the assembly was dismissed, Elder Parker came to the wagon and requested me to notify an appointment for him at early candle-lighting, at the house of a son-in-law of his, in the immediate neighborhood—"Not," he said, "for a lecture; but I have some communications that I wish to make to the people." The notice was accordingly given out, and the house was filled at an early hour. The Elder gave a pretty elaborate history of his Christian experience; and indeed, with an avowal of his conversion to the faith of the final restitution—the ultimate purity and happiness of the whole human family.

The next day, the members of the society assembled at the school-house and transacted the business of their social community; and at my suggestion, they gave Elder James Parker a letter of fellowship and commendation as a preacher of the everlasting Gospel which God preached to Abraham, saying, "And in thy seed shall all the families of the earth be blessed."

Of the four other speakers already named, two of them, Ross and Moore, made little or no proficiency in the ministry. Mr. Billinghurst was already an old man; and although he had been, for several years after his conversion to the faith, very zealously engaged in the ministry, he was now becoming infirm, said it injured his health to preach, and in a year or two after this, relinquished it entirely. He was a European, an Englishman by birth; and in England united with the order of the general Baptists, and became a preacher among them. He was always, no doubt, liberal in his religious opinions, for he might be so in that denomination, without subjecting himself to the ordeal of excommunication, or even censure, as several of the most eminent and learned preachers of that Order were avowed Universalists, and boldly advocated the sentiment; but Mr. B. was not a Universalist when he left England. He emigrated to America in 1795, and within the course of a few years settled in the town of Boyle, now Pittsford, Monroe county. But previous to his settling in Boyle, he told me, if I mistake not, he became fully convinced of the truth of the doctrine of God's universal, efficient grace, and firmly established in the faith of the final holiness and happiness of all intelligent beings; and he added, "so overjoyed was my heart at the discovery of this glorious truth, that, like Paul, I stopped not to confer with flesh and blood, but immediately began to publish the glad tidings to the world." Mr. Upson was a convert from the Methodists; he had been a licensed preacher in that denomination. He had already received a letter of fellowship from that society, and subsequently received similar testimonials from the "Western Association of Universalists in the State of New York;" and he continued for a number of years to preach the doctrine to some effect, and remained firm in the faith, I believe, until the day of his death. I was also informed that there had been a preacher among them of very respectable talents, by the name of Badger, a convert from the Presbyterian, or rather Congregational denomination, and a clergyman of that order, who, some years before came from Massachusetts; and whose labors had done much for the planting of the cause in that country. The memory of this man was held very dear by Universalists generally; but he had "finished his course" a short time before this, not to exceed a year, I think, and gone to receive his "crown of righteousness, which the Lord hath laid up for all who love his appearing and kingdom." All these had labored with more or less zeal and success, amid other avocations, and succeeded in effecting such organization as I have before named. But Mr. Billinghurst and Mr. Badger were, by far, the most able and efficient laborers in this section of the Redeemer's vineyard. I gave then, at this meeting, a circumstantial account of the planting of the doctrine in Central New York—of its establishment and progress; of the organization of the Western Association, and its union with the General Convention in New England; and cordially invited them to unite with the Western Association for mutual strength and encouragement in our endeavors to extend the knowledge of the great TRUTH we were publishing to the world. They listened with much gratification to the account I gave them; for they scarcely knew that there was another body of Universalists, as numerous as themselves, constituted in the wide world, and thereupon passed a resolution to appoint a delegate to attend our association, with instructions to ask the fellowship of that body; and Elder Parker was chosen. But for some reason, probably on account of the remote place of its meeting, he did not attend the next session; but the year following, he, in company with Mr. Knapp, who had then settled in the county of Ontario, attended the Association in New Hartford. Their petition was then laid before the council ; and the "First society of Universalists in the county of Ontario" was received into fellowship,and from thenceforth became a flourishing branch of this spreading vine.

From the meeting in Gorham I went home with Mr. Billinghurst and his company, for many came down with him to "this feast;" and here I found a settlement, almost exclusively of English people, consisting of forty, fifty, or more families compactly situated ; and a more intelligent, pleasant, and harmonious neighborhood, I never found. Mr. Billinghurst's settlement in this place while it was entirely new, almost a wilderness, constituted a nucleus around which they naturally gathered as they emigrated, one after another, from the mother country. And whether they were Universalists or not when they came, their national attachment, and the confidence they reposed in Mr. Billinghurst, induced them to attend his meetings ; and at the time I visited them, there was scarcely an exception to their unity of faith in the Great Salvation. It was most refreshing and exhilarating to preach among them, to witness their profound and devout attention, and the manifest effect the word was exerting upon their feelings. Oh, how widely different are the feelings of the preacher under such circumstances ; when every word seems to take effect, to carry conviction to the understanding, and sensibility to the heart; from what they are when addressing a congregation who manifest no interest in the doctrine advocated ; who merely look at outward appearances, and only listen to his words as they would to a sunset songster, or a farce acted upon the stage ; when his words bound back upon himself like a ball thrown against a rock, which constitutes as great a restraint upon his feelings, and almost as effectually forbids the expansion of his ideas, and flow of utterance, as though he were addressing a yard of cabbage heads.

They were a people, too, who practiced the least duplicity of any that I ever associated with. If they discovered a fault in you, they were sure to tell you of it, and to do it in an affectionate and kind way ; and they were equally as sure to tell you of your virtues, if you possessed any, and how well they liked you, without the least reserve.

I delivered several discourses in this settlement, with unbounded satisfaction to myself; and I never felt myself more at home in any society of people I ever associated with. The females as well as the stronger sex were uniformly in the faith, and Mrs. Billinghurst in particular. She was in advance of her husband, having embraced the doctrine of Universalism before she left England—Heaven made her constitutionally a Universalist. The dogma of endless misery never for a moment found a resting-place in her capacious soul; she was a devout worshiper, a practical Christian, and one of the most intelligent and worthy women I ever found in all my extensive travels.

I remained seventeen days in the county of Ontario; and in the course of that time delivered twenty-one discourses in eleven townships, as follows: Benton, Gorham, Boyle, Perrinton, Penfield, Westown, Bloomfield, Seneca, Middlesex, Canandaigua, and Phelps. And by their earnest solicitation, I made them another visit of two weeks, the winter following, and delivered sixteen discourses, preaching in most of the places where I had held meetings on my former tour, and extending my ride this time as far as Honeoye Lake.

On my return home from the Genesee country, in the fall of 1811, after crossing the Cayuga Lake where the upper bridge now stands, I traveled up, on the east side of the lake, to Ithica, at the head of the lake, and from thence to the town of Spencer, now Danby, to make Dr. Beers a promised visit. In this region I remained several days, and delivered a number of discourses in the vicinity, and at the house of Dr. Beers; I then returned home through the town of Homer, where I also delivered an evening lecture. I had been from home twenty-nine days, had traveled four or five hundred miles, and delivered twenty-five discourses.

For about four years after my removal into the town of Hamilton, the winter season was employed in teaching school. To this course I was driven to provide the necessaries for an increasing family; but this, however, did not prevent me from preaching on the Sabbath, and I frequently delivered lectures on week-day evenings. After this lapse of time my little farm became more productive, affording me greater rewards for my labor; and calls for preaching becoming more extensive, requiring a much wider extent of itinerancy, I relinquished the profession of pedagogue entirely; and, from henceforth depended, under the never-failing care of a gracious Providence, upon the productions of my little farm, under the culture of my own hands, and the pittance I received for my ministerial labors, for our support. And although I never accumulated wealth, my family never knew what it was to do without *bread*, nor did they ever suffer for the absolute necessaries of life.

CHAPTER XI.

Association in 1812—Mr. Miles—Dr. Ellis—Mr. L. Knapp—Long tour through Canisteo and Genesee—Pleasant Incident—Meetings in LeRoy and Batavia—Genesee Falls—Funeral at the landing—Hard day's ride—Mr. Sherman's ordination—Association in 1813—Mr. James Gowdy—Mr. Seth Jones—Mr. S. R. Smith—Association in 1814—Meeting-house refused—Meet in a Barn—The effects of the refusal—Dr. Green—Mr. Pitts—Genesee branch—Chaplain in the Militia—Amusing anecdote—Campaign in the service—Sackett's Harbor—Immoralizing effects of a military campaign—Visit to Ellisburgh—Close of campaign, and return—Association in 1815—Mr. Root—Mr. Underwood; admission into connection—Mr. Whitnal—Mr. Cook—Theological Seminary—First session of Genesee branch—First Universalist meeting in Auburn—Severe fit of sickness—Sectarian slander—Visit to Mr. Person, Greenfield—Ague and fever—Association in 1815—Cold season—Journey to Sea-coast—Clam-bake—Capt. Martin—Sail on the bay at New Bedford—Lecture at the head of the River—Rochester—Deacon Foster—A religious maniac—Visit to Newport, Rhode Island—Lecture in the State House—Elder Green—Meeting in Dana—Return home.

We met in annual Association in 1812, in the town of Duanesburg. Mr. Stephen Miles, who has long been known as a worthy member of our denomination, and a devoted and faithful laborer in the ministry, accompanied me to the meeting. He was a resident of Augusta, and had been a member of Elder Morton's church, (the same Elder M. who has already received so much attention in these memoirs,) and was a recent convert from the Baptists. I had become acquainted with him; and he freely expressed to me his strong desire to preach the Gospel, and that he had an unconquerable presentiment that it was his imperative duty to devote his life to it; and I invited him to attend the Association and become acquainted with the ministering brethren. From this time, so great was his ardor for the cause, and his indefatigable zeal and industry, that, notwithstanding he had a large family on his hands for a young man, and had no other means for their support than the daily labor of his own hands, he surmounted all these difficulties; and in less than a year from that time launched forth as a laborer in the vineyard of the great Husbandman, to which he has faithfully devoted his life up to the present moment.

We were now apparently and indeed really, gaining strength every year, in our ministerial connection, as well as receiving new societies into the fellowship of our Association. Although Mr. Dean did not meet with us on this occasion, having gone a journey to Vermont, yet two other preachers, who had never before met with the Association, were present; and also the same individual from the General Convention who came as a delegate the preceding year. Dr. J. H. Ellis, one of the preachers alluded to above, was an Irishman by birth, and a convert from the Baptist denomination. We had learned by the published proceedings of the "Northern Association," in Vermont, that he had received the fellowship of that body, and this was all the knowledge we had of him until he met with us at this time. A few months previous to the meeting of this Association, he had removed to the town of Duanesburg, and was supplying the society at that place; we therefore cordially greeted him as a member of the council, and congratulated ourselves on the acquisition of an able and worthy member. But, alas! he was of no advantage to the cause of truth. For, besides being one of the most singular, eccentric characters on the stage of action, which essentially injured his public usefulness, and a most disgusting pedant, he was at that very time, though unknown to us, under admonition by the "Northern Association" for gross immoral conduct, which resulted in his expulsion from that body the next year; and, consequently, although he continued to preach, in his way for many years afterwards, yet he never sat as a member of our council, nor was he ever recognized as a Universalist preacher. Mr. Liscomb Knapp, the other individual to whom I have alluded, was a young man; he came from Vermont, had preached some in that State, and received a letter from the "Northern Association;" and after Mr. Dean's removal to New Hartford, he came to that place for the purpose of studying with him. This was the first time he met with our Association, and he was a valuable acquisition to our little band. He was a man of very good talents, of becoming zeal, and his daily life and conversation were a practical comment upon the superior excellency of the doctrine he inculcated. He cheerfully devoted his life of more than ordinary duration, to its service, through many trials and severe labors, without faltering, and died rejoicing in the faith.

It was during this year, if I mistake not, that Mr. Underwood, whom I have before had occasion to name, came out into the open profession of his faith in the final Restitution; but although he did not hesitate to own and to defend it, both in private conversation and in his public discourses, still he did not see fit immediately to unite with the Association.

In the fore part of this season, soon after the meeting of the Association, Mr. Knapp made me a visit. And, knowing the extreme solicitation of the brethren in Ontario county to have an active and efficient preacher of Universalism settle among them, (for they had most earnestly urged me to do so, and once addressed a very pathetic letter to the society in Hamilton, requesting them to assent to it,) I proposed to Mr. Knapp to take a tour through that country, to see if he would not like the location, and find an encouraging field of labor. To facilitate this object, I offered, on condition he would supply my place in Hamilton and vicinity, to take a tour as a pioneer, and leave appointments for him—a schedule of which I would hand him on my return. On mature reflection he consented to do so. I immediately wrote to friends through all that region of country, and made arrangements for a more extensive tour than I had hitherto taken. In this way, I made appointments in all the principal places I had heretofore visited, leaving intervals, however, to be filled up casually on my way; made my calculations for the length of time I should be absent, told my family the day they might look for my return, Providence permitting; and on the last day of July I left home on my devious journey. On this tour, I pursued a different route from what I had formerly pursued, traveling through Homer, Virgil, and Dryden to the residence of Dr. Beers, in Spencer, (Danby,) where I remained one day to talk to the people. From thence I journeyed through Ithica, at the head of Cayuga Lake; Catharine's, at the head of the Seneca, to the town of Benton, where I again made a stop for a single day. From thence, passing through Gorham, Manchester, and Victor, I arrived at Boyle, (Pittsford,) where I made another short pause. From Pittsford, I returned through Canandaigua to Benton, where Elder Parker joined me, and accompanied me up to Crooked Lake and through Bath to the residence of Mr. Upson, in the town of Canisteo.

Quite a pleasant incident occurred as we were traveling near the margin of Crooked Lake. The country was very little cultivated, the land hard and rocky, principally timbered with oak, and densely covered with fern, or whortleberry bushes;

the inhabitants were sparely scattered along the road, with small improvements and log houses. It was a little past the middle of the day, and the meridian sun beat down with unwelcome rays upon our heads; we had talked ourselves weary, and were jogging lazily along between sleeping and waking, when two women appeared in sight at a considerable distance before us, tripping along with their utmost speed the same course we were pursuing. My first impression was, that they were on a whortleberry excursion, and so spoke to Br. P.; but, on nearing them, I discovered they were dressed in their holiday suit; and then remarked to Br. P., "These women are not after berries—I apprehend there must be a meeting of some sort ahead." We soon overtook them, and I inquired the cause of their haste. They replied, "There is a meeting to be held at the next house, and we are fearful of being too late." "What kind of meeting, madam?" "Preaching." "By whom?" "A Methodist circuit preacher." After we had passed them a few yards, I said to Br. P., "We have rode some distance, and it will do our horses no injury to breathe a few minutes; and, as we are entire strangers, we may perhaps enjoy the privilege of a meeting without being abused, or having our feelings wounded by a malignant attack upon our sentiments. What if we should stop long enough to hear the discourse." The proposition was accepted; and, by the time we had made our arrangements, we came in sight of the house. A few people were standing in front of the house; we rode up to the fence, dismounted, tied our horses, and joined the company; but, alas! we were betrayed; for as soon as we reached the place where the men were standing, one of them called the Elder by name. We told the man that we were on a journey, and having just been informed that there was a meeting to be holden in that house, we concluded it would do our horses no injury to rest a little, and as it might do us some good to hear preaching, we would stop long enough to hear the sermon. The man looked pleased, politely invited us into the house, and furnished us with seats. I looked around for the preacher, but saw no person I felt willing to recognize as such; and, in answer to my inquiry, was informed that he had arrived, and would be in soon, for it was about time to commence service. The building was constructed of unhewn logs, consisting of a single room, not very capacious, and it was soon very well filled. In a short time a young man entered, came directly to Elder P. and myself, and, with a smile, cordially gave us his hand, and took his seat by a stand on which a Bible and hymn-book had already been placed. He had no doubt been informed who we were, although no formal introduction had been given. He soon arose, opened his meeting by their usual ceremonies, and took for a text the words of Pharaoh, when the people came to him in the time of the seven years of famine, crying for bread; "Go unto Joseph." He undertook to show the analogy between Joseph and Christ, and succeeded to some extent, though he made some trifling mistakes; one of which was, that "Joseph was a keeper of his father's flocks, and Jacob sent his sons to find him," &c. However, we got along with this well enough, and so did he, for he did not discover his error. But, although he displayed no great talent in sermonizing, he exhibited that which was far better, *great charity*, and no disposition to misrepresent and abuse the opinions of others. He was also very brief, occupying probably not more than twenty or twenty five minutes in his sermon; and closed his discourse by saying, "A few words spoken by a bungler is certainly better than a great many, without any meaning." He then looked at Elder P., and asked him if he had any remarks to make. The Elder seemed to feel rather dull, and he replied that he had not. He then asked me the same question. And I answered in the affirmative, and arose on my feet. Although I had not been highly captivated with the eloquence of the speaker, yet I had been extremely gratified with the privilege, once in my life, of hearing a discourse from a Partialist without being abused—had been pleased beyond measure, and my feelings warmed up almost to a boiling point, by his charitable language and demeanor. The Elder cast at me rather a repulsive look, but I heeded it not. I proceeded, and gave an exhortation in conformity to the doctrine the young man had designed to advance. I had not spoken five minutes, when the preacher clapped his hands with all his might, and shouted aloud, "Amen." He had now set them an example, and it was instantly followed by almost the whole congregation; and, for a moment, I was nearly stunned by the noise, and actually embarrassed. I was not accustomed to such acclamations; and it came, too, totally unexpected. I however soon recovered, and finished my exhortation, amid loud shouts of "Glory to God," and "Amen," from every part of the room, the preacher being sure to raise his voice the highest. When I had resumed my seat, he asked me to close the meeting by prayer; I did so, and the deafening peals of shouting were kept up, or, if possible, increased until the closing "Amen." The young man seemed animated beyond measure; and the complacent smile that lighted up the countenances of the congregation, was an unmistakeable evidence of the happiness they felt. The young man had said not a word about the wrath of an offended God, hell, or future misery. He had endeavored to portray, as well as he could, the benignity of the divine character—his care for mankind, even while alienated from him by wicked works, in the ample provision he had made for every soul; and to direct the attention to the medium he had prepared, by which they could come and obtain it; and all I had to do was, to illustrate, commend, and enforce his arguments. At the close, the preacher, and many of the congregation, gave us their hands most warmly and affectionately, and we separated happier than when we met; and the Elder and I "Went on our way rejoicing." It was peculiarly consoling to me, amid the trials and conflicts I was destined almost every day to encounter, to have, once in a while, such an unexpected season of refreshing—it enabled me to "Thank God, and take courage."

At Canisteo, Elder P. left me, and returned back; and I had to perform the remainder of my journey alone. I remained a few days with Mr. Upson, and delivered several discourses in different parts of the town of Canisteo, when I resumed my tour. Crossing the Allegany ridge, I struck the head waters of a creek, called, I believe, Conhocton, and following its course reached Dansville, thence north to Geneseo, thence down the Genesee river to Avon, there crossed the river, and continued my travels west as far as Batavia, stopping at Le Roy. Mr. Billinghurst had written to a friend in Le Roy, notifying him of my intended visit, and the time I might be expected there. I called at Ganson's tavern; and, on entering the house and inquiring for Mr. Ganson, an old gentleman, sitting alone in the bar-room, looked at me and said, "If you are the man I expect you are, I was once acquainted with your father." I replied, "My name is Stacy." "Ah!" said he, "the very same," and he caught me in his arms, and hugged me as he would a baby. He was a native of New Salem, Massachusetts, and, in his younger days, well acquainted with my father's family. I preached in LeRoy one Sabbath, and delivered several lectures; and was accompanied to Batavia by a number of the friends in that place, where I delivered one discourse in the Court-house. On my return, I delivered another discourse in LeRoy, and solemnized a marriage; and then returned through Avon, Bloomfield, and Mendon, to Pittsford, where I again tarried a few days, and delivered several discourses.

On this tour, I saw the Genesee Falls, for the first time. It was a jaunt of about eight miles from Mr. Billinghurst's, which he and another friend by the name of Sawens and myself performed on a leisure day, merely to view this stupendous cascade, although such days very seldom occurred with me, at that period of my life and labor. At that time, where the city of Rochester now presents its splendid and richly ornamented structures, its well-paved streets, its crowded marts, its numerous houses of worship, with their gilded spires glittering in the sunbeams, and its population of more than thirty thousand, there was, on the west side of the river, only a small tavern-house, a miniature store, and not more than one or two other buildings. At this tavern, we obtained refreshment for ourselves and horses; and, while it was being prepared for us, we took our ramble to the Falls, in doing which we were compelled to clamber over fallen trees, crawl through briars and tangled underbrush, and bruise our limbs by coming in contact with unseen rocks; but, although somewhat scratched and bruised, we were amply compensated, by beholding this mighty sheet of water take its awful leap of nearly one hundred feet, far below the common level of the surrounding country, into a deep channel excavated by its own power through a bed of limestone for more than three miles, running smoothly along in a surpentine course until it passed beyond our vision. Soon after our return to the tavern, which stood a little west of the bridge, a messenger called in pursuit of Mr. B. to preach a funeral discourse on the death of a child, at what they called the Landing, three miles below. I felt much gratified on account of their application to him, thinking by this providential occurrence I should enjoy the pleasure of hearing a sermon from him, which I had never experienced. But, alas! I was doomed to disappointment; he refused, and referred the messenger to me; and, in despite of all my remonstrances and efforts to avoid it, "The lot fell on Jonah," and I was compelled, on this solitary day of leisure, to ride some three miles farther, making my ride in the course of the day nearly twenty five miles, and the labor of preaching. The unexpected additional ride, together with the funeral services, made the day fatiguing, and brought nightfall some time before we reached the hospitable dwelling of my attendant host.

Discourses were delivered on this tour in most places I had previously visited in the western country, besides the additional places I have already enumerated; and in most of them I left appointments for Mr. Knapp. The last meeting was holden in the Court-house in Canandaigua, which left me but two days to ride one hundred and ten miles, and reach home on the appointed day. I made a tolerably early start in the morning; but my way for a short distance lay through the midst of acquaintances and friends, and the numerous salutations I received, and the repeated questions which pressed so hard upon me for answers, retarded my progress so that at noon I found myself but ten miles on my journey. After taking dinner with a friend, I said to him as I seated myself on the saddle, "To-morrow night, God willing, I see my family." "You can't do it," he said. I replied, "I shall 'salute no man by the way'—set my face like a flint, neither turning to the right nor to the left—I will recognize no friend and battle no foe until I see my family, which I have promised to do to-morrow night;" and I fulfilled my promise. That afternoon I traveled some miles beyond Auburn, continuing my ride until I had to call a tavern-keeper from his bed to put out my horse. The next morning I again called him from his slumbers to get my horse and receive his pay; and before I slept, through the mercy of God, I entered my own rustic dwelling. I had been from home between five and six weeks; and in my tour—my zig-zag wanderings through the country—I had traveled not much short of six hundred miles, had delivered twenty five or thirty discourses, and returned to my family on the day I appointed when I left them. Heaven blessed me with good health, with fine weather, and pleasant traveling; and amply rewarded me for my toil in a consciousness of having, according to the best of my ability, discharged an important duty. I gave Mr. Knapp a schedule of the appointments I had made for him on the circuit, and he immediately went to fulfil them; and from that time made his residence in that country.

The doctrine of God's Universal Grace now began to make some greater progress in its steady, onward march in this State, and several preachers as well as laymen came over to its help in some degree, though rather cautiously, who loved the doctrine but feared the name; and among the number a man by the name of Sherman, who, I believe, had been a Baptist. The Partialists had employed every means in their power to render the *name* of Universalism odious; and had so succeeded as, in numerous instances, to almost prevent individuals, after they became thoroughly convinced of the truth of the ultimate holiness and happiness of the whole human race, from acknowledging that they were Universalists. They appeared actually afraid of the *name*, and would try to adopt some other in order to shield them from the odium—would wrangle about it, and, as Pope says, act like

> "Fools at war about a NAME,
> Which often has NO meaning, or the SAME."

"Why do you not call your doctrine by some other name," said an old gentleman to me one day, after he had exhausted his vocabulary of anathemas against Universalism and Universalists, "Why don't you call your doctrine by some other name—you'd have as many again hearers." I replied, "I never gave it the name; but, whether given by friend or foe, I like it *well*, and do not wish to exchange it, because it is so appropriate, and so definitely distinguishes my denomination from all the ramifications of the Partialist church.

Mr. Sherman was considerably troubled with timidity. He firmly believed the doctrine, loved it with all his heart, and was quite zealous in persuading others of its truth. He established a meeting in the neighborhood of his own residence, in the town of Manlius, collected a little band into church organization, and preached to them; but never extended his ministerial labors much beyond his vicinity. His church desired to enjoy the privilege of receiving the Christian ordinances, and applied to Mr. Dean and myself to confer ordination upon their pastor. We accordingly went there; and finding a little band, united by the strong ties of Christian brotherhood, well established in the faith of the final reconciliation of all mankind to God through our Lord Jesus Christ, evidently "Adorning the doctrine of God our Savior in all things," and reposing the utmost confidence in their pastor, who truly appeared every way worthy of their reverence and esteem; who, although he would prefer to be called by some other name, either Unitarian, Restorationist, or Unitarian-Restorationist which pleased him rather the best, yet desirous of receiving ordination at our hands, we solemnly set him apart, according to our usual forms, to the work of the ministry of reconciliation, and as pastor of the church of his own planting. But he never formally joined our Association, nor were his labors extensively useful to the cause of Universalism in our region of country.

At the session of the Association it 1813, which was held in New Hartford, several valuable accessions to the ministry were received, besides the addition of the first Universalist society in the county of Ontario, with its clerical members. Mr. Knapp, and Elder James Parker, were the only delegates from that society, as it appeared they had not seen cause to appoint lay delegates; but no delegation was received this year from the

General Convention in New England. Letters of fellowship were granted this year to Seth Jones, and James Gowdy, both converts from the Baptist clergy, also to Stephen Miles, whom I have had occasion to name, and to S. R. Smith, a young man who had been, for a short season, studying with Mr. Dean. All these were good men, and valuable members of our community ; but the labors of some were far more efficient, in the advancement of the cause, than others. Probably Mr. Gowdy's ministry was more circumscribed, and of less celebrity and utility, than either of the others. Mr. Jones, although an illiterate man, (I think he told me he never went to school but five days in his whole life) was, nevertheless, one of the most successful itinerant preachers our State ever produced ; and for many years he traveled extensively, and preached with the zeal of a Paul, and the eloquence of an Apollos. I have never seen a crowded congregation more captivated, more enamored, sit with more ease, under the preaching of any living man, than under him, in a discourse of two or three hours long. But of all the preachers who received the fellowship of the Association at this session, or indeed, had ever received a letter of fellowship from its council, S. R. Smith was, by far, the most important acquisition. He had never belonged to any Partialist denomination ; his mind had never been imbued nor soiled with the false theology of the schools. His first religious breath was drawn in the pure and uncontaminated atmosphere of the Gospel of Christ ; where its great and glorious doctrines fell upon a soil free from thorns and noxious weeds, and of sufficient strength to bring forth "an hundred fold." He had not, I believe, publicly addressed a congregation previous to that time ; but so well acquainted with him were many of the members of the council, and such confidence they had in the correctness of his opinions, in the strength of his faith; the stability of his character, his integrity, and moral worth, in his studious habits, his indefatigable zeal, and the expanding powers of his giant mind, that, unsolicited by him, a letter of fellowship was proffered to him by the unanimous voice of the council, which he modestly accepted. Time has shown the correctness of their judgment, and how fully their anticipations have been realized, and more than realized, by his extensive and valuable labors. He stands justly, and his name ever will stand, upon the faithful page of history, at the head of the Universalist clergy in the State of New York. This is not fulsome panegyric ; it is the solemn conviction of one who has been intimately acquainted with him from the commencement of his ministerial labors up to the present moment. And it is said without meaning the least disparagement to the numerous learned, pious, and able divines who now grace the ranks of the Universalist clergy in that State.

Our earnest and long-reiterated prayers for more laborers in the vineyard seemed now measurably answered ; and as an increasing family demanded my utmost endeavors, and most prudent and economical management to meet their necessary calls, I was obliged to curtail my peregrinations as much as possible, and apply my hands diligently to the implements of husbandry. During this year, therefore, I traveled but little abroad ; I mean by abroad out of the counties of Madison, Chenango, Otsego, Herkimer, and Oneida ; but I by no means relinquished preaching every Sabbath ; and frequently attended evening meetings during the fall and winter seasons.

In 1814, the Association met in the village of Sherburne. Our friends, when they applied for this meeting the preceding year, had encouragement of obtaining the Presbyterian meeting-house for its accommodation ; but when the time arrived, bigotry prevailed, and the door was bolted against us. Our friends were, therefore, driven to such an expedient as was often necessary to resort to in those days of superstition and sectarian bigotry, and prepared a barn very comfortably for our accommodation. On entering it for service, on the morning of the first day, a manuscript poem was handed me, written for the occasion, by an aged sister, Mrs. Skinner ; in which she greeted us with Christian affection, and welcomed us to the *barn ;* that, although the "Inn" afforded us no room, it was no disgrace for the followers of Him who was born in a stable, to meet for his worship in a barn. It was read to the congregation immediately before the commencement of worship, and had a thrilling and salutary effect ; for, while it enstamped the blush of shame upon the brow of bigotry and intolerance, it animated and cheered the faithful, and well prepared the heart for spiritual worship. It was ordered by the council to be published with the minutes of the proceedings. It has been published several times in our different periodicals ; and had I a copy of it, or could I distinctly remember it, I would insert it here.

By the good providence of God, all the unhallowed means resorted to by the enemies of truth, for the purpose of discommoding us, and crushing the cause they dare not openly and manfully oppose, were turned to our advantage, and served to advance the truth they designed to suppress. It was peculiarly so in this case. Their meeting-house stood unoccupied through the whole of the session ; and their conduct excited the indignation of the non-professor, and, indeed, of the liberal part of their own community. Our meeting in a barn, together with the pathetic address of our venerable sister on the occasion, excited their sympathy, and disposed many to attend and listen to what was said and done, who, otherwise, in all probability, would have paid no attention to the meeting. Our season was, therefore, a refreshing one, and brought additional numbers to our ranks.

Mr. C. G. Person had, a little previous to this, removed from Vermont into the State of New York ; and settled with a society in Greenfield, Saratoga Co., and for the first time met with the Western Association; and two others, Dr. Archelaus Green, a convert from the Baptists; a worthy man, and an old and approved preacher in that order; and Lewis Pitts, a convert from the Methodists, and a licentiate in their ministry, received letters of fellowship. Dr. Green was a useful member, and devoted the major part of the remainder of his long and active life to the ministry, as faithfully as he could, in connection with his professional avocation as a physician, and died triumphant in the faith. But Mr. Pitts, although at that time he manifested great zeal and devotion to the cause, soon passed off into another hemisphere. He was a neighbor to Doctor Beers; and by reading his books, and having free personal intercourse with the Dr., soon embraced the visionary theory of Swedenbourg; and not possessing much strength of intellect, nor having the leaven of Christian meekness and love that Dr. Beers possessed, he became cold, and indifferent, soon abandoned the ministry, and left our ranks.

It has already been observed, that the first society of Universalists in Ontario county, in which Mr. Knapp had settled, was received into fellowship. Mr. Knapp had been nearly two years settled in that county, and his labors were blessed in extending the knowledge of the truth, in forming new congregations, and organizing new societies ; and he was instructed to ask, at this session, for the establishment of a branch of the Association, which should hold an annual session in that region. It was not expected nor desired to establish an independent body, nor by any means to be considered a distinct Association ; but the distance of their location from Central New York, where the Western Association ought uniformily to hold its annual meetings, rendered it extremely difficult for many of them to attend, and the utility of those meetings in the region where they were holden, rendered it very desirable to have an annual session in that department of the vineyard, which should be pretty sure to have a large delegation from the parent Association. They therefore wished to be considered as still belonging to the Western Association, and to have their body denominated, "The Genesee Branch of the Western Association." The plan was readily and cordially approved of, and a committee appointed to meet with the preachers and delegates from societies in that section, and organize the Genesee branch Association. This was the germ of the Genesee Association; for in a few years afterwards, their growing numbers and strength rendered it proper and advisable to choose them as an independent association.

The militia law of the State of New York required a resident commissioned chaplain within the beat of each regiment. When I settled in Hamilton, Mr. Hosmer, pastor of the Baptist church in that town, held that office. In 1812, or early in 1813, he died, leaving the office of chaplain in the regiment vacant; and in the fore part of September, 1813, I received a letter from the commandant of the regiment, informing me that he had led his officers to the choice of a chaplain, and that they had unanimously cast their votes for me; and he very politely, but earnestly, requested me to accept of the office, and desired me to officiate with the regiment, on field day, that fall. On sober reflection—as it would require but little time, three days only, in each year; and as it would introduce me more intimately to the acquaintance of men of some influence in society, and thereby enable me, perhaps, to be more extensively useful in advancing the cause, which was the paramount object of all my labors—I came to the conclusion to accept the office. It will be recollected, that at this time our nation was engaged in a second war with Great Britain; and this circumstance rendered military office, even among the militia, of more importance than usual. I accordingly attended the battalion and regimental reviews, and officiated as chaplain, on parade. In the course of religious service, on one of the days, at a battalion training in the town of Madison, a petition was offered, which produced some excitement; and which was laid hold of, by the vigilant enemies of Universalism, as an evidence of the blasphemous presumption of the preachers of the order, a total disregard of divine instruction, and a vile perversion of Scripture language! The petition, in substance, was, That we might be inspired with a pure spirit of patriotic devotion—that when our liberties were menaced, our shores invaded, our towns and our cities in flames, our possessions wrested from us, and our sons and our daughters carried into captivity—we might be willing to "beat our plough-shares into swords, and our pruning-hooks into spears, and let the weak say I am strong." "There," they said, "that is your Universalist chaplain! see how he perverts scripture. The Bible says the time will come, when they shall 'beat their swords into plough-shares, and their spears into pruning-hooks'; but he prays for the reverse: that the people may beat their plough-shares into swords, and their pruning-hooks into spears!" The flame of excitement was blown by the breath of the Presbyterians, with the clergyman at their head, who were, in general, equally opposed to Universalism and the existing war with Great Britain; for they now flattered themselves that they had obtained an efficient weapon with which to crush Universalism, at least, in that place. "I was much pleased with Mr. Stacy's services," said Major M. to Col. C., "but am very sorry he made use of that expression, although it was truly appropriate." "Why, you fool," said Col. C., "don't you know that it is Bible?" "O, no," answered the Major, "the Bible says, they shall beat their swords into ploughshares, &c." "Well," said the Col., "I'll bet you a bottle of wine, that I can find the very words he made use of, in the Bible." The bet was taken; and the Col. took the bible, and turned to the third chapter of the book of Joel, and put his finger on the passage. "I'm glad I've lost the wine," said the Major; "I'll have them now." The very next Sunday, Major M. attended the Presbyterian meeting. When the morning services closed, before the preacher had time to leave the desk, he walked deliberately up the pulpit stairs—his movement excited the attention of the whole congregation, for Major M. seldom attended that meeting; it was surprising to see him there; and still more wonderful what business he could have in the desk; and their amazement created profound silence—but he walked up with as much dignity as a priest; and without speaking to the clergyman, took the Bible, and with profound solemnity, opened it, and read in a loud, clear, and distinct voice, the condemned words of the Universalist chaplain, naming the book, chapter, and verse. Such a shock upon a congregation of people, he said, he never before witnessed. The preacher looked ashamed, and hung his head; his congregation looked stupified, and left the house without uttering a word in his hearing; and the Major walked, with a triumphant air, out of the house.

This turned the scale of triumph, and converted their vile machinations into means for the promotion of truth. All this took place at my expense, without the least suspicion, on my part, of having given cause for crimination, until some weeks afterwards, when I was informed of it by Col. C.

The winter following, I received a commission, from "Our beloved Daniel D. Tompkins, Governor of our said State," and was, consequently, duly installed into office. In the summer of 1814, a detachment of militia was called for, to organize, and stand ready for actual service, for six months in the course of the year; and Col. C. was assigned to the command of a regiment of six months' militia. He, by dint of authority vested in him, assigned me to the office of chaplain, in his regiment; and notified me to stand ready for actual service, at a moment's warning; and it was in vain that I expostulated; he would receive no denial. Before the detachment was thoroughly organized, the fortress of Sackett's Harbor, on Lake Ontario, which had already received one attack from the British forces, on the opposite side of the Lake, was again menaced; and the militia, *en masse*, from all the surrounding country, were called out for its defence. This swept the whole country, within 100, or 150 miles of the fort, clean of every man enrolled in the militia, unless he procured a substitute, or stayed at home in defiance of the order; but they were encouraged with the promise of being discharged, as soon as the detached troops should reach the post; these hopes, however, proved fallacious. The detachment was organized with all possible expedition, and marched to the post; but the commanding General, from the threatening attitude of the British, upon the opposite side, and the manœuvering of the fleet upon the Lake, was panic-struck, and refused, upon any pretence whatever, to discharge a single individual, and kept the whole, mass and detached militia, on the ground, until they were relieved by the arrival of General Brown's army, from the west, late in the month of November.

I arrived at Sackett's Harbor about the 22d of September, and remained there until the troops were discharged; and it was one of the most, and I may say, with safety, *the most* disagreeable season of my whole life. The weather was extremely unpleasant; the heavens, shrouded with murky and impervious clouds, poured down torrents of rain, or drizzled their contents upon the earth in "one eternal storm," which covered the whole country as with a bed of mortar, into which the feet of our horses would sink, until they reached the solid rock; (that whole country is imbeded with an unbroken stratum of lime-stone, from six to two or three feet from the surface of the earth)—and if we could walk from one cantonment to the other, without sinking above the tops of our boots in the mud, we thought ourselves very fortunate. There were not five fair days during the whole of our two months' campaign!—add to this the sickness that prevailed, particularly among the mass militia, owing to their unpreparedness for the season, having been drawn out without a moment's warning to make preparation; their disappointment in not being discharged according to promise, and their consequent dissatisfaction and despondency, which terminated in more or less deaths almost every day. This is but a faint sketch of the scene before my eyes for two months; yet here you have a picture before you, enough to enstamp a fearful gloom upon the most buoyant and cheerful heart. There was but one Sabbath during the whole campaign, when the weather would permit of parading the regiment to hear a discourse; and then, both officers and soldiers were obliged to stand in the mud something less than knee deep. The regiment, however, was uniformily paraded after roll-call in the morning, for prayers; and I also often officiated for a regiment of mass militia which had no chaplain.

My time was very busily employed in visiting the sick, in attending at the burials, and following the poor fellows who died to Briar-hill, the place of interment; and in getting permits for such as were able to ride, to go a little way out into the country, to take the purer air, and to get a little more suitable food than the barracks afforded them; and in furnishing them with a horse for the excursion. I enjoyed an ample reward in the consciousness of being enabled, in some degree, to mitigate the sufferings of these disappointed, gloomy, and disheartened fellow-mortals. But my feelings were much more deeply affected, mortified, and chagrined, on another account, than any thing that I have yet named; and that was, to see men of the best habits, men of integrity and of the first respectability, so instantaneously metamorphosed into ruffians—totally reckless of their appearance, their language, and their demeanor. They were, in too many instances, no more like the men I had known at home, in the circle of their friends and acquaintances, and in the ordinary walks of life, than a demon of the nether regions would be like an inhabitant of the celestial sphere. Had they been strangers to me, had I never known them under other circumstances, I should actually have considered them as the dregs of the human race, as out-laws from all civilized society; but I was personally acquainted with hundreds of them, and had intimately associated with very many of them in private life, and felt myself honored by their friendship —and now to see them here, to witness their change of character, their recklessness, their want of civility, their total disregard of every moral principle, made me groan in spirit, and cry, if this be the immoral consequence of war, may the Sovereign Lord, in great mercy, save America from another rupture with any nation of the earth!

But my situation was comparatively pleasant and agreeable to that of the officers and soldiers in general. I was intimately acquainted with the commanding general, Oliver Collins, he being one of the first individuals who signed the constitution of the first Universalist society in Whitestown, in 1805. And as soon as I had reported myself to my Colonel, on my arrival at Sackett's Harbor, I made General Collins a visit. From him I learned that a mutual friend of ours resided within a mile of the encampment, and kept a public house; and I obtained permission to make that my boarding-place during the campaign. Consequently, I drew a soldier from the ranks as a servant, entered my horse in the public stable, gave it in charge to him, and took up my quarters a mile out of the encampment. My servant brought my horse to me each morning, and awaited my return to my quarters; so that I could ride to the cantonment, and from place to place, where it was difficult to walk; and when the duties of the day were performed, return to my boarding-house.

Although I could preach very little on parade, I delivered lectures frequently, in the adjacent country; and once delivered a funeral discourse for a soldier, who died two miles out in the country.

During this military career, I never once forgot the great object of my sacerdotal mission; and in all my pursuits, I ever considered that paramount to every other consideration; and, consequently, at every opportunity, published, with the best powers I possessed, the doctrine of the great salvation. While out on this campaign, I obtained a permit of absence for one week, and visited the town of Ellisburg, to which two or three families of my acquaintance had removed, from Whitestown; and spent one Sabbath with them, besides delivering several lectures, in different parts of the town. Mr. Winslow had previously visited this region, once or twice; and I believe he was the only Universalist preacher who had ever delivered a discourse in all this country.

Late in the month of November, General Brown's army marched into our quarters; and a more besmeared set of reptiles were never seen crawling out of the mud. They had marched from the Niagara frontier, through incessant rains, which covered the whole country with a bed of mortar, almost up to their knees; and their tattered and filthy garments looked more like the habiliments of beggars—much more, than like the neat uniform of regular troops; and they were completely worn out and dispirited—indeed, many had to be left by the way, being totally unable to proceed on their march. But their arrival was hailed by the most welcome cheers of the disheartened and exhausted militia, who were eager to leave this bed of mire, and scene of wretchedness. The militia were all now discharged; and those who had escaped the ravages of death, were permitted to return once more to the bosom of their families. Few, very few, who were out on this campaign, escaped sickness; and those who were sick while out, and lived through it, were, in general, the most fortunate; for the sickness which followed, was far the most malignant. My health, during the time I was at Sackett's Harbor, was good—I thought, never better; but I evidently imbibed the germ of a disease, which, in about a year afterwards, prostrated me on a bed of sickness, and brought me near the grave. This campaign commenced and closed the service of the six months' militia; for before another season opened, a treaty of peace was effected between the belligerant powers, and peace once more beamed on the United States of America.

Once more at home, in the bosom of my family, I realized the sweets of domestic life with an infinitely greater relish, after the dreary campaign from which I had just escaped, than I ever before experienced; and most devoutdly did I pray, that the peaceable intercourse of our nation with the different governments of the world might never again be interrupted. But, alas! I have lived to see our nation engaged in another war; and though far removed from my retired and peaceful abode, the alarming reports of infuriated conflicts, of "confused noise, and garments rolled in blood," of ensanguined fields, and human butchery, of the widow's wail and the orphan's hopeless tear, reach even this secluded spot on the foot-stool of God, awakening the deepest sympathies of the heart, and disturbing the evening of my days. And, oh, may the great Arbiter of nations, the Father of us all, in great mercy interpose his sovereign arm, wrest from the hands of his infatuated children the implements of death, smother their rage, soothe their temper, and, restoring them to reason, to justice, and to truth, inspire them with kindred sentiments of friendship; that they may be disposed to "Beat their swords into plough-shares, and their spears into pruning-hooks," that gentle peace may extend her olive wand "From poll to poll, and from the river to the ends of the earth."

Resuming my labors, on the field of peace, which now seemed doubly delightsome, not extending my travels to any great distance, I spent the winter cheerfully; and the season rolled pleasantly on, and brought about the time of our annual convocation, when our tribes should again go up to Jerusalem, with their yearly offerings to the Lord.

Our Association met, in June, 1815, in the town of Homer, Cortland County. (But I shall not be able to designate every place of its meeting up to the time in which I removed from the State, for the want of authentic memoranda, which I was too busy or too negligent to make.) This was peculiarly a season of congratulation and encouragement, from the circumstance that it brought together a greater number of preachers than had ever before congregated in this State.

Mr. Isaac Root, formerly a Baptist, but who had labored in the cause of God's Universal Grace successfully for several years, in New England, met with us, and gave us encouragement of taking up his abode in this country; which he did in the course of the season. Mr. Underwood, of whom I have heretofore spoken, also attended this session, and received a letter of fellowship; and Mr. Isaac Whitnall, an Englishman by birth, who had emigrated to the United States a few years before this as a Baptist preacher, had embraced the faith of a world's salvation, commenced proclaiming it with the zeal of an enthusiast, appeared also at this Association, and received a letter of fellowship. These were important acquisitions; which, while they invigorated our hopes and strengthened the band of our union, presented a more formidable front to the opposing ranks of the enemy. These accessions commanded a degree of respect from them, although unwillingly, which gave greater consequence to our labors, and obtained for us a more general attention from the mass of the community. Mr. Person, of Saratoga county, again attended, and brought with him a friend by the name of Cook, whom he recommended as a profitable laborer in the vineyard, and asked for him a testimonial of fellowship, which was also granted. Besides those already named, there were several others, of less note, who united with us at this session; and who, although ultimately of no advantage to the cause of truth, served to swell our ranks, on this occasion, to an enviable number.

Mr. Dean who had previously removed to Boston, and settled as colleague with the venerable Murray, made this Association a visit at this time. He came on a special mission. I had, some time during the previous year, received a circular letter from a committee appointed for the express purpose of soliciting subscriptions for the establishment of a theological seminary in Massachusetts. The circular stated one important provision of the proposed institution, which was quite objectionable in my estimation; and that was, the education, gratuitously, of indigent young men for the ministry; and I therefore used no influence in its favor. Mr. Dean now came authorized to lay the subject before the Western Association, and guaranty to us that whatever sum we would furnish toward carrying the object into effect, should be faithfully refunded whenever we should see fit to establish such an institution in our own State. He privately opened his business to me, inquired if I had received the circular, what success I had met with; and wanted I should second his efforts in the Association. I told him I had duly received the circular, and had met with all the success I desired—that I was perfectly willing he should lay his business before the council, but I should conscientiously oppose him. He appeared astonished at the stand I took—said that we certainly needed a better-educated ministry; and that it would render our denomination more popular, which was certainly a very important consideration. I replied that I was sensible, very sensible, we needed a better-educated ministry; I felt every day the need of a better education myself, and would exert every faculty I possessed to establish a *literary* institution, free from the shackles of sectarianism and the trammels of human creeds as possible, for the education of young men; but I would have them go alone to the school of Christ—to the holy Bible—to obtain their divinity, and not to human, theological institutions. Moreover, there was, to my mind, a very objectionable feature in the proposals of the circular, which was the gratuitous instruction of indigent young men. It laid a temptation before idle and unprincipled youngsters to make a profession for the sake of getting an education, and acquiring a living without labor—without the least sentimental regard for the cause they would espouse. It had already proved deleterious to other denominations, many instances of the truth of which had come under my own personal observation, and it would surely be so to us. As to the unpopularity of the order, I had less to fear from that circumstance than I should have from its popularity. I knew very well that we were unpopular—I had suffered enough myself to learn that fact. So was primitive Christianity unpopular, but its unpopularity was its guaranty against imposition and imposture. I wished the doctrine of Universalism to become popular only by its own intrinsic merits, and not by any external splendor that might render it pleasing to the people. These were the sentiments of my heart, at that time; and I have never had occasion to change them. We have been accused of propagating licentious doctrines—doctrines which have fostered crime, and filled our penitentiaries with convicts. This charge has led to the examination of the penitentiaries in several States; and we have honestly and justly boasted that not a single individual who had ever professed to be a Universalist could be found there; while multitudes of professors of almost every other denomination, with a full proportion of those who had been preachers among them, occupied the cells. While passing through the State prison at Auburn, I was once told by the overseer who conducted me, that he had thirteen preachers confined there under his tuition; but there was not a Universalist, either preacher or layman, in the prison. But, once let the denomination dazzle with the splendor of this world, let it hold out inducements to the unprincipled to enter its ranks for the sake of its popular applause, the indulgence of an indolent and lazy habit, or the acquisition of wealth without industry, and we should no longer be able to boast exemption from legal conviction, nor of that tranquillity which has hitherto distinguished us; but crime would destroy the peace of our church, and disorder and anarchy would sever the cord of affection that now binds us in one celestial brotherhood. Mr. Dean finally said, if I was resolved to oppose him, he would not introduce the subject into the council; and consequently did not.

At this Association, Mr. Jones, Mr. Underwood, and myself were appointed delegates to attend the Genesee branch Association, which was to hold its session in the town of Benton, on the 4th Wednesday and Thursday in August; and through the blessings of God, we were all enabled to fulfil our mission. We found the cause prospering under the faithful labors of Mr. Knapp, with the trifling assistance he received from Messrs. Billinghurst, Upson, and Parker, and the casual visits of some other preachers. The session was well attended by preachers and delegates, and a large congregation attended religious worship in a barn; and both preachers and people were encouraged and strengthened thereby in their race. I remained some two weeks or more in that country, and preached in Gorham, Canandaigua, Victor, and Pittsford; and on my way home delivered a lecture in Auburn, another in Camillus, and preached a Sunday in the village of Nine-mile Creek, in Marcellus. Auburn, which now takes rank, in point of magnificence and population, with the most splendid inland cities, with its hundreds of merchants, its elegant mansions, its numerous and splendid churches, and other public buildings, and with one of the most numerous Universalist societies in the State, possessing a large and commodious meeting-house, was then but an indifferent hamlet, affording but two or three families who dared to manifest any sympathy for the doctrine of Unlimited Grace. A small school-house was the only building into which a preacher of our faith could be admitted, to speak of the good things of the kingdom of God.

For the whole of this season, after the opening of spring, my health and spirits had been on the decline; and during this tour, especially, I had experienced a lassitude, an unaccountable stupor, dulness of spirit, and drowsiness, that marred my enjoyment, and rendered it almost impossible for me to arouse up and acquire spirit enough to address a congregation. I however completed my intended tour; but when I had delivered my last discourse on Sunday, at Nine-mile Creek, such was my solicitude to reach home, that, notwithstanding the heavens looked threatening with portentous, black, and rolling clouds in the western hemisphere, I refused to listen to the reiterated entreaties, persuasions, and expostulations of friends, to remain over night, but called for my horse, determined to ride ten or twelve miles that night, that I might, without severe labor, reach home the next day. I had not proceeded over four miles before the rain broke upon me in torrents, and before I could reach a public-house, I was completely drenched to the skin on every part of my body. I put up for the night, dried and refreshed myself, and retired to bed; but not to rest, for, in addition to the racking pains which were fast gathering upon this frail tenement, the *rats* were troublesome companions, often disturbing my broken slumbers. In the morning I found they laid siege to my possessions, had actually gnawed through my coat-pocket, and made some incisions upon my pocket-book.

I arose from my bed in the morning, racked with excruciating pains through my whole frame, even to the extremity of every limb. But what should I do? I could not think of remaining there to be sick; and it did not appear possible for me to mount my horse, or ride a step if I were on his back. I sat for a few moments in deep and melancholy thought. I then arose, saying, "This will not do—I must reach home—Landlord, give me a glass of brandy." I drank it, and it soothed my pain. I then buttoned my overcoat tight around me, mounted my horse and rode thirteen miles. When I had accomplished this, I could sit on my horse no longer. I stopped, drank another glass of brandy, fed my horse, and tried to eat some breakfast. But, alas! a trifle—an insignificant mite—was all that I could eat or did eat, until I entered my own dwelling. But I persevered, soothing my pains with brandy when I could bear them no longer; and, on that dreary day, I rode more than sixty miles, reaching my own residence between ten and eleven o'clock in the evening. In three days from that time, I was entirely helpless, and had to be lifted by others from my bed. More than forty days, I lay prostrated under what the physicians called a "A lake bilious fever." The germ of the disease had, undoubtedly, been taking root in my frame from the time of my campaign at Sackett's Harbor; and the drenching rain to which I exposed myself gave it a thrifty and fearful growth. About three weeks of the time I was somewhat deranged, although I have some indistinct recollection of particular events. But, although my case was for weeks considered hopeless, my faith was not in the least degree shaken, but remained firm and abiding when I was capable of realizing my situation.

An incident occurred, for the knowledge of which I am wholly indebted to my wife. The physicians—two of whom were punctual in their visits two or three times each day during my sickness—strictly prohibited any conversation with me on the subject of my faith, or any other exciting subject. I was quite inclined, (I was told,) while in an unconscious state, to be muttering something to myself, generally unintelligible, but sometimes a word or two could be understood. One day a very kind neighboring woman, who had watched over me much, and with much tenderness, was sitting by my bed-side, and caught a word which led her to say to my wife, "That man is concerned about his soul." The woman was a rigid Calvinistic Presbyterian; and my wife was very unwilling to have such a report circulated, unless there was real ground for it. She therefore came and sat down by me, and spoke calmly to me until she thought I was fully awake, and as intelligent as I could be under the disease, and then asked me if I felt any concern about my future state. She said I looked around, and seeing Mrs. B. sitting near the bed, addressed myself directly to her, and spoke for several minutes with greater strength than I had done since I had been sick, and in such a manner as led the woman to say, "O, no; he has no concern about the salvation of his soul—his faith is not shaken."

My sickness produced considerable excitement, especially among the Partialists; and gave rise to many uncharitable remarks, and some slanderous reports. A near neighbor to me started from home one morning, and, after riding sixteen or eighteen miles, stopped to feed his horse at a public house in the town of Nelson. While there, he heard one man ask another, "Have you heard that Mr. Stacy is dead?" "No," said the other, "is it so?" "Yes." "Well, how did his faith hold out?" "O, he renounced his doctrine, and died in despair!" My neighbor inquired, "How came you by that intelligence?" He replied, "By a man who has just arrived from Hamilton—no doubt it is correct." "Well," replied my neighbor, "I know it is false—every word of it. I am a near neighbor to Mr. Stacy, and saw him this morning. He is very sick, but we begin to have hopes that he will recover; and, as to his having renounced his doctrine, it is as false as the report of his death. I presume that he has never given occasion to any person to suspect, that a shadow of doubt has ever come over his mind." He subsequently informed me, that while one of the men looked pleased, the other hung down his head and appeared disappointed; and my friend rather concluded he was sorry that the story did not prove true.

One good, pious old Presbyterian lady, after inquiring of my physician how I was, and receiving for an answer, "Very sick," with a woeful countenance and a deep pious sigh, remarked, "I think it most probable he will never recover; and it would probably be a great blessing to the world, and especially to the church of God, if the Lord should see fit to remove him out of the way." The Doctor was not a Universalist, though my particular friend, and a great enemy to sectarian bigotry; the old lady's remark excited his indignation a little, and he replied, "You need not felicitate yourself with the prospect of his death—he shan't die. I would rather lose every other patient I have than to lose him—he shan't die."

My physicians were as faithful as friends could be, as skilful as the country afforded, and employed the best means within their knowledge; but, alas! their remedies proved more painful than the disease they combated. They subdued my fever with calomel; and I was actually sensible of more acute pain from a sore mouth than from the fever I had endured; but, during a large share of the time I was prostrated, I was quite insensible to pain. Every tooth in my head was loosened, and they have never been firm since. For weeks after I was able to walk about the house, and even to ride out, I was compelled to hold a napkin to my mouth to absorb the water that constantly issued from it; and, when it eventually healed, a tendon was so contracted on one side of my mouth, that I could scarcely introduce my little finger between my teeth. "There," said a kind Presbyterian friend, "if the Lord has not killed Stacy, he has shut his mouth—he can never preach again." "Well," repled a Universalist, "he has left him a head and hands—he can write, and perhaps do as much good by writing as he could by preaching." But, by the use of proper remedies and exercise, I became able to talk moderately though indistinctly; yet I did not soon acquire the fluency and ease of articulation I previously possessed. Nevertheless, I slowly gained strength, so that before the middle of January following I commenced holding meetings.

My recovery was extremely slow, having little or no appetite for food; and, during the whole winter, it required the utmost exertions of my strength to harness my horse and drive him. It was suggested that a journey might be beneficial. Arrangements were accordingly made, and about the middle of January, I left home with my wife for a visit to my native land; but in about two days the snow left us, or rather we left the snow, and struck upon the bare *terra firma*. This induced us to diverge from our direct course, and make a visit at Brother Person's, in Greenfield. Here we waited for snow some two weeks; but the heavens continued serene, the stars, on each returning evening, twinkled with unusual brightness, not a cloud overcast the azure vault, nor a flake of snow fell to relieve our anxious feelings. After waiting until the season had so far advanced as to render it hazardous to proceed any farther from home with my cutter, even if sufficient depth of snow should fall, I sold it, purchased a wagon and returned again to my family. But, notwithstanding the feebleness of my health, I was enabled to deliver two discourses while in Greenfield, and one in Otsego on my roturn home.

My health was in no degree improved by my journey, but, on the whole, I was not as well. I felt my strength declining on my return home, and could obtain no nostrum that seemed to have any restorative tendency. I met with the society but two Sabbaths after my return, before I was seized most violently with the ague and fever. I was wholly unacquainted with the complaint,and under the first paroxysm I verily thought I was dying, or, at least, must be on the verge of dissolution. I talked with my wife on the subject, gave her the best counsel I could, particularly in regard to our infant family, and made up my mind that I should soon try the realities of my faith. I sat for hours and shook like an aspen leaf in the blast of a hurricane, incapable of realizing the least warmth from fire, or all the clothing that could be applied; and then lay as much longer, burning over a fever as hot, it appeared to me, as Nebuchadnezzar's furnace; when the perspiration broke forth in torrents more nauseous than the fumes of Gehenna! Surely, this was tremendous—beyond any thing, as I supposed, that any mortal being had ever before experienced; and what the result would be, short of death, I could not divine. I had so far recovered from the last stage of this strange phenomenon, as to feel tolerably comfortable, and sit in a chair, when a special friend made me a visit. He inquired about my health, and I informed him that my last hour was evidently drawing nigh, and described the symptoms of my disease, the extraordinay manner in which I had been treated under it, &c. But, to my utter astonishment, instead of a gloomy countenance, and a sympathy suffusing his face with tears, he broke out into a most hearty laugh, and exclaimed, "I'm glad of that—now you'll get well. It is the ague and fever that has been hanging about you, which has kept you down so long—you'll have another fit to-morrow or next day." And sure enough I did; and continued to have this loathsome and discouraging disease, having fits every or every alternate day; when I had four regular fits, passing through the different stages of shaking, fever, and sweating, in forty eight hours; until I was reduced to a mere skeleton, with just strength enough to totter about the house.

Mr. Kneeland, of whom I have already spoken, came into the country that spring, (1816,) and settled with the society in New Hartford; and in the latter part of May made me a visit, remaining a week or more in the town, and preaching several times. My ague-fits had so far subsided, that I concluded that I could get to the Association with his assistance. It met this year, in Cooperstown, forty miles from me. I had never missed a session; and, although I was incapable of taking an active part in the council, or the devotional exercises of the occasion, I felt, nevertheless, a strong desire to be present. He, therefore, took charge of my team, helped me in and out of the carriage, and by taking two days to accomplish a journey of forty miles, we safely reached the place. A very respectable council, both of preachers and lay-delegates, were in attendance, and a large congregation assembled in the Episcopalian church, which was obtained for our accommodation. This was an unparalleled cold season. The Association was invariably holden on the first Wednesday and Thursday in June; and on both days of its session this year, snow fell almost with the violence of a wintry storm, so that, on Friday morning, the snow lay from one to three inches deep over the whole face of the country, presenting the appearance of a winter morning. Although I had reached the place of meeting, I was only able to attend the session of the council, or the exercises of public worship, about half of the time, and the other half sat shivering over a fire, or lay on a bed, burning with a fever. But it was a source of spiritual refreshing, notwithstanding: I saw the brethren—I heard their encouraging reports—I witnessed their devotions—and, although cold in the outward man, yet the inward man was warmed and invigorated; and, with the assistance of the delegates from Hamilton, I reached home without suffering any serious injury.

Col. N. Haskel, of Brookfield, an intimate acquaintance and friend, who had been in the habit, for several successive seasons, of visiting the sea shore for the benefit of his health, was again about to start on a maritine excursion, and suggested to me the probability that it would recruit my health to accompany him, kindly offering to wait upon me by the way, and assist me all in his power, if I would do so. It struck me forcibly that it might be my best course, and I readily accepted the proposition. By the latter part of June, we had all things in readiness. I took my own horse and wagon, and the Colonel rode with me, drove, and took care of the horse as far as Albany. When we had reached this place, my health had very sensibly improved, and I felt strong enough to drive my own horse; and as he desired to go down the river to the city of New York, we separated, agreeing to meet again at a particular point on the sea-board. The remainder of the journey I performed alone. I traveled through my native town, where I stopped a few days to rest and visit my parents; and then proceeded to the town of Attleboro', where Mr. R. Carrique was settled as pastor of a Universalist society. After spending a few days with him, he accompanied me to the village of Assonett, on Taunton bay, where I met Col. Haskel, who had arrived a few days before. Mr. Carrique delivered a discourse, on the great doctrine of the Gospel of Universal Grace, to the inhabitants of the village, who, I believe, had never before enjoyed such a feast, and then returned home. We remained here several days, and took some short excursions in a boat on the bay ; and, on the fourth of July, I enjoyed one of the most delicious treats I ever had, on that or any other day, with what the inhabitants called a Clam-bake. From thence, we went to New Bedford, where an incident took place, sufficiently amusing to me, and vividly illustrating the power of habit. The Colonel stopped among some relatives, but I put up with Capt. Martin—a mile from the head of the river. I was very anxious to take a ride on the bay, and the Captain very kindly offered to give me one. He was a sea-faring man, had commanded a vessel of some description for many years, but, at this time, happened to be at home. He went to the head of the river, and on his return told me he had engaged a good boat for the excursion. He said, the next morning we would take a wagon and ride down to the river, where all things would be in readiness for our voyage. The next morning I told his young man to harness my horse, and hitch him to my wagon. He did so ; but when the Captain came out to get into it, he suddenly stepped back and said, "I dare not ride in that wagon—we shall overset." "Why, sir, I have rode in it a great many hundred miles, over all kinds of roads, and have never overset once." "But," said he, "it is so narrow, we shall certainly overset before we get to the head of the river—I dare not get into it." I had a common, New York, one horse wagon ; but all I could say to him would not persuade him to get into it ; but he, having a wagon of Yankee construction, with axles of the same length as an ox-cart, would have the wagons exchanged. When we arrived at the head of the river, the boat was in readiness. It was about the size of the long-boat of an ordinary vessel, schooner rigged ; and into it the Captain jumped with great animation and hilarity—down the river we sailed—called at the village—took the Colonel on board, and out into the bay toward Nantucket, under a brisk wind, which, to use the Captain's own phrase, "careened" the boat sometimes so as to dip water ; but he was not in the least afraid that *she would overset*, nor did he apprehend the least possible danger. We remained in this place two days only; but, feeble as I was, I had to deliver one lecture in the dwelling-house of Captain Martin. From thence we went to Rochester, called on the aged Deacon Foster, brother of my old friend, Nathan Foster, of whom I have before written, who, in his old age, after serving as deacon of a Partialist church for half a century, had been "born again" into the full liberty of the Gospel of Christ, and then rejoiced exceedingly in the faith of an unlimited salvation; but his wife—poor woman—was in delirious despair, and had been in that state for many years; which was occasioned by the awful apprehension, that she and her husband had both committed the unpardonable sin, and were inevitably doomed to endless punishment. It was in vain that I talked with her. She seemed not to comprehend what I said—to realize nothing but her intense misery. She would sit the whole day, and most of the night, wringing her hands, and groaning. Oh, what indescribable wretchedness that blasphemous creed has brought upon suffering humanity! From thence, we made a short visit to Middleborough, and then went to Mr. Carrique's, in Attleborough, where the Colonel left me, and returned home. After remaining a few days with Mr. C., he accompanied me to Providence; and from thence to Newport, Rhode Island. In Newport, I found one of the most delightful situations I ever visited in all my travels. It is surrounded by the ocean, whose invigorating breath seemed to impart new life and animation to my emaciated frame. It was supplied with all the luxuries of the sea and land, and peopled with the most unaffectedly polite and hospitable class of inhabitants I ever became acquainted with, in any section of our humane country. We remained in Newport a week; and I delivered a single lecture in the Court-house to a crowded congregation, which not only filled the Court-room, but the stairway and hall, as compactly as they could stand. During our stay in the city, we could not get an opportunity to expend a cent—all our wants were anticipated and supplied, and more than supplied; and, on leaving the place, they gave us funds sufficient to defray all our expenses, from the time we left Attleborough until our return. During our visit there, I was introduced to Mr. Green, a Baptist preacher, who made a remark that I have often thought of, and which I think it would be well for all pugnacious, theological controvertists to remember. The Elder, in a very mild and friendly way, inquired about my peculiar doctrinal views, to which I readily and frankly replied; and, in return, I made similar inquiries in reference to his faith, which he as ingenuously answered; and then, instead of bolting upon me by an acrimonious condemnation of my sentiments, which was often the case with Partialist preachers, mildly and pleasantly remarked, "Well, I never had religion enough to quarrel about."

After our return to Attleborough, I remained a few days with Mr. Carrique, attended meeting one day, delivered one discourse, and then set my face once more toward the home of my family, where my anxious thoughts had often wandered. On my return, I again passed through my native town, made another short stop with my parents, and preached one Sunday in the town of Dana. I arrived at home in the fore part of the month of August, having been absent about eight weeks, with improved health, but not well. I had been afflicted, during the whole summer, with a bloating of the stomach, attended with the most excrutiating pain, which I could only mitigate with the use of opium or laudanum. Shortly after my return, I fell in company with an aged physician, of long experience, as well as celebrated skill, and requested him to examine my case, and prescribe for it, if he could help me. He complied; and, in the course of a few weeks, by the use of the means he recommended, which was one of the most simple things in nature—a tea-spoon full of pulverized mustard-seed, in a glass of wine, three times every day, I was entirely relieved from that difficulty, and enabled to dispense with my opium. In about thirteen months from the time of my first attack with the fever, I was restored to perfect soundness of health, with the exception of the effects of mercury in my system, which has troubled me, more or less, to the present time. Hence, I could again answer the question, "How do you do?" by saying, "I AM WELL."

CHAPTER XII.

Ancient treatise, "The world unmasked, or the philosopher the greatest cheat" —Publishing a book, an unfortunate enterprise—Judge Flagler's conversion—Lecture at Judge Flagler's—Judge F. commences preaching—Colchester settlement—Journey to Connecticut——Meeting in the city of Hartford—Reception at Colchester—Remarks of a friend on Sunday morning—Meetings in several towns and societies—Return through Duchess county, New York—Tour to Buffalo—Session of Genesee Branch—Calvin Morton—Anecdote of Mr. Whitnall and a Scotch-Presbyterian clergyman—Extraordinary excitement—Conference meetings—Feelings of other denominations on the subject —Presbyterians and other sects attend—Methodists unite in the meetings—Mr. M., the Congregationalist clergyman—Correspondence—Mr. M.'s course in conferences—Time of conference meetings changed—Mr. M.'s vexation and wrath—Interview with the Methodist presiding Elder—Quarterly meeting—Mr. M. attends church-meeting—Communion-Address of a Methodist sister-Mr. M. comes into a Universalist meeting, and his errand—Union meeting in the Congregational church—Mr. M.'s ecstacy and zeal—General excitement, Conference—Opposition of the Congregationalist clergy—Mr. M.'s retraction and the consequences—A dream—Water-baptism—Another dream—Mrs. Pierce—Mode of preaching and exhortation of the Methodists during the revival—Peculiar sensitiveness at an evening lecture in a remote part of the town—Church organized in Madison—Baptism of Rev. C. G. Person, in the winter season, by immersion—Result of the awakening—Numbers united to the church—Mr. Job Potter—Mr. Oliver Ackley—Increased diligence in reading the Scriptures—Presentation of texts—Inspiration.

I need not inform my acquaintances that I was never a good financier, for they have had too many opportunities of demonstrating the fact, to be ignorant of it. Often, very often, my zeal for the advancement of the cause led me headlong into expenses, which drew the last cent from my scanty purse, and left me in debt. In an early day, such debts were incurred by publishing the minutes of our Association. But the worst dilemma of tho kind—the most distressing to my family, and the most trying to my conscience—I must, as a faithful historian, record, however repugnant to my feelings.

Some few years after my settlement in the State of New York, I found, in the hands of a friend who had recently emigrated from Massachusetts, an ancient treatise on the doctrine of the final restitution, entitled, "The world unmasked, or the philosopher the greatest cheat, in twenty four dialogues; to which is added, the state of souls separated from their bodies," &c.; in two volumes. The first volume contained the dialogues; the second, the dissertation on the state of souls, &c., in a series of familiar letters to a friend. The work was originally written in French; and the volumes which I found were printed in London, in 1743; being the second English edition, and translated from the second edition, in French. The antiquity of the work excited my curiosity. I purchased it, and read it with much greater satisfaction than I anticipated, when I first took it into my hands; especially the second volume, which treated upon the doctrine of the universal purification and salvation of all souls. This volume I circulated as far as I had opportunity; and it produced a valuable effect, not only by the correctness of the sentiment, the soundness of the argument, and the brilliancy of the illustrations of the great doctrine of the final Restitution, but by showing that Universalism was not a "New-fangled scheme." It presented the fact, that it had been embraced and ably advocated as a distinct theory for a period of more than a hundred years prior to that age, even in a land where superstition, bigotry, and Popish intolerance vindictively resisted its onward progress. As books on the doctrine of Universalism were exceedingly scarce, I was repeatedly and earnestly solicited to get the second volume reprinted. After a partial recovery from my long sickness, my friends, no doubt from the best motives, redoubled their importunities, urging its publication by two important considerations: First, to advance the cause of divine truth; and, second, to repair the misfortune and attendant expenses of my sickness by the anticipated profits arising from its publication, which, they entertained no doubt, would meet with a ready and extensive sale. At the same time, a printer who was a very partial friend to me, and was publishing a weekly newspaper in the village of Cooperstown, voluntarily offered, if I would furnish the paper, to do the printing, and not call on me for any remuneration, until such time as all other expenses should be liquidated, by the sale of the books; and, if that could not be effected, he would never demand any thing. Over-persuaded by such arguments and propositions, though having serious apprehensions that I was not adapted to such an enterprise, I finally agreed to make the trial. I went to another friend, who was a manufacturer of paper, contracted for a sufficient quantity to make two thousand copies, reviewed the work, added a few notes, where I thought the idea was a little obscure, wrote an advertisement and a short preface, and placed them in the hands of the printer. He immediately issued a prospectus, gave it quite an extensive circulation, and obtained ample encouragement for the work, which was offered at one dollar per copy.

But, alas! in every pecuniary speculation, I was destined to be unfortunate. When I contracted for the paper, soon after the close of the war, and amid those cold seasons which approximated the nearest to a famine that our country ever experienced; every article of produce and all kind of labor, especially mechanical labor, bore an unprecedented high price. The printer, being disappointed in help which he had engaged, was under the necessity of postponing the work one whole year beyond the time stated in the prospectus; and then a very important change had come over the face of things—money had become very scarce—produce, labor, and every thing else had fallen to a low price—and, consequently, when the books were ready for delivery, hundreds of subscribers felt the pressure of the times so hard, they refused to take their books. They complained of the price, as being too high in proportion to other things; and they considered themselves absolved from their engagement by the delay of its deliverance, and therefore justified in refusing to take the book. But there was no deliverance for me—I could not so easily discharge my liabilities. Although I never had but one thousand copies bound, yet I was involved in a debt of seven or eight hundred dollars, and had no prospect of liquidating it in any way but by the sale of the books And, to add to my embarrassment, my printer removed to Albany, established himself in business there but soon failed; was obliged to make an assignment of all his property—my account with others—to his creditors, and I was immediately called upon for payment. He wrote to me on the subject, manifested great mortification and regret, yet there remained but one alternative—to pay it. He also exerted his influence with the creditor into whose hands the account against me fell; and induced him to show me that lenity which, together with my utmost exertions, barely enabled me to escape legal prosecution. And, to satisfy the paper-maker, I gave him a mortgage on my little farm, which, however, in progress of time I was able to redeem. But the whole of this business was a source of the greatest vexation, mortification, labor, and anxiety, that I ever endured. It troubled me by day and by night. I could suffer temporal privation without repining—could endure hunger and cold, labor hard, and all the while rejoice in the spirit; but to be dunned—to have my creditors call for their just demands, call, and call again, and I nothing to satisfy the demand, wounded my spirit, and drove me almost to despair. It was a long and tedious struggle. But I employed every means that I could command—my creditors saw it—and they were unusually lenitive, and put me to no unnecessary expenses. But years rolled round before I had so far extricated myself from that burden, that I could breathe easy; and the last of that debt was never fully cancelled until I removed to Michigan. A true and faithful friend gave his note to the book-binder for me, for one hundred dollars, which he paid when due, and gave me time to pay him. I paid him some, and renewed the note several times, adding to it the interest, before I left Madison county; and continued to renew it as often as I visited that country. After removing to Michigan, I paid two hundred and forty dollars on that note, from the avails of my farm which I had sold in Columbus, canceling for ever that unfortunate debt, and removing a burden from my mind, which had oppressed it for thirty years. But this enterprise, although afflicting in the extreme, taught me a lesson that I have never forgotten, and I trust I never shall forget; and that is, never again to involve myself in another such debt by tampering in the publication of books, and incurring responsibilities with no other means to satisfy the same than the sale of books.

In the fall of 1816, having recovered my health and spirits, I resumed my ministerial labors with renewed zeal. It seemed as though I had lost time in my Master's employ; and I felt under special obligation to redeem it as soon as possible. Although I was generally engaged on the Sabbath with the society in Hamilton, and laborers had so multiplied in that country as to supply all the organized societies a portion of the time at least, yet I traveled, during the latter part of the fall and in the winter, several times over most parts of the counties of Madison, Chenango, and Otsego; and more or less in Oneida and Herkimer, delivering lectures and holding conferences in different towns and neighborhoods; and an increased interest was manifested in most places. In the town of Norwich, particularly, there was more than ordinary attention given to the preached word, and a very important conversion in one instance, at *least*, was effected. John S. Flagler, Esq., one of the judges of the court in Chenango county, and who has long since been known as an able advocate of the doctrine of unlimited grace and salvation, had been a most bigoted Calvinist, and a violent and bitter opposer of Universalism. But, from some cause, he was induced to attend the meetings, became interested, his prejudices wore away, entered earnestly into an investigation of the doctrine, trying it by the only infallible standard; found it to be a revealed truth, and embraced it with a full heart. He requested me to deliver a lecture in his house; and, in the month of April following, (1817,) I was enabled to comply with his request. He had the influence to collect a pretty numerous congregation; and, at the close of the discourse, he arose and addressed the people, with great animation and zeal, nearly as long as I had spoken, advocating the great principles of the doctrine, illustrating its moral influence, and urging the importance of an examination into its merits and claims. After the congregation had retired, he said to me, "Brother Stacy, not three years ago," (he was living in a house probably about three years old,) "not three years ago, I said that my doors were open, and my house free to hold meetings in for any denomination, except Universalists; but they should never darken my doors: now God, in his providence, has so ordered it that you are the first preacher who has ever holden a meeting in my house." Immediately after that, Judge Flagler appointed conference meetings in his own house, and in different places in the neighborhood, in which he uniformly took the lead. His meetings soon began to excite quite an interest, and he extended them to a greater distance, discoursing more freely and expansively until he got to preaching in good earnest; and, if my memory is not too treacherous, he received a letter of fellowship within two years as a preacher of that "faith which he once destroyed."

There was a large and thrifty neighborhood in the town of Hamilton, settled principally with emigrants from Colchester, in Connecticut; so much so that it received the cognomen of Colchester. A large majority of these people became early attendants on the Universalist meetings. They "Heard the word with all readiness of mind, and searched the Scriptures daily, to see whether these things were so," consequently embraced the doctrine, and constituted a large and valuable portion of the Universalist society. They were an affectionate, friendly, social people, and often made visits to, and received visits from, their native land. And whenever their friends from Connecticut made them visits, they were very sure to induce them to attend religious service with them. By that means, in the course of the twelve years that I had resided in Hamilton, a very considerable number of converts had been made of persons who resided in old Colchester; and they had importuned me to make them a visit, and introduce this strange doctrine into that "land of steady habits." Several letters had passed between us on the subject. I had referred them to preachers much nearer them, and of far superior talents, but to no purpose; they had never heard any one but myself preach the doctrine of Universal Salvation, and hardly believed any other person could preach it. I eventually came to the conclusion, notwithstanding the distance was over three hundred miles, and, in a manner, in the vicinity of older and abler preachers, that it was possible the Lord had a work for me to do, even in Connecticut; and I would therefore "Take up my cross and follow" on. I wrote to them, and made an appointment. Consequently, after the session of our Association, which met this year, (1817,) in Marcellus, I arranged my concerns for the tour, and started on my mission.

On my way, I called and spent one Sunday with Mr. Flagg, who was then preaching to the society in Hudson, and received from him a letter of introduction to a gentleman in Hartford. I arrived at Hartford about noon on Friday; and, on presenting my letter, was requested to give them a discourse. I informed the friend of my engagement in Colchester on the next Sabbath, but if he could get a congregation that evening, I would cheerfully give them a discourse. He said there was sufficient time, he would send a messenger to a few friends out of the city, notify a few more in the city, and then, by ringing the bell, there would be a good congregation at early candle-lighting. They held the meeting in what they called the South Presbyterian meeting-house. In the afternoon I walked with him through the city, and was introduced to a few friends. No Universalist society had ever been organized in Hartford, although they had had occasional preaching from the days of Winchester, who finished his valuable life in that city; and there were quite a number of believers in and about it. In due season the bell rang, we repaired to the church where a numerous congregation was in waiting, and I very gladly delivered my message. Early the next morning I proceeded on my way. But, on my return, I was not a little amused to hear the remarks which had been made about me and my discourse, by those who had heard it.

There were not probably twenty persons, in the congregation of several hundred, who had any previous knowledge of my sentiments. I delivered a pointedly doctrinal discourse, as was my general custom in those days, but did not distinctly call it Universalism. My congregation was a mixture of all sects; and they all claimed the discourse as the annunciation of their own doctrine, and me as a preacher of their own order. The Presbyterians were confident I could be nothing else but a Presbyterian, the Methodists knew the doctrine was genuine Methodism, the Baptists felt certain I was a Baptist preacher, and the Universalists, whether they had any previous knowledge of my sentiments or not, were well satisfied with the discourse. My friend, who was rather humorous, had made himself some sport with it, and wanted very much that I should deliver another discourse; but my time would not allow of it. I told him to tell the people that names were indifferent things with me; if they liked the discourse they were welcome to baptize it by the name which best pleased them; all I would ask was for them to practice its moral teachings.

I arrived at the house of the friend with whom I had corresponded in Colchester on Saturday afternoon; and it relieved his mind of great solicitude. He had given extensive publicity to the appointment, not only in Colchester but in the adjacent towns, which had created considerable excitement, and he gave himself some uneasiness lest providential hindrance should disappoint their expectations. No meeting-house could be obtained for the Sabbath, but he had appointed the meeting in a large dwelling-house, which would accommodate double the number of people that could find room in any school-house in all the country. Sunday morning opened fair—the second Sunday in July—the sun shone with brilliancy, and nature, clothed in her richest summer livery, inspired cheerfulness and thanksgiving to the great Author of our being. My friend was under great excitement—early clad himself in his Sunday habiliments, and walked the floor, impatient for the hour of meeting to arrive. At length he stopped in the middle of the floor, and turning to me said, "Such a morning as this never before dawned on old Colchester." "It is truly a very pleasant morning," I replied. "But," said he, "that is not what I mean. We have had many as bright and as pleasant mornings as this, in respect to weather, but there never was a day before when the TRUTH was to be preached in Colchester!" The to-him-tardy hours rolled along, and at length brought the time of service. We repaired to the appointed house, where a very large congregation assembled from all the surrounding towns, and filled every space in the lower part of the house; so that I had to stand as near the center as I could find a spot, and raise my voice to its utmost pitch, to enable the people in the different rooms to hear. Not a tithe of them ever heard the doctrine preached before, or even had anything about it; but they had heard that there was a preacher of some new and strange, passing strange doctrine going to hold forth that day, at the house of Capt. Pratt, in Colchester, and curiosity had drawn together this multitude, and fastened their attention during the whole exercise; and strange to relate, I met with no attack at the close of the exercise, and heard no scolding nor grumbling! This was the first discourse ever delivered in Colchester, by a Universalist.

I remained in this section long enough to preach in Colchester three Sundays, and in the intermediate days lectured in several different neighborhoods in this town, and in the towns of Hebron, Lebanon, and West Hampton; and on my return, I delivered lectures in Glastenbury and Winstead, Conn.; preached one Sunday in Amenia, Duchess Co., N. Y.; and lectured in the town of Northeast, and in the city of Hudson. But before leaving Colchester, I engaged, Providence permitting, to make them another visit in the course of the next year.

I had but a few days to remain at home with my family, before it became necessary to start on another tour of two hundred miles to the west. The "Genesee Branch" was to hold its session on the first Wednesday and Thursday in September, at Buffalo. Mr. S. R. Smith, young, ardent, zealous, and faithful, had penetrated into this country, and even as far as Chautauque county, publishing the glad tidings of the Great Salvation; and had planted the standard of God's Universal Grace in that new, but then fast settling country. In Buffalo, which was then just recovering from its conflagration and total desolation in the late war, he had collected a small band who had applied successfully for the session of the Association, and I had given encouragement of attendance; and, about the 25th of August, started on this journey. Mr. Calvin Morton, who had a few vears before this moved into the State of New York, had taken up his residence in the south part of Canandaigua, and was itinerating and preaching in that country. I called on him, and he accompanied me. In Le Roy we found

Mr. C. G. Person on his way thither; and subsequently fell in company with Mr. Root, and Mr. Whitnal—we then traveled in company to Buffalo, where we met Mr. Smith.

I may here correct a prevailing error, in regard to Mr. Morton, as well, I think, as to let it always remain uncorrected. By some unaccountable means, our brethren have obtained an idea that Mr. Morton was a Baptist preacher before he embraced Universalism; such was not the case. Mr. M. and I were natives of the same state, and from adjacent towns. He began his ministry about the same time as myself, preaching occasionally in the town of New Salem, where he married his first wife, with whom I was acquainted. He commenced a Universalist. I will not dare *affirm* that he never belonged to a Baptist church, but I am strongly impressed with a belief that he never did. For some reason he did not see fit to devote his whole time to the ministry, as I did, at that time. For some years he was out of my knowledge, and until he buried his first wife. After he lost his first wife, who was educated a Baptist, and I conclude never became a believer in his doctrine, he resumed his ministry, worked his way from Vermont, where, it appears, he had resided for some years, into this State, and eventually reached the region of my residence. He remained in this country some time, and having become acquainted with a widow lady, a good woman, whom he desired for a companion, with her consent I united their hands.

An incident occurred while on our journey to Buffalo, sufficiently amusing to occupy a brief space in these memoirs, while it illustrates the principles with which some professed preachers of the Gospel enter upon that solemn and holy vocation. A scotch Presbyterian clergyman, somewhat past the meridian of life, fell in with our company, and traveled with us the major part of one day. At every place where we stopped to refresh ourselves or animals, he also stopped, and was very sociable; made many inquiries about our doctrine, our denominational order, &c., and long before night manifested a pretty strong faith in the final holiness and happiness of the whole human family; and we began to congratulate ourselves on the accession of an able and learned divine to our ranks. He and Mr. Whitnal were on horse-back, and the rest of us rode in carriages of some sort; they, consequently, could have conversation while traveling; and toward the latter part of the day, after he had pretty well satisfied himself in regard to every other matter of our order, he inquired of Mr. Whitnal what pecuniary encouragements a man of talents would be likely to find, by entering our denomination as a preacher.

Mr. W. had become pretty well aware that he was following more for the sake of the "loaves and fishes," than for any love of the truth; and had learned that he was destitute of a situation, and was then in search of one. He answered by telling him, that if he could afford to clothe himself, furnish his own means of traveling, and bear his own expenses, and preach every day without receiving a cent for his labor, he would do for a Universalist preacher, but not without. "Ah!" said the old gentleman, "I'll not join ye then;" and soon left our company.

During this tour, which occupied about one month, besides attending the Association in Buffalo, I held meetings in the towns of Le Roy, Bloomfield, Riga, Pittsford, Penfield, Ontario, Bristol, and Manchester, besides attending two funerals, one in Pittsford and the other in Manchester.

This and the following year, (1817–'18,) were remarkable for one of the most extraordinary movements ever known among Universalists, in Central New York, or perhaps in the United States of America, or even in the known world. From our earliest organization in Hamilton, we had been in the habit of holding social evening conferences, in the fall and winter, when the evenings were of sufficient length, for singing, prayer, and exhortation, and for religious discussion. At times we adopted the practice of giving out, at the close of the meeting, a passage of Scripture for examination at the next meeting; and, at other times, let each or any individual introduce such passage as struck his mind at the time. These meetings proved vastly profitable, by enlightening the minds of inquirers, confirming the wavering, strengthening believers, and enlivening and exhilarating all. They were generally well attended by Universalists, and not unfrequently engaged the attention of non-professors, and sometimes even of opposers. They were generally held at the center of the town, or in the neighborhood of my own residence, one mile from the center. In the fall of 1817, as usual, our conferences were commenced. No unusual excitement was at first manifested, and no uncommon exertions made to induce people to attend. But in the course of a few weeks an unusual interest seemed to prevail, large numbers flocked in, and a greater freedom of speech was abundantly manifest. Requests were frequently made for meetings of the kind to be held in other parts of the town. Soon the report became circulated, to the astonishment of the other sects, that there was a revival of religion among the Universalists! Such a thing had been confidently denied, by the professedly religious world, as ever having taken place, and as confidently pronounced impossible, under the preaching of that doctrine. Curiosity, therefore, if nothing else, prompted people of other sects to come in and see what was being done; and the Methodists soon caught the true spirit of the meeting, and joined, heart and hand, in the exercises.

They lost all the obnoxious points in their sectarian creed; no terrors, no thunderings of Almighty wrath, no flashings of hell-flames, nor groans of hopeless despair from the dark regions of the damned, were heard, either in their exhortations, or in their prayers or songs; but all was love, the boundless love of God to sinners, the universal atonement of Christ, the unchangeable will of God for the salvation of the whole world, the amplitude of Divine grace, &c. "The middle walls of partition" were completely broken down between us; and so pleased, edified, and animated, and so perfectly at home in our meetings were they, that they even attended our services on the Sabbath, expressed their approbation of the doctrine they heard, and many of them united in communion. Some of the Baptists came in, but were a litttle more cautious; and the Presbyterians, after a few casual calls, came *en masse*, with their clergyman at their head.

I had lived long enough in Hamilton to witness the third Presbyterian* clergyman settle there, as pastor of the church. Mr. Moulton, their present pastor, was an emigrant from Massachusetts; and, when he settled in Hamilton, promised them that he would very soon explode Universalism, and annihilate the church and society in that place; and his ostentatious bragadocia produced a correspondence between him and myself, which resulted in a more friendly course than either of his predecessors had pursued. But now he came into the conference meeting, took a dictatorial attitude, seating himself on the table, and without any invitation from those who had previously and constantly attended the meetings, assumed the head of the services; and was not so careful in withholding doctrines conflicting with Universalism, as the Methodists had been. His conduct grieved many, and highly offended our Methodist friends; and on Sunday morning, several of them came to me and re-

* The government of the church was Congregational—the doctrine Calvinism.

quested that I would appoint a conference on some other evening of the week, especially for Universalists and Methodists; hoping thereby that Mr. M. would take the hint, and not interfere with our services. I told them, I could not do it. But if they wished, I would appoint a conference on another evening in the week, though I could not be exclusive; it must be open for all who wished to attend; I therefore made the appointment, saying at the same time it was for Methodists, Universalists and everybody else who wished to attend, professor or non-professor, of all denominations, or no denomination.

It had the desired effect; for neither Mr. M., nor any of his church attended that meeting nor any subsequent meeting of the new conference. Mr. M. kept up the old conference for a short time; but the Methodists immediately abandoned it, and the Universalists and those of no sect dropped off one after another, until it entirely dwindled away; Mr. M. became vexed, and called it all the work of the devil, declared he would never attend another conference, and raved like a madman. The other conference meeting increased in interest and numbers; conferences were also held weekly in other parts of the town; and I had frequent requests to deliver lectures in different neighborhoods, all of which were attended to overflowing. The Methodists would come in crowds, and their preachers, at every possible opportunity, would cheerfully lend a helping hand, maintaining the strictest caution, in all their services, not to advance a single sentiment conflicting with the doctrine of God's universal grace. Indeed, they neither felt nor thought of opposition. Their whole theme was love; and they dwelt upon it with all the fervor that the superabounding love of God in the soul inspires. We felt, we talked, and worshiped, for almost two years, as one people. During this union season, the presiding Elder of the district, Mr. Barnes, called on me, saying he wanted to hold a quarterly meeting in Hamilton, and asked if I thought the Congregationalist meeting-house could be obtained for the occasion. I told him I thought it doubtful; but said I, "Although it will do no good for me to intercede for you, or show any favor to you on the occasion, you may still offer them the school-house where we hold our meetings for the Sabbath, which will amply accommodate their congregation; for we shall hold no separate meeting, but worship with you." He applied for the meeting-house, but, as I anticipated, was refused—"Don't give up the ship," said a bigoted old member, and they all heartily responded to the sentiment.

But a barn, in the neighborhood, was nearly empty, which was obtained for the Sunday meeting, although it was the first part of the month of March. They held their watch-meeting and previous exercises in the school-house; and the day being warm and pleasant for the season, a vast concourse assembled in the barn on Sunday to attend preaching. The whole church and society of Universalists met with them, and not one word fell from the lips of a single individual, grating to the feelings of the most fastidious of our sect. I was requested to give an exhortation after the Elder's sermon, which I did, and a pretty lengthy one, with heart and soul.

In such harmony we lived—and thus we should have lived, for aught I could see, time without measure, had not a good old pious (?) Methodist preacher, (Elder Dewey,) from a distance, come along, and "rebuked them sharply" for their temerity, and told them that they were beside themselves—they would all soon be Universalists—and shut up the bars, charging them not again to pull them down on their peril. But the poor man was a little too late; for by leaving them down as he had, a large number of his sheep had escaped from the fold, which he could neither call, nor drive back; they had found a safer fold, and richer feed which they would not leave for the scanty and unsavory fare they had heretofore tried to live upon.

But the climax of the story is not yet completed. After Mr. Moulton's conference had dwindled away, and he had entirely abandoned it, I could hear of his making very uncharitable remarks about myself, and the Methodists, our meetings, &c.; but I saw nothing of him until one Saturday previous to communion in the Universalist church. It was our practice, uniformly, to hold a preparatory meeting on Saturday before communion, which was opened by a short discourse, and then a social conference ensued, in which every member took a part, and generally, without exception, had something to say. It was early in the month of February, a cold, stormy day, and few, if any, besides members of the church were present, and not all of them were present. I commenced service in the usual form; and at the close of the first prayer, I noticed a man standing with his head leaning against the mantle, who looked like Mr. M. I felt quite surprised, having so frequently heard of his invidious expressions in reference to us, and our meetings, and kept my eye upon him until he turned around—and seeing it was the identical man, I spoke to him, and invited him to take a seat by my side. This, however, he modestly declined, and seated himself near where he stood. While proceeding with my discourse, I noticed that Mr. M.'s countenance was very expressive of emotion, and tears often gathered in his eyes. The discourse closed, and I observed, "There is now opportunity for remarks, or exhortation; and I hope that freedom of utterance may be given, and improved. Mr. M., this is a free meeting; if you have aught on your mind, any thing to say to us, I hope, sir, that you will use your liberty." He very civilly thanked me, and said he surely would. Some one called for the reading of the church platform and covenant. It was complied with, and Mr. M. gave very serious attention to it. On the first establishment of the church, the profession of faith adopted by the General Convention in New England was adopted by the church; but subsequently that had been expunged, and the short apostolic creed, "We believe that Jesus Christ is the son of God," substituted; and this, and nothing else—no more—constituted the only written creed of the church. This attracted Mr. M.'s special attention. He made several inquiries, appeared rather pleased, and seemed well satisfied with the answers given to his inquiries.

The conference was a lively one—the brethren and sisters felt a great degree of freedom, though our numbers were comparatively small, and there was no "silence," not even "for the space of half an hour," in our meeting. Mr. M. manifested quite a degree of sensibility through the whole meeting, but said no more until near night, when he arose and spoke nearly to the following effect: "Brethren"—this was a new appellation to us, when addressed by a Presbyterian, especially Mr. M., who had been so free in the use of opprobrious epithets, and it aroused feelings to the highest pitch of astonishment—"Brethren, I arise simply to say, that I am under the necessity of leaving the meeting; I have business to attend to, and it is nearly night. I have troubled you with this remark, lest any one should think I left the meeting dissatisfied. It is not so; I have been edified, and should like to stay longer, but I can not; and, brethren and sisters, we have all a duty to do for ourselves; it is our duty to worship God, and let us all see to it that we worship him acceptably." He then left the house, with tears in his eyes. Some remarks were made concerning him, but all were satisfied that some unusual work was going on in his mind; and none could divine what would be the result.

The next day was fair and pleasant for the season, the

sleighing good, and at an early hour the house was thronged—crowded to excess. It was our uniform custom to attend the communion at the close of the morning service. The bread had been broken and the elements distributed, and a hymn had been read with which to close the festival; the choir were standing with books in their hands, when a Methodist sister, who had partaken with us, having received Scripture measure, *full and shaken down*, it *ran over*, and the tongue of eloquence had to relieve the surcharged heart. She spoke of her feelings when she first removed into the town, for she had been a resident in it but a few months; of her inveterate prejudices against Universalism; of her unwillingness to settle in the midst of such an immoral, and irreligious people; of the fears of the demoralizing influence of their doctrine and example upon her family; of the extreme horror, of the thought that any member of her family should, by accident or otherwise, be induced to attend one of their meetings, and of the alarm she felt, when she first learned that one of her family had ventured into that conventicle of infidelity and profanity! But thanks be to God, she had ventured in herself, and instead of hearing profanity, and witnessing crime, she had heard the Gospel of the blessed God, the word of eternal truth, which had filled her soul; and instead of meeting a set of infidels, scoffers of religion, and despisers of holy things, she had met a band of the true followers of Christ, united alone by the cords of Divine love, and practicing its fruits in works of pure and undefiled religion; and here she had found a home, a home dearer to her soul than she had ever before found on earth. Every soul was full; and the house continued crowded; very few, whose situations were peculiarly uncomfortable, had left. Every heart was moved by the earnestness of her discourse, and the pathos of her manner; a tear of gratitude glistened in each eye, and a smile of complacency beautified each countenance. In the midst of her discourse, I noticed a movement at the door; the people near it drew back, the congregation pressed still closer together, as if to make room for others. I soon saw Mr. Moulton enter, attended by a number of the most influential members of his church—thoughts, wild, confused, heterogeneous, passed like lightning through my mind, which stretched itself beyond measure to divine the cause of their unexpected and strange adventure. "Perhaps his visit is designed as a finale to warn us for the last time, and exhort us to repentance; and if we will not take heed, to anathematize us, in the presence of those who attended him, in the name of the God of Calvinism! Well, be his message what it may, Heaven has prepared us for it, it can not deeply wound us." But when I got a fair view of his face, and called to remembrance his visit the day before, I became satisfied that his message would not be of an unfriendly character. When fairly within the door, he stopped until the woman had closed her discourse, and then addressing me, with tears flowing freely from his eyes, he said, "It is impossible for me to describe the feelings I have experienced for the last twenty-four hours"—His emotion choked his utterance, and there was not a dry eye among the hundreds that filled the house—recovering, he resumed, "I have called this the work of the devil—I have felt hard, and said many hard things against it; I have been stubborn, and struggled long against it. Forgive me, brethren, I have seen my error; God, in mercy, has shown it to me, and convinced me that this awakening, this reformation, is his work, and that these are his children; and that the children of God should meet together, they should not be divided. I have not attempted to preach today, but have been endeavoring to show my people that this is a reality, and, I trust, have in a good measure succeeded; and have obtained their consent to have a union meeting in the meeting-house this afternoon. I have called a vote in my congregation to decide the question, and all except one individual voted for it; and we will not be angry at that brother, but pray for him." He had hardly closed these remarks, when a shout, seemingly from every voice in the house, that appeared to reach the heavens, went up, of "*Glory to God in the highest.*" After a moment's pause, Mr. M. resumed, "I wish, sir, if you favor this movement of my own, that you would call a vote in your congregation, to ascertain whether they will agree to it, and come over to the meeting-house. I propose the meeting-house because it will hold all the people; whereas, the school-house will not. I do not mean for preaching, but for a social conference, for prayer, and for exhortation; and to speak of the great things that God has done for us." I replied, Br. Moulton, I have no occasion to call a vote, I vouch for every individual who attends my meeting; it is what we all have long desired, and for which we have devoutly prayed. God willing, we will meet you this afternoon.

Both congregations assembled in the meeting-house in the afternoon, with the exception of a very few of Mr. M.'s church; for he was deceived, there were three or four of his church, who were opposed to the union meeting, and did not attend it. Our meeting that afternoon was a season of spiritual devotion ; no root of bitterness was permitted to disturb the unity of our feelings, "Every plant that our heavenly Father had not planted," was at that time "plucked up." Mr. M. and myself sat side by side, in the "unity of the spirit and in the bonds of peace," while our exhortations and our prayers were manifestly influenced by the same spirit and embraced the same subjects ; and it was evidently one of the happiest seasons for both congregations that they ever enjoyed. Mr. Moulton took occasion, in the course of the afternoon, to say, "I would have no one infer, from the course I have taken, that I have changed my faith ; but I am beyond particular creeds, and am resolved to unite and worship with the children of God, wherever I can find them, irrespective of their peculiar opinions." And so he was, at that time, infinitely beyond the creeds of all limitarians ; he had followed his celestial conducter into the "waters above his loin," and was now delightfully bathing in the boundless ocean of God's Love. Oh, the bare retrospection of the scenes of that blessed day, though at so distant a period, fills my heart with emotion, and starts anew the fountain of my soul!

The news of the miraculous events of this day flew like wild fire, through the instrumentality of both friend and foe. The disaffected part of Mr. M.'s church dispatched messengers to all the neighboring clergy of the denomination, informing them of his defection, and the disorganizing step he had taken, in opening the door and inviting the enemy, in full force, in upon them! And shouts of joy and exultation, and angry and bitter execrations, came mingled upon every passing breeze. A letter of affectionate congratulation was addressed to Mr. M. and myself from an eminent and learned friend, who was then a preacher in another denomination ; and it seemed, for the moment, that all the walls which separated the different denominations tottered to their very foundations.

We enjoyed one, and only one more union meeting. The next Wednesday evening was our weekly conference at the centre of the town. We began to assemble at the school-house, as usual, but soon saw the necessity of a larger building, and resorted to the meeting-house, which was soon filled with scores, more than could find comfortable seats. The Baptists, forgetting for the moment their close communion, united with the rest; Mr. M. was yet in the spirit, and the Methodists were alive in the good work. One preacher, at least, of each denomination, and scores of laymen, and females of all denominations, lifted up their voices in praise and thanksgiving to the common Father of all, and but one spirit pervaded the whole assembly—the spirit of love to God and love to man. The joys of this blessed season amply repaid me for all the toils, the privations and sufferings I had experienced, in proclaiming the word of life to the world.

But, alas for my friend Moulton! Little did he think, in that season of transport and spiritual enjoyment, of the portentous cloud which was already gathering, and so soon to burst with its seven-fold thunders upon his devoted head. He was then sincere, honest with himself, with God and with man. He verily believed he was following the dictates of the spirit of God—and so he was; but the spirit of God, and the spirit of Calvinism, are very different things. Had he possessed the fortitude to have breasted the storm, he would soon have out-rode the tempest, into the calm and clear light of eternal TRUTH ; and no doubt would have been a zealous and faithful laborer in the unlimited field of universal philanthrophy. But alas! he had not the moral courage necessary for a soldier of the cross ; and was, therefore, driven back, by the fury of the tempest that assailed him, again into the frigid regions of Partialism ! The very day following the conference, he was called upon to attend an association of clergymen in a neighboring town, and there dealt with ; and the only satisfactory atonement he could make for his dereliction of duty, was to read a written confession of his guilt, and retraction of his crime, imputing all to the instigation of the devil, before his church on the very next Sabbath. But it proved a death-blow to Mr. M. and the church. He soon after this left the town, and wandered from place to place, never remaining long in one location, until he died.

Some of the members of the church, and many of the congregation immediately separated from that meeting, and entirely from the denomination ; and although they settled another minister after Mr. M. left them, they never recovered from the stroke, but continued to dwindle away, until there were not enough left to support preaching. And they have long since become entirely extinct as a church, and their meeting-house pulled down and removed to another part of the town ; and a Universalist meeting-house has been erected near the place where it stood.

I do not believe this to have been the time spoken of by Joel, the prophet—" When your young men shall see visions, and your old men shall dream dreams, &c., for two reasons: first, because I do not consider the events of sufficient importance to be distinctly seen by ancient prophets; and secondly, and more surely, because the inspired Peter has informed us, that was the time of the miraculous pouring out of the spirit on the day of pentecost, immediately after the ascension of our Lord. And I am ready to appeal to those who have been best acquainted with me, for the establishment of the fact, that I am not a visionary; although possessing something of an excitable temperament, yet I was never subject thereby to be thrown from the balance of reason, and brought under the superstitious influence of signs and omens, so as to be terrified with fearful forebodings, or fanatically elated with future prospects. Nevertheless, I must confess that I had dreams, immediately preceding and during the progress of the events which I have recorded, which made vivid impressions on my mind at the time—unusually so—and it so accurately received fulfilment in subsequent events, that I should violate my consciousness of duty did I not mention them.

Elihu, the Buzite, says, "For God speaketh once, yea twice, yet man perceiveth it not. In a dream, in visions of the night, when deep sleep falleth upon men, in slumberings upon the bed; then openeth he the ears of men, and sealeth instruction." But the prophet, although he has by no means forbidden the relation of dreams, has cautioned us against putting too much confidence in them. "The prophet that hath a dream, let him tell a dream; and he that hath my word, let him speak my word faithfully: what is the chaff to the wheat? saith the Lord."

I shall not, then, be considered, scripturally, superstitious if I relate a dream. And I will preface it by saying, that I was never in the habit of putting the least confidence in dreams, or relating them; and for this good reason, especially after I arrived at adult years, I could scarcely ever remember one distinctly; if I recollected any thing about them, they were a heterogeneous mass, and generally connected with previous thoughts, meditations, purposes, or business, and usually broke off abruptly, or changed into something of entirely different shape without ever coming to any regular termination. But not so with this; its commencement and conclusion were clear and distinct, and its progress not interrupted by any thing extraneous; and so vividly were the scenes impressed upon my memory, that after awaking I could hardly realize that they were not realities ; nor have I, through the subsequent changes of my life, lost a single feature of them ; but they appear as fresh before the eye of my mind now, as in the morning that I awoke from them.

Some time previous to any of the events last recorded, I dreamed of preparing fishing-tackle and going a fishing. (This was uncommon business for me ; I seldom employed an hour in angling.) I repaired to a place that I never before saw, where I was compelled to fish with a very long line from an exceeding high and bluff bank, or ridge, into a stream which ran in a deep gulf or ravine far below the surrounding shore. At the spot I was soon joined by Mr. Moulton, who also came with his fishing apparatus. We greeted each other very cordially ; no one else was present ; and we soon began our fishing operations at a very short distance from each other. I soon began to draw out fish, rather small at first ; but soon I caught one of a monstrous large size, so heavy that it required all my strength to draw him up to the spot where I stood. Mr. M. all this while had no luck, and had not caught a single fish. He had been looking rather enviously at me, while I was drawing out the small fish ; and when he saw that monster flounder upon the bank, he threw down his pole and line, and came to where I stood, and insisted upon having the great fish. We stood and argued upon it for some time ; but on my peremptory refusal to give it up to him, he became very angry, declared he would fish with me no longer, and left the place. I will leave the reader to draw his own conclusion, from the analogy of the dream with the subsequent events.

Said Joseph to his father and brethren, "Behold, I have dreamed a dream more"—and I, also, must be indulged in relating one more ; nor have I the least fear that I shall suffer such consequences, for my temerity, as that poor youth suffered from his cruel brethren.

This dream, however, may not be considered quite as singular as the foregoing, because it might, in some measure, have received its shape from immediately preceding occurrences ; still it is characteristic enough to entitle it to a place among extraordinary visions.

Quite a large number of converts under this revival desired water baptism. And as I ever considered this, as well as all other external ordinances, as a matter of conscience with the candidate rather than the administrator, I never attempted to dictate in regard to it. I was always ready to give my opinion when requested ; and ever felt it a solemn duty to throw what light I could gather on the subject from the word of inspiration ; and then exhorted each individual to act conscientiously for himself, as to the utility and importance of the ordinance, and its mode of administration. There were, in the course of these two years, some fifty or sixty who received water baptism ; and a large majority, forty or more, received it by immersion, the others by effusion or sprinkling. And previous to the dream I am about to relate, I had administered water baptism by immersion to a number of candidates. But now for the dream:

In a dream, in a vision of the night, when deep sleep was upon me, I found myself beside a stream in a well-known neighborhood in the town of Hamilton, and in the center of the first Methodist class, or society, ever organized in that town. But an appendage to the place, although it caused no marvel in my vision, was added to the reality—a Methodist meeting-house, with a very tall, square steeple porch, such as was, in ancient times, attached to one end of the meeting-houses in New England, but far the tallest I ever saw, and entirely detached from the building by about one rod; and on its top, in the ordinary place of balls above the cupola, appeared a figure or statue of a woman, in full size, standing upon a small platform. I was about to administer baptism, by immersion, to a number of candidates, who stood near me ; and a large congregation, as usual, stood around to witness the ceremony. I kneeled down to pray, with my face directly toward the meeting-house, when some person in the congregation cried out, "*She is coming!*" I opened my eyes, and behold, the steeple was inclining, very slowly, directly toward the place which I occupied. I remained upon my knees, however, until it came fully down to the ground, without any crash, or even noise, and placed what I supposed to be a statue, directly by my side ; and to my utter astonishment, instead of being a piece of human mechanism, it was a being of flesh and blood, a living woman ! As she struck the ground, she raised herself up, and addressing me, with a smile, said, "I am glad I am down." I inquired if she had received any injury by the fall. She answered, "None." I then made several inquiries of her, as to how long she had been in that situation.—Whether she had not suffered much with cold, especially in stormy weather and in winter.—How she obtained food ; &c., &c. She informed me, that she had been there several years—that her situation was rather uncomfortable in cold weather, but not insupportable—and that they raised food to her by means of a rope and pulley. But she expressed great satisfaction that she was at length relieved from the predicament she had so long been in. We had quite a long conversation; and marriage between us was proposed; but before it was consummated, the vision VANISHED!

Several years previous to this, there was a family by the name of Pierce removed into Hamilton, originally from the town of my nativity, both the man and his wife, and with whom, in my younger days, I had had some acquaintance. The woman was a very zealous Methodist, of good colloquial powers, and was esteemed by the whole denomination, within the circle of her acquaintance, as a *saint*, although she never united with the church in this place; but stood a little aloof, and rather seemed to look *down* upon them.

As the result of our former acquaintance, and the intimacy of our parents in former days, we exchanged visits; but her sectarian zeal and bigotry frequently rendered our visits unpleasant. I have often seen her face livid with passion while talking on the subject of religion, and have received from her the most severe reproofs and censures I ever received from mortal lips; and she kept entirely aloof from our meetings until long after almost every other individual of the Methodist denomination, in the country near, united with us. But after a long season, and when she saw she must be left without company if she so rigidly adhered to her prejudices, she ventured into the meeting; and when once the enchantment was broken, she became a constant attendant both at the conferences and on Sundays. She was careful, however, to say nothing on the subject of doctrine, until one Sunday, in the summer of 1818, when a number of candidates were baptized by immersion. She attended at the water, and appeared considerably affected during the ceremony; and after retiring from the water to the house of a friend, to which we also repaired, to adjust our apparel before going to church, she, in conversation with one of our sisters in the church, who remarked, "Mrs. Pierce, I believe every soul, when born into the kingdom of Christ, is born a Universalist," replied, "I believe so, too; indeed, I know it must be so, by my own experience." And from that time, henceforth, she avowed her firm belief in the ultimate holiness and happiness of all mankind; and she appeared as happy, and as much relieved from her former confinement, as did the woman who had been so long elevated upon the pinnacle of the cupola, whom I saw in my vision. She, however, never united with the church; and in the course of two or three years, the family removed some hundred or more miles to the west. But I saw her several times afterwards; and in January, 1829, I made the family a visit, and delivered a discourse in the neighborhood. I always found her strong in the faith, rejoicing in the hope of universal salvation, with a full assurance that it would bear her up in the approaching hour of mortal dissolution. And in all probability she has, ere this, tried the strength of her faith in that solemn hour.

The period to which I have alluded was by far the most extraordinary, and the events which occurred the most unaccountable of any that I ever witnessed. There were certainly no extraordinary efforts made by me, nor any other individual, to produce excitement at the commencement; nor, during the whole period, to keep it up, except what our Methodist friends had made; and theirs were of an entirely different character from their usual course, both before and after. Not a word was heard from them, at any time, about "Divine wrath"—the "vengeance of an angry God"—"sinning away the day of grace;" "probationary state"—and "no alteration after death,"—"the hopeless state of the finally impenitent;" no fearful descriptions of hell, nor appalling representations of the "great day of final judgment," escaped their lips. They were indeed, enthusiastic, and made zealous efforts to excite sympathy and produce effect upon the passions; but it was all done by the spirit of love; "The love of God to man, to a sinful and a guilty world!" "The love of Jesus"—"The great things He hath done for us," —"His groans, his sweat and blood in the garden, his condemnation, his stripes, his crown of thorns, his crucifixion, his bleeding side, his last prayer on the cross,—all, all to testify, that his love was stronger than death—to show his willingness, his fervent desire, that all should be saved, and to open up a way for the salvation of the world." Such was their theme; not an exceptionable word was heard in their sermons, their exhortations, or their prayers. And such discourses produced effect; but a very different effect from that produced in ordinary exciting operations. It produced no slavish fear, no terrific apprehensions of endless misery, no groans of despair, no delirium. But it softened the heart, melted it down into the most perfect contrition for sin; it produced a wide, expanding charity, and a sympathy that ran from heart to heart, and caused tears of love to flow, like rivers, from surcharged souls.

It was astonishing to see how easily, and how undesignedly these effects were produced. At all times, and in every place, in congregations of every description, they were visible. I had a call to deliver an evening discourse in a remote part of the town; and several of the Universalist brethren accompanied me—not a single Methodist attended the meeting. I commenced with no peculiar emotion, but rather in an unusually dull manner. I was rather fatigued, and was not so pathetic as was common in those days, during my whole discourse. The congregation was respectable, and mainly composed of young people, who, living remote from the usual place of meeting, had seldom attended. I had proceeded but a little way in my discourse, before I discovered a visible emotion among my hearers; and soon thirteen youths, of both sexes, were bathed in tears, and audibly sobbing, and remained so until the discourse closed. I then took occasion to converse with them separately; and inquired of them, Why this emotion? Whether or not they feared that God was an enemy, and about to cast them off for ever, &c. No, no,—they had not even thought of any such thing. They had not thought of hell, or future misery; but they found there was something to which they had not attained, a reality in religion which they had never before discovered, and which they had never sought for; that while God had been good, gracious, and merciful to them, they had been indifferent about religion—ungrateful for the blessings he had so bountifully bestowed—slighted his divine favors, and sinned against him. In short, they were not as they desired to be; but no such thing as fear of hell, wrath of God, or endless misery, entered their minds, until I made the inquiries. This is the substance of what each expressed, as I conversed with them; there was little or no variation in the description of their feelings to me. The effect was lasting upon their minds. Several of them afterwards united with the Universalist church, but two or three, who lived in the midst of a little Baptist community, were after that converted to Calvinism, and joined the Baptists.

Nor was this revival confined exclusively to our town; but the spirit seemed to extend, in some degree, through the whole fraternity of Universalists in Central New York, and even farther. The town of Madison shared quite largely in it. Conference meetings were holden, preaching obtained as often as possible, and converts multiplied to such an extent, and so much engagedness realized by the believers, that Mr. S. R.

Smith and myself were called to assist in the organization of a church; and on that occasion, numbers came forward and related their experience, and eight received baptism by immersion.

But probably the most extraordinary occurrence, of those ex-extraordinary times, has yet to be recorded.

In the summer of 1817, I received a letter from my beloved brother, Cornelius G. Person, a fellow-laborer in the vineyard of Christ, in Greenfield, Saratoga Co., of whom I have several times spoken in these memoirs; informing me, that after a careful and prayerful examination of the subject, he had become conscientiously convinced that it was his solemn duty to receive baptism by immersion. And as he considered all who named the name of Christ as Christians, whatever might be their distinctive sectarian opinions, he had felt no scruple about receiving the ordinance at the hand of any authorized administrator, in any branch of the Christian church. He had, therefore, offered to receive it by the hands of both Baptist and Methodist; but neither would baptize him, unless he would renounce his faith in Universal Salvation. This he had no power to do; for the evidences were so strong, that he increased in faith every year, and every day of his life; and he requested me to make him a visit, and administer the ordinance. I replied, that my engagements were such, during the summer and fall, that I could not come; but, God willing, I would make him a visit the ensuing winter, and if his faith was then strong enough, I would most cheerfully admister the ordinance. I accordingly obtained help of the Lord, and fulfilled my promise to him. I found his faith "strong in the Lord and in the power of his might;" and on the 15th of February, as cold and stormy a day as I ever experienced in that season of the year, we had a hole cut in the ice, and I baptized him "In the name of the Lord Jesus Christ," and we went to his house rejoicing. We sang a hymn, and invoked the divine blessing before going into the water; and as soon as we came out, stepped into his cutter, and drove to his house, about a mile distant, without experiencing the least inconvenience.

Had we, during the period of this excitement, entered into that regular system of proselytism uniformly practised by other denominations, we might, unquestionably, have swelled the ranks of our church to triple or quadruple the numbers who united with us; but this I never could conscientiously consent to do. I never desired one to profess a belief in God's universal grace, until he felt the vital efficacy of that faith; and I never desired one to unite with the church under a brief excitement, nor until he had arrived at years of discretion, until his judgment was matured, and he had sufficient time to examine the subject coolly and deliberately; and become understandingly and conscientiously convinced of his duty for himself. Therefore, while I gave the candidates fairly to understand that it would be grateful to my feelings, and cause of unspeakable joy to my soul, to have them come forward, I never failed to express my opinion on the importance of the step they were about to take, and caution them to do nothing precipitately. But without any extraordinary efforts on my part, or by any of the old members of the church, between sixty and seventy were added to the church in Hamilton; making the number of communicants to exceed a hundred.

Whether any lasting or permanent benefit resulted to the Universalist denomination from this extraordinary movement, I leave for others to determine; but be the result what it may, I could never accuse myself of using any unwarranted exertions to produce it, or to continue it; nor of taking undue advantage of it to swell the ranks of nominal Universalists.

That some beneficial results for a time certainly were realized, I think must be acknowledged; for from this very awakening in Hamilton, arose two faithful laborers in the vineyard of the great husbandman—Mr. Oliver Ackley and Mr. Job Potter, who, ever since, have successfully devoted their time, and talents, which are by no means of an inferior kind, to the promulgation of the blessed Gospel.

Mr. Potter, though quite a young man when I moved into the State of New York, was a prominent member of a Baptist Church, in the immediate neighborhood of my first location; but he soon became convinced of the truth of the doctrine of Universalism, and either withdrew voluntarily, or was expelled from the church.

He soon, however, became indifferent to the subject, married a wife, took up pettifogging for a livelihood, and lost all sympathy for religion, in any form. He had frequently changed his place of residence, removing from one place to another, without abiding long in any one location; and just before this awakening commenced, he had fixed his residence in the town of Hamilton. He was an early subject of the awakening—came forward at the meetings—made a most pathetic and humble acknowledgement of his back-slidings, avowed the renewal of his faith, of his religious devotion, and his determination now to persevere—made application for membership in the church, and, for the first time took a place among us. He exhorted much in our meetings, and soon began to appoint meetings for himself, in which he took the lead; and, shortly, from exhortation he began to sermonize, and to preach to the great acceptance of our friends. He is now extensively known among Universalists as a venerable father in Israel.

Mr. Ackley was quite a youth when I removed to Hamilton, and usually attended my meetings; but made no pretensions to religion until the time of this revival; he, too, was an early convert, and one of the first individuals who received baptism by immersion. He had an uncommon talent of natural eloquence, and improved it successfully in our conferences. At length he was invited and urgently requested to hold meetings abroad, in the neighboring towns, which after repeated solicitations, together with my influence, he with great modesty and manifest reluctance consented to do. And so edifying were his improvements, so confident were the people of his great usefulness as a preacher of the everlasting Gospel, that he was persuaded, eventually, to take upon himself the solemn responsibilities of an evangelist. And how well he has sustained the dignity and the sacredness of that high and holy vocation, I need not say; for he is well and extensively known to the denomination as a devoted Christian, and an able advocate for the truth, and enjoys the undivided confidence of all his acquaintances; and is greatly beloved by all who know him.

Still another benefit I delight to record, and which may probably be considered of as great vital utility as any one yet mentioned; and that is, it produced a faithful engagedness in reading, and a careful and diligent examination of the Scriptures; and this was general, among almost all classes within the compass of my field of labor. The excitement, itself, did not fully satisfy the ardent desires of its subjects. From what they saw, heard, and felt, they were led to believe there was a reality in religion; but they wanted a more thorough knowledge of the foundation on which it rested—of the source from whence this hope sprang, and their feelings proceeded. And they were carefully exhorted, at least by one, not to take up with excited feelings—with a sympathy, however fervid and pleasing, in experimental operations, as a substitute for faith, or as a foundation for religious hope; but to go to the *Bible*, and try their experience by that infallible standard. And while they paid respectful attention to the opinions of others, treating no man's religious creed with contempt; yet never to receive my word, nor that of any other fallible mortal, as truth on the subject of religion, until they had carefully tried it by the touchstone of divine revelation; to be careful to submit all creeds, and all opinions offered them, to that ordeal before putting unqualified dependence on them; and to believe that they were capable of judging for themselves, and to have the moral courage to do so. And this they did. They read, and they compared Scripture with Scripture; they were fond of consulting together, and exchanging thoughts and opinions. They wanted mine; and, probably for one whole year, I did not myself select five texts to preach upon, in the town of Hamilton. Both male and female, youthful and gray-headed, would come with their texts, and solicit me to speak from them; and frequently I had half-a-dozen on hand at one time. But I felt happy to accommodate their feelings, and turned none away; for sincerity and inquiry characterized their applications, and I served them each according to the order of application. Having assumed the solemn vocation of a teacher of religion, learned or unlearned, qualified or unqualified, I realized all the awful responsibilities of that sacred station; and therefore felt under a solemn obligation to give a reason for my faith, and to render my opinion on any passage of the inspired word, either in private or in public, whenever respectfully called upon to do so.

I know not that I ever refused discoursing upon a text handed me by any person in a kind manner, believer or unbeliver, professor or non-professor; and I have a number of times, in the course of my ministry, had texts handed me after I had commenced the services of the meeting. They were, generally, subjects which I had studied and matured my judgment upon previously; but whether I had methodically arranged them or not, I never declined to use them. And I have enjoyed some of the most happy seasons of my life, under such circumstances. The excitement was just enough to relieve me from all embarrassment, to expand and invigorate my mind, and enliven and interest my feelings; and I do not know that I ever failed to engage the profound attention of my auditory, and, at least, to satisfy myself. Let not the sceptic say that the hand of the Lord was not in this; my experience contradicts the assertion, and my soul gratefully acknowledges Divine aid. Still I claim no miracle in my behalf, no extraordinary outpouring of the Divine spirit. It is the ordinary arrangement of Divine wisdom; the inspiring influence of Divine TRUTH, firmly believed and fully appreciated, upon those intellectual powers with which God has endowed his moral offspring; and it ever has been, and ever will be, the case with the faithful and devotional servant of the divine Master. He told his disciples that they should be brought before kings and governors: "But when they shall deliver you up, take no thought how or what ye shall say; for it shall be given you in that same hour what ye shall speak."

CHAPTER XIII.

Association in 1818—Accession to the ministry—Second visit to Connecticut—Anecdote of Mr. H. Foot—City of Hudson—Universalist meeting-houses—Previous and ordinary places of worship—Prosecution for preaching in a meeting-house—Singular interview with a singular man—Interview with Esquire J———n; his experience, scepticism about miracles, and the miraculous birth of Christ; the result—Association in 1819—Rev. Tho. Gross—"Gospel Advocate"—Dr. Adams—History of the Order—Tour to Jefferson County—Conference—Sackett's Harbor—Mr. Luff—Meeting-house and Society—Tour to Northern Pennsylvania—Sheshequin—Athens—Widow of Noah Murray—Mr. Park, his widow, and family—Impostors—Esquire Streeter and David Gibson—Second visit to Pennsylvania—Third visit to Pennsylvania—Fourth visit to Pennsylvania—Elder Whipple—Session of the Genesee Branch—Hollis Sampson—Alfred Peck—Prosperity of the Cause—Conference—Organization of Chenango Association—Proposition for a State Convention—Delegates appointed—Proposition for Convention meets an unfavorable reception in Genesee Branch; also in Central Association—Change of sentiment on the subject—Establishment of a State Convention.

In 1818, if my memory serves me correctly, (but I have had no memoranda on which I can confidently depend,) our Association met in Hamilton; and if so, at least three individuals received testimonials of fellowship as preachers of the everlasting Gospel, viz: Mr. Flagler and Mr. Vanderburg, of whom I have before spoken; and Mr. Amos Crandall, who closed a short but active life in the ministry a few years afterwards, in the town of Brooklyn, Susquehanna County, Pa.

Our Zion was now beginning to "enlarge the place of her tents, and stretching forth the curtains of her habitation;" she was "lengthening her cords and strengthening her stakes, and breaking forth on the right hand and on the left;" for although several, who had had a temporary residence and location in our State, had removed to other States, our clerical band had increased to seventeen or eighteen, and societies and congregations were multiplying; and an increased interest to hear the preached word prevailed through the length and breadth of the field of our labors.

In September of this year, in accordance with my engagement, I made a second journey to Colchester, Connecticut, and spent three more Sabbaths in that town. On this tour, meetings were holden in all the places I had before visited in that section, with some additional places; and we made an excursion to a place called Rope-Ferry, in the town of Waterford, on the sea-coast, where I delivered one lecture. The cause I found progressing—the seed had not fallen on unproductive ground. A greater interest was manifested, and larger congregations generally collected than on my former visit, and loud and earnest requests were made and reiterated for lectures and meetings in other towns and neighborhoods. The distance for me to travel was so great, that the friends could not expect that I would visit them often; it would have been unreasonable to ask it; and they promised me, that they would make application to other preachers, who were much nearer to them, and would endeavor to establish stated preaching in the place; which promise, I believe, they fulfilled not long afterwards.

On this visit, an anecdote, not a little amusing, was told me, of an aged gentleman by the name of Foot. He had, from early life, been a member of the Presbyterian church in Colchester, and was now the oldest member in the society; but he appeared, notwithstanding, to be less bigoted than many others. Curiosity, or something else, prompted him, in the course of my former visit, to leave his own meeting on one Sunday and attend mine. This was a crime which could not be lightly passed over; and the old gentleman was forthwith called before the church, to answer for his offence. He pleaded, that he did not spend the Sabbath in unlawful labors, nor in a riotous manner—that he attended divine service; and he had yet got to learn that there was any command of God to confine his religious worship to one place, or with one congregation, or exclusively to hear one man preach—that he met with a civil congregation, and heard nothing in either of the discourses repugnant to the Gospel of Christ. But it was a Universalist meeting; and Universalism was a damnable heresy; there could be nothing in Universalism but what was contrary to the Gospel; there was not a word in the whole Bible in favor of it. "Why," said the old gentleman, "it is one *thing* to believe that a part of mankind will be saved, is it not?" Why, yes. "Well, it is another *thing* to believe that all will be saved, is it not?" Why, to be sure. "Well, 'charity believes *all things*,' so the Bible says; is not that in favor of Universalism?" But this subterfuge would not clear him. He had broken covenant—he had given offence; and he must make a retraction. But what should he do? He could not conscientiously say he was sorry he went to the meeting, for he actually was not; and all he could say, was, that he was very sorry that any members of the church were grieved about it. But this would not quite satisfy them; it would do, however, if he would promise he would never go again. And after parleying with them a long while, he finally consented to say he would not *go* again to hear the wicked Universalist preacher. "Will you be fully satisfied, brethren, if I say I will never *go* again to hear Mr. Stacy preach?" Yes, yes; that would give complete satisfaction; that would mend the breach; they would require nothing more. "Well, now, brethren, I want you to understand what I have promised, and *all* I have promised; and that is, that I will not *go* to hear Mr. S. preach. But if Mr. S. should come to my house and preach, I have nor promised to leave the house, not stop my ears, nor shall I do so." They saw they were caught, but made no reply, and the matter was dropped. And the old gentleman actually made calculation to have a discourse delivered in his own house, on my second visit; but it was inconvenient for me to do so, and fulfil my other engagements. I made him a short call, however, and became satisfied that he was a full believer in the doctrine.. But he was an old man; and did not wish the evening of his life disturbed by theological controversies. A year or two after this, he visited his friends in the State of New York; (he had a son, and other relatives residing in our vicinity;) and during his stay, attended my meeting every Sabbath, —whispering in my ear, at some time, "Perhaps the church will never hear of this."

On my return from Connecticut, I called at the city of Hudson, where I found Mr. David Pickering. Within two years, I believe, from the time they first had any efficient preaching of this gospel in the city of Hudson, they had formed a society, built a good meeting-house, organized a church, and Mr. Pickering was now settled as pastor. Mr. Mitchel, of the city of New York, made a visit first, I believe, and delivered a few discourses; Mr. Kneeland, previous to his settling in New Hartford, spent a short time with them; and Mr. Flagg one year. During the time of Mr. F.'s ministry, they completed their organization, and erected their house of worship, and were now sustaining preaching every Sabbath.

The meeting-house in Hudson was the second Universalist meeting-house ever erected in the State of New York. In this remark, however, as well as all of a similar character, I exclude the city. Mr. Mitchel had been preaching there for some years, had a large church, and, of course, a meeting-house; but Mr. M., for some cause known only to himself, I presume, never saw fit to join our Association, although he devoted his brilliant talents to the promulgation of the doctrine of the universal, ultimate purity and happiness of all mankind. The society in Whitestown, then more generally known as the New Hartford society, but the second society ever organized in the State of New York, in 1805, built the first meeting-house ever erected by Universalists, exclusively, in the State, in 1815, just 10 years after their organization. Previous to this, and in most cases for many years afterwards, our meetings were generally holden in dwelling-houses, school-houses, sometimes in barns, and, not unfrequently, in God's magnificent *temple*, with the verdant foliage of the forest for its ornaments. Occasionally, but rarely, we could be admitted into a meeting-house, some times peaceably, and some times amid rather disagreeable contention. The only crime for which I ever had a legal precept served upon me, was for preaching in a Presbyterian meeting-house. This took place in the town of Littlefield, Herkimer Co. After Mr. Underwood's conversion to the faith, there was a society gathered in that town, in his immediate neighborhood, and he agreed to supply them two Sabbaths in each month for one year; and one half of that time was to be supplied by exchanges with other preachers. He made arrangements for regular exchanges with Mr. Potter and myself. Their place of worship was an old building originally erected for an academy, but dilapidated, and totally unfit for such a use. Immediately in the vicinity stood a Presbyterian meeting-house, which was occupied with preaching only half the Sabbaths; and the Universalists, by calculating the amount of their property in the house, according to the original subscription, ascertained that they, of right, owned about one half of the house. The house, when built, was erected by a legally-organized Presbyterian society; but many, who were not even then Presbyterians, subscribed for its erection, and quite a respectable number of those who were then Presbyterians had now become Universalists. They laid the case before the Presbyterian society, and claimed the right of occupying the house a part of the time; and especially as the Presbyterians were unable to support preaching in it the whole of the time; but the society refused to give up the use of the house to them even for one day. The Universalists then offered to sell their property in the house to the Presbyterians; but the idea was hooted as an absurdity; as though they were invited to purchase their own property! The house was a Presbyterian house—they already owned it. They then offered to buy out the Presbyterians; but they would not sell. The Universalists then informed them that they should occupy the house on a certain day, being careful to appoint a day on which, according to ordinary arrangements, the Presbyterians had no preaching; and it happened on the day that I was to exchange with Mr. Underwood. All this I was informed of when I arrived in town. I regretted the course they had taken, and so told them. I was no warrior, and regretted very much to have any such kind of contention. They justified themselves, however, on account of right of property and privilege. They had made fair and even generous offers, but all had been refused, and their claims treated with contempt. They expected a law-suit would be the result, and they were prepared to meet it; and had taken this step because they chose rather to be defendant than plaintiff in the case. A number of the most respectable and influential inhabitants told me not to apprehend any trouble from a prosecution, as they would defend me; and they had no fears of any disturbance on the Sabbath.

On Sunday morning, while walking to church in company with several of the most reputable inhabitants in the town, having arrived within fifty or sixty rods of the house, we met a gentleman, who very civilly accosted us with, "Good morning," and with a smile, gave his hand to each of us, and turned and walked with us. I supposed, from his appearance, he was a friend who had come to attend meeting; though I did not recognize him, he evidently did me, for he called me by name. After a few common-place remarks, however, he turned to me and said, "Mr. Stacy, are you going to preach in this house today?" I replied, "I understand the meeting is appointed here." "Well," said he, "I forbid your going into the house." I then understood the object of his errand, and merely replied, "I shall go, sir, where my friends conduct me." He then turned to the others, severally, and forbade their entrance into the house. This was all done in as pleasant a manner as such an errand could be performed; and he continued to walk with us until we reached the house; here he took his stand at the door, and forbade as many as he thought necessary, I suppose, and then retired; and this was all the disturbance that we experienced that day. After services, the same gentleman came to me, and inquired how long I expected to remain in town? I told him I should remain over the next day, but did not know that I should longer. He said he wished to do a little business with me before I left; but he thought probably that would give him sufficient time. I assured him, if it would not, if he would be so good as to inform me, I would try to accommodate him with any reasonable length of time he desired. He thanked me very civilly, and bade me good-bye. On Tuesday morning, while at Mr. Underwood's, I was waited upon by an officer, who served upon me a supreme writ. They had associated my name in the writ with eight others, and company, too, that I had no reason to be ashamed of, and prosecuted us in the name of the Presbyterian society; but they served it on me only, before they discovered some defect in the writ, and destroyed that and took out another, leaving out my name, probably not wishing to travel twenty-five or thirty miles for the pleasure of reading it to me. This writ they served on the others; but alas! before it came to trial, they found that they had no authority! They had prosecuted in the name of a body which had become defunct. The society, in its first existence, was incorporated according to statute; and by neglecting to attend to the legal provisions of the statute, they had lost their corporation, and the Presbyterian society had lost its existence. This the Universalists had been careful to ascertain before they took the step they did; and therefore felt no alarm at their threats, or prosecution. They then withdrew their suit, paid up their cost, and settled with the Universalists for their right in the house; and here the matter ended.

But where have I wandered? I had started to conduct the reader home from my second visit to the "land of steady habits;" but in my wild and fanciful excursions, have carried him to Littlefield, several years afterwards, where I got a supreme writ on my back, and was well-nigh committed where my good friends had often wished me—in the penitentiary! But the only apology I am disposed to offer, is to ask his patience, and invite him to accompany me back, to a brief conclusion of my tour.

Suffice it to say, that after leaving Hudson, I spent one Sunday in Rensselaerville, where I delivered three discourses, and then returned home from my second and last visit to Connecticut.

I have traveled several times, in the course of my peregrinations, through the region of country lying between Cherry Valley and the city of Hudson, but never delivered a discourse in that region except the time above named. One or two years after this, (I have now no means of making the date certain) while traveling in company with Mr. Ackley, to attend the general convention, which met in Hudson that year, I had rather a singular interview with a singular character. Perhaps the anecdote is worthy to fill a brief space in these memoirs, as it will serve to show the diversified modes of attack we were destined to meet with from various quarters. We were riding in the town of Durham, near the middle of the day, when we were unexpectedly saluted by an old acquaintance. We had known him in the county of Chenango, and were apprised of his removal from that place, but had never become acquainted with his whereabouts until we here met with him. He pointed to his house, a few rods distant, and invited us to stop and refresh ourselves, and team; and as it was about the right season, we gratefully accepted his hospitality. As we entered his house, we were introduced, as Universalist preachers, to a Dr. ———. He was a large, corpulent, coarse-looking man, and proved as coarse and blunt in his demeanor as his physical appearance indicated. After a little conversation of a general and common character, during which he eyed me with a great deal of attention, and apparent disdain, addressing himself directly to me, he said, "Are *you a preacher?*" drawing out the last word to a lengthy and disdainful emphasis. I answered, "I sometimes have the temerity to address a congregation on the subject of religion." "Well, you don't look much like a *preacher.*" "I honor your judgment, sir," I replied. "No; a preacher should be a great pursy, big-bellied fellow, who can fill up a great armed-chair: such a *little, insignificant, diminutive* looking fellow as you are, surely don't look much like a *preacher.*" And he went on immediately to say, that he had no great reverence for preachers of any order, nor had he any faith in any of their stuff. And according to the account given of Jesus Christ, in the Bible—indeed, according to the account he gave of himself—he considered him one of the worst men that ever lived on the face of the earth. I remarked, that he had taken entirely a new position. I had met with men who disbelieved the Bible, and several who said they entertained very serious doubts that there was ever such a personage on earth as Jesus Christ; but all with whom I had before conversed, had readily admitted that the character attributed to him by his professed biographers, was good, even the most unexceptionable character they ever heard delineated; that he was the first man I ever met with, who ever charged Jesus Christ with folly or crime. Well, it was so, and he would prove it by Christ's own words; for Christ said he came not to send peace on earth, but a sword; that he came to set a man at variance with his father; and the daughter should be against her mother, and the daughter-in-law against her mother-in-law; and a man's enemies should be those of his own household. "Now," continued he, "the man who is wilfully and knowingly guilty of such conduct as this—who purposely stirs up intestine strifes, and promotes discords, must be a very bad man." I soon discovered that he was a captious fellow; and to attempt to offer an argument, or to reason formally with him, would be of little or no use. But I was very unwilling to have him go off exulting, as I presumed he had been been in a habit of doing; and after a moment's reflection, I said to him, "Sir, are you a republican?" He answered, "Yes, I am a thorough-going one." "Well, sir, I am glad of that—I thought you were." "Then, sir, you are a friend to our country, and to the civil institutions of our government; you believe we have a good government, do you not, sir?" "Yes, the best that was ever established on the face of the earth." "Well, sir, do you think the men who planned and achieved our separation from Great Britain, and established our independence, were wise and good men?" "Yes, as good men as the world ever produced." "Well, sir, I will direct you to a single individual—Washington—do you believe he was a good man?" "Yes, I consider him the best man that God ever made." "Well, sir, when Washington accepted the office of Commander-in-Chief of our revolutionary army, and resolved to conduct the country to independence, peace, and prosperity, could not he have said, with the utmost assurance, that he should thereby set the son against the father, and the father against the son, and that a man's enemies would be those of his own household? and was it not so? Not that these results were the prime object of his mission, far from it; but this would necessarily and unavoidably take place in the struggle for the revolution, and the attainment of these great and glorious results which you so highly prize." The Dr. dropped his head, and seemed to sit in deep thought for a few moments, and then, looking up, very pleasantly said, "I'm down, sir—I'm down—I give it up." By this time it became necessary to pursue our journey; we bade the eccentric Dr. and our benevolent friend farewell, and left them to their own reflections and meditations. I ever supposed that the Dr. took this rough and uncouth course to try me, and see if he could not brow-beat the "little, insignificant-looking" preacher down: but I never afterwards saw him.

I may as well here record another more interesting interview which I had with a sceptical man, but a man of more solemnity and dignity, about those days. I have in possession no means to fix the date exactly; but it was not far from this period.

A well-known and highly-esteemed friend of mine called on me one afternoon, and introduced a respectable-looking gentleman, by the cognomen of Esquire J——n, of Paris, Oneida County. He said, that Esquire J——n having a strong desire to converse with me, and being a stranger, had requested him to accompany him to my house, which he had very cheerfully complied with. I put up their horses, and they remained with me until the next morning. The Esquire introduced the conversation by frankly relating his experience. He was educated strictly, in the school of Calvinism; but very early became dissatisfied with the manifest inconsistencies and contradictions of the theory, and disgusted with the injustice, partiality, and cruelty that it ascribed to the Supreme Creator; and supposing that the Bible supported that doctrine, he had thrown it aside with disdain, as unworthy to be accredited as a revelation from the Great Parent of moral nature. He believed in a God; for he could not resist the evidences of the existence of infinite intelligence, or infinite wisdom, power, and goodness, so clearly displayed on the face of the visible creation; but Calvinism appeared to him as totally unworthy of, and actually repugnant to, every attribute of a God. He had read the Bible much; but he had read it exclusively in the light, or rather in the darkness, of Calvinism; and solely for the purpose of detecting its discrepancies, and furnishing himself with arguments against its truthfulness, and with weapons with which successfully to battle Christians; and he sought every opportunity to do so. It made no difference with him to what denominations they belonged; they were all alike fanatics, in his estimation; and nothing pleased him better than to get hold of a preacher, throw obstacles and difficulties in his way, and confound him upon his own ground; and he boasted of being able to silence any preacher, learned or unlearned, of any denomination. But a very great change had come over his feelings, a change he could not satisfactorily account for, upon his former hypothesis; and coming upon him from such a source, so unexpectedly, it had proved a theme of profound thought, of unexampled solicitude. It had caused him many sleepless nights; and having been the least acquainted with the theory of Universalism of any system of Christianity, he felt so anxious to learn something more about it, and ascertain whether it was free from the absurdities which he invariably detected in other theories, and whether it presented the character of God in a more amiable light, that he had sought this opportunity to have an interview with me.

He then proceeded to relate, circumstantially, the steps by which this extraordinary change of feeling came upon him. He was at work with a neighbor, a very honest, inoffensive man, but, as he considered, a very ignorant and very superstitious Christian. While at work, as was his wont, he took pleasure in teasing and hectoring this man on the subject of his religion, who at length put a question to him—(the Esquire did not tell me what the question was)—which he answered; but on reflection, although the answer received no rejoinder from the man, he was not well satisfied himself with the answer he had given; and it bore with such weight upon his mind, that before they separated, he acknowledged to the man that he was not satisfied with his answer to the question, and said he, "I am going to think on it more, and if I can not give you a better answer than I have given, I will acknowledge myself beat." But the more he reflected on it, the greater were the difficulties he met with; and his feelings became quite excited on the subject. He always meant to be honest with himself, and not settle down on a theory that was indefensible; he therefore formed a resolution to re-examine his whole theory—for he had one, as he thought, well digested—beginning at the foundation, and faithfully trying all its parts; and, if he found a flaw in it, a single idea which would not bear strict scrutiny in the light of reason, to reject it. He therefore began his examination: *First*, "There is a God." This was a self evident truth; all nature declared it; and this was the foundation of all truth on which all must rest. *Secondly*, "God must be a fountain of infinite intelligence, and must possess communicable attributes, and these could be nothing else than wisdom, power, and goodness; and these must be essential properties of the divine nature, and must be infinite, unlimited; he could therefore be subject to no change, nor any passion conflicting with these essential attributes." And so reasoning on, step by step, very cautiously, and, as he designed, impartially examining every inch of ground that he passed over, so as to be perfectly sure that it would bear the severest criticism, until at length a flood of light, which overwhelmed him with amazement, and with glory, burst upon his mental vision, and almost deprived him of mortal respiration. And to use his own words, "Had I been as superstitious as Saul of Tarsus, I should have been smitten to the ground as suddenly and as violently as he was." He saw that God, not only possessed communicable attributes, but that it was consistent with those attributes to make a special revelation to mankind; and he felt fully convinced that he had done it; and did it not to display his wrath, but as a means to carry into effect his designs of infinite goodness. "Why," said he, "I saw the holy city, the New Jerusalem, descend from God out of heaven; I saw it perfected, and all moral nature made holy and happy in that blessed region!" He was a new man—had new sources of thought and meditation, new feelings, and inexpressible joys. He read the Bible with different feelings, and with a different design from what he ever did before, for he began to think it was most probable that it did not contain a revelation from God. He became satisfied that it contained much truth, certainly, but there were difficulties still in his way of receiving it as an unadulterated revelation; and he had sought this interview to see if I could clear his mind from those difficulties and doubts. He firmly believed in Jesus Christ, that he was a great Prophet, and Teacher of Divine truth; but he was afraid that his biographers had interlarded the history of his life with unfounded and unreasonable fables. He could not believe in miracles; nor could he consent to the account of the miraculous birth of Christ. "Well, Esq. J—n," said I, "What is a miracle?—What do you understand by miracles?" "Why something contrary to the laws of nature; such as raising the dead, or curing diseases with a word, or a touch, &c." "And what do you mean by the laws of nature? Are they the laws by which God arranges and governs the physical universe?" "Yes, surely," said he. "Well, are you so well acquainted with those laws as to be able, in all cases, to analyze their operations, and determine what is, and what is not, in accordance with those laws?" "No," said he, "I do not profess to be." "Well then, how can you determine that your definition of the miracles of Jesus is correct? They were certainly extraordinary, uncommon, and strange works, but whether they were absolutely *contrary* to the laws of nature, remains yet to be proved. I suppose that he, who gave nature her laws, is able, at pleasure, and when it will conduce to the accomplishment of his own divine and gracious purposes, to modify and accommodate those laws to the object he designs to effect. Nor do I discover any greater power requisite in raising one from the dead, or any greater perversion of the laws of nature, than there is in causing a spire of grass to spring from the seed and grow from the ground. The only difference is, one is common to our observation; we see it performed every year, and we do not wonder at it; while the other occurs only on particular occasions, and manifestly to show that He who makes the grass grow, has power also, without violating his own laws, to raise the dead; and is able therefore to do all things; and that he is able, and will fulfil, all his mighty promises. Now, I will suppose a case, and a possible one, where a miracle would be wrought, in the view of an individual, as strange and unaccountable to him, as it would be for him or you to see one rise from the dead by the speaking of a word, which to you would excite no wonder. Take an individual from the torrid zone, where winter is never known, where the earth is covered with perpetual verdure, where blossoms succeed to fruit, and fruit to blossoms, without intermission, who shall have no possible knowledge of the geography of the earth, no acquaintance with any other clime save that within the circumference of his own sensible hemisphere, and in the dead of winter, transplant him to our cold region, and bid him look around. He sees nothing green, nothing alive; one dreary reign of desolation and death meets the widest stretch of his wondering gaze, from every quarter. The earth covered with a cold white mantle, which will forever prohibit vegetation; the streams have ceased to flow, and no water can be obtained to slake his thirst; the trees of the forest are stripped of the last vestige of foliage, and extend their naked branches to the frigid blasts of the north wind, and no signs of vegetable life appear on the face of the earth. Now tell him, that in a few weeks, this fleece of snow shall be dissolved and gone, that the earth shall put on a green carpet, and be covered with vegetation; that these trees shall put forth leaves, and blossom and bear fruit; and he would tell you that it was impossible—that it was contrary to the laws of nature. He had seen trees stripped of their leaves, but they never again put forth more, they were dead. But let him wait only a short time, and all this strange, this wonderful work is actually accomplished in his presence; a miracle, in his view, as astonishing, as incomprehensible, as it would have been to you, to havestood by the tomb of Lazarus, and heard Jesus call him from the dead! We nowhere read in the Bible, as I am aware of, that miracles are a violation of, or contrary to the laws of nature. They are truly extraordinary and wonderful occurrences, and are used only to confirm immediate Divine agency in the establishment of a special revelation from God. And surely, I can discover no more improbability in this special manifestation of Divine agency, and I see not why it requires any greater stretch of credulity to admit of it, than it does to believe in a special revelation, which you say you are convinced of."

This reasoning, if it did not convince him that the miracles of Christ might be true, stopped all further objections to the account of his ordinary miracles; but there was yet one insurmountable difficulty in his way; and he was sure, that *could not* be removed consistently with the received history of Christ; and that was, the account of his miraculous birth—this he considered an utter impossibility. No human being could ever be ushered into the present mode of existence out of the course of ordinary generation. "Well," I said, "I am strongly suspicious now, Esq. J—n, that you are 'straining at a gnat while swallowing a camel.' Permit me to ask you one question; which, I am sensible, you can and will frankly and honestly answer; do you belive there was ever a first pair of our race? I do not mean to ask whether you believe the Bible account of the creation of Adam and Eve; that would make no difference in the result. I only ask, did our race ever have a beginning? Was there ever a first pair?" "Why, certainly," said he. "Well, sir, how did the first pair come into existence? Not by ordinary generation, surely. And would it not be easier, if one thing could be easier than another with infinite Majesty, to produce a second individual in the way Christ is said to have come into our world, than to produce a first pair?" The Esquire dropped his head a few minutes, and then acknowledged that there was something new in that argument; something he had not thought of. He did not know but the account of the birth of Christ might be true after all; and he would give this subject a more careful and dispassionate examination, and from that time he never again opposed Christianity. Not many years after this he removed from the town of Paris, into the western country. But during his residence in Paris, I repeatedly called on him; and he always, while within the compass of my knowledge, attended Universalist meetings when any way convenient, and ever appeared engaged in patronizing and supporting them, and highly to enjoy his privilege.

In 1819, the Association held its annual session in Lisle, Broome county. A small society had been gathered there, principally, I believe, under the labors of Dr. A. Green. We held our meeting in a barn, and a large congregation was in attendance. At this time we received an important accession to the ministry in the person of Rev. Thomas Gross, a man past the ordinary meridian of life, and a convert from Presbyterianism. He was an educated man, and in early life had been settled as pastor of a Presbyterian church in the town of Hartford Vt.; but some years previous had removed into this vicinity, where he continued his ministry up to that time. However, God, in the dispensations of his grace, and much, I believe, through the instrumentality of Dr. Green, caused the light of Divine truth to shine into his understanding, "Giving him the light of the glory of the knowledge of God," in the universal reconciliation of all moral intelligences, through Jesus Christ our Lord; and he met with us here for the first time, and received a letter of fellowship from the council. He delivered a very excellent discourse from the words of the venerable Simeon; "Now lettest thou thy servant depart in peace according to thy word; for mine eyes have seen thy salvation"—which he very appropriately and most pathetically applied to his own case; and he did it with effect upon his audience.

He subsequently removed to Cortland village, where he for some years preached, and taught an academy. From thence he removed to Buffalo, where he started a periodical, entitled "The Gospel Advocate," which he conducted for some years; which then went into the hands of Mr. Everett, and ultimately passed into the hands of Mr. D. Skinner, and was united with the "Evangelical Magazine," of which Mr. S. was then publisher, in Utica. Mr. Gross certainly lived to an advanced age; but whether he has yet united with the great congregation of the dead, I have no means of determining; yet presume he has long since entered upon the fruition of those joys which he so ardently hoped for, and so firmly believed in, as the ultimate portion of all God's moral offspring. At this Association I also became acquainted with Dr. S. Adams, who was then in the practice of physic in the town of Lisle, but who shortly after this left, in measure, his prescriptions for physical ailments, and commenced administering the "precious balm of Gilead" to diseased moral nature; and who has ever since been known as a devoted and faithful laborer in the vineyard of Christ.

It would be impossible for me, without subjecting myself to vastly more labor and expense than the importance of the object would justify, to trace the Western Association through all its operations, to designate all the places of its meetings and record its important proceedings, up to the time when I removed from the State; nor is it by any means necessary. I have brought up the history of Universalism in the State of New York from its first budding, circumstantially enough, to the time when it became an object of some notoriety and consequence, and began to assume, in despite of all the obloquy which its enemies tried to heap upon it, a respectable standing among the Christian denominations in the country;—to where its history is more generally known, and its publication has been commenced, and will, no doubt, be prosecuted, by a far abler pen. The further historical incidents and anecdotes of the order will, therefore, be such only as are inseparably connected with my labors, and are indispensably brought in, in order to make out a faithful auto-biography of my life.

In August, 1821, I made a tour to Jefferson county. Mr. C. G. Person had removed to Ellisburgh, and Mr. Pitt Morse was preaching in the town of Henderson and vicinity. The cause of divine truth was prospering abundantly under the well directed labors of those faithful servants of the divine Master, with the occasional assistance of some others who had visited that region. A conference, or two days meeting, was holden in Henderson, which afforded ample evidence that the hand of the Lord was among them, and that their exertions and labors met with divine approbation. On this tour I delivered two discourses in Henderson, lectured in three different neighborhoods in Ellisburgh, and pursued my travels as far as Sackett's Harbor. I had not visited this place since my dreary campaign in 1814; and when I consented to visit the place, which I did with reluctance, the thought was appalling, and actually made my frame shudder; but my astonishment, on arriving at the place, was beyond anything of the kind I ever before experienced. When I left Sackett's Harbor, I bade an everlasting adieu, as I thought and intended, to one of the most filthy mudholes I ever was compelled to wallow through, covered with dilapidated barracks, smarming with ruffians, under the appellation of common soldiers; the common dwellings of the inhabitants not much better than the barracks, weather-beaten, old, and dirty in the extreme, and, with very few exceptions, the inmates equally as rough and uncivilized as the soldiers, lost to every feeling of common humanity and common courtesy, possessing nothing, scarcely, in common with the civilized world except physical formation. But the place, with all its appendages, had undergone a most thorough renovation. The mud had given way to spacious and handsomely graveled streets, with flagged side-walks, ornamented with handsome shade trees, and flowering shubbery; the filthy barracks and weather-worn buildings were replaced with handsome dwellings and splendid edifices; the spires of several churches glittered in the sunbeams, and an evident taste, and utmost neatness were manifest in the whole scenery. The former inhabitants, if any remained, were completely metamorphosed, or were succeeded by a polite, civilized, and refined people. True, there was yet, and probably always will be, while this continues to be a frontier port, a standing force of regular troops stationed here; but they had splendid brick barracks, inclosing three sides of a large square, or garden laid out with the finest taste, with neat gravel walks, adorned with the most beautiful shrubbery and cultivated in the best manner, open to the bay, where lay the shipping, and affording one of the most pleasant promenades imaginable; and both officers and soldiers not only exhibited the utmost neatness in their dress—their equipments glittering with silver brightness—but, in their manner and demeanor, the civilian and the gentleman. Here, also, I found a small Universalist, or rather Restorationist (for I choose to call things by the names their possessors best relish) society and meeting-house. Many years before this, a gentleman from Europe, (England,) by the name of Luff, if my memory serves me, settled in this place—(I think he had a partner in his work of benevolence; but the name if ever I had it, I have lost; nor will I be very positive that I have got the name of this gentleman right)—and preached the doctrine of the Final Restitution, and, at his or their own expense, built a small meeting-house. He was an acquaintance of Mr. Billinghurst; they either formed an acquaintance in their native country, or in consequence of their nationality and sympathy in religious sentiments, formed an acquaintance in the new world; and they often exchanged compliments, and sometimes visits. The meeting-house was standing in an unfinished state at the time of my campaign, and was used as a hospital. I often visited it, and found it filled, both the body of the house and the galleries, with the poor sick and dying soldiers; and almost every day followed some poor fellow to his final resting-place in the bosom of our "mother earth."

Whether Mr. L. was in the place at that time, I knew not; I heard him spoken of by some of the inhabitants, but did not see him. If he was absent then, he returned after the war, and finished his meeting-house in good style; he collected a respectable congregation, and administered to them "All the words of this life;" and on my visit to Sackett's Harbor at this time, I enjoyed the happiness of delivering an evening lecture in that house. I found Mr. L. a very pleasant and well-informed man; but a man of considerable eccentricity, and possessing very peculiar doctrinal opinions, of which he was very tenacious. Although he called himself a Restorationist, and zealously and boldly advocated the doctrine of the final holiness of all mankind, still he could not have full fellowship with our denomination, and never, to my knowledge, attended any of our Associations.

From Sackett's Harbor I went to Brownville, and Watertown, and delivered a discourse in each of those places; and another in the village of Tayburgh, on my way home.

I have traveled and labored very considerably in Northern and Western Pennsylvania. My first visit to this State was made in February, 1822. A friend of mine, residing in the town of Eaton, had relatives living in the town of Warren, Bradford county, who became extremely anxious that the doctrine should be introduced into that region, where it was scarcely known even by name, except by two or three individuals; and through his importunity in their behalf, I consented to make the tour, by his agreeing to accompany me. I had learned, some years previous, that there had been a respectable and flourishing society in existence, in the town of Sheshequin, which had formerly enjoyed the labors of Mr. Noah Murray, and subsequently of Mr. Park, both of whom were then dead; and the probability was, the society had had no preaching for a long season; I therefore made arrangements to visit them also, on my tour. I found the doctrine was entirely new to most of the people; no preacher of the order ever having visited that place. But the opposition was by no means as violent as in most new places I had visited. Indeed, it was not violent enough; those who did not believe it, seemed to pay but little attention to it; there was not opposition enough to produce any excitement, and nothing could be done to produce any permanent or lasting effect. I delivered several discourses in Warsaw, one in Pike, and one in Orwell; and on my way from thence to Sheshequin, I gave a lecture in Wysox. I lectured also in Sheshequin, and Athens, Tioga Point; and on my way home, in the town of Fabius, New York.

In Sheshequin and Athens, I had large congregations, and found some of the most repectable and influential inhabitants strong and bold in the faith. And, indeed, how should it be otherwise, when for years they had enjoyed the labors of some of our most able divines. Athens was the residence of the venerable Noah Murray, when he united with our denomination; and to which he returned after his tour, at that time, through New England, and where much of his preaching was employed, until he was called home to enter upon his higher life. He had died a few years before the time of which I speak, but his widow, and most or all the surviving members of his family, resided here, whom I had the pleasure to visit.

Mr. Murray had been instrumental in converting to the faith of Universal Grace a Baptist minister, of good talents and extensive influence, by the name of Park, who resided a neighbor to him, and who, for a season after his death, administered to these people the same "spiritual meat." But Mr. Park had, also, before my visit to the place, been called from his earthly labors. He also left a widow, and quite a numerous and highly respectable family, with whom I formed a happy acquaintance. But a curse had fallen upon that people in the shape of impostors, which had depressed their spirits and almost fatally discouraged them.

During the last sickness of Mr. Park, Squire Streeter, a young man of prepossessing appearance, and of good speaking talents, visited that place, and for a season preached with them to great acceptance. They were captivated with his eloquence, and reposed unbounded confidence in him; but alas! he sailed under false colors. He had, some years before this, received a letter of fellowship from the Association in the State of New Hampshire, I think, but had been guilty of sad misdemeanor, for which he was expelled. About the time of his expulsion he left New England, and traveled west, and keeping a little in advance of the notice of his crime, and excommunication, imposed on several societies for a season; and the last place of his resort, within the limits of my knowledge, was Sheshequin. Two or three days only before the intelligence of his character and standing reached that place, he took a sudden and unexpected leave of the people, and of Mr. Park, then on a sick bed and near his final exit; stepped aboard of a boat, and went down the Susquehanna river, leaving his friends in wonder and sad disappointment. But their amazement was of short duration; a few days explained the whole of his conduct.

Their next visit was from David Gilson, a man, also, of superior speaking talents, and who had once received a testimonial of fellowship from the Western Association; but his character became such that he retained his standing but a very short time. They received him with some caution; but he ingratiated himself into their favor by a prudent course for a short time, until he gained their confidence, and obtained some substantial pecuniary favors, when he gradually began to throw off his mask, and indulge in his old habit of intemperance,—disappointed their hopes, and left them in a complete state of discouragement. So much disheartened were they by the impositions which had been practiced upon them, that they had resolved never again to give countenance to a stranger. The widow Park said to me, "Br. Stacy, had not your name been here long before you came, you could never have got up a meeting in this place; it was your *name*, not your talents, which procured you such respectable congregations. We have been so abused and imposed upon by vile characters under the garb of the Gospel, that we had nearly resolved never again to put confidence in any man who came in that pofession, nor encourage him enough to attend meeting. But we had long heard of you; and when your name was announced, it aroused us from our despondency, and inspired hope."

The cause had flourished heretofore, in this region, under the ministry of Mr. Murray and Mr. Park; not only in Sheshequin and Athens, but in Towanda, the county seat, and in the adjacent towns; and they very much wished to see the revival of truth once more in that region. They solicited, most earnestly, another visit; and my own feeling pleaded so strongly in their behalf, that before I left them I made a promise to improve the first opportunity that a kind Providence should grant, to renew my visit and spend a longer season.

Another opportunity, however, did not occur to visit Sheshequin until a year from the June following, (1823). I was then enabled to make a second tour in that region, and spend three Sabbaths; one in Sheshequin, one in Athens, and another in Towanda; and in the intervening season, besides delivering lectures in all the above-named towns, I held meetings in

Litchfield, Burlington, Troy, Lansingburgh, Sugar Creek; and in Jackson, Tioga county; and on my way home after leaving Tioga Point, I lectured in Owego, Union, and Windsor.

My third visit was made in August, 1824. At that time I spent two Sabbaths with them, and lectured in most of the places I had visited on my former visit.

The society in Sheshequin had now thoroughly revived, had reorganized, and sent delegates with me to the Chenango Association which met this year in the town of Hopbottom, (now Brooklyn,) Susquehanna county, and by application obtained the appointment for its next session in Sheshequin.

My fourth and last visit to that interesting people was made at the time of the session of the Association, September, 1825. At that time we enjoyed an interesting and a profitable meeting. No meeting-house had been erected in the place by any denomination; but an extensive booth was prepared for the occasion, in front of the dwelling-house of Esq. Kinney, grandfather of the celebrated and lamented Mrs. J. H. Scott; and a congregation assembled more than could be accommodated in the house and this temporary apartment. A large number of preachers, for the time and that part of the country, attended the session, and among them were Mr. Potter, and a very promising young man, just entered upon the clerical profession, by the name of Doolittle, who has, from that period, successfully devoted his time and talents to the promulgation of the Gospel, and now holds a prominent position among the ablest preachers in our denomination. At this session, also, a letter of fellowship was granted to Elder Whipple, a convert from the Baptists, who also proved an active and profitable laborer in the vineyard, and who, but a short time since, closed a long and industrious life, rejoicing in the faith of Universal Salvation.

My wife accompanied me on this journey; and we visited a brother of hers, who had, a few years before this, removed from Vermont into the town of Jackson, Tioga county. Here I delivered a discourse; and on our way home, we held meetings in Union, and Binghamton, where large congregations assembled, especially in the last-mentioned place.

In the autumn of 1822, I attended the session of the Genesee Branch, which held its annual meeting in the town of Hopewell, formerly a part of Gorham, and in the vicinity of the first general meeting I ever attended in that country; and it was exceedingly gratifying to see the change which about ten years had wrought in the aspect of the cause. Societies and preachers had multiplied, and a wide-spread interest was abundantly manifest from the multitude which thronged the courts of the Lord on this occasion. One able preacher had, by emigration, been recently added to the faithful little band whose labors had already accomplished so much. Mr. Hollis Sampson, a man of sterling pulpit talents, who commenced his clerical functions in connection with the Methodist denomination, and, seceding from them, had been once settled as pastor of a Congregationalist church in Wilmington Vt., still persevering in his theological researches, and growing from "one degree of faith to another, embraced the doctrine of the final Restitution, and boldly entered on its ministry. A little before this, he had penetrated into this section of country, and fixed his residence in the town of Stafford, Genesee county, and was doing a great work in the upbuilding of the Redeemer's kingdom in this part of his heritage. Mr. Alfred Peck, who had spent some little time in my family when quite a youth, and who had, with untiring patience and perseverance, through obstacles insurmountable to ordinary minds, pursued a resolution formed when a boy, until he had become an acceptable preacher of the Great Salvation, had also taken up his residence in this country. He accompanied Mr. Sampson to the Association, and was here set apart by solemn ordination to the work of an evangelist.

On this tour, I spent one Sabbath in Le Roy, one in Pittsford, and lectured in Batavia and Stafford; and on my way home delivered one discourse in the town of Galen, on the canal, in Wayne county. It was most exhilarating to my feelings, while traveling through the Genesee country, to witness the advancement of the cause of divine truth, the increase of laborers, and springing up of societies; the engagedness manifested to hear the word and inquire after truth, where, ten or eleven years before, I had found, in a doctrinal sense at least, a howling wilderness.

The first meeting (conference) for the purpose of deliberating on the propriety and expediency of organizing another association, comprising the counties of Chenango and Broome, and the northern counties of Pennsylvania, adjacent, was holden in Norwich, Oct. 31st, 1822. It was resolved, at that meeting, that it was both expedient and necessary that such an association should be organized; and that it should be denominated *The Chenango Association of Universalists*, and should hold its first meeting in the village of Oxford, in Sept., 1823. Hitherto we had kept up a communication between the different branches of our association, and, as far as possible, with the General Convention of New England, and with sister asociations, by visiting committees, as we chose to call them, or delegates appointed from one to the other. But we were now increasing to that degree, two or more branches of the Western Association being already organized, and several more in agitation, which very soon would necessarily receive a separate existence, that I began very seriously to apprehend a great inconvenience, and, indeed, an impracticability, of keeping up any thing like a general intercourse through these temporary committees; it would require too much time, and would infringe too much upon our engagements with societies. Still an intercourse, and a regular communication from one branch of the great body to the other, was not only desirable, but appeared to me absolutely necessary, not only for mutual encouragement and support, but to maintain wholesome order and discipline in our ranks; and the thought suggested itself to my mind, that this might be most easily and successfully done by the organizing of a State Convention, composed of delegates from each Association, which should hold a yearly meeting for that purpose. No such body yet existed in our denomination. All those bodies which had yet been formed, by whatsoever name they were designated, associations or conventions; were nothing more than the simple association, or meeting of the churches or societies by delegation. I once proposed, at a session of what was called the General Convention, (though in fact it was nothing more than an ordinary association, composed of delegates from individual societies and churches,) holden in the city of Hudson, to have that body change its constitution into a convention, to be composed of delegates exclusively from associations; and prevailed on Mr. Carrique to make a motion to that effect. But it met with opposition, and the motion was withdrawn. Nevertheless, I thought that such organization would become necessary, as our borders enlarged and our associations increased in numbers; and I thought this a proper season to begin with it in our own State.

I had no idea of creating a hierarchy, of investing this body with supreme or superior prerogatives, whereby it could impose creeds or rules of discipline on churches, societies, or associations. I considered all power, under the great Head of the church, to rest originally with the people; that any number, therefore, of the people, who felt disposed to unite for mutual aid and religious improvement and worship, had the inalienable right to adopt such constitution and form of government as they considered adapted to their circumstances, as Christians—to choose their own teachers and officers, and ordain them—to change them at pleasure, and, in all cases, to deal with their own members. But, if they saw fit, for their own convenience or safety, to do these things or any part thereof by meeting in association with any other churches, through delegates chosen directly by themselves, and from their own body, they had an indisputable right so to do; though their delegates should possess no rightful authority to transfer the trust or power committed to them by the church to another body, in which the church has no direct representative. This was my view of the subject then; and it is so now. The convention which I proposed was simply designed as a center of communication, where delegates should meet together, once a year, from all the branches of the great body—bring in the joyful intelligence of the prosperity of the cause throughout all its ramifications—consult together for mutual improvement and the adoption of such general measures as might be believed would promote the best interest of Zion; and diffuse from this center, or heart, the life-blood through the proper channels, or arteries, to all the members of this ecclesiastical body. No ecclesiastical power was to be invested in it, not even the power to grant letters of fellowship, or to confer ordination; as these powers belonged originally and exclusively to the churches; and this body was too far removed from the churches to exercise, rightfully, any authority of the kind. All the power it could of right exercise was merely appellatory or advisatory. It might hear appeals from contending associations, and, as an arbitration, settle differences between preachers and associations; and it would properly give counsel, and determine as to the expediency of organizing new associations, and determine their territorial limits.

I therefore suggested to the council of the Chenango Association, at its first session, the idea of a State Convention; explained my views of the character of such a body, as well as I could, and the utility and importance of it; and it met the undivided approval of the whole council. Steps were then taken to try the feelings of the other associations on the subject, and delegates were chosen to meet, on a certain time the next season, if the other associations approved of the plan, to more fully discuss the subject, and, if thought advisable, to prepare a constitution for such a body; and the delegates to the other associations were particularly instructed to lay the subject before them at their next meeting.

Mr. Ackley was appointed delegate to the Genesee Association, which would hold its meeting next in order. But, he either did not himself fully understand the character of the body designed to be organized, or he could not make that council understand him. They obtained totally a wrong idea concerning it; construed it into an ecclesiastical hierarchy; branded me, as being the mover of it, with the epithet of Pope, and spiritual tyrant—as seeking to be lord over the heritage of God; and spurned the idea with disdain. I was appointed to lay the subject before the Western, the parent association. But the breeze, or rather *gale*, which had been raised by some of the members of the Genesee Association, and their misunderstanding of the character of the body proposed to be formed, had produced such a prejudice against it, that before I had an opportunity of introducing it before the council, I was satirically rallied upon it; and the idea was treated with ridicule and even levity by those who, in less than one year afterwards, saw the necessity of such a body I merely replied to their ridicule, that under such circumstances I would not introduce it at all, but would let the matter rest until they saw the necessity of such an organization; and I assured them that they would, ere long, see such necessity, and would then treat the subject with more seriousness: and sure enough they did. From that time it became a subject of serious reflection among the most intelligent of the denomination; and the very next year the subject was brought up in the Western Association; and those very same individuals who had treated me with ridicule because of it, the year previous, became its most zealous advocates; and it was never again abandoned until a convention was permanently established. The struggle, however, was rendered long and hard by the opposition, and even obstinacy, of some of the members of the Genesee Association; one of whom, in particular, has not, even to this day, abandoned his inveterate enmity to it. It has undergone several modifications since its first organization; but it is not now, in my estimation, as good, as profitable, and as safe a body as I first proposed.

CHAPTER XIV.

Organization of Black River Association—Warren Skinner—A text given—The discourse—Tour to Genesee and Cayuga Associations—Disaffection—Mr. Flagler's opposition—Further views of the powers of the Convention—Digression; and Mr. Flagler's course at the Genesee and Cayuga Associations, in 1823—W. J. Reese—Meetings in Onondaga and Manlius—Supplies the desk for a short time for Mr. Smith, in Philadelphia—Journey—Reception—Mr. P. Morse—State of society—Habits—Jewish Synagogue—4th of July—Congress Hall, 1776—Death of Ex-Presidents John Adams and Thomas Jefferson—Address on the occasion—Bishop White—Return journey—Visit in New York city—In Hudson—T. F. King—Chenango Association—Meeting-house in Nelson—Engagement to preach in Nelson—Mr. E. M. Wooley—Journey to Vermont—General Convention—Meeting with Mr. Ballou—Meeting in Fort Ann—Arrival at Bridgewater, Vt.—My mother—Barre—My wife's sister—Our reception—Northern Association—Mr. Williams; his defection—Meeting in Barre—In Bridgewater—Return—State of the cause—Engagement in Sanquoit—Associations—Dr. J. B. Pierce—Visit to Lyons—Three Sabbaths in Lyons—Hon. Myron Holley—Newark.

The Black River Association was organized in 1824, and its first session was holden in Brownville, Jefferson county. No ordinary consideration prevented me from attending all such meetings within reasonable limits; not only because of the importance attached to them, but because of the high gratification and the indescribable happiness it afforded me, in beholding the enlargement of the boundaries of our Zion, and hearing the soul-rejoicing reports from the messengers of truth, brought in from its various branches. Few could realize and enjoy what I did. I had seen one little society stand tottering alone, within the whole compass of territory containing more than fifty societies at that time, and then organizing its fourth association; and the small figure 3 would number all the preachers within the limits which then required fifteen times that number to count. To *me*, this did not look like "The day of small things;" for the "Stone taken from the mountain, without hands," in its onward roll, was gathering velocity and magnitude infinitely beyond my most sanguine anticipations. At this meeting, I became first acquainted with Warren Skinner, Esq., who resided in the village of Brownville, and who, shortly after this, began his proclamation of this great salvation, and who now holds a conspicuous standing among its most able advocates.

On the last day of the session a request was sent in, by some person, to have a discourse delivered from the 22d verse of the 13th chapter of Ezekiel: "Because of lies ye have made the heart of the righteous sad," &c. It was supposed, at any rate, to have come, originally, from an opposer of the doctrine, who considered it peculiarly applicable to the preachers of our order; and many manifested a great solicitude that it should be attended to. But to deliver a discourse from it that day would materially interfere with the arrangements of the speakers, and especially with mine, and I did not consider the subject appropriate to the occasion; and as I had agreed to improve the following Sabbath in Watertown, I informed the messenger that if I could have the use of the meeting-house we then occupied, (it belonged to some Partialist denomination; the Baptists, I believe,) I would deliver a discourse from the text, on the Sabbath following, at 5 o'clock, P. M., if that would satisfy. The proposition was accepted, the use of the house insured, and the appointment given out at the close of our services.

The time arrived, and the house was filled to overflowing. In the first place, I endeavored to give a brief history of the text, showing the then condition of the Jewish church, and the proper original meaning of the prophet, and the application of the text to the false prophets in Israel. And in the next place, dwelt upon the gross perversion of the text, by those who were in a very constant habit of using it, and lugging it entirely out of its connection, and pressing it into a service the most distant from any meaning the inspired penman could possibly have attached to it; and then, by "turning the tables," I applied it, with all the power and severity I was master of; by showing the analogy between the characters of the false prophets of Israel, who "dealt partial in the law," who "prophesied for reward," who "looked every man to his gain from his quarter," who could "bite with their teeth while they cried peace," and "prepared war against every one who would not put into *their* mouths," and a certain class, or classes, of professed prophets in the Christian church, who arrogated to themselves all temporal and spiritual immunities; and made the "hearts of the righteous sad"—desolate, by producing scepticism, darkness, unreconciliation, despair, delirium, and death.

They had voluntarily put a weapon into my hands, and I felt justified in using it. The audience gave profound attention, and I could discover visible manifestations of surprise on many countenance. What effect it ultimately had, I am not able to say. But opposers generally satisfied themselves, in those days, with the trite remark, "The devil always helps Universalists."

Besides the places already mentioned, I delivered discourses, on this tour, in Field's Settlement, Watertown, Sackett's Harbor, and Richland.

I remained at home but two Sundays after returning from my last visit to Bradford County, Pa., in 1825, before starting on another tour to the west. The Ontario Association, formerly the Genesee Branch, held its session in Parma, Monroe County, on the third Wednesday in September, 1825; and the Cayuga Association met in Marcellus, on the fourth Wednesday in the same month; and my calculation was to attend both. The Sunday previous to the meeting in Parma, I preached in Pittsford, and on the Sunday following in Hopewell, and lectured on my way out in Henrietta, and on my return in Rochester, Canandaigua, and Waterloo.

Up to about that time there had never anything taken place to cloud the sun-shine of our associational meetings, to cause dissension in our council, or disturb the perfect unanimity of action and harmony of feeling; we seemed to have but one object in view in all our deliberations, and one spirit pervaded the whole; but now a cloud was coming over us, and the thunders began to roll. And what grieved me the most was, that I had been the first cause of disturbing the elements. I have previously mentioned the proposition for organizing a State Convention—the incipient steps that were taken—the feelings with which it was met, the opposition it encountered, and so forth. It had by this time become a subject of serious importance; several Associations had adopted the plan; many who at first treated it with indifference, and even with ridicule, had now espoused it with a zeal more fervid than I ever felt, and were pursuing it with more strenuous measures than I could desire; and the convention had already been organized by three or more associations, and had holden one or two meetings.

The subject was brought before the council in Parma, and a motion made to unite with the convention and appoint delegates for that purpose. But as I was Moderator of the council, I neither made the motion, nor advocated it; but I was under the absolute necessity of trying to defend myself. For although there were now many more zealous advocates for it than myself, still I was known as the first mover of it; and therefore the whole weight of the oppressor's vengeance fell on me. Mr. Flagler was a member of the council; and I have already stated that he took a violent stand against it. He was a man of large stature, strong mind, and profound argument—at least in one respect, for he *never yielded.* You might as well stand and argue with the mighty waters of the cataract of Niagara to cease their roar, as to attempt to remove him from a position he had taken. And by his untiring perseverance, his bold, dogmatical, overwhelming, and endless declamation, he had acquired a complete ascendancy over many minds in that region, and awed others into a servile submission to his own measures. And now he came out with all his artillery not only against the measure, but against me as its author. I was represented as an ambitious aspirant, seeking to establish a hierarchy, to rule as lord over the heritage of God, impose creeds, confessions of faith, and rules of discipline, and the next thing would be a *holy inquisition.* One of his proselytes, a good lay brother and member of the council, who probably never contributed a dollar towards defraying the expenses of those who had devoted their whole lives, their strength and talent—who had willingly sacrificed their temporal comforts and ease, and family endearments—encountered the buffetings of the elements, and the more soul-trying storms of human passions and prejudices—who had suffered cold and heat, hunger and thirst, and expended their last cent to proclaim far and wide the doctrine *he* professed to believe as the truth of God—called me *Pope,* and *Bishop,* and charged me with cupidity! It was in vain that I explained my views of the character and powers of a constitution. That I had never desired it to be clothed with ecclesiastical power, nor did I think it consistently could be, not even to decide upon the qualification of candidates for the ministry, nor grant letters of fellowship, nor even expel a disorderly preacher—that these powers belonged to the churches in their individual capacity, in the first place; and secondly, in their associate capacity, as, for instance, in this council; much less could the convention impose creeds, or rules of discipline upon churches and societies—that all the powers which the convention was designed to exercise, according to my plan, were merely advisory. It might give counsel to associations, or serve as an arbitration to settle differences between associations, or between churches and associations, or associations and preachers, when appealed to by an aggrieved party; but the only object that I had in view in proposing such a body, was to create a center of communication for the whole body of Universalists in the State, for mutual edification, encouragement, improvement, and *liberty* of the whole—not to tyranize over, nor in any shape to infringe upon the rights or principles of associations, churches, or individuals. "Surely, brethren," said I, "in my labors in this country for twenty years past—itinerating through its length and breadth—coming and going at your call, through storms and sunshine, heat and cold, hunger and thirst, by day and by night, serving you without fee or reward—surely, I must have given you some very strong evidences of personal ambition and cupidity!" But all this was to no purpose. Feelings had been awakened, and —(I would forever obliterate this part of the history of our order, could I do it with justice to community)—unkind feeling which rebutted every appeal to reason or to sympathy. Ah! Universalists are nothing but men, after all; and are subject to like passions with other men.

Mr. Flagler had taken his stand; and all the power and influence he possessed were called into requisition to crush the convention in its bud. He rallied all his forces, and attended every association possibly within his reach for several years; and never, to this day, gave up his opposition; but being overpowered by the operation of the convention, and the diffusion of light to other minds on the subject, he at length was compelled to "sit and grieve alone."

Something of the feelings of Mr. Flagler may be discovered from the treatment I received from him three years afterwards. He kept some two or three of the western associations from uniting with the others in convention for several years; and consequently we kept up, as far as possible, a communication with them by our old means, of visiting committees. In 1828, I received an appointment from the Central Association, (such was the name given, after a number of other associations had sprung up around it, to the old Western Association,) to visit the Ontario Association, which was to hold its session in the town of Victor. On my arrival, I stopped at the house to which I was directed by our friends, and while standing on a platform in front of the door, Mr. Flagler drove up. As his carriage stopped, I stepped to him and offered him my hand, and inquired after his health and that of his family ; but all I received in return was merely a cold touch of the hand, with the icy, laconic answer, "They are well," without a return of the compliment, or even another word ; he then descended from his carriage, and, without any further notice of me, passed by me into the house. I had known Mr. F. from his first conversion to the faith, had encouraged his entrance upon the ministry, had recommended him to our societies and brethren, and indulged all the warm and friendly sentiments of a brother toward him ; and this treatment from him, on an occasion like this, when we had not met for some two years or more, and where we were in the habit of greeting each other with undissembled cordiality, wounded my feelings prodigiously, and overwhelmed my soul with a gloom which I could not shake off during the whole tour ; and he persevered in this coldness and neglect during the whole session. At a suitable time, he, as a leading member, called on the preachers and delegates to repair to the council-room in another part of the building—all done in my presence, but without asking me to accompany them, or intimating that my presence would be acceptable. The meeting was called to order, and I was told, (for I was not present,) that some brother nominated me for moderator, which Mr. F. objected to, had the motion recalled, and got appointed himself. However, after the council had organized, and, as I was informed, entered on business, I ventured into the room, and at a suitable time arose and asked the privilege of addressing a few words, which was coldly granted. I stated to them, in substance, that by appointment of the Central Association I made them this visit, to present the congratulations of that body ; and to inform them that the cause of Zion was prosperous in that region, and the manifestations of Divine approbation were apparent in the addition of churches, societies, and laborers, in the course of the past year ; and that the Association to which I belonged desired a reciprocation of the like favor, &c. And all the reply that I received to my address, and all the notice that was taken of it, was merely a groan from the moderator. And so perfectly under the control of that individual were the whole council, that there was not a motion made to invite me to a seat in the council, which was a civility uniformly extended to *all* visiting brethren, and considered indispensible in case of a visiting committee ; and I was never invited to participate in any of their deliberations. The committee of arrangements, however, applied to me to deliver a discourse, and urged their suit with so much earnestness, that I reluctantly consented; but I surely felt little like preaching, and I presume my discourse was as cold and lifeless as was their conduct toward me. That Mr. F., on subsequent reflection, felt some compunctions of conscience, I had pretty good evidence, from some remarks he made to Mr. Ackley, as well as from the course he pursued at the Cayuga Association, which met the week following, at Sempronius. My mission extended to these two Associations; and notwithstanding the cold reception I had met with at the Ontario, I could not conscientiously forego my obligation to fulfil my whole mission. I therefore repaired to the next Association, expecting I should probably meet with similar treatment; for Mr. F.'s influence was nearly as great in that as in the Ontario; and I expected he would be there. But his manner was completely changed. He sought the earliest opportunity to speak to me, and even tried to be sociable. He was again appointed moderator, and the first act of the council, by his suggestion, was to pass a resolution inviting me to a seat in the council, and sending out a committee to inform me, and requesting me to come in. But he was too stubborn ever to make an apology to me.

But again I have rambled with you, kind reader; you must now accompany me back. We started to attend two Associations; but the portentous cloud which broke upon us at the first, and the hurricane which followed, have blown us away amid troubled waters, to two other Associations, at a much later period, and nearly bewildered us. You must now allow me to conduct you back to the Cayuga Association, in 1825, where a happier season awaits us, a richer feast is being prepared, and where we shall in some measure forget the bitterness of that unsavory cup we have been compelled to drink.

At this meeting, among many other excellent brethren, I found my highly-esteemed friend and brother C. G. Person, whose soul always mingled with mine, and whose spirit ever drank at the same fountain. It was a happy meeting; and perhaps appeared doubly so to me, who had borne a heavy load at heart for several days past. No dissensions arose in the deliberations of the council. "The hand that soweth discord among brethren" was not there. The evidences of the enlargement of our borders, and the prosperity of the cause afforded subject of congratulation, and encouragement, and hope. At this Association, our young, gifted, and highly-esteemed, but now deeply-lamented brother and fellow-laborer, Wm. J. Reese, whose short, active life was so faithfully employed in the service of his Divine Master, even to the very last moment, received ordination; and I enjoyed the pleasure of delivering his ordination sermon, from St. John, 15: 16.

On the day following the Association, in company with Mr. Person, I attended a meeting in Onondaga, and the Sunday following preached in Manlius; and on Monday returned home once more in peace to my family. My oldest daughter accompanied me on this excursion, as well as on the other alluded to, in 1828, which, in some degree, assisted to dispel the gloom and despondency to which I was exposed.

I remained pretty steadily at home during the remainder of the fall, the ensuing winter, and spring, fulfilling my engagements with the societies in the immediate vicinity, and made no excursions to any great distance; and gave my attention more immediately to the concerns of my family, to try, if possible, to relieve my wife of the cares, labors, and anxieties which too heavily pressed upon her; for in my zeal for the cause, I was too much in the habit of neglecting those duties, and throwing vastly too heavy a burden on her.

Mr. S. R. Smith and Mr. P. Morse had, a year or more before this, settled as pastors of the churches in Philadelphia; Mr. Smith with the Callowhill, and Mr. Morse with the Lombard St. Church. And one day, about the middle of June, 1826, a little past the middle of the day, I was much surprised to see Mr. Smith enter my house, not having heard a word from him for months, and supposing him to be in Philadelphia. He ever had a feeble appearance; but now he looked unusually sallow, emaciated, and feeble, and manifested, on his first entrance, an uncommon degree of solicitude. He had come on an express, which he said was imperious. His health had failed him to that degree, that his usefulness, if not his life, depended on his relinquishing his city labors for a season, of retiring for a season and taking more exercise in the unpolluted air of the country than he could possibly enjoy in the city; and he had left Philadelphia with the express stipulation, that if I was alive and well, I should go and supply his place for a few Sabbaths; or in case of failure, he was to return immediately. I was, indeed, taken by surprise; but he pleaded so earnestly, and his pale and haggard countenance appealed so eloquently to the sympathies of my soul, that I could not deny his suit; and therefore determined to break off thus abruptly from my own societies, and try to satisfy them the best way I could, after my return, and to go to Philadelphia. Hasty preparations were made, and I repaired to Utica, where I took passage in a stage coach for Albany, on as dark and rainy a night as is ever seen in that season of the year; from Albany to New York I got passage in a steam-boat, and from New York to New Brunswick, in N. J.; from thence by land in stage-coach to Trenton, and thence by steam-boat to Philadelphia, where I arrived on the next Saturday after Mr. S. came to my house. Before leaving the steam-boat, I descried, among the crowd collected upon the wharf, Mr. Morse, peering through the multitude to examine the passengers; although his eye caught mine, and a smile of recognition relieved his visible anxiety; he conducted me to his dwelling, and I boarded with him during my stay. I remained in Philadelphia six Sabbaths; during the time, made several exchanges with Mr. Morse, but preached none on week days. The doctrine seemed wholly confined to the city; few or none attended meetings from the surrounding country, nor could I learn that any one beyond the suburbs of the city professed the least knowledge of Universalism. But I found here an intelligent and good people, plain and unostentatious in their manners, just and upright in their deal, temperate in their habits, and social, kind, and benevolent in their intercourse. The meetings were well attended, and the members of both churches manifested a strong attachment to their pastors. The members of the Callowhill church expressed great solicitude about Mr. Smith, most ardently desired the recovery of his health, and his return to his pastoral charge. I enjoyed good health during my residence, but in order to secure it, I was obliged to be a little eccentric in my habits. Half of their preaching, even at that season of the year, (July,) was done in the night. One discourse at 10 in the morning, and another at candle lighting, was the invariable custom in most churches of the city, I believe, and certainly so in both Universalist churches; and all their social parties were holden after candle-lighting. They, therefore, scarcely ever retired to bed until after 12 o'clock, nor rose in the morning until 8 or 9. A conformity to this practice would never answer my purpose. I was always an early riser; and after the light of day had penetrated my chamber, there was no more "sleep to my eyes, nor slumber to my eye-lids," let the time of my retiring be what it might. I therefore adopted the same practice in the city as at home, of rising before the sun, and taking a walk out into the country, to breathe the salubrious and refreshing air of the morning. And while I crept stealthily away from the snoring multitude, and inhaled the invigorating breeze of the morning, these lines of the immortal Thompson would always occur to my mind:—

> "Falsely luxurious! will not man awake,
> And, springing from the bed of sloth, enjoy
> The cool, the fragrant, and the morning breeze,
> To silent meditation due, and sacred song?"

Having taken my morning excursion, generally of a mile or more out of the city, I could return with a good appetite for breakfast, spend the forenoon in my study, take a season of repose after dinner, and be ready for a social interview in the evening; and although the weather was unusually warm, for me, I nevertheless found, in this course, the means of preserving my health, and keeping up my spirits.

While in the city, I had the privilege, for the first and only time in my life, of going to a Jewish Synagogue, and witnessing the forms of Hebrew worship. There was little in it interesting to me; not being a Hebrew scholar, I could not understand much they said "out of the law," nor "say amen," as they spake "in an unknown tongue:" I could only see their formulas, in which I discovered very little solemnity.

A still more interesting occasion to me occurred, which I enjoyed the pleasure of witnessing. On the 4th of July, the old Congress Hall of '76 was thrown open, and I had the privilege of hearing an address delivered from the very stand where the venerable President, John Hancock, sat when the Declaration of Independence was adopted; where a full-size statue of Jefferson, in marble, with the roll of independence in his right hand, stood directly behind the speaker. The discourse was not great; but the association of ideas and feelings produced by the scene was thrilling and captivating. On this day, too, one of the most remarkable, solemn, and interesting events occurred, that belongs to the history of the United States. Two of the Ex-Presidents, John Adams and Thomas Jefferson, both of whom were active members of that Congress, and members of the committee who prepared and brought in that everlasting document which sealed the independence and glory of the United States of America, on the 4th of July, 1776, departed this life, probably within one hour of each other. It might be said of them, as in the lameniation of David over Saul and Jonathan, "They were lovely and pleasant in their lives, and in their death they were not divided." And before I left Philadelphia I heard (or rather saw, for few could hear) an address delivered on the occasion. A staging was erected, in front of the second story of the Old State House, for the speaker; and the whole garden, or green, thirty rods square, in front of the building, was densely crowded with people; the staging was hung with mourning, and the whole scene was one of great solemnity. The venerable Bishop White, who, I believe, was chaplain to the Congress of '76, and also a chaplain in the revolutionary service, made his appearance on the stage, his thin, snow-white locks gently waving in the breeze, and read prayers on the occasion.

At length Mr. Smith returned with his family, (for when he left Philadelphia, he felt so sure of securing my labors, that he took his family with him,) with improved health, to the great joy of his parishioners. I had been treated with great cordiality and respect during my sojourn with this kind people; and, receiving an ample reward for my labors, at their liberal hands, I took an affectionate leave of the city of brotherly love, and, with a beating heart, set my face once more toward my family. I returned in the same manner and by nearly the same route that I went, but a little more leisurely. I spent a short time in the city of New York, and made Mr. Kneeland the first, and the last, and the only visit I ever made him in his family; and it was at this time that he accompanied me forty miles up the river with his little necromancer, in search of Captain Kidd's gold!

I also called at the city of Hudson, where our much-lamented brother, T. F. King, was settled as pastor of the church. At his earnest request, I remained with him over the Sabbath, preached for him as well as I could, and administered the elements of the Eucharist to the church. I found the cause prosperous under his well-directed labors, and the church enjoying spiritual life. We truly enjoyed a happy season. From thence I traveled by steam-boat to Albany, stage to Schenectady, canal-boat to Utica, stage to Madison, and reached the bosom of my too-much-neglected family on the 11th or 12th day of August.

I arrived home from Philadelphia in season to attend the Chenango Association which met this year, on the 4th Wednesday in August, in the town of German, but made no more extensive excursions until the fall of 1827.

During the year 1826, the inhabitants of Nelson Flats, town of Nelson, Madison County, without distinction of sect, united and built a meeting-house, and finished it off in good style, which they mutually agreed should be free for all denominations, without any other restriction than, that no denomination should make appointments in it to interfere with the regular appointments of another. They got their house completed and ready for occupancy early in the spring of 1827, and in April of that year applied to me to hold a meeting in it. I complied with the request, and entered into an engagement to preach with them once a month for a year. This was the first engagement for regular preaching in the house.

A spirit of universal liberality seemed to prevail; and the inhabitants, without distinction of sectarian opinion, generally turned out to meeting and filled the house; and a spirit of inquiry was soon awakened. Among those who seemed to take deep interest, was a young man by the name of E. M. Wooley, a resident of the village, a young man of superior talents, but a zealous opposer of the doctrine; and, as I desired, he was very eager to oppose it, and seize every opportunity to battle with me. He was very constant at meeting, affable and polite in his manner, and notwithstanding our difference of opinion, we soon contracted a strong friendship. One day, when he was battling me with all his might, I said to him, "Brother Wooley, you may now fight this doctrine hard as you please; but I now tell you, and I wish you to remember it, that strong as your prejudices now are against it, you have got yet to believe it, and to *preach* it to the world!" And I now feel quite willing to let the world decide upon the evidences of my being a true prophet; for before the year of my engagement closed, he became a happy believer in the truth of the doctrine, and within about three years, commenced its promulgation, to which he has zealously, faithfully, and successfully devoted his time and talents up to the present time; and he stands now among the most able advocates of the blessed truth.

More than seven years had elapsed since we had visited any of our relatives in New England; during which time several had been called from these mortal shores, and nearly all of them scattered from the land of our birth; not a single member of my father-in-law's family remained in New Salem, nor a relative of his except sister's children; and I had only a brother and a half-sister, with some remnants of their families, that remained in our native town. My father died in Feb., 1824; and soon after his decease my mother took up her residence with my youngest sister, in Vermont, where I had another sister, and where my wife also had two; Vermont, therefore, instead of the land that gave us birth, had now become the object of our solicitude. But although my mother had become far advanced in years, and filial as well as fraternal affection drew me strongly to that point, I had an additional inducement for the visit this fall. The General Convention was to hold its meeting in September, at Saratoga Springs, which I should necessarily pass on my journey. I had, for many years past, seldom enjoyed the privilege of meeting with that body; and I could also so arrange my travels, without interfering with our visits, as to attend the Northern Association, which met at Calais, Vt., on the first of October. Accordingly, about the middle of September, 1827, in company with a widowed sister and a niece, we left home, and made our first visit to a brother of my wife, in Charleton, Saratoga County, where I left my company, and proceeded to the Convention.

My feelings were highly exhilarated in meeting many of my old co-laborers in the proclamation of the "Common Salvation," and beholding the members who had engaged in the holy cause since I last enjoyed the happiness of attending a session of the convention; and more especially of once more meeting my spiritual father, Hosea Ballou, and hearing "words of truth" from his experienced lips. Three young men were, at this session, set apart to the work of the ministry by solemn ordination, in the solemnities of which a part was assigned to me. This was the last time that I have enjoyed the privilege of attending a meeting of the convention, and this was the last time—and I fear it will be the last time—that I have ever seen the man under whose ministry I have enjoyed some of the happiest hours of my life, and whom I have styled, with the utmost propriety, my spiritual father. At the request of a few friends from Fort Ann, who attended this meeting, I sent an appointment to that place for the next Sabbath. The next day I rejoined my company, and we proceeded on our journey to Fort Ann, where I found a numerous congregation on Sunday, who listened with great attention to the message I had to deliver to them. After remaining a single day in the town of Fort Ann, to visit my relatives who still resided in that place, we pursued our journey through Whitehall to Rutland, Vt., from thence crossing the Green Mountains, through Sherburne to Bridgewater, where my mother resided. It was cause of inexpressible happiness to find my venerable parent, now advanced to four score years, in the full enjoyment of all her physical and intellectual faculties, as bright and as vigorous, almost, as in the days of my youth; and my sisters and their families in good health, and surrounded with all the necessary comforts of life. It was necessary, however, to make but a short stay here, as the time for the meeting of the Association was approaching; and reserving the major part of our visit for our return, I left my sister and niece, and with my wife pursued our journey to Barre, Washington County, where she had a sister residing, and near the place of the meeting of the Association.

These sisters had lived remote from each other from early life, had not met for more than thirty years, and had seldom heard from each other; all the correspondence they had ever held was a single letter which I addressed them soon after our marriage, by the hand of Mr. Farwell, who resided a neighbor to them, but to which we never received a reply. It was night before we arrived there; but the weather was mild, and the moon's full orb, with her silver, mellow, solemn beams, brilliantly lighted our path-way, casting a sombre hue upon the rich, variegated face of the vegetable world. But we knew nothing of the temporal circumstances of those we sought, whether we should find a shelter for our jaded beast—for we had driven fifty miles over the mountainous roads of that country—or accommodation for ourselves. We made inquiry, and found we were approaching their habitation, and were conversing on the total uncertainty of the manner of our reception, the fare that we should meet with, and the pleasure of our visit; but concluded that if we were so fortunate as to find them alive and in health, we should not regret the weariness of our journey—when, emerging from a small strip of wood-land, our road opened upon a broad, extensive improvement, exhibiting a large farm in a high state of cultivation, with good fences and handsomely-arranged lots, which bore indubitable testimony that the hand of industry and agricultural skill was there; while in the distance we could discover two large barns in close proximity, and a very good frame dwelling-house, that appeared to belong to the premises. "Well," said we, "if these are Mr. Lawson's premises—if this farm and these buildings belong to him, we need not fear for accommodation from lack of means; but how shall we make ourselves known?" We drove up in front of the house, where we saw a man in the entry-way, (the door being open,) churning by the light of the moon, in a churn half as large as a common cider-barrel; reining my horse near the door, I hailed him with, "Good evening, sir; can you entertain strangers for a night?" An answer in the affirmative was unhesitatingly given; and we were requested to alight and walk in, while preparations were made to take care of our horse and carriage. We walked into the house, and took off our over-garments; but no symptoms of recognition were discernible. Nor was it surprising; they had never known me; and the sisters, who were young when they last met, had now become old women. After having a little conversation, however, by way of prelude, we made ourselves known; and, that we were received with grateful feelings and joyful hearts, the tears, which coursed in showers down their cheeks, gave ample witness. And to add to our gratification and pleasure, we found them in affluent circumstances. Their full barns and granaries afforded rich living for our horse, and their chambers, and larder, and cellar, all the necessaries and even luxuries of life, for us. Oh! how blessed it is, while traveling the rugged, and often dark and cloudy paths of life, to find, here and there, some sunny and pleasant spot!

One day only was allowed us to remain with our friends, at this time, before the association, about fifteen miles distant. We repaired thither, and enjoyed a happy and profitable meeting. Very few whom I had before seen were there; but I had seen their names enrolled as soldiers under the "Captain of our Salvation;" and although strangers in the flesh, we were intimate associates in the spirit. We had learned the tongue, and could familiarly converse in the language of Zion—we had drunk at the same fountain, and could bathe together in the same impassable "River of Life." Surely, such convocations as these are prelibations of future joys! I found many here whom I never before met in the flesh, and whom I shall never meet again until I meet them in heaven. There were preachers and delegates here from almost every part of the State, and some from the Queen's dominion; but none with whom I had associated in this region, in the infancy of my ministry; they had all wandered to other parts of the world, or gone to a better.

I here formed an acquaintance with a preacher from Ohio, by the name of Williams, who, with his lady, was making or rather had made the tour of New England. He was about returning to Ohio, and at my request, promised to make me a call on his way. This he did; and remained with me several days; and preached one Sabbath, to the great satisfaction of our people. It was late in the fall, the traveling had become very bad, and his wife in a very poor state of health; and feeling much solicitude about them, we extracted a promise from him to write as soon as he reached his habitation. No letter came from him, however, and I began to entertain fears that they had got cast away upon the Lake. But my anxiety in this respect was relieved, a few months afterwards, by learning that he, and several others, had been shipwrecked by the tempest of a more boisterous sea, and cast upon a desolate and barren desert! Mr. Williams, and several other preachers, (all then in the region of the Western Reserve, Ohio,) except a single individual, I believe, all at one and the same time, while assembled at a general meeting, as though by previous concert, which probably was the case, took one bold retrograde step back into the ranks of the "disciples" of Alexander Campbell. I will here state, that the individual excepted is our venerable brother Beals, who alone breasted the shock, and maintained his standing upon the ROCK OF AGES, where he still abides in safety; and through all the raging and strife of the elements around him, has never ceased to blow the trumpet of the Gospel, to give notice to the benighted mariner of the haven of safety and peace.

From the association in Calais, we returned to our friends in Barre. I delivered one lecture in Montpelier; and on the Sunday after the association, preached in the elegant brick Universalist meeting-house in Barre. The congregation was numerous, filling the house to overflowing, and the season was rendered captivating to me by the attention of the audience, but more especially by the superior performance of the choir, led by that king and queen of singers, Mr. Waters and his lady, who had given spirit and life to the association in Calais. The Tuesday following, we took leave of our friends in Barre, and returned to Bridgewater, where we spent another week. Here I delivered a lecture in one part of the town, and preached one Sunday in another; and found the cause in this, as also in other parts of the State that I had visited, in a steady, onward course. On the Monday following, we bade farewell to our mother, sisters and their families; and, without meeting with any occurrence worthy of particular notice, returned once more to our home in the State of New York.

The first societies that were organized in the country arose up promiscuously over a great extent of territory, frequently, and, indeed, very generally, quite remote from each other. But as years rolled on, and preachers multiplied, those intermediate sections began to be visited, new places for meetings were opened, new interests awakened, and new congregations established; which brought our societies into nearer proximity to each other, and increased the density of our fraternal connection.

I had holden meetings repeatedly in the town of Nelson, in

several different neighborhoods, as well as in the adjacent towns, before the erection of the meeting-house at the Flats, but had never preached in this village; but now the largest and most respectable congregation, and the most flourishing society existed here, of any in all that region of country. And late in the fall of this year, another door was opened in the midst of surrounding societies. In a very early day of my settling in the State, I had had occasian to deliver some lectures, and attend one or two funerals on the Sanquoit creek, in the east part of the town of Paris; but no great interest was manifested in the doctrine of Universalism, until then. I had now a very urgent request to make an appointment there, which I complied with; and so much interest was manifested—so numerous and increasing were the congregations, that after a few meetings I engaged to preach with them one half of the Sabbaths for the ensuing year, which arrangement was renewed at the close of the year, and so continued until I left the State of New York.

In the year 1828, I attended the Central Association, in Fly Creek settlement, in Otsego county; the Black River Association, in Ellisburg; as well as the Ontario and Cayuga Associations, which I have before mentioned. While at the Ontario Association, I received, by the hand of a friend, a very handsomely-bound pocket-testament, as a present from Dr. J. B. Pierce, of Lyons, son of the lady whose conversion from Methodism, in Hamilton, I have noticed, with a request from the donor that I should call and deliver a discourse in Lyons, on my return. Having no engagement for the Sabbath intervening the Ontario and Cayuga Associations, I returned an answer that I would be at Lyons on that day. Extensive notice was given, and a congregation filled every seat in the court-house on the occasion; many of the most respectable and influential citizens attended, and among them, the Hon. Myron Holley, of considerable celebrity in the political world. This led to a request for me to visit them again the ensuing winter, and spend a few Sabbaths in succession with them, as the distance from my residence, being nearly one hundred miles, would render it very inconvenient to go for a single Sabbath at a time. Arrangements were accordingly made, and in the month of January following, (1829,) I spent three Sabbaths in Lyons. The houses of Myron Holley, Esq., and Dr. J. B. Pierce, were freely opened to me, and in their kind, hospitable families I received every civility and attention I could possibly desire, during my stay. The court-house, which we occupied for our meetings, was quite a spacious building, for a country town, and was uniformly well filled on each Sabbath; and the meetings constantly increased in popularity and in attendance. Appearances were then certainly promising for building up a respectable society, and permanently establishing the cause in that place; and I very much regretted that I could not comply with their earnest solicitations to remain longer; but my other engagements forbade it. I left them, however, with some hopes of being able to make them another visit; but subsequent circumstances rendered it impossible ever to enjoy that privilege.

Mr. Holley was a man of much popularity; but although a firm and avowed believer in Universal Salvation, and a real lover of the truth, he would much prefer the name of Unitarian. He had some personal acquaintance with the celebrated Dr. Channing, of Boston, extolled him very highly, and said that Dr. C. was as firm a believer in the ultimate holiness and happiness of all mankind as I was, although he was denominated a Unitarian; and Mr. Holley thought that the cause would flourish better under that name, than Universalism. Oh! how names will sometimes frighten men of sound abilities, and of great boldness in other respects. But Mr. H. was a constant attendant on my meeting, and treated me with the utmost respect and cordiality, and probably contributed the most liberal for my support of any individual who attended the meeting.

The parents of Dr. Pierce resided in the town of Rose, some twelve or fifteen miles from Lyons. They attended meeting in Lyons one Sunday; and, during my sojourn, I made them one visit, and delivered one discourse in their place. During the time I remained in this country, I delivered several lectures on week days, or rather evenings, in the adjacent towns, and among the rest, one in Newark, where now is a flourishing society, and an elegant meeting-house. But Newark was then but an indifferent hamlet. One public-house, and a few other buildings were all that could be counted where the village of Newark, with its splendid churches, its numerous stores and houses of entertainment, its spacious streets and ornaments, its tasteful and sumptuous dwellings, and its thousands of inhabitants, now graces the banks of the grand canal.

Having finished my mission here, for the present season, and received from the hands of my friends a liberal reward for my labors with them, and from their lips the heart-felt valedictory blessing, I bade adieu to this romantic and delightful little village; and have never since set my foot within its borders.

CHAPTER XV.

Retrospection—Present state of the cause—Ephemeral preachers—J. S. Thompson—Laborious itinerations—Remunerations--Approaching storm—Anti-Masonic excitement—Anarchy in churches generally—Agitation in Universalist societies—Disaffection in the church in Hamilton—Mr. H—— —Church meeting—Address—Bernard's " Light on Masonry"—Elder Blain ; his course at a Masonic funeral—Thoughts on removal—Correspondence with societies—Visit to Brooklyn, Pa.—Proposals from Columbus, Pa.—Visit to Columbus—Brokenstraw country—Capt. D. Curtis--Village commenced—Further arrangements—Return—Disposal of property in Hamilton—Visit to Vermont—Mr. Freeman's visit and settlement—His ministry and death—Farewell discourse—Removal—Arrival at Columbus—Gift of a village lot—Winter arrangements—Sickness of my wife—Organization of a society and church—Calls for preaching—One preacher in all this country—State of the cause—Extensive itinerancy—Societies organized—Our family—Severe trial and bereavement—Intense feeling—Divine power of faith—Commencement on a farm lot—The oldest son returns to his trade ; the other chooses a profession, and farming abandoned—Death of Capt. Curtis—Temporal misfortune—A periodical, " Genius of Liberty"—Mr. Z. C. Todd's indifference of order ; his course and his defection.

We have now arrived at a point in the history of my life, as well as that of Universalism, where it will be proper for us to pause, and take a brief retrospective glance. And, standing upon the verge of the year of our Lord 1830, having seen more than half a century, an elevation to which, in my youth, I never expected to attain—I can look back with sensations of devout gratitude to the great Author of my being, and to the prime minister of his government, our Lord Jesus Christ, and with mingled feelings of complacency and regret upon my past life. There are many scenes of my life, and many actions that I can call to recollection with conscientious approval ; but many, alas ! too, too many, that I could wish obliterated from Jehovah's book !

In regard to the doctrine, or rather the *Order* of Universalists in America, I have seen it, in its infancy, oppressed by the cruel hand of a gigantic enemy, throwing obloquy and contempt, calumny and detraction upon its cradle, and using every unhallowed means to smother it in its childhood. But, I have seen it, under the fostering care of the great Head of the church, arise through all these impediments, and gradually, but surely, acquire the stature of a man ; and, with the strength of a Sampson, tear asunder the "cords" and the "withes" with which they attempted to bind it; and, with becoming dignity, command the respect of surrounding denominations. In the State of New York, I have witnessed its first breathings, its infantile struggles, its youthful fears and hopes, and ardent longings and anticipations, until it assumed a manly dignity. I have been with it from before the organization of the second society, at a time when only three of the feeblest of the feeble advocates of its cause were engaged in its behalf; with nothing but the approving smiles of high Heaven and the approbation of their own consciences to encourage them in their arduous and thankless task. I have—and I record it with feelings of unmingled gratitude to Almighty God—beheld its advancement until it comprises within its expanding embrace nearly two hundred societies, and between eighty and one hundred preachers, ten associations and a general State convention ; and all this within twenty-five years.

During the period we have reviewed, there were quite a number who appeared in our religious hemisphere, either as transient visiters from other spheres, or were kindled up with the combustible elements of our own, like meteors, whose ephemeral glare served only to make the darkness more visible in the region of the path they traversed ; but who soon passed off into other spheres, or dispersed in common air. Among them may be named an Ellis, a Lisher, a Thompson, a Brownson, a Gibson, a Streeter, a Jacobs, a Goodwin, a Shannon, and perhaps some others. But the most remarkable was John S. Thompson. He was a European by birth, a man of professed erudition, and of good speaking talents. He came to America in the character of a Methodist preacher, but, as I was informed, became converted to Universalism by disputing with Mr. Kneeland in the Berean Society, in the city of Philadelphia. But, alas ! though a theoretical Universalist, he knew not its spiritual vitality ; he appeared wholly destitute of the stamina of pure religion. He was a man of strong, turbulent, and unchastened passions, and of towering ambition ; and, no doubt, entered the ranks of Universalists, with a design to be an oracle and a leader; but although they venerated his learning, and appreciated his talents, they could not succumb to his dictatorial arrogance; and becoming dissatisfied, he flashed and passed from our orbit. He was a man of keen, satirical wit, and his petulancy frequently led him to make a severe use of it, when speaking of opposing denominations. A lady in the village of Auburn once told me an anecdote of him, quite amusing: He was speaking of the dogmas of Trinitarianism and endless misery, and trying to make them look as ridiculous as language would admit of, and becoming passionately disturbed with the disgusting subject, he broke out in his true Irish brogue, "Why, there's yer great God, the Father, he is *willing* the salvation of all men; and there's yer great God, the Son, he is inthercedin'; and there's yer great God, the Holy Ghost, he is dhrawin'; but that little black man, down there, *out-pulls them all!*"

In regard to myself—my life, thus far, since I entered upon the ministry, has been exceedingly laborious. My travels, in all seasons, through all kinds of roads, amid all sorts of weather, and amidst almost all the variety of character that human nature is capable of sustaining, have been excessively fatiguing. I have itinerated from the shores of the Atlantic to Lake Erie, and from the borders of Lake Ontario to the city of Philadelphia; and my remunerations, taken in the aggregate, have been scarcely sufficient to defray the necessary expenses of my peregrinations. But for the greatest share of the time, Heaven has blessed me with good health, and with increasing vigor of constitution; and in addition to the consciousness of using my utmost endeavors to discharge a solemn and imperative duty, I have been encouraged and sustained by the smiles and the friendship of a few individuals who, in spite of the frowns of a domineering and bigoted church, the anathemas of a proud and pampered priesthood, or the sneers of a thoughtless, a soulless, and a selfish world, have dared to stretch forth the helping hand, and to stand firmly by me through good and through evil report; and, until within a short time past, I have enjoyed the heart-sustaining consolation of living in the most perfect harmony with the church of my most special charge, as well as with all the societies to which I have had the pleasure of ministering. I am not conscious that there ever was, until quite recently, the least distrust, jealousy, or unkind feeling existing in the head or heart of a single member of the church or society in Hamilton toward me; or that a word, a look, or an action, ever for one moment interrupted our cordiality and perfect harmony. But a change came over the scene; and were it possible, with justice to the reader and to the world, I would "seal up what the seven thunders uttered," I would suppress this portion of the history of my life, and try to sink in everlasting oblivion those events which pain my soul to record. But I have promised to give a faithful and true history; and however painful to me, or unpleasant to others, the task must be performed. And I pray God, that it may prove a salutary monition to religious bodies, to let no popular excitement intrude upon their consecrated ground, and sow acrimonious discord among the brethren.

Everybody knows what havoc the anti-Masonic excitement made of churches, societies, and associations, and of religious bodies of every description, and of every denomination, through the length and breadth of the State of New York, and even much farther—in almost every State in the Union. And what scenes of discord it produced through all ranks of society, from the highest to the lowest. Political aspirants, demagogues, and partisans, laid hold of it to accomplish their disorganizing purposes—religious hypocrites who had joined the Masonic fraternity to clothe themselves with a respectability that they were unworthy of, and to gain an influence which their moral character, together with their religious profession, without it could never acquire, and never deserved—took advantage of it, by renouncing Masonry, whose principles they never understood nor appreciated, to hoist themselves into popular favor, and fan the flame of discord to gratify their unhallowed ambition, and viler passions; and by these means, the most bitter and malignant spirit that ever characterized the most violent political factions, found its way into the church. "Fire-brands, arrows, and death," were hurled with relentless fury, until the peaceable kingdom of the Redeemer almost became an Aceldama.

It was to be hoped that the liberality of Universalists, their detestation of spiritual tyranny of every description, their admiration of unrestricted liberty of opinion, thought, word, and action, would be a guaranty against any important inroads of this mover of seditions within the peaceable precincts of their fraternity. But, alas! the hope was fallacious; Universalists are but men, and the contagion was most insidious.

Nearly all the Universalist preachers in the state of New York were Masons, as well as vast numbers of the clergy of other denominations. Before I ever came into the state, I united with the fraternity; and I here feel under a solemn obligation to state, that during all the trials, the obloquy and the perscutions I experienced on that account, I never, for a moment, regretted the step I had taken. But this hydra-headed monster,

> "Whose tongue outvenoms all the worms of Nile
> Whose breath rides on the posting winds and doth
> Belie all corners of the world,"

found its way into our ranks, sundering the cords of fraternal affection, which had proved invulnerable to the attack of every other enemy, and shook many societies to their centre, if it did not entirely prostrate them. Large numbers who had professed an unshaken faith in the doctrine, who had been the most ardent friends of our preachers, and among their most liberal supporters, left the meetings and withdrew their patronage from every preacher who was a Freemason; and instantaneously discovered in the characters of those they had extolled as super-human—as almost angelic—all the appalling deformities of a demon of the lower regions.

There were but a very few in the church and society in Hamilton who entirely abandoned our meetings; but "the love of many waxed cold," and this was a sore trial to me. My soul was formed for friendship; and the manifest frigidity of those cords which bound the people of my charge to me, cooled the ardor of my feelings, and I felt confident would render my labors among them a mere nullity.

Among my anti-Masonic brethren and sisters, (for this was an excitement in which females took a very active part,) were a few who had been among my warmest friends and most liberal supporters; one particularly, a Mr. H., who several years afterwards confessed to me, that anti-Masonry overset his reason and destroyed his religion, during its reign. This man was an active member of the church; he had been one of my most devoted friends; but the anti-Masonic excitement had produced a complete aberration of his reasoning powers, and converted him into a most stupid and superstitious fanatic. He told my wife once, in conversation with her on the subject of Masonry, that he did not believe I was *willingly* and *wilfully* guilty of murder, but he had no doubt that numerous instances of *murder had been committed in the lodge,* while I was present. But Masons possessed the infernal power of casting a mist before the eyes of whom they pleased; and knowing that I would not approve of deeds of murder, the leaders blinded my eyes while the dreadful act was done; for he believed they uniformly put to death all who violated their oaths. He labored very earnestly and faithfully with me, to have me renounce Masonry; but, being unsuccessful, he at length told me, with tears in his eyes, that he must conscientiously leave my meetings, and withdraw his support from me.

On a certain Saturday, at a preparatory meeting previous to communion, Mr. H. desired a little private conversation with me before the services of the meeting. We retired; and he then asked me, how I felt in regard to Masonry, and if I did not consider it my duty to renounce it. I told him that my feelings had undergone no alteration on that subject since my first acquaintance with the institution, and I could not renounce it until I saw something in it different from what I had been able to discover; and that was hopeless, as I had taken all the degrees that belonged to it, and knew as much about it as any other man. He replied, that he was very sorry, and that under such circumstances he could not commune with me. I answered, "This is hard, Brother H., but you and I must act for ourselves; and let us try to be honest with ourselves, in the fear of God." He further remarked, that he should have something to say in our church meeting; but as he desired not to hurt the feelings of any one more than he could help, he wished to have the other members speak first. I told him, he should certainly enjoy his privilege, and at such time as would be most agreeable to him.

The meeting was opened in the usual form, by a short lecture, the members of the church had all expressed their feelings very freely, and some of them with considerable animation. Mr. H. was quite deaf, and as the sisters generally spoke without rising, he was unable to determine whether or not they had spoken, or indeed were speaking; I therefore said to him, "Brother H., I believe we have heard from all the brethren and sisters but yourself; if you have a word for us, we shall be happy to hear from you." He instantly arose, and spoke with a good degree of warmth of the strength of his faith, his love of the Redeemer's cause and kingdom, his determination to persevere, &c.; and exhorted the brethren and sisters to be faithful, and persevere unto the end. "But," said he, "there are two brethren in the church, Brother Stacy and Brother Lord, that, under existing circumstances, *I can not* commune with. They belong to a society which, I believe, had its origin in heathenish darkness; which has for its object the destruction of religion and civil government, and which has been supported by *blood and murder* from its commencement up to the present time." And after inveighing, for several minutes, against Masonry in the strongest language he was master of, Mr. H. took his seat. I then arose, and addressed them, in substance, in the following language :

"Brethren and sisters, I rise not to attempt a vindication of Free Masonry against the charges which have been brought against it. I am extremely sorry to be under the necessity of saying one word on the subject. I had seriously hoped that *Universalists*, at least, would have the liberality to let people settle matters which solely belong to their own consciences without interfering—matters *exclusively* between their own consciences and their God. But I have risen to ask you, what you want of me. You know me as well as it is possible for you to *know a man*. Twenty-five years I have had the pleasure of preaching to you, and twenty-two years I have lived in your midst; so that you are under no necessity of inquiring of any man concerning me, for you yourselves know all about me that can be known by man. You are acquainted with my private character as well as my public fame, with my daily walk and conversation as well as my public labors; and, if I am guilty of any crime, of any immorality, or misdemeanor, *you know it*—you need no other evidence than your own personal knowledge, for you know all about me that *mortals can know*. And you know that I was a Free-Mason before you ever saw me—before I ever came into this country. If Masonry, therefore, has led me into bad company, if it has imbued my soul with bad principles, with a malicious, vindictive spirit, and led me into the commission of crime, it can not be hidden from you. I have never said any thing to any of you on the subject of Masonry, as I can recollect, unless by your request; and then I have fully and cheerfully explained to you its principles, without reserve. I have never said it was Christianity, nor equal to Christianity; but I have said, and I now say again, that there is nothing in Masonry, either in its principles or in its formulas, incompatible with the purest religion, or that should prevent the most devotional and fervent Christian from uniting with the order—that it enjoined the same rules of moral life—that the great *square*, by which it requires its votaries to try all their actions, was the golden rule of our Savior: "All things, whatsoever ye would that men should do unto you, do ye even so unto them." I as much disapprove of, and condemn, the conduct of those concerned in the abduction of William Morgan, as any of you *can*; and I know no more about it than you do; nor have I any other means of knowing about it than you have; and I would use all the means in my power, as readily as any of you, to bring the perpetrators of that crime to justice. But one thing I do know that you do not, and that is, that the act was a total violation of the principles of Masonry, and must have been committed by men, though nominal Masons, who were criminally ignorant of its moral principles, and were influenced by a blind and perverse fanaticism, or, perhaps, by selfish and more criminal motives.

"But, I ask again, what you now want of me? Do you want that I should tell you, that for twenty-five years, while I have been advocating religion in your presence, and professing to be a warm admirer of the civil institutions of our beloved country, and an ardent supporter of good government, that I have all this time, been a base hypocrite? and been combined with a set of vile knaves and rascals for the overthrow of both, as Brother H. says I have? Or do you wish me now, for the sake of gratifying some splenetic mind, to become a hypocrite? Do you wish me to say that Masonry is a vile institution, when I know better? Now if you want either of these, my brethren and sisters, you *can not* have them. Thus far I have been an honest man; and, by the help of God, I'll die an honest man. I hold myself responsible to you for my conduct, and not only to you, but to the world—to the least child that walks on God's footstool. Point out to me a crime—a wrong that I have committed against any living being, that is tangible, that can be investigated, and I will crawl on my hands and knees, if I can not walk on my feet, until I make reparation. If you can not sit under my ministry, tell me so, and I will use my best endeavors to procure you a preacher who can edify you; or if you will hear me preach, but can not receive the elements of communion at my hands, tell me whom you would choose to break the bread for you, and I will exchange with him if within my power. All these things I will freely and cheerfully do for you; but do not ask me to renounce Masonry, for I WILL NOT DO IT. And I now say, for once and for all, *you have no business with it—you have no right to complain of me about, nor be grieved with it*—it is a matter exclusively between my own conscience and my God; and *I feel no accountability to you on the subject.* I will enter into no compact with you about it, nor agree not to sit in a lodge. I will do so if I please, and as often as I please, without asking your liberty. I will have my liberty in this respect; and while I cheerfully accord to you equal liberty, I beg of you never again to let this subject be brought into the church."

When I resumed my seat, there was not a dry eye in the house; I felt myself deeply moved. The subject was a tender one, and when I arose I resolved to make a finish of it—to never have it again introduced into church-meeting—and it never was. As soon as the power of speech was recovered, several voices exclaimed, "We do not want Brother Stacy to renounce Masonry now—it is certainly too late."

But the wound, though probed, was not thoroughly healed; there were too many influences against it. Anti-Masonic tracts and periodicals were profusely scattered over the country—churches of every denomination were fanatically calling many of their pastors and members to an account, and fulminating their anathemas against such as would not renounce—acrimonious denunciations against the order by professed seceding Masons were zealously circulated—Barnard's "Light on Masonry" was hailed as an oracle—and anarchy and misrule, among churches as well as society in general, were the order of the day. Some preachers, in order to retain their standing and salary, would compromise with their churches, by agreeing never again to attend a Masonic meeting; and it was considered an act of great liberality and condescension in a church to accept of such a condition. I was a witness to one disgusting scene arising from such a compromise. There was a Baptist clergyman by the name of Blain, pastor of a church in Madison, a man of reputed superior talents, and a truly fluent speaker, became a very zealous Free-Mason. He delivered several festival sermons, one or more of which was published, in which he extolled Masonry vastly beyond what I conscientiously could do, not only as the handmaid of Christianity, but almost its mistress, and certainly above every other institution known among men. It so happened in the midst of the anti-Masonic excitement, that a member of the lodge to which we both belonged died; and, on his death-bed, requested the lodge to bury him, and me to deliver the discourse. The lodge met on the occasion, proceeded to the house of the deceased, took charge of the body, and conveyed it to the meeting-house, where I met Brother Blain, and invited him into the desk. He cheerfully accepted the invitation, and at my request made a prayer. It was in the winter, and on a cold day; and the master of the lodge concluded to perform as much of the funeral rites in the church as would possibly be consistent, because it would be very uncomfortable standing long at the grave. Therefore, as soon as the pulpit services closed, he began the Masonic. I heard a noise at my side—looked around, when Br. Blair had seized his hat, and was running from the desk as though a lion was at his heels. He had made such a covenant with his church. From my soul, I pitied the man, while I despised his conduct.

Very few of the church or society in Hamilton, except Mr. H., entirely withdrew their patronage; but they became quite remiss in attending meetings, and cold and distant in their demeanor toward me. These things I could not endure; and I resolved, for my own peace and tranquility, as well as that of the church and the good of the cause, to change my residence. I made known my determination—indeed, I had made several trials, years before this, to get the society willing for my removal, believing that the change would be profitable to them. if not to me; but hitherto they had effectually opposed every movement of the kind. Now, however, although a majority manifested great reluctance to the proposed measure, yet they could not help seeing that the present state of feeling was an ample justification of my course.

After it became known abroad, that I would remove from Hamilton, I received several calls to settle in old societies; one from Sullivan, Madison county; one from Barre, Vermont, which, with the utmost difficulty and not without nearly or quite offending them, I [illegible]sisted; and one from Brooklyn, Pennsylvania, which I once visited in the course of the negotiation, and where I probably should have removed, had it not been for rather a singular incident, which eventually changed my course to another place. I had been in the habit of preaching, more or less, in the town of Columbus, Chenango county, New York; and quite a respectable number of my friends had removed from thence and the adjoining towns into a new country on the Brokenstraw creek, Warren county, Pennsylvania, where they had settled a township with families who had nearly all emigrated from those parts, and in honor of the town of their former residence had given it the name of Columbus. In the winter of 1828, while on a tour in Columbus, I visited one evening with two families who had sold their property, and were about removing to

Brokenstraw; and, in the course of the conversation, they said to me, "What would induce you to move into our new country?" I carelessly replied, "Give me a hundred acres of land, and I'll go." This led to some further remarks, and they again asked me, "If we should offer you a hundred acres of land, would you agree to move to Brokenstraw?" I replied, "If you want any thing serious about it, I will seriously tell you what I will do. If you will make me the offer, so that I can feel *sure* if I accept of it, I will certainly make you a visit, if life and health will permit; and if, after seeing it, I like the country, I will remove there. But the land must not be a consideration for preaching, but a donation for becoming a settler among you. I will not be under obligation to preach one Sunday for the land; if I preach, that must be another consideration." "Well," they replied, "we believe you will have the offer." Here the matter was dropped. In the following spring, these families removed to Brokenstraw, and I thought little or nothing more about it. In the mean time, the correspondence with the societies above alluded to, took place; and I made one visit to Brooklyn with pretty strong anticipations of accepting the call from that society. But wholly unexpected by me, early in the spring of 1829, I received a package from Captain David Curtis, then postmaster in Columbus, Warren county, Pa., containing the offer of one hundred acres of land in that township, upon the exact conditions I had named to my friends, with the legal vouchers to make it sure, in case I accepted the offer; and giving me two years to make preparations, and remove there. Hence, I was then under obligation to fulfil on my part, so far, at least, as to make them a visit.

The society in Brooklyn were immediately informed of the circumstance, and advised to seek some other preacher to supply their desk. I made arrangements with as much despatch as circumstances would admit; and, about the middle of June, in company with a man who married our neice, and who wanted to find a home in some new country, started on this journey of about three hundred miles. I had previously written to friends in Lockport and Buffalo, which I designed to visit on my way, and given appointments for a week-day lecture in Lockport, and the usual services on Sunday in Buffalo; and when I arrived in Jamestown, I was immediately called on by a gentleman who had attended my meetings in Otsego many years before, and almost forcibly detained to preach with them on Sunday.

After traveling about ten miles from Jamestown, Chautauque county, we entered a wild and almost entirely uncultivated country, where the road was merely cleared of the trees and fallen timber, the streams roughly bridged, but in other respects left in a state of nature, and almost impassable with our carriage. These things afforded rather a gloomy prospect; but we saw indications of strong soil in the unparalleled size and height of the trees of that dense and dark forest; and occasionally we passed a small improvement, where the products of cultivation confirmed this indication. In the winding course of our road at that time, we had to travel about sixteen miles over a rough no-road to reach our destination. My friends had been apprised of our approach, and were prepared to receive us, and did receive us with every demonstration of gratification. This township and the immediate vicinity were entirely new; although within fifteen, twenty, and twenty-five miles on either hand were old settlements, and some populous towns. The first settlers of this town from the east, had been there but five years; and they were the first who had made any permanent improvements. There were, many years previously, some squatters from other parts of Pennsylvania, settled down in several parts of this and adjacent towns, remote from each other, who had cleared off some small spots, but made no other improvement—not so much as to cut the trees from the road wide enough for an ox-sled to pass, or make even a rude bridge across a single stream, or erect any kind of mill, or establish any kind of mechanical business; and all the intercourse they held with each other, or any of the rest of the world, was by means of walking and wading through streams of water. But becoming discouraged, and finding they could not hold the land merely by possession, which they anticipated when they first settled down on it, they had all left but two or three families, before our eastern people came into the country. But the present population was of Yankee origin—hardy, industrious, and enterprising—and many of them had made large improvements, had opened roads and made bridges across the streams, had erected large barns and out-houses, and astonished the "natives" by their zeal, activity, and enterprise. They had already drawn a plot for a village at the confluence of the Coffee-creek with the Brokenstraw, embracing extensive water-power, where a grist-mill and two saw-mills were already erected; and they had commenced putting up other buildings, and some eight or ten families had collected there.

The first business after our arrival was to have a meeting; and the next to show me the country. My friend, Captain Curtis, devoted his time to this object, conducted me over the township, and out in every direction to the surrounding settlements. Although the country was mostly in a state of nature, and the roads intolerable, still I was pleased with it. It evidently possessed great strength of soil, with the heaviest growth and the greatest variety of timber I had ever seen, or have since seen, thrown together in any one place. The country was neither level nor mountainous, but just undulating enough to produce a salubrious air, and pure and lively streams of water, sufficiently large for all ordinary hydraulic purposes, and to float off their lumber down to the Allegany, thence to the Ohio, and to the western and southern markets. Capt. Curtis was well qualified to show me the country; for he was a practical land-surveyor, and was employed by Huydekoper, the general agent of the Holland company, who owned the greatest part of this township and the adjacent country, to survey and dispose of these lands; and he devoted two weeks, principally, to make me acquainted with it.

The village, as I have already remarked, was laid out at the confluence of the Coffee-creek with the Big-Brokenstraw, on lands belonging to Luther P. Mather and Capt. Curtis; and besides the buildings already mentioned, there was a building erected for a public house, another for a store, and shops for a blacksmith, shoemaker, wagon-maker, and some other mechanics.

After I had had sufficient time to view the country, and become acquainted with its relative position in regard to the market places, and the other surrounding towns and settlements, my friends inquired how I liked it, and whether or not I felt disposed to accept of their offer. I told them I liked the country well; and although I was sensible it would subject me to many hardships and privations which, in all probability, I might avoid by accepting either of the other calls I had already received from other societies, nevertheless, I felt disposed to accept of their proposal, inasmuch as I had three sons whom I wished to make farmers, if I could excite in them a taste for it; and I would use my best endeavors to dispose of what little property I had at the east, and remove my family among them. The man who accompanied me was so well pleased with the country, and the location of the contemplated village, that he purchased a village lot, with a determination to settle there. He was a mechanic—a cabinet-maker.

We returned home; and, in the course of a few months, I had an opportunity to dispose of my little place in Hamilton; and I then began in earnest to make preparations to leave the State of New York.

The following winter, in company with my eldest son, who had then become of age, I visited my venerable mother for the last time; although she lived seven years after that time. As my new home placed me at least five hundred miles from her, and as, before her death, I had removed to the State of Michigan, three hundred miles farther from her, that was the last time I saw her.

In the spring following, Mr. Porter, the man who accompanied me to Brokenstraw, removed thither, and my eldest son went with him. It required the ensuing summer for me to settle my affairs, and make the necessary preparations for removal; and, on the first of September, all things were in readiness. Previously to my removal, however, I prevailed on the church and society in Hamilton to authorize me, before I left them, to give some one of our preachers a call to settle with them, being aware of the probability at least, if I left them in their present state of feeling, destitute of preaching, they would sink down into such a condition of coldness and apathy, as would result in their disorganization and death, from which they might never recover; and as the society in Madison was destitute of preaching, I persuaded them to unite with the society in Hamilton in giving a preacher a call who should serve both societies. I named several preachers who, I believed, might be obtained, and, from the number, they selected Mr. John Freeman, of Saratoga. I wrote to him, informing him of the wishes of the two societies, and requested an immediate answer, so that in case of his refusal I might make another application, as I very much wanted to see a preacher settled with them before my removal. But, instead of writing, he made us a personal visit, preached at least one Sabbath to each society, besides some lectures; and gave such satisfaction, that they engaged his services, and made immediate preparations for the removal of his family. This relieved my mind of very serious, and even burdensome solicitude. I felt extremely reluctant to leave them in that divided and lukewarm state, with no one to break to them the bread of life. They had grown up under my feeble ministry, and I felt for them the solicitude of a father for his beloved children. And, although the separation, at best, was a sore trial, the sting was greatly blunted, when I obtained the assurance they would not be left destitute; but would enjoy the benefits of the labors of one who would, if within the power of man to accomplish it, soothe the asperity of their feelings, and heal the unhappy division which was sapping the foundation of their peace: And Mr. Freeman did so, certainly to a very great extent, and the society flourished under his ministry while he lived with them; but, alas! he "finished his work," and closed his valuable and useful life in their midst, in less than four years from his settlement with them.

The time for my leaving Hamilton at length arrived, all necessary preparations were made, and the trying hour of of separation came. On the last Sabbath I met with them, the house, and to a great extent the surrounding common, were densely crowded; a window was taken from the house, and my pulpit embraced the aperture thus formed, In the morning, I addressed the youth, from 2d Tim., 3: 14, 15; and, in the afternoon, the church and society, from Acts 20: 27. At the close of the meeting, my friends crowded around me, and even those who had forsaken my meetings, Mr. H. among them, and wept like children. The scene nearly overpowered my fortitude; but the die was cast, and, on the eleventh day of September, 1830, with all my family, I bade adieu to Hamilton, where I had resided twenty-two years and five months; and, on the 29th day of the same month, we arrived in the town of Columbus, Warren county, commonwealth of Pennsylvania.

My son, who had preceded us, had purchased a village lot, cleared off the timber, and erected a frame and partly enclosed it for a small dwelling-house. We finished this with as much despatch as possible, so far as to make it habitable for the winter, and removed our family into it. I now selected my hundred-acre lot, which they gave me the privilege of doing from any of the Holland company's unsold lands, or any land belonging to Capt. Curtis; and I made a selection of a good lot, within one mile of the village, from the company's land. In addition to this, and over and above the donation the society had made me, Capt. Curtis gave me one of the best village lots his possession afforded, adjoining my son's lot, on which I erected a barn that fall. We were, therefore, soon settled in our new habitation, with all the comforts a new country could furnish around us, and should have felt a contentment, and indeed a happiness, which the broils and confusion arising from the excited state of society we had left, rendered impossible, had it not been for the sickness of my wife. But either before we left Hamilton, or on our way thither through the unhealthy part of the State of New York, which lay in our way, she imbibed the incipient elements of the ague and fever, (a disease wholly unknown in Columbus,) and on our arrival was immediately taken down with it, and which prostrated her nearly three months.

One, and no inconsiderable object in my estimation, which I had in view in removing to Columbus, aside from getting a farm for my sons, (which I never could have procured the means to purchase in the country from which I removed,) was to lessen my own travels, which had heretofore uniformly kept me from my home and family. I supposed I could nurse up a society in this place; and I designed to confine my labors principally or solely to them, while I assisted my boys in improving and cultivating a farm, which should afford us sufficient sources of subsistence. And the almost impossibility of traveling in this country would certainly favor my object—the excessive badness of the roads would afford sufficient excuse for declining to make appointments abroad. Our friends immediately took steps to organize a society; and the ensuing season a church, consisting of about twenty members, was also organized.

We made every possible arrangement during the winter, to commence making improvements on our farm-lot the ensuing spring. My eldest son, although of age, and a mechanic, agreed to lay aside his trade, at least for a season, and take hold with the rest of us until we could get our farm in a state of cultivation; and I would turn a deaf ear to calls for preaching if any were made from abroad, and lay off the clerical garb mostly, and be captain of my little band of laborers. But notwithstanding my firmly fixed resolutions of selfishness, my assumed stoicism to the condition of others; in despite of the almost impassableness of the roads through all that country, and the excessive fatigue and even danger in traveling over them, I could not steel my heart against the pathetic calls for the preached word, by souls famishing for the bread of life.

There was only one preacher of our order in all that extensive country, including Chautauque and Cattaraugus counties in New York, and all Pennsylvania west of the Allegany mountains, and that was Mr. L. C. Todd, who resided, I think, at that time in the town of Chautauque. I might have excepted Mr. Todd's father, who then resided near him, and who was in fellowship with our denomination, but who had preached very little, if any, for several years. There had been other preachers in Chautauque county; Mr. S. R. Smith had itinerated in the western part of the county in an early day of his ministry; Mr. Alfred Peck had once resided there, and and an Association had once been organized; but all the preachers except Mr. Todd had left the country, the societies all, or nearly all, had become disbanded, and the Association had not held a meeting for several years. Mr. T. was, at that time, though possessed of sterling talents and sound arguments, rather a cold preacher, and manifested no zeal for religious organization or order of any kind, and very little for the advancement of the cause. I was compelled to stop and give them a meeting in Jamestown, and another in Busti, at the time of my removal, before I reached Columbus; and they extracted a promise from me, to visit them again as soon as I could make it convenient after getting well settled in my new habitation. While on my first visit to that country, I had delivered a single lecture in Warren, our county seat; and while at Erie after our furniture, which we sent by water to that place, I found an individual who had heard me preach in Madison county; and he extorted a promise from me to make him a visit at some future day, and deliver a lecture in that borough. The news that a Universalist preacher had removed into the country was soon circulated in every direction; and as individuals of our faith were scattered promiscuously over it, in nearly every town in the counties of Erie, Crawford, and Venango, in Pennsylvania, as well as Chautauque and Cattaraugus, in New York, before I could fairly get rested from the fatigues of removal, and my family settled in their new home, the most earnest, plaintive, and pathetic solicitations to "come over and help us," were borne, as it were, on the "wings of every wind." How could I resist those appeals? It was not in my nature to do it. I loved mankind, and I loved the cause too well to resist them. And, notwithstanding the firm resolution I had made, not to listen to calls from abroad, but to pursue my secular concerns—notwithstanding the infirmities of age which I felt fast creeping on, and the fatigues I must encounter, by day and by night, before the year rolled its round it found me traveling at least two hundred and fifty miles a month, over roads that would make a man's bones ache to look at, to fulfil my regular engagements; besides diverging at almost every corner to attend casual lectures; and, within the year, societies were organized in Columbus, in the borough of Warren, in Oil Creek township, Crawford county, Mill Creek township, Erie county, and respectable congregations collected in many other places.

But we had trials awaiting us, more poignant and heart-rending than any we had ever yet been called to experience. When we removed to Columbus, our family consisted of eight children, three sons and five daughters. We had always been highly favored on account of sickness among our children; they generally possessed good constitutions; and, as we at least thought, were quite as promising as families in general. Death had never made inroads upon our family, and we looked forward with pleasing anticipations to the time when we should see them all settled around us in this new but improving country, and in the decline of life realize their social and sustaining influence. But, alas! how uncertain are all our earthly blessings, how fragile the foundation of all our temporal hopes, and how soon our fondest anticipations may be blasted! In one short day, we were plunged from this enviable eminence to the depth of darkness, and almost despair! On the morning of the 14th of May, 1831, the spring after our removal to Columbus, I directed my two youngest sons to remove some lumber sixty or seventy rods, to a place where we were erecting a school-house; part of the boards were in the saw-mill, and while in the act of taking them away, my youngest son, then in his fifteenth year, fell through a hole broken in the floor the preceding day, into a floom, called the bull-wheel floom, containing about eight feet of water; and that beloved child, who, in the morning, was as healthy, as cheerful, as full of hope, of life, of activity, as any child of his age ever could be, was a cold corpse before the sun had sunk behind the western hills. He was taken from the water, and resuscitated so as to breathe freely; but his reason—his senses returned not; a few incoherent words were all he uttered; all means to get any thing into his stomach were resisted, and he shortly sunk into a stupor from which he never revived. There was a beam over the floom immediately under the hole through which he fell, on which it is supposable he must have struck, and received some undiscovered injury; for the instance of one being taken from the water, and then dying in the manner he did, I know not to be recorded on the page of history.

That was a stroke I found myself ill prepared to bear. He was the hope of my declining years, the staff on which I anticipated leaning my faltering steps as I approached the grave. It came upon me with such *force*—so sudden, so unexpected—that it seemed like the breaking up of the foundation of creation—like the crash of worlds—the heavens seemed shrouded in gloom, and angry thunders growled their approaching peals—the vernal season was clothed in sackcloth, and the feathered songsters uttered dirges of inconsolable woe—I slipped; but my feet struck, and remained steadfast upon the "Rock of ages"—I tottered and reeled, but the hand of infinite mercy caught, and sustained me erect. Oh, where should I have found consolation, had it not been for the sustaining power of that faith which embraces a God of infinite, unchangeable wisdom, power, and *love*; and a life of immortal blessedness for all the posterity of Adam, "through the redemption which is in Christ Jesus." It now appears to me, that unutterable despair and raving madness must have been my inevitable doom. But God, in mercy, smiled upon me from behind the howling tempest, cleared the skies at length, restored peace to my soul, confirmed my confidence anew, and by this tremendous stroke drew me still nearer to him, to take shelter under the wing of his divine protection, and enkindled a more ardent zeal for the cause of his truth.

With mournful and smitten hearts, we pursued our contemplated object with as much engagedness as we could command; but my zeal for temporal enterprise was essentially checked, and a gloom hung around every improvement I had before contemplated in such glowing colors. We, however, made some improvement on our farm-lot, and erected a house on our village-lot; and, during the summer following, we continued to exert ourselves to enlarge our improvements on our farm, until we had between twenty and thirty acres under cultivation, and a house and barn erected thereon. In the mean time, my eldest son married, and settled on the farm; but, after remaining something more than a year on it, he became tired of farming, and chose again to return to his trade. This left me with a single son, seventeen years of age, small in stature, being only; about my size who, although a faithful and good boy to work, appeared unequal to the Herculean task of grappling with the mighty forest which covered the lot, and, single-handed, convert it into a "fruitful field." I therefore requested him to take it into serious consideration; and if the result was, that he would choose to follow farming, we would try to finish paying for the lot—the society, notwithstanding their engagements with me, were unable to fulfil all their stipulations—and I would help him all I was able to bring it into a state of profitable cultivation; but, if he chose some profession, we would sell the farm the first opportunity, and I would help him all I was able. He weighed the subject according to his judgment, and came to the latter conclusion. Before leaving Hamilton, he had enjoyed some privilege in the academy in that town; I now sent him to the academy in the borough of Erie for a season. On my removal to Michigan, in 1835, he accompanied me, and entered upon the study of law, which he completed while there, and received admittance at the bar before we returned again to Pennsylvania. But to return from this digression.

It is an old remark, that misfortune and trouble never come alone; and my experience, in those days, abundantly attests the truthfulness of the observation. I was soon called to part with one of the most efficient and faithful friends I was ever blessed with in mortal man. Capt. David Curtis was the efficient instrument of my removal into this country. He stood at the head of our little society, and, as it were, was the temporal foundation of its prosperity. He had the right of the disposal of the land I had selected, but designed to make no writings in regard to it, until the money was all collected, so that the land could be procured at cash price, which was two dollars per acre; whereas, to article the land would add one third to the price. While the land was in his hands we considered it perfectly safe, and with the assurance of security from his word, I went on to it and made the improvements above named. But it pleased the allwise Disposer of events, in the inscrutable disposition of his government, to remove him from the society of his earthly friends, and bring another deep, dark cloud over the sunshine of our joys. He sickened in the spring of 1832, and in the month of July, that year, he left these sublunary and mortal shores for a brighter world and a more exalted life. But notwithstanding he was in the vigor of manhood, having seen but forty-six years, a man of indomitable perseverance and enterprise, had accumulated a property in this new location, by his own industry, worth fourteen or fifteen thousand dollars, and contemplated great improvement in the country, and in his village in particular—had a beloved companion, and a large family of young and dependent children ; still he complained not of the dealings of his heavenly Father, nor repined at the hour of approaching dissolution which he perfectly realized ; but trusting in God, with a well-established faith in the Son of his love, and a well-grounded hope in the ultimate purity and happiness of all moral intelligences, he met his end with the most perfect cheerfulness—called his afflicted family around him but a few moments before he breathed his last, gave them a husband's and a father's counsel and blessing—and then requesting to be laid in the middle of his bed, that he might freely stretch his limbs, in two or three minutes, without a struggle or a groan, yielded up his spirit to God who gave it. Oh, how blessed is that faith which can thus reconcile the soul to God, and illuminate its passage through the "valley of the shadow of death."

But this dispensation left me under embarrassments. My friends had subscribed a sufficient sum to pay for the land they donated to me, could it have been purchased at cash price, which was their intention and expectation ; and part of the subscriptions had already been paid into the hands of Capt. Curtis ; I, with his responsibility, had made several hundred dollars' worth of improvements upon the land. But now I was liable to have the land sold out from under me, at any moment, without any guaranty for what had been paid ; or for the improvements I had made upon it ; and there was no way of safety now, but to pay for the land without delay, or take an article from the general agent. The first was beyond my power without help from the society ; and that help the society could not afford then : the latter, therefore, was the only feasible course. What money had already been collected and paid into the hands of Capt. Curtis, was paid over to the general agent, and I took an article for the land, which gave me eight years to pay the remainder, with the addition of one dollar upon an acre from the cash price. And this was all that was ever paid by me, or for me, for the land ; for before the time had half expired, I sold my betterments and transferred the article to the purchaser.

These bereavements and disappointments, severely as I felt

them, did not, however, produce the least inclination to relinquish or relax my ministerial labors, but rather spurred me on with additional zeal; for in this alone I found my solace and my spiritual support. The more the world frowned—the more its atmosphere darkened, its proffered blessings vanished, and the fragile foundation of its hopes trembled, the brighter did the Sun of Righteousness shine above the work of death—the more glorious did the imperishable foundation of eternal realities display itself, and "durable riches and righteousness" present themselves to my eager grasp.

Soon after my removal into this country, Mr. L. C. Todd removed to the village of Jamestown, and issued a prospectus for a periodical, to be published weekly, in that village, devoted to the cause of Universalism, and to be entitled "*The Genius of Liberty.*" The ultimate fate of that paper, and the course which Mr. Todd pursued, are too well known to need further notice in these memoirs. Suffice it to say, that Mr. Todd's mental and religious aberrations were of but few years' duration; and though the trial was a severe one to him, and very painful to his friends, it was, nevertheless, attended with a happy result. He is now more firmly established in the faith of the Great Salvation, more zealous in the cause, more devoted to useful order and ordinances, and wholesome discipline—and is again enrolled in the family of the faithful, a better preacher and a better man than he was before he passed through this "furnace of affliction."

After Mr. Todd commenced publishing his paper, I used all the influence I had with him, to argue upon a suitable time and place, and give notice through the medium of his paper, for a grand conference meeting of our brethren and friends, with a view to revive the Chautauque Association. But although he did not directly oppose such a meeting, he manifested no interest in it. He would put me off, from time to time; and, indeed, never found leisure, nor opportunity to attend to it. His time was wholly occupied in teaching a select school and publishing his paper. He preached but little in Jamestown, or elsewhere; and seemed to feel no farther interest in the cause than what was immediately connected with his publication. There was no other preacher in all that country with whom I could confer; and to assume the whole responsibility of appointing such a meeting myself, was a step I felt diffident about taking; and therefore deferred it until Mr. Todd and his periodical both ceased to be organs of our denomination.

CHAPTER XVI.

Prosperity of the cause in Hamilton under Mr. Freeman—Erection of a meeting-house—Visit to Hamilton—Central Association—Greeting of old friends—Brother H.; his change of feelings and confession—Dedication—Visits among friends—Meetings during the tour, and prosperity of the cause Mr. Bond removes to Carroll—Mr. J. E. Holmes to Westfield—Conference in Carroll—Resuscitation of the Chautauque Association—Heavy affliction—Death of a beloved daughter—A scrap—Tour to Ohio—Western Reserve Association—Meetings in several towns—Chautauque Association—Circuit proposed—Mr. W. E. Manley—Circuit conference—Tour for establishment of circuit—Administration of Capt. D. Curtis' estate—Tour to Virginia—Voyage on a raft—Visit to Marietta, O.—Introduction—Meeting—Visit to relatives up the Muskingum—To Belpre—Mr. Chappel—Meetings—Sunday at McConnelsville—Return journey—Meeting at Beaver, Pa.—Arrival home—Call from Michigan—Tour—Passage up the Lake—Detroit-Ann Arbor-Society—Meeting-house—Reception—Meetings—General appearance of the country—Engagement—Return—Close of executorship—Removal to Michigan—Journey through Ohio—Storm—Steam-boat voyage—Arrival at Detroit—At Ann Arbor—State of society in Michigan; habits and institutions—Two Universalist preachers, A. H. Curtis and Thomas Wheeler—Lectures in different places—Organization of association—Preachers present—Church organized—Interesting anecdote of the conversion of Deacon John Williams—His sickness and trial of faith—The church approves of his public improvements—Receives a letter of fellowship from the association—Opposition of the clergy—Invitation for a discussion-Address to the clergy—Article published in the "State Journal" and "Michigan Argus"—Rev. Mr. Marks' article—His second article—Reply—Course of lectures.

I have already had the pleasure of recording that the society in Hamilton, after I left them, prospered under the labors of Mr. Freeman. As I had fondly anticipated, he had the unspeakable happiness of calming the asperities of their feelings, in a very great measure, and of reuniting them in one congregation. His meetings were well attended, and additions were made to his congregations, until the "place became too strait" for them; and their old house, too, becoming dilapidated and unfit for use, they were really under the necessity of providing a more ample temple for the service of God. They therefore purchased a handsome lot in the center of the town, in the immediate vicinity of their former place of worship, and erected a convenient meeting-house; and both pastor, church, and people united with one voice in an earnest appeal and request for me to attend its dedication, and deliver the dedicatory sermon.

This arrangement gratified me; although I never approved of the practice of sending for another preacher to dedicate a church where a society had a settled pastor; still I was gratified with this call on two accounts; one was, it would afford me an opportunity of visiting a people in whose prosperity I felt deeply interested—whose happiness was inseparable from my own; and another was, it afforded me an evidence of attachment and confidence on their part, which the unhallowed excitement, that had been a principal cause of our separation, had not utterly destroyed. I apprehended that I fully understood their feelings, and appreciated their motives in calling for me. It was not for the sake of procuring brilliant talents, or making a display of great pulpit eloquence on the occasion; for had this been their object, besides their pastor, there were numbers of others much nearer them than myself, with whose superior endowments they were well acquainted. But they had a more noble feeling to gratify, and a more commendable object to accomplish. From my lips they, or the most of them, had received the very first intimations of the existence of that glorious truth that had freed their souls from the bondage of darkness; and they had sat under my ministry for years, feeble as it was, until they had acquired the strength of men. These circumstances had produced an attachment not easily obliterated, and which neither the untoward events that had separated us, nor time, nor distance, had effaced or weakened. It was to gratify these feelings of friendship, to assure me of their abiding existence, and show to the world their unimpaired confidence, that led them to call for me to dedicate their house of worship. And a reciprocation of these feelings and sentiments, led me as cheerfully and as readlly to comply with their call.

My wife must accompany me on this tour; for her attachment to the people and the place was certainly as strong as mine, and was as faithfully reciprocated by our friends in that country.

About the middle of May, 1833, we left home to answer this call; and traveling by stage and canal, with making some stops on the way to hold meetings, we arrived in Hamilton just in season to attend the Central Association, holden in that town on the first Wednesday and Thursday in June. On Tuesday evening we stopped with a friend in our old neighborhood, and early on the next morning repaired to the house where the council were to greet, eager to meet our well-remembered and long-cherished friends; and among the earliest on the ground was my old Brother H., of whom I have been obliged so often to speak, who, without being able to utter a syllable, clasped me in his arms and wept like an infant.

He was, like the man among the tombs, again "clothed in his right mind"—clothed in the "beautiful garments" of Christian meekness and humility, and had the same "mind in him which was in Christ Jesus." Oh, this was to me a happy meeting! and it was on this visit that he made the confession that I have before mentioned.

The dedication of their meeting-house took place on the 27th of June. The house was well filled on the occasion; and Mr. Potter, Mr. Freeman, and some others, assisted in the services of the consecration. Great solemnity prevailed, much sensibility was manifest; but none, probably, felt the solemnity of the scene, or were, deeply interested, as myself. I had seen this society in its infancy struggling for existence, amidst sneers, scoffs, derisions, and persecutions. I had seen them meet in a little band, in a small school-house, near the spot where now they had erected a respectable house of worship, while the proud steeple of a Presbyterian meeting-house, with its still spiritually prouder inmates, looked down upon them with every demonstration of contempt. I had seen them struggle on, bearing with Christian meekness all this contumely and persecution, cheered only with the conscious assurance of the divinity of the truth they had embraced, and that "Truth was mighty, and would prevail." I had witnessed their increasing, and the decline of their proud and boasting enemy, until the scene had become reversed. The Presbyterian church had gradually dwindled away, until they were no longer able to support preaching, and their house was forsaken; while the "Fruit of a handful of corn in the earth, upon the top of the mountain, had been made to shake like Lebanon—and they of the city to flourish like grass of the earth." And now their congregation filled a house of respectable dimensions, the fruit of their own industry; and here in this memorable day, they, with Christian meekness and fervor, consecrated this pious labor of their hands to the God they loved, and dedicated it to the worship of Him who is the Father of the spirits of all flesh, and the SAVIOR OF THE WORLD.

We were absent from home on this tour about three months, during which time we visited many of those dear friends with whom we had spent the strength of our days; and the cordiality with which we were received, gave ample testimony that time and distance impaired not the strength of those attachments consummated in the morning of life.

On my journey eastward, after leaving the borough of Erie, I delivered lectures in Ripley, Westfield, Fredonia, and Silver Creek, Chautauque county; preached one Sunday in Buffalo, and lectured in Lockport, Rochester, and Perryville; and during our stay in Central New York, I held meetings in a large number of the towns and places of my early labors, besides attending two associations, the Central and the Mohawk River. And the advancement of the cause—the additional societies that had grown up, the number of efficient laborers who had entered the field, and the numerous meeting-houses that had been erected, afforded cause of inexpressible gratification, and fervent gratitude and thanksgiving to Almighty God. "A little one had become a thousand, and a small one a strong nation."

It was while I was absent on this eastern tour, that Mr. Todd renounced Universalism, wound up the publication of his periodical, and withdrew from the connection. Not long after my return home, Mr. Ami Bond removed into Carroll; and Mr. John E. Holmes, a young man of very promising talents, from Madison county, who had just commenced the ministry of reconciliation, came into this country, and soon became established in Westfield. Therefore, although the defection of Mr. Todd left me alone in this country, it pleased Heaven, in a very few weeks, to send two faithful laborers to occupy the field which he had abandoned.

On the removal of Mr. Bond into Carroll, I opened a correspondence with him on the subject of taking measures to revive the Chautauque Association; he very cordially approved of the measure; and on the 20th of February, 1834, a general meeting was holden in Carroll for that purpose; and from that time to the present, the association has never failed of its yearly communications. Encouraged by the additional laborers the great Husbandman had employed in this section of his vineyard, I felt under renewed obligations to redouble my exertions to prune and dress the vines.

But clouds and sunshine intervene through the whole day of mortal life; and behind the fragrant roses which bestrew our path, the sharp thorn is ready to wound our flesh. The ways of Heaven are inscrutable to us, frail mortals; but the voice of sovereign wisdom and love is heard above the hoarse howlings of the approaching storm. "Be *still* and *know that I am God.*" The chastening hand of a provident and tender Father was already mingling for us a cup of deep affliction, and was about to probe to the bottom an unhealed and incurable wound. Our third daughter—Oh! too much our idol—then in the 16th year of her age, after a short sickness, not exceeding three weeks, on the 23d day of March, was taken from our arms! But we enjoyed the blessed consolation of ministering, as far as parental affection and skill could minister, to her every possible comfort—of witnessing her patient resignation to the Divine will—of receiving from her dying lips the last seal of filial affection—and of beholding her—more than cheerful—her triumphant deliverance from the dominion of death, when her pure spirit wended its heavenward way.

But notwithstanding our confidence in the Divine government—our unshaken and abiding hope—our knowledge, and our *thankfulness* that the "Heavens do rule"—notwithstanding the sweet consolation that her dying hour afforded, yet a "sword pierced" the parents' hearts, inflicting a wound which language is too lean, *too barren* to describe; leaving a sad, an awful vacuum therein, which time can never, never fill. Eternity, only—reunion in eternal life, can alone heal and replenish the heart.

I had been with numerous—with hundreds of friends in seasons of bereavement; I had seen parents bowing with indescribable agony over the pale and lifeless forms of beloved children; I verily thought I could feel their sorrow of heart, could sympathise in their sufferings—my heart has been melted into compassion, until my emotions have obstructed utterance. I have appealed to the Gospel of Christ to administer consolation. I have directed their attention to the numerous evidences of the "Great love wherewith God loved us"—to the unchangeability of his nature, to the designs of his government, to the merciful tendency of his chastenings. I have urged the strong, overwhelming evidences of future life, the destruction of sin and death, and the reconciliation of all things to God. I have appealed with pathos to the bleeding Savior on the Cross, as a commendation of the love of God to sinners—to his triumphant resurrection from the dead, as a Divine pledge of the resurrection of our whole race, and a re-union with the dearest objects of our hearts' affection. And I have, upon these considerations, fervently exhorted them not to mourn. But never, until high Heaven taught me by sad experience, did I realize the feebleness, and even the *mockery*, of such exhortation. But now have I learned that it is my privilege to mourn; it is a solace I would not be deprived of by the cruel kindness of my friends. I would not murmur, I would not complain of the dealings of Heaven—but I would *feel* my bereavement—I would appreciate my loss—I would dwell with mournful recollection, each evening and each morning, upon the names and the excellencies of the beloved ones I can behold no more.

The reader will surely pardon my inserting here a scrap written on the first anniversary of the death of my beloved Mary Adaline, in the little chamber where she breathed her last:—

In this lone room, my dear, departed child,
Where thy sweet life its glimmering taper closed,
I sit a solitary mourner; wrapp'd,
Still wrapp'd in sable weeds of deepest woe!
  Though through besetting toils and scenes vexatious,
Business of earth involving urgent cares,
Or fears of ill, or hopes deferred, I wade;
Yet nought of earth, nor cares, nor hopes, nor joys,
Can draw my thoughts from hence---from thee, nor loose
My mind from those heart-chilling, withering scenes
Which tenderest cords of fond affection wrung,
When parents' warmest, elevated hopes,

In one sad hour, sunk to the darksome tomb!
Oh, no! nor can, nor would I e'er forget
The sweet, complacent, soothing smile which dwelt
Perpetual on thy fading lips, affection's
Token, evidence divine of inward
Joy, and resignation to high Heaven's will.

I see it now, or seem to see, and feel
The warm, though tremulous grasp of thy soft hand,
So oft extended mine to meet, as to
Thy bed, with all the fond solicitude
A parent feels, to minister some cordial
For relief. But vain illusion! Heaven
Decreed thy short, thy earthly pilgrimage
Should close! And I again should feel the sharp,
Invenom'd spear of death plunged deeper into
This lacerated breast, far deeper than
The call had been my own!

Vain are all words!—All human language vain!—
Vain the attempt the feelings to describe,
The deep sensations this sad heart endured,
When from thy dying lips was seal'd on mine
Filial affection's last, deep, lasting pledge!
Ten thousand pointed, barbed arrows shot
With ruthless rage, making as many deep
Incisions in this heart, from whence pure streams
Of vital gore incessant flow. Not dark,
Deep clouds, portentous, with peals of thunder
Seven-fold, bursting with horrid crash upon
This devoted head—nor earth, deep groaning
With fierce volcanic fires, its jaws expanding
Millions to devour, could so intensely
Sink this soul to woe!

But, oh! 'tis past! Twelve months, this night, have closed,
Have closed their gloomy round, and find me here,
Still pondering o'er the scene, indulging still
In bitterness of woe!—And still I'll mourn;
It is the solace of the soul to mourn;
Not murmur, not repine at Heaven's will,
But mourn MY loss, mourn my lov'd children gone—
Cut off in life's bright morn, in hope's full bloom,
Torn from my bosom, numbered with the dead!
I'll follow from their death-bed to their grave,
There weep, and kneel, and pray, and let this heart
Vent all her flood of woe!

Then rising, view the Gospel's glorious plan,
Where God's unpurchased love 's reveal'd to man;
Where, through the Savior's resurrection power,
Immortal life illumes death's darkest hour;
Where death, at last, his wide domain resigns,
And Christ shall reign with power and love divine;
Where all shall meet on one immortal shore,
Friends re-unite, and death divide no more.

COLUMBUS, MARCH 23, 1835.

In the month of May, 1834, I made my first tour in the State of Ohio. The Western Reserve Association held its annual session that year, in the town of Olmstead, Cuyahoga county. This meeting I had the pleasure of attending, where I formed an acquaintance with the few preachers of Universalism in that region, and among them was our venerable Brother Beals, whose stability and fidelity enabled him to outride the tempest which, but a few years before, engulphed every other preacher, within the limits of that association, in the dark whirlpool of Partialism. But the Lord had provided him a few coadjutors now, one of whom, a Mr. Tracy, soon followed his unhappy predecessors; and another, Mr. Wadsworth, after a few years of faithful and efficient labor in the vineyard of the great Husbandman, has been admitted to the enjoyment of a higher life. During this tour, besides attending the association, I preached in the towns of Paris, Middlebury, Akron, Carlisle, Cleveland, Painesville, Madison, Saybrook, and Ashtabula.

On the 21st of August, this year, the Chautauque Association held its annual session, in the town of Westfield; and at the earnest solicitations of delegates and friends from the various societies and neighborhoods in the counties of Chautauque and Cattaraugus, N. Y.; and Warren, Erie, and Crawford, Pa.; measures were adopted to try and establish a regular itinerancy, or circuit preaching, through these several counties. Mr. W. E. Manley, a young man of uncommon talents, and a scholar, who had recently entered the field of labor with an indefatigable zeal, had penetrated into this section, and was ready to use all his influence and labors for the accomplishment of so desirable an object; and he did so, with all the faithfulness and ardor of an inspired Apostle, until he broke down his health and manly constitution, and was actually under the necessity of retiring from the field, and resting from his labors for a year or more, I believe, to recruit his health. It was truly astonishing to witness the zeal, and to see the amount of labor performed by that excellent young man, in so short a space of time. Mr. Holmes was also ready to enter upon the circuit; and so sanguine was the belief of the friends generally, in the feasibility and the success of the enterprise, that a committee was appointed to draft a constitution, bye-laws, and regulations for a circuit conference, and a time and place for its first meeting appointed, to carry the object into effect.

The first meeting of the circuit conference was holden in the court-house, in Warren, on the 15th and 16th of October. The constitution and bye laws were reported and adopted, and measures taken to commence operations. It became necessary that each place where stations for preaching were to be established should be visited, and classes, as we styled them, be organized; and subscription-papers issued, to raise funds for the support of circuit preachers. This involved a vast labor in the introduction; but this labor, with the help of Mr. Manley, I engaged to perform. I, therefore, on the 8th of December, started on the circuit—traveled upwards of 200 miles, through the counties of Chautauque and Cattaraugus, N. Y.; and Warren and Crawford, Pa.; and formed classes and issued subscription papers at twenty-two diff rent stations therein: this occupied about one month. We eventually succeeded in getting our circuit very regularly established, and were successful in raising ample funds for the salary of two circuit preachers, who were to succeed each other at regular periods, at the several different stations on the circuit; and I felt a comfortable assurance that it would be a means of giving a renewed and powerful impulse to the spread of the truth. Indeed, although for the want of a thorough acquaintance with its system of operation, by those whose special business it was to direct its affairs, but more from the delinquency of some of our circuit preachers, who could not be brought under the implicit subordination of Methodist discipline, it continued but a short time; still much good was eff cted by it; and it was in quite successful operation when I removed to Michigan. But when I returned back to this country, after five years' absence, to my great sorrow the conference was disorganized, and the enterprise abandoned.

During the last sickness of my lamented friend, Capt. D. Curtis, he called on me to assist him in arranging his temporal concerns, and preparing the necessary writings for the settling of his estate; and at his irresistible request, I consented to become one of the executors of his last will and testament—fully believing, however, at the time, that his sickness was not unto death, (though he considered it so,) and that the labors and responsibility would never devolve upon me. But infinite wisdom had otherwise determined. My friend died; and amid the cares of my own family, and the labors and solicitudes of my clerical profession, requiring a vast amount of labor, both of body and mind, the heavy responsibility of settling his estate came upon me. His business was extensive for the amount of property he possessed; and being broken suddenly off, in the midst of his activity and success, leaving his schemes and enterprising arrangements in an unfinished state, rendered the settlement of his estate both laborious and perplexing, aud in despite of the best skill, prudence, and economy of the executors, subjected it to real loss; the estate, which in his own hands would have been worth sixteen or seventeen thousand dollars, with all our care and prudence, did not leave to the heirs over about twelve thousand. His property lay mostly in wild lands, and the will was so constituted as to authorize and require the executors to sell all, except the home farm, and pay the legacies to the heirs, out of the avails arising therefrom, as they became due.

He was joint partner with two others of a tract of three thousaud acres of land in Tyler county, Va.; but the title to the whole tract was vested in him. Already had one, and the only surviving original partner, thrown it into the Court of Chancery, in order to obtain a division of the land. It became necessary, therefore, that one at least of the executors should go to that State and attend to it, as well as to make proof of the will of the deceased, in order to get possession of the land and expose it for sale; and, as usual, the "Lot fell on Jonah." It became necessary, also, to take the journey in the month of April, a season of the year when traveling generally is the most intolerable; but a friend of mine, who was in the habit of running lumber on rafts down the Allegany and Ohio rivers, proposed to me to make the trip down on his raft, from which he could land me at Sistersville, only about twenty-five or thirty miles from the place of my destination. Of this privilege I gladly availed myself; and on the 8th of April, 1835, I took passage on board his raft, at Warren, with my horse, amply provided with hay and oats for the voyage, and like Noah's Ark, "Went upon the waters," moving with the current of these majestic and romantic rivers, down the Allegany and Ohio, in their serpentine course, four hundred miles; from which I was taken by a ferry-boat, and landed at the village of Sistersville, Tyler county, Va. It was, on the whole, one of the most pleasant voyages I ever made. The weather was fine, and the romantic scenery through which the Allegany finds its course, cutting its way through mountains whose pointed summits seem to penetrate the cerulean canopy, and mingle with the upper world, and carrying the astonished passenger to every point of compass on the dial—sometimes apparently thrusting him with violence against the base of an almost perpendicular and inaccessible mountain, through which he sees no aperture nor possible turn of the stream, until the forward end of his frail craft almost presses upon the ledge which threatens his destruction, when a sudden turn of the river, perhaps making an acute angle to the right or left, seems hastening back from whence he came, captivates the feelings of the lover of the sublime, and affords abundant subject for wonder and meditation. Sometimes you discover a small improvement, and occasionally a little hamlet; and once in a while, at the mouth of some stream, where the interval widens out to a greater extent, a pleasant little village, with its church or churches, its pretty painted houses, its mills and its work-shops, affords a change of scenery. But it appeared to me that there was but a small proportion of the lands upon the borders of the Allegany suitable for cultivation, until you approach near its junction with the Monongahela, forming the Ohio. Down the Ohio the scenery is somewhat different. But the very high banks of the river prevent the passenger on a raft—which places him down to the water's surface—from having a fair view of the handsome, cultivated farms, and splendid villages, in many places scattered along the "Banks of the pleasant Ohio." But the motion of the raft is so gentle and still, that you can read or write with as much ease as though under no motion at all. I wrote letters to my family, and some other friends, and prepared necessary writings for the facility of my business, with as much ease as though I had been in my study.

I was fortunate in the transaction of my business about the land, and accomplished the object of my mission in about one week. Having long cherished a desire to visit Marietta, Ohio, the first place in the State settled by civilized inhabitants, among whom were some of my own blood-kindred, therefore, on my return to Sistersville, finding myself within about thirty miles of the place, I could not well resist gratifying my inclination. Having so successfully accomplished my secular mission, I concluded to take a little time to myself, and my divine Master. Accordingly, I crossed the Ohio river, and made my way along its romantic bank to the desired place. It was night before I reached the city; and, although I was aware that there was a Universalist society in the place, yet being an entire stranger, and wearied by traveling, I put up at the first respectable-looking tavern. Of the landlord, I learned that evening, that none of my relatives remained in the city. The few who formerly resided there had removed about nine miles up the Muskingum to a place called Rainbow; but I made no inquiry about Universalists. In the morning, having written a line to a friend in McConnelsville, which was about forty miles up the Muskingum, notifying him of an intended visit, and giving him an appointment for a Sunday, I went to the post-office to deposit it. This led me quite to the opposite side of the city; and, on leaving the post-office, I fell in company with a citizen, and after exchanging civil compliments, the following dialogue, in substance, ensued:

Stranger. You have a handsome little city here, sir, very pleasantly and romantically situated; and I should judge, from the number of churches I discover, that you are quite a religious people.

Citizen. Yes; we are generally emigrants from New England, and are quite fond of attending meeting somewhere.

S. I should conclude, from the number and appearance of the meeting-houses, that they belonged to different denominations.

C. Yes; (pointing to one, and then to others, as he spoke,) that is a Presbyterian house—that a Baptist—that a Methodist —that an Episcopalian, &c.

S. Among your different denominations of Christians, I

conclude you have none of that strange sect, called Universalists.

C. Oh, yes; many of them—there is quite a society of them in the city.

S. Astonishing! What, Universalists here? Why you must be very unfortunate. Can you keep your property and your lives secure among them? Why, I have been told that they are the most immoral, and the most dangerous people in the world.

C. Oh, sir, you have been wrongly informed; some of our very best inhabitants are strong and decided Universalists.

S. Indeed, sir! Is that possible? Can you show me a likely, good, moral man who is a Universalist?

C. Certainly, sir. Why, there is uncle Jo Holden, one of the best men in the world; and there is Esquire Fish; both Universalists; and many others.

S. Well, sir, if you will have the goodness to show me either of the gentlemen you have named, you will confer a great favor; for I have a strong desire to see a *likely* man, who calls himself a Universalist.

C. Well, sir, just walk with me to Mr. Holden's store, and I'll show you such a sight with much pleasure.

After walking a few rods, we arrived at the store, but Mr. Holden was absent. My companion informed his clerk, that a gentleman wished to see Mr. Holden. The clerk replied, "He has just stepped out, and I will look for him." He soon returned, and said, "I could not see him, but he will most certainly return to the store in a few minutes." I said to my friend, "You named another gentleman—is it far to his residence?" "Oh, no; Esquire Fish is doubtless in his warehouse. He keeps that cabinet ware-house," pointing to a building near by. "Well, sir, will you have the goodness to walk there with me?" He cheerfully complied, for he began to manifest some curiosity about my engagedness to see a likely Universalist. We found Esq. Fish in his shop, and my friend addressed me, as we entered the room, with, "This is Esq. Fish." I bowed to the Esq., and said, "I have requested this gentleman to accompany me here, sir; and, although an entire stranger, I will take the liberty of introducing myself to you, as a Universalist preacher, by the name of Stacy." Esq. Fish extended his hand, saying, "You are no stranger, sir, we know you very well, and are very happy that you have given us a call—your name is familiar to us all." I then turned to my kind conductor, who manifested some little surprise in his countenance, but at the same time no displeasure, and thanked him for his politeness and attention, and he left us. I told Esq. F. that I had merely called to make an introduction; for I designed to go that day to my friends, up the Muskingum. "No," said he, "you can't go to-day—we can't spare you—you must preach with us to-morrow." (It was Saturday morning.) "But, have you time to give sufficient notice?" "Yes, plenty of time; and we are truly hungry for the bread of life." "Well, I'll stay then." We immediately went to Mr. Holden's store, where we found him. My horse was sent for; and every comfort that warm hearts, willing hands, and full purses could supply, was provided for me. Information was circulated through the city, and adjacent country; and, at an early hour the next day, the Court-house was thronged with a large congregation of interested and interesting hearers.

An appointment was sent from here to Belpre, sixteen miles down the river, for the next Sunday; and most of the intervening time I spent with the surviving members of Col. William Stacy's family, a few of whom I found in the place before named, called Rainbow, nine miles from Marietta. Col. Stacy was a revolutionary officer, and one of the company who made the New England purchase, and commenced the settlement at Marietta, about the year 1788. I found two of his children only, a son and a daughter, and the widow of another son with a small posterity, remaining. Many years had elapsed since we had met. Those who were then rejoicing in the pride of manhood, were now tottering on the brink of the grave; and we who were their children had long since passed the meridian of life, and were fast hastening on to the same destiny. This, though it awakened melancholy reminiscences, and stirred up mournful feelings, was nevertheless hailed as a happy season, and acknowledged as such with gratitude to the great "Preserver of men." I was very happy in finding the younger branches of my revered uncle's family in the faith of the Great Salvation; and I enjoyed the privilege of delivering to the old and young the message of eternal life. From thence I returned back to Marietta, and accompanied by a young man, of the name of Chappel, who shortly afterwards became a preacher himself, and who still remains "faithful to Him who called him," repaired to Belpre, delivering one lecture by the way. In Belpre I found a flourishing society of faithful and devout worshipers, with William Pitt Putnam, a descendant of General Putnam, of revolutionary memory, at its head. They had in progress of building a meeting-house, which they have long since completed and enjoyed.

After delivering my message here, I proceeded to McConnelsville, Morgan county, delivering two lectures by the way; which place I reached on Friday evening, and found the friends in expectation of my arrival. My letter had been duly received, and information of the meeting widely circulated; so that on Sunday the Court-house was amply filled. On Monday morning, taking an affectionate leave of my friends, and bidding adieu to a country I had never before visited, and which I never expected to see again, I directed my course through one of the most romantic, though not one of the most productive, countries I ever traveled in, to Wellsville, on the Ohio river, some thirty miles below Beaver, in Pennsylvania. I arrived in Beaver on Friday, and stopped with a friend over Sabbath, where I delivered two discourses to very respectable congregations, comprising several persons who had probably never before heard a discourse delivered by a Universalist; but they gave me profound attention, and I am happy in believing that my labor was not wholly in vain. On Monday morning, I again set my face toward my family, whom I reached on the Wednesday following, being a little past the middle of May. I had been absent about six weeks, and, including my voyage on the raft, had traveled nearly one thousand miles.

Early in the spring of this year, (1835,) I received a letter from the Clerk of the Universalist Society in Ann Arbor, Michigan, giving me an invitation to remove into that country, and take the pastoral charge of the society in that place. I had been then four years and a half itinerating and pioneering this wild and trackless country; and although improvements in roads, as well as in agriculture and every thing else pertaining to civilization, were progressing with as much rapidity as could be rationally expected, still it was almost impracticable to travel with carriages of any kind, and it was truly a severe task to perform my monthly labors. And considering my advanced years, and increasing infirmities, I felt justified in changing my position, so that I might enjoy, at least, a temporary release from the extreme fatigues I had so long endured. Several families who had been my hearers in Central New York had fixed their residence at Ann Arbor, and were members of that society; and it was through their recommendation that I had received the call. They informed me that they had already a convenient meeting-house—that Mr. P. Morse, who had been to see a brother in that part, had made them a visit, and dedicated the house; and they felt able to sustain constant preaching, and were anxious to secure my services. After taking the matter into deliberate and prayerful consideration, I wrote them that I would make them a visit early in the month of July, Providence permitting—would spend four Sabbaths with them, and would then give them an answer. Knowing that I had the journey above described to perform, I put off my visit a sufficient length of time to accomplish it. After returning from my Virginia tour, I made preparation for my journey to Michigan, and on the sixth of July started for the then "far west." I took passage in a steam-boat at Erie, for Detroit. This was the first time I had ever crossed this inland sea, and it was quite an interesting voyage; and although we had somewhat of a rough time, and a little sea-sickness disturbed for a short time the equanimity of my feelings, still I enjoyed it well for the most part; and about thirty-six hours brought us safely to the city of Detroit. A few years before this, several of my wife's relatives, (brother's children,) had removed to this place; I remained here, therefore, over one day to make them a brief visit; and while here, one of the leading members of the society in Ann Arbor called on me. He informed me that my letter had been received—that they had given information of my intended visit, and circulated notice for a meeting on the next Sabbath. Taking passage in a stage the next morning, a ride of forty miles over a very bad road, for at least half the way, brought me a little before night-fall to the place of my destination.

Ann Arbor is the seat of justice for Washtenaw county. It is pleasantly situated on both sides of the Huron river, which disembogues into the Straits of Detroit, near the head of Lake Erie. The river is very rapid near this section of it, affording excellent mill-seats, at convenient distances, for twenty miles or more, with sufficient water for all mechanical purposes. A convention had recently been in session in Detroit for the framing of a State constitution, which was subsequently adopted, and at the following session of Congress the State of Michigan was received into the family of the republic; and Ann Arbor became the seat of the State University.

On my arrival, I found a Universalist Society, of respectable numbers, legally incorporated, comprising a portion of the most respectable and influential inhabitants, and possessing the only meeting-house, in a finished state, in the village. My reception was cordial and hearty, and the meetings well attended. I remained with them four Sabbaths, and, during the intermediate time, I visited the adjacent towns, and delivered several lectures in different places. The country, though new, exhibited evidence of a rich and productive soil, and was fast advancing in agricultural improvements; and, although it had been reputed as unhealthful, yet to me it bore the appearance of being healthful—the surface handsomely undulating, the streams of water pure and lively, the atmosphere serene, and the climate sweet and salubrious; and I concluded it would, at least, answer for a temporary residence for my family. Therefore, at the close of my probationary term, I agreed to settle with them for a season; and if I could possibly bring my secular business to a final adjustment, a considable portion of which was still on my hands, I agreed to remove my family the ensuing fall.

I then returned home, applied myself with the utmost diligence to accomplish a final settlement of the estate of Capt. Curtis, and succeeded as far as it could be completed until the heirs severally became of age; when I delivered all the books, papers, and writings belonging to the estate into the hands of a co-executor, resigned my commission, and was in readiness to start with my family on the first of November.

The season had so far advanced, and the autumnal winds were generally making the lake so rough, that navigation had become perilous, and regular trips of steamboats had ceased—although boats continued to navigate the lake, as they always do at irregular intervals, until obstructed by ice—that I concluded to take my family by land the most part of the way. Therefore, having sent our furniture to Erie to be forwarded by water to Detroit, we provided ourselves with a good team and light pleasure-wagon, and proceeded by land as far as the port of Huron, in Ohio. We stopped here with a design, if possible, to get a steam-boat passage just across the head of the lake, which would not only save a great distance in travel, but also save us the journey of thirty miles through what was called the Black Swamp, where teams, at that season of the year, were frequently unable to make ten miles a day. We arrived at this port on the tenth of November, in the latter part of the day; and on that very night a most tremendous storm of wind and snow was experienced on the lake, which drove every vessel, of all descriptions, into the nearest port they could make, and precluded any attempt to put out again for several days. The port of Huron was swept of its waters, which receded to the depth of six or eight feet, leaving the few vessels and water-crafts in the port high and dry. We were here weather-bound, therefore, three or four days—could neither travel by land, nor find passage by water. But a kind Providence, uniformly, "after a storm sends a calm;" and after waiting with some anxiety for several days, the lake became smooth, the waters returned to their wonted bed and equilibrium, and the sight of a steam-boat, puffing into port, relieved our solicitude. She proved, however, to be an old crazy boat, and heavily laden; but the Captain assured us she was safe, and he could make room for us; and the uncertainty of another boat, and the great probability that another storm would not succeed this violent blow until we should have time to reach Detroit, encouraged us to take passage; and committing our case and ourselves to the care of the great "Preserver of men," we went on board. The boat was loaded to the water-brim, the engine poor, and she lugged very slowly through the water; so that our passage merely across the head of the lake, occupied more time than it generally takes to navigate its whole length, from Buffalo to Detroit. But under the watchful care of an ever-wakeful Providence, no disaster occurred, the lake retained its peacefulness, the heavens smiled above us; and a little after dark, on the second evening of our voyage the brilliant lights which appeared on our larboard quarter, announced our approach to the city of Detroit. Our friend and kinsman, Cornelius Clark, was at the wharf when we landed, and conducted us to his hospitable habitation, where we found a resting-place from the fatigues of our journey, as well as all the charities of life that the hands of kind friends could provide. After remaining two days with our friends in the city, we proceeded on our journey to Ann Arbor.

The first settlement of Detroit bears date nearly with that of the city of Philadelphia. It was an old French fortress, and a fur-trading establishment. It passed into the possession of the English on their conquest of Canada, and eventually, by the Revolution, fell into the hands of the United States. At the time of my removal, quite a large proportion of the citizens were descendants of the original French settlers, and the Roman Catholic religion was in the ascendant. But other parts of the State were peopled, and were then rapidly settling with emigrants from the eastern and middle States, as well as from Europe. Many Irish and German inhabitants were to be found there; but a majority probably were from the State of New York, or those who had made that State a stopping-place for a season, in their western progress. Society, therefore, might be considered in a state of disorganization—the people had not yet assumed a sectional character—their manners and their habits, educationally so different from each other, had not yet had time to assimilate. The leading habits were those of the citizens of the State of New York; and their State-constitution and laws modeled accordingly. They were divided into all the sects that were known in the Christian church, but in most cases less bigoted, and more liberally and charitably disposed toward each other than in older countries, and under long-cherished and permanently-established institutions. Hence, in most cases where a Universalist preacher should appoint a meeting, he would get a respectable congregation. A very few of the preachers of the Great Salvation had briefly visited that country, but there were only two who devoted their time to the ministry, residing within the limits of the State. Mr. A. H. Curtis had been there some two or three years; he had been successful in getting up congregations in several towns and counties in the State; and to his labors, unquestionably, the society in Ann Arbor were considerably indebted for their prosperity. He had been instrumental in organizing small societies in Tecumseh and in Adrian, Lenawee county; and one in Blissfield, where he had settled with his family. Mr. Thomas Wheeler removed into the State sometime in the course of the summer before I removed my family, and had fixed his residence in Macomb county. There were two others who had received letters of fellowship, as preachers in our denomination, Mr. J. Lockwood, in Lenawee county, and Mr. Daniel Walker, in Jackson county; but both were engaged in secular employments, and paid little or no attention to the ministry. Four societies were all that existed under any form of organization, and that in Tecumseh scarcely merited the appellation of a society; and nothing as yet had been done toward organizing an Association. Mr. Curtis soon visited me after my settlement at Ann Arbor; but Mr. Wheeler I saw not for more than a year.

Although my labors were confined on the Sabbaths to one society, I soon began to ride and lecture on week-days in the adjacent country, and very shortly had several regular stations for weekly lectures—one in Plymouth, sixteen miles distant. Mr. Curtis had preached there, more or less, as well as in several others where I was called to lecture, but no organization had been effected. Mr. Curtis and myself had had some conversation, from time to time, on the expediency of organizing an Association, and concluded to make a trial. At the annual meeting of the society in Ann Arbor, holden in April, the subject was laid before the society, and they passed a resolution inviting an inceptive meeting for that purpose, to be held in that place.

Accordingly, on the first Wednesday in June, 1836, just thirty years from the organization of the first Association in the State of New York, we assembled at Ann Arbor, State of Michigan, and organized the first Universalist Association in that new State; and as in New York, so in Michigan, but three societies were duly represented by legally appointed delegates. The reader will very easily imagine that reminiscences of a peculiar and interesting character were awakened in my mind.

Previously to that meeting, Mr. J. E. Holmes came into that State; and a young man by name Richard Thornton, subsequently known as the able editor of the "Primitive Expounder," had just entered upon the ministry, and had been itinerating for a short time in that region. Mr. D. Biddlecom had settled with the society in Perrysburg, Ohio; and Mr. K. Townsend was at that time on a tour through that country. All these met with us on that interesting occasion, who, with Mr. Lockwood and Mr. Curtis before mentioned, made out rather an imposing phalanx of Universalist preachers for the first session of an Association in that remote, western limb of the great Husbandman's vineyard. The Association was organized in due form, by the name and title of the "Central Association of Universalists in Michigan," a constitution was adopted, and Mr. Thornton received a letter of fellowship as a preacher of the "everlasting Gospel." That was the germ of the regular organization of Universalists in the State of Michigan. In the course of that month, June, a church was organized in Ann Arbor, consisting of about thirty members; and another in Adrian, where, at a conference for its recognition, Mr. Curtis received water baptism and ordination, and became its pastor for a season. Several other preachers soon moved into the State, and settled in different parts of it, believers were multiplied, societies sprang up in various places, and the cause began to assume a promising and encouraging aspect.

One incident, which may be well connected with the establishment of the church in Ann Arbor, is certainly worthy of a place in these memoirs.

Early after my arrival with my family at Ann Arbor, while waiting for the arrival of our furniture from Detroit, and we were yet quartered upon our friends; in a conversation upon the existing and prospective state of the cause in Ann Arbor, and the country in general, with two of the leading members of the society, Messsrs. Fuller and Kellogg, partners in the mercantile business, they mentioned several influential men, who, if converted to the faith, would be strong pillars in the church; and among them they named Deacon John Williams, of the adjacent town of Webster. They had known Deacon W. from their earliest remembrance. He emigrated from the same place with themselves, and they entertained a high regard for him as a man and a Christian, although in theory he was a bigoted Calvinistic Presbyterian. He was a man in the decline of life, about my age, affluent circumstances—a fore-handed farmer, and had been a professor of religion, and a member of the church from the age of sixteen years. He had uniformly holden the office of deacon, or elder, or both, for thirty years, or more; had associated much with the clergy, was a correct theorist in the Calvinistic school, and a most zealous and persevering advocate of its doctrines. He subsequently told me that one important consideration of his removal into Michigan, was the establishment of a church in the true faith, and the propagation of those doctrines which he so firmly believed to be the truth of God, and so necessary to be embraced in order for salvation by the multitudinous emigrants thronging into that country. He was a man of sound judgment, of powerful natural talents, and extensive influence; and he employed all, and was not sparing of his wealth even, in the cause of the religion he had embraced. Therefore, although they ardently desired his conversion, yet, considering his long-standing religious connection and habits, his unyielding tenacity to his creed, and his zeal for its propagation, they considered, very rationally, that the case was hopeless.

A few days after that conversation, having rented a house, and received part of our furniture from Detroit; and while arranging it so far as to get my family together once more, I stepped into the store in a hurry to get some article I needed, and was there introduced to Deacon Williams. Although I knew not how to spare a moment, we must nevertheless have some conversation. We were invited into the counting-room with the two friends before named. I found the Deacon a very reasonable man, familiar and pleasant, and by no means so rigid and overbearing as I had anticipated; and not inclined at that time, at any rate, to enter into a doctrinal discussion. After some half-hour's conversation, I began to excuse myself on account of my particular business of the day, when the Deacon addressed me nearly in the following language:

"Mr. Stacy, I have long had two passages of Scripture on my mind, containing, as I think, very important doctrine, that I have desired to hear some able divine discourse from. I have several times requested ministers of my own denomination to preach from them, but as yet have never been gratified. I was mentioning it the other day to our friends, Fuller and Kellogg, and they thought you would be willing to preach from them; and I told them if you would, I would come and hear you." "Well, Deacon," I said, "I always feel under obligation to give my opinion on any passage on which I have an opinion formed, when presented in a friendly manner; and I have so closely made the Scriptures my study for many years, that I have formed an opinion, satisfactory to myself at least, on most passages; and I always esteem it a privilege to do so in private, or to make the passage a subject for a discourse in public, if it be suitable for such a use. If you will have the goodness to name the passages, I will tell you at once whether I will or will not do it." He observed, "I do not propose them as special objections to *your* doctrine; but believe they contain very important doctrine which ought to be carefully discussed and fully understood. I have a great desire to hear some others." He then repeated the passages, —*First*, Acts 4 : 27, 28, "For, of a truth, against thy holy child Jesus, whom thou hast anointed, both Herod and Pontius Pilate, with the Gentiles and the people of Israel, were gathered together; for to do whatsoever thy hand and counsel determined before to be done." *Second*, Acts 2: 23, "Him being delivered by the determinate counsel and foreknowledge of God, ye have taken, and by wicked hands have crucified and slain."

I felt not a little surprised when he named the texts, for I had anticipated some passages about the "tremendous day of final judgment" or the "awful retributions of eternity." But I felt at once gratified, and a hope was at once enkindled in my soul that some good might be done. I thanked the Deacon, and told him that I should be highly gratified with the privilege of discoursing upon those texts in his presence. "But," said I, "I have this day begun to try to get my family together—part of our furniture is here, and part yet in Detroit. It will require several days to get in our household furniture, and arrange the concerns of my family, so as to enable me to give any attention to study. And although I shall probably find nothing, in the re-examination of the texts, to alter my opinion in regard to the doctrine, which, to my mind, is very clear. Still, to do justice to the subject, to you, and to myself, a little time for reflection and arrangement is necessary." "Oh, I am aware of that," said the Deacon, "take your own time, and when you get ready, just name it to your friends, F. and H., and they will send me word; and, Providence permitting, I will come down."

In about three weeks from that time, I told our friends they might notify Deacon W., that on such a Sunday, (setting the time two Sundays in advance,) I would, God willing, preach from his texts, one in the forenoon and one in the afternoon. I had, just before this, set up Sunday evening lectures, discoursing upon controversial subjects; such as were deemed, by Partialists, insurmountable objections to Universal Salvation, and of giving out my text a week beforehand; and it was producing considerable excitement, and collecting large congregations to the evening meetings; and at the request of Mr. Kellogg, I named to him the text for the evening of that day, that he might inform the Deacon, with a hope that he might be induced to remain in the evening and hear what a Universalist could say on the parable of the rich man and Lazarus.

The day arrived, and the Deacon was there in good season. He paid profound attention to the discourses; and after meeting, he took occasion to thank me for compliance with his request; observing, "I presume I have been as attentive a hearer as you have had to day, Mr. Stacy; but whether as profited a one or not, remains yet to be determined." "Well, Deacon," said I, "I hope I have been successful in conveying my ideas to your understanding." "Oh, I understood you well, I think; you made it very plain; and, as far as I could see, I agree with you; but I am resolved to examine the subject more thoroughly." "Well, Deacon, I believe, if you will dispassionately and carefully examine the subject in the light of the Scriptures, you will see that the inferences I have drawn are unavoidable and true. The Deacon felt so much interested in his meeting through the day, that he concluded to stop with friend K. for the night, and attend the evening lecture. The evening discourse filled him with astonishment. It was something new in all its relations—something he had never before thought of; and he talked almost all night about it. The next morning Mr. Fuller put into his hands "Smith on Divine Government," and asked him to read it. He promised he would; for his feelings had become somewhat excited, and he felt now ready to read any thing that would throw light on the subject. In two or three Sundays after this, the Deacon (whose residence was about eight miles from Ann Arbor,) was down again, and attended meeting all day, without any special invitation. A less time again elapsed, and he was there again; and, from a little conversation with him, I discovered that his Calvinism was a "gone case." From that time, he became a constant attendant; and in June following, when a church was organized, John Williams was elected first deacon of a Universalist church.

Never was a man's conversion more astonishing, save that of Saul of Tarsus—nor more thorough. He came out into the full sunshine of eternal truth, perfectly theorized in all its branches; no cloud, nor shadow of doubt on his mind—and his rejoicing was beyond measure. It constituted the theme of his meditation by day and by night, and the subject of his conversation at all times, and in all company. "Oh," said he, "how unaccountably strange it is, that I have lived in darkness so long, when truth shines so divinely bright on every page of the inspired word!—how much I have lost! I was happy in religion, at times, when I could contemple on the love of God through Christ, and keep my theory behind my back; but when that came up—when Calvinism presented itself, it cooled the ardor of my feelings; it chilled the blood in my veins, and made me groan in bitterness of soul. Indeed I felt no safety for myself. How could I *know* that I was so happy as to be a chosen vessel of mercy? And if I were, surely it was not probable that all whom I loved, that even all my own family could share eternal glory with me; and how could I be reconciled to the eternal separation, and to their endless burnings? Oh, I was compelled to banish the thoughts from my mind, as quick as possible, to save my soul from despair—from distraction. But now, blessed be God, I have obtained permanent relief from those agonizing, tormenting fears. I can clearly see in the great plan of salvation under the Divine government, a safety for myself, for my family, for all I hold dear, *for the whole human family!* I see it plainly; I see it straight—there is no darkness on the way, no obstruction in the path—I can see the third marked tree clear through the woods. In my former system, I could never see but one marked tree before me; and when I arrived at that, I was obliged to stop and look, first to the right, and then to the left, and had to angle about, and often to meet with stumps and quagmires which I had to get around or over as well as possible. But now, thank God, I can see the third marked tree, as straight as a line can be drawn, and have neither stump nor bog in my way."

Deacon Williams' wife, and a majority of his family were, together with himself, members of the Presbyterian church; and his conversion produced much excitement in his family, as well as among the members of the church generally. They were alarmed, and called him crazy. He said he gave them some cause for alarm; for during nearly three months, he neither worked nor slept much, but read and meditated day and night. He would say to himself, "Well, I will now go to bed and sleep." But as soon as he laid his head on his pillow some portion of Scripture would come into his mind, and on reflecting upon it, others would present themselves; and out of bed he would bound, light his candle and get his Bible, and perhaps before he would again think of sleeping, the day would break upon him.

And, to try the strength and power of his new faith, God, in the dispensations of his Providence, brought him to a test. In the summer of 1837, if I mistake not, he was visited with an alarming disease, vulgarly called the Black-tongue. His tongue swelled so that it protruded from his mouth, and he could not speak a word for several days, nor even swallow any thing except the purest liquid, nor even that without the greatest difficulty. He was able, however, the whole time to sit up, and walk about his rooms; but all communication, even with his own family, had to be done, on his part, by writing, or by signs. He, as well as his physicians and friends, concluded he must die; and during this sickness he arranged his temporal concerns, made his *will*, and as far possible settled all his business. I visited him in the course of this trial, and though he could not speak, he could hear, and answer questions by writing. I soon learned from him that his faith was not in the least shaken; indeed, he wrote on a slip of paper which he handed to me,—"I have a desire to again get the use of my tongue, that I may use it more faithfully in praising God, and proclaiming his great Salvation." And it pleased God to restore him again to health, and once more grant him the use of his tongue.

As soon as he was able to ride, he was again in his seat in the church; and on the first Sunday after his recovery, at the close of service he arose and addressed the congregation with much pathos,—"It is a common remark," he said, "among the opposers of our holy faith, that Universalism will do to live by, but it will not do to die by; but I know better, for I have tried it." And he continued saying, that after he had given up all possible hopes of recovery, his first concern was to make arrangements in regard to his temporal business, and get the care of that from off his mind. Then he passed, in review, his whole life, and entered into a close and critical examination of his religious creeds; first, his former creed, under which he had passed the greatest part of his life; and the more he brought it into the light of the holy Scriptures the darker and the more appaling its features appeared! But on the contrary, the more critically and closely he examined the doctrine of God's Universal Grace, the more he tried it by the unchangeable word of God, the brighter it shone, the more glorious and worthy of God it appeared; "And I know," said he, with tears streaming from his eyes—"I know it *will* do to die by, for I have tried it!" And he exhorted the members of the church to a constant perseverance, and faithful obedience to the faith, and to let their light shine before men.

Deacon Williams was not an educated man, but he was a man of a studious mind and deep thought, and possessed a happy talent of communicating his thoughts, in his way, with ease and perspicuity; and he was most faithful to his calling. He would go from place to place, through his own and the adjacent towns, and get up meetings. And being generally known—his acknowledged piety, his proverbial integrity, his universal benevolence, together with his recent, and almost miraculous change of sentiment, and his untiring zeal in the cause he had espoused, produced quite a general excitement; and his weight of character—for his life was a living exemplification of the superior excellency of his faith—gained him an attentive hearing wherever he went; and after producing a sufficient interest, he would give out an appointment for me, generally naming the text I should preach from. And in this way, for several months, he kept as much business on my hands as I could possibly attend to, and was instrumental in introducing the doctrine into many places where otherwise it would scarcely have gained a hearing. So thoroughly were the church convinced of his usefulness in the cause of divine truth, that they voluntarily offered him a letter, testifying their approbation of his public improvements, and recommending him to the fellowship and kind attention of the churches, societies, and brethren, wherever God, in his Providence should call him, which he modestly accepted; and a few years afterwards the Association gave him a letter of fellowship, as a preacher of the Gospel, which he held and honored until the close of his active and useful life.

The progress of the doctrine, the increase of preachers, the organization of societies, and the establishment of an association in the State, alarmed the clergy. The whole country was full of them, of all the Partialist denominations; and they came out, not in open and manly controversy, but with misrepresentations, slanders, and denunciations, and virulent condemnations of the doctrine, both in their pulpits where they felt safe from attack, and in private circles where they felt pretty sure they would meet with no well-informed Universalist; and quite an excitement on the subject prevailed through all the surrounding country, among almost all classes of people.

After the transaction of the business of the society, in Ann Arbor, at the annual meeting in March, 1837, Mr. Fuller arose and addressed the meeting, in substance, as follows:—"I wish to have something done that will stop the mouths of gainsayers, and silence the tongue of slander which is busy and loud against us from every quarter. I can not walk the streets without meeting with some ridiculous assault from some ignorant block-head on the subject of a doctrine which he knows nothing about, and is too shallow-pated, or too superstitious, to learn. I am willing to meet an honorable antagonist, and am ready to defend the doctrine, if I can have a fair opportunity; but this is not allowed. The clergy will ensconce themselves behind the ramparts of their own pulpits, where they have no fears of a reply, and there discharge their volleys of slander and misrepresentation, and furnish their ignorant and superstitious hearers with missiles to dart at every gentleman they meet, who may chance to favor the doctrine of Universal grace. I want to let them have a chance for open and manly combat, if they dare to enter the arena. In a word, I want the glove thrown down, and let them take it up, if they dare."

I replied: "Brethren, I am willing; nay, I should esteem it a privilege to have an opportunity to defend the doctrine of the Great Salvation, in a public discussion with any clergyman of ability, in good standing with his religious sect, who feels disposed to enter upon such a contest; or to meet him in any other form, upon reciprocal arrangements; but I have never given a challenge. I have conscientiously avoided it; but I should never refuse accepting one, if given by an honorable antagonist." "I do not want *you* to give a challenge," Mr. F. said; "but I want this society, at this meeting, to pass a resolution requesting you to give an *invitation* to the clergy, in Ann Arbor, to enter into a fair, Christian, and amicable discussion of the distinguishing doctrines of your sects, that is, endless punishment and universal salvation, upon reciprocal grounds. To offer them the use of this house to preach against the doctrine of Universalism, and vindicate that of endless misery, provided they will give you an opportunity of replying in their presence, and engage to use their influence to have their hearers also attend; or, for you to deliver a discourse in either of their desks in proof of your doctrine, and let them have the opportunity of replying; or, should it please them better, to hold an oral discussion with either or all of them, upon fair and equitable principles." "Well," I said, "if the society pass such a resolution, I shall certainly comply with it, if my life and health are spared."

The following preamble and resolution were consequently drawn up and passed by the unanimous voice of the society; and that, with the article annexed, was immediately published in both newspapers printed in the village, the "State Journal" and "Michigan Argus."

"*Resolution* passed by the first Universalist society in Ann Arbor, at their annual meeting on the 27th of March, 1837.

"*Whereas*, There is excitement manifested on the doctrine of final restitution by the orthodox clergy in general, and especially in this region; and its demoralizing and degenerate tendency made the subject of pulpit declamation, not only in their revival meetings, but also ordinarily on the Sabbath; and

"*Whereas*, The members of this society feel as deeply interested in knowing the truth as others can feel; and being sensible of the imperfection of man—of the powerful influences of the prejudices of education on his judgment—and also of his liability to form opinions hastily and inconsiderately; and feeling not disposed to affirm dogmatically, without a fair and liberal investigation, that they will continue to maintain and support the doctrine they now verily believe to be the truth of God, whether right or wrong, and consequently shun all further investigation of the interesting and important subject; therefore

"*Resolved*, That this society respectfully request Mr. Stacy, their present pastor, cordially to invite the clergymen of Ann Arbor to enter into a candid and Christian investigation of the doctrine; and to offer them the use of the Universalist church for that purpose, provided that he shall have the privilege of replying to them in their presence; or to meet them, upon reciprocal principles, in their own houses of worship—and that this invitation be given through the medium of the public journals published in this village."

"To the Rev. Messrs. *Beach, †Marks, ‡Calclazer, and §Miller, clergymen of Ann Arbor:

"Gentlemen: My apology for addressing you in this way is found in the foregoing resolution. Nothing else conceivable can be so desirable, to the seriously inquiring mind of mortal man, as a knowledge of religious truth, and no exertions more commendable than endeavors to attain it. And while such a variety of opinions are published to the world as *religious truth*, and so many of them so directly opposed to it, and irreconcilable to each other, all professedly having their foundations laid in the oracles of God, and advocated by honest and conscientious believers, and professedly instructed and 'called' preachers of the 'everlasting Gospel,' it is certainly one of the most reasonable things in the world, that the honest inquirer after truth should desire to hear a charitable and candid discussion of those discordant opinions, and an investigation of their respective claims on divine authority for support; and it is by no means strange that they should invite the professional advocates of these different opinions to a conference.

"It is but justice to the society and to myself to say, that the resolution originated not with myself, nor was it procured through my influence with the society; but it unquestionably originated in the sincere desire of the members of the society themselves for the *knowledge and propagation of the truth, as it is in Jesus.* And although they *verily believe* the doctrine they now profess to be the truth of God, yet knowing that *truth* can never suffer by investigation, and realizing that nothing but *truth* can be of any moral benefit to them or to the world, they are not only willing, but desirous of submitting it to the most rigid and critical investigation.

"Nor is the subject a matter of indifference with myself. Many years have rolled over my head, and I feel myself standing upon the verge of the eternal world. The subject

*Presbyterian. †Episcopalian. ‡Methodist. §Baptist.

of religion has been dear to my heart from my youth up. And with the feeble powers God hath given me—with the means He hath kindly placed within my reach, I have sought for TRUTH, as for the 'One thing needful,' and trust in God *that I have found it.* I believe, without the shadow of a doubt, in the final 'Restitution of all things which God hath spoken by the mouths of all his holy prophets, since the world began;' I believe it to be expressly revealed in the word of God, (without contradiction,) which has been a subject of my meditation and prayerful examination for more than thirty-five years. And I hesitate not to say, that with critical examination, and increase of years, my faith strengthens, that 'The God of our Lord Jesus Christ, the Father of glory,' will, in the *fulness of time,* and by his own appointed means, bring the whole wandering posterity of Adam to a state of holiness and happiness immortal.

"And so far from this faith having an immoral tendency, I believe it is the *only safe* doctrine to carry fully into practice. But still it is irreligious presumption in any man, to say that he *positively knows* aught that passes beyond the curtains of time: 'We walk by faith, and not by sight;' hence the reasonableness and the importance of keeping up a constant inquiry after truth; and the man who convinces me of an important error in my religious faith, confers on me an invaluable favor, and lays me under a debt of everlasting gratitude.

"Therefore, in obedience to the request of the society, I respectfully and affectionately invite you, brethren, any or all of you, to enter upon the glorious work; and offer you the use of the Universalist church, in this village, for that purpose. You may preach a discourse against the doctrine of Universal Salvation, or in support of endless misery, which are the great questions between us; and I will reply in your presence, and in the presence of the congregation, or as many of them as are disposed to hear, either immediately, or at an appointed time, as circumstances may warrant; and we will repeat the exercises from day to day, or from time to time, as long as it may seem good to you and to the people to attend. Or if it please you better, I will deliver a discourse in either of your places of worship, in proof of the doctrine I believe, provided you will use your influence to have your ordinary hearers attend, and you shall have the privilege of replying. Or, if it still better suit you, we will hold a public discussion, and each alternately speak on a question involving the main doctrinal point of difference between us, endless punishment or universal holiness and happiness, under such regulations as we may mutually agree upon.

"I can not persuade myself, brethren, that you will neglect the present respectful invitation; but you will avail yourselves of the opportunity now offered, in the good providence of God, to discharge an imperious and solemn duty you owe to God and man, by exposing a radical error, in your own estimation, which, undoubtedly, you honestly believe, involves infinite consequences; and of using your arguments and influence to undeceive the bewildered, and snatch a desiring people from the vortex of endless and irretrievable perdition.

"I await your reply in such a way as may suit your convenience. And with all due respect, and Christian charity, I am, gentlemen,

"Your obedient servant, for Christ's sake,

"N. Stacy."

Within a few days after the annual meeting of the society, at which the resolution was passed, the foregoing article, verbatim, appeared in both the newspapers published in Ann Arbor. It produced much excitement, and elicited many opinions in regard to the final result; but the clergy were quiet as pampered babes. I was personally acquainted with all of them, and occasionally, during this period, passed a compliment with them; but not one word escaped their lips to me on the subject. An old Baptist Elder, residing in a neighboring town, said to me one day, "I have seen your invitation to the clergy of Ann Arbor." "Well, what do you think of it, Elder T." "I think it is a very reasonable and Christian-like invitation; I don't see how the clergy can get around it, and not accept."

I could hear it whispered round that the clergy held meetings in conclave, on the subject; that Mr. Beach, the Presbyterian, proposed to accept of the invitation, and wrote to a distant clergyman on the subject, who advised him to be still. But I will not vouch for the truth of any of these reports. At any rate, nothing was said, or written to me, nor to the society on the subject; and after a few weeks the excitement died away. I waited between two and three months; a sufficient time, in all conscience, for the clergy to make up their minds about it, and then came out with the following article, which was also published in the "State Journal," and also, at my request, copied into the "Argus:"

"E. Lawrence, Esq., Editor of the 'State Journal:'

"Dear Sir: Will you have the goodness to give the following a single insertion? It is far from my design to invite, or to wish, a religious discussion in the columns of the *Journal.* I know full well that it would be discordant with the design and character of the paper, and would be dissatisfactory to your patrons. But inasmuch as a respectful invitation to the clergy of this village, to enter into an honorable, and charitable, and Christian investigation of those doctrines that are being published to the world as religious truth, for the benefit of an inquiring community, has been given through the columns of the *Journal*, by your sufferance and kindness, and the clergy have seen fit to pay no attention to it whatever—I sincerely wish, as a lover of the souls and bodies of men, to give the people as fair an opportunity as the circumstances will render possible, to hear an investigation of the all-important subject.

"Very respectfully yours, N. STACY."

"It will be remembered, at least, by those who felt sufficiently interested, (and surely nothing should more deeply interest the human family than an inquiry into religious truth,) that, in the 'State Journal' of April 6th, in conformity with a resolution passed in annual meeting of the first Universalist society in Ann Arbor, in March last, a friendly, respectful, and affectionate invitation was given to the clergy of this village, to enter, upon honorable and liberal terms, into an investigation of the doctrines of *Endless Punishment*, and *Universal Salvation*; and to try, by all the means Heaven has placed within our reach, the respective claims of each on divine authority for support. Nearly three months have rolled away, and nothing has been heard from any of the gentlemen addressed on the important subject. The feelings of those who are *honestly* and *seriously* seeking after truth—who are *sincere* in their *professions*, are not satisfied. If the endless destiny of man depends on his religious faith in this world—and such is the uniform representation of the clergy—and the clergy are truly sincere in their professions of the love of souls—if they view them in such imminent danger of endless perdition in consequence of heretical opinions, and honestly believe that those errors are so easily exposed, and the whole system so readily exploded as they pretend—the people are at a great loss to account for their supineness and indifference; especially when so fair an opportunity has been offered them; and when they certainly *know* that *truth* can never suffer by investigation—that it is error and evil only that 'hateth the light,' while 'he that doeth the truth cometh to the light, that his deeds may be made manifest that they are wrought in God.'

"But we wish once more to bring this subject before the public—we have not yet done with it. Having waited a sufficient time for the clergy to make up their minds on the subject, and hearing nothing from them—and feeling an ardent desire for the knowledge and advancement of religious truth, we propose, and wish hereby to give notice to the clergy and the public, that we design to enter into the *investigation* ourselves. Consequently, if God permit, a course of lectures will be commenced in the Universalist church, on Sunday, the 22d day of July next, at 5 o'clock P. M., and continue from Sunday to Sunday, as long as the object shall require, embracing the following topics:

"1st. A Scriptural illustration and defence of the doctrine of Universal holiness and happiness.

"2d. Removal of objections founded on the representation of its immoral and licentious tendency; in which it will be shown that it is not only not immoral in its tendency, but that it is the only theory of religion which can be safely carried *fully* into practice.

"3d. Removal of objections founded on the particular construction of certain passages of Scripture which, according to their ordinary application, are supposed to be irreconcilable therewith. On this department of the lectures, both friends and opposers of the doctrine are invited to present such passages as they wish to have brought under examination, with the assurance that if presented with a spirit of candor, they shall receive all the attention that the ability of the writer is able to give them, in the fear of God.

"4th. An examination of the orthodox doctrines of Christianity, so called—showing,

"1st. Their irreconcilability with the revealed character and perfections of God.

"2d. Their irreconcilability with the clearest testimonies of Divine revelation—and,

"3d. Their demoralizing and dangerous tendency upon human society.

"Those who feel interested are affectionately invited to attend; and they may rest assured, that by Divine assistance, the whole shall be treated with all that candor, charity, and forbearance that the nature and solemnity of the subject requires. N. STACY.

"ANN ARBOR, JUNE 17, 1837."

This last brought out the Episcopalian clergyman, in two articles; first in the "State Journal," and second, in the "Michigan Argus." And in justice to Mr. Marks, as well as to all concerned—and to show the feelings and the manners of the man, I feel under obligation to record them.

The following appeared in the "State Journal" of July sixth:

"Mr. Editor: Mr. Stacy has spoken twice of the clergy of Ann Arbor, in your paper, relative to discussing the doctrine of endless punishment. In the second communication he says, 'We wish once more to bring this subject before the public. Having waited a sufficient time for the clergy to make up their minds on the subject, and hearing nothing from them, and feeling an ardent desire for the knowledge and advancement of religious truth, we propose and wish to give notice to the public, that we design to enter into the investigation ourselves.'

"If Mr. Stacy has such an 'ardent desire for the knowledge of the truth' as he professes to have, I for one of the clergy, will use all possible means for his indoctrination, provided he will seek it as all pupils do, by resorting to my own kind house. I have a Greek grammar, Testament, and Parkhurst's Lexicon; but if he should change the scene and say, I come in the character of a teacher, to instruct the benighted ministers of Ann Arbor, in the principles of theology, I wish him to know, that I have made the writers of olden times my masters, and am perfetly easy in my mind. I wish not to be considered one of that number, who are *ever* learning, and *never* come to the knowledge of the truth. It is often said by opponents, I am open to conviction; but, I fear, that so great is the opening of the mind, that the *truth* goes through without any effect.

"I shall not, Mr. Editor, compliment Mr. Stacy for the apparently kind style of his piece. Well-bred gentlemen always challenge their opponents to single combat, in the most courtly manner. *☞ Were it not sir, for several amiable gentlemen whose misfortune I deem it to be of Mr. Stacy's way of thinking, and for whom I entertain the highest and kindest regard, I assure you sir, I would not put you to the trouble of putting these lines into type. From the formal manner in which the challenge was got up, it would appear that the downright theological murder of the clergy was intended. It would be uncourteous treatment of the framers of the resolution 'passed in annual meeting of the first Universalist society in Ann Arbor, in March last,' to discuss 'the doctrines of endless punishment and Universal Salvation,' to pass it over without notice. In a hasty manner I give the reason for not entering upon the debate, although at the same time, it is in the face of my better judgment; and it is more than probable, will cause me to be faulted by my congregation for giving this brief notice in your 'Journal.'

"Were men, my dear sir, fully aware of the extent of their transgressions against a holy God, there would be less wonder that they should suffer eternally for sin; and more, that the Deity could, or would do otherwise than condemn them to perpetual banishment from his presence, and the holy angels. Painful as this truth may be, to those who differ from me on this subject, (the reiterated challenge is certainly to blame for it) I will not suffer the present opportunity to pass without a strong expression of my opinion. I doubt whether the scheme of Universal Salvation, as inculcated, be not far more dangerous than open Deism itself. It does not shock us, like barefaced infidelity; we feel no pain, and suspect no evil, while it stands like 'water into our bowels,' like 'oil into our bones.' Reason teaches us that God may punish sinners as long as they continue to sin, and there is no reason to suppose that those who die impenitent will never produce a holy one. Sinners, too, will always deserve to be punished. God may, therefore, punish them for ever. With respect to the duration of future punishment, mankind are not proper judges, for they know not the full demerit of sin. This, God alone can determine, and he speaks of it in the Scriptures as 'eternal,' 'for ever,' 'for ever and ever.' We must there-

* I have added the index, because I thought the sentiment deserved it. N. S.

fore *renounce* the Bible, or believe the doctrine of endless future punishment. My object sir, in this article, is to say, that it is not fear of being unable to sustain the doctrine of endless punishment, that I, as one of the four clergy challenged to enter the arena with Mr. Stacy, declined. No, sir, I act by the counsel of one competent to advise in such matters ; 'the beginning of strife is as when one letteth out water ; therefore, leave off contention.' When, Mr. Editor, the proverb says, 'before it be meddled with'—I am now, thank God, so far as I know, on good and pleasant terms with Christians of other than my own communion, and, as far as it is possible, mean to live peaceably with all men. I shall not be the first to offer a lance, nor will I fear, on a suitable occasion, to break over with an aggression. It does not appear to me, that the village of Ann Arbor is in any great danger, from the inculcation of anti-endless punishment doctrine. For one, I can truly say, that I have unbounded confidence in the good sense of young ladies and gentlemen ; and believe that it will be very difficult to turn from their course the senior part of community ; therefore, I conclude that it is best to let well enough alone, and that a defence of Scriptural doctrines, at this time, is altogether uncalled for. With good wishes for Mr. Stacy and a desire to be on kind and good terms with his congregation, I again refer them to our proverb, as a cogent reason for my refusal to meet him in public debate. Of the truth of my doctrine I have not the shadow of a doubt, and if any doctrine of the Bible can be reduced to mathematical certainty, that of eternal punishment may be. Fearful is that man's responsiblity, who has the courage to say to his congregation, in the face of the 9th verse of the first chapter of the second of Thessalonians, 'Who shall be punished with everlasting (in the Greek it is eternal) destruction from the presence of the Lord and from the glory of his power'—that eternal punishment is not a Scriptural doctrine." "Yours,

S. MARKS."

I have transcribed it *verbatim et literatim, et punctuatim*, as it appeared in the "Journal."

The language of the piece was so ungentlemanly, so uncivil ; and the attack upon Universalism so ungenerous, so dastardly, where he knew he could not receive a reply ; where he knew we had been denied, properly denied the discussion of any doctrinal question ; and when he had received so fair and generous an offer—not a challenge, as he invidiously called it, but a brotherly invitation, to come out like a man and a Christian, and enter into an amicable and charitable investigation ; that I felt perfectly disgusted when I saw it, and concluded it was entirely beneath my notice. But the very next week there came out another article in the "Argus," over the signature of S. Marks, which led me to conclude it best, if I could do it in a very brief article, to silence his pen, and save him from the extreme mortification, if he had any sensibility, of reviewing any more such testimonials of his own incivility.

Here follows his second article :

—

"For the "Argus."

"I am sorry to discover, Mr. Editor, that our fellow-citizen, Mr. Stacy, is so determined upon the discussion of his doctrines with those he ironically calls the *Orthodox* clergy. Mr. Stacy has always been represented to me, as a very worthy man, and so far as my intercourse has gone with him, I can bear witness to his good breeding. I confess to you, sir, that I deeply regret the course he has pursued toward the clergy of Ann Arbor ; and especially toward myself. I never gave him, nor any of his friends, provocation—that is, I never directly attacked their doctrines. My intention, when I came into town, was to cultivate the friendship of every man, woman, and child. Experience has taught me, that without the heart and confidence of community, a man may be as wise as Solomon, as meek as Moses, and as eloquent as Appollos, without being able to do a particle of good. I have had nothing to do with public discussion of any kind, without the pale of our church; nor do I propose to have, unless dire necessity brings me into it. I consider a debate on the subject unnecessary and uncalled for. The Orthodox denominations are getting along very well, and I, for one, think we should be thankful for well-enough, and let it alone. The learned have long since put the question at rest—I should have said Jesus Christ, the Evangelists, and Apostles. I wish Mr. Stacy well. For many of his flock, I have a *warm* and special regard. It is not through fear I abstain, but *from* a firm belief, that my Master's cause would not be benefited from the controversy. I conclude with an anecdote of

Dr. ——, and a Restorationist. The Restorationist after hearing the sermon, observed—'I have heard you preach, and now I wish you to prove your doctrine.

"Dr.—I thought I did by the Bible.

"R.—You had much to say about hell and eternal punishment.

"Dr.—Well, what do you believe?

"R.—That a man should lead a good life, but, if he dies impenitent, he will be punished according to the deeds done in the body, and then go to glory.

"Dr.—Well, I believe in two things—first, That Jesus Christ died for sinners—secondly, That there is a straight road to Heaven—now, if you have a mind to go through hell to get to heaven, you may, but I shall take the straight road.' Every man has his choice. "Yours, S. Marks."

—

The next week, I handed to the publisher of the "Argus," the following, which was immediately inserted:

"Mr. Editor,—When I first cast my eye on the article over the signature of the Rev. S. Marks, in the last week's Argus, I did not discover that it demanded any more notice from me than his communication in the Journal a few weeks since; as I had no personal controversy with Mr. Marks, nor any expectation or wish to enter into a religious discussion in a political Journal, nor any more inclination for a 'newspaper squabble' than I have, in my old age, to become a 'pupil' to the profound erudition and theological lore of the Rev. S. Marks, obtained, doubtless, from his 'masters of olden times,' probably of the eleventh or twelvth century, in his 'own kind house' where 'all pupils' get their instruction; but on looking it over a second time, I discovered an insinuation which might mislead a stranger, and therefore beg leave to correct it.

"Mr. Marks says, 'I deeply regret the course he (myself) has pursued toward the clergy in Ann Arbor, and especially toward myself;' as though my course had been marked with some egregious impropriety toward all the clergy, but more especially toward him. Now in regard to what he alludes to, Mr. Marks knows that my course toward him has been marked with no peculiar characteristic to distinguish it from that toward the others, unless it be forbearance.

"My personal acquaintance with the clergy of Ann Arbor

has been very limited, and my intercourse, as far as I know, perfectly harmonious; for it has consisted simply in a passing compliment, except in two or three instances, and those of the most friendly kind. I have, indeed, spoken to them through the Journal, not *twice*, as Mr. Marks says, but *once*; and that in obedience to the earnest request of my friends, and in discharge of a solemn duty I owed to God on their behalf. And I now challenge—I have not challenged before—but I now challenge Mr. Marks and the world, to point out, in that address, a single disrespectful word, one uncandid, arrogant, unpolite, unchristian, or uncharitable expression. I spake as I felt, as far as I could find words to express my feelings; for the subject was a momentous one, and of equally deep interest to my friends, to myself, to the clergy, and to the whole human family. But with Mr. Marks, I have had very lttle personal intercourse whatever, either in private or in public. I am not conscious of ever having treated him unpolitely, or of ever having spoken of him to others, either in private, or in a *public newspaper*, disrespectfully, not even so much as to *represent him totally beneath my notice, were he not associated with others much more respectable than himself*; but have hitherto entertained for him the most kind and charitable feelings. And notwithstanding I am led to regret he has not given so high an evidence of his Christian candor, meekness, and charity, as I could desire, I am resolved to cherish still no other sentiment toward him. And while I readily accord to Br. Marks the unquestionable right of 'choice,' I do most devoutly pray—and pray in the full assurance of faith—that he may ultimately 'choose the path of heavenly truth' and wisdom, which is a sovereign remedy for *imperious arrogance*, which leads to Christian meekness and humility, and which is the only 'straight road' to heaven; and that we may yet unite in songs of grateful praise with a redeemed world. "Very respectfully yours,

"N. Stacy.

"July 25th, 1837."

From this time I heard no more from the reverend gentleman; he even appeared to shun me. If I were likely to meet him on the side-walk, he invariably found business on the other side of the street; whereas, he had formerly met me with a smiling countenance and a warm hand. Not long after this, I called at his house on business sent from Mr. Morse, of Watertown, N. Y., which more properly belonged to him than to myself; but he was not at home. Shortly after, I happened to meet him at the door of a store which I was entering the moment he was coming out, and got hold of his hand—but it was a cold one—and reminded him of my call, requesting him to return it, and interest himself in the business I called about. That was the last time I recollect of ever speaking with him ; not long afterwards he left Ann Arbor, and another clergyman supplied the desk.

Notwithstanding the ebullition of Mr. Marks' feelings—for he was the only individual I ever heard of, either clergyman or layman, who ever attached any incivility, blame, or uncharitable or unchristian conduct to the society, or myself, in regard to the proposed investigation—I pursued my course, unawed by his frowns and unannoyed by any further interference from any quarter, and, agreeably to the notice given, commenced a series of lectures which were continued until thirty were delivered. They excited much interest and were well attended. In the course of the third department, several passages of Scripture were presented which were carefully investigated—indeed the whole course received more than ordinary attention and care, and were all fully written out ; so that in case of misunderstanding, or controversy, we might refer to the notes, and re-examine the subject. Their publication was called for, but a want of means, and a consciousness that there was nothing very extraordinary in them, has, thus far, excluded them from public notice ; although I should have been perfectly willing to have submitted them to public examination, as they fully contain my theory of religion, as clearly as I could explain it ; my mode of defending the doctrine of the Great Salvation, and my views of the unscripturality and absurdity of the leading doctrines of Partialism. One of the lectures, that on Heb. 9 : 27, 28, was printed at the request and expense of my friends, during the season of a protracted meeting of the Partialist denominations in Ann Arbor, and handed freely about among clergymen and laymen ; but it never elicited any reply, nor any particulur remarks from opposers, that I ever heard of. But the whole course we pursued evidently resulted in good ; not only in extending and diffusing the knowledge of the true doctrine of the Gospel, but also in exhibiting the absurdities and incongruities of human creeds, and their deleterious influences upon the human mind, and also of softening the asperities of many limitaians who had the liberality to attend the lectures ; and especially in making the opposing clergy a little more modest in retailing their slanders, and in their assumption of judicial authority to fulminate their anathemas against every one who had the temerity to doubt their divine inspiration.

CHAPTER XVII.

Unsettled state of citizenship in Ann Arbor—Burden of support on a few—A means of spreading the truth—Speculating mania—Extortionate prices—Duration of residence in Michigan—Reasons for returning to Pennsylvania—Losses by bank failures—Expenses exceeding income—Society-meeting—Making up arrearages—Anonymous articles in the "Magazine and Advocate"—Dr. T. C. Adam—Propositions to enter the ministry—Correspondence—Dr. A. makes an appointment—His success—His second appointment and his fitness for Ann Arbor—The society give Dr. Adam a call to settle with them—He accepts for one year—Salary raised—The author's dismissal—Farewell discourse and separation—Session of the Association—Three additional laborers—State of the cause—Number of our preachers—Dr. A. enters upon his charge—His character and habits—His ill health, and subsequent relinquishment of the ministry—Ill health of my wife—Removal from Ann Arbor—Dr. A.'s benevolence—Further reasons for returning to Pennsylvania—Providential favors—Leaving Michigan—Journey through Ohio—An eccentric man, and singular theory—State of the cause in Pennsylvania—Lake Erie Association—Judah Babcock—Reports concerning him, and his withdrawal-His certificates and restoration-Subsequent circumstances, and investigation—Complaint against him—His suspension—Visit and letter to the author—His expulsion—Doings of the Blue River Association, Indiana.

The meetings in Ann Arbor were generally well attended, the church frequently crowded to overflowing; but the congregation was by no means permanent. It was a time of the most rapid settlement of the State—the greatest influx of emigrants. Very few of the inhabitants, comparatively, could be considered permanent residents—hardly stationary; for a vast many families only made it a temporary stopping-place, until they could have time to look around the country, and find a location to their liking; and those who first took up a residence in the village, or vicinity, were ready, upon any advantageous offer, to change their abode. The village was, therefore, constantly changing inhabitants, and very little dependence for support could be placed on a great majority of those who made up the congregation. The whole, or nearly the whole burden of supporting a constant ministry, as a consequence, devolved on a very few. There were a number of liberal supporters in the society, and I must say the most liberal, according to their means, that I ever found in any place. There were three, and they were not what the world would call *wealthy*, who during the whole of my residence in Ann Arbor never subscribed less than fifty dollars each, annually, and often more, besides paying me nearly as much more in some instances to make up the deficiency of subscription-list; and quite a number of others subscribed from fifteen to forty dollars, which must certainly be accounted liberal in a new country, where no large fortunes had been accumulated. The fluctuation of inhabitants, too, rendered the stability of the society doubtful. Converts were made—members were added, but no sooner was the bird caught than he had flown; nevertheless there was one abiding consolation—he had carried with him the seed of divine truth, which was planted in his heart there to be conveyed through him, and scattered around his new habitation. That gratified my highest ambition; for my object had ever been to advance the cause generally, to spread far and wide the knowledge of the truth, rather than to build up one splendid society, or surround myself with the appendages of earthly opulence.

There were other difficulties we were doomed to encounter. It was the time of that speculating mania, whose veneficial contagion infected the whole moral atmosphere of America, diffusing itself into all places, among all ranks and orders of society, and evincing a moral disease which paralyzed almost every truly industrial operation, prostrated many of the heaviest capitalists in our country, bringing bankruptcy, poverty, civil disorder, and moral degradation in its wake. It even vitiated legislative halls, corrupted their proceedings, so as to lend aid to schemes of vile peculation. Banks arose up in almost every hamlet, without a cent of capital—without the semblance of responsibility, issuing vast amounts of their *mockery* of a circulating medium, giving momentary facilities to wild and unprincipled speculators, until business was deranged, confidence destroyed, and society and government nearly reduced to a state of anarchy. People would not be satisfied with the slow proceeds of useful manual labor—mechanical shops were deserted, farms were neglected, and suffered to overrun with thorns and thistles—all rushed to the banks to obtain an irredeemable currency for the gratification of their avaricious desires, until, alas! too late, a reaction convinced them that, instead of accumulating affluence to themselves, or increasing the wealth and respectability of society, they had only been employing means of pauperism and degradation.

The effect of this was felt through the ranks of Society, down to the most humble day-laborer. This country being new, and a vast congregation thronging in, whose chief business was the purchase of the necessaries of life; and agriculture being neglected for the sake of "buying and selling to get gain," the necessaries of life had risen to an enormous price, most of which had to be imported from other States; which placed them almost beyond the reach of the poor, and required the greatest prudence and management with those who did not see fit to enter into schemes of speculation, to support their families. For some years after I removed into the State, flour ranged from six to ten dollars a barrel; butter, in firkins, from twenty-five to thirty-seven and a half cents per pound; cheese, from twelve to eighteen; pork from twelve to sixteen; beef from eight to twelve; and I have paid twenty dollars a ton for hay, and a dollar per bushel for oats; and nothing in the shape of a cow could be purchased for less than thirty dollars;—I have known a good cow sold for sixty. The times changed, however, before I left the State; and produce and stock were reduced to reasonable prices.

I remained in Michigan five years, or nearly that length of time. When I removed there, I by no means calculated on making it a permanent residence, or there to close my days; but having become weary of traveling over the rough roads of Western Pennsylvania and New York, I considered it but just and reasonable to seek a little respite; and believing, too, that I might for a while be of some service to the cause of religion in that fast-settling country, I was induced to make the trial. Our three eldest children were married, and two of them, at least, permanently settled in the country we had left. And although my eldest son had removed his family to Michigan, the spring after we arrived there, it had become evident that neither he nor his family could enjoy health there; for after the first season, his family had not been free from sickness, at any time, for the space of one month, and they were frequently all sick at the same time; and he had wisely concluded to remove back to Pennsylvania. Moreover, what little property I had, was in Columbus, Pa. I had, indeed, sold my farm; and with the avails, cleared myself from an old debt, and expended the remainder in subsisting my family in Michigan. But my village lot and buildings, which constituted the sum total of all my worldly wealth, remained unsold, and I concluded it would be most proper, and most prudent for us, to return back and spend the remnant of our days in the midst of our children; inasmuch as the three now immediately attached to our family, would return with us.

From the brief detail given above, of the exorbitant prices of the necessaries of life, together with the spurious and worthless character of the greater part of our circulating medium, which subjected the bill-holders to constant hazard and frequently to actual loss—(for if one took a bill one day, he ran great risk of losing the amount by keeping it over night, so constantly were these mock banks breaking down) —it will readily be perceived that a man required a considerable income to support a moderate family in such a place, and at such a time. Indeed, I actually did lose between thirty and forty dollars, even in my small dealings, by way of these spurious banks. At the close of my fourth year, notwithstanding the punctuality of the members of the society in paying up their subscriptions, and the great liberality of a number of friends in "free-will offerings," over and above their subscriptions, I had actually expended, for the support of my family, between one and two hundred dollars more than I had received from the society.

Before the close of the year I made known my condition to the trustees, and my design to leave the country and return back to Pennsylvania. A society meeting was called, but they would listen to no such proposal. They would raise my salary, and use more vigilance to increase support and collect dues. Indeed, this was necessary; for, although living was at that time far less expensive than it had been for years past; yet money, or a good circulating medium, had become quite scarce, and consequently subscriptions in general were not so liberal. Two of the most liberal supporters, however, threw in their notes for fifty dollars each;—another would board me and my wife, and keep my horse, the ensuing winter, while our two daughters were on a visit among their friends in Pennsylvania; and I must at any rate stay another year. My mind, however, was fixed, and my resolution to leave the country unalterable, so soon as it could be done without breaking down the society, or inflicting a wound upon the cause. And a kind Providence, in the course of the ensuing winter, opened a door.

Shortly after my settlement in Ann Arbor, a series of articles appeared, under a fictitious name, in the "Magazine and Advocate," which had a wide circulation in that country, entitled, "Notes on Sacred Subjects; addressed to Adelia." They were dated Lenawee county, Michigan; but who the author was, neither the publisher of the paper nor any of our preachers in all that section of country could divine. It was evident that the author was a man of high literary attainments, and deep theological and biblical research. We made all the inquiry that lay in our power; but the author kept himself so closely incognito, that months and even years rolled away before we were able to unveil him. It was, however, at length discovered, more by stratagem than any other way, that Dr. T. C. Adam was the author of them; and not long afterwards, Providence directed my way to make an acquaintance with him. Dr. Adam was a foreigner by birth—a Scotchman—and received his education at the University of Edinburgh. I found him all that I anticipated in respect to erudition, high intellectual powers and culture; but to my great disappointment I found him one of the most unassuming, and even bashful men, I ever met with; so great was his diffidence that he actually appeared awkward, and almost incapable of expressing himself explicitly in the presence of a stranger. But, on becoming acquainted with him and treating him with familiarity, his diffidence was overcome, and he began to show himself in social conversation; and I soon discovered that he had not only a talent, but an inclination for preaching. While he was on a short visit at my house, in 1839, the fall before I left Michigan, I proposed to him to enter the ministry. But had I struck him with my fist, the color could not have rushed to his face sooner, nor he have manifested more surprise, or received a more unexpected shock. I immediately apologized as well as I could—told him I knew he possessed talent and learning equal to the calling; and if I had not been greatly deceived, I had discovered in him a taste and inclination for it; and it was my candid opinion that he never would feel satisfied and at ease until he entered upon the work. But he repelled the idea with some degree of feeling, and the subject was dropped. Not many weeks elapsed, however, before I received a letter from him, acknowledging that the proposition which I had made to him, together with my remarks, had been a source of much, and, in some degree, painful thought. He confessed that he had ever from his youth felt deeply interested in the subject of religion—that since coming to America, and indeed within a short time past, he had become fully and unhesitatingly convinced of the doctrine of the final Restitution, and his heart and soul were engaged in it—that his most ardent desire was for its propagation and advancement in the world; and could he be made to believe that his talents and influence would advance the cause—that his character was, or could be made, such as to give weight and force to his labors, nothing would gratify his feelings, or contribute so much to his happiness as to engage in the ministry; and he requested me to write to him on the subject. This led to a correspondence, which resulted in an appointment from him to deliver a discourse in the Universalist church in Ann Arbor; and on the fourth Sunday in January, 1840, he delivered his first discourse to a very full congregation. He evidently suffered much with embarrassment, but both the matter and manner of the discourse were of the first order. Never before, I presume, was there so eloquent and finished a discourse, or one delivered with more pathos, or one that more strongly riveted the attention of an audience, delivered in that house, or perhaps in the village of Ann Arbor. It was received with the highest applause, and most hearty commendation; and it inspired him with courage. At my request, he had prepared two discourses, and was persuaded to preach again in the afternoon; and at the united importunity of myself and the society, he left another appointment for two weeks from that time. After preaching three Sabbaths to full and increasing congregations, he in a great degree overcame his diffidence, so that they had a fair specimen of his ministerial capacity; and their admiration of his labors, and their confidence of his great usefulness in the high and holy calling being freely expressed, I discovered a way by which I could be relieved from my pastorship, and immediately set myself about it. There was a man exactly fitted for that station. Ann Arbor had become the seat of the University, and would, of course, be the focus of the literati of the State; and the society needed a pastor who, in regard to literary attainments, could compete with the most eminent professors of the institution; and Dr. Adam was that man. I so represented it to the society, and urged it to give him a call; and to do it immediately, before he left the State. He was by no means calculated for an itinerant preacher; but his talents, learning, and habits were calculated for a settled pastor in a populous city; and if they did not secure his labors immediately, he would be gone to Boston, New York, or some other of our eastern cities; for there was no other location in Michigan that would be adapted to his genius, and none that would think of giving him a call—that they, equally with me, would wish to retain him in the State, and that to employ him would be the only feasible means of doing it—that it was presumable he would not demand a salary above their means, inasmuch as I was satisfied there were numbers who would subscribe for him, who would not set their names to paper for any other man they could procure. Some of the society objected to it at first, no doubt out of personal respect for me, and wished me to remain. But being told that my mind was fixed—that I should leave at the close of the year, at farthest, they consented to make the trial, and authorized me to enter into a negotiation with him on the subject. I immediately opened a correspondence with Dr. Adam, informing him of the wishes of the society, and I united with them in urgently pressing him to accept the call. At first he repelled it, as an infringement upon my rights—as superceding me. But being assured that I was determined to leave whether he accepted or not; and being made to believe that such was, in fact, my real and unalterable intention, he finally consented to settle with them for one year—he would not give encouragement for any longer period. My next business was to ascertain the necessary amount of salary, and to see that it was raised. After making several propositions to him, he at last told me, that five hundred dollars was all he would accept of, which would support his family, and he had no wish to make the Gospel a burden to the people, nor a subject of pecuniary speculation.

As I had succeeded thus far, I resolved that no effort of mine should be wanting to settle Dr. Adam in Ann Arbor; and therefore went about raising his salary, which was accomplished in a short time. I entrusted the business to no hands but my own. I had never the confidence to ask subscriptions for myself, to sustain my labors in any society, and hardly to ask for the payment of sums voluntarily subscribed; but I could freely and boldly do it for Dr. Adam. Accordingly, after preparing the papers, in one or two days, at farthest, I obtained on subscription the whole amount required. No individual subscription was unusually large, but numbers, as I anticipated, freely subscribed for him who had never before put their names to such a paper. I then went to the trustees of the society, put the papers into their hands, and took from them an obligation guaranteeing the payment of the amount of the subscription in equal quarterly instalments to the Doctor, provided he fulfilled the stipulations on his part; and that obligation I delivered to Dr. Adam; when I congratulated myself on the work being done.

I now had the satisfaction of having accomplished some good for the cause in Michigan. Whatever my labors hitherto had been, or might yet prove in their effects, I considered my last efforts in influencing Dr. Adam to enter the ministry, and obtaining his settlement in Ann Arbor, as being far above all the rest, in promoting the growth and advancing the prosperity of the cause in the State. One trying scene, however, remained for me, and, I doubt not, for my friends to pass through; and that was, to dissolve our connection—to take leave; and the last Sunday in May this trial was endured. It was the last day I ever met with them as pastor of the society and church; and the last discourse I delivered was on the words of the apostle to the Elders of the church at Ephesus, Acts, 20: 26, 27. At the close of the service, by a request of Deacon Williams, I took a stand on the first step of the pulpit stairs, near the entrance of the house, so that as many as chose might take my hand as they passed. The congregation was large, the house densely filled, and every man, woman, and child took my hand as they passed, for they all took the trouble to pass out at one door, and I know not that there was a dry eye passed from the house that evening. I had ministered to them a little over four years and a half; and nothing had taken place during that time to interrupt our harmony, or in the least degree to impair confidence; and though our relation of pastor and people had been brief, many strong attachments had been formed, and consequently a separation, although no doubt best for both parties, was, nevertheless, painful in the extreme.

The following week being the first Wednesday and Thursday in June, was the time for the meeting of our Association, which held its session that year in Ann Arbor; when Dr. Adam, together with three others, viz., Dr. I. Smead, D. K. Lee, and William Hard, received letters of fellowship as preachers of the everlasting Gospel. Dr. Adam delivered the last discourse on the occasion, which more than sustained the recommendation that I had given him, and inspired the strongest hopes and confidence in the breast of preachers and delegates —of believers and inquirers after truth. That was the last time I ever met with the Association in that State; and although attended with some melancholy sensations, arising from the great probability that it was the last time I should ever meet the brethren in my earthly tabernacle, still it was to me, "a feast of fat things," and my cup of "wines on the lees," was filled to overflowing. It was the fifth session of that body, including the one at its organization. Then there were only three preachers present who could be considered residents of the State, and but three societies duly represented; and within the short period of four years, amid all the discouragements and opposition which Universalism is uniformly doomed to encounter in its infantile struggles, in almost every land, numerous societies had grown up, whose delegates were there in council, and ten preachers besides myself were residents of the State, viz., A. H. Curtis, T. Wheeler, E. Gage, J. Billings, S. S. Curtis, A. Sweet, I. Smead, T. C. Adam, D. K. Lee, and W. Hard; and there were several other preachers in different parts of the State, who did not attend the Association that season. It will not be difficult, therefore, for those who feel interested in the prosperity of Zion, to judge of the feelings of one, under such circumstances, who had devoted a long life exclusively to the promulgation of the same Gospel. Oh, with what fervent gratitude to the "Father of spirits" should our hearts be filled, although there are many severe trials to be experienced in our life's "rough and rugged" path—many dark hours to overshadow us on the road from the land of "bondage" to the "Jerusalem" we seek, yet he mercifully affords us many brilliant seasons of heart-felt enjoyment; and, to give us strength and encourage faithful perseverance, spreads occasionally before us such a divine repast of good things.

On the first Sunday in June, Dr. Adam commenced his labors with the people of his charge. I attended meeting with him on the first day, formally introduced him to the church, as the pastor of their choice; and, at the altar of our common Lord, laying my hand on his head, installed him, informally, into his sacred, holy, and responsible office.

But all my anticipations were not fully realized. I had not the least doubt, when Dr. Adam settled in Ann Arbor, that, at the close of the year, he might demand almost any amount of salary, and it would be raised for him, without the least hesitation, and without difficulty. But his labors proved too severe for him; his health became impaired; and he was compelled to retire for a season from the ministry. And, at two separate trials since that time, in the city of Boston, Massachusetts, where he had a call, he has preached himself sick, and has been compelled to relinquish the duties of the ministry almost entirely. Hence, I very much fear, that our cause must wholly lose the valuable labors of this great man. Dr. Adam was rather fastidious in regard to the diction and logic of his discourses—nothing must go out of his hands in the least degree unfinished; and his extremely diffident feelings caused him to tremble, through fear of committing some error. He, therefore, applied himself to study with such intensity—not giving himself time for relaxation, and sufficient muscular exercise to keep up any thing like an equilibrium—that by the time he had prepared his discourses for the Sabbath, and delivered them, his whole physical system would be completely prostrated; and were a week twice as long as it is, it would be still too short for him to prepare his discourses, agreeably to his literary taste and refinement. I had thought, and hoped, that time and experience would have overcome his squeamishness, (as I once bluntly told him it was;) but I have pretty much given up his case as hopeless.

During the last year of my residence in Michigan, the health of my wife became very much impaired, and no medicine seemed to have any effect toward a restoration. Her disease appeared to have its seat in the nervous system; and traveling and suitable exercise, which we tried as far as circumstances would enable us, and which generally is the most successful in affording relief from such complaints, proved wholly ineffectual. This, had no other consideration been presented, would have afforded sufficient inducement for me to leave the country, and return back among our children. Having closed all my engagements, and arranged things at Ann Arbor according to my most ardent desires, I turned all my thoughts and attention to preparations for finally leaving the State. I had preparations to make, and some pecuniary affairs to settle, which would necessarily occupy some time, in all of which it became necessary to study and practice prudence and economy as far as possible, inasmuch as I had, by no means, increased my funds by removing into the State. Accordingly, accepting a very liberal and voluntary proposal of Dr. Adam, I removed my family, in the month of July, into the house he had vacated, in the town of Franklin, Lenawee county, which he generously offered to let me occupy, together with as much of his farm as I chose to improve, free of rent as long as I was disposed to stay on it. While making preparations for removal, I still continued to hold meetings in the surrounding country, and had several encouraging offers to settle with different societies, and remain in the State. But these proposals, however flattering, afforded no inducement to remain, under the circumstances of the ill health of my wife, and the desire of spending the evening of our days in the immediate society of our children. We were becoming old—our sun had long since passed his meridian, and was fast declining to his occidental hiding-place; and we began seriously to feel the infirmities of age, and the importance of seeking such repose as that feebleness so imperatively demands. I had devoted the strength of my years, most willingly and joyfully, to the cause of my great Master—I had sought the advancement of his cause rather than my own ease, or the affluence of this world's goods; and he had blessed us through the whole period with the absolute necessaries of life, with a good share of health, and, above all, with kind, dutiful, and affectionate children. As, therefore, by removing back to Pennsylvania, we should place them all in the same neighborhood, where in all probability they would quietly remain, so no earthly consideration, nor even the prospect then before us of being longer useful to the cause in that region, could interpose a sufficient inducement to change my mind.

A kind and watchful Providence, "who tempers the winds to the shorn lamb"—who never forgets those who trust in him ; who had mercifully sustained us thus far in our journey through life, dispelling the darkness which had often gathered in our path-way, often providing for our returning wants in some unexpected, and not unfrequently in an almost miraculous way, was still mindful of us ; and through the liberal exertions of some of our friends, and the ready, though unexpected sale of such articles of household furniture as we wished not to remove, furnished us with the means of returning in a comfortable manner to the place we desired. And on the second day of September, we bade farewell to our friends in Michigan, and set our faces to the east.

We entered our furniture at a forwarding-house in the village of Clinton, marked for Erie, Pennsylvania—from whence we proceeded to Toledo, where our son and our eldest daughters took passage in a steam-boat. I had provided myself with an able horse, and a carriage sufficient for the purpose, and took my wife and youngest daughter by land, through the State of Ohio. We were blessed with an excellent fall for traveling, fine weather, and good roads—and took our journey leisurely, journeying through the counties of Wood, Sandusky, Huron, Lorraine, Medina, Summit, Portage, Trumbul, and Ashtabula. We found many old friends, even some who had immigrated from New England recently, and formed some new acquaintances on our way—visited a good number of societies, held meetings in sundry places, and arrived at the place of our destination, now our own humble home, on the second day of October, just one month from the time we started ; having traveled, by the circuitous route we pursued, between four and five hundred miles.

One important object I had in view in making the journey by land, was the improvement of my wife's health, which was in a good measure effected, although she was very feeble when we started, and indeed experienced much sickness on the route. Still, after a sufficient season for resting from the fatigues of the journey, she enjoyed better health than for many months before ; and about a year afterwards her health was so recruited, that she has enjoyed, most of the time since, as good health as the generality of people of her age. Indeed, we have great cause of gratitude to the

Author and Preserver of our being, for the amount of health we have both enjoyed through a long and laborious life.

On our journey through Ohio, I delivered an evening lecture in the town of Florence; and at the close of meeting, a man was introduced to me, or rather introduced himself, who made extraordinary pretensions to religion, but had formed in his own whimsical imagination a most singular and peculiar theory, such an one as I never before found among all the variety of characters whose whims and phantoms had been regarded as religious truth, in this whimsical and superstitious world. It seemed to be a compound of Platonism, Judaism, and Christianity, and the Lord knows what else; but whimsical and eccentric as it was, it was surely more consistent with itself than any other system of Partialism I had ever before heard explained. The man had been a zealous Methodist; but in the labyrinths of that "bottomless" system had evidently become bewildered, and had seceded from them; and from the various materials he had picked up among the rubbish through which he had groped his way, had framed a theory without having much regard to anything but his own vitiated taste and bewildered imagination, to which he had tenaciously wedded himself.

He said he believed in two uncreated, self-existent, eternal principles or beings, one good and the other evil, whom he called God and Devil—that God took care of all his children, all he created, and would finally save them; but God created none but the Jews;—and that the devil created all the Gentiles. But the children of God and the children of the devil had become so amalgamated, so intermingled, that it was almost impossible now for infinite wisdom to trace the dividing line—that Jesus Christ came into the world to save the children of God, and would finally accomplish it; and that if possible, (and indeed he thought it quite probable,) he would succeed in saving some that the devil had created.

I had but a few moments conversation with the man. He was quite a fluent talker, and appeared perfectly sane on every other subject, and I was told, a respectable man; but whether he had ever succeeded in making any proselytes to his theory, I did not learn.

On my return to Pennsylvania, I found the cause of Divine truth in a gradually progressive state. Several new societies had grown up, while some that were measurably in a state of organization had been dissolved; but on the whole there had been an increase. Some two or three young men had embarked in the ministry, and two or three preachers had removed into this section ; and a new Association, (" The Lake Erie Association") had been organized in Western Pennsylvania. But I found a burden of very considerable weight lying upon the cause, which essentially retarded its progress in this region ; and I undertook, painful as was the task, to search it out, and, by the help of God, to remove it out of the way.

A man by the name of Judah Babcock, residing some where in Allegany county, New York, a short time before I removed to Michigan, had seceded from the Free-will Baptist connection, professed conversion to the faith of Universalism, and obtained from the Allegany Association a letter of fellowship as a preacher. He was an illiterate man, but possessed a certain kind of speaking talent which captivated a particular class of community, and produced considerable excitement wherever he went, which rendered him quite popular. After I left Columbus he came into this region, and for a season, preached to good acceptance in Columbus and the surrounding country ; and even made arrangements to remove his family into the town of Columbus. But while these measures were in progress, reports derogatory to his moral character, and reproachful to the cause in which he was engaged, were put in circulation, which not only led to some unhappy feelings in the society at Columbus, but brought a stain on the cause wherever his name was connected with it. Some steps were proposed to investigate these reports, but, as it too evidently appeared, in order to avoid investigation, he in a private and informal manner returned his letter of fellowship to the clerk of the Association, and said he thereby withdrew from the connection, and denied the authority of the Association to deal with him.

In the course of the year, however, he obtained certificates of certain individuals of respectable character, but who were not of our denomination, nor professors of religion, and had no sympathy for Universalism more than any other sentiment, stating that they did not *know*, and had no special reason to *believe* the reports in circulation—which was the amount of the certificates obtained ; and at the next session presented these certificates, and requested the restoration of his letter of fellowship, which was restored to him. This was the position of Mr. Babcock when I returned to Pennsylvania from Michigan.

While on a visit to this country the year before I removed back, I learned something about these difficulties; and also, that Mr. B. was not then in fellowship. But seeing, in the printed minutes of the next year's session of the Allegany Association, that his letter of fellowship had been restored, I of course was led to believe that all difficulties were satisfactorily settled; and I greatly rejoiced that harmony again was restored to the church in this section. Nor was anything said to undeceive me on this subject until the session of the Lake Erie Association, in June, after my return. Mr. B. attended that Association on his way to Ohio, and the Western States; and I was greatly astonished that one of our delegates from Columbus, as well as of some other individuals whom I expected at the meeting, were not there. On inquiring the cause of their non-attendance when I returned home, I was informed it was because they had learned that Mr. B. would be there, and they could not conscientiously sit in council with him. I then set myself about the business in good earnest to ascertain what had been done in his case, and how far the breach had been healed; but, to my astonishment and mortification, I found *nothing* had been done, or nothing effectually, to satisfy an aggrieved brother or sister, or wipe away the stigma from the denomination. On inquiring of some of the leading members of the Association, why Mr. B.'s letter of fellowship was restored to him, while the stain of impurity was unwashed from his character; I was told, that while dispossessed of his letter of fellowship, he denied the authority of the Association to call him to an account for his conduct, or to investigate the reports in circulation concerning him; and their object in granting him fellowship again, inasmuch as he continued to preach and call himself a Universalist, was to place him within the reach of discipline. "Well, why have you not done it, seeing the reports are not contradicted by the authority, nor the burden removed from the aggrieved party?" They answered, "because no one has entered a complaint against him." I then told them, that plea should no longer suffice for their delinquency; that if ground for a complaint existed, it should be made, and that soon, for I resolved that the cause of God and humanity should no longer groan and cripple under this unnecessary burden. If Mr. B. was slandered, he should have an opportunity, and help too, to clear himself from those vile calumnies,—or, if he was guilty, he himself should be made to "bear his own burdens." I spent weeks, therefore, in traveling over the counties of Warren, Chautauque, Cattaraugus, and Allegany, visiting those who were grieved with the conduct, or the reports of the conduct, of Mr. Babcock, examining the nature of the charges, and getting the evidences on which they relied for support, and embodied the whole in a written complaint, which I presented to the committee of discipline of the Allegany Association.

Mr. Babcock remained at the West, and we could by no means learn the place of his address; but every means in the power of the committee or myself were resorted to in order to inform Mr. B. of the transaction, and urge him to attend it. Notice was given through the medium of our Western periodicals, and the examination put off from time to time, but to no effect—he appeared to take no notice whatever of our proceedings. At length it was necessary for the prosperity of the cause that something should be done, and at the session of the Association, held in Yorkshire, Cattaraugus Co., in June, 1843, a patient, careful, and charitable examination of the evidences was attended to, which resulted in the suspension of Mr. B. for one year, with a request that he should attend the next session, and defend himself against the charges preferred.

In the course of this year, while I was on a visit in New England, Mr. B. made a visit to this country; but took no notice of the proceedings in his case, never called on the committee of discipline, nor made any arrangements to vindicate himself. All the notice he did take of the case, as far as I could learn, was to address a lengthy menacing letter to me, which he left in the hands of a friend in Columbus, to be delivered on my return. This letter I forwarded to the council of the Allegany Association, at their session in 1844, and the final step was then taken, by withdrawing the hand of fellowship from him. Thus ended the unhappy affair. It was truly a painful task for me, and brought down some vials of wrath, not from Heaven, but from Mr. B, on my devoted head, and also some not very friendly innuendoes from the "Blue River Association," Indiana, headed by Mr. Kidwell, who, in council, condemned my proceedings, and the doings of the Allegany Association, and justified Mr. Babcock; pronounced him an able and worthy preacher of the Gospel, and in good standing. After the publication of the doings of the Association in which Mr. B.'s expulsion took place, I received a letter from Mr. Kidwell, making inquiry in regard to the charges brought against him, &c. I replied to him at length, all I could write on three sheets of foolscap, giving him an impartial and circumstantial history of the whole transaction from its commencement to its termination. This letter he laid before the "Blue River Association," and the result was as above stated. Mr. K. sent me the proceedings in his "Encyclopædia."

CHAPTER XVIII.

Physical improvement of the country—Views and expectations on returning to Pennsylvania—Mr. Paine—Calls and labors—Mr. Paine's removal—Engagement in Columbus—Extent of monthly travels—Arrangement for a tour to New England—Journey—Allegany Association—Boston—Buffalo—Niagara Falls—Lockport—Gaines—Rochester—Organization of a church—Newark—D. K. Lee—Geneva—Arrival in Madison county—Journey to Vermont—Charleton, Saratoga county—Arrival in Bridgewater My mother's grave—Inscription—Woodstock—Barre—Meeting and separation of friends—Return through Northfield—Visits in Woodstock and Bridgewater—Rev. R. Streeter—The farewell—Improvement of the country, and roads-Journey from Woodstock to New Salem—Rude inscription on a monumental stone—Reminiscences—Visit to our native town—Pleasingly melancholy reflections—The cemetery—Visit to my brother's family —To Mr. Flagg, Dana—State of the cause—Meeting in the old Congregational house—Reminiscence of ancient times—Rev. Joel Foster—Universalist preacher settled in New Salem—Disappointment—Journey to Madison county, New York—Brattleborough—S. Elliot, Esq.—Rev. Mr. Ballou—Wilmington—Rev. Mr. Bailey—Conference—Bennington—Snowstorm—Duanesburg—Rev. Mr. Lyon—Cooperstown—Rev. Mr. Whiston —Arrival at Hamilton—Meeting and parting with a brother—His death—Labors of the winter—Conferences and funerals—Mr. D. Dunbar and his wife—Her death—Remarkable coincidence—Return home—Providential favors—Reflections.

During the five years of my absence from Western Pennsylvania, great improvements had been made in the roads through the country, as well as in almost every other respect. I could now travel very comfortably in every direction in a carriage, and through almost every town and neighborhood. Although I had received no special call from Columbus, nor any other society particularly in this country, yet I had no idea of relinquishing my ministerial labors. The field was sufficiently large to require the labors of all who were in it, indeed it required many more to supply its demand; and calls had always increased, within the compass of my observation, in proportion to the increased means of supplying them. I returned to Pennsylvania because that was my home; and I was disposed to make it so during the remainder of my earthly pilgrimage. But while kind Heaven granted me health and strength, I was resolved to employ my time, as far as I could, and at the same time procure the means of subsistence for my family, in proclaiming the word of salvation. Mr. L. Paine was settled in Columbus when I returned, and supplied that society, and one in Westfield, Chautauque county, New York; and I had no expectation or desire to supercede him, nor in any manner to infringe upon his privileges. I had no desire or expectation of being employed as pastor of the church in Columbus; but felt a gratification in becoming a neighbor to Mr. Paine, and of associating my labors with his, as far as consistent, so as to be mutual helps to each other. I therefore, as soon as I could arrange my affairs, and get my family into any thing like a comfortable state, commenced making appointments in answer to calls in the surrounding country, and frequently, in Mr. Paine's absence, in Columbus also. Nor could I well be idle, had I the inclination; for more earnest and urgent solicitations were made from organized but destitute societies, and from places where organization had never been effected—vastly more than I was able to supply; and my time was very soon wholly employed.

In the course of the following year Mr. Paine closed his engagements in Columbus, and removed his family to Chautauque county, where he had uniformly employed a part of his time during his residence in Columbus; the church and society therefore being destitute, I once more accepted the pastoral charge; and from that day to the present I have devoted a portion of my time to their service; but during the same period I have had engagements with other societies, which have generally subjected me to the necessity of riding from fifty to one hundred miles a month.

Many years had elapsed since we had seen any of our surviving relatives in New England, and still more since we had visited the country of our childhood; and age admonished us, that if we would realize our wish to enjoy such a visit and interview, it must be accomplished soon. We were both among the youngest of our fathers' families—our parents had long since fallen asleep, leaving but a small remnant of their immediate posterity, and they were all far advanced in life. My wife had two sisters in the State of Vermont, who, with herself, were all that survived of her father's family. I had also two sisters in Vermont, and one brother, and a half-sister in Massachusetts. Therefore, after once more getting our family comfortably settled in Columbus, and seeing the two oldest, who had hitherto remained as immediate members of our domestic circle, married and settled in the world, we concluded that kind Providence had now afforded us an opportunity to accomplish so desirable an object. Consequently, providing ourselves with a good safe horse and a comfortable carriage, so as to travel independently of public conveyance, and enable us to pursue our journey as leisurely as we were disposed, diverging from a direct course when it became necessary to visit friends, and stop, and go at our own bidding; we left home in the latter part of June, 1843. I had in view, not only to visit our friends and relatives in New England, but to make a very general visit in the field of my early labors in Central New York, as well as to visit many friends, and some societies on our way. We left home, therefore, without giving any encouragement of returning short of a year.

We first steered our course to Cattaraugus county, made a short stop with our daughter in Farmersville, and attended the Allegany Association, which held its session in the town of Yorkshire. Thence, we proceeded to Boston, where I preached the following Sabbath; thence to Buffalo, where we tarried only one day with our friends, at that great port and outlet of immense inland seas; and thence to Niagara Falls, where we stopped another day to gaze and wonder at this sublime and matchless work of Him, "Who created all things by the word of his power." I had visited that place before, but will never attempt a description of a wonder which has defied the skill of infinitely more vivid imaginations than mine. All I will attempt now to say is, that with every successive visit to that stupendous and unparalleled cataract, astonishment increases, and the soul is overwhelmed with wonder, awe, and reverence. From thence we proceeded to Lockport, where we stopped two nights, one with an old acquaintance, and the other with Mr. B. B. Bunker, who had recently removed into the village, and settled as pastor of the Universalist church. From Lockport, we proceeded to Gaines, where we tarried over the Sabbath with Mr. S. S. Curtis, and I preached in the morning and afternoon, in the Universalist meeting-house. Our next stopping-place was the city of Rochester, where, and in the vicinity, we spent nearly one week. The Sunday following, at the earnest solicitation of Mr. C. Hammond, who was then settled as pastor of the society in Rochester, I spent with him and Mr. S. Miles, in the city; when, for the first time, a small church of believers was organized, and recognized—and a happy day it was to them. From Rochester we proceeded to Newark, where many years before I had delivered a single evening lecture to a few individuals in a private house; but we now beheld a populous and thriving village, situated on both sides of the Erie canal; and with it a very respectable Universalist society, who had built a very neat and convenient meeting-house, and settled Mr. D. K. Lee, one of my Michigan boys, as its pastor. Mr. Kneeland Townsend had previously preached there, and his family then resided in the village We spent about twenty-four hours in the place. We next proceeded, diverging from our direct course, to the village of Geneva, at the outlet of the Seneca lake, and made a short visit with another of my boys, Rev. O. Ackley, who resided there, and had been many years a successful laborer in the vineyard of our Lord. After spending one night only with him, we again resumed our journey, and, on the twenty-eighth day of July, reached Madison county. To meet our calculations, some time was necessarily required to be spent there; but as the season was advanced far beyond what we intended it should have been before reaching that place, it became quite an important consideration, whether we should make our visit in that region during the remainder of the summer and autumn, and spend the winter in New England, or proceed immediately on our journey, and return there for winter quarters. The latter, however, was finally agreed upon; and after visiting in a limited circuit among our friends, which occupied, however, about four weeks, we set our faces toward New England; and as the largest number of our relatives then resided in Vermont, that, of course, became the object of our first desire. We traveled with as much expedition as we conveniently could, making a short visit on the way, in Charleton, Saratoga county, where resided several children of a deceased brother of my wife, and arrived at the house of my brother-in-law, in Bridgewater, Windsor county' on the fifteenth of September. It had been fifteen years since my wife had visited her friends in that country, and between thirteen and fourteen years since I there, at that very house, took the last parting farewell of my revered and aged mother. She there spent the last days of her long and useful life; and her remains sleep in a little rural cemetery in the neighborhood, with a very humble monumental stone to mark the place of her interment, on which is the following inscription, prepared by my own hand and forwarded to my sister, soon after her death.

IN
Memory of ANNA, Relict of
RUFUS STACY,
WHO DEPARTED THIS LIFE, FEB. 26TH, 1837;
IN THE 92D YEAR OF HER AGE.

Long was she spared, by Heaven's kind behest—
In virtue's path her friends and children bless'd;
Her hope, triumphant, soar'd o'er death's dread gloom,
That Christ should wake her slumbers from the tomb!

I visited the spot; and penetential tears coursed down my cheeks, at the remembrance of my ingratitude to the tenderest and best of mothers; and that my youthful waywardness should have caused her so many anxious thoughts and heartfelt pains. Oh, what hoards of sorrow do thoughtless and wayward youth lay up for themselves in riper years!

But time waited not for us—the season was rolling rapidly on, and we had to hurry our visits much faster than we desired. My other sister resided in the town of Woodstock—she was then a widow, having buried her husband previous to my former visit, and now lived with her eldest son. We made her but a short visit at this time, but proceeded immediately to Barre, Washington county, where one of my wife's sisters resided; we had already called on her other sister on our journey hither, but as we could stop at her residence on our route back to New York, we made her a temporary call. Though many years had elapsed since we had met our brothers and sisters in Barre, yet recognition was by no means difficult; and we were extremely happy in finding them in health, though laboring under the weight of man years.

We spent about one week with them; and I enjoyed the privilege of once more announcing the word of life to a large congregation in the Universalist meeting-house, on Sunday. I also went to the village of Montpelier, in order to make a short acquaintance with Rev. Eli Ballou, editor of the Watchman, but had the misfortune to find him absent.

Painful as the task was to take each other by the hand, in all probability, for the last time, (as it has actually proved in the case of brother and sister Lawson, for both have departed this life,) it must be performed; and, grateful to God for the privilege of meeting once more in the flesh, but with painful feelings on separation, we performed the solemn and melancholy ceremony, and commenced our returning steps. We however took a circuitous route on our return, to visit three of my sister's sons who resided in the town of Northfield; but on the day following we again reached Bridgewater. In this town, and in Woodstock, we spent another week; and for the first and last time in my life, I took hold of the hand of Rev. Russel Streeter. I was informed that he resided at Woodstock Green, and thither I went on purpose to see him; for he seemed like an old acquaintance, although we had never seen each other's face in the flesh. It was little past the middle of the day when I reached his residence, and inquired for him without giving my name. His lady invited me to a seat, and said she would call him. He had evidently been lying down; for he entered the room rubbing his eyes, and approaching me, said, "I believe this is brother Stacy." Our hands met in the paternal warmth of long intimacy, and a short season was happily improved; but it was short, as all my visits were necessarily obliged to be during that journey.

Sunshine and clouds are uniformly interspersed through the atmosphere of human life. Pleasure and pain are man's alternate companions, and joy and sorrow are mingled in the cup that Providence places in his hand. We had experienced the sunshine, we had enjoyed the pleasure, we had quaffed with delightful gust the surface of our cup, but the clouds now began to lower, at the painful necessity of draining its bitter dregs! Time sped, on its everlasting, untiring wings, and brought the day of our separation. And although our hearts throbbed with emotions of profound gratitude to God, for the hitherto prosperity of our journey and the inestimable privileges we had enjoyed, still an indescribable *pain shot* through the latent fibres of the soul, when our hands, probably for the last time, grasped the hands of our separating friends! We turned our faces, quick as possible, to conceal the emotion we could not suppress, and drove off with as much speed as prudence would allow, to try, by the interest new objects would excite, and the anticipations of pleasure still in reserve in visiting our native country, to overcome the gloom of the present moment.

Our way lay through one of the most romantic regions of that mountainous State, through ravines excavated by the everlasting flow of the mountain streams, among bold and lofty eminences whose cloud-capt summits often defied the penetration of our sharpest gaze; but when the sunbeams had dispersed the fog, and thrown the night-cap from the heads of these gigantic hills, we could easily discover upon their precipitous sides, and even on their summits, handsome plantations and splendid buildings, which, however, would seem to require the wings of an eagle to reach them. Often at a short distance ahead, it appeared that our course must be obstructed by an inaccessible mountain, through which no possible pass could be found; but ere we reached the spot a sudden turn in the road would discover a pass which nature had formed, and the untiring search of man had found; and whose ingenuity and skill had converted into one of the most level, smooth, and safely guarded roads, that I ever traveled in my life. We passed on leaving South Woodstock, where we parted with the last of our relatives through Reading, Weathersfield, and Springfield, and crossed Connecticut river on Cheshire bridge.

While riding in the town of Reading, I discovered by the way-side a roughly-wrought stone, with some inscription on it. Curiosity led me to descend from the carriage and examine it. It purported to have been erected to the memory of Capt. James Johnson, who, with his family, were taken prisoners by the Indians, in August, 1754, and brought to that place, then a dense and howling wilderness; and within half a mile of the spot where the stone is erected, his wife was delivered of a child! Upon the stone, just above the inscription, was rudely carved an Indian in his savage costume, with his tomahawk in hand.

The weather was pleasant, roads excellent, and we traveled

from Woodstock, Vermont, to New Salem, Massachusetts, a distance of one hundred miles, in two days. But although our speed was rapid, thought was equally as active.

Reminiscences of an interesting character were awakened in passing through nearly every town. Forty years before this, I had passed for the last time through this region of country, although, previously, I had frequently traveled the road. After crossing Connecticut river, we passed through Charlestown, Walpole, Surrey, Keen, and Winchester, New Hampshire; Warwick, and Orange, Massachusetts. In Winchester, I received my letter of fellowship, as a preacher of the Gospel. In Walpole, I had supplied the desk for a Congregationalist clergyman, Rev. Thomas Fessenden, one Sabbath—in Surrey, I had lectured in the house of the venerable Zebulon Streeter; and, all along our route, I had formed acquaintances with aged fathers in our Israel, whose counsel I delighted to listen to, but who had long since bade adieu to earthly associations and toils.

We arrived in New Salem on the 4th day of October; but, alas! though the land of our nativity, it afforded a gloomy resting-place for us. Twenty-three years had rolled away since we set foot upon our native soil; and those years had swept our kindred and acquaintances from the land, or wrought such changes upon them as to render them entire strangers to us, except in a very few instances. None of our relatives, not any of the children or the posterity of our fathers remained, except an aged half-sister of mine, eighty-five years old, and a son and daughter of hers, and three children of a sister of my wife, who were *little ones* when we last saw them. Time had so changed the few that remained, with whom we had associated in early life, that we gazed at each other in apparent astonishment when we met. Nevertheless, there was a thrill of melancholy pleasure when we stepped on our native soil, and retraced the paths of our youthful gambols—when we viewed the streamlets to whose ripples we had listened in childhood, the pastures whither we had driven the cattle to their morning's repast; the meadows where we had gathered the delicious strawberry; the hills we had climbed to pick the sweet-whortleberry, or collect chestnuts from the burrs which the chattering squirrel would drop down to us; or the smooth rock on which we sat under the mellow light of the full-orbed moon, to listen to the plaintive notes of the whip-po'-will. Even the barren pitch-pine plain, over which we had rambled to gather winter-greens and blue-berries, and, at the rustling of a leaf, would startle lest we should come in contact with the poisonous fangs of the rattle-snake, which often concealed itself beneath some old moss-covered log ; the sight of the ponds on whose waters we had often paddled the rude canoe, to gather the virgin lily, which whitened its surface, or angle for the sportive fish which played beneath—inspired thoughts and awakened up remembrances of the most thrilling character, and led us to repeat with a little variation, the well known stanza :

> " How dear to our hearts are the scenes of our childhood,
> Each streamlet, each hillock, each mountain and dell ;
> The plain and the meadow, the pasture and wild-wood,
> And e'en the rude bucket that hangs in the well."

But above all, here reposed the remains of our fathers, and very many of the dear ones with whom we associated in early life. The place seemed sacred to their memory ; we felt, when approaching the little mounds which marked their resting-place, as though we stepped " on holy ground," and must " put off our shoes from off our feet," nor utter a word " above our breath." But alas! when I entered the cemetery where the succeeding generations of my native town had been gathered, and where the mortal remains of very many of my early associates slept in everlasting repose, and where I knew that the remains of my father were deposited, having no one to guide me, I was unable to find the spot.

We remained in this region thirteen days only. My eldest brother had, a few years previous, removed from that town to Phillipstown, about sixteen or eighteen miles from that place ; and during the period above stated, we made his family a short visit, but found him absent. About the time we left Madison county, he started for that place, to visit his children there, and spend the winter among them. Although disappointed, I did not regret the circumstances, inasmuch as we were calculating to return immediately there, it would afford me a much longer time to enjoy his company. We also called on Rev. J. Flagg, in the adjacent town of Dana, whose family we found in deep mourning—four days before this, he had buried his wife.

I found the cause of divine truth progressing in every place I visited, but in none more so than in the town of my nativity. Many years ago, when the interesting questions of Trinitarianism, and Unitarianism became subjects of discussion in the Congregational, or Standing Order churches in New England, and produced the existing division among them, a majority of the church in New Salem, with their pastor, Mr. Harden, took the ground of Unitarianism and consequently professed great liberality. But although the Universalists held meetings in the town, often, if not regularly, none of the Standing Order church, either preacher or layman, associated with them, but kept as great a distance as the most rigid Orthodox. I had always held meetings in the town whenever I visted my parents, and often in different neighborhoods; but, with very few exceptions, none of the members of the Congregational church had ever been at my meetings; but now I found a great change in that respect. The generation that had formerly taken the lead had passed from the stage, and their posterity had been reared up under more liberal sentiments than were their fathers, and began to bring their principles more fully into practice. Universalist preachers had been invited into the old parish meeting-house, and the "good seed" had fallen upon a favorable soil. I was now requested, earnestly requested, to preach in the old parish church. But one Sabbath was all that I could spend in the town, having engaged to preach one in Dana. Although Mr. Harden preached now but half the Sundays in New Salem, that was the day of his meeting; and, whether he would give up the house for the day, or any part thereof to me, was still, in the opinion of a number of his parishioners, quite problematical. The experiment, however, they said should be made, and if he refused, a meeting should be held in the town-house, in the immediate vicinity. It so happened, however, that Mr. Harden exchanged that day with a young man from Northfield, and he very readily consented to let me occupy half the day. We were introduced on Sabbath morning, walked to the church together, and, at his proposal, (I mention this in commendation of his liberality) took seats together in the desk. I prayed for him in the morning, and he prayed for me in the afternoon. Whatever effect my discourse had on him, I can not say, but I was much edified with his; there was not a sentence, nor a word, that I could not conscientiously respond to. That day, however, was a season of profound and thrilling sensibility to me. I was now in the house where, in my boyhood, I had uniformly attended religious service; where the congregation were all known to me, both the gray headed and the youth; where I listened to the eloquent words of Rev. Joel Foster, the earliest preacher I ever heard, whose flexible, musical voice always captivated me; and it seemed, when I entered the house, as though I should see him; and my imagination painted the scene in such vivid colors, that I could easily fancy I heard his voice, in its musical and measured tones, still ringing in my ears! So lively was the picture in my imagination, that I could not avoid alluding to it in my introduction. Joel Foster was settled in that parish in my infancy. He was then a young man, and, I believe, the second clergyman ever settled in New Salem, (the first was a Mr. Kendall)—and he continued as pastor of the church until I became of age, and began to wander about the world. It was not strange, therefore, that visions of him should haunt my imagination when I entered the church; but solemn reflection reminded me that his voice was long since hushed in death! When I looked around upon the congregation—for the house was well filled—there were but four faces besides my wife's that looked familiar; and one of them was that of Mr. Flagg, who came from Dana purposely to attend the meeting. But I suppressed my emotions as well as I possibly could—and profound attention was given to my message—so much so, that my associate preacher took notice of it, and, although he expressed no opinion in regard to the discourse, yet he remarked "You can not complain that you did not receive *good* attention." This whole circumstance, together with the reflection that it was the residence of my progenitors, and the home of their graves—the parish of my nativity, and the school of my first religious instruction and impressions, awakened in my soul a peculiar interest in the well-being of the members of that parish; and I was made unspeakably happy in hearing, less than two years from that time, that that same parish had actually settled a Universalist preacher as pastor of the church.

We experienced no little disappointment in one respect—when I first anticipated this tour, after our removal from Michigan, I intended to have prosecuted our journey much farther, and have visited Boston, and many other places on the Atlantic coast. My intention was to leave in the fall, spend the winter in Central New York, and employ the whole of the following warm season on the tour of New England, which would have afforded us sufficient time to gratify our wishes to the utmost extent. But a wise Providence seemed to indicate that my calculation was not best; and by throwing obstacles in our way, prevented us from starting until the opening of Spring; then, by unavoidable hindrances, we were detained till near midsummer before we got fairly started. This brought it so late in the season by the time we reached our native place, that we dare not push our journey farther, nor tarry long here, lest the snow upon the Green Mountains, over which we had to pass on our return, should effectually obstruct our passage. Consequently, on the 17th day of October, we bade farewell to our friends, and probably a long farewell to the land that gave us birth, and set our faces once more for the west. We shaped our course for Brattleborough, designing to cross the mountain from Wilmington to Bennington. In Brattleborough I had a cousin, Samuel Elliott, Esq., the only surviving member of the family of a beloved aunt, and in age about two years my senior, with whom I had spent many days in youthful plays and gambols, but whom I had not seen for many years. We reached his residence just before nightfall on the day we left New Salem, and found him in health, and surrounded with all the comforts of life, and very pleasantly employed in assisting his young wife, the third he had married, in nursing and fondling their young child. We could remain with him but one night—the next morning we made a momentary call on Mr. Ballou, a Universalist preacher who ministers in that place, and pursued our journey, through cold and chilly winds, and over rugged hills, to Wilmington, and stopped with Mr. Bailey, the Universalist clergyman, for the night. Nearly forty years had elapsed since I had been in that town to make a visit, and not one of my former acquaintances remained. But the cause had flourished—a good society had grown up, and they enjoyed steady preaching. We found in Mr. Bailey and his companion fervent and faithful believers, persevering and zealous advocates of the Great Salvation, and affable, and kind-hearted companions. He had a conference meeting appointed for that evening, in a remote part of the town, several miles from his residence; and notwithstanding the fatigues of my journey, I accompanied him and his lady to the meeting, and at the earnest request of the Assembly delivered them a discourse. The next day we crossed the Green Mountains to Bennington, where we spent one day with the family of a nephew of mine; and the day following reached the residence of the sister of my wife, heretofore mentioned. By this perseverance on our journey, we just escaped the dreaded mountain storm; for before reaching the residence of our sister, a storm began which lasted several days, and several inches of snow covered the ground; and which detained us in this neighborhood a full week, before we could pursue our journey. We now pursued our course leisurely; for we had to buffet with rough roads and cold weather. We spent one Sabbath in Duanesburgh, where Mr. Lyon was then settled; and I had the pleasure of meeting his society and delivering them a discourse. The next Sunday we spent in Cooperstown, where Mr. Whiston was preaching. This was within the field of my own labors for many years—the day we spent there was quite stormy, the snow several inches deep, and still falling, the congregation small, and but very few of my old acquaintances present. But the cause was prospering under the ministry of our excellent brother Whiston, and the prospects were encouarging. The Tuesday following we again started on our journey; and by steadily persevering in my course over the hills, and wallowing through drifts of snow, at some places, nearly as high as the hubs of our carriage wheels, we arrived at Hamilton, Madison county, after two days' traveling, on the 16th of November. We had been absent on our eastern tour two months and eleven days. We considered our journey ended for the present—we expected indeed to travel much through the winter, but it would be merely through the neighboring towns. No long tours were contemplated, and we calculated to take time for our peregrinations, and improve the most comfortable weather a kind Providence should afford us.

We soon found my brother, among his children, and during the winter we were much together. The circumstance of his having come into that country to spend the winter with his children, without having the most distant anticipation of my contemplated visit there, and the disappointment I experienced in not finding him with his family in New England, I set down as one among hundreds of instances, in the course of my life, where a kind Providence has thwarted my own calculations, to bless me with privileges I should surely have deprived myself of, had I been permitted to pursue my own inclination; and these events have abundantly taught me to be reconciled to any and every providential derangement of my own calculations, and inspired my soul with confidence in the divine government. Had I found him at home, our visit must have been very brief, not exceeding forty-eight hours; but now we were permitted to be often together for nearly five months, and it was the last meeting we ever had, or ever can have in the flesh. I took his hand for the last time, in the city of Rochester, in April following, whither he had preceded me to visit two of his children who resided in that region. Soon after this he returned to his residence in Massachusetts, where, in December following, he was gathered to his fathers!

Although we made no long journeys through the winter, we nevertheless were constantly on the move. Our familiar acquaintances were scattered over the counties of Madison, Chenango, Oneida, Herkimer, and Otsego, and urgent calls for visits and meetings were made and repeated in rapid succession, as soon as it became known that we designed to spend the winter in that country. In the course of the winter, I attended four conferences, or two days' meeting; one in Sherburne, one in Cedarville, one at Richville-springs, and another in Columbus; and besides preaching in Hamilton on every Sabbath we spent in that town, I held meetings in the towns of Lebanon, Brookfield, Eaton, Smithfield, Richfield, Bridgewater, Columbus, New Berlin, Sherburne, Smyrna, Marshall, Litchfield, and Fenner; delivered a discourse to an immense congregation on Christmas eve, in Lebanon, and officiated at seven funerals. Among the funerals I was called upon to attend, there was one that deserves special notice. Mr. David Dunbar and his wife were among my earliest and most devoted friends in the town of Hamilton—among the very first members of the society organized in 1805, and the most regular attendants on our meetings, until she lost her health, so that for the most part of the time, for more than thirty years, she was confined to her house; but after that sad calamity, he and his family were never absent from our church until I removed, when able to attend. In 1829, the year before I removed to Hamilton, they lost a beloved and very promising son, in the twenty-second year of his age, under the most afflicting circumstances. Mrs. Dunbar had then been confined for many years to her house, though not to her bed, and had borne her sufferings and privations with the most Christian fortitude and resignation; and even under that heavy additional affliction she complained not, but, being sustained by the well-grounded hope of immortality, and a faith of assurance in God's universal grace, she was cheerful and happy under that tremendous shock! Her composure, her resignation, appeared to me truly miraculous! Oh, how severely rebuked I felt for my spiritual leanness, when I witnessed with what calmness she bowed to the will of God, and with what confidence and cheerful resignation she reposed in the arms of infinite Mercy. Not many days after, while in conversation with her on the subject, she expressed an opinion that she should not long survive, said she had been selecting a text for me to preach from on her funeral occasion, taking the Bible which she always kept within her reach, for it was her daily companion, and showed me a text, requesting me to remember it. The next year, I removed to Pennsylvania, and subsequently to Michigan, and the circumstance became substantially obliterated from my memory. When we arrived at Hamilton, on our journey to New England, however, we found Mrs. Dunbar alive, and as little changed, in every respect, as any person, young or old, that we found among our numerous acquaintances; and although she was deprived of the privileges of public worship, and hearing the preaching of the Gospel, she nevertheless abode steadfast in the faith, and strong in the Lord. She could read, and did read the Bible—her consolation and support—and from its sacred pages she extracted the bread of life, which daily supplied her with renewed strength. Thus we left her when we started for New England, and thus we found her on our return. But while I was absent, in the month of February, attending an appointment in the town of Litchfield, she was suddenly and violently seized with an epidemic, then prevalent throughout the country; and on my return to Marshall, where I had left my wife, I was informed that she was evidently at the point of death. We hurried as fast as possible to Hamilton, but just before we reached her habitation, she breathed her last. After the emotion occasioned by our entrance of the house at that pecular period had subsided, her daughter brought the Bible, and said, that her mother, just before she died, requested her to get the Bible, so as to be sure no mistake could be made, and mark with a pencil the text she had selected for me so many years ago, and remind me of it as soon as I arrived. Fifteen years had elapsed since she had selected the text, and requested me to preach from it at her funeral. Most of that time we had resided three hundred miles apart, and a part of it over five hundred; but a mysterious Providence had sent me there in season to comply with the request of his sainted handmaid. The text is recorded in 1st Corinthians 15: 51, 52, 53, 54. The occasion of her funeral was solemn and interesting almost beyond a parallel. Multitudes asembled, for she was universally esteemed; and I never saw more intense sensibility manifested by a whole congregation at any funeral; and I firmly believe it was blessed to the spiritual benefit of many who attended. One man—one who had never professed faith in the doctrine, who seldom attended my meetings while I resided in Hamilton, and who followed her to the unseen world about the time I left Madison county—came to me after the discourse, and, taking my hand, said, with tears in his eyes, "I bless God that I have heard your voice once more."

The winter passed off very pleasantly, and, we hoped, not unprofitably. But we had children at home; and, although we had often heard from them, by keeping up a correspondence in writing as often as once or twice a month during the whole season of our absence; still, as the returning sun freed the earth of its white mantle—as the "flowers appeared upon the earth, and the time of the singing of the birds" came, our hearts felt an irresistible yearning to meet our offspring once more. Accordingly, as soon as the roads became sufficiently settled, which was quite early that year, we, on the twenty-second of April, took leave of Madison county, and our almost countless friends in that region of country, and began our journey for home. We made but short calls on our way, and on the second day of May we reached the residence of our daughter, in Cattaraugus county. There we remained a short time to rest ourselves, and recruit our horse; and on the tenth of that month reached our own dwelling.

To us, that was one of the most interesting tours we ever

made; and the remembrance of it, as long as we are tenants of this mundane sphere, will afford us the highest gratification, and cause the most devout aspirations of gratitude to Almighty God. It seemed to be wholly Providential in all its bearings. We had been absent about eleven months, had traveled in all our devious wanderings more than two thousand miles, and never met with a single accident—not so much as to lose a pin from our carriage, or a shoe from our horse. We had enjoyed unusually good health, seen vast numbers of our highly esteemed and beloved friends, visited numerous societies which, under God, owed the germ of their existence to my feeble labors, and who were not forgetful of the circumstance, but greeted us with the affection and attachment of grateful and obedient children. We had witnessed the advancement of the holy cause of redeeming grace, not only in the field of our early labors, but also in the land which gave us birth, and in various other parts of the Redeemer's heritage. We had visited most of the surviving posterity of our fathers, and many of them for the last time. And, had we delayed our journey two years longer, that gratifying but melancholy reflection could not have mingled with the reminiscences of future years. When we arrived at our home, my wife had a sister and her husband living in Vermont, I had a sister in Hamilton, and a half-sister and brother in Massachusetts, with all of whom we had enjoyed happy and pleasant visits; but who have all since that time been numbered with the congregation of the dead! And a vast many more, who were bound to us by strong and endearing ties of consanguinity and affection, with whom we spent many happy hours during that season of our peregrinations, we can never meet again on this side of the grave; for the great destroyer of our race has been busily at work among them.

On our return home we found all things as we desired—our children and their families well, our friends in health and prosperity—few or none had been removed by death, and they gathered around us with their usual affectionate greetings. How well and freely then could we pour out from our surcharged hearts, most devoutly, the libations of gratitude and praise to the great Author of our being and enjoyments, in the language of divine inspiration: "Bless the Lord, O my soul, and let all that is within me bless his holy name. Bless the Lord, O my soul, and forget not all his benefits ; who forgiveth iniquity ; who healeth thy diseases ; who redeemeth thy life from destruction ; who crowneth thee with loving kindness and tender mercy ; who satisfieth thy mouth with good things, so that thy youth is renewed like the eagle's."

CHAPTER XIX.

Inquiry about the memoirs of my life—Renewed resolution to try to overcome obstacles—hindrances—Commencement—Slow progress—Restless temperament—Arrangements for a tour to Michigan—Marriage of our youngest child—Lake Erie Association—Legitimate powers of an Association—Mr. L. C. Todd restored—Journey to Michigan—Disaster and fright on the lake—Arrival at Detroit—Mr. J. Stebbins—State of the cause, and religious character of the citizens in Detroit—Reception at Ann Arbor—Improvement of the place—Sensations on entering the church—Condition of the society—Mr. Miles—State of the cause in general—Additional Association—State Convention—Periodical visits and meetings—Dr. T. C. Adam—Penitentiary—Mr. Billings chaplain—Terror ineffectual to prevent crime—Mr. Ring's influence—Reformation of convicts—Return home—Reflections Conclusion—Number of States visited and preached in—Number of discourses delivered—Number of funerals attended—Number of marriages solemnized—Valediction.

The inquiry was often made, in almost every region we visited on our eastern tour, in reference to the memoirs of my life—when they would be forth coming. For by some means an impression had gone abroad, even to the most remote country we visited, that I had promised to give to the world a history of my life; and the solicitude that was manifested on the subject led me almost to think, that my life had been of some consequence in the world. Many whom I would have supposed to have better judgment, insisted on my doing it without delay; and urged, as a reason, that the denomination had a right to demand of me a history of the rise and progress of Universalism in the State of New York, which no other individual could give with equal accuracy; and personal friends, who were very numerous, would never feel satisfied without the memoirs of my whole life. I concluded, therefore, if I should once more reach home, onerous and irksome as the task might be, I would surely begin it; and if Heaven saw fit to lengthen out my days to a sufficient period for that purpose, I would give the history of my life to the friends I might leave behind. Therefore, I concluded to make as few engagements as possible, and devote the most of my time to the object. I was not made a Mr. Rogers, to itinerate every moment of my life, and at the same time to write volumes on volumes for the public; nor a Mr. Whittemore, to superintend an extensive printing establishment, edit a large weekly paper, preach every Sabbath, lecture almost every day in the week; and, at the same time, write an elaborate history, make music books, publish extensive commentaries on the sacred Scriptures, and almost numberless other volumes on theology; neither my brains, nor my muscles were constituted for such labors.

But my resolution, sincerely as it was made, was, like many others of a similar character, not very strictly adhered to. I was at home again; and the little world in which I moved soon found it out, and began to call, and call loudly, for my labors. Besides the society in Columbus, other societies with whom I had labored insisted on a renewal of engagements; and towns and neighborhoods, where the doctrine had never been introduced, became agitated on the subject; the doctrines of Partialism no longer satisfied the yearnings of the soul—they wanted to hear something else—to learn if there was not in the volume of Revelation something more satisfactory to the cravings of the immortal mind. My nerves are such that I never can withstand like urgent appeals. I therefore soon found myself engaged, agreeably to former practice, traveling from place to place, and preaching with as much earnestness and zeal as the infirmities of my age would possibly allow me to do.

However, at the beginning of the following year, I commenced writing, and during the winter was enabled to make some progress. But although I had not, like the apostle, the "care of all the churches," I felt, nevertheless, deeply interested in the advancement of the truth, and a sincere commiseration for the unhappy condition of the doubting and unbelieving; and my heart most sensibly deplored the prevalence of scepticism and infidelity—the legitimate offspring, as I verily believe, of the popular dogmas and the artful and delusive measures employed by crazy fanatics, not to say unprincipled deceivers, to spread their heart-withering tenets, and replenish their sinking churches—and I could not devote my time to any thing that would essentially interfere with the great and leading object of my life.

In that way three years were passed—writing when I could, but traveling and preaching more; when my restless spirit began again to move me to go abroad. How others are made I know not. God, undoubtedly, constitutionally fits each man for the sphere in which he designs he should move, and bestows upon him those moral and intellectual endowments which, by proper culture, qualify him for his assigned post, in the great machinery of the moral universe in which he designed him to act. And he has bestowed on me a restless spirit which can not long be satisfied with confinement to one spot—to confine my labors to one congregation of people, and witness only the advancement of truth in the circumscribed limits of one community. To hear from abroad, excites in me an irresistible desire to see, to be a partaker of the joy, and share in the labors and perils of those engaged in the arduous work of extending the knowledge of the truth, and advancing the cause of the Redeemer; and especially in a region of my acquaintance, and in a field where a portion of my labors have been employed; in which Providence has always seemed to favor the gratification of this wandering inclination.

Six years and a half had elapsed since we left Michigan. When we parted with our friends there, they extorted from us a promise that we would visit that country once more, if circumstances would permit; and we had been repeatedly reminded of that promise by letters during the intermediate period. At length a kind Providence seemed to indicate, that we might redeem that promise without injury to ourselves or the cause, or the violation of any obligation we were under to any individual or to community. My wife and I were left alone in our family—our last and youngest son having married and gone away from us—and our children no longer required our guardianship, and no longer needed any thing at our hands. We were in possession of pretty good constitutions for people of our age, in the enjoyment of comparatively good health; and, looking around upon the existing state of things, I said to my wife, as Paul said to Barnabus, "Come, 'Let us go again, and visit our brethren where we have preached the word of the Lord, and see how they do.'" Therefore, in the spring of 1847, we made preparations for a tour to Michigan, the last, quite probably, we shall ever make to that country; but "God only knoweth." It must be postponed, however, until after the session of the Lake Erie Association, which met that year on the fourth Wednesday and Thursday in June, in the village of Conneaut, Ohio; for I had a strong desire to attend that meeting. I have always felt deeply interested in the doings of our Associations, much more so than in those of the State Convention, or that of the United States; because I consider their proceedings vastly more important, in regard to necessary order and discipline in our ranks. They, being composed of immediate delegates from the churches and societies—being, in fact, the assembly of the churches and societies through their only proper representatives in council—possess the only legitimate authority to establish rules and regulations for the government of the order; to grant letters of fellowship, determine the qualification of candidates, confer ordination, discipline offending members, withdraw fellowship, and *do all things* pertaining to the government of the church. All other ecclesiastical bodies, more remote from the churches, rightfully possess only advisory, or appellatory powers, and always transcend their authority, whenever they presume to do more.

I was peculiarly happy, at that Association, in meeting Mr. L. C. Todd for the first time since he resumed the ministry of universal reconciliation. But he was there, "sitting at the feet of Jesus, clothed in his right mind," and in the full stature of a man; and I had the unspeakable pleasure of hearing the words of life flow from his lips in far sweeter strains than before his aberration. From my first acquaintance with Mr. Todd, I considered him a man capable of being extensively serviceable to the cause of divine truth, and I mourned sincerely over what I regarded his fall, watching with much solicitude his movements; because, for some undefinable reason, I ever indulged a presentiment, and a strong hope, that he would again be "restored to the great Shepherd and Bishop of souls," and become more extensively useful in the cause of the divine Master; and that hope then seemed ready to be fulfilled.

Immediately after the Association, we made all necessary preparations for our journey, and on the last day of June we left home. It would have been extremely gratifying to us, to have again taken our own conveyance, and leisurely pursued our journey over-land through the State of Ohio, visiting our friends and the societies in that region; but the shortness of time we could be allowed to be absent, admonished us to take a different course. We proceeded to Erie, took passage in a steamboat for Detroit, and from thence to Ann Arbor by rail-road. We were fortunate in obtaining good boats, and polite and accommodating captains and officers, both in our out and return passages. But the first disaster that ever happened to a steam-boat in which I was a passenger, took place during our voyage up the lake. We left Erie at eight o'clock in the evening of the first of July, in the splendid new boat, Missouri, which was in the most perfect repair; and one of the most pleasant seasons I ever saw—weather fair, the lake perfectly calm, and as still as a sea of molten lead. But while puffing along at a rapid rate, about three or four hours above Cleveland, a sudden and violent crash with the instantaneous stopping of the boat, brought all the passengers to their feet, and the cry of FIRE threw a death-like paleness over every countenance. In a few moments, however, it was ascertained that there was no imminent danger. The shaft had broken, and one wheel was shivered to pieces, rendering it entirely useless; and the cry of *fire* proceeded from some terrified individual, without other cause than a bewildered imagination. The confusion produced by the alarm soon subsided, and the passengers became measurably calm; but the boat had become so crippled, that she could not proceed on her trip. Consequently, she was compelled to put about, and go halting, like a man with one leg, back to the port of Cleveland. My nerves, I believe, were not so irritable as some, or even as they once were; or else, from the want of feeling, I was insensible to danger; for, amid all the confusion, I felt no alarm; nor even could I realize a single tremor of the nerves, notwithstanding there had been recently some shocking disasters on the lake, and, by the burning of steam-boats, a lamentable loss of human life. I felt almost angry with myself because I could not feel as others did, and could assign no other reason for my indifference only that I must be a person of great insensibility.

After remaining at Cleveland about two hours, the new and excellent steamer, Michigan, came into port bound for Chicago. We obtained a passage on board of her, and arrived at Detroit about the middle of the second day after leaving Erie. In Detroit my wife had distant relatives, children of her eldest brother, and their families; we therefore concluded to spend some little time with them before proceeding further. I there spent one Sunday with Mr. J. Stebbins, who had collected a small society of Universalists in the city, and was ministering to them. But Detroit was a hard place for Universalism, or any thing that appeared like liberality in religious sentiments. Roman Catholicism and orthodox Protestantism predominated, and the inhabitants, absorbed in the speculations of the world, appeared content to let their priests and clergy attend to all matters of religion—to think and believe for them, as well as to preach and pray for them—not having time to spare from their devotions to mammon, nor much inclination to do either for themselves. During my whole residence in Michigan, I never delivered but one discourse in the city of Detroit, and that was at the time of the session of the legislature; and my congregation was composed principally of the members of that body.

After remaining in Detroit a few days, we proceeded to Ann Arbor, our former place of residence while in that State. We were warmly received by our friends, and felt almost as though we had once more arrived at home. Ann Arbor had improved very considerably in every respect, during the period of our absence. Many splendid buildings had been erected, extensive additions made, especially in what was called the Upper Town; churches, that were then in progress, completed, and others built; a number of new stores added, as well as mechanic's shops; and, finally, the village exhibited tokens of prosperity.

When I entered the little church, on the first Sabbath after my arrival, where I had labored constantly for nearly five years, and where I had enjoyed some of the happiest seasons of my life, although a very respectable congregation were in waiting, my nerves underwent a more sensible tremor, and my feelings were excited to a much higher tone, than when the alarm was given on the steam-boat. I could indeed see many familiar faces—many with whom I had intimately associated—who had been my constant hearers and liberal supporters, who had borne with me "the burden and heat of the day," who had stood by the cause and defended it with their arguments and their influence, in despite of the scoffs of the proud and the malignity of bigots, and denied not their Savior before men; but in vain did I look for others whose seats were never vacant when I entered that house before. Where was Deacon Williams? Where was Colonel Thayer? Where was Mr. Durren? Where were many others that my eyes wandered after? Alas! the shafts of death had reached them —their spirits had flown to a more exalted temple, and earth had received its own! That gave a melancholy reflection for the moment, but my regret was soothed into reconciliation by the faith, that our loss was their gain. While we were left here to battle with the world for a season longer, and meet with the buffetings of these disturbed elements, they had entered upon the fruition of anticipated joys.

I found the society in Ann Arbor not in as prosperous a condition as I fondly anticipated, when I left them, they would be at that time. When I had once got Dr. Adam settled there, I indulged a very strong hope in the permanent growth and prosperity of the cause in that important station; but although the cause had by no means retrograded, yet the society did not exhibit that life and spirit—that zeal and faithfulness which I so ardently desired to see. After Dr. Adam's year had expired, and he had left them, as I have had occasion to remark, they engaged the labors of Dr. Smead for a season; but the hand of death removed him. Since then, they had enjoyed the occasional preaching of some others, and at the time of our visit, Mr. S. Miles was laboring with them; but he was drawing toward the close of the second year, and, from what I could learn, I obtained the impression that he would conclude his labors with them at the expiration of his engagement; which was actually the case.

In the State, we found the cause in as prosperous a condition as we could reasonably expect, although it fell short of fully gratifying all our impatient desires. A very considerable number of preachers had been added to their ranks, a second Association had been organized, a State Convention had been established, and a periodical, the "Primitive Expounder," had been started by Mr. Billings, which then had a good circulation, increasing in patronage and influence, under the able, judicious, and faithful editorial management of Mr. R. Thornton. The appearance of our cause, therefore, when we could coolly and rationally look at it, was truly encouraging. During our continuance in the State, I made visits, as extensively as I well could, among our acquaintances and societies. In Lenawee county I had relatives residing, the widow and surviving children of Dr. C. H. Stacy—my eldest brother's son; there, of course, we made something of a visit. We also visited Jackson and Livingston counties, besides Wayne and Washtenaw, already mentioned; and besides preaching three Sabbaths in Ann Arbor, and two in Detroit, I held meetings in the villages of Clinton, Manchester, and Jackson, and in the town of Marion, Livingston county. We also visited Dr. T. C. Adam and his family, whom we found residing on his old place, four miles west of the village of Clinton; and we were very happy to find them in comfortable health, except the Doctor, who was in a condition barely enabling him to perform a limited ride in his medical profession. His faith, however, was strong; his soul was ardently engaged for the prosperity of Zion, and he suffered depression of mind from his physical inability to engage in his divine Master's employ. But, alas! I feared he would never be able to enter the field again; or, if he were, that he would never be able to pursue the work to the full gratification of his ardent and capacious soul.

The State penitentiary of Michigan is located in the village of Jackson. On my visit to that place I found Paul B. Ring, Esq., an overseer of one of the departments, and exercising an immense influence. Mr. Ring was a devoted and zealous Universalist; and the superintendent and several of the other overseers were also men of liberal sentiments. They had just elected Rev. J. Billings, a Universalist preacher, chaplain for the prison, and Mr. Billings had entered upon the duties of his office a week or two before my visit. Therefore, I had the privilege of visiting the State prison, and attending divine service with Mr. Billings in the morning of the Sunday I spent in Jackson; and I was gratified beyond measure, in witnessing the devout attention given by the convicts to the discourse, and the manifest influence the law of kindness was exerting upon their moral feelings. This doctrine they had not been in the habit of hearing; for, strange as it may appear, no Universalist has ever yet broken into the State prison, though some have been let out from it—at least from that in Jackson. The rod, the prison, and the halter—the wrath of an angry God, and the fire of an endless hell, have been resorted to as the only efficient means to prevent crime, and reform the wicked; and they have ever proved ineffectual to do either, and always will, so long as any relation exists between cause and effect: for, as philosophically and as religiously true as it is, that "love begetteth love," so it is equally true, that wrath worketh wrath; and the greater the harshness and vindictiveness exhibited in the administration of the divine government, or the execution of the laws of the land, the greater will be the hardness and obduracy of the criminal. Civilized society is beginning to learn this truth, in respect to civil government, at least; and to practice accordingly. Corporeal punishment is being laid aside in most instances, I believe, in our penitentiaries; and milder means, exhibiting kindness, employed in order to maintain a proper order in our prisons, and effect a reformation in the offenders; and especially was this the case in the penitentiary at Jackson. Mr. Ring had carried with him practically, in the government of his department, all the benevolence of his Universalist principles; and he exerted thereby a wide influence, not only in his own jurisdiction, but through the whole prison. Every thing appeared in good order; the convicts cheerfully attended to their duties, kindness beamed on every countenance, and the utmost confidence was manifested between overseers and laborers. Several important reformations had then taken place. I was introduced to a young man at Mr. Ring's, who had been pardoned only a few days before. He was a young man of prepossessing appearance—appeared truly humble and penitent, and imputed the whole of his reformation to the influence of Mr. Ring and his doctrine; and appeared to manifest as strong filial attachment to Mr. Ring, as the most affectionate child could do toward a parent. He was educated a Partialist—never heard of a God of *infinite goodness* and *universal benevolence*, until he learned it from the lips of Mr. Ring; and he saw, in his conduct toward the erring inmates of the penitentiary, a practical illustration of the influence of the doctrine; and so powerful was the effect upon him, that it regenerated him, and made him a new man. He had come out of prison strong in the faith, and bade exceedingly fair to be a blessing to society. Nor is that a solitary case. Mr. Ring had others under his tuition, in whom, aided by the daily and weekly labors of Mr. Billings, I had a strong hope that a successful illustration of the superior influence of the doctrine of God's universal grace—of the law of heavenly kindness toward the erring and the guilty, would be given to the world.

We enjoyed an exceedingly pleasant visit with our numerous friends in Michigan, and received from them many tokens of friendship which wlll not be forgotten. But the most pleasant seasons we are permitted to enjoy on mortal shores must be at a close. The time came for our separation. Was it a final separation? Were we never again to meet in the flesh? It was painful indeed to think so, although we felt a divine influence, and at the time of our separation seriously realized the truth, that we shall all meet in a happier clime ere long; but to make the separation as little unpleasant as possible, we promised, if Heaven sees good to grant us the opportunity, to visit them again; nor was that promise insincerely made to them.

After spending between six and seven weeks in the State, among numerous friends and several societies, and "hearing and telling," not exactly like the Athenians, "some new thing," but "things new and old," drawn from the inexhaustible store-house of the blessed Gospel, we took the hands of our beloved friends with sorrowing though grateful hearts, and turned our faces toward HOME. We had been absent about two months; and on our return we found all things to our satisfaction, under the guardian care of Him who "doeth all things well."

Since our return from Michigan, I have remained pretty quietly at home, laboring in the little field of my allotment, according to the strength given me. But I feel that my days are waning, that I can no longer encounter all kinds of weather and traveling, nor perform the amount of exercise that I once could endure. And in order to retain my strength, and enable me to perform my duty as long as I can in any manner be useful, I have, for a season past, confined my labors in most cases to one discourse in a day. I still continue to travel to the amount of about eighty miles a month to attend my regular appointments.

I have now, kind reader, given you a few of the many incidents of my life; and with a few words will take my leave. A little more than forty-six years have passed since I lifted up my feeble voice in proclamation of the Great Salvation, which was then a new and strange doctrine to the world. I need not inform the reader, if he has had the patience to read the preceding pages, that my life has been a laborious one, and attended with many severe trials and temporal privations; but I may conscientiously say, that it has been a happy one, notwithstanding. I have never been ambitious for worldly wealth or grandeur. I have never envied any man his gold, his silver, his splendid equipments, or his renown. If I have ever for a moment felt a passion bordering on envy, it has been toward those who could preach so much better than myself, and consequently be so much more influential in advancing the cause of the Redeemer; I have wanted their talents—I have wanted their eloquence and power. But these feelings were silenced in a moment, on reflecting that it required a variety of members to make up the great body. And the smallest member was equally as necessary as the greatest, and equally honorable, if it kept within its own proper sphere, and did not try to perform a part that belonged not to it, so that "The eye can not say to the hand, I have no need of thee; nor the head to the feet, I have no need of you."

With profound gratitude to Almighty God, I realize—very sensibly realize—that I have experienced vastly more health than sickness, more joy than sorrow, more happiness than misery, more hope than despondency; but with this acknowledgement I *aver*, that my religious faith and hope have been at the foundation of all I have enjoyed. It is to these, and to these alone, I am indebted for all my cheerfulness—all my happiness; deprive me of this faith and hope, and life would not be worth having—*I could not be grateful for it.* But with this faith and hope—this religion—amid the greatest labors I have been called to endure, I have found strength. This gave me light amid darkness, and saved me from despondency. This cheered me under the greatest conflict with an opposing world, under the still more severe conflict with my own passions, and assured me of victory. This, in the bitterest hour of affliction, under the most severe bereavements, afforded permanent consolation, and reconciled me to the government of God. And, if I have been restrained from the commission of crime, it is this faith in the paternity of the divine character, this hope in the triumphs of infinite mercy toward all, even the greatest sinner in the universe of God, and the ultimate purity and immortal blessedness of all intelligent beings, that has exercised that restraining power. Oh, may God grant, that this faith and hope may universally prevail. This alone can reform the world. This will annihilate crime, and demolish the gallows, prisons, and penitentiaries. This, and this alone, will abolish slavery, bring war to an end, and introduce the reign of universal peace. And all our ingenious contrivances, and wise-laid schemes, without a living, active faith in the Gospel of the blessed God, will for ever prove abortive. THIS IS A TRUE PROPHECY.

Should the curiosity of the reader excite him to inquire in regard to the extent and amount of my labors in the ministry, I will here inform him—not by boasting, for hundreds have done more—that I have preached more or less in ten States of the Union; have delivered, up to the present time, December, 31, 1848, four thousand seven hundred and forty-nine discourses, which I have minutes of, and many of which I have kept no minutes; have officiated at three hundred and sixty-eight funerals, and solemnized two hundred and twenty eight marriages. And here I take leave of my readers, in respect to the events and incidents of my life. What there is yet before me to perform, to enjoy, or to endure in mortality, I know not—God only knoweth. But my desire is, to stand in my lot—to be found ready to discharge every duty which may devolve upon me, according to the best of my ability; and with patience and resignation to the divine will, "Wait all the day of my appointed time, until my change come."

APPENDIX.

In two Parts.

PART I.

EXHIBITING THE AUTHOR'S PECULIAR DOCTRINAL VIEWS.

CONTENTS.

Impossibility of perfect unity of opinion—Former opinions—Calvinism extended—Inconsistencies and absurdities—Universalism defined—Different opinions create no schisms—Present views stated under five propositions.

PROPOSITION I.—OF MAN.

Man is the moral offspring of God—He possesses freedom of moral action within his sphere—is not bound in a state of passivity by the fatality of divine decrees—Has actions which are properly called his own, and for which he is accountable, rewardable, or punishable.

PROPOSITION II.—OF SALVATION.

Salvation is not a deliverance from deserved punishment, nor a mere transition from one mode of existence to another—nor does it exclusively consist in a deliverance from sin—but it does consist in purity of soul produced by that knowledge of the divine character, and the moral government of God, which inspires confidence in the divine wisdom, reconciliation to the divine will, supreme love to all the divine attributes ; and assimilates the whole moral man to the divine character.

PROPOSITION III.—OF CHRIST, AND THE MEDIATORIAL KINGDOM.

Christ is the Son of God in a more exalted sense than Adam, or his posterity —He had an individual existence previous to the works of creation—was the agent of the Father in the creation of the visible universe—The mediatorial kingdom of Christ, called in the Evangelists the kingdom of heaven and the kingdom of God, is not the kingdom of immortal blessedness, but preparatory—This kingdom is not confined to any mode of existence, but includes the future as well as the present—This kingdom is not a state of probation, but of discipline and instruction.

PROPOSITION IV.—OF PUNISHMENT.

Punishment, under the government of Christ, is not vindictive, nor retaliatory —But is disciplinary and emendatory.

PROPOSITION V.—OF THE RESURRECTION.

The resurrection of the dead, as argued by the apostle, in the 15th chap. 1 Cor., is not a resuscitation of these material bodies, the bodies which die ; but a rising, or resurrection, of the whole body of the church from the intermediate state, or from the preparatory kingdom to the immortal kingdom.

INTRODUCTION.

Having given the reader the memoirs of my life, with a history of my ministerial labors, he, perhaps may be curious to learn something of my peculiar opinions. And as every man who has the moral courage to think for himself on the important subject of religion, and believes his own opinions to be the most consistent with Scripture, reason, and the nature and fitness of things, and the best and safest for the world to believe; it will not be deemed strange that I, also, should be desirous of placing my peculiar views before the world.

In this imperfect state it is not to be expected, nor is it morally possible, that there should be a perfect unity of opinion among those who investigate the subject for themselves. Where the church assumes infallibility, and dictates by sovereign authority, in written creeds, exactly what doctrines its members must embrace, what opinions they must maintain, there may be unity of opinion; or rather there is *no* individual opinion at all—nothing can be properly considered as personal faith. But when once a people have extricated themselves from ecclesiastical tyranny, and denied the right of the church, or any man or body of men, to dictate to them their personal faith, and abjured all written creeds and confessions of faith, and learned their own moral strength and their own personal responsibility, and resolved to believe for themselves, making the Scriptures alone the standard of their faith, without a human creed to measure it by—they will most assuredly arrive at different conclusions on many points, and especially so, under the influence of an early religious education. Such was the case of those who embraced the doctrine of Universalism, at least in the days of its infancy. They seceded from all denominations; and although they arrived at one point in regard to the great and glorious doctrine of the Final Restitution, they brought with them their peculiar prejudices in regard to points of minor doctrinal consideration, as well as to external ordinances. And while those who make the Scriptures of the Old and New Testaments exclusively their guide are, unquestionably, coming nearer into proximity with each other's sentiments, there will be a diversity of opinion maintained among them "while the world standeth;" nor is it desirable that it should be otherwise. Diversity of opinion excites investigation, and investigation elicits truth; and while those opinions are maintained under the influence of that charity which the great doctrine of the paternity of God and the universal brotherhood of man inculcates, they can never be an injury, but rather a blessing to the church.

Universalism, as it is now well defined and understood, at least by its votaries, embraces a faith in *one God*, who has made a special revelation of his nature, character, and purposes, in the Scriptures of the Old and New Testaments; which revelation he has established and confirmed by miraculous displays of his divine power, and, consequently, an *unequivocal faith* in the divine authenticity and authority of those Scriptures, in all matters of faith and practice; and in Jesus Christ, as the only personal Mediator between God and man, being the true and perfect moral image of the Father, possessing "All the fulness of the Godhead bodily"—an embodiment and complete exhibition of all the divine perfections, so that "He that seeth the Son seeth the Father"—that the Father has made him the mediate administrator of the divine government, having "Put all things under his feet," and "given him all power in heaven and in earth," for the express purpose, that he should "Reconcile all things to God," and save the world. Thus far Universalists perfectly agree; but there is a diversity of opinion in regard to the time of the accomplishment of this great, this glorious, and unchangeable purpose of our God, and also, in some measure, in regard to the diversified means which infinite wisdom employs to consummate and perfect it. Nevertheless, this diversity of opinion, of itself, has hitherto created no schism in their ranks. They have considered the great doctrine of the Final Restitution as paramount to all others, and as the grand fundamental theme of pulpit labors; and they could thereon meet, heart, hand, and soul, and, with all the feelings of Christian love, bid each other "God speed." But should any, in their investigations and researches, find other revelations which they believe more consistent and authentic than what *we* call the *word of God*; and in consequence become sceptical in regard to the authenticity and authority of the Scriptures, whatever views they may entertain on the subject of the final destiny of the human race—while we cheerfully accord to them the perfect right of investigation, and the adoption and promulgation of their own free and uncontrolled opinions, we do say, that it is but reasonable and proper that they should withdraw from the ranks of Universalists, and assume a name significant of the opinions they adopt, and not impose upon the world by appearing under the name which, in the present age, unerringly defines a sect with whom they have little or no sympathy.

Among other thinkers, I too have thought, and my object now is to give the reader, briefly, as clear a view of the results at which I have arrived as my language will enable me. I am not about to argumentatively defend the positions I take, but merely to state my opinions, give some of the reasons why I entertain them, and a few passages of Scripture which I believe sustain them.

When light first broke upon my mind, amidst the impervious darkness which had so long enveloped it, I saw, as it were, the grand system of divine grace, summarily. Calvinism taught me, that "The decrees of God are his eternal purpose, according to the counsel of his own will, whereby, for his own glory, he hath fore-ordained whatsoever comes to pass;" and I discovered that the most prominent decree of God, according to the Bible, was the eternal salvation of our whole race, through Jesus Christ our Lord! This was enough, for it satisfied my soul; for I well knew, as surely as there was a God, that what God had purposed and decreed, was as unalterable as his own nature, and that "His purposes should stand, and he would do all his pleasure." I stopped not to inquire how or when this purpose of God was to be perfected; it was enough for me to know that it was *His purpose*, and that it could not fail. God had said, I "*will have all men to be saved*, and come unto the knowledge of the truth;" and I said in the language of the poet:

"Here stop, my soul, no farther seek to go;
What God's reveal'd is quite enough to know."

The belief of this, reconciled me to all the dealings of the Divine hand—removed all slavish fear, and filled my soul with "joy unspeakable."

All the theory I had was "Calvinism improved," or rather extended. I had received my early education among Calvinists, and all my first religious impressions were purely Calvinistic. Calvinism taught that God had unalterably decreed the salvation of the elect without any *foresight of faith or good works;* and the very first lesson that I learned in this new school, was, that his decree of salvation embraced all mankind, and that the salvation of *all* was just as secure as the salvation of the Calvinistic *elect*, and that it would be effected by the same instrumentality, and in the same manner—that Christ had taken upon himself our sinful nature; had suffered, in our stead, the penalty of the divine law; satisfied, *fully* satisfied, divine justice, appeased the wrath of God, by the shedding of his own blood, upon the cross ; purchased the love of God for the sinner, and reconciled Him to man. This atonement was complete, and was universal, inasmuch as Christ had "tasted death for every man," and became a "propitiation for the sins of the whole world."

But when I gained time and inclination to review my theory, to examine its various ramifications, I discovered, or thought I discovered, irreconcilable discrepancies, and blasphemous imputations to the divine character. While we maintained that God was unchangeable, we ascribed to him the most puerile mutations. God was pleased, in the first place, with all his works and pronounced them "*very good*;" but under the influence of his own decrees, which embraced every thought, word, and action of all his creatures, they had, by their transgressions, so changed his feelings, that He became infinitely angry with them—hated them with perfect hatred, and raised his almighty arm to send them all to an endless hell!—but paused a moment, in the midst of his awful wrath, and concluded to take flesh and blood himself, (for Calvinism teaches, that although there are three persons in the God-head, there is but one God, and that Jesus Christ is "*very God!*") to assume our sinful natures, suffer, and die on the cross to satisfy the demands of his violated law, and purchase his own mercy for our fallen race!—that by so doing he changes his feelings a second time ; and from a wrathful, vindictive enemy, he becomes a God of boundless compassion, of mercy, and love! All moral agency, too, by this theory, is denied to moral beings. They became infinitely sinful, in a state of passivity, without any possible will or action of their own—(for, saith the Catechism, "All mankind sinned in, and fell with, Adam in his first transgression, and were *so* made liable to all the miseries of this life, to death itself, and the pains of hell for ever")—and are also saved in a state of equal passivity ; for being totally morally depraved, they can neither think a good thought, nor do a good work, until the irresistible power of the spirit of God does it in them, and for them.

When I discovered these glaring absurdities, I was led to doubt the truth of Calvinism, not only in its decree of reprobation, but in all its ramifications; and turned with renewed engagedness to the Bible, by the careful examination of which I was compelled to reject, in toto, all the appendages and dogmas that belonged to that mother of scepticism; for if it contained any truth, it was so interlarded with falsehood, that it "changed the truth of God into a lie!"

In the word of divine inspiration I could find nothing about a "trinity of persons in the God-head," nor "triune God;" but I learned that there is "but one God, the Father, of whom are all things, and we in him; and one Lord Jesus Christ, by whom are all things, and we by him;" that there is "one God, and one Mediator between God and men, the *man*" (not God) "Christ Jesus"—that a "Mediator is not a mediator of one, but God is one"—that to ascribe original deityship to Christ was to deny the *existence* of a Mediator. I learned, therefore, that Christ was not God, in the highest and purest sense of the term, but the Son of God—"The only begotten son of the Father." I also learned that God was *infinitely immutable*, was "of *one mind*," and none could turn him—"without variableness, or *shadow of turning*"—that His nature was uncreated, underived, and therefore infinitely *above* all possible extraneous influences, or the possibility of the slightest semblance of a change; and that *that* nature was LOVE!

I learned consequently that the mission of Christ was not to appease divine wrath, nor suffer the penalty of the divine law as a substitute for the sinner; nor to influence God to love mankind, to reconcile God to the world, or purchase salvation for our race; so far from this, the uncreated, unpurchased love of God was at the bottom of the whole. The plan of salvation originated in the divine nature;—"Herein is love, not that *we* loved God, but that ***He loved us***, and sent his Son to be the propitiation for our sins." (1 John, 4, 10.) "For God *so loved the world*, that *He sent* his only begotten Son," (John 3: 16.) Hence, so far from Christ's "purchasing our pardon," or salvation, (as sung by the Methodists) he was simply the messenger, the bearer of it; He receives the gift from the hand of the Father, and brings it down and bestows it on man.

Here surely was a great advance from Calvinism, or, at least, a wide departure from its teachings. But, thus far I believe our whole denomination in America have gone. There are few, or none, who have studied the Scriptures—and this, thank God, is a prominent characteristic of Universalists —who will dissent from the above position. But there are other points wherein there exists a diversity of opinion; and some of these points, most important in my estimation, I am now about to contend with. I am not, however, going to combat, nor even attempt to state the opinions of others; but merely to advance my own, with some brief reasons for entertaining them. In doing this, I shall omit further notice of the position taken above in respect to the divine character, and the ultimate object of the mission of the divine Mediator; although I may more fully explain my views of the character of our Lord Jesus Christ. And I shall probably state my views explicitly under the five following propositions.

PROPOSITION I.—OF MAN.

Man is the moral offspring of God ; he possesses freedom of moral action within his sphere ; is not bound by the fatality of divine decrees, but has works which are properly called his own, and for which he is rewardable or punishable.

That man is the offspring of God, I learn explicitly from the revelation God has made to the world, wherein He is called, " The Father of Spirits"—(Heb. 12 : 9 ;) and "The God of the spirits of all flesh"—(Num. 27 : 16 ;) and by the teachings of Christ, wherein he instructs us so to denominate Him in our supplications ; as well as by the inspired apostle, who declares that " God hath made of one blood"—(i. e. one fountain of life)—" all nations of men, for to dwell on all the face of the earth ;" consequently " we are also his offspring" —(Acts 17 : 26, 27, 28 ;) and because the New Testament writers, every where, make use of the appellation of *Father* to express the relation which God bears to man.

As the moral offspring of God created in his likeness, man must possess the image of his moral attributes ; and one of those attributes, or rather the basis of *all*, must be thought, and volition, which are indispensible properties of intellect, and infinite freedom of action—to determine and do what he pleases. Man, therefore, must have freedom within *his* sphere, he must be endowed with the power of thought and volition. God is infinite, man is finite. And although God enstamped upon man the image of his own eternity of duration, by the indissoluble relation of father and child, he left but the impress of his moral attributes, limited and finite, and therefore capable of endless improvement. Man's actions, therefore, though free, are necessarily limited, and can not involve infinite consequences.

But I not only infer man's moral freedom from the very nature of his being; I also learn it from the whole teachings of divine revelation.

The Scriptures every where speak of man as a moral agent, as a being who enjoys moral freedom of action, unrestricted by irresistible decrees—who does works properly called his own, and for which he is rewardable or punishable. I need not particularize; take, for example, this passage which is perfectly consonant to the whole teachings of the word of God: "Say ye to the righteous, it shall be well with him; for they shall eat of the fruit of their doings: Woe unto the wicked, it shall be ill with him; for the reward of his hands shall be given him." Isa. (3: 10, 11.)

Let it not be said, that this view of the subject destroys the sovereignty of God, nullifies his decrees, and deprives him of his foreknowledge.

I dislike the term *decrees*, when applied to the moral government of God; nor is it a common term of Scripture. There was formerly more said about the decrees of God, in the course of one sermon, than can be found about them in the whole Bible. I dislike it because it seems to imply the existence of a secret, irresistible power, exerting itself over every thought, word, and action, as the weight of a clock, or of water, upon the wheel which propels the machinery attached to them; and seems to make man a similar passive machine under the irresistible impulse of the decrees of God; and so Calvinists, times without number, have defined it. God's foreknowledge comprehends all events, not because he decrees them, but because "He declares the end from the beginning, and from ancient times the things that (to us) are not yet done." (Isa. 46: 10:) But they *are*, and always *were*, and always *will be* done, in the view of Him, with whom there is no succession of time—with whom there is nothing old and nothing new!

As I have said, man is limited in all his powers; he can not act, nor feel, nor *think* above his sphere. He can no more *think* infinitely than he can feel or act infinitely. We speak of infinite extension and infinite duration; but after all we have no just conception of either; our thoughts are limited, we fix a centre and boundary to infinite space, and an end to infinite duration—we *can not* avoid it. When man attempts to contemplate the subject, he becomes lost in the immensity of thought, and at length is compelled to

"Drop into himself and be a fool!"

How God foreknows all events, is a question man, with all his ingenuity and wisdom, has never been able to solve, and never will be; and it is sufficient for me to believe that *it is so*. An infinite intelligence must be infinite; and this is saying all, in a few words, that man should presume to say.

Moreover, divine revelation informs us, that "His understanding is infinite," (Ps. 147: 5;) but it is the Westminster catechism, not the Bible, which says, "God fore-ordained whatsoever comes to pass."

The sovereignty of God consists in his ability to accomplish his *will*, to do his pleasure and perfect his purposes in despite of all opposition, and in his wisdom to make the free-will actions of his creatures subservient thereto. For an illustration take the case of Joseph and his brethren, recorded in Genesis, chapters 37, 39, 40, 41, 42, 43, 44, and 45. God had revealed to Joseph a certain purpose, through the medium of a dream, which he related to his brethren; and the brethren undertook to defeat the accomplishment of that purpose. Never did a set of men act more freely or more wickedly; and never were men more successful, in their own estimation, in accomplishing their wishes to their full extent. They as effectually prevented his exaltation, in their own belief, and according to the keenest perception of human foresight and wisdom, as though they had actually shed the blood which they made their father believe the wild beasts had spilt.

But although they acted with perfect freedom, without the least restriction of their liberty, accomplished all they then desired to accomplish, there was, nevertheless, a power above them which took the action out of their hands—when they had done all that finite beings could do, and with that very action, by which they designed to defeat his will, perfected his own divine plan. Here, then, is fully illustrated the sovereighty of God ; not in making his creatures machines, nor slaves, but in making them free agents, and super-abounding and super-controlling that freedom by his own power and wisdom.

PROPOSITION II.—OF SALVATION.

Salvation is not a deliverance from deserved punishment, nor a transition from one mode of existence to another, nor does it exclusively consist in a deliverance from sin ; but it does consist in purity of soul produced by that knowledge of the divine nature and moral government of God, which gives confidence in the divine will, supreme love to all the divine attributes, and assimilates the whole moral man to the divine character.

Salvation can not be a deliverance from deserved punishment, because deliverance from deserved punishment would rather have a tendency to make men reckless of their conduct than to reform them ; moreover the Scriptures abound with declarations to the contrary ; "God will render to every man according to his deeds, and there is no respect of persons with God ;" (Rom. 2: 6, 11,)—"He that doeth wrong shall receive for the wrong which he hath done ; and *there is no respect of persons* ;" (Col. 3 : 25)—"Though hand join in hand, the wicked shall not be unpunished ;" (Prov. 11 : 21,)—"The Lord God, merciful and gracious, long suffering, and abundant in goodness and truth ; keeping mercy for thousands, forgiving iniquity, transgression, and sin ; and that will *by no means clear the guilty*." (Ex. 34 : 6, 7.) Now the atonement of Christ is certainly a means which God makes use of for the salvation of man. But according to the declarations of Almighty God, it will not clear the guilty ; it will not deliver from deserved punishment ;

therefore, deliverance from deserved punishment *is not salvation*, nor a means of salvation.

Salvation is not a transition from one mode of existence to another, because it consists in a moral condition. Therefore, an alteration of local situation, unless that alteration produces a moral change, can have no effect to produce salvation. Nor does salvation consist exclusively in a deliverance from sin, because there may be instances of perfect innocency—of sinless purity, with incapacity to enjoy salvation : witness the infant and the idiot. Salvation is not a *negative*, but a positive state. But the salvation which Christ came to effect and administer is a *state* of supreme felicity, with the soul filled "with joy unspeakable and full of glory ;" and this can only be effected by the highest state of intellectual improvement, and a perfect devolopment of all the moral powers, which are emanations of the divine perfections. Salvation is a progressive work, and is effected only by divine instruction. Christ is emphatically called the Teacher ; and this is the most significant of his character, as mediator and Savior, of any appellation that can be given him. He expressly informs us that teaching the truth was the great work of his mission ; "To this end was I born, and for this cause came I into the world, that I should bear witness unto the *truth* ;" (John 18 : 37,)—and that truth concerned the divine character. "The gift of God is eternal life (eternal felicity—for life, in the religious acceptation of the term, is happiness) through Jesus Christ our Lord." (Rom. 6 : 23 ;) "And this is life eternal, that they might know thee, the only true God, and Jesus Christ whom thou hast sent." (John 17 : 3.) "This gift Christ confers by revealing the Father, of whom he is the true moral image and likeness ;" (Heb. 1 : 3,)—"by doing his Father's will ;" (John 6 : 38,)—"by performing his Father's works ;" (John 4 : 34) "by publishing his Father's doctrine, or purposes ;" (John 7 : 16)—and in all things, and in all ways, through his whole ministry, in teaching us of the Father. And he is the *only* medium through which we can come to the knowledge of God—"For there is none other name given under heaven among men, whereby we must, (or can) be saved;" (Acts 4:12)—"No man knoweth the Father save the Son, and he, to whomsoever the Son will reveal him;" (Matt. 11:27.) The Bible was not given, neither did Christ come, to teach us that *there was a God.* The evidences of that truth were inscribed, in bold relief, on the face of the visible creation, that "elder scripture writ by God's own hand." But the Bible was given to teach us something about God; and the anointed came to unfold to us all the adorable perfections of the divine nature, and by that means to raise us, step by step, from the labyrinth of darkness, in which we were involved, and from the dominion of sin, and to excite in our souls supreme love, reverence, and adoration for the divine character—to assimilate that character, and prepare us for exalted beatitude in the resurrection state.

PROPOSITION III.—OF CHRIST AND THE MEDIATORIAL KINGDOM.

Christ is the Son of God in a more exalted sense than Adam, or his posterity. He had an individual existence prior to the works of creation—was the agent of the Father in the works of creation. The Mediatorial kingdom of Christ, called in the Evangelists the kingdom of heaven, and the kingdom of God, is not the kingdom of immortal blessedness, but preparatory to the immortal state. This kingdom is not confined to the present mode of existence, but includes the future as well as the present. This kingdom is not a state of probation, but of discipline and instruction.

It is unnecessary for me to attempt any further exposition of my views in respect to the unity of God, or the sonship and dependence of Christ; as I have already been sufficiently explicit on that subject in my former remarks. The application of the term, *God*, to Christ, is in a subordinate sense, as it was applied to Moses and to the Judges of Israel: so the divine Redeemer himself argued, in reply to the accusation of blasphemy: "Is it not written in your law, I said, ye are gods? If he called them gods, unto whom the word of God came, and the scripture can not be broken, say ye of him, whom the Father hath sanctified, and sent into the world, thou blasphemest; because I said, I am the Son of God?" (John 10: 34, 35, 36.) But I desire to make a few further remarks on the character of Christ, and his pre-existence; because it is a subject on which there is a variety of opinions in Christendom, and even among Universalists.

I learn the superior sonship of Christ from the fact, that he is called, "The *only begotten* Son of the Father," John 1 : 14, and elsewhere. I here leave out the account of his miraculous conception, because it has been rejected by many learned and pious minds as spurious; though I unhesitatingly acknowledge, that their reasons for rejecting the account are by no means satisfactory to me. I learn his priority of existence from the fact, that he is called, "The beginning of the creation of God," (Rev. 3: 14,) and that he was "Before all things." (Col. 1: 17.) I come, therefore, to the very reasonable, and clearly, as I believe it will appear from what follows, the only Scriptural conclusion, that *Christ was the first production of the energies of creative power*, and the only being that the supreme God did immediately, (I mean, without a Mediator—without an Agent,) create. I also learn the fact of his priority of existence from his own divine teachings. He says, "I came down from heaven." (John 6: 38.) Hence, he surely existed in heaven before he came on earth. Again, "Before Abraham was, I am." (John 8: 58.) And in his prayer, (John 17: 5,) he says, "Father, glorify thou me with thine own self, with the glory which I had with thee *before the world was*." That he was the Agent of the Father in the work of creation, and consequently always stood as a Mediator between God and his works—as the medium through whom all communications were ever made from the self-existent Father to the intelligent world, I learn from the plain, unambiguous, and unequivocal language of inspiration: "All things were made by him; and without him was not any thing made that was made." (John 1: 3.) Again, "God created all things by Jesus Christ." (Eph. 3: 9.) Once more; "For by him were all things created that are in heaven, and that are in earth, visible and invisible; whether they be thrones, or dominions, or principalities, or powers; all things were created by him, and for him; and he is before all things, and by him all things consist." (Col. 1: 16, 17.) It appears to me utterly impossible for any person to frame language, that will more clearly express the position I have taken, than the foregoing passages of Scripture; nor can I see the possibility of avoiding the conclusion to which I have arrived, without the most perverse departure from the words of inspiration. Besides, I do not discover that the views I have taken reflect any dishonor upon the character of God, or of the divine Mediator; but rather add a lustre to the character of that invisible Divinity, who thus so clearly reveals all his adorable perfections to the intelligent world, by him who is declared to be "The image of the invisible God, and the first born of every creature."

That the mediatorial kingdom, or kingdom of God, mentioned by the Evangelists, is not the kingdom of immortality, I learn from the fact that it is to be given up, or the authority resigned, when a certain event shall be accomplished, and to be succeeded by another state of things. It was established for a specific purpose, and that purpose embraced the subjugation and reconciliation of all things to God. The prophet says, "And a kingdom was given to him, that all people, nations, and languages should serve him." (Dan. 7: 14.) The apostle says, "Then cometh the *end*, when he shall have delivered up the kingdom to God, even the Father; when he shall have put down all rule, and all authority, and power. For he *must reign*, till he hath put all enemies under his feet. And when all things shall be subdued unto him, then shall the Son also himself be subject unto him that put all things under him, that God may be ALL IN ALL." (1 Cor. 15: 24, 25, 28.)

This kingdom is so denominated, perhaps, because Christ rules in it supremely, as Lawgiver, King, and Judge; but there is very little analogy between his kingdom and the kingdoms of this world. We would, I am persuaded, in the present age of the world, set forth a more correct idea of it, if we should denominate it a school; for it is a school of divine instruction, as has been before demonstrated, of which Christ is the divine Principal and Teacher; and he has established such modes of teaching and discipline, of which we shall have occasion more fully to speak hereafter, as are calculated to accomplish the great purposes of its establishment. This kingdom extends, not only over the present mode of existence, but also over the future. The dissolution of this mortal body, simply, can not, according to the views I have presented, and which I believe are the only views sanctioned by the Scriptures, fit and prepare the soul for the possession and enjoyment of the immortal inheritance. Nor can I conceive that an unconscious sleep, from the death of the body to the resurrection, can have a more salutary effect. Therefore, there is an intermediate state of instruction, between the dissolution of the body and the consummating event, called "the resurrection of the dead." And that there is a continuous conscious state, between the death of the body and the resurrection of the dead, I learn most clearly from the declaration of our Savior, where he says of God, "He is the God of Abraham, the God of Isaac, and the God of Jacob. For he is not a God of the dead, but of the living; for all live unto him." (Luke, 20: 37, 38.) I also learn it from the appearance of Moses and Elias at the transfiguration of Christ on the mount; from the circumstance of the appearance of *many* at the time of the crucifixion; as well as from numerous declarations of the inspired apostle, which, to me, would be meaningless without the existence of such a state: such, for example, as "To live is Christ, but to die is gain;" and, "It is better to depart and be with Christ." See Philippians, 1: 21, 23, and many other passages.

The amplitude of the kingdom and the mission of our Savior, is abundantly confirmed by every prediction of "God's holy prophets," who have spoken of his coming, "and the glory that should follow." Hear a few of them. "I will declare the decree, [Ah! here is a decree; but it regards the purpose of God—not the actions of men,] Thou art my Son, this day have I begotten thee. Ask of me, and I shall give thee the heathen for thine inheritance, and the uttermost parts of the earth for thy possession." (Ps. 2: 7, 8.) "He shall have dominion also from sea to sea, and from the rivers unto the ends of the earth." (Ps. 72: 8.) "It is a light thing that thou shouldst be my servant to raise up the tribes of Jacob, and to restore the preserved of Israel; I will also give thee for a light to the Gentiles, that thou mayest be my salvation unto the end of the earth." (Isaiah 49: 6.) It is also confirmed by the testimony of John the Baptist, who says, "The Father loveth the Son, and hath given *all things* into his hand." (John 3: 35.) The unerring word of the Son of God assures us, that "All things are delivered unto me of my Father." (Matthew 11: 18.) "All power is given unto me in *heaven*, and in *earth*." (Matthew 28: 18.) But to be *in* this kingdom implies, to be under the immediate instruction of Christ, or under the influence of the institutions and means which he has appointed to be employed in this divine school; and to be out of this kingdom, is to be excluded from those privileges. Hence, Christ says to the Jews, who had heretofore been under the more immediate and efficient means of divine instruction, "The kingdom of God shall be taken from you, and given to a nation bringing forth the fruits thereof." (Matthew 21: 43.) "Many shall come from the east and west, and shall sit down with Abraham, and Isaac, and Jacob in the kingdom of heaven: but the children of the kingdom shall be cast out into utter darkness." (Matthew 8: 11, 12.) "There shall be weeping and gnashing of teeth, when ye shall see Abraham, and Isaac, and Jacob, and all the prophets, in the kingdom of God, and you yourselves thrust out." (Luke 13: 28.) This view explains and harmonizes many expressions of the Savior, which otherwise would be enigmatical; such as taking away the keys of knowledge—taking the kingdom of heaven by violence—shutting up the kingdom of heaven—and, especially, the gift of the keys of the kingdom of heaven to Peter, who by this special favor was authorized and empowered to open this new school, both to Jews and Gentiles.

That the authority and mission of Christ extend over the future as well as the present mode of existence, I learn from the inspired apostles. They denominate him, "The Judge, [*i. e.* Ruler and Teacher,] of the quick and the dead." (Acts 10: 42; 2 Tim. 4: 1; 1 Peter 4: 5.) Once more: "Whether we live, we live unto the Lord; and whether we die, we die unto the Lord; whether we live therefore or die, we are the Lord's. For to this end Christ both died, and rose, and revived, that he might be Lord both of the dead and living." (Rom. 14: 8, 9.)

That the kingdom of which I have been speaking is not a state of *probation*, is obvious from its very nature, and the object for which it was established. *Probation is not a term of Scripture*; nor is it applicable to any state or condition of man under the government of Christ. Christ did not come to try men—to see if they were fit for the kingdom of glory; but, by suitable and proper instruction and discipline, to make them so. The state of man, therefore, through the whole reign of the kingdom of Christ, both in the present and future modes of existence, is a state of discipline, instruction, and improvement.

PROPOSITION IV.—OF PUNISHMENT.

Punishment, under the government of Christ, is not vindictive, nor retaliatory ; but disciplinary and emendatory.

Nothing reflects so much dishonor on the divine character —so tarnishes the divine glory, as to ascribe vindictiveness, or a spirit of retaliation, to God! This representation of the divine Being, together with the other absurdities of Calvinism, once almost drove me into the " bottomless pit " of infidelity. In the whole administration of the divine government, in all its ramifications, there is, there can be but one ultimate purpose and design ; and that is the willing subjection of all moral intelligences to the *will*, and their assimilation to the character of God, thereby making them " partakers " of the felicity " of the divine nature." Does any one say, " God governs for his own glory?" I answer, " This is for the glory of God." The glory of God is displayed in the revelation of his adorable perfections, and in the accomplishment of all his divine purposes ; and in no other way could he appear glorious. All the divine attributes harmonize—there are no conflicting demands between them. What justice demands of the sinner, mercy pleads for ; and the stripes that justice inflicts, mercy approves and sanctifies. What else could the Psalmist mean when he said, " Unto thee, O Lord, belongeth mercy ; for thou renderest to every man according to his work." (Ps. 62 : 12.) We know that justice demands an equitable retribution—a suitable punishment, according to our sins ; but unless it has a still further demand—has an eye on the consequences of that punishment—if it be satisfied with the mere infliction of pain, it becomes *revenge*, not justice. But God says, under the solemnity of an oath, that he has no pleasure in the punishment itself—in the pain inflicted; but in the effect designed to be produced thereby: "As I live, saith the Lord God, I have no pleasure in the death, [punishment,] of the wicked; *but that the wicked turn from his way, and live.*" (Ezekiel 33: 11.) Punishment, in order to be just and equitable, and not vindictive and unmerciful, must be a *means*, and not an *end*; and just enough to accomplish the *end* designed, and no more; and by *that* the quantity of punishment must be measured, and not by the magnitude of the offense. In all human penal codes there is something vindictive. We graduate the punishment by the magnitude of the offense, and not by the effect produced. We say, if a man steal so much, he shall be so long confined in the common jail; if he steal so much more, he shall go to the penitentiary for one year; and if he steal still more, he shall go for a longer term, &c., without any regard to his moral reformation. It is not so with God; he says, "When the wicked man turneth away from his wickedness which he hath committed, and doeth that which is lawful and right, he shall save his soul alive." (Eze. 18: 27.) Nor is it so with an earthly parent. To illustrate: A parent has two sons; both commit offenses against his government which merit correction; but the crime of one is very trifling, just enough to make correction necessary; while that of the other is most heinous. The parent calls both to an account; and according to human laws, and the ordinary opinions of mankind in regard to the demerit of sin and the demands of justice, one must receive a very severe punishment, while a slight correction is all the other deserves. But the parent is influenced by parental feelings and sympathies. He does not punish for the sake of gratifying vindictive feelings, but to reform his sons—to bring them to repentance. He takes no pleasure in the pain they endure; but, although painful to himself to chastise them, he is encouraged to do it, and consoled for the pain he endures only by the hope of the beneficial effects it will produce upon his wayward children. He begins with the greatest offender; and before he has inflicted the fifth stripe, the child falls on his knees, asks pardon for his offense, and promises amendment.. It is enough —the object is attained—he has received all he deserves, and to inflict another blow would be cruelty. The parent then calls up the light offender, and commences with him; but he is as stubborn as a bull, and receives as many as the ancient Jewish law could inflict, forty save one, and perhaps more, before he yields. Now this last has received no more than he deserved, although he has received ten times the amount of the great offender, because he has received no more than was necessary to produce the desired effect; and to have stopped short of this would have been both unjust and unmerciful. Here, then, are justice and mercy blended, and satisfied—justice in the retribution awarded, and mercy in the effect produced; and this I consider a fair illustration of the retributive government of our heavenly Father. And this, we surely learn from Holy Writ; for when God threatened the most severe punishment conceivable upon Israel, he said, "By this, therefore, shall the iniquity of Jacob be purged; and this is all the fruit *to take away his sins*; when he maketh all the stones of the altar as chalk-stones that are beaten in sunder, the groves and the images shall not stand up." (Isa. 37: 9.)

From the view I have taken of this subject we discover, that there is no such thing under the divine government as penal punishment FOR sin; that is, so much punishment because of such an amount of transgression, but a punishment IN sin. God makes the way of the transgressors hard, not because they HAVE SINNED, but because they DO SIN; and this is done not to gratify a vindictive spirit, but to convince them of the mistake they have made, dissuade them from sin, turn them from an evil course, and, with other means, to "heal all their backslidings." Neither is there any reward FOR obedience, but IN obedience. IN keeping the commands there is great reward; (Ps. 19: 11,) IN the elevated enjoyment which the soul received *in* the very act of obedience; and this is reward enough. My friend invites me to a feast; I accept the proffered hospitality, and luxuriate in the gratification and pleasure of the entertainment. But with what astonishment and surprise would he stare at me, if, after I had enjoyed his kindness and partaken of his bounty, I should step up to him, and demand pay for what I had received? Equally absurd is the general notion of being rewarded *for* our acts of righteousness.

Punishment—I use this term because it is a common one, although I dislike it; for, according to the general acceptation, it always carries with it a notion of vindictiveness—but punishment, under the divine government, is not, therefore, vindictive, but disciplinary and emendatory; and this discipline, if I am right in my views concerning the kingdom of Christ, is extended through every department of that school, and will necessarily continue until his pupils have completed their primary education, and are prepared for a higher sphere. Suffering will only be proportionable to our obstinacy, or the darkness we have involved ourselves in by transgression. That man will commit sin in a future state I argue not—believe not. But I see no inconsistency in supposing that he may suffer the consequences of sin, through the darkness which he has brought upon himself by transgression, and by his neglecting to improve the means of instruction in the present life. And such, it clearly appears to me, is the doctrine of the apostle, where he says, that "Christ being put to death in the flesh, but quickened by the spirit, went and preached to the spirits in prison, which were sometime disobedient, when the long-suffering of God waited in the days of Noah." (1 Peter 3: 18, 19, 20.) Every other exposition of this passage that I have ever seen advanced, appears to me to be far-fetched, strained, and irrelevant.

I formerly—a great many years ago—reasoned, that as all sin originated in our earthly natures, our animal propensities being alone vulnerable to temptation, and sin being the only cause of misery; when our bodies were dissolved, our animal propensities destroyed, all temptation to sin would cease, and sin, which is the cause of misery, consequently would come to an end; and as the effect must cease when the cause is destroyed, therefore there could be no misery or suffering after the dissolution of our mortal bodies: not considering the fact, that a consequence may remain long after the cause which produced it has ceased to operate. My body may be prostrated by a burning fever, (as it has been,) near to dissolution—that fever may yield to medical treatment, and be entirely expelled from the physical system; yet it will take a long while after the fever is removed, with careful nursing and strict regimen, to restore one to health and strength. Again: The parent provides a school for his son, and furnishes him with all the means necessary to obtain, during his minority, a competent education to transact the business of life when he becomes a man; but the son, through idleness and inattention to the means afforded, reaches his majority in a state of profound ignorance. And although he now sees his folly, and deplores his neglect, he nevertheless is compelled to suffer the consequence, and loses time and happiness by being obliged to prosecute studies which he had neglected during his minority.

PROP. V.—OF THE RESURRECTION.

The resurrection of the dead, as argued by the apostle 1 Cor. chap. 15, not a resuscitation of these material bodies ; but a rising, or resurrection of the whole body of the church from the intermediate state, or from the mediatorial or preparatory kingdom to the immortal kingdom.

The doctrine of the resurrection of the dead is placed, by the apostle, as the fundamental doctrine of the Christian faith—as that on which the whole fabric rests; a denial of which represented the apostles as bearing false witness of God, and overthrew the validity of the whole revelation that God had made to man. It has always been considered by divines, in every age of the church, as an indispensible article of the Christian faith, necessary to be believed in order to secure salvation. But the diverse and conflicting opinions which have obtained, in regard to what body should be raised, as well as the nature of the resurrection state, have very clearly proved to me, that "they understood not what they said; nor whereof they affirmed." The habit of applying the word resurrection, in all cases where they find it, to a single point, has led many into the most absurd inconsistencies and contradictions; and compelled them to represent that state, wherein Christ said there should be no more death, but all its subjects should be "equal unto the angels, and be children of God, being children of the resurrection," as a state of endless impurity and death! Others, who have obtained a more correct notion of the resurrection state, seem at a loss about the subject of the resurrection, and the time and manner of its occurrence. One maintains that there is no inherent principle of immortality in man—that conscious existence is alone the effect of material organization—that at the death of the body man falls into an unconscious sleep, and so remains until the time of the resurrection of the dead, when all shall be raised at one and the same time, and receive the bodies identical they put off at death, in a refined and indissoluble nature, and resume a conscious existence. Another maintains that the general resurrection of the dead means the resurrection of all, but not at one and the same time; and that the resurrection is progressive as the demise of our race is progressive, one after another; and that the body which man lays down, "is not that body which shall be, but God giveth it a body as it hath pleased him," at the time of putting off this body of flesh; and he immediately arises, and enters into the resurrection state. Others, who have learned, or think they have learned, from the words of the apostle, that the resurrection of the dead, and the simultaneous change of the living, is an event that is to take place at a specified point of time; that it is the closing event of the mediatorial mission; and also that there is an intermediate state of conscious existence—that death is not an unconscious sleep of the soul—that the soul exists in some form, and must therefore have a spiritual body, or vehicle; seem to be at a loss about what will be raised. The soul already has a body, exists in a higher state than it did in this mortal body, and, according to common phraseology, is already in eternity, and inherits immortality. What, then, can be raised? What beneficial change can it experience? These are questions which seem difficult to answer upon this hypothesis.

I have felt deeply interested in this research, having never found a theory published by uninspired man that did not, in my estimation, involve inextricable difficulties. But I do think that Heaven has opened my understanding to see the theory of the inspired apostle, on this all-important subject, which is not only reconcilable with itself, but in perfect harmony with the general thread of divine revelation on the subject of the resurrection of the dead. And now, with all due deference to the opinions of the learned, and to those thinking heads who have, certainly on most subjects, thought longer and more deeply than myself, I will venture "also to give mine opinion."

The primary meaning of the word *anastasis*, translated resurrection, according to Parkhurst, is not a resuscitation of this mortal body, nor the bringing of any dead thing to life; but a rising up from a lower to a higher state, or situation; and consequently may imply, advancing forward, or higher in a moral condition; as I am satisfied it often does mean. Parkhurst says, "*anastasis*, from *anistemi*, to rise," signifies "a standing on the feet again, or rising, as opposed to falling. It occurs, though figuratively, in this view, Luke 2: 34. (Comp. Isa. 8: 14, 15.) In the LXX it is twice used, Lam. 3: 62, Zeph. 3: 8; in both of which texts it answers to the Heb. [word] to stand up, rise, and in the former is opposed to sitting." (*Parkhurst's Greek and English Lexicon.*)

From the word itself, then, we can neither learn the nature, nor the subjects of the resurrection. It should be remembered, that the apostle, both in the 15th chapter of first Cor., and 4th chapter of first Thess., uses the terms *dead* and *asleep*, not necessarily as implying a state of unconsciousness, but in opposition to life in the flesh—to distinguish those who have departed from those who remain in the flesh. The subjects, therefore, of the resurrection of which he speaks, may have as active an existence, or more so, than men in the flesh; but are not in as high a moral or spiritual state as they can arrive at. It should also be noticed, that he uses the terms *Adam* and *Christ*, the first and the second man, as representatives of the two states or conditions of man, the earthly and the spiritual. The body of Adam is the whole body of man in the flesh; the body of Christ is that whole body redeemed and delivered from the flesh: and the state to which that whole body is to be ultimately raised, is a state "like unto his *glorious body*." But the glorious body of Christ did not appear unto the disciples at his resurrection from the tomb of Joseph; but only to Peter, James, and John, at the mount of transfiguration, and afterwards to John, on the isle of Patmos.

Having premised the foregoing particulars, I am prepared to enter into a more careful and critical examination of the important subject.

In the 15th chapter of 1st Corinthians, which contains the most elaborate argument the apostle uses in all his writings on any individual subject, we find four positions distinctly defined, and attended to; first, the *fact* of the resurrection of the dead; second, the *order* of the resurrection, in point of priority and time; third, the *manner* of the resurrection, and character of the body raised; fourth, the consequence, or the resurrection state. That this august event, which includes the simultaneous resurrection of all the dead, and the change of all the living, takes place at the same identical instant of time, is expressed in as strong and as plain terms as it is possible to use, in 51st and 52d verses: "We shall not all sleep, but we shall *all* be changed, *in a moment, in the twinkling of an eye*, at the last trump; for the trumpet shall sound, and the dead shall be raised incorruptible, and we shall be changed."

Of the *order* he says, "Christ the first-fruits;" and then no more until the consummation—until the coming which the apostle particularly describes in 1st Thessalonians, 4th chapter, and which is parallel with the declaration of the angels to the disciples at the time of his ascension, (See Acts 1 : 11,) when he "shall have put down all rule, and authority, and power;" and when "all things shall be subdued unto him," (vs. 23—28,) then shall all the members of his body be raised up; all that die in Adam, the earthly body, shall be made alive in Christ, the spiritual body." (v. 22.)

In the whole of his description of the manner of the resurrection, and the nature and character of the body to be raised, the apostle is careful to use the singular number when he speaks of the body. "But some man will say, how are the dead raised up? and with what *body*, (not bodies,) do they come?" And when he leaves similitude and metaphor, to describe expressly the character of the resurrection body, he uses the singular pronoun, *it—it*, the one whole body—"It is sown in corruption, it is raised in incorruption." (v. 42.) Compare this with Rom. 8: 23. "And not only they, but ourselves also, which have the first-fruits of the spirit, even we ourselves groan within ourselves, waiting for the adoption, to wit, the redemption of our BODY." This *body* was the whole creation, which the apostle had before said, "Was made subject to vanity, not willingly, but by reason of him who hath subjected the same in hope;" that is, it was "sown in *corruption*, in *dishonor*, in *weakness*, *a natural body*." But God had not left them without a hope, and with this hope, although they could not suppress a groan, they were waiting for it to receive a deliverance "from the bondage of corruption into the glorious liberty of the children of God;" that is, for it to be "raised in incorruption, in glory, in power, a spiritual body," where all the members would be "equal unto the angels and be children of God, being children of the resurrection;" and until which, not one could be perfectly blessed, because "While one member suffers, all the members suffer with it." (1 Cor. 12: 26.)

The apostle often makes use of the metaphor of the physical human body to illustrate the connection of the members of the church, and the relation which exists between Christ and the church. "I would have you to know that the head of every man is Christ." (1 Cor. 11: 3.) "Now are ye the *body* of Christ, and members in particular." (1 Cor. 12: 17.) "For we are members of his flesh, and his bones." (Eph. 5: 30.)

Should we admit that this body, or any of the members thereof, have already been exalted to the highest state of spiritual glory, and have been made partakers of the full fruition of the immortal inheritance, it will not only militate against the simultaneous resurrection of all the dead, but will render unintelligible a vast many passages of the inspired word; such, for instance, as the one above quoted; "While one member suffers, *all* the members suffer with it." Besides, the inheritance is a joint inheritance. "And if children, then heirs; heirs of God, and joint-heirs with Christ." (Rom. 8: 17.) And of a joint inheritance, the eldest can not come into full possession until the youngest heir becomes of age.

The body to be raised, therefore, is a body already in existence, not extinct, nor unconscious, yet not in its highest and most exalted state. This appears to be plainly the doctrine which Christ taught to the Sadducees. He seemed to predicate his argument for the resurrection of the dead upon the fact, that the subjects of that resurrection were not extinct, but still lived: "Now that the dead are raised, [and as I understand it, the present tense of the passive verb, *are raised*, in this connection, has a future signification, the same as *are to be raised*, because all present understood the subject of the resurrection of which they were speaking to be *future*, if there could be any such event,] Now that the dead are raised, even Moses showed at the bush, when he called the Lord, the God of Abraham, and the God of Isaac, and the God of Jacob; for he is not a God of the dead, but of the living." (Luke 20: 37, 38.) Now the argument, as I understand it, is this: Because they are not dead, but still live, we have proof that

God will raise them. Moreover, we have positive proof that, when Christ was upon earth, not one individual member of this body had been exalted to the highest heavens. " And *no man* hath ascended up to heaven, but he who came down from heaven, even the Son of man which is in heaven." (John 3: 13.) And again; the apostle Peter says, " For David is not ascended into the heavens." (Acts 2: 34.)

People are in a habit of using the terms, "immortality" and "eternity" familiarly, as applicable to that state into which the soul enters immediately at the death of the body, as simply signifying a continuous perpetuity of existence; but it certainly appears to me, that the inspired penmen had a higher, a more refined, and a more exalted meaning in the use of these words. The term "eternity" is used but once in the whole Bible, and is there called the habitation of God. " For thus saith the high and lofty One that inhabiteth eternity." (Isa. 57: 15.) The apostle says, "Life and immortality are brought to light through the Gospel." (2 Tim. 1: 10.) This must mean that the Gospel reveals a future life, and an immortal inheritance to be enjoyed in that life; but I do not understand that he means the same thing by *life* as by *immortality*. He says, that God " *only hath immortality*, dwelling in the light, which *no man* can approach unto." (1 Tim. 6: 16.) Eternity, therefore, is the habitation of the infinite, divine mind; and immortality is the blessedness of that nature. Man, therefore, only enters eternity when he unchangeably approximates the divine mind, delivered from all extraneous influences of a lower nature; and he puts on immortality when every member of the great body is so exalted as to deliver him from all those sympathies which can in any degree impair the lofty felicity which results from the onward and upward exploration of the endlessly-unfolding divine perfections.

It appears to me, therefore, strong as demonstration, that

there is an immediate, future state; that all who have entered that state, as well as all in the present state of existence, are subjects of the mediatorial or preparatory kingdom of Christ; and are, or will become, pupils in that school under the tuition of the divine Teacher, in such institutions, forms, and circumstances as are adapted to their conditions; and will enjoy all the advantages of their improvement, that is, increase in blessedness as they increase in divine knowledge, wisdom, and holiness; and suffer all the consequences of obstinacy and misimprovement. Were I to indulge a conjecture, I would apprehend that the future department of this school was the higher department, with greater facilities for advancement in divine wisdom and divine life; but man must be free there as well as here, because no mind can be *compelled* to be happy contrary to its will, nor can he be so without free, voluntary exercise; for mental advancement and moral improvement constitute the basis of all that can be properly called felicity.

We then necessarily come to the conclusion, that the human family—the posterity of the earthly Adam in the aggregate—constitute that church which "Christ loved, and gave himself for, that he might sanctify and cleanse it with the washing of water by the word, that he might, [at last,] present it to himself as a glorious church, not having spot or wrinkle, or any such thing; but that it might be holy, and without blemish." (Eph. 5: 25, 26, 27.) And when all this shall be accomplished, "Then cometh the end"—then the trump will be sounded—then the "Lord himself will [again] descend from heaven with a shout, and with a voice of the arch-angel and the trump of God"—the living will be changed—the departed and the living be united—"Christ will deliver up the kingdom to God, even the Father;" and, united to this one mystical body, raise it from this preparatory or mediatorial kingdom into the eternal and immortal kingdom;

and into the perfect fruition of the immortal inheritance where "God is ALL in ALL." Amen.

Then will be heard the grateful and triumphant song, bursting in sublime symphony from the united voices of a redeemed universe: "O death! where is thy sting? O grave! where is thy victory? Thanks be to God, who giveth us the victory through our Lord Jesus Christ." Halleluiah! Amen. "The Lord God Omnipotent reigneth!" Amen, and Amen.

PART II.

MISCELLANEOUS POETRY.

For my own amusement, and for the gratification of particular and valued friends, I have indulged occasionally in the muses with such gifts as have been bestowed upon me. I have never considered myself a poet, nor claimed sublimity of fancy or depth of thought for my poetical productions ; but they have served to fill up a niche in the versatility of a busy life, and have gratified some of my *partial* and very highly esteemed friends ; and for the sake of such, I have consented to introduce a few pieces to such of my readers as are disposed to read them, at the close of my book. They are not introduced to gratify the delicate spleen of the connoisseur ; nor is any one compelled to read them whose fastidious sensibility may be wounded by the roughness of the numbers or the rudeness of the rhyme.

THE BLOOM OF SPRING.

Written in the year 1800; and designed as a counterpart to the "Gloom of Autumn," a popular song in those days.

Join with me, ye youthful songsters,
   Sing the blooming, fragrant spring—
See all nature's beauties brighten,
   See all nature smile again!

Long has earth been bound in fetters,
   Nature's beauties stood aghast;
But returning spring now flatters
   That the rage of winter's past.

See the limpid waters pouring
   From the lofty mountain's side,
From their icy fetters roaring,
   Through the valley smoothly glide.

See the woods in verdant clothing;
   Feather'd songsters cheer the plain;
View the landscape, how it brightens—
   Meads and mountains robed in green.

See the lambs, their gambols playing
   Round their bleating, anxious dams;
The swain, through verdant groves a-straying
   With his lover hand-in-hand.

See the huntsman briskly bounding
  With his hounds, the wilds to rove;
While his mellow horn he's sounding,
  Chase the roe-buck through the grove.

See all vegetation springing—
  All with beauty spring adorn;
Fruit-trees, white as lilies blooming,
  Sweet perfume the vernal morn.

Such scenes are worthy our attention—
  Pleasant, beauteous—Oh, how fair!
They lead our minds to contemplation—
  Transient, fading still they are!

While we mourn these short-lived pleasures,
  Quick they come—how soon they're o'er!—
Consider, there's a richer treasure
  Where life's winter is no more.

Here we're bound in mortal fetters,
  Here confined in one cold clod;
But soon this broken band shall let us
  Return, like spring, to nature's God.

There are everlasting pleasures;
  There is one eternal spring;
There reigns our Savior—blessed Jesus!
  There his praises angels sing.

There all nations shall adore him;
  There before his throne shall fall;
And, in one united anthem,
  His redeeming grace extol.

These are pleasures worth all trouble—
  Jesus stands our heavenly Friend;
This repays us, more than double,
  Though these short-lived pleasures end.

Haste, O, haste our quick returning!
  Blessed Jesus! call us home;
Free us from this vale of mourning,
  To thine arms bid us return.

ELEGIAC LINES.

Written in the year 1802, *by request of special friends, Mr. and Mrs. M.———, of New Salem, Mass., who were bereaved of a very promising daughter, aged about three years.*

List, friends! and hear the solemn sound!
The gloom-wrapt heavens, and woe-smit ground,
  In awful trembling stand!
While down the mission'd angel rode,
Arm'd with the shafts of death, by God,
  To fulfil his dread command!

But where, great Arbiter of fate,
Thy angel send? Thy great mandate
  Who must obey, and go?
Must hoary age the summons hear?
Those who have pass'd the golden year?
  Or those in manhood? No.

Who, then? Oh, mournful to declare;
My trembling muse, in half despair,
  Doth scarce assistance bring;

The orbs of light in splendor fail,
All nature joins the solemn wail,
While mournfully I sing.

In Salem sprang a lily bright,
Just open'd to the morning light,
Dear Nancy's emblem proved ;
At this the shafts of death were thrown ;
The lily's cropp'd, and Nancy's gone
To brighter worlds above.

Her infant form too fair appear'd
To dwell in clay, with mortals here,
So Christ hath call'd her home,
To deck the fields of heaven above,
Where all are fill'd with heavenly love,
And love fills every song.

But O, the agonies and smart
That rend the tender parent's heart,
To part with that dear flower !
Scarce did their eyes her beauty trace,
And their affection on her place—
She's gone, to be no more.

With drooping hearts they view the urn
That holds the tender, death-like form,
And kiss the sleeping clay ;
And, weeping, cry, O cruel death !
Oh, why so early snatch her breath,
And hurry her away.

But cease, fond parents ! cease to mourn,
And let your peace again return,
And worship, praise, adore ;

The hand who gave the stroke is God!
Then bless the power, and kiss the rod,
And sigh, and weep no more.

Know that he will a Father prove,
And all his ways are truth and love—
He's call'd your child to bliss,
Where you will soon her partner be,
Beyond this world of misery,
Complete in happiness.

There death no more can friends divide,
There all our sorrows will subside;
We'll spread immortal wing,
And in a song of triumph say,
"O grave! where is thy victory,
O death! where is thy sting."

Then humbly wait the glorious hour,
When Christ shall save you from the power
Of death, the king of dread,
And wing you to felicity,
Where all our ransom'd race shall be
United with their Head.

EXPERIENCE---IN TWO PARTS.

In the early part of my ministry I was very often requested to relate my experience, especially by my Partialist friends. Dear souls! they loved me, and earnestly desired my salvation, and were exceedingly anxious to find some ground to indulge a hope for me! but they could not find a peg to hang the least hope on, unless they could find it in my experience; for they always look there for the foundation of hope, rather than in the revelation that God hath made of his unchangeable purpose—

" The oath and promise of the Lord."

Therefore, to save a stale prosaic repetition, I put it in homely verse, so that I could repeat it with more facility, or sing—sing! Why, did you ever attempt to sing?—Yes, indeed; in those days, I used to *strain* up my voice, and try to make a noise like singing.

The first part was written in 1803, soon after I commenced preaching, and the second part about thirteen years afterwards. I have used metaphor; but it is expressive of my feelings, and will be readily understood.

In seeking for pleasure, I fancied a treasure
In youthful diversions I surely should find;
So, bent on such folly, determined to follow
All the vain dictates of a fantastic mind.

My liberty gained; then all that remained
Was roving the country in search of my prize;
But soon I perceived that I was deceived,
For roving's a pleasure which ne'er satisfies.

In vain recreation I found only vexation;
Such pleasures are short, and of no solid worth:
In sober reflection, I found an objection
To spending my moments in frolicsome mirth.

My days fast departing, my life so uncertain,
That something more worthy I thought to pursue;
My determination was then education—
The paths of bright science to visit and view.

But here I discerned the great and the learned,
The wise and the good, kings and nobles, all died ;
Death over all reigned, and learning here failed ;
"Ah, there is no happiness here," I cried.

In darkness and horror, my soul sank in sorrow ;
Soon, soon I must die, and there is no reprieve ;
Friends e'er so united must soon be divided,
And all earthly comforts must finally leave.

In anguish I groaned, and sadly bemoaned
My fate, as a tenant of this gloomy world ;
While sadness oppress'd, a voice me address'd,
Saying, "Why these complaints, poor ungrateful child."

The voice, though alarming, still sounded most charming ;
Such music enliven'd, and gladden'd my soul ;
I turn'd to invoke it, 'twas wisdom that spoke it ;
A bright form stood by me in laurels of gold.

With love near she drew me, and spake these words to me,
"Blame not your Creator, nor say he's unkind,
But take a flight with me, and quickly you shall be
Where peace, sweetest comfort, and joy you shall find."

My hand then she seiz'd, and bore me, releas'd
From this dismal posture of stupid surprise,
O'er valley and fountain, till high on a mountain,
Transparent as sunbeams, we soon did arrive.

On this elevation she planted my station,
And then she extracted the scales from my eyes ;
The prospect was glorious, all nature harmonious,
No discords nor jarrings could ever arise.

I view'd my Creator as a Father and Savior;
  All his dispensations are kindness and love;
There's no contradiction in his divine system,
  No invading schemes his intentions can move.

He's founded his system in infinite wisdom,
  He's measured the whole by his infinite love;
He has raised his tower with infinite power;
  His chain is eternal, no link can remove.

He's fixed the station of human creation
  On this ball of earth, but a space to remain;
Though troubles assail us, yet God does not fail us;
  His love will here reach and restore us again.

Though sunk in corruption, though seeking destruction,
  And wandering far from the fields of delight;
Though vain and false-hearted, from wisdom departed,
  His soul all enshrouded in darkness and night;

Yet Christ, the Anointed, by Heaven appointed,
  Descended to earth, and was veiled in flesh,
To reconcile man to the law of his Maker,
  Raise up his soul from the bondage of death.

The spirit of wisdom, descending from heaven,
  Reproveth mankind for the sins they have done,
And worketh salvation through regeneration,
  And purifies them by the blood of his Son.

When this she'd revealed, my heart then she sealed,
  And into my hand a bright trumpet did give;
"Go, face opposition in every condition,
  And sound this loud trumpet, that sinners may live."

Great Spirit! attend me; and wisdom befriend me,
  That I may obey the command of my God;
Though friends all should fail me, and malice assail me,
  I'll march a bold soldier in wisdom's bright road.

PART SECOND.

Obedient to the solemn word,
  I left my friends, my parents dear;
I left the land of my abode,
  To spread the Gospel far and near.

Through foes within and foes without,
  Through hunger, thirst, and pain I trod,
To sound the Gospel-trump about,
  That sinners might return to God.

O'er mountains, desert, wild, and bleak;
  Through scorching rays and stormy winds;
Where'er the lamp directs my feet,
  Or where the spirit me commands;

With weeping eyes for sinners lost,
  With anxious groans and care I cry,
And show the price salvation cost,
  And point to mansions in the sky.

O sinner, sinner! hear the sound!
  Behold your Savior bleed and die!
Think of his sorrows—count the wounds
  Which he received on Calvary!

For you he bore the cruel pains,
  That you eternal life might have;
From death he rose, and lives, and reigns,
  That he a guilty world might save.

Then turn to God with all your heart,
  Implore a Savior's pardoning love;
His hand will every grace impart,
  To raise your souls to heaven above.

There shall you taste unmingled joy,
With all the numerous, ransom'd throng;
And love and praise be your employ,
While endless ages roll along.

LINES INSCRIBED TO WIDOW C.------

During my itinerancy in the Onion River country, in the winter of 1802–3, I became acquainted with a young widow, C.—— She was a native of Massachusetts, a daughter of a Mr. J——, of Brookfield, with whom I had a limited acquaintance. When quite young she married a Dr. C.——, who settled in practice in the town of Essex, Chittenden County, Vt.; but soon died, leaving his excellent young wife with an infant son. She was a deep, and almost inconsolable mourner. I had much conversation with her, gathered a description of her intense grief and sufferings, as far as she was able to express them, and strove to draw her soul to the fountain of Gospel consolation; and I had reason to hope, that I was not altogether unsuccessful. After I had taken leave of her, and just before I left that region of country, which I have never since visited, while walking one day, in a natural and beautiful grove, to which I often resorted for meditation, her case was vividly presented to my imagination; and seating myself upon a moss-covered log, with a pencil I sketched the following lines, which I afterward transcribed, and left in the care of Br. Babbit to be presented to her.

Hail, long-forgotten muse! I claim thy aid.
Hast thou no charms to cancel fell despair?
Must sympathy lie lurking in the shade,
When virtue calls? No; with her thou shalt share.
Hark! What's that sound from yonder lonely cell?
Some weeping angel in distress appears!
She strikes the mournful lyre—What does it tell?
O God of love! her face suffused in tears!

Her looks deject, and bordering on despair;
  Her harp some dirge to human greatness plays;
She mourns—Ah! reason, too, has she to care,
  Her friend, her partner, lies entomb'd in clay.
With plaintive steps, and slow, she treads the ground,
  While in her arms an infant son she bears;
At length, she stops—then casts her eyes around—
  The youthful bloom still on her cheek appears.

She steadfast downward fix'd her streaming eyes,
  On that lone spot, the dear remains enshrin'd;
Her feeble voice, though audible her cries,
  Spoke lamentations torturing to the mind.
"O hapless youth! how can I tread
  The path which Heaven has design'd for me?
How can I bear this unremitting load,
  O dear departed friend! untried by thee?

Once, on thy soothing bosom could I pour
  My fond desires, and ease my troubled breast;
But now, alas! that heart can beat no more,
  And lies encircled in the arms of death.
Do I not dream? Does not my consort live?
  Will he not come to give my heart relief?
Methinks, e'en now, I see him nimbly move—
  Away, false shade! thou canst not stay my grief!

Beneath this heap, and free from strife he rests;
  Nor would I call him from his peaceful home;
No ruthless troubles here invade his breast;
  The scene he's tried where all must shortly come.
But O my infant! O thou orphan dear!
  My grief I can not stay—come, welcome tears—
No father hast thou, O the thought most drear!
  To guide thy steps, and guard thy infant years."

Then up to God she turns her longing eyes,
  Kind Heaven's benediction to implore:
"O God! all bounteous, faithful, true, and wise,
  The widow's God, Father to orphans poor!
Grant thy benignant smiles to cheer my days;
  May meek submission to thy will be mine;
Oh, lead my infant in sweet virtue's ways,
  And may he in the courts of wisdom shine."

Then sighs obstruct her speech—she's bathed in tears,
  The briny flood her burden'd heart to free,
When suddenly a soothing voice she hears,
  "Fair angel, weep and sigh no more for me."
'Twas not dread thunder, nor fierce glaring fire,
  Nor rattl'ing hail, nor storm, the silence broke,
Nor apparition, ghost, nor spectre dire;
  A calm and welcome voice, like reason, spoke.

"Dry up thy tears; nor let grim discontent
  Pall on thy soul, and tear thy heart in twain;
Thy days of trouble shortly will be spent,
  Then we shall meet no more to part again.
Pine not for friends—One thou art sure to have,
  More dear to thee than earthly friends can be;
Oh, how hath he express'd unbounded love,
  Who bowed his head, and died on Calvary.

He's human nature's glorious, guardian Friend,
  Bound by those ties which death and hell can't loose;
He'll lead, direct, and guide thee by the hand;
  In his dear bosom there is sweet repose.
Thy infant he doth in his arms receive,
  As the good Shepherd, keeps him near his heart;
His spirit everlasting comforts give,
  His love doth life and energy impart.

He'll guide his ransom'd flock to endless day,
   All Adam's race are purchas'd by his blood;
In lucid robes of spotless purity
   He'll clothe and own them for his chosen bride.
There all shall meet, and join the choral song,
   All who inhabit air, or earth, or flood;
All glory, honor, praise, and power belong
   To our Almighty, glorious Savior, God.

There we shall meet, in that harmonious throng,
   With all mankind, in sweet felicity,
And join the eternal, new, and glorious song
   So weep and sigh, dear girl, no more for me."

SEARCH THE SCRIPTURES.

The following was written for, and published in 1811, *in the "Religious Inquirer," a contemplated periodical, of which I have spoken in my Memoirs.*

Go "search the holy Scriptures" saith the Lord,
   In them, ye think, eternal life you'll see;
They are my work, the record of my word,
   "And they are those that testify of me."

My spirit shall illuminate your path,
   Make truth with heavenly lustre on you shine;—
Shall break the bonds that chain you down to death,
   And raise your souls to life and peace divine.

There can you read the sacred promise sure,
Immortal life unfolding to the view,
There find for sin and woe a sovereign cure,
And wisdom's path with rapturous joy pursue.

How vain, O man, to seek for perfect joys,
In earthly honors, fame, or stores of gold ;—
To grasp, with anxious mind, earth's fleeting toys,
And grovel in the earth for peace of soul !

Essential bliss is not of earthly birth ;
Here rust corrupts, and moth corrodes our gain ;
Souls wedded to this world will feel a dearth,
Which blasts the joys they fondly would obtain.

Seek, then, O man ! thy treasure in the Lord,
And let thy soul his gracious promise prove ;
Pursue the written pages of his word,
That sacred record of unchanging love.

There will you find unsullied joy and peace,—
There streams of bliss from heavenly fountains roll ;
There, in God's mountain, find a sacred feast—
While strains immortal, swell th' enraptured soul !

These joys, O man ! the world can not impart,
Nor all united powers of earth remove ;
Though troubled billows may assail thy heart,
'Twill stand unshaken on God's mount of love.

LINES

Written with a pencil at the grave of a son, on the first anniversary of his interment, May 16th, 1831.

Again, my son, to thy lone grave I come,
Still deeply groaning 'neath this ponderous blow,
On this dread day, o'ercast with deepest gloom,
Sad anniversary of a father's woe!

Twelve lingering months have roll'd their tedious round,
Since to the Power who gave, thy breath resign'd—
Since here thy weeping friends, this spot around,
To the dark vault thy precious form consign'd.

Nor day nor wakeful hour has pass'd along,
But thy lov'd image floats before my sight;
I see thee as thou wast, in time that's gone,
Nor would I lose, for worlds, the vision bright.

Those sparkling eyes with fire celestial glow,
When cherish'd by a father's fond embrace;
Thy words, to me, like heavenly music flow,
And smiles seraphic sit upon thy face.

But oh, when 'neath correction's bitter smart,
I hear thy cry, and see thy tearful flow,
Ten thousand pangs assail this bleeding heart—
I groan,—I faint,—I sink beneath the blow!

"Forgive," I cry, "O dear departed shade!
A father's frowns, or words that cruel seem;
From this torn heart, with drops of vital blood,
Each precious tear he gladly would redeem.

G—G

"Spare, spare the torturing sight! Oh, let a tear
  Repentant blot the scene from memory's page!
Yet with thy soothing smiles, sweet cherub, cheer
  The remnant of my earthly pilgrimage.

"May thy lov'd form still keep within my view,
  In all the charms of youth and beauty bright;
This mournful solace let each morn renew,
  And dreams of thee dispel the gloom of night."

But what is this? Oh, see the dismal pile!
  Mark where that form lies mouldering back to clay
No more those limbs can move, nor lips can smile—
  Then burst my heart, and stream my eyes away!

Hush! hush! rebellious heart!—I hear a voice;
  "Be still, vain mortal! know that I am God."
Father, I hear; though sorrowing, still rejoice,
  That thou, not man, lett'st fall the lifted rod.

I know thy wisdom, power, and boundless love
  Whate'er is best for mortals will perform;
Though rebel man must thy chastisings prove,
  Yet mercy smiles above the raging storm.

No; not a murmuring thought would willing rise
  Within this torn, this lacerated breast;
Yet, O my Father! while these streaming eyes
  Look up, and seek in thee my only rest,

O still permit a father so bereav'd,
  Unnoticed by the world, to come alone
To this retired, this sacred spot, and grieve,
  And breathe to sighing winds his peaceful moan.

The grave my baser passions shall chastise,
  Ambition, avarice, envy, pride, deceit;
Death's dread, resistless power shall make me wise,
  And bring me, conquer'd, at thy sovereign feet.

For here the great must lie, the wise, the brave,
  The rich, the poor, in undistinguished clay;
The master's dust must mingle with the slave,
  Till Gabriel's trump proclaims immortal day.

ACROSTIC.

During the last sickness of my beloved daughter, Mary Adaline, her teacher, whose school she had attended until she was prostrated on a bed of sickness, made her a call, and presented her a book, "The Life of Dr. Franklin," which he had promised as a premium for good behavior and scholarship. She was highly pleased with this token of approbation, and although unable to read, yet she would often request to look at it, and hold it in her hand; and to add gratification to pleasure, I promised to write an acrostic on her name, upon a blank leaf of the book. And although she was taken from my arms before it was accomplished, yet I, nevertheless, performed the mournful task, with conscientious devotion.

Mysterious are thy ways, O God of love!
And may I bow submissive to thy will;
Resolv'd, though chasten'd, still thy grace to prove,
Yield to thy rod, and bid my heart be still.

Ah, my loved child! how dear thou wert to me!
Did virtue dwell on earth, 'twas in thy soul,
All meekness, patience, and from envy free;
Love's gentle spirit did thy mind control.
I knew thy worth; but worth and virtue die!
No; Heaven translated thee to worlds above;
E'en yet I'd hold thee prisoner from the sky.

Such was my fondness—my misguided love!
Thy time had come; nor skill, nor parent's love
Around thy life entwined with strong desire,
Could still the voice which call'd thee from above,
Yonder to join in Heaven's seraphic choir.

ELEGY

On the death of Erastus Ransom, son of Robert and Lucy Ransom, of Fenner, Madison county, New York, who died after a short sickness of eight days only, in the State of Illinois, August 19th, 1838; also alluding to the demise of a daughter, their youngest child, who departed this life, January 13th, 1839. They had previously buried two daughters. Written by the request of his parents.

'Tis done; alas, the fatal blow is given!
His spirit's flown, and fondest hearts are riven!
Erastus ne'er again our eyes will meet,
No more his voice our listening ears shall greet,
No more his hand the friendly grasp impart,
His lyre* no longer soothe the aching heart.
That lyre, which oft with Gospel music rang,
Lies silent now, its golden chords unstrung.
Heaven touch'd his heart, and form'd him for its own;
Hope cast her anchor near the eternal throne;
His faith embraced the promises of God,
He saw salvation's triumphs spread abroad;
Not for himself alone the Savior's grace,
But from all sin to purge the human race:
This taught his heart her strains of heavenly love,
And ripen'd his young soul for bliss above.

* He possessed a poetical genius.

Still one lone waste our mourning souls must feel;
We weep with smart no human aid can heal!

But late we saw him healthful, blithe, and young,
His course on earth with prospects fair begun,
With bright'ning hopes of usefulness in view,
He bade the mansion of his sire adieu;
And westward shaped his course to stranger lands,
Nor dream'd life there must burst her feeble bands.
But vain is human skill 'gainst Heaven's decrees,
T' arrest the aim of mortal, fell disease!
The word from Heaven went forth; on wings of love
Bright angels bore him to the courts above;
There, free from mortal cares or storms of woe,
T' resume those strains of love begun below,
And chaunt the praise of our victorious Lord,
Till death's dark reign and kingdom be destroyed.

But look! the western sky is dark'ning fast—
Hark! that sad knell, with hollow, mournful blast,
Sweeps o'er the hills, and, strength'ning in its course,
Strikes kindred hearts with overwhelming force.

As some old oak, which long the storm defied,
Now quakes and reels beneath the whirlwind's tide,
Whose yielding roots can scarce their hold maintain,
Or help the stock its equilibrium gain;
So reel these parents, reft of limb by limb,
Beneath the strokes of death, fell terror's king!
For not one falls alone; that western knell
Is echoed back—another droop'd and fell!
Severe, still more severe the blasts succeed;
Open'd afresh, the wounds more freely bleed,
Till sinking nature, verging to the grave,
For succor calls, "O God of mercy, save!"

Nor calls in vain; one all-sustaining power
Saves from despair in this distressing hour;
One root, deep center'd, strength divine affords,
The root of faith in God's unchanging word!

Here rest you, then, my friends! here fix your trust;
Though tempests rage, though worlds are dash'd to dust,
Though lightnings flash, and dismal thunders roll,
No terrors here can overwhelm the soul.
Nor mourn——But no, I mock a parent's woe;
'Tis man's sad fate to mourn and weep below.
Though blest the lot of him whose spirit's fled,
Our hearts still twine around our kindred dead.
Oh, yes; I know it. Sacred drops are blest
That wet our cheeks, tho' from the heart they're press'd
In vital blood, until life's flickering lamp
Seems near extinguish'd with their chilling damp.
Though we mourn not with blasted hope, nor fear;
Though faith in Christ brings heaven and glory near,
Yet woes our viler passions shall chastise,
And form our souls for mansions in the skies.

Then wait we on; with mournful pleasure wait,
Through this short sojourn of our mortal state,
Till our change come—our spirits take their flight,
To meet our loved ones in the realms of light.

A CARD.

On being presented with a splendid Camel's-hair cloak, by my friends in Erie, Pennsylvania.

Benevolent friends! accept my warm regard,
My thanks for your kindness, (a meagre reward.)
The cloak you present me, so ample with wings,
Oh grant it may not be a "cloak for my sins;"
A shield to my frame from the cold, chilling snows,
Thro' valley, o'er mountain, when boreas blows—
To sound the loud trumpet of free Gospel grace,
Through Christ, the Redeemer, to Adam's lost race.
But yours be the meed, ye loved of the Lord!
And be the prize of virtue your reward.
While your kind hearts your willing hands thus lead,
To clothe the naked, and the hungry feed,
Be mine the humbler task to speak his name,
And his salvation to the world proclaim,
Till we shall meet in realms of light above,
Wrapp'd in the boundless *mantle* of his love.

A CARD.

On receiving a donation from friends in Ann Arbor, Michigan, comprising every article necessary to constitute a complete suit of apparel, together with a wig, and several dollars in money.

Kind brethren, or friends, (take the term that you love,
As shall best please the mind, or the heart's kindly throe,)
And brethren we are, for our great Sire's above ;
But our works, not profession, our friendship must prove.

But how can I doubt, when this body around
  Is array'd in the rich garb of charity's boon?
Not a niche, nor a spot, from the sole to the crown,
  But the sweet buds of friendship incessantly bloom.

E'en the locks, which the scissors of time long had shorn,
  Or relentless disease with her hand torn away,
Are replaced; and new ringlets this sear'd brow adorn,
  Which the channels of time and of care still display.

But why all this care for this vile lump of clay?
  This clod of pollution, corruption, and crime?—
Hold there, vile traducer! nor dare thus to say,
  Since its Author's the fountain of wisdom divine.

For erst from the ocean of chaos it sprang,
  God survey'd all its parts with an infinite eye;
And this curious machine, which in wisdom began,
  By his omnific word was perfected on high.

It was made to be cherish'd, be clad, and adorn'd,
  Not hated, degraded, abus'd and despised;
To be honor'd and bless'd, if to wisdom conform'd;
  Protected and lov'd; but if sinful, chastised.

Then I'll bow, dearest friends, with a heart that o'erflows,
  Both grateful to you and to God ever bless'd;
For the vestments with which this frail frame you inclose,
  And the dignified sentiment thereby express'd.

For pure religion's here exemplified,
  Approv'd of God, and safe for fallen man;
To bless the world with which a Savior died,
  And sublimate of grace Heaven's wond'rous plan.

No monk austerity, nor hermit gloom,
No self-tormenting with a scorpion rod;
No hateful pilgrimage, nor penance doom,
To sate the vengeance of a ruthless God!

But kindred minds can mingle here in love,
In imitation of the God of grace,
Whose light and rain, descending from above,
Illume and bless the whole of Adam's race;

Can seek the wretched, gild the heart of woe
By timely aid, search the lone widow's cot,
The orphan's cell, and blessings there bestow,
Till joy shall triumph, sorrow be forgot.

How doubly blest—the heart alone can tell—
To see the hungry fed, the naked clothed,
The vile reform'd, the wayward turn'd to dwell
In wisdom's sacred palace, and beloved;

To see the eyes, so late suffused with tears,
Beam forth with gratitude, and joy, and love;
The heart, the seat of dark despair for years,
Lit up with hopes of peace and joy above;

To gain th' assurance of a grateful heart,
Untuned to flattery's art, unused to guile;
And feel the bliss those heavenly works impart,
Which raise o'er earthly woe the joyful smile.

Such bliss is yours, my friends, while thus you prove
Obedient to the Savior's great command;
While strangers, friends, and foes can *feel* your love,
In blessings scatter'd with a liberal hand.

Go on! th' reward is sure ; your treasures lie
  Beyond the reach of *moth*, or *rust* or *thieves* ;
Peace on the earth, and hopes beyond the sky—
  These are the treasures which the soul receives.

Go on! remember the sure word of grace!
  The voice that promises will surely give
Garments, whose lustre time can not efface,
  But through revolving ages shine and live.

Yes; sin shall die; darkness shall cease to reign ;
  The last deep groan of anguish die away ;
Then Christ will burst death's adamantine chain,
  And raise a *universe* to endless day.

Hail, sacred morn! when Christ shall raise the dead,
  Clothed in rich vestments of primeval light,
And crowns of joy grace each triumphant head,
  With stars of love, most dazzlingly bright!

Angels will shout; powers and dominions bow ;
  All intellectual beings prostrate fall ;
Wreaths of immortal glory grace a Savior's brow ;
  Infinite bliss shall reign, and "God be all in all."

A CARD.

On finding a splendid new harness on my mare, New Year's morning, before day-light, 1846.

In the year '46, on the very first morn,
  E'er the sun had illumin'd the east,
I repair'd, lamp in hand, to my humble barn,
  To see that all things were at peace ;

Where, behold! my old Doll, (she's the pride of her race,
And her heart is as white* as her skin,)
Stood proudly array'd in a shining new dress,
And her eyes spake of pleasure within.

With wonder I gazed; then, approaching her side,
Found a billet quite fairly display'd,
From St. Nicholas' self, without boasting or pride,
Attach'd to the gift he had made.

My heart felt a thrill; for direct from above
It descended, it seem'd to profess;—
Still, why should I doubt that the spirits of love
Delighted poor mortals to bless?

But his servants on earth were his agents in this,
And their kindness of heart I revere;
Though all I can do is to pray for their peace,
And to WISH THEM A HAPPY NEW YEAR.

---

* Her color is white.

www.ingramcontent.com/pod-product-compliance
Lightning Source LLC
LaVergne TN
LVHW021307110826
845150LV00003B/509

* 9 7 8 1 4 2 5 5 5 9 4 2 7 *